autoCAD

A CONCISE GUIDE TO COMMANDS & FEATURES

For Release 13 for Windows

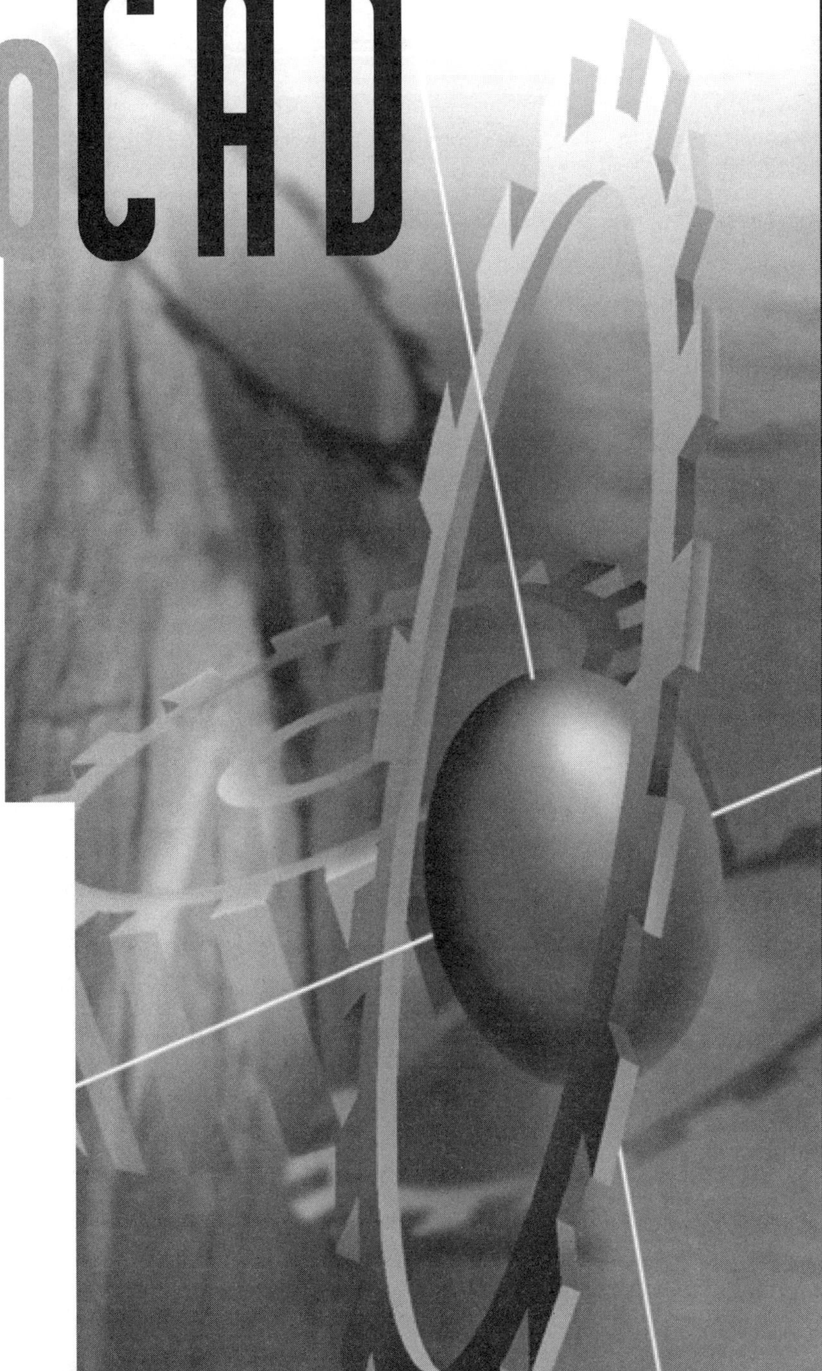

autoCAD

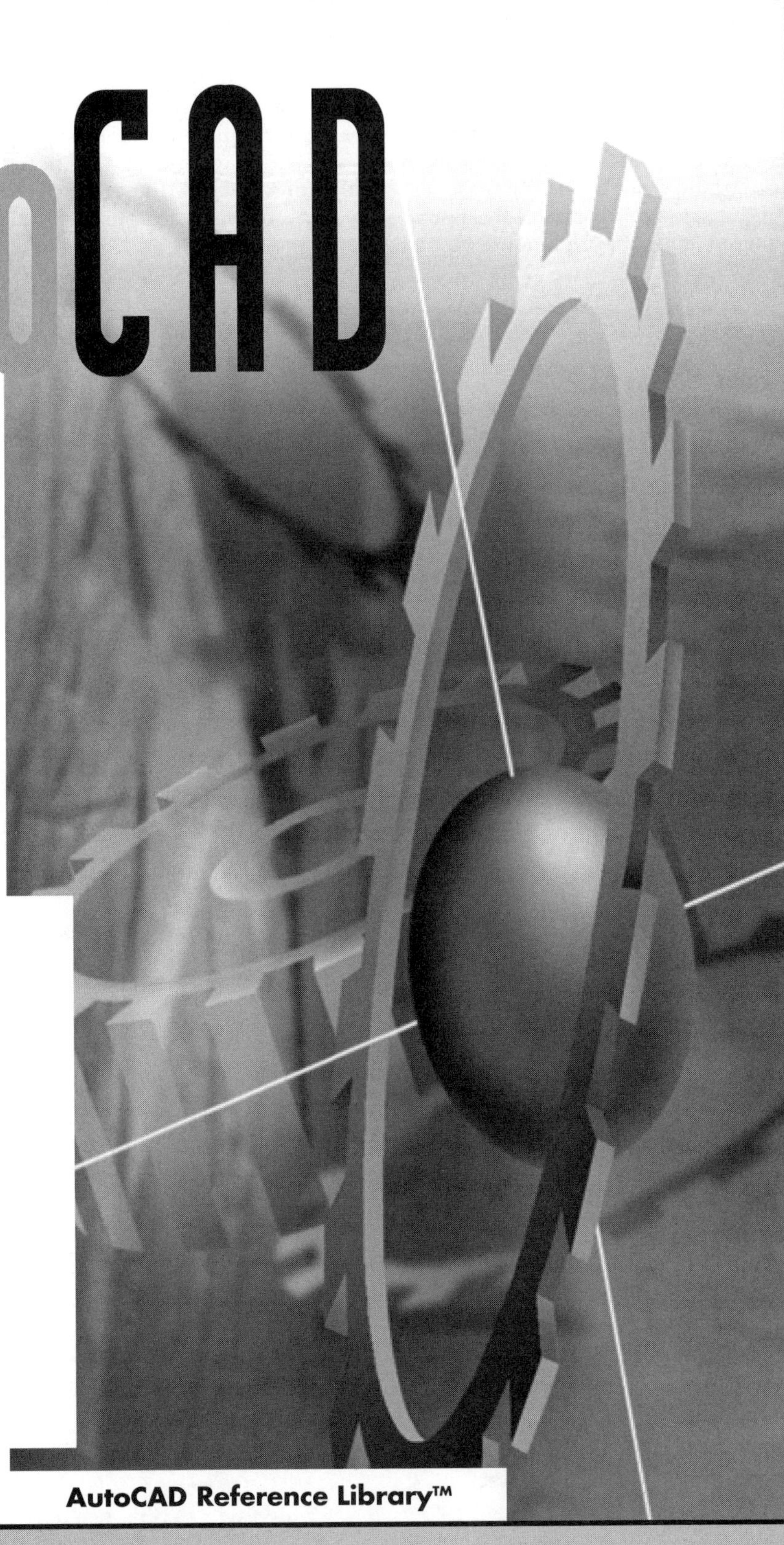

A CONCISE GUIDE TO COMMANDS & FEATURES

For Release 13 for Windows

Fourth Edition

Steven D. Elliott
Ronald W. Leigh
Brian Matthews

VENTANA PRESS

AutoCAD Reference Library™

AutoCAD: A Concise Guide to Commands & Features - For Release 13, Fourth Edition

Library of Congress Cataloging-in-Publication Data

Elliott, Steven D., 1960-
AutoCAD: a concise guide to commands & features for release 13 / Steven D. Elliott. -- 4th ed.
p. cm.
Rev. ed. of: AutoCAD / Ronald W. Leigh. 3rd. c1993.
Includes index.
ISBN 1-56604-139-2
1. Computer graphics. 2. AutoCAD (Computer file) I. Leigh, Ronald W. (Ronald Wilson). AutoCAD. II. Title.
T385.E466 1995
602'.0042'02855369--dc20 94-25298
CIP

Book design: Marcia Webb
Cover design: *series concept:* Tom Draper Design; *adaptation:* Mike Webster
Index service: Stephen Bach
Technical review: Brian Matthews, Architectural Technology Dept. Head, Wake Technical Community College
Design staff: Marcia Webb, Dawne Sherman
Editorial staff: Angela Anderson, Walter R. Bruce III, Tracye Giles, Lynn Jaluvka, Martin Minner, Nathaniel Mund, Pam Richardson
Production staff: Wendy Bernhardt, Cheri Collins, John Cotterman, Dan Koeller, Jaimie Livingston
Proofreader: Martin Minner

Fourth Edition 9 8 7 6 5 4 3 2 1
Printed in the United States of America

Ventana Press, Inc.
P.O. Box 2468
Chapel Hill, NC 27515
919/942-0220
FAX 919/942-1140

Limits of Liability and Disclaimer of Warranty

Trademarks

About the Authors

Steven D. Elliott recently accepted a position at Autodesk, Inc., as lead writer for 3D Studio documentation. Prior to that he was an independent consultant and instructor on the use of computer graphics in the design professions. He has consulted with Autodesk on educational issues for both AutoCAD and 3D Studio, and has taught AutoCAD and Multimedia seminars at the Autodesk Authorized Training Center at Moraine Valley Community College in Palos Hills, IL. Mr. Elliott is a registered architect and holds advanced degrees in both architecture and computer science.

Ronald W. Leigh is ranked "Master Teacher" in the Drafting/CAD Technology Program at Indiana Vocational Technical College, an authorized AutoCAD Training Center at Fort Wayne, IN. He is also an AutoCAD and AutoLISP programmer and consultant.

Brian Matthews is coauthor for this book and technical editor for all of the books in the Ventana Press AutoCAD Reference Library. He heads the Architectural Technology department at Wake Technical Community College in Raleigh, NC, and directs the college's AutoCAD Training Center. For the past nine years, he has been responsible for organizing and creating AutoCAD and AutoLISP courses, which are taught as part of a two-year engineering technology curriculum. He has also coordinated and taught several AutoCAD Industrial Extension Service programs at North Carolina State University.

Readers with technical inquiries can reach Brian Matthews by phone at 919-662-3476, by fax at 919-779-3360, or by e-mail on the Internet at *bmatt@wtcc-gw.wake.tec.nc.us*.

Contents

SECTION III: ADVANCED

SECTION IV: APPENDICES

INTRODUCTION

Autodesk, Inc., has said that it sees the future of AutoCAD moving toward Windows, and Release 13 clearly charts that course. Indeed, many of the Release 13 features are available only in the 32-bit Windows version of AutoCAD, and not in the DOS version.

Completely rewritten for Release 13 for Windows, this book starts with basic procedures and leads you through AutoCAD's drawing and editing commands, images, rendering and Windows applications to help you produce more efficient drawings.

The authors have tried to keep the content as straightforward as possible so new AutoCAD users can begin to draw without wading through complex material on database extraction, AutoLISP programming and other powerful features reserved as advanced treatments.

When you have mastered the basics, you may wish to explore AutoCAD's more advanced capabilities. Several excellent references are available, including complementary books published by Ventana Press: *The AutoCAD Productivity Book*, *The AutoCAD 3D Companion*, *1,000 AutoCAD Tips & Tricks* and *AutoLISP in Plain English.*

What's Inside

AutoCAD: A Concise Guide to Commands and Features serves two main objectives. First, it's a learning guide to help you master AutoCAD's drawing and editing commands. The book is arranged so that new users can advance from easiest to more difficult skills. Second, after you've learned AutoCAD, it will serve as a reference book for looking up details you don't use often enough to remember.

Consider the *AutoCAD Reference Manual* supplied with AutoCAD—an excellent source of information, comprehensive and well organized. Yet because the manual is organized by major subject areas, some advanced and difficult commands are often grouped with simple commands. Thus, advanced topics such as meshes and 3D polylines appear early in the manual, while basic topics such as snap and zoom appear later.

This sort of organization works well for a reference manual but makes learning difficult. In contrast, *AutoCAD: A Concise Guide* organizes commands and topics into much smaller groupings and lists them under 45 chapter headings, following a logical sequence through dimensioning, polylines and attributes and then onto some of AutoCAD's more complex features. By looking at the table of contents, you'll see that the more basic sections appear at the beginning of the book, and each section builds on the earlier sections.

Start at the beginning and carefully work through each section, and you'll build a solid understanding of AutoCAD. Chapter 34, "Solid Modeling," and Chapter 36, "Rendering," provide overviews of these exciting new features in Release 13. Chapters 44 and 45 provide hands-on exercises to help you get up and running. And the appendices offer supplementary information on tablet menus, overlays and attributes.

Finding Material

A reference book is useful only if you can find what you're looking for. There are two ways to find material in *AutoCAD: A Concise Guide*.

First, all commands and subjects are listed in the table of contents, and related commands and subjects are grouped under appropriate headings. Basic commands and topics appear first.

Second, the index in the back of the book is thorough enough to let you find most any topic that comes to mind.

The Companion Disk

To get the fullest use from *AutoCAD: A Concise Guide*, you'll want to use its Companion Disk. This self-installing diskette unpacks a library of drawing files, drawing and editing exercises, and custom menu files. All drawings for the hands-on exercises in chapters 44 and 45 are included, as well as the drawings for Appendix A and Appendix B.

As a bonus, the disk includes fourteen 2D and 3D AutoLISP utility programs that will enhance your productivity; instructions on using each program are included in the MANUAL.DOC file on the disk. For general instructions on installing and using the disk, see the INSTALL.DOC and README.DOC files.

A Note on AutoCAD's Tutorial

AutoCAD comes with useful tutorial exercises that expose you to about one-third of the AutoCAD commands. If you have access to that tutorial, it can introduce you to the general flavor of AutoCAD and explain some of the basic concepts on which AutoCAD is built.

Although the exercises in AutoCAD's tutorial are organized in different order from the material in this book, they may also be used quite effectively with the hands-on exercises in chapters 44 and 45.

You're on Your Way . . .

. . . to learning how to use one of the most powerful, exciting computer applications ever written. Every step you master using AutoCAD will save you hours and hours of drawing time down the road. You'll draw faster, design more efficiently and explore a new way of problem solving that will change forever the way you think about your craft.

Let's get started.

Section I

BASIC

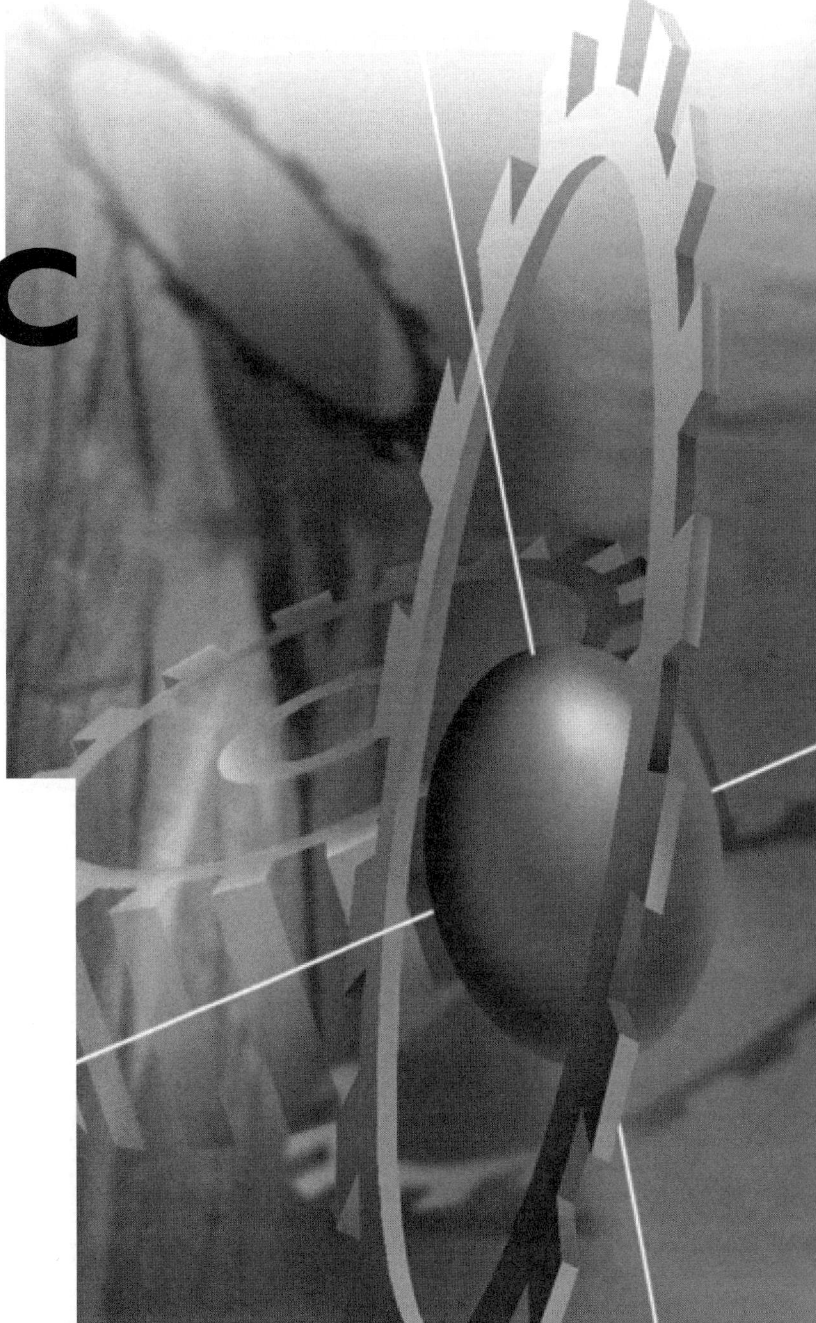

CHAPTER 1

Preliminaries

Welcome to computer-aided drafting and design. You'll find AutoCAD is a flexible computer drafting program that lets you create two-dimensional drawings, three-dimensional models and rendered images for a wide variety of applications.

This book, completely rewritten for AutoCAD's Release 13 for Windows, begins with the most basic concepts and procedures; leads you through all of AutoCAD's drawing and editing commands, including image rendering; and finally shows you how to customize AutoCAD to produce your drawings more efficiently.

How to Use This Book

This book assumes that you have already installed Windows and AutoCAD Release 13 for Windows on your computer.

Chapter 1 provides basics about using Windows and managing files and directories. It also covers what to do if you encounter problems, such as a system crash or a locked or corrupt file. Chapter 2 explains how to enter and exit AutoCAD and takes you through a sample drawing. Chapter 3, "In the Drawing Editor," provides an important introduction to new Windows-style graphical elements in Release 13 as well as to the drawing editor. The rest of the book is organized topically by groups of related commands, from the most basic to the more complex.

Autodesk has said that it sees the future of AutoCAD moving toward Windows, and Release 13 clearly charts that course. Indeed, many of the Release 13 features are available only in the 32-bit Windows version of AutoCAD, and not in the DOS version.

In this transitional stage, the Windows version adds the user-friendly features that have made Windows popular. But it also keeps open the familiar option of command-line entry. If you wish, you can type a command instead of using the Windows-style icons and menus.

To initiate a task in Release 13, you often have several choices:

Clicking on an icon or series of icons.
Selecting from pull-down menus.
Typing a command at the command line.

In *AutoCAD: A Concise Guide*, we present commands by their most familiar names. The command names as you would type them on the command line are also included. For example, Chapter 13 introduces the DISTANCE command this way:

DISTANCE Displays distances & angles between two points
COMMAND LINE: **dist**

Following this heading is the Distance icon, which you can click instead of entering a command at the command line. With the icon is information about how to find it:

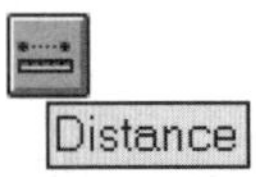

Figure 13-3: The Distance icon from the Inquiry flyout of the Object Properties toolbar.

Here and throughout the book, we may give you a number of possible starting points. From there, the step-by-step instructions for carrying out the task are the same. For the POINT STYLE command in Chapter 5, for example, you may either enter **ddptype** at the command line or choose Display from the Options pull-down menu and then choose Point Style.... In either case, the following dialog box is displayed:

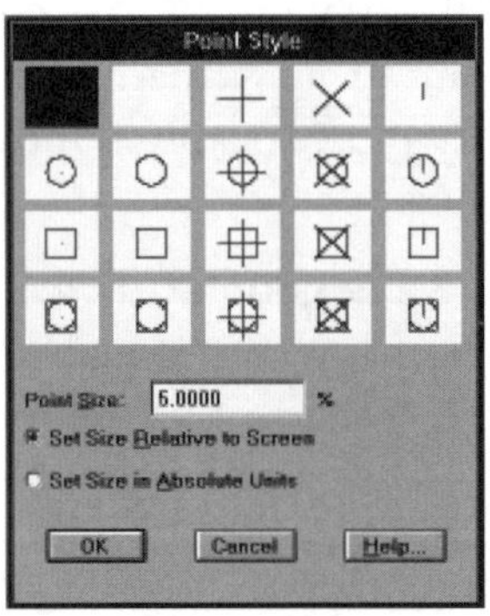

Figure 5-7: The Point Style dialog box.

The Companion Disk

To get the fullest use from *AutoCAD: A Concise Guide*, you'll want to use its Companion Disk. This self-installing diskette unpacks a library of drawing files, drawing and editing exercises, and custom menu files. All drawings for the hands-on exercises in chapters 44 and 45 are included, as well as the drawings for Appendix A and Appendix B.

As a bonus, the disk includes fourteen 2D and 3D AutoLISP utility programs that will enhance your productivity; instructions on using each program are included in the MANUAL.DOC file on the disk. For general instructions on using the disk, see the INSTALL.DOC and README.DOC files.

Using the Windows Program Manager

When you start Windows, the Program Manager window usually appears, as shown in Figure 1-1. This the primary window where you'll find and launch your application programs (such as AutoCAD).

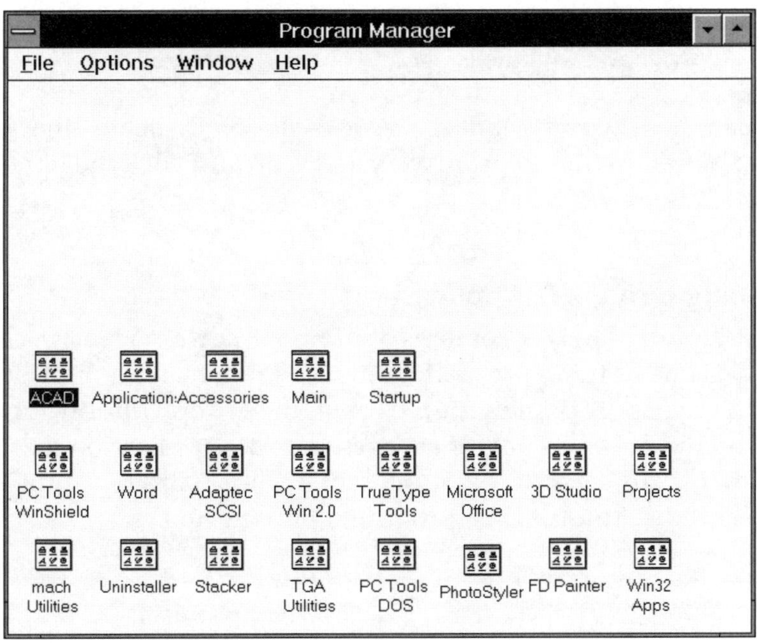

Figure 1-1: The Program Manager window.

Some systems are set up so that Windows starts with the Program Manager minimized and displayed as a small picture, or icon, at the bottom of your screen, as shown in Figure 1-2:

Figure 1-2: Windows with the Program Manager minimized.

To open the Program Manager, *double-click* on the icon—that is, position your pointer on the Program Manager icon and click the left mouse button twice.

Opening Groups & Applications

The Program Manager contains a number of group icons, each of which contains one or more program items. To launch an application, double-click on the appropriate group to open the group window. Then double-click on the program item that represents the application that you wish to launch. Figure 1-3 shows a number of groups with the AutoCAD group open and the AutoCAD 13 program item selected.

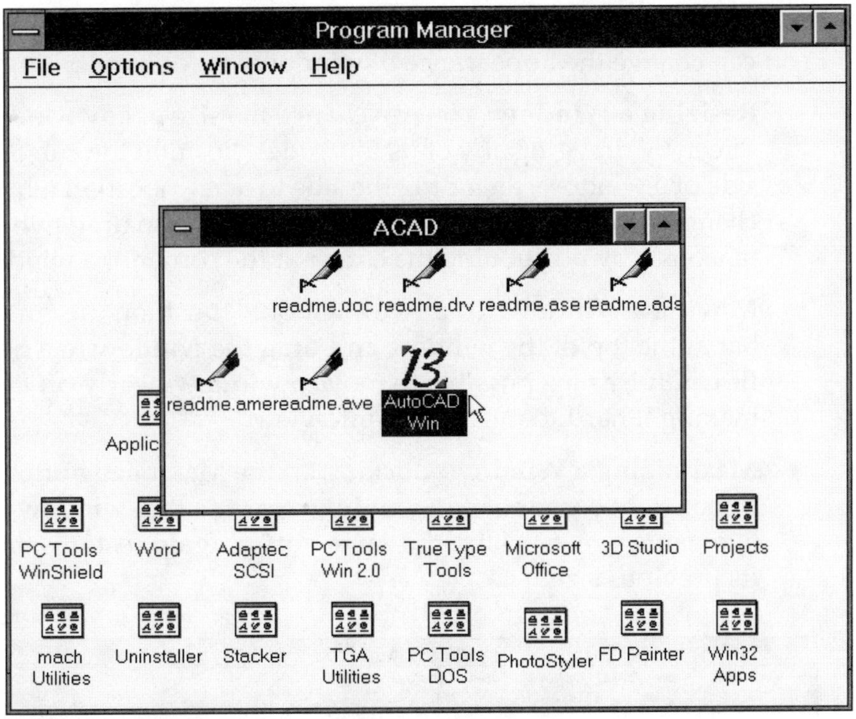

Figure 1-3: Selecting the AutoCAD program item.

Using the Mouse

When the instructions in this book involve use of the mouse, the following terms are used:

Click means to position the cursor over an object and quickly press and release the left button on your mouse or digitizer.

Right-click means to press and release the right button of your mouse or digitizer.

Double-click means to click on a mouse or digitizer button (normally the left button) twice in rapid succession.

Drag means to position the cursor over an object and then press and hold down the left button while moving the mouse. This technique is most often used to move an object from one part of the screen to another.

Manipulating Windows

You can change the appearance of windows as follows:

Resizing a Window: You can change the size of any window on your screen by dragging any of its four sides. Position the cursor near the side of a window, then drag the side to a new location when the cursor changes to a double-headed arrow. You can also drag two sides simultaneously by positioning the cursor at the corner of a window.

Moving a Window: To move a window, position the cursor in the title bar at the top of the window and drag the window to a new location. Be careful, as it's possible to move a window nearly off the screen, making it hard to move back into view.

Maximizing a Window: Clicking on the Maximize button in the upper right corner of any window expands that window to its largest allowable size. Clicking the same button again restores the window to its previous size.

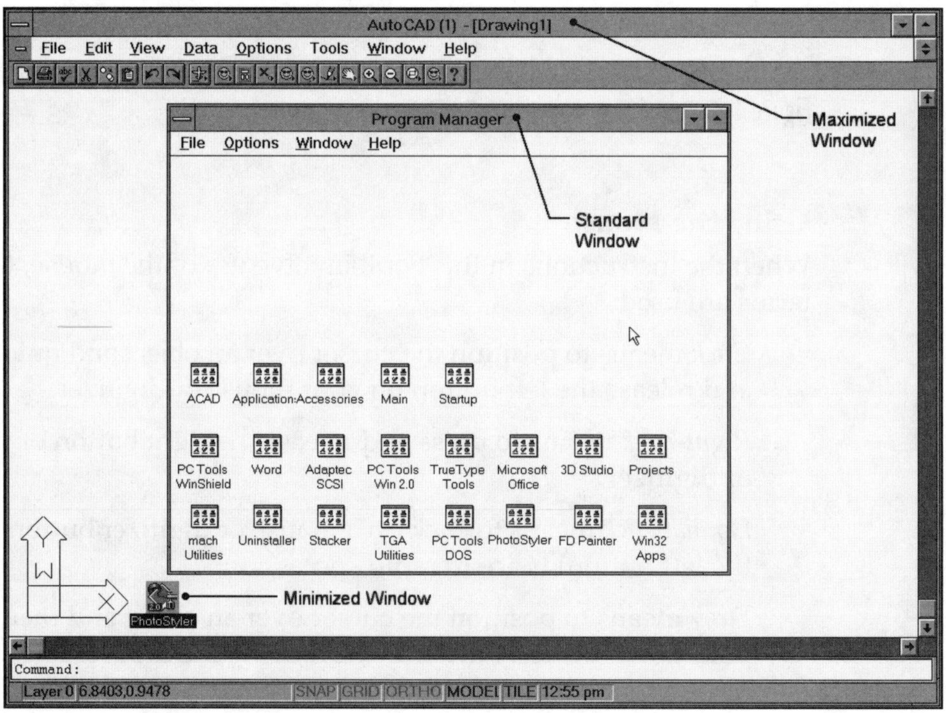

Figure 1-4: Standard, maximized and minimized windows

Minimizing a Window: Clicking on the Minimize button, just to the left of the Maximize button, shrinks a window to an icon. Double-clicking on the icon restores the window to its previous size. Figure 1-4 compares a standard window with maximized and minimized windows.

Closing a Window: To close a window, double-click on the Close button in its upper-left corner. Closing a window has different meanings for different types of windows. Closing a group window just minimizes it to an icon. Closing an application window is the same as exiting the program. Closing the Program Manager ends your Windows session.

Bringing a Window to the Front: It is possible to have many overlapping windows displayed on your screen. To display a window that is partially covered by one or more windows, just click on any visible part of the window that you want to see.

Using the Window Menu: The Program Manager and most applications have a pull-down menu called Window. Selecting this menu displays a list of window names. You can then select the name of the window you want to display.

Switching Between Applications

Windows allows you to have more than one application open at the same time. To switch between them, first minimize your current application. Then select the other application's window, or double-click its icon. You can also display a list of open applications by pressing Ctrl+Esc to open the Task List window. From the Task List you can select the application you want and click on the Switch To button.

Ending a Windows Session

You end your Windows session either by closing the Program Manager window or by selecting Exit Windows from the Program Manager File menu. Windows will attempt to clean house for you by closing all open applications and checking whether any files need to be saved, but it is best if you do that yourself before attempting to exit Windows.

Using the Windows File Manager

The File Manager is a Windows program that displays your directory and file structure and allows you to manipulate files. The basic installation for Windows places the File Manager icon in the Main group.

To open the File Manager

1. Find the Main group in the Program Manager and double-click to open the Main window.

2. In the Main window, find the File Manager icon and double-click on it to open the File Manager.

As an alternative, you may

1. Choose Run from the File menu of the Program Manager.

2. Type **winfile** in the dialog box as shown in Figure 1-5.

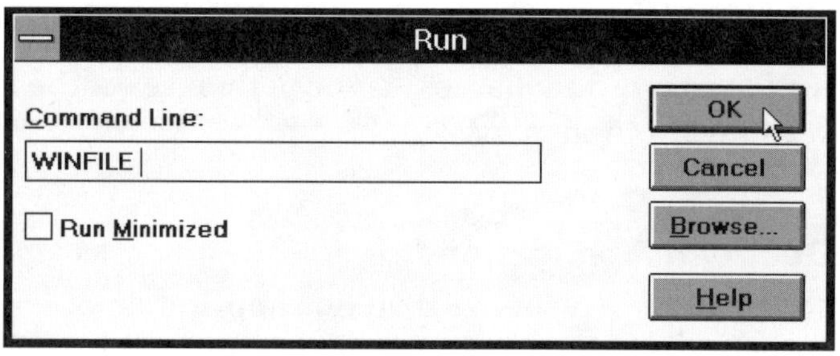

Figure 1-5: Starting the File Manager with the Run command.

To go to the File Manager from Windows

1. Click on the Minimize button in the top right corner of the AutoCAD window.

2. Launch the File Manager.

3. After you've completed your file management tasks (as described later in this chapter), return to AutoCAD by double-clicking on the AutoCAD icon.

NOTE: The File Manager does not know about AutoCAD's temporary files. Take care that you do not delete any files from the ACAD13 directory or root directory or otherwise change any files that AutoCAD might be using. In general, you should not perform any housekeeping tasks or deletion of unnecessary files unless all your applications are closed.

About Files

As you draw with AutoCAD, the program builds a database containing all the information in your drawing. This database is constantly updated in the computer's memory during the drawing and editing process. You store the information permanently by saving it to a file on either a hard disk drive or a floppy disk.

On a DOS system, each drawing within the same directory must have a unique name of eight characters or fewer. Here are some sample drawing file names using combinations of letters, numbers and a few other selected characters. Notice that there are no spaces within the file names.

BRACKET

PROJ_1

When AutoCAD saves its drawings to disk, it automatically adds a .DWG file name extension. When you're entering file names in AutoCAD, you don't need to enter the extension; AutoCAD automatically takes care of it. However, when you're entering file names in the Windows File Manager, enter the complete file name including the three-letter .DWG extension.

File name extensions identify the type of job a file does. Here are some other common extensions and their file types:

.BAK	Backup drawing file
.DWG	Drawing file
$__	Files whose extensions begin with $ are usually temporary files that AutoCAD creates and then erases when you exit AutoCAD in the usual way.

About Directories

A hard disk drive holds many more files than a floppy disk. Managing all these files requires that you divide the hard disk into a number of directories and subdirectories. (On some computers, these are termed *folders*.) An example of a simple hard disk drive organization is shown in Figure 1-6.

Let's look at how this organization is achieved. The files in each directory are identified by a path name. For example, the path name

C:\ACAD13\SUPPORT\ACAD.MNU

identifies drive C:\ as the root directory. The directory \ACAD13 is followed by the subdirectory \SUPPORT and finally the file itself, \ACAD.MNU (one of AutoCAD's menu support files).

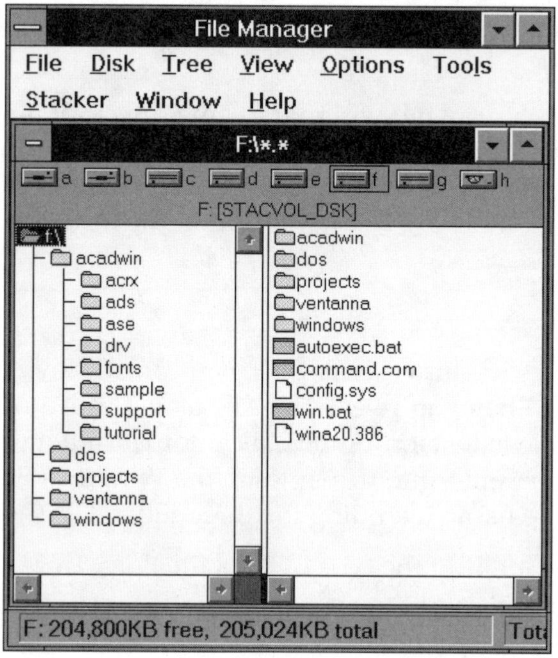

Figure 1-6: A sample directory structure on a hard drive.

Always place your working files in a separate directory, such as the \PROJECTS directory in Figure 1-6. This technique allows you to manage your files easily and prevents the nightmare of trying to separate your working files from the program files that AutoCAD needs to operate.

In industry, drawings for each project are permanently stored in different directories on the hard disk. Businesses that use a computer network might store drawings on one computer that acts as a file server for all the other computer workstations.

In an educational setting, a different approach may be taken. With many students using the same workstation, the hard disk would quickly become cluttered and drawing security would be difficult to maintain. Therefore, students generally keep all their files on their own diskettes, using the hard disks only for temporary storage while working on their drawings. If the school uses a computer network, students can be assigned private directories on the file server to safely store and access their files from any workstation on the network. Even so, it's a good idea for students to save their files on diskettes as a backup, just in case the network crashes or a power surge downs the system.

Controlling the File Manager Display

Here are instructions for manipulating the display of files and directories in the Windows File Manager.

Choosing a Drive to Display

To select the drive you want to view, click on the appropriate drive icon at the top of the window. You can also choose the Select Drive command from the Disk menu. This command displays a dialog with a list of all available drives. You then select the drive that you want and click on OK.

Selecting Directory or File Display

The default display shows the directory structure (called the Tree) at right. The files in the selected directory are shown at left. From the View menu, you can specify that Windows display any of the following:

Both the directory tree and the directory files (Tree and Directory)
Only the directory tree (Tree Only)
Only the files in the selected directory (Directory Only)

Controlling File Display

From the View menu, you can also control how much file information is displayed in a directory file window. The first two choices immediately update the file display.

Name displays only the file names and file extensions.

All File Details displays the names, file size in bytes, the date and time that the file was last modified, and the file attributes.

The third choice is Partial Details, which displays in the dialog in Figure 1-7. Using this dialog, you can choose the information you want displayed in the directory files window. Notice there is no choice for file name, as file names are always displayed.

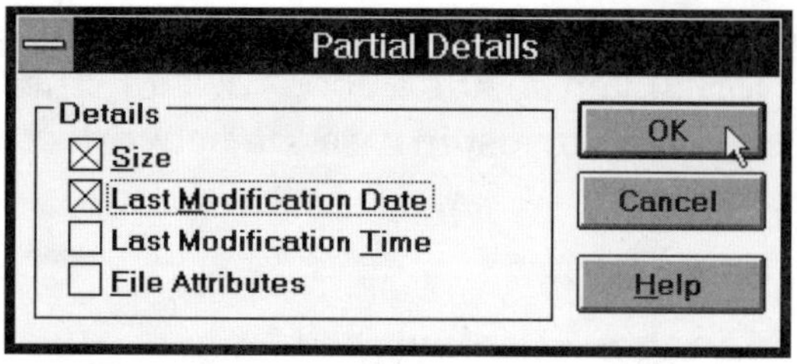

Figure 1-7: The Partial Details dialog for file display.

Sorting the Display

When a window with a file list is displayed, you have a number of options for sorting the display of the files. Select the File menu to choose one of the following options:

Sort by Name	Sorts the files in ascending alphabetical order based on their eight-character file names.
Sort by Type	Sorts the files in ascending alphabetical order based on their three-character file extensions.
Sort by Size	Sorts the files in descending order based upon their file size from the largest to the smallest.
Sort by Date	Sorts the files based on the date of their last modification. The sort is in descending order, from most recent to the oldest.

File & Disk Management

File management plays an important role in AutoCAD use. The following descriptions tell you how to perform basic file management with the Windows File Manager.

Creating Directories

Creating directories is essential to your file organization. Many novice computer users store all their files in a single directory. This is similar to taking all the notes, drawings and magazines that you have ever used and piling them into a big box. Imagine trying to find one specific drawing in that mess!

A directory is like a file folder, and Windows uses a file folder symbol to represent directories. To create a directory, take these steps: In the Tree window, select the directory you want to add to. Then choose the Create Directory command from the File menu. The command displays a dialog where you'll type the name of the new directory and then click on OK. Windows then creates the new directory and inserts it inside your selected directory.

Renaming Files & Directories

Directories and files are both renamed using the same command. Select the file or directory that you want to rename, and choose Rename from the File menu. A dialog appears containing the original name and an area where you can type the new name. Click on OK to complete the command.

Selecting Multiple Files

You may select a single file by just clicking on it. For multiple files, you have two other options.

First, you can select a block of contiguous files. To do this, select the first file in the block and then hold down the Shift key while clicking on the last file in the block. In this way, you select all the files listed between the first and last picked files.

Second, you can select a group of files that are not contiguous. To do this, hold down the Ctrl key while clicking on files. This allows you to select files scattered throughout your directory while skipping the files listed between them.

Copying Files & Directories

Copying files and directories is quite easy in the Windows File Manager. After selecting the files you want to copy, position your cursor over one of the selected files, press and hold the Ctrl key, and then drag the selected files to the disk or directory icon where you want the copies placed. Windows displays a dialog asking if you really want to copy the files, and you confirm the command by clicking on Yes.

If you do not press and hold the Ctrl key while dragging the selected files, Windows decides for itself whether to copy or move the files to the new location. The Windows default is to copy the files if they are placed on a different disk and to move the files if they are placed in a different directory of the same disk. Pressing the Ctrl key overrides this default and always copies the files.

Moving Files & Directories

Moving files and directories works just the same as copying except that you hold down the Alt key to force the files to move.

Deleting Files & Directories

You can quickly delete files and directories by selecting them and then pressing the Del key. Windows displays the Delete dialog and asks you to confirm the deletions. After you click on OK to confirm the delete command, Windows plays it safe by displaying the Confirm File Delete dialog shown in Figure 1-8. This dialog allows you to confirm the deletions one file at a time, confirm all deletions immediately or back out by canceling the command.

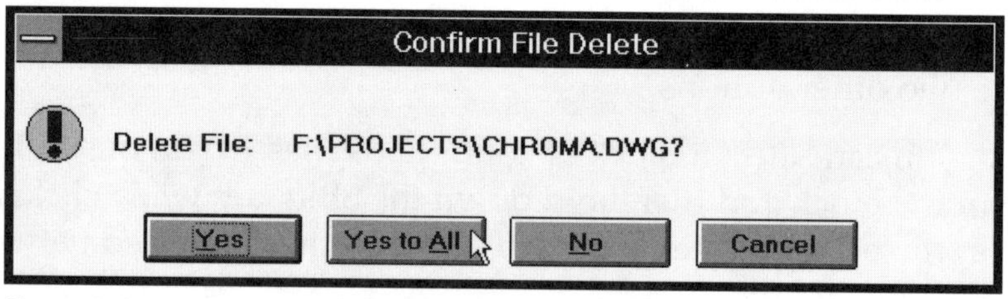

Figure 1-8: The Confirm File Delete dialog.

Searching for Files & Directories

Sometimes you don't know where a file is located on your disk, and this is when the Search command on the File menu comes in handy. Choosing Search displays the Search dialog shown in Figure 1-9.

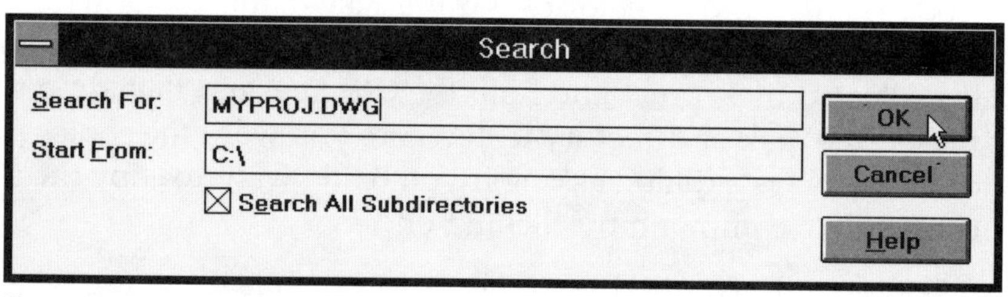

Figure 1-9: The Search dialog.

The most common way to use the dialog is to enter the file name that you want in the Search For field, enter the root directory of the drive in the Start From field (such as C:\) and enable the Search All Subdirectories check box. This causes Windows to search the entire disk for the desired file. Once the search is complete, it displays all the files with that search name in a single window.

What to Do After a System Crash

When a misbehaving program or a hardware error causes your system to stop operating, or "crash," you will need to restart the system. There are several ways to restart the computer: soft boot, hard boot and cold boot. The method you choose will depend upon the type of crash you experience. The order in which you should attempt to restart a crashed system is as follows:

1. To perform a soft boot, simultaneously press the Ctrl, Alt and Del keys. Under Windows, this terminates the crashed program without requiring that you restart the whole system. If Windows believes it can successfully terminate the program, you'll see a prompt that describes available options. Usually, pressing the Enter key will terminate the crashed program and return you to Windows. If you press Ctrl+Alt+Del a second time, the system reboots.

A soft boot reloads the operating system and the system configuration files, but it should skip the hardware and memory checks that are performed when the system is first turned on. Since this technique is actually an attempt to run the computer's restart program, it's possible for a system crash to disable the soft boot to the system. In that case, you must try one of two other options.

2. To perform a hard boot, press the Reset button on the front of the computer. Most modern desktop computers now have a Reset button that immediately terminates all processes running on the CPU and restarts the computer as if it had just been turned on. Pressing the Reset button is preferable to turning the power off and back on again because it spares the computer the stress of the power-on voltage surge. Think of how a light bulb burns out; it almost always happens when you first turn on the power.

Sometimes a system crash is so severe that the Reset button has no effect or the system fails to restart properly. In those instances, your only choice is to turn off the power.

3. The term "cold boot" refers to turning off the system power and then turning it back on. You should always wait at least 30 seconds before turning the system back on. This minimizes stress to the system and allows the voltage to drop to zero in all the components. A good rule of thumb is to wait for all sound produced by the fan and the spinning hard drives to stop before turning the power back on.

Handling Locked or Corrupt Files

At times you may not be able to load a file because it is either locked or corrupt.

If file locking is enabled (which is the AutoCAD default), AutoCAD prevents other users on a network from loading your drawing file while you are working on it. Sometimes, if you hang your system or otherwise abnormally end AutoCAD, your drawing file does not unlock properly. If you try to access a drawing that AutoCAD reports locked, and you are sure no one else is using the file, you can use the Unlock File command to gain access to it. For instructions, see Chapter 9, "Files."

If a file is corrupt, you can analyze and correct it using the Audit & Recover command, also covered in Chapter 9.

Moving on

So far, you've reviewed the preliminaries for file directory structure and file management. You've also learned a little about how to get around in Windows and manipulate files in the Windows File Manager. It's important that you feel comfortable in moving through the directory structure and finding files before going to the next chapter. And always remember the directory in which you store your files.

The next chapter gets you started with AutoCAD itself. You'll learn various ways to start AutoCAD and open and save files. The rest of this book will help you quickly move into the AutoCAD drawing environment.

CHAPTER 2

Entering & Exiting AutoCAD

There are many ways to start AutoCAD, use prototype drawings and name and save drawings. The Quick Start sample in this chapter is an easy sequence that illustrates just one way to create and save your drawings.

If you're new to AutoCAD—particularly to Release 13—you'll want to try this sequence. It leads you through creating and saving one drawing, editing that drawing, starting a different drawing, and then returning to edit the original drawing.

After you feel confident that you can get in and out of AutoCAD and save your work, study the procedures explained in the following sections so you can use AutoCAD's flexibility to your advantage.

Remember, in Windows, you can use the Esc key to back out of any command. If you feel you've made a mistake and want to start over, the Esc key will return you to AutoCAD's command prompt. You can also use Esc to exit a dialog box or halt a screen regeneration.

Quick Start: A Sample Sequence

1. Start AutoCAD. From Windows, open the AutoCAD group and double-click on the AutoCAD icon. This will take you directly into AutoCAD's drawing editor.

2. Name your drawing. Choose Save... from the File menu. AutoCAD displays the Save Drawing As dialog box, shown in Figure 2-1. Make sure your \PROJECTS directory is highlighted in the Directories window. Then type **d1** in the File Name window. Click on the OK button to complete the command.

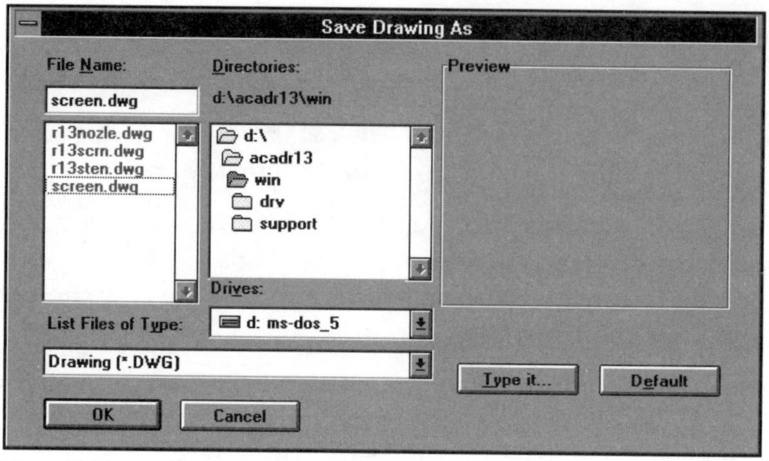

Figure 2-1: Entering information in the Save Drawing As dialog.

3. Place a few lines in the drawing. Select the Line icon from the Draw toolbox, as shown in Figure 2-2. Then pick a few points on the screen. Right-click the mouse button when you want to end the LINE command.

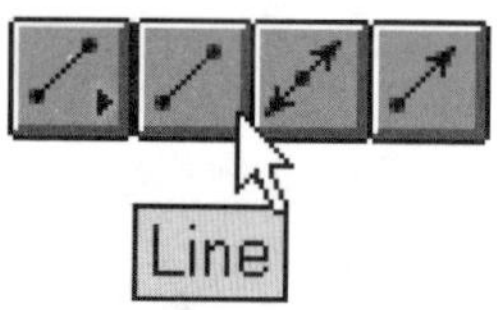

Figure 2-2: Selecting the Line icon in the Draw toolbox.

4. Save your drawing and stay in the drawing editor. Choose Save... from the File menu again. Notice that this time no dialog box appears. Once you have given your drawing a name, AutoCAD automatically continues to save your work to that name.

5. Reselect the Line icon and place a few more lines in the drawing.

6. Save the drawing again and stay in the drawing editor. (Don't quit.)

7. Start a new drawing called D2. Choose New... from the File menu. When the Create New Drawing dialog box appears, click on the New Drawing Name button. When the Create Drawing File dialog box appears, select your \PROJECTS directory from the Directories window. Enter **d2** in the File Name field, then click on OK. Click on OK again when the Create New Drawing dialog box reappears, as shown in Figure 2-3.

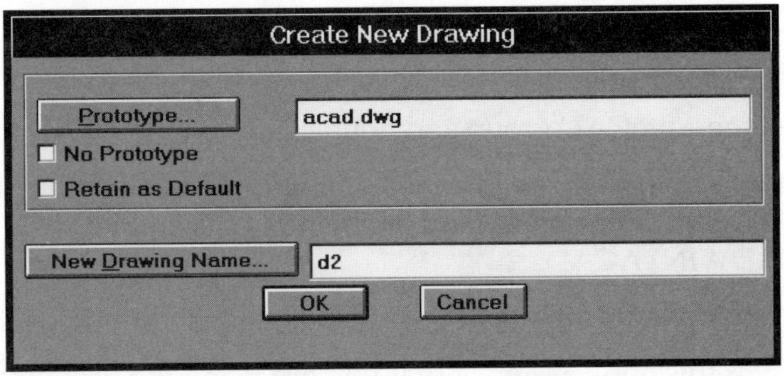

Figure 2-3: Entering the file name in the Create New Drawing dialog box.

8. Place a few circles in this new drawing. Select the Circle icon from the Draw toolbox, shown in Figure 2-4. Then pick the center and radius points on screen. Create several circles in the drawing.

Figure 2-4: Selecting the Circle icon in the Draw toolbox.

9. Save the drawing, but don't quit AutoCAD.

10. Open your first drawing, D1. Choose Open... from the File menu. When the Select File dialog box appears, select D1 from the File Name window and click on OK. Your first drawing, containing a few lines, will appear.

11. Add a few more lines to the drawing.

12. Save and end your drawing and return to Windows. Choose Exit... from the File menu. AutoCAD displays the Save Changes dialog box shown in Figure 2-5. Click on the Yes button to save your work.

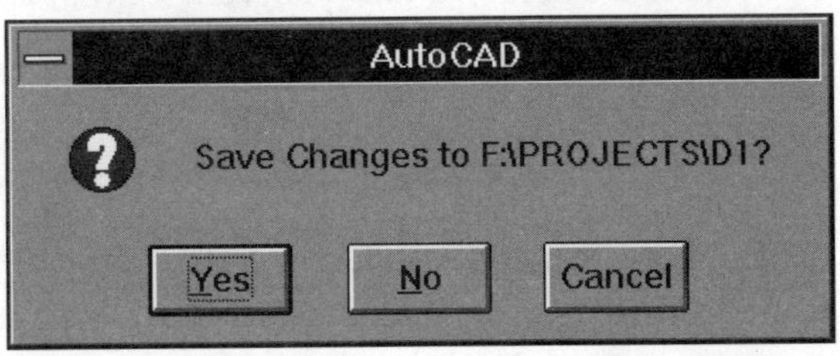

Figure 2-5: Saving your work with the Save Changes dialog box.

Starting AutoCAD & Selecting a Drawing

In Windows there are three ways to launch AutoCAD:

1. Open the AutoCAD group and double-click on the ACAD program icon.
2. Choose Run... from the File menu and type the full path to the ACAD.EXE file in the command line field. For example: C:\ACADWIN\ACAD.
3. Find the ACAD.EXE file in the File Manager and double-click on it.

The rest of this book assumes that you are using the first method to start AutoCAD. This method is preferable because Windows allows you to specify a default working directory as part of the program item properties. The other two methods make your working directory the same as AutoCAD's directory, which we've already explained is not desirable.

You can change your default working directory by editing the program item properties for AutoCAD. From the Program Manager, click to select the AutoCAD program icon and then choose Properties... from the File menu. When the Program Item Properties dialog appears, as shown in Figure 2-6, you can enter the full path of your default working directory in the Working Directory field.

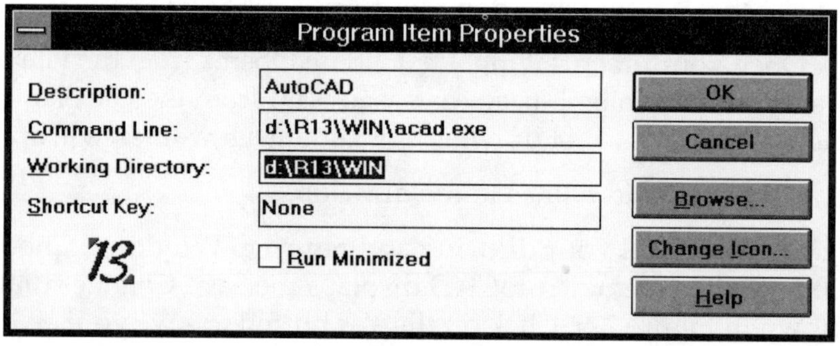

Figure 2-6: Changing the Working Directory under Program Item Properties.

Starting a New Drawing

If you've entered AutoCAD without preloading a drawing file as described above, you're in an empty drawing. You now have a couple of options: either assign a name immediately and then begin your drawing or begin drawing and then assign a name when you decide to save your work. Either way you name your drawing by choosing Save... from the File menu and then typing the name in the File Name field.

Figure 2-7: The New icon from the Standard toolbar.

If you are already working on a drawing and wish to create a new drawing file, choose New... from the File menu, or click on the New icon. If you have not yet saved the work in your current drawing, AutoCAD displays the Save Changes dialog as shown in Figure 2-8. You can click on one of three buttons at this point:

Yes	Saves your work in the current drawing and then displays the Create New Drawing dialog.
No	Throws away your work since the last save and then displays the Create New Drawing dialog.
Cancel	Forgets you ever asked for a new drawing and returns you to your current drawing.

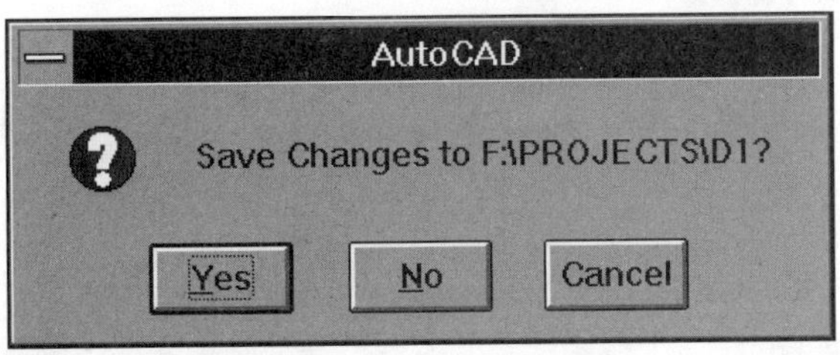

Figure 2-8: The Save Changes dialog.

If you choose Yes or No, AutoCAD displays the Create New Drawing dialog. We will discuss the prototype options in the top of the dialog later in this chapter. Right now, you have two options in naming your new drawing file:

1. Your first choice is to type the name in the New Drawing Name field. Remember that currently a file name can have only eight characters and that you do not need to enter the extension .DWG. If you type just the eight-character file name, your drawing is placed in your current working directory as shown in Figure 2-9. Otherwise, you can type the entire path along with the file name to force the file to any directory on your hard drive.

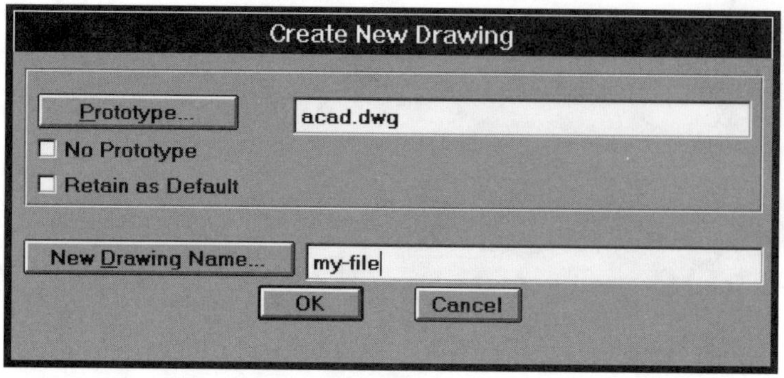

Figure 2-9: Naming the drawing.

You can also create a new empty drawing by clicking on OK without specifying any name in the New Drawing Name field.

2. Your second option is to click on the New Drawing Name... button to the left of the New Drawing Name field. This button displays the Create Drawing File dialog as shown in Figure 2-10. This dialog allows you to navigate through all of the drives and directories accessible through your workstation. Once you have selected a directory in the Directories window, you type the name of your new drawing in the File Name window and click on OK. This method is the preferred way to create a new drawing in a specific directory.

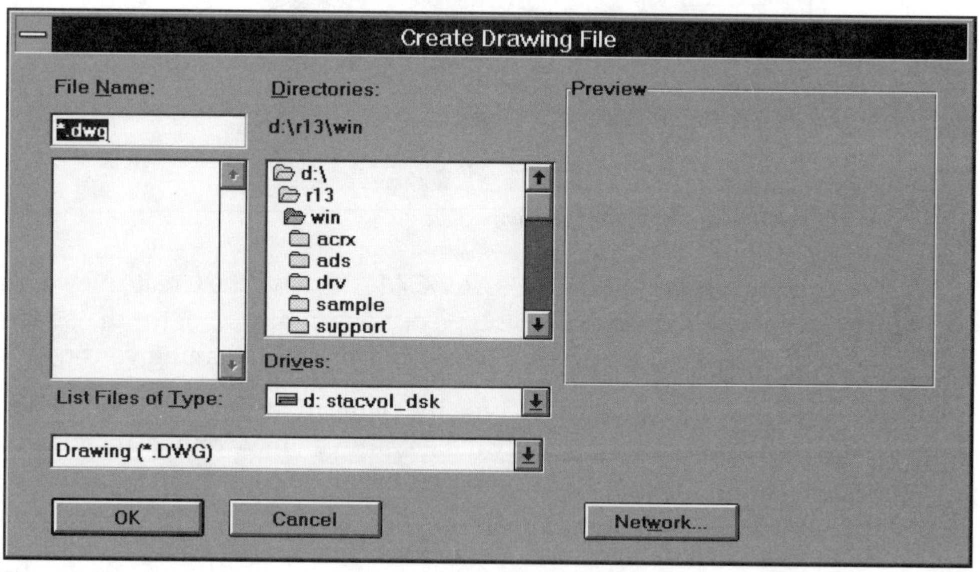

Figure 2-10: Creating a new drawing with the Create Drawing File dialog.

Naming & Saving Your Drawings

As mentioned earlier, you choose Save... from the File menu to name a previously unnamed drawing. There are actually three commands to save a drawing. Two are available from the menus, and one is an old command available only from the command line. The names of these commands are QSAVE, SAVEAS and SAVE. All three use the same dialog (shown in Figure 2-11), so it's important that you pay attention to which command you're using. Here's a comparison of the commands:

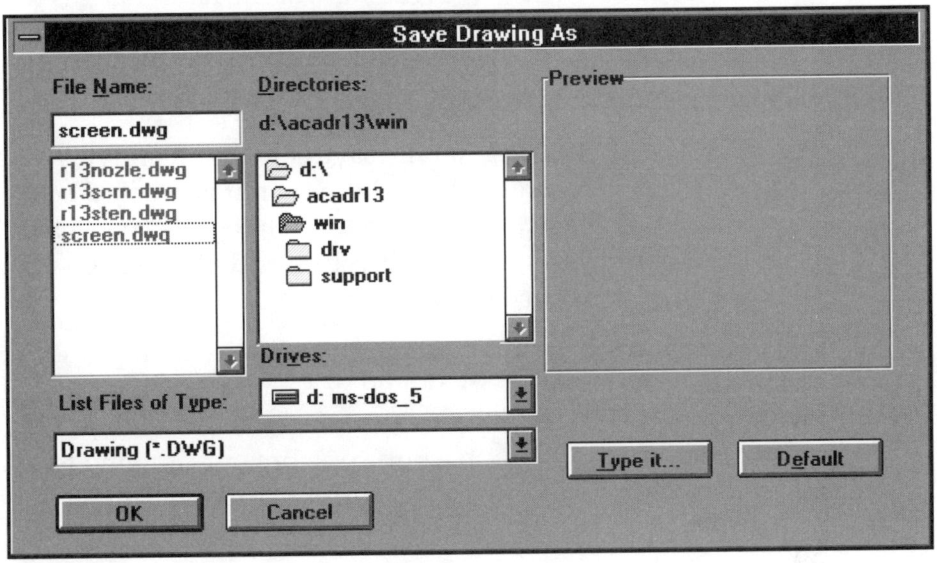

Figure 2-11: The Save Drawing As dialog.

Figure 2-12: The Save Icon from the Standard toolbar.

QSAVE is executed when you choose Save... from the File menu or click on the Save icon. The most useful feature of this command is that it only displays the Save Drawing As dialog if you attempt to save an unnamed drawing. If your drawing already has a name, QSAVE quickly saves the drawing to disk without further input from you. That is why its name is QSAVE, for Quick SAVE. Choosing Save... from the File menu is the preferred method for saving your work.

SAVEAS is executed when you choose Save As... from the File menu. This command displays the Save Drawing As dialog and lets you save your current work to a new file name and then immediately begin working with the new file.

Let's assume that you are working on the drawing D1 from the exercise at the beginning of this chapter. You decide to save a copy of the file D1 as "D2" so you can add new information to drawing D2. You choose Save As... from the File menu and type D2 in the File Name: field. AutoCAD then closes file D1 without saving any of the new changes to the file. Your current work is saved under a new file named D2, and D2 becomes your current working drawing. This technique is useful for saving incremental versions of your drawing as you work.

SAVE is AutoCAD's original file save command, and it is available only from the command line. Although this command could be considered obsolete, it does have a unique feature. The SAVE command allows you to save your current work to any directory and file that you wish, but it leaves you in your current drawing.

If you entered **save** at the command line in the example above (instead of using SAVEAS), your work would be saved to the new file (D2), but you would be left with D1 as your current working drawing. This technique is sometimes used to save a backup copy of your drawing to another disk or directory without affecting your current working drawing or directory.

Automatically Saving Your Drawings

You can also instruct AutoCAD to automatically save your drawing periodically. You control this feature by entering **savetime** at the command line and setting it to the number of your choice. Setting SAVETIME to any value greater than zero specifies the number of minutes between automatic saves. After the specified number of minutes has elapsed, AutoCAD triggers an automatic save as part of the next command. In other words, if you set SAVETIME to 20 minutes and then leave your workstation 18 minutes later, nothing will happen until you return and enter a command. As soon as you enter that command, AutoCAD will first save your drawing before proceeding with your command.

The automatic save feature of AutoCAD does not save your drawing to its original file name. If it did, it might overwrite your drawing with changes that you really didn't want to save. What AutoCAD does instead is to put automatic saves into a special file with the name AUTO.SV$. This file is a regular AutoCAD drawing with a funny name. If you rename the file to have an extension of .DWG, AutoCAD will open it just like any other drawing.

The purpose of SAVETIME is to provide you with a safety net in case you forget to use one of the save commands above. It is not a replacement for saving your files manually. Here is how SAVETIME should be used:

1. Decide the maximum amount of time you are willing to lose in the event of a system crash, and set SAVETIME to that amount. Many users find that 30 to 60 minutes is a good trade-off between the security of automatic saves and the brief interruption of work when AutoCAD saves the file.

2. Work on your drawing as usual, remembering to manually save it from time to time. A good rule of thumb is to manually save a drawing whenever you have performed enough work that you would be upset to lose it all. Some days that may take hours, and other days you will save every 10 or 15 minutes.

3. When you can restart your computer after a system crash, find and rename the file AUTO.SV$ (for example, to SAVEFILE.DWG).

Do not launch AutoCAD until you have renamed AUTO.SV$! The reason is that the SAVETIME variable is still active. If you launch AutoCAD and do not exit before the number of minutes in SAVETIME has expired, the AUTO.SV$ file will be overwritten, destroying your chance to recover any lost information.

4. Launch AutoCAD and compare the renamed AUTO.SV$ file with the drawing you were working on when the system crashed. The file that contains the most recent information will depend on whether an automatic save or a manual save was performed closest to the crash.

5. If the renamed AUTO.SV$ file has the most recent information, use the Save As... command from the File menu to save the file back to your original drawing name.

Remember, the SAVETIME system variable is a backup safety net only. You should still manually save your drawings using either Save... or Save As... from the File menu.

Opening an Existing Drawing

Figure 2-13: The Open icon from the Standard toolbar.

Choose Open... from the File menu, or click the Open icon, to view or edit an existing drawing. Figure 2-14 shows the Select File dialog box, which lists directories and drawing files. The Select File dialog is a special case of the generic file dialog box used by many AutoCAD commands (for more detail on the generic form of dialog, see "The File Dialog Box" later in this chapter). You select the drive, directory and file name from the lists. Once you have selected a file, AutoCAD displays a thumbnail image of the drawing to help you confirm that it is indeed the file that you want.

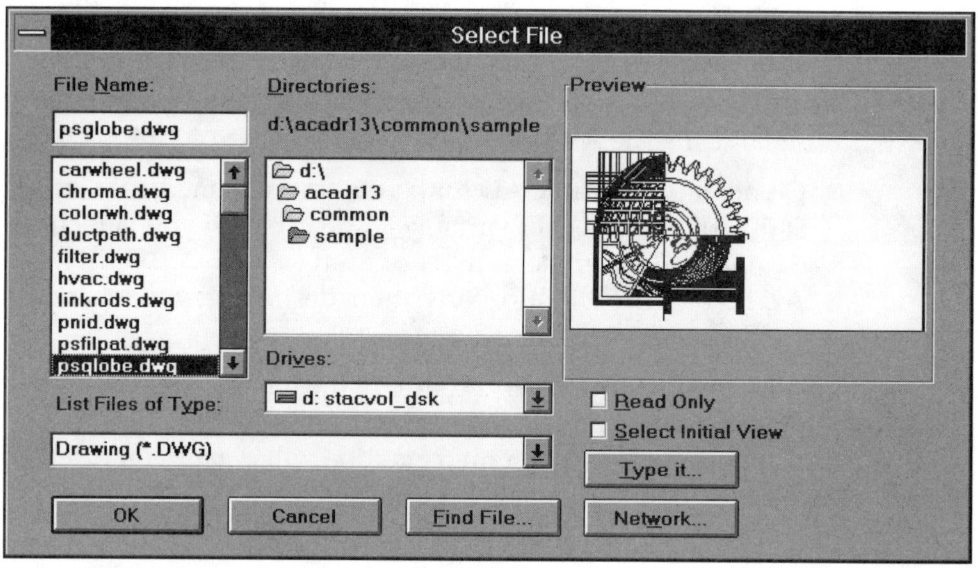

Figure 2-14: The Select File dialog box.

The Select File dialog includes two other unique features. First, you can activate the Select Initial View check box. If this check box is selected when you click on the Open button, AutoCAD will begin to open your selected drawing and then stop and display the Select Initial View dialog. This dialog contains a list of saved views available in the drawing, followed by

M for a Model Space view and *P* for a Paper Space view (see Chapter 11, "Looking Around," for details on saving views). You then select the desired view and click on OK. If the Select Initial View check box is not selected when you open a file, the initial display will be the view displayed when the drawing was last saved.

Second, you can activate the Read Only mode option. This option allows you to view a drawing but doesn't let you save any changes you make to the drawing. If, after opening a drawing in Read Only mode, you decide that you want to edit the drawing and save the revised version, you can enter **dwgwrite** at the command line and set its value to 1. This cancels the effect of opening the drawing in Read Only mode and allows you to save the changes you make to the drawing.

Ending a Drawing Session

Choose Exit... from the File menu to close your drawing file and terminate AutoCAD. If you have made changes to your drawing and haven't yet saved them, AutoCAD displays the Save Changes dialog discussed earlier. Select the appropriate button to save your changes, discard your changes or cancel the Exit command.

If you have been working in a new, unnamed drawing and you click on the Yes button, the Save As dialog appears so that you can name your drawing before AutoCAD terminates.

Using Drawings From Earlier AutoCAD Versions

AutoCAD Release 13 can read drawing files from Release 12 and earlier, but older AutoCAD versions cannot read drawing files saved with Release 13.

If you need to save your drawing in AutoCAD Release 12 format you can enter the command SAVEASR12 at the command line. Note that R13 information in your drawing will be lost when it is saved in R12 format.

The File Dialog Box

Many commands require you to enter a file name. File dialog boxes for this purpose vary somewhat from command to command but share many common features. Figure 2-15 shows the Select Slide File dialog, which is remarkably similar to the Select File dialog that we discussed earlier.

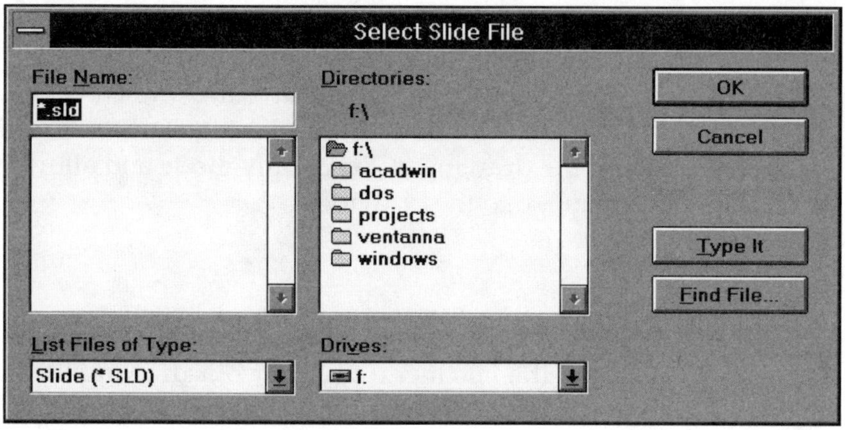

Figure 2-15: The Select Slide File dialog.

At the top-left of the dialog is the File Name field. This contains the display pattern for the file list box below. For example, if *.SLD is in the File Name field, only files with the extension .SLD are displayed.

If the pattern is changed to M*.SLD, only files whose names begin with *M* and end in *.SLD* are displayed. Below the file list box is the List Files of Type list. Clicking in this list displays a list of file types commonly used by AutoCAD. Figure 2-16 shows this list displayed under the Select Slide File dialog. You can quickly change from a list of slide files to a list of drawing files by selecting file types from this list. Note that even though you can list and select a drawing file from the Select Slide File dialog, AutoCAD will return an error because drawing files are not valid inputs to slide commands.

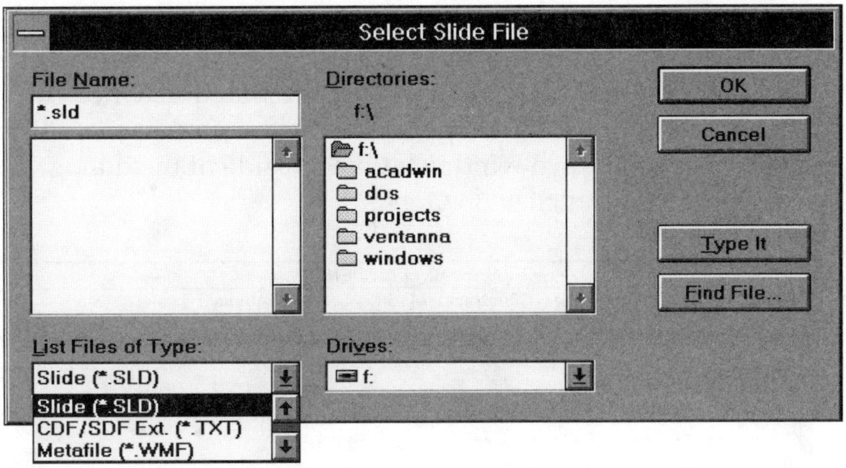

Figure 2-16: The List Files of Type list.

To the right of the file list box is the Directories list box. This list displays the directories available on the current drive. Each directory is displayed as an icon of a small file folder. The current directory and any of its parent directories are displayed as open folders, while all others are displayed as closed folders. You select a folder to open by double-clicking its icon. Selecting directories above and to the left of the current directory moves you up the directory tree toward the root directory. Selecting directories below and to the right of the current directory moves you deeper into the directory tree.

Below the Directories list box is the Drives list. Clicking in this list displays a list of all the drives accessible to your workstation. To make another drive active, click on its name in the list.

The scroll bars at the right edges of the Directories and File Name lists allow you to scroll up and down to see additional listings. You can click on the up arrow or the down arrow to scroll the listing one line at a time, or you can drag the slider box to quickly scroll through the entire list. Since the listings are alphabetized, you can also press the first letter of a directory or file name to immediately jump to that section of the list.

Once your desired file is highlighted, you can double-click on its name, press Enter or click on the OK button to accept the file.

If you are not sure where the file you want is located, click on the Find File... button on the right side of the dialog. This displays the Browse/Search dialog in Figure 2-17. The Browse/Search dialog lets you specify search parameters based on file name, file type, and time and date created. You can also instruct AutoCAD to search only specific directories or to search all drives accessible from your workstation. Once you click on the Search... button, AutoCAD performs the search that you specified and lists all the files found in a window at the left side of the dialog. You then select one of the files and click on Open.

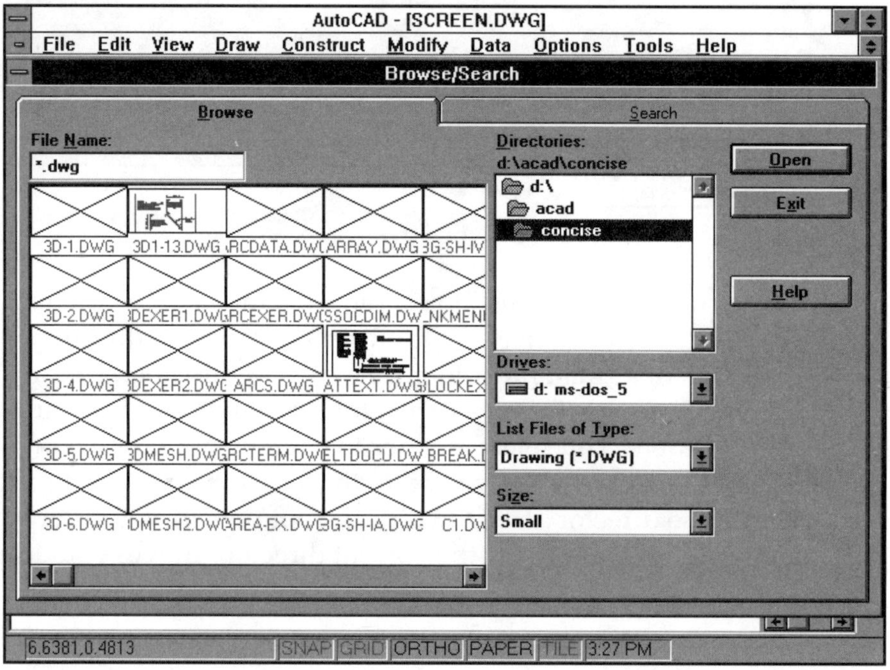

Figure 2-17: The Browse/Search dialog.

Finally, if you really prefer to type the name of your file, click on the Type It button in the Select Slide File dialog. This will hide the file dialog and allow you to type the full path and file name on the command line.

Choosing Prototype Drawings

Prototype drawings are used as the basis for new drawings. Any drawing can serve as a prototype. It can be empty, it can have a border and title block, or it can include settings for limits, grid, snap, layers, etc. It can reside anywhere on disk. You can edit prototype drawings just as you edit any other drawing (for more on these drawings, see Chapter 17, "Understanding Limits & Prototype Drawings").

You choose a prototype drawing when specifying a new drawing file. The prototype controls are found in the top of the Create New Drawing dialog shown in Figure 2-18.

When you first install AutoCAD, you are asked to specify a default prototype drawing as part of the configuration process. If you specified a default, that file name will appear in the field to the right of the Prototype button in the Create New Drawing dialog. The prototype controls include two optional check boxes. The first check box is No Prototype. Selecting this check box instructs AutoCAD to create a completely empty, untouched file. The second option is Retain as Default, which instructs AutoCAD to continue using your selected prototype as the permanent default.

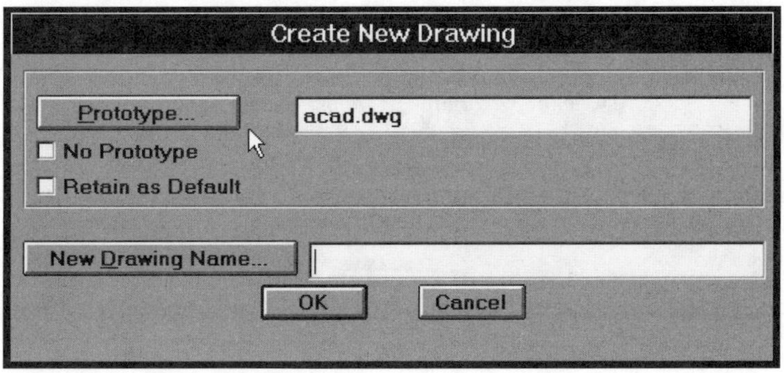

Figure 2-18: The Create New Drawing dialog and its prototype controls.

There are a number of ways that you can select other files to use as a prototype. The two most common methods are described below.

First, with the Create New Drawing dialog onscreen, you can click on Prototype to display the Prototype Drawing File dialog box. Then you can pick a prototype drawing from the list.

Second, you can type its name directly in the prototype blank in the Create New Drawing dialog box. This method only works if the prototype can be found in AutoCAD's search path. It is much better to use the first method.

The ABOUT Command & ACAD.MSG File

The ABOUT command displays the AutoCAD banner and the ACAD.MSG file, as shown in Figure 2-19. The banner contains six lines of basic information about your software, including the AutoCAD version and serial number. These are the same six lines that appear in the graphics window when you start AutoCAD.

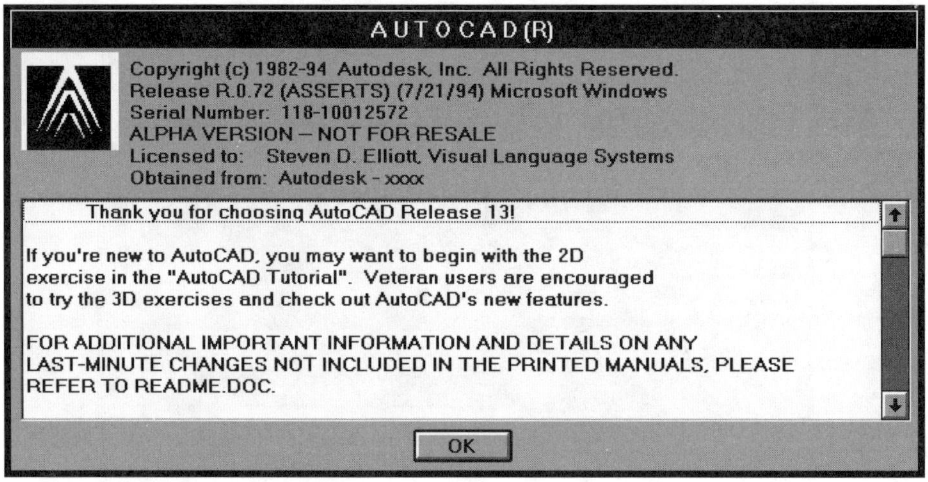

Figure 2-19: The About dialog.

The ACAD.MSG file is displayed in a scrolling window underneath the banner. This file is located on the \ACADR13\SUPPORT directory under the directory holding your AutoCAD program files. You can click on the up or down arrows or move the slider box to scroll the file.

When you first install AutoCAD, the ACAD.MSG contains a brief introductory greeting from Autodesk. It is a standard ASCII text file that you can erase or modify with a text editor. If you have text information that you want readily available while you are drawing, consider placing it in the ACAD.MSG file so you can display it simply by entering **about**.

Configuring & Reconfiguring AutoCAD

This book assumes that AutoCAD is already configured and running on your system. When you first run AutoCAD, the configuration procedure runs automatically. However, from time to time you will change a device such as a digitizer or printer and will need to reconfigure AutoCAD. The

CONFIG command does this. When you enter **config** at the command prompt, a listing of the current configuration is displayed. Press Enter, and a menu appears to let you set up AutoCAD to use a different video display, digitizer, plotter or printer plotter. You can also set certain operating defaults.

To use the CONFIG command as described above, you must be able to enter the drawing editor. If something prevents that, you can go directly to the Configuration menu by altering the command line entry for the AutoCAD program icon as follows.

1. Click on the AutoCAD icon to select it and choose Properties… from the Program Manager File menu.

2. In the Command Line field, add **-r** to the end of the line. Your command line entry should now look something like this:
C:\ACADR13\WIN\ACAD.EXE -R.

3. Click on OK and double-click the icon to start AutoCAD. You will now be taken immediately to the Configuration menu rather than to the drawing editor window.

After reconfiguring AutoCAD, be sure to remove the -R from the command line field.

Another, possibly easier, technique is to simply delete the ACAD.CFG file. The next time that you start AutoCAD you will automatically go through the configuration process.

You will find a complete discussion of configuration in the *AutoCAD Interface, Installation, and Performance Guide.*

Setting User Preferences

Once you have configured AutoCAD and are in the drawing editor, you can further control AutoCAD's behavior through the Preferences command. Choose Preferences… from the Options menu to see the Preferences dialog shown in Figure 2-20. See Chapter 40, "Customizing AutoCAD," for more on the Preferences settings; also refer to the *AutoCAD Interface, Installation, and Performance Guide.*

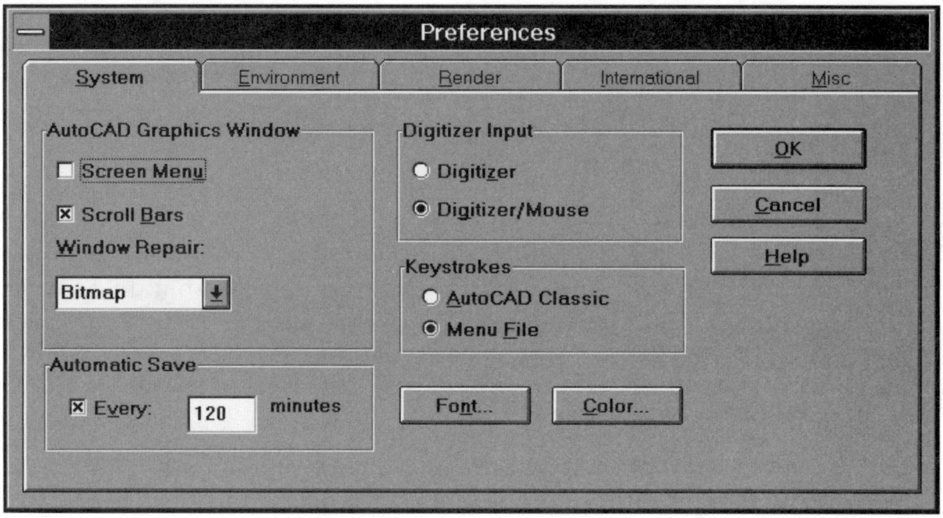

Figure 2-20: The Preferences dialog.

Reinitializing AutoCAD

If you sometimes run programs in a DOS window, use other software that alters the display or I/O ports, or edit your ACAD.PGP file, you may need to reinitialize your system. Use the REINIT command to reread or restart parts of AutoCAD that may not be functioning properly. This command displays the Re-initialization dialog shown in Figure 2-21.

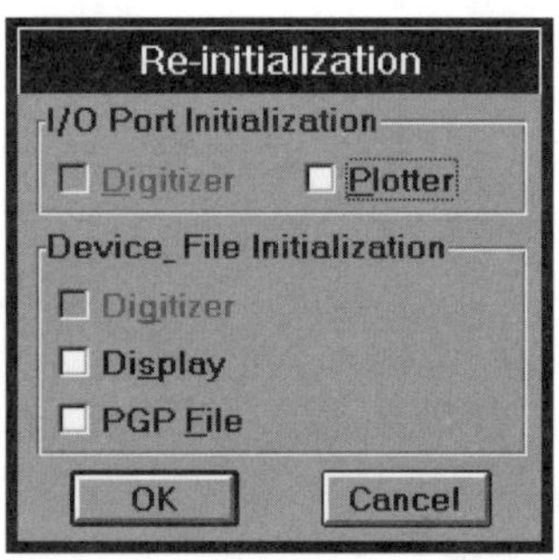

Figure 2-21: The Re-initialization dialog.

When you choose Re-initialize... from the Tools menu, or enter **reinit** at the command prompt, a dialog box appears to let you select one or more of the following check boxes: Digitizer port, Plotter port, Digitizer, Display or ACAD.PGP file. When you click on OK, the selected items will be reinitialized.

Obviously, if your pointing device or display is not functioning properly, it may be difficult to use the Re-initialization dialog. In that case you can also reinitialize by entering **re-init** at the command prompt (notice the hyphen between RE and INIT). When prompted for the new value, enter **31** to reinitialize all of the areas listed above.

Moving on

This chapter showed you how to start AutoCAD and create or load drawing files. You also learned about various ways to save your files and received a brief overview of AutoCAD's configuration.

Chapter 3, "In the Drawing Editor," introduces you to AutoCAD's drawing editor. You'll familiarize yourself with AutoCAD's user interface, the coordinate systems and the command structure.

In the Drawing Editor

The drawing editor is the heart of AutoCAD. When you start AutoCAD, you're placed there, to create and revise drawing geometry. When you run AutoCAD, you're almost always in the drawing editor.

The looks of the drawing editor have changed in Release 13, which features the addition of many Windows-style GUI elements. For example, there are now 50 *toolbars*—sets of picture icons from which you can activate commands or display *flyout* toolbars with additional choices.

You may access the same features in various ways:

Through the toolbar icons.

Through menus that you "pull down" just long enough to make a selection.

Through commands entered at the command line, as AutoCAD users have traditionally done. But now the command line appears in a floating command window that can be moved and resized on your screen.

Through an optional, more traditional "screen menu" that you can keep onscreen.

This chapter provides the basic information you need to use the drawing editor. It begins by describing the screen organization. It then covers data entry and how to use the screen elements such as toolbars, command prompts, icons, dialog boxes and menus.

Later, Chapter 40, "Customizing AutoCAD," provides a more in-depth view of these features as you become an advanced user.

The AutoCAD Screen

Figure 3-1 shows the parts of the Release 13 screen and its setup. The main central section, referred to as the drawing editor, is where you'll create your drawings.

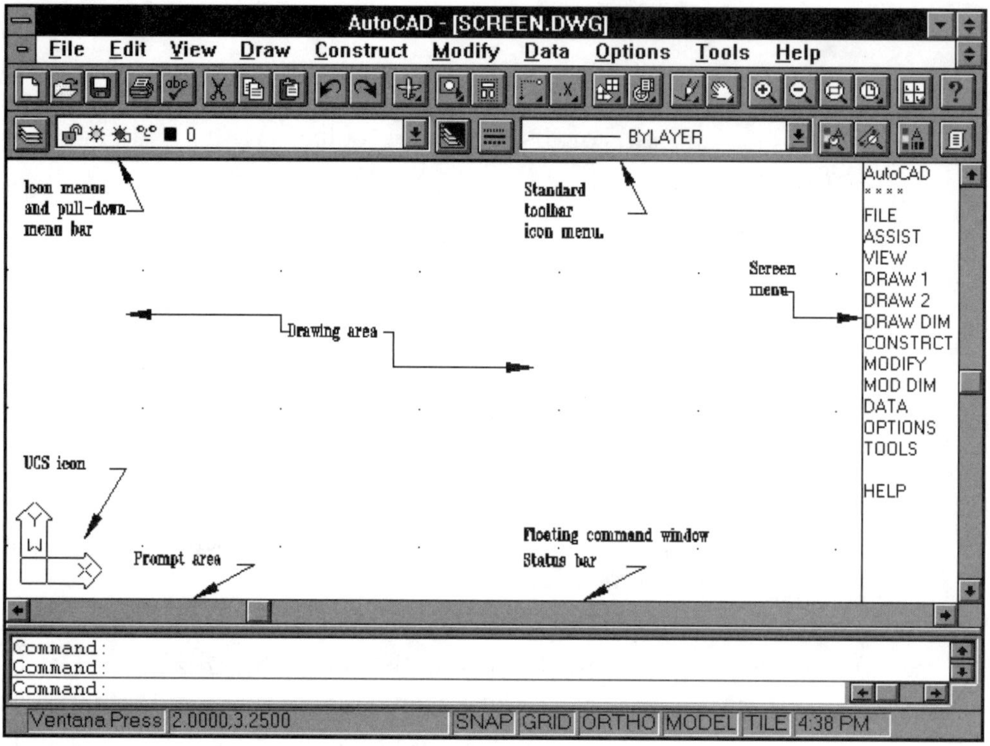

Figure 3-1: Elements of the AutoCAD screen: the menu bar, standard toolbar, drawing area, UCS icon, floating command prompt window and status bar. The picture also shows the more traditional "screen" menu at right, which is by default turned off.

The Title Bar

The title bar at the very top of the screen shows the program name (AutoCAD) and the name of your current drawing.

The Menu Bar

Below the title bar is the menu bar. The labels that appear across the menu bar are the titles of pull-down menus. By clicking on the title, you can pull down a menu and click on an item to select it. When you select a menu item that's followed by an ellipsis (...), AutoCAD displays a dialog box from which you can make further entries or selections. If the menu item is followed by a forward arrow (>), a submenu appears. If the menu item has neither an ellipsis nor a forward arrow, it directly activates an AutoCAD command.

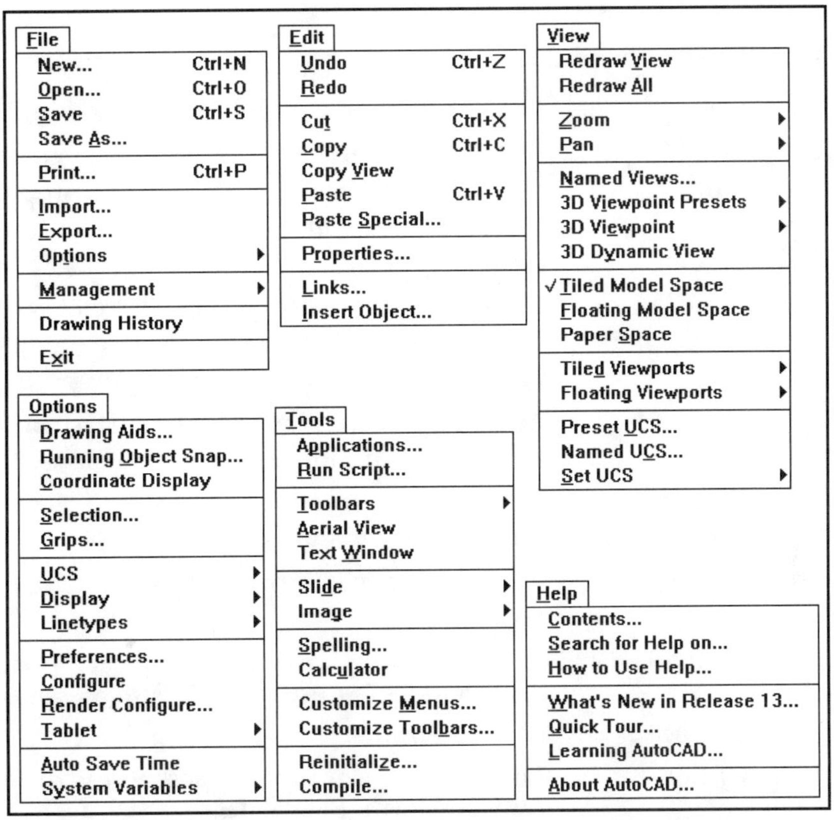

Figure 3-2: Selections on the standard Release 13 pull-down menus.

The menu bar in Figure 3-1 (on the preceding page) includes three options that do not appear on the menu bar that AutoCAD displays when first installed. But these options—the Draw, Construct and Modify pull-down menus—are available, and they offer you added flexibility in issuing AutoCAD's commands.

To display this version of the menu bar (which is named Acadfull), just enter **menu** at the command line (located in the floating command prompt window at the bottom of your screen). Then use your mouse or digitizer to select Acadfull in the dialog box that appears.

To switch back to the simpler menu bar, enter **menu** and select Acad.

NOTE: *You may wish to display Acadfull now, since the hands-on exercises that appear in chapters 44 and 45 use these three menus.*

Briefly, the pull-downs have the following purposes:

File	Provides options for creating, saving and otherwise managing files.
Edit	Lets you undo commands, edit the properties of objects in a drawing—for example, cut, copy and paste objects—and set up variables.
View	Controls coordinate systems and views of the drawing. For example, you may use the menu's options to zoom in and out and to set up viewports.
Draw	Lets you draw any object, use surface and solid commands and put in text and dimensions.
Construct	Provides construction options such as mirror, copy, offset, chamfer and fillet.
Modify	Provides ways to move, rotate, stretch, trim and edit objects.
Data	Lets you set up variables for object creation, such as units, layers, multiline style, dimension style and drawing limits.
Options	Lets you set user preferences, access drawing aids and configure AutoCAD.
Tools	Activates toolbars and lets you hide, shade or render 3D objects and create images.

NOTE: *The screen menu, shown at the right side of the drawing screen in Figure 3-1, is by default turned off; however, you can display it by checking the Screen option in the Preferences System dialog, as described in Chapter 40.*

Using the Standard Toolbar

The standard, out-of-the-box icon toolbar is an important feature of AutoCAD Release 13 for Windows. In keeping with other graphical user interface environments and industry standards, it resembles other Windows-based software applications, such as Microsoft's Excel, Powerpoint and Word for Windows.

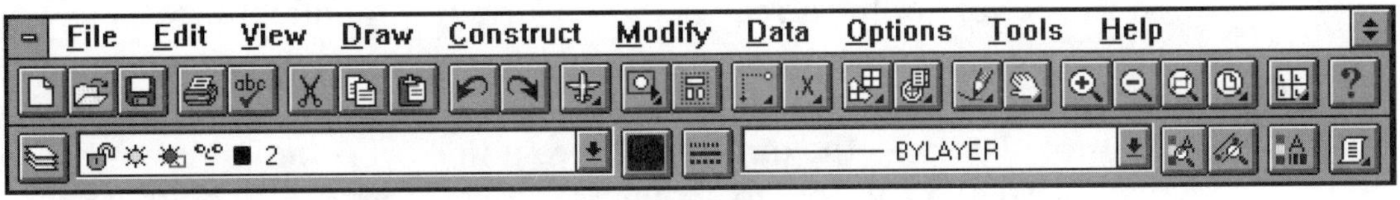

Figure 3-3: The Standard Release 13 toolbar.

New with Release 13, the toolbar contains icons you can click to activate editing and drawing management functions. From left to right, the 25 icons allow you to do the following:

Start a new drawing.

Open a drawing.

Save a drawing.

Plot a drawing.

Spell-check text.

Cut, copy and paste.

Undo and redo commands.

Move into an aerial view window.

Select objects.

Choose an object group or an object snap.

Set the coordinate system.

Select a view.

Redraw the screen.

Pan, zoom in or out or choose a zoom option.

Enter Paper Space.

Access the help window and on-line help screen.

Choosing Tools and then Toolbar lets you access the Standard Toolbar and many other icon toolbars within the Toolbars dialog box. Chapter 40, "Customizing AutoCAD," provides a more in-depth view of these features, with a look at icon customization and window controls.

Floating Command Window

At the bottom of the screen is the floating command window. Here, you may type in commands as an alternative to clicking an icon or making a menu selection. As a default, AutoCAD displays three lines of "command prompt history"—the three most recent lines of commands entered. You may resize the window to show more, or you may click on the scroll bar at its right edge to scroll up or down through the history.

UCS Icon

In the default ACAD drawing, the User Coordinate System (UCS) icon appears in the lower-left corner of the drawing area. The icon lets you tell at a glance which coordinate system is in effect: the World Coordinate System (if a *W* appears in the icon, as in Figure 3-1) or a coordinate system created by the user (see Chapter 30, "Coordinate Systems," for details). You can remove the UCS icon by entering **ucsicon** at the command line, and then **off**.

NOTE: *When certain editing tools are activated, AutoCAD also displays an aperture box (or pickbox) on the crosshairs. The crosshairs appear, for example, when you are using object snap or grip mode.*

Entering Data

You will often have to type in data in response to a prompt or to enter a command using the keyboard.

Text

Although commands are referred to in uppercase letters in this book, you may use upper- or lowercase letters for anything you type in AutoCAD.

If you've mistyped information and want to correct it, use the Backspace key to return to the mistaken character, then continue typing.

To cancel all characters when using the command line AutoCAD, press Esc (the Escape key). To cancel all characters in a dialog box, position the cursor at one end of the line and then press and hold the mouse pick button while dragging across the offending characters. Then you can simply type in new information to replace the old. Or cancel the dialog with the Esc key.

Using the Spacebar

Pressing the Enter key signals AutoCAD to execute the command you've typed or to accept the data you've entered. As alternatives, you can send the same signal by

Pressing the Spacebar.

Pressing the left mouse button or button 2 on your digitizer.

Naturally, when you enter text (within the TEXT, DIM, ATTDEF commands, etc.), the Spacebar works in the usual way.

Cartesian Coordinates

In the basic 2D X-Y construction plane, you input 2D coordinates as X and then Y values, separated by a comma but no spaces: **x,y**. The lower-left corner of the screen is set to 0,0 in the standard Cartesian coordinate system (see Figure 3-4). A more advanced coordinate system, which lets you place an X-Y construction plane anywhere in space, is described in Chapter 30, "Coordinate Systems."

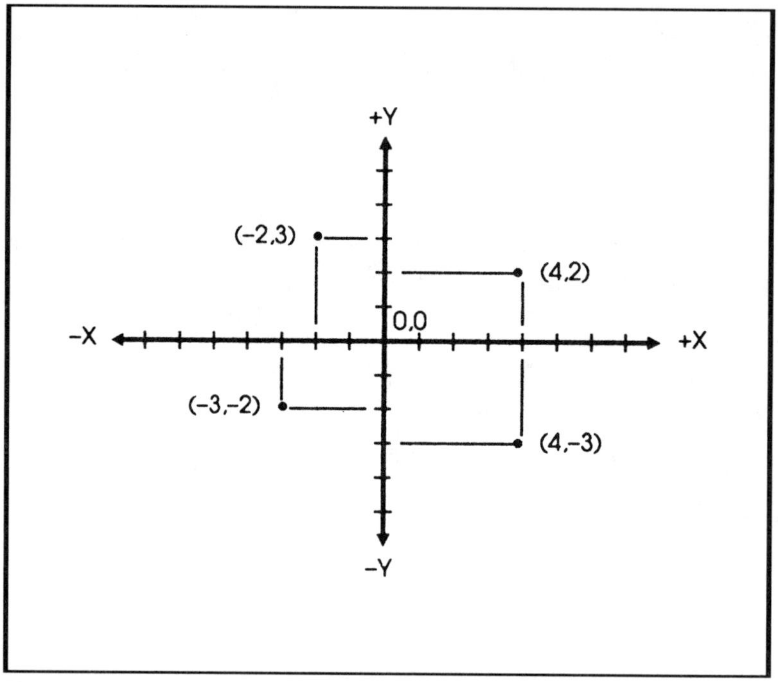

Figure 3-4: Default drawing area quadrants.

Although you can draw in any of the four quadrants, the upper-right quadrant is the default drawing area. Thus, 0,0 is located in the lower-left corner of the screen, and all locations have positive coordinates. (See "LIMITS" in Chapter 4, "Setup," for other setup options.)

2D Coordinate Points

A prompt will often ask you to locate a point. You can do so either by entering the point's coordinates at the keyboard or by moving the pointer to the desired position and pressing the pick button. Whenever you enter points from the keyboard, you must type in both the X and Y coordinates (X first) and separate the coordinates with a comma (no spaces) like this: **3.75,2.125**.

3D Coordinate Points

For 3D points, AutoCAD requires three coordinates (X,Y,Z) separated by commas but no spaces. If you only enter an X,Y coordinate point, AutoCAD automatically assumes the third coordinate is 0 (zero).

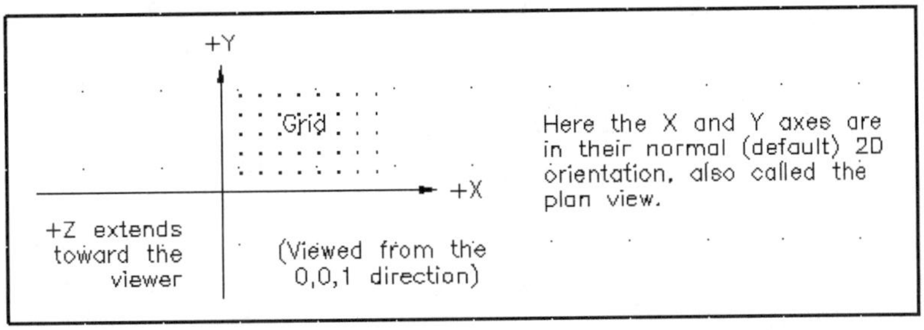

Figure 3-5: Entering 3D coordinates.

Angles

The standard conventions for angles are described below.

Angles are normally measured from the positive X direction.

Positive angles normally revolve counterclockwise.

Negative angles revolve clockwise.

Use polar coordinates to enter angles. For example, suppose you enter the LINE command and start from point 1,1, and you wish to place the next point 2 units away in a vertical direction. To do this, you would enter **@2<90**. The @ symbol tells AutoCAD to start from the last known pick point (in this case, 1,1). The 2 is the distance, and <90 indicates an angle of 90 degrees.

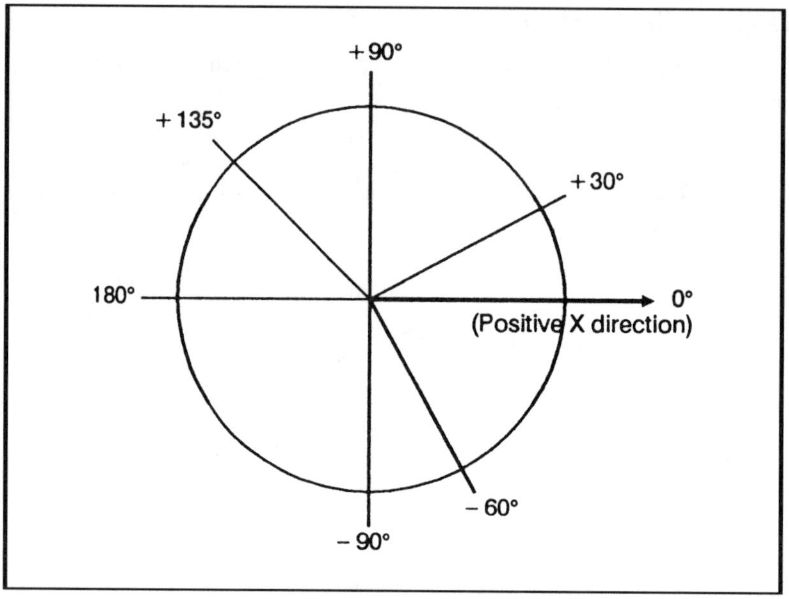

Figure 3-6: Default angle orientation.

However, you can select any angle as the zero-angle, and you can select either counterclockwise or clockwise as positive rotation (see "UNITS" in Chapter 4).

Entering AutoCAD Commands

You can enter AutoCAD commands in several different ways. Through the graphical user interface you may choose an icon, a pull-down menu or a dialog box. You may also use the keyboard. And, depending on your platform configuration, you may pick from a screen menu or from a tablet menu.

Object Properties Toolbar

Directly beneath the Standard toolbar is the Object Properties toolbar (see Figure 3-3). At far left is the Layer icon, which you click to create, select or rename a layer of your drawing. In the drop-down list field to its right, AutoCAD displays pictures that represent properties associated with the layer. You can click on the down arrow to list all of the drawings layers and associated properties; from this list, you can also select a different layer to work on.

In the center of the toolbar are icons for controlling color and linetype.

Completing the Object properties toolbar are the following:

The linetype control drop-down, which lets you display and select linetypes by object type.

The Object Creation Modes icon, which lets you set up color, layer and text style for a current object.

The Multiline style icon.

The Properties icon, which displays the Modify dialog and lets you modify a selected object's properties.

The List icon, used to display database information about selected objects.

Status Bar

At the bottom of the screen is the status bar. You can display the status bar in a number of ways. First, as your cursor passes over an icon or a menu item, the labels disappear (gray out); and help text appears to advise you on its use. Try moving your cursor pointer to any icon in the Toolbar, and you'll see a short, single-sentence explanation of that chosen icon in the status bar. Isn't that elegant?

Figure 3-7: The status bar, beneath the command window.

Second, separate horizontal label areas display numerical and angular coordinate data as well as on/off parameters for snap, grid, ortho, Model/Paper Space and tilemode status. If you double-click in any of the label areas of the status bar, the function of your choice turns on or off. Alternatively, you may use the functions keys to this effect, as described under "Function Keys" later in this chapter.

The status bar also displays the time.

In the Floating Command Window

The command prompt at the bottom of the screen has been an integral part of AutoCAD, but the three-line floating command window is a new feature. When you use the keyboard to enter coordinates, angles or text, this is the area you view as you enter the commands and await AutoCAD's display prompts and messages. The window is resizeable, and you can scroll through it.

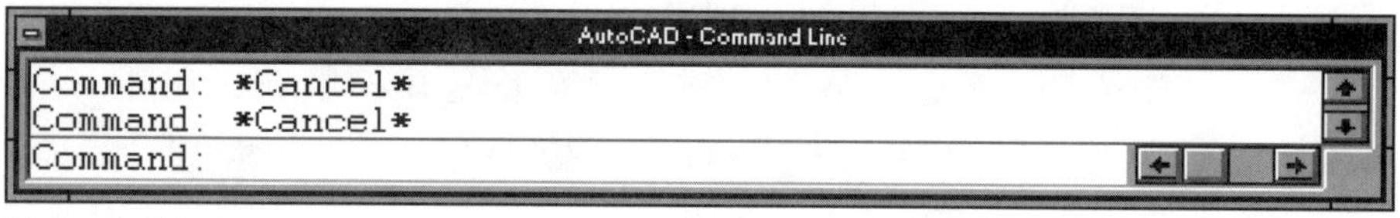

Figure 3-8: The floating command window.

If you want to use the keyboard, you may type the command in uppercase or lowercase letters at the keyboard, and then press Enter. Be sure that you're in *command mode* before you enter a command. Command mode is active whenever you're in the drawing editor and the command prompt is displayed.

NOTE: If you're using the side screen menu you can enter any command from the keyboard as long as you're in command mode. It doesn't matter what page of the screen menu is currently showing. (See "Preferences" later in the chapter on how to activate the screen menu.) You can return to command mode at any time by pressing Esc.

Most users choose to leave the floating command window at its default location. But you may float the window to any area of screen you choose. To do so, click in the naming bar across the top of the window and hold down the button as you drag the window to another location. Then release the mouse or digitizer button.

Displaying Command History

To scroll through the command history, click on the up and down arrows in the scroll bar at right. You can also resize the floating command window.

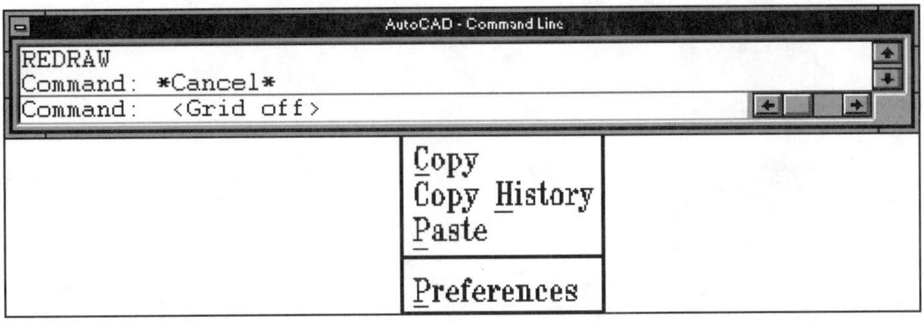

Figure 3-9: The command prompt "cursor" pull-down menu.

You can click in the floating command window to display the "history" cursor menu, which offers the following options.

Copy	Use this option to copy selected text (text that you have highlighted) to the Windows Clipboard (for example, to insert it into a script file).
Copy History	Use this option to copy the entire history to the Clipboard.
Paste	Choose Paste to paste the copied text to another location in the command history.
Preferences	Displays the Preferences dialog, which lets you set preferences about the system environment (for details, see Chapter 40, "Customizing AutoCAD").

Floating Toolbars & Flyouts

Floating toolbars contain icons used to activate commands and related tools. Out-of-the-box, AutoCAD provides the Draw and Modify floating toolbars.

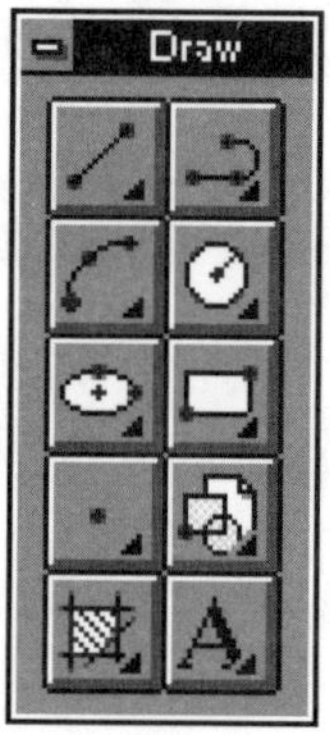

Figure 3-10: A floating toolbar.

As toolbars are activated, you can place them to the side or float them in the drawing editor. Rows and columns can be resized in numerous width/height combinations, such as 1 x12, 2 x 6 or 3 x 4. They can be hidden when you have finished the task.

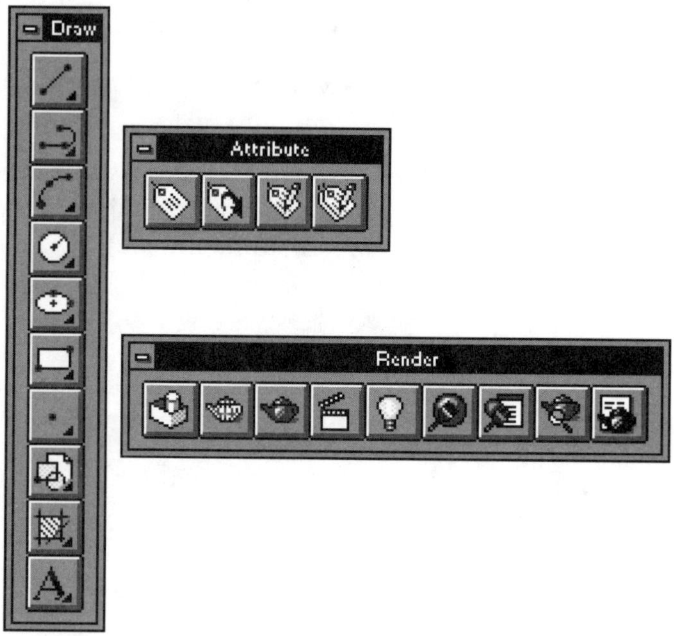

Figure 3-11: Three typical configurations for a toolbar.

Flyout toolbars supplement functions on the floating toolbars, providing further access to related tools. Take the LINE command, for example. Typically, it includes an extra set of icons as three attached tools of ENDpoint, INTersection and MIDpoint flyouts.

Figure 3-12: A flyout toolbar.

Not all commands have flyouts. If an icon has an arrow in the lower-right corner (pointing diagonally to the right), it has a flyout. To access the tools of a flyout, position your pointer on the icon, hold down the pick button and drag along the flyout. The available tools then pop up. Release the button when you reach your choice.

Pull-down Menus

To display the pull-down menu bar, move the crosshairs into the status line at the top of the screen. Click on its title in the menu bar, and then make a selection.

Dialog Boxes

Dialog boxes appear onscreen when you select certain options from AutoCAD's standard pull-down menu and toolbar icons. They are explained in a separate section later.

More on Command Entry

The rest of this chapter explains aspects of AutoCAD command entry options that are common to most of the entry methods mentioned above.

Answering Prompts

After you enter a command, AutoCAD prompts you for more information to complete the command. Read these prompts carefully in the floating command window. The most recent prompt always appears on the bottom line of the prompt area, and the previous prompts scroll upward until they disappear. By reading this bottom line carefully, you'll know what AutoCAD expects you to do. In many cases, you can enter options from the keyboard, the screen menu, the tablet overlay or a dialog box. Remember, you can also scroll through your prompt history using the scroll bars.

Default responses appear in corner brackets *<like this>*. When these brackets contain numbers or letters, you may enter the default simply by pressing Enter. For example, if you use the SNAP command, AutoCAD displays a default of <1.000> in the floating command window. You may either accept the default of 1.000 or enter a different number.

When the brackets surround one of several options, AutoCAD expects you to enter information in response to that option, or to select one of the other options (usually by entering its first letter).

The Screen Menu

If you have activated a screen menu (the side menu), use your mouse pointer to pick the command from the menu that appears on the right side of the screen. If your screen menu is not activated, see "Preferences" later in the chapter on how to do so.

The screen menu contains two kinds of command items. Command menu items followed by a colon enter a command and call up a different page of the menu. Command menu items not followed by a colon merely call up a different page (submenu) of the menu. Some submenus occupy two pages. Notice that most screen menu items are in alphabetical order.

Tablet Menu Overlay

Use the pick button on the pointer to enter the command from a tablet menu overlay. Before you can use AutoCAD's standard tablet template, you must configure the digitizing tablet using the TABLET command. See Chapter 40, "Customizing AutoCAD." Also see "Standard Tablet Overlay" later in the chapter.

Dialog Boxes

Dialog boxes are another type of graphical user interface. They appear onscreen when you select certain *dynamic dialog*-style commands from AutoCAD's standard pull-down menu and icon toolbar. If a pull-down menu item is followed by ellipses (...), it leads to a dialog box.

The boxes are user friendly, allowing greater ease of use with multiple choice options. To save your settings in a dialog box, press the OK button. If you make a mistake, you may simply write over the mistake or press Esc or the Cancel button as an option and start again. Often, a dialog box has a second and sometimes a third dialog box layered below it. Press each OK button as you finish with each dialog box, or if you have no input press Esc to cancel out.

Commands that display dynamic dialogs from the command line begin with the letters ***dd***.

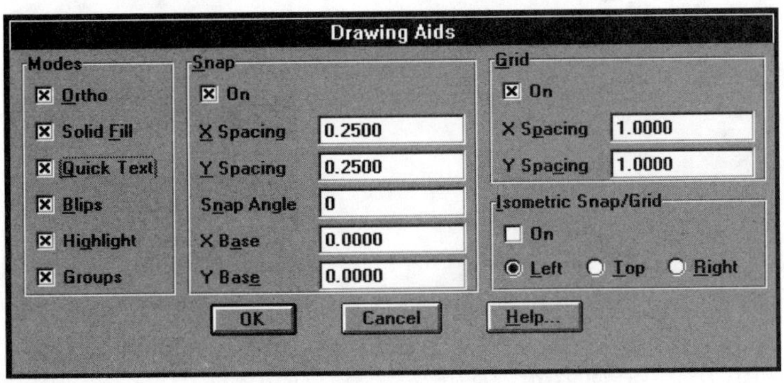

Figure 3-13: Typical dialog box.

You can repeat any command simply by pressing Enter (or the Spacebar or right mouse button) when you're in command mode. Also, you can type **multiple** before entering a command (for example, **multiple arc**). This repeats the arc command automatically until you either press Esc to stop the repetition or select another command from one of the menus.

Pointer Buttons

You can use a mouse or digitizing device to choose or activate commands. When you use the pointer (mouse or digitizer) to enter commands from the icon-bar menu, a screen menu, a tablet menu overlay, a pull-down menu or a dialog box, merely place the pointer at the appropriate location and press the pick button.

On a two-button mouse, the left button (button 1) is the pick button; it is used to make a selection. The right button (button 2) is like the Enter key; use it to enter the command or accept the entered data. Simultaneously press Shift and the right mouse button to display the cursor menu.

On four-button pointers (digitizers), the buttons are assigned as follows:

Button 1	Pick button (selects).
Button 2	Enter button.
Button 3	Displays the cursor menu.
Button 4	Cancel (same as Esc).

Figure 3-14: Pointer button numbers for a four-button puck.

When you use the pointer to enter a 3D point (three coordinates), the X and Y coordinates are taken from the position of the pointer, and the Z coordinate is taken from the current elevation. The default is usually 0 in the current UCS. (See "ELEV" in Chapter 32, "3D Objects," on how to set 3D elevations).

Function Keys

You can also use function keys to perform various tasks. In the Windows version of Release 13, the following are available:

F1	Displays the HELP window.
F2	Toggles between a full-screen text window and the drawing window.
F3	Is not used.
F4	Or Ctrl+T. Turns Tablet mode on or off after calibration.
F5	Or Ctrl+E. Toggles through isometric modes of top, right and left.
F6	Or Ctrl+D. Makes the coordinate display in the status line at the bottom of the screen active or inactive, or switches display from polar to rectangular coordinates, etc.
F7	Or Ctrl+G. Turns grid on or off.
F8	Or Ctrl+L. Turns ortho on or off.
F9	Or Ctrl+B. Turns snap on or off.

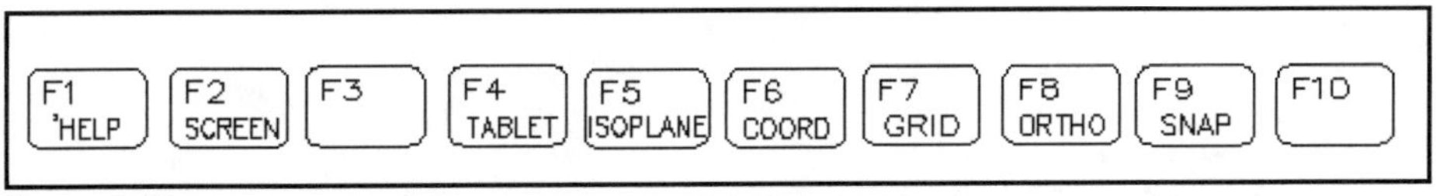

Figure 3-15: Function key uses for AutoCAD for Windows.

Other Ctrl key functions are as follows:

Ctrl+O	Open
Ctrl+P	Plot
Ctrl+A	Group
Ctrl+S	Quick save
Ctrl+C	Copy Clipboard
Ctrl+V	Paste Clipboard
Ctrl+N	New drawing
Ctrl+\	Cancel

The Cursor Menu

The cursor menu appears where your cursor is currently located when you click the right mouse button or Shift-Button 2. The cursor menu includes osnap modes and a submenu of point filters. (Both are explained later: object snap modes in Chapter 12, and point filters in Chapter 19).

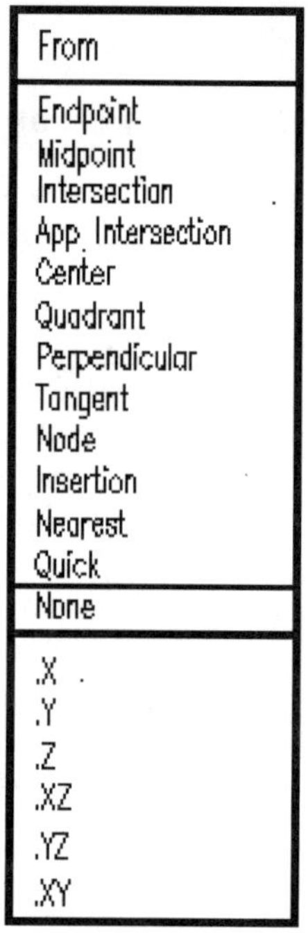

Figure 3-16: The cursor menu.

When you pick an item from the menu, the menu clears from the screen. You can also clear the menu by picking any point outside the menu. To customize this menu and the button that displays it, see Chapter 40.

If you display the cursor menu while working in the floating command window, a small history menu appears, as shown in Figure 3-17.

Figure 3-17: The history cursor menu.

The Standard Tablet Overlay

AutoCAD's standard tablet overlay contains four menu areas, shown in Figure 3-18:

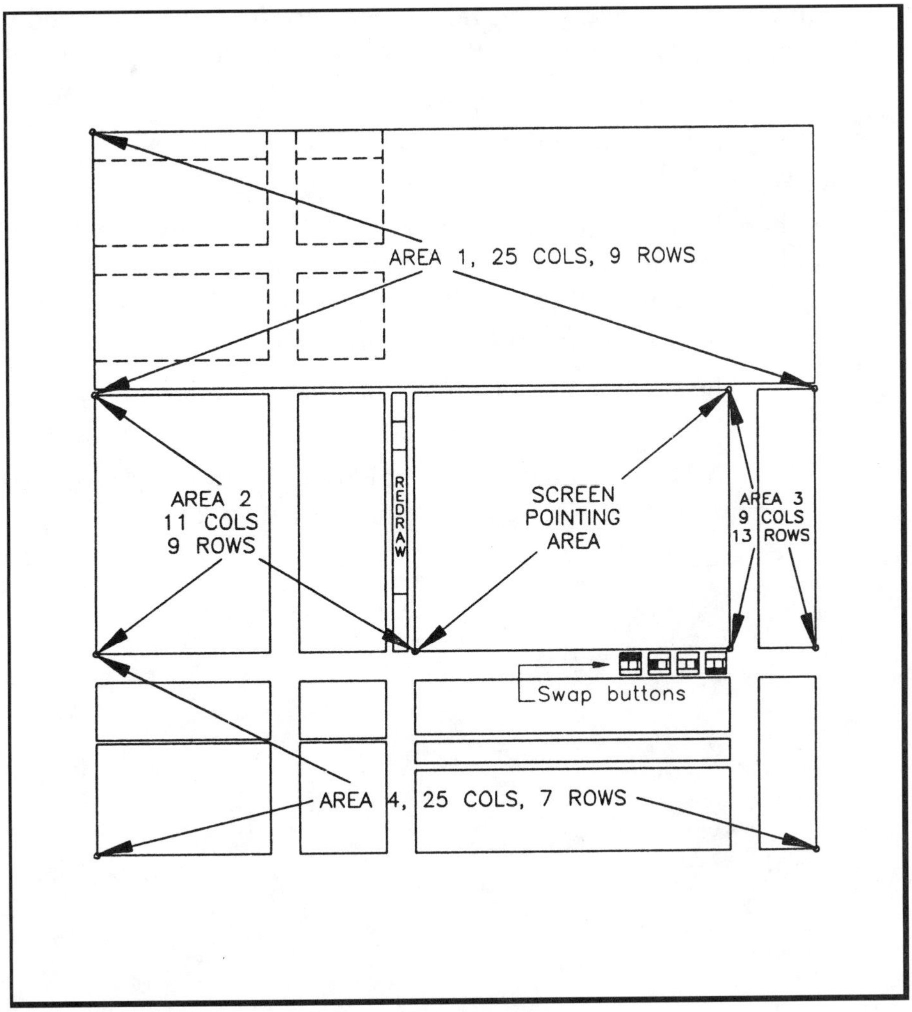

Figure 3-18: AutoCAD's standard tablet menu areas.

After the tablet overlay is secured to the digitizing tablet, it can be configured as follows:

At the command line, enter **tablet** and then **cfg**, and follow the prompts onscreen. For each of the four tablet menu areas, pick the points shown above and enter the number of columns and the number of rows. Then enter **y** to designate the screen pointing area and pick its lower-left and upper-right corners. This tablet menu configuration is saved with your configuration files rather than with the drawing.

When the standard tablet area 1 menu is operating, it is a blank menu area that you can customize as you like. Third-party developers use this area to customize their specific programs.

When the standard tablet area 2 menu is operating, the ZOOM and PAN commands are transparent when picked from the tablet. (They can be used in the middle of other commands.) Also, VPOINT and DVIEW switch temporarily to the World Coordinate System.

When the standard tablet area 3 menu is operating, the upper item in each cell is enabled.

When the standard tablet area 4 menu is operating, the osnap options in this part of the menu function as immediate overrides.

Displaying Online Help

Figure 3-19: The HELP icon.

You can display online help by choosing the HELP ? icon, pressing the F1 key or entering **help** at the command line. A Help information window appears which allows you to enter the name of a specific command or pick a command from a scrolling index.

If you enter **'help** (note the apostrophe) while you are in the middle of a command, the Help information window immediately displays information pertinent to that command. When you finish viewing the information and pick the EXit button, you may continue in the command you were using.

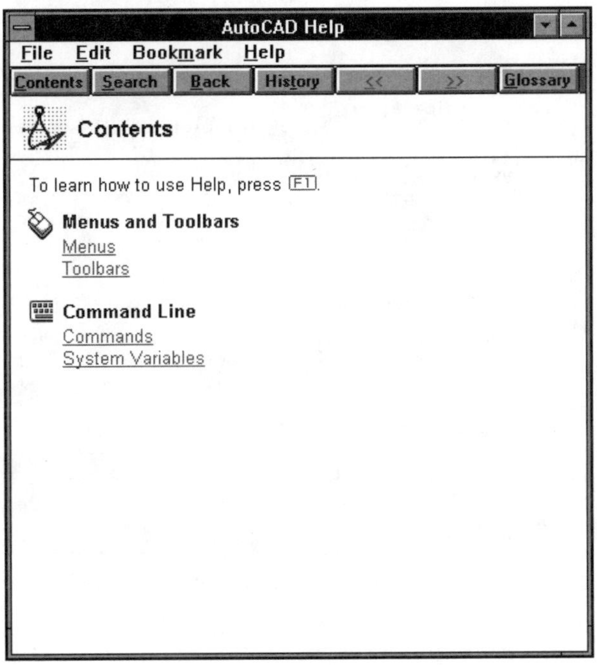

Figure 3-20: The HELP window.

Displaying Time-Related Statistics

Choose Time from the Data pull-down menu. In the text screen, AutoCAD displays time-related statistics including the current time, the time when the drawing was created and last updated, the total editing time, if an elapsed timer was switched on, and when the next automatic save is due to be activated.

When prompted, you may enter

d to update the display.

on to turn the elapsed timer on.

off to turn the elapsed timer off.

r to reset the elapsed timer to 0.

To return to command mode, press Esc, press Enter or click in the AutoCAD window.

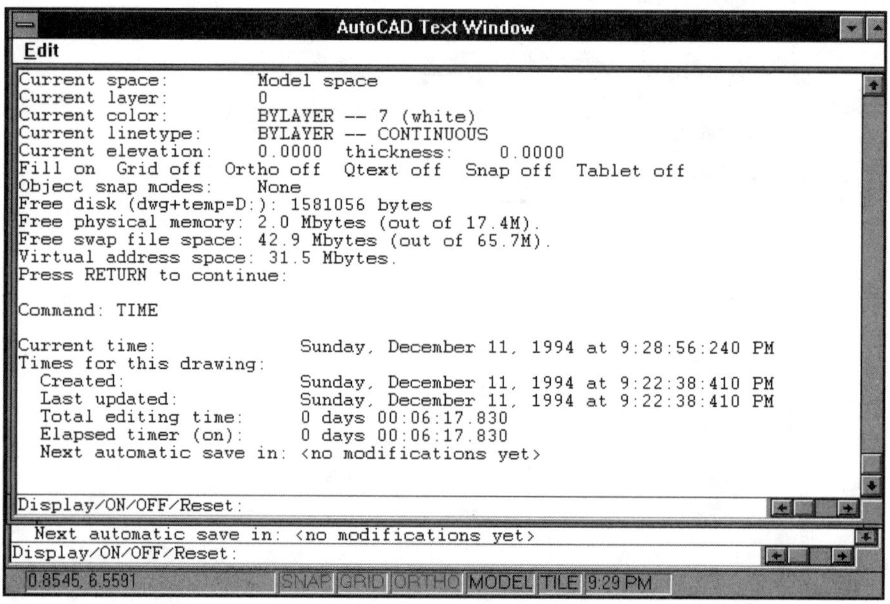

Figure 3-21: Time-related statistics in the AutoCAD Text Window.

Turning on Auto Save

You can have AutoCAD automatically save your drawing periodically by activating SAVETIME. To do so, choose Auto Save Time from the Options pull-down menu (or, at the command line, enter **savetime** and then enter a number of minutes).

The SAVETIME command is preset to <120>. Simply enter a new number such as 15, and your drawing is automatically saved every 15 minutes.

If you have named the drawing you are working on, it is saved as a named drawing file. If you have not named it, it uses the AUTO.SV$ naming as an option. You may also set the savetime feature through the "Preferences" dialog. See "Setting User Preferences" later in the chapter.

Loading a Menu

At the command line, enter **menu**. When prompted, enter the name of the menu file. Do not include the extension .MNU or .MNX. If the file hasn't been compiled, AutoCAD will compile the .MNU file and create a new file with the same name but with extension .MNX.

When you save a drawing, the name of the most recently used menu file is saved with that drawing. The next time the drawing is edited, that menu file is loaded automatically, assuming it resides in the default directory or the directory with the AutoCAD program files. You can also access and activate the screen menu through the Preferences System dialog box. See "Setting User Preferences" below.

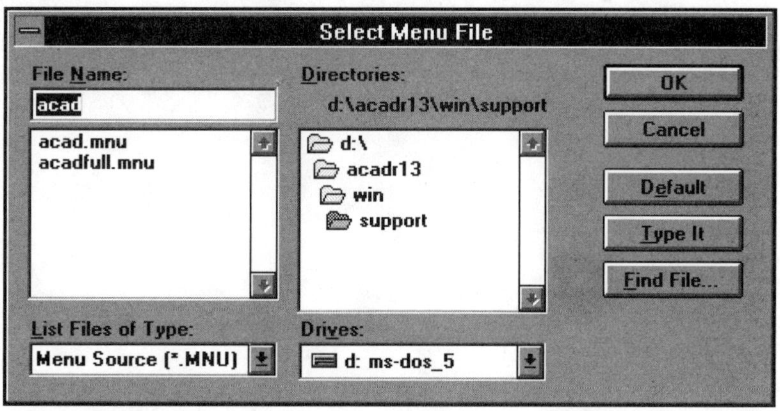

Figure 3-22: AutoCAD's menu dialog box.

Setting User Preferences

Think of Preferences as the equivalent of the Windows Program Manager, the way you set the environment for Windows. But in this instance you configure system and environment settings for AutoCAD to run optimally in Windows. Its settings simply inform AutoCAD where to find certain files and directories. AutoCAD will automatically configure its own operating environment and will not need to alter any settings.

To activate the Preferences dialog, choose Preferences from the Options pull-down menu (or, from the floating command window, click the right mouse button to display the history cursor menu and then select Preferences). You can change such settings through the Preferences dialog as described in Chapter 40, "Customizing AutoCAD."

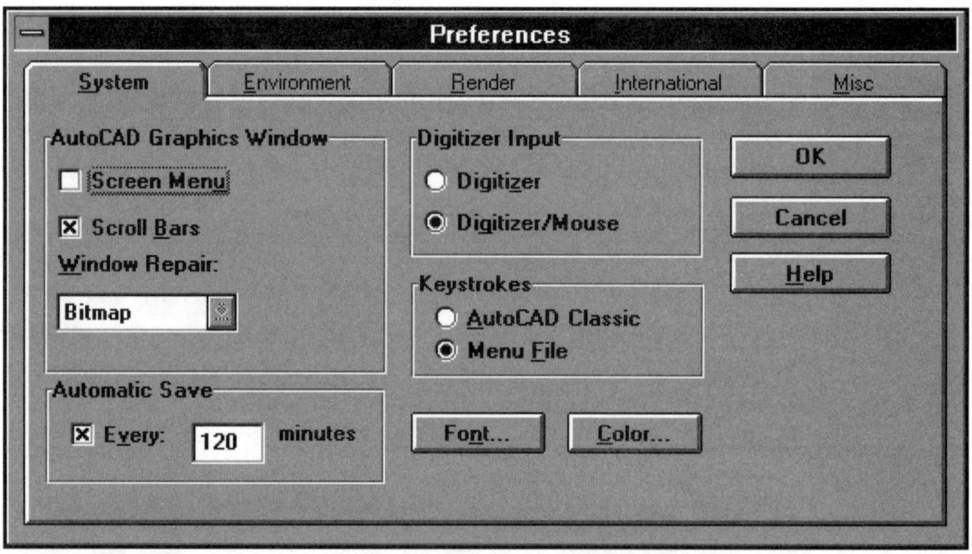

Figure 3-23: The Preferences dialog, with its five subdialogs.

Moving on

One of the most basic but often puzzling operations a new AutoCAD user has to understand is establishing paper size and drawing scale. In Chapter 4, "Setup," you'll look at how to set up a drawing for units, scale and limits.

Setup

Whether you draw on the board or with a computer, a certain amount of setup is required. On the board, that might include selecting a certain sheet size and a scale. In AutoCAD, it includes providing settings for units, limits, snap and grid. When you start AutoCAD it uses default settings from the ACAD.DWG file. This acts as a prototype drawing in order to let you start drawing.

For more information on setup, see Chapter 17, "Understanding Limits & Prototype Drawings." Also see the setup exercise in Chapter 44, "Hands-on Exercises."

UNITS Helps set up the drawing format

COMMAND LINE: **ddunits**

To set the format and precision for display of coordinates and angles, choose Units... from the Data pull-down menu. Figure 4-1 shows the Units Control dialog box.

Figure 4-1: The Units Control dialog box.

Setting up Linear Measurement

There are five formats for linear measurement: scientific, decimal, engineering, architectural and fractional.

1. Scientific
   To display: 1.8603E+03
   Enter: **1.8603E+03**

The base is always between 1 and 10, and the exponent following the E indicates how many places to move the decimal point to the right (positive) or left (negative).

2. Decimal
   To display: 14.375
   Enter: **14.375**

AutoCAD will also accept 14-3/8 entry format.

3. Engineering
   To display: 4'-2.75"
   Enter: **4' 2.75"** (no spaces, inch designator optional)

You may enter only feet and inches with decimal fractions. Numbers entered without a unit designator are assumed to be inches.

4. Architectural
   To display: 2-7 3/8"
   Enter: **2′7-3/8"** (no spaces, inch designator optional)

You may enter only feet and inches, with decimal fractions. Numbers entered without a unit designator are assumed to be inches. AutoCAD will also accept fractional feet, such as **12.5'**.

5. Fractional
   To display: 27 3/8
   Enter: **27-3/8** (no spaces)

Notice that only the engineering and architectural formats are locked into particular units of measure. The other three formats can be used with any unit of measure, such as microns, millimeters, inches, yards or miles. A metric engineering drawing would typically use the decimal format.

Setting up Angle Measurement

There are also five possible formats for angular measure:

1. Decimal degrees (360 degrees in a full circle)
   To display: 15.230
   Enter: **15.230**
2. Degrees-minutes-seconds (360 degrees in a full circle)
   Example: 15d13'48"
3. Grads (400 grads in a full circle)
   To display: 16.922g
   Enter: **16.922**
   1 grad = .9 degrees (exactly)
   1 degree = 1.111111 grads
4. Radians (2-times-pi radians in a full circle)
   To display: .26584
   Enter: **.2658**
   1 degree = .01745329 radians
   1 radian = 57.29578 degrees
5. Surveyor's units
   To display: N 74d46'12" E
   Enter: **N74d46'12"E**

AutoCAD lets you enter angles in a unit other than the unit set by the UNITS command. For example, while UNITS is set for degrees, you can enter an angle in radians or grads by placing **r** or **g** after the number, as in **1.2r** or **50g**.

You can also force units to be displayed in the same format you enter them by entering the system variable **unitmode** and setting its value to 1.

The zero-angle direction is normally to the right (east, or 3 o'clock), but you can set it to any other direction. Positive angles are normally measured counterclockwise, but you can set them to be measured clockwise.

You can alternate between the available linear formats, levels of precision and angular formats at any stage during the drawing process. For example, if you're using an angular zero-direction other than east, you can force decimal degrees, zero east, by using a double-angle symbol (as in **@3<<45**). Or you can use a triple-angle symbol to force zero east but retain current angular units (as in **@3<<<.07**, where the unit is radians).

When you save a drawing, the options you selected are saved with the drawing, so they'll be the same the next time you open and edit the drawing.

Setting Units Defaults

If you're a new user, here's an easy format for learning. Set up your units defaults as follows:

First, choose Units... from the Data pull-down menu to display the Units Control dialog box, shown in Figure 4-2.

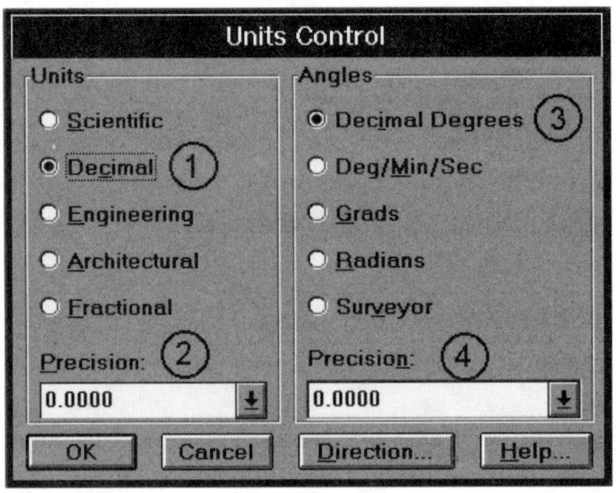

Figure 4-2: Setting units through the dialog box.

1. Click on the Decimal radio button for the decimal units format.

2. Click on the Units Precision pop-up list, and choose 4 decimal places of precision.

3. Click on the Decimal Degrees radio button for the decimal angle format.

4. Click on the Angle Precision pop-up list, and choose 4 decimal places of precision.

Now, click on the Direction button to display the Direction Control dialog, shown in Figure 4-3.

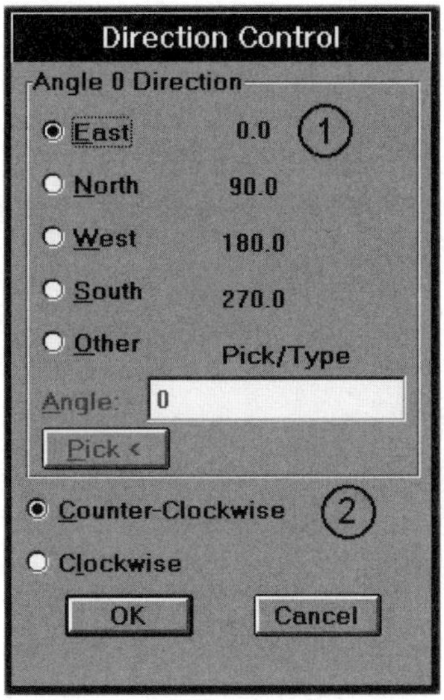

Figure 4-3: Setting your angle direction.

1. Click on the East radio button to orient the zero angle in the positive X direction (AutoCAD's standard 3 o'clock orientation).

2. Click on the Counter-Clockwise radio button so that positive angles will rotate counterclockwise.

3. Finally, click on the OK button to close the Direction Control dialog, and click on OK again to close the Units Control dialog.

Using & Setting Metric Units

Suppose you want to draw in millimeters rather than inches. Drawing in units other than inches is just as easy as drawing in inches—you don't need to convert every dimension. However, there are several things you should do.

Remember that when UNITS is set to scientific, decimal or fractional, AutoCAD doesn't use specific units such as inches, feet, miles or meters. It works only in pure units, which may represent any form of linear measure from inches to miles or microns to light-years.

If you're going to draw in millimeters, take these steps:

1. Reset the drawing aid values. For example:
SNAP 1 or .5 GRID 10

2. Reset the dimensioning variables that govern visual size to their metric equivalents (or set DIMSCALE to 25.4).

3. Set LTSCALE to approximately 25, and then adjust it as needed. If you've been using text styles with fixed heights, change their heights to the metric equivalents.

You can make these changes part of your metric prototype drawings. When you plot, select millimeters, then set the size of the plotting and the pen width to their appropriate values.

Blocks that were created in inches and then written to disk can easily be reused in a metric drawing. Simply insert them at a scale factor of 25.4.

LIMITS Sets the onscreen rectangular drawing area

COMMAND LINE: **limits**

You can set the rectangular drawing area and enable or disable the limits check by choosing Drawing Limits from the Data pull-down menu.

When prompted, enter the coordinates of the lower-left corner of the desired drawing area (often 0,0). Then enter the coordinates of the upper-right corner. Remember that you can enter the default values displayed in corner brackets simply by pressing Enter.

To enable or disable the limits check, enter **on** or **off**. When the limits check is on, AutoCAD won't let you enter points outside the limits.

If you've changed the limits and want to have the entire drawing area displayed on the screen, choose Zoom from the pull-down menu. Then choose A (for All). See "ZOOM" in Chapter 11, "Looking Around."

You can reset the limits any time while you're working on a drawing, without affecting any of the objects you've already drawn.

NOTE: *LIMITS uses separate settings for Model Space and Paper Space. See Chapter 31, "Model Space & Paper Space," and Chapter 32, "3D Objects."*

SETTING THE GRID Controls grid display

COMMAND LINE: **ddrmodes**

Choose Drawing Aids... from the Options pull-down menu. This displays the Drawing Aids dialog box, which contains controls for the grid display.

Figure 4-4 shows the Drawing Aids dialog with the cursor near the controls.

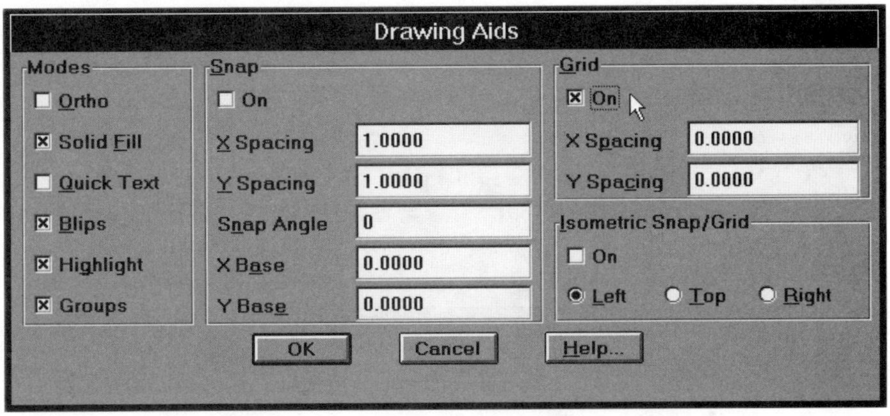

Figure 4-4: Controlling the grid through the Drawing Aids dialog.

The Drawing Aids dialog box lets you adjust the spacing of the visible grid and also turn the grid on or off. With it, you control the following grid features:

On — Activate this box to display a grid of dots in the drawing window according to the X and Y spacing.

X Spacing — Enter a number here to set the distance along the X-axis between grid dots. A value of zero sets the grid spacing equal to the Snap spacing (see "SNAP" in Chapter 5). Note that any entry you make in this field is automatically copied to the Y Spacing field. AutoCAD assumes that you want to use a square grid.

Y Spacing — If you want to create a rectangular grid, enter a value in the Y Spacing field that is different from the X Spacing value. Remember to set your X value first since it always replaces the Y value.

You can also quickly toggle the grid on and off by pressing function key F7 or by double-clicking the GRID field in the status bar at the bottom of the screen.

When grid is on, the grid displays only within the drawing limits. The rotation and style of this visible grid always match the rotation and style of the invisible snap grid. If the grid spacing is set at 0, it automatically adopts the snap spacing (see "SNAP" in Chapter 5).

STATUS Displays information about a drawing

COMMAND LINE: **status**

Choose Status from the Data pull-down menu to display a drawing's name, limits, actual space used, parameters and other statistics, as shown in Figure 4-5.

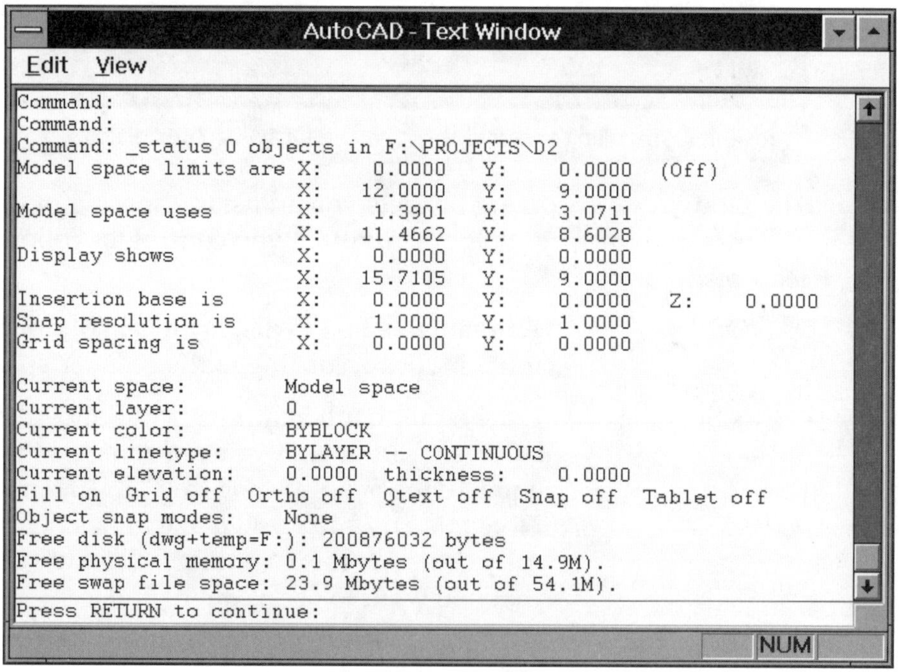

```
AutoCAD - Text Window
Edit  View
Command:
Command:
Command: _status 0 objects in F:\PROJECTS\D2
Model space limits are X:     0.0000    Y:     0.0000   (Off)
                       X:    12.0000    Y:     9.0000
Model space uses       X:     1.3901    Y:     3.0711
                       X:    11.4662    Y:     8.6028
Display shows          X:     0.0000    Y:     0.0000
                       X:    15.7105    Y:     9.0000
Insertion base is      X:     0.0000    Y:     0.0000    Z:     0.0000
Snap resolution is     X:     1.0000    Y:     1.0000
Grid spacing is        X:     0.0000    Y:     0.0000

Current space:         Model space
Current layer:         0
Current color:         BYBLOCK
Current linetype:      BYLAYER -- CONTINUOUS
Current elevation:     0.0000  thickness:     0.0000
Fill on  Grid off  Ortho off  Qtext off  Snap off  Tablet off
Object snap modes:     None
Free disk (dwg+temp=F:): 200876032 bytes
Free physical memory: 0.1 Mbytes (out of 14.9M).
Free swap file space: 23.9 Mbytes (out of 54.1M).
Press RETURN to continue:
NUM
```

Figure 4-5: Drawing status displayed in the Text Window.

Use the scroll bar at right to examine the information displayed in the scrolling Text Window. To return to the drawing, choose the Close box of the Text Window or click in any visible part of the drawing window.

Moving on

You're now prepared to draw with AutoCAD. You've named your drawing, chosen your drawing units, considered the size of the drawing area and established a planning grid.

The following chapters describe using AutoCAD's powerful drawing and editing commands. Chapter 5, "Points," starts you off.

CHAPTER 5

Points

AutoCAD has so many features that some of them may be confusing at first. If you're new to AutoCAD, you'd be wise to disable certain features so they won't distract you from the basics.

Before you begin drawing objects, you may want to disable both the UCS icon and the grips. The UCS icon appears by default in the lower-left corner of the screen editor. It's used primarily in 3D modeling and is discussed in Chapter 30, "Coordinate Systems." To turn it off, choose UCS from the Options pull-down menu, then choose Icon.

Grips provide an alternate method of editing objects and are discussed in Chapter 14, "Editing—Group One." To disable grips, choose Grips... from the Options pull-down menu, uncheck the Enable Grips check box and then click on OK.

You'll reenable both the UCS icon and the grips later, after working more with AutoCAD.

POINT Places points in the drawing

COMMAND LINE: **point**

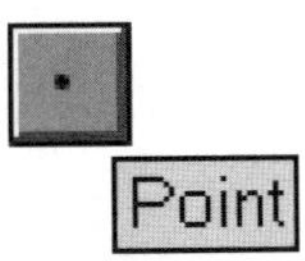

Figure 5-1: The Point icon from the Draw toolbar.

When you're prompted for the point, enter the X, Y coordinates separated by a comma (no spaces). Or move the pointer to the desired location and press the pick button. A point may be entered with all three coordinates: X, Y and Z. (See Chapter 32, "3D Objects.")

NOTE: *Don't confuse these points (which are separate drawing objects) with the points you must locate to define a line, a circle or another object.*

Entering Points

When you place points, lines, circles and other objects in a drawing, you'll need to enter the points that define their location, direction and size. There are several ways to do this. Each method described in the following paragraphs applies to both point objects (when using the POINT command) and to the points used to define geometry, such as lines, circles and so on. (See also "Using Point Filters" in Chapter 12.)

The following paragraphs describe common ways of entering points using Cartesian coordinate methods (see "Cartesian Coordinates" in Chapter 3). Other coordinate systems used with AutoCAD are described later in the chapter.

Cursor (Mouse)

Move the cursor to the desired location and click. This method should always be used with snap on or with an osnap mode. (See "SNAP" later in this chapter and "OSNAP" in Chapter 12, "Object Snap.")

Keyboard Absolute Coordinates

Enter the precise coordinate location, such as X, Y and Z values from the 0,0,0 origin. For example, **4.25,3.875** describes a point 4.25 units along the positive X-axis and 3.875 units along the positive Y-axis from the origin. If a Z value is not specified, AutoCAD assumes it to be 0. You may also enter the fractions in the above example as **4-1/4,3-7/8**.

Keyboard Relative Coordinates

Type the relative sign @ preceding your coordinates to convert them to relative coordinates. Relative coordinates describe the X, Y and Z offset from the previous point picked. Using the same example as above, **@4.25,3.875** specifies a point 4.25 units along the positive X-axis and 3.875 units along the positive Y-axis from the previous point.

Try the following example to compare absolute versus relative coordinates:

Choose the Line icon. At the prompt, take these steps:

1. Type **4.25,3.875** and press Enter.
2. Type **@4.25,3.875** and press Enter.
3. Press Enter again to complete the command.

Figure 5-2 shows the result of this example. The first endpoint of the LINE command is at the absolute coordinate X, Y location of 4.25,3.875. The second X, Y endpoint of the LINE command is at 4.25 units to the right (X) and 3.875 units up (Y) from the first point, or at the absolute coordinate location of 8.5,7.75.

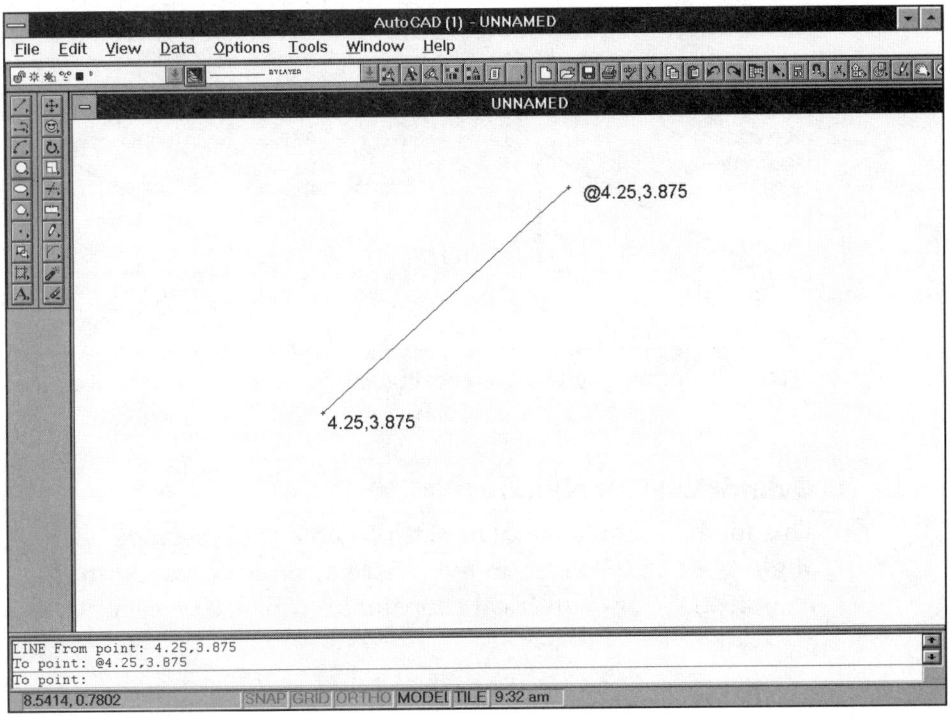

Figure 5-2: Comparing absolute to relative coordinate entry.

It's important to understand the difference between absolute and relative coordinates. Much of the geometry you create will be specified as an offset from an existing point (relative coordinate entry) rather than as an absolute coordinate from an origin.

The methods of absolute and relative coordinate entry also apply to other coordinate systems, as described below.

Polar Coordinates

Polar coordinates are the second-most-used method of entering points. The polar method lets you specify a point as a distance and angle from another point. Figure 5-3 compares relative rectangular coordinates with relative polar coordinates. The format for these coordinates is the distance, the angle symbol < and the angle (as in absolute polar coordinates of **3<45**, for example). Your polar coordinates can also be relative, as in **@3<45**.

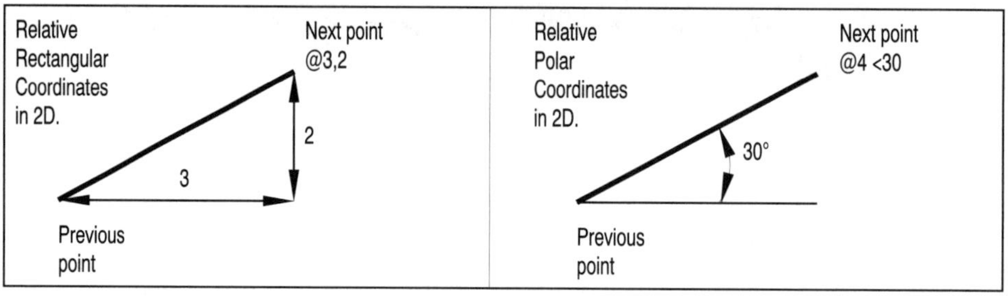

Figure 5-3: Comparing relative rectangular to relative polar coordinates.

Cylindrical Coordinates

This method applies only in 3D. You enter the distance from the origin, the angle symbol, the angle in the X-Y plane, a comma and the Z coordinate (as in **3<45,2**). Your cylindrical coordinates can also be relative, as in **@3<45,2**.

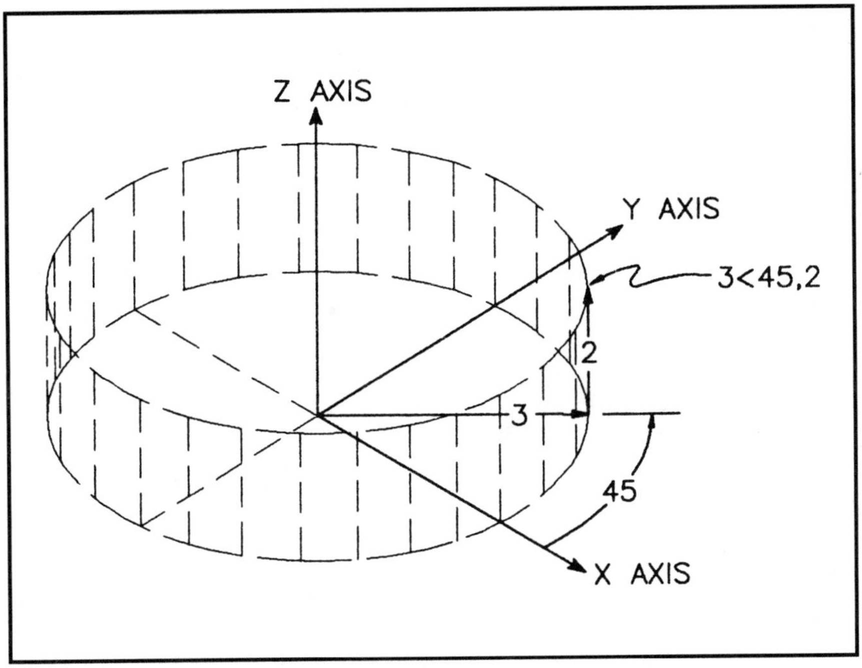

Figure 5-4: Entering cylindrical coordinates.

Spherical Coordinates

This method applies only in 3D. You enter the distance from the origin of the UCS, the angle symbol, the angle in the X-Y plane, a second angle symbol and the angle from the X-Y plane (for example, **3<45<20**). Spherical coordinates can be relative, as in **@3<45<20**.

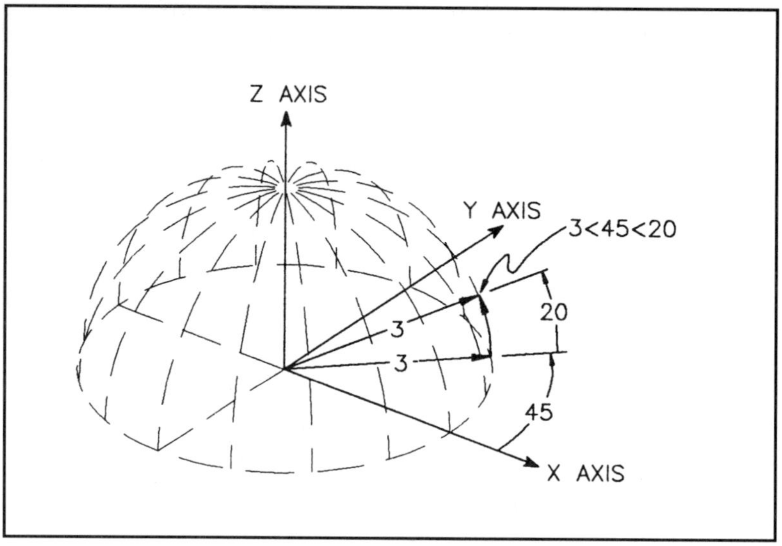

Figure 5-5: Entering spherical coordinates.

SNAP Adjusts snap spacing & angle; turns snap on & off

COMMAND LINE: **ddrmodes**

You can set the snap spacing and angle and turn snap on and off by choosing Drawing Aids from the Options pull-down menu.

The snap grid is invisible (see "GRID" in Chapter 4, "Setup"). When you're locating a point with the cursor, AutoCAD rounds the location to the nearest snap point if snap is on.

From the Drawing Aids dialog (shown in Figure 5-6) you can control the following snap features:

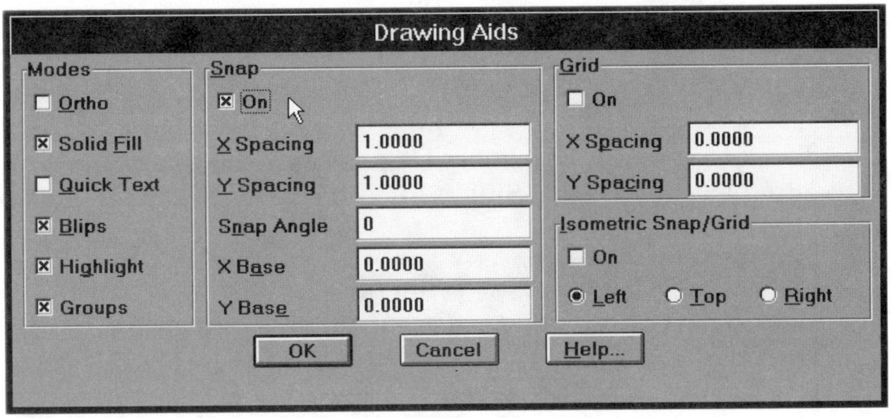

Figure 5-6: Snap control in the Drawing Aids dialog box.

On	When this box is checked, snap is active.
X Spacing	Enter a number in this field to set the distance along the X-axis between snap points. You'll notice any entry you make in the X Spacing field is automatically copied to the Y Spacing field. AutoCAD assumes that you want a square snap grid.
Y Spacing	If you want to create a rectangular snap grid, enter a value in the Y Spacing field different from the X Spacing field. Remember to set your X value first, since it replaces the Y value.
Snap Angle	Enter an angle to rotate the snap grid about the snap base point.
X Base	Enter the X coordinate for the snap base point.
Y Base	Enter the Y coordinate for the snap base point.

The snap grid extends to infinity in all directions. The importance of the snap base point is that the snap and grid measurements begin there. You can adjust the snap and grid to match up with any point in your drawing by entering the coordinates of that point in the X Base and Y Base fields.

You can also quickly toggle snap on and off by pressing function key F9 or by double-clicking the SNAP field in the status bar at the bottom of the screen.

POINT STYLE Sets the style for the type of point you require

COMMAND LINE: **ddptype**

To set the point style, choose Display from the Options pull-down menu, and then choose Point Style.... This displays the dialog box in Figure 5-7.

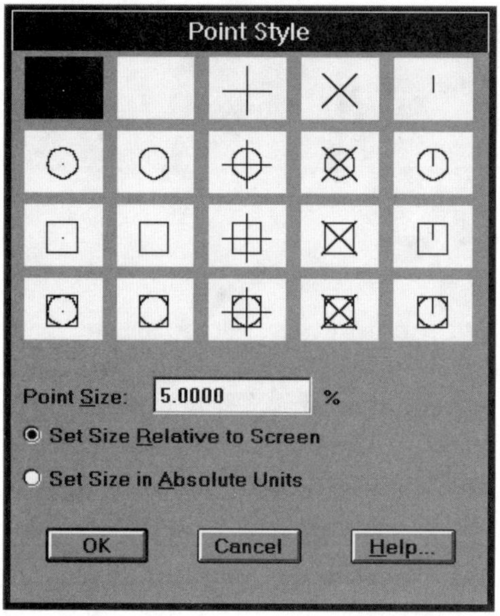

Figure 5-7: The Point Style dialog box.

The top half of this dialog presents 20 icons representing the modes AutoCAD can use to display points. Click on the icon for the mode you prefer. Note that the empty icon (top row, second from the left) makes points invisible. Invisible points cannot be selected with regular selection commands or snapped to with osnap modes.

The bottom half of the dialog controls the point display size. The meaning of the Point Size field varies depending on which of the two radio buttons below it are active.

If the Set Size Relative to Screen button is active, the Point Size field represents a percentage of the screen height. After a the screen is regenerated (usually with a REGEN command), the points will always display at the same size on your screen regardless of how far you have zoomed in or out.

If the Set Size in Absolute Units button is active, the Point Size field represents the actual unit height for the point display. The points will display at a fixed height like other objects.

Both the display mode and the display size are global. After a regeneration of the screen, all point objects are updated to the current settings.

Moving on

In this chapter you learned about basic point and coordinate entry methods. You'll use the absolute, relative and polar methods frequently.

In Chapter 6, "Lines," you'll work through AutoCAD's variety of line commands and methods of entry. You'll also learn more about AutoCAD's linetypes and their placement.

CHAPTER 6

Lines

Creating a line is the most fundamental objective in any CAD program. AutoCAD has numerous types of lines to perform different tasks. This chapter, split into three parts, reviews lines, multilines and construction lines.

This chapter notes the differences among the three types of lines, yet points out that they all serve the same purpose: providing the drafter/designer with the tools to convert rough sketches into accurate working drawings on time.

For more advanced line use, see "PLINE" in Chapter 28, "Polylines & Splines."

Line Commands

To draw all your basic objects, use the LINE command. As you start AutoCAD, you'll use this command the most. You can use ORTHO with LINE to force new lines to be horizontal or vertical.

To draw multiple lines at one pass, use the MLINE command. An architectural designer, for example, could use it to create a total wall system, including the outer walls (with pen width), the cavity, the brick hatch detail, the insulation hatch detail and the center line of studs.

And if you need to substitute a new part for an old part, use the XLINE and RAY construction line commands to work up the design.

LINE Creates a straight line or series of straight line segments

COMMAND LINE: **line** or **l**

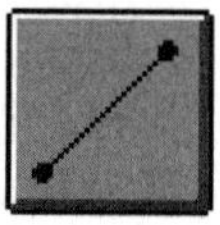

Figure 6-1: The LINE icon from the Draw toolbar.

Choose the Line icon, or enter **line** (or just **l**) at the command line. (If the screen or "side" menu is displayed, you may choose Line and then Draw1.)

When You Are Prompted for a From Point...

Locate the starting point of the line. Do this by entering X-Y coordinates at the keyboard or by moving the pointer to the desired location and pressing the pick button.

When You Are Prompted for a To Point...

Locate the end of the line or the next point in the series of lines, using the keyboard or the pointing device.

While the LINE Command Is Active...

You may also use the following options:

> If you make an input error, enter **u** to undo the last line segment drawn in this series of lines. You may enter **u** to undo as many times as you require. Or press Esc to cancel the command, and then start the LINE command again by pressing the Spacebar.
>
> Enter **c** to close a polygon and return to command mode. Entering **c** joins the line back to the start point.

To End a Series of Lines...

Press Enter to end the series and return to command mode.

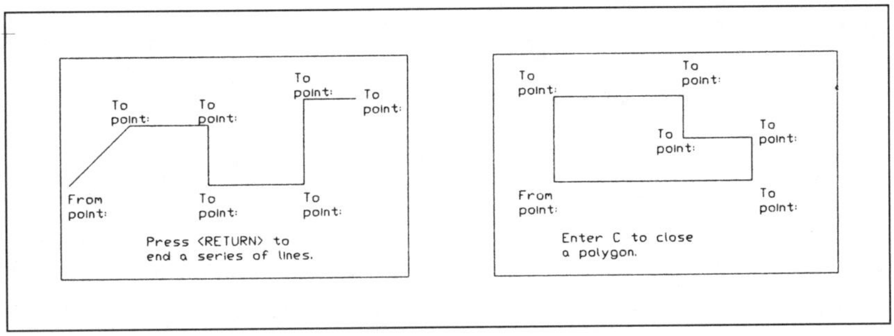

Figure 6-2: Using the LINE command.

If You Have Just Created a Line or Arc Onscreen...

You may press Enter to begin the line at the end of the most recent line or arc. (If you're starting from the end of an arc, the direction is already set and you need enter only the length of the line.)

Although you'll often use the LINE command to produce regular 2D X-Y lines, it also accepts the Z coordinate. If you enter only X and Y or select the location with the pointer, AutoCAD adopts the Z location from the current elevation, usually in the current UCS (see "ELEV" in Chapter 32, "3D Objects").

You can use relative rectangular coordinates that include all three coordinates, such as @2,3,4. However, relative polar coordinates specifying distance and angle, such as @3.25<45, operate only in the X-Y plane. You can also use 3D cylindrical and spherical coordinates as explained in Chapter 5, "Points."

NOTE: To extrude existing lines in the Z direction, use the CHPROP command. To set extrusion thickness for subsequent lines, use the ELEV command.

See Chapter 44, "Hands-on Exercises 1," for three simple exercises involving 2D lines.

ORTHO Forces new lines to be horizontal or vertical

COMMAND LINE: **'ortho** or **ortho**

To turn ortho on and off, choose Drawing Aids from the Options pull-down menu.

Or at the command line, enter either **'ortho** (transparent) or **ortho**. When prompted, enter **on** to enable ortho (to make all subsequent lines orthogonal) or enter **off** to disable ortho (see Figure 6-3).

To turn ortho on and off more conveniently, press function key F8. Or double-click in the ORTHO label of the status bar at the bottom of the screen. You may do this at any time during a series of line inputs.

When a line's endpoint is entered from the keyboard, it's not affected by ortho.

If the snap grid has been rotated, newly created orthogonal lines will also be rotated. If the snap style is isometric, orthogonal lines are always parallel to one of the three isometric axes.

***NOTE:** Ortho also affects the displacement in the MOVE and COPY commands.*

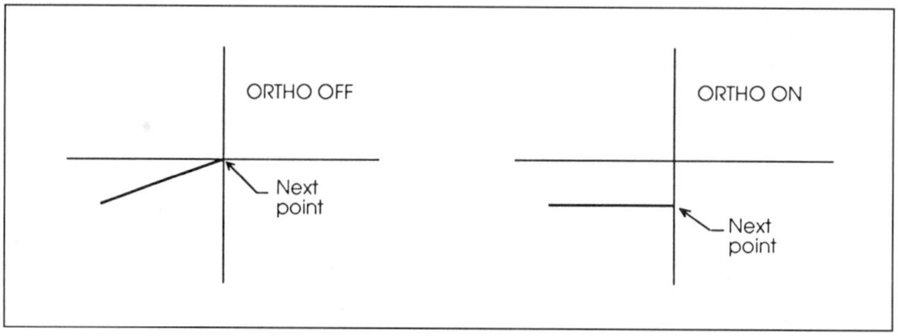

Figure 6-3: Ortho, off and on.

Multiline Commands

Multilines are a useful new feature of Release 13. Using multilines, you can create composites of multiple parallel lines, each with different spacing, linetype patterns, colors and background fill.

With the MLSTYLE command you first create multiline styles or select an existing style. You may then use the MLINE command to draw multilines and the MLEDIT command to edit them. All three commands are described below.

MLSTYLE Creates & sets multiline styles

COMMAND LINE: **mlstyle**

Figure 6-4: Multiline Style icon from the Object Properties toolbar.

Before you can use the MLINE command to draw multilines, you must create or select a multiline style. The Multiline Styles dialog box lets you do this.

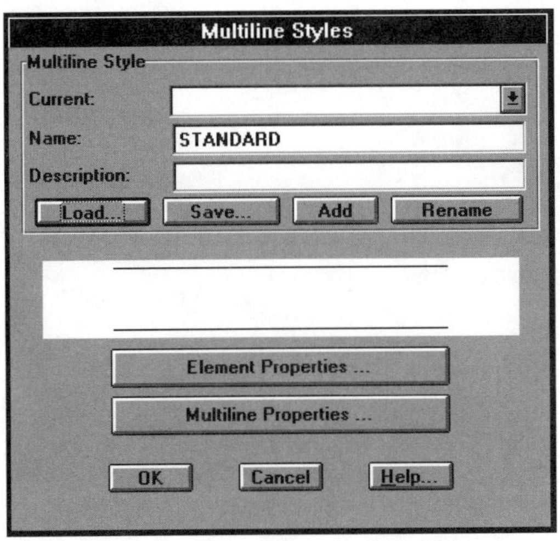

Figure 6-5: The Multiline Styles dialog.

From the Options pull-down menu, choose Multiline Style.... The Multiline Styles dialog box lets you define, view and edit multiline styles. Use the dialog's options as follows:

Current	To select a style from the pop-up list.
Name	To name a new multiline style.
Description	To describe the style.
Load...	To choose a style to load from an external file.
Save...	To save a style to an external file.
Add	To add a new line style to the current multiline style.
Rename	To rename a current style.

The Multiline Properties Dialog

To set the properties for all lines in the multiline, choose the Multiline Properties button. This dialog controls the end cap parameters between different sets of joints, lines and backgrounds.

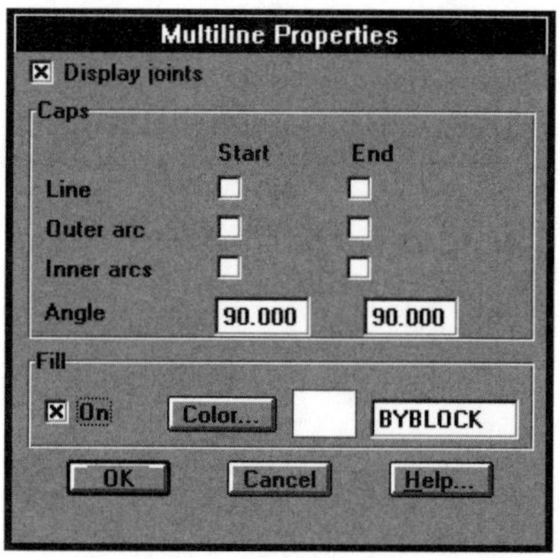

Figure 6-6: The Multiline Properties dialog.

In the Multiline Properties dialog you may use these options:

Turn on Display joints to display a miter line across all segments of the multiline.

Choose Caps to activate control between the Start cap and the End cap.

Use the Line setting to create a straight line cap to the Start or End of the multiline.

Outer Arc creates an arc between the two outer lines of the multiline.

Inner Arc creates an arc between even-numbered lines inside the two outer lines.

Angle sets an angle for the Start and End caps. The end caps can be arcs and/or lines.

Fill controls background fill of the multiline. Use the check box to turn Fill on or off. Use the Color option button to display the standard AutoCAD color swatch and select a color.

Element Properties Dialog

To set properties for individual lines, choose the Element Properties button. Each line object has an offset value defined relative to the 0,0 origin—the center of the multiline. A negative value offsets a line below the center origin, whereas a positive value offsets a line above the center origin point.

To set up a line, pick the offset number in the list box. Then alter the number in the Offset box. Remember 0.00 is a center line. Positive numbers are above the center line and negative below. You may add up to 16 lines to your multiline style.

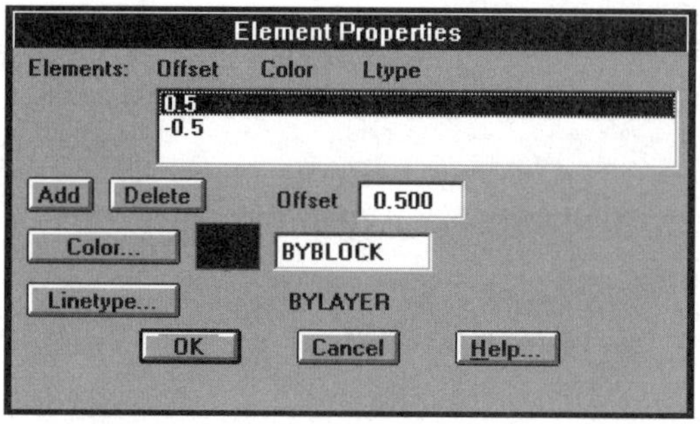

Figure 6-7: The Multiline Element Properties dialog.

Elements	Lists the individual offset objects making up the current multiline style. Remember, the offset list starts at 0,0 origin for each line defined and includes color and linetype.
Add	Allows you to add up to 16 new lines.
Delete	Erases a selected line from the current style.
Offset	Lets you alter the position of the selected line.
Color	Lets you choose and control the color of a selected line.
Linetype	Lets you choose and set a specific linetype pattern.

MLINE Allows you to draw multilines previously created with MLSTYLE

COMMAND LINE: **mline**

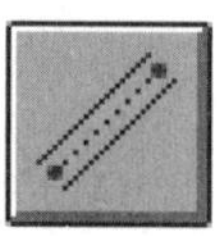

Figure 6-8: The MLINE icon from the Polyline flyout of the Draw toolbar.

Use the MLINE command to draw multilines once you have created a multiline style or styles. You can assign different properties to individual lines. You can also control the end cap of the lines to have your multilines end with a line, an arc or an angle.

MLINE Control Factors

The MLINE command has three setting factors: drawing control, scale factor and style name.

Justification provides drawing control, Scale provides scale factor control, and Style provides style name control. (See "MLINE Setting Variables" below.)

The input of MLINE is similar to the LINE command previously mentioned. You simply pick points in X-Y coordinates. You may justify (set) the multiline to draw from the top, the center or the bottom. As you enter the MLINE, there is onscreen input information to indicate the current control and justification of the three settings.

The prompt sequence is

```
Justification = Top, Scale = 1.00, Style = STANDARD
Justification/Scale/STyle/<From point>:
```

Justification Control

Choose Justification to define how the multiline will be produced. As you see from the prompt sequence above, it defaults to Top. You specify points from right to left. The justification options are

```
Top/Zero/Bottom<top>:
```

Top allows you to draw from the top of the multiline. An architectural designer, for example, would use this default method if the design involved outer walls of brickwork or CMU (where the design must to conform to standard or modular brick/CMU sizes.)

Use Zero to draw from the center (the 0,0 origin) of the multiline.

Or use Bottom to draw from the bottom of the multiline.

Scale Control

Choose Scale to control MLINE width. The scale is set to 1.00 as a default.

Scale Examples

1. A scale setting of 0.5 produces a multiple line pattern that is half the width of the defined MLSTYLE command. Or it would be twice the width if it were set to 2.0.
2. A negative scale factor mirrors the multilines.
3. A zero scale setting produces a total collapse of the multiline into a single line.

STyle Control

Choose STyle to control a specific MLINE style. Remember it must be created first before it can be used. You'll use MLSTYLE to create it.

MLINE Setting Variables

MLINE has three setting variables that accept new defaults for MLINE drawing control, scale factor and style name as you set them at the on-screen prompt.

You do not need to set these variables; they will be established as you set up MLINE for use.

Here are brief descriptions of the variables:

CMLJUST provides drawing control to accept the Justification setting of MLINE.

CMLSCALE provides scale factor control to accept the Scale setting of MLINE.

CMLSTYLE provides style name control to accept the STyle of MLINE.

MULTILINE EDIT Allows you to edit multilines

COMMAND LINE: **mledit**

Figure 6-9: The Edit Multiline icon from the Special Edit flyout of the Modify toolbar.

Use MLEDIT to edit multilines. Take these steps:

1. Enter **mledit** at the command line (or click the Edit Multiline icon) to display the Multiline Edit Tools dialog, shown in Figure 6-10.
2. Double-click one of the 12 image tiles in the dialog box and press Enter.
3. Pick the multiline segments you want to edit.
4. Press Enter again to return to the dialog box.
5. Continue editing or press OK to accept your edits.

NOTE: *You cannot edit multilines with the normal AutoCAD editing commands of BREAK, CHAMFER, FILLET, TRIM and EXTEND. But you may use SNAP, COPY, MOVE, MIRROR, STRETCH and EXPLODE.*

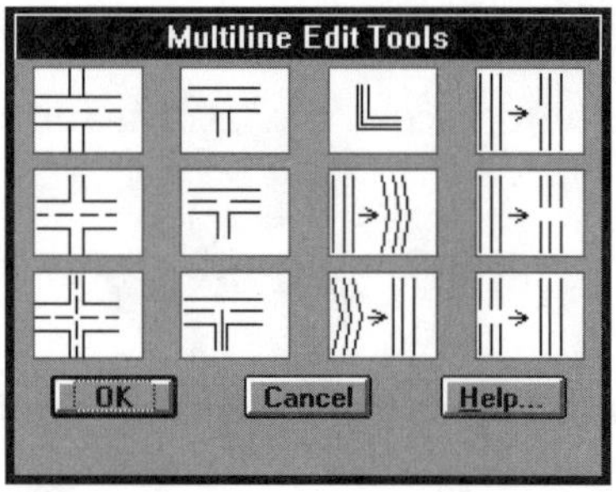

Figure 6-10: The Multiline Edit Tools dialog.

The Multiline Edit dialog has built-in editing tools. The 12 tiles in Figure 6-7 initiate operations that connect corners, form crosses or tees, cut or join lines and add or delete vertices of a multiline.

Editing Corners

Choose Corner Joint to edit corners. Double-click the corner tile, then choose the multilines to connect into joints. The operation trims any two overlapping multiline segments to form a single corner element.

There are two formats for intersection editing: cross and tee. Both cross and tee editing allow further options of closed, open and merged.

Editing Cross Intersections

Three cross edit options let you edit the crossed intersections. The three edit types are closed cross, open cross and merged cross. Choose a tile and then select the multilines to edit. Press Enter to return to the dialog, and choose OK to accept the edits.

Three tee edits let you edit tee intersections. The options of closed, open and merged are similar to cross editing. Again, choose a tile, select the multilines to edit, and press Enter to return to the dialog. Choose OK to accept the edits.

Editing Lines

Three Line Edit options (cut single, cut all and weld) let you edit straight multilines. Use cut single to break or erase a single segment from your multiline element. Use cut all to break or erase all the elements in a multiline segment.

NOTE: *Whether you cut single or cut all, the multiline is still a single object. You join or restore a multiline segment using the weld option.*

Editing Vertices

To add or delete vertices, choose the add or delete tile. Pick the multiline segments you want to edit then press Enter to return to the dialog box. You may edit further or click OK to accept your multiline edits.

Construction Line Commands

Prior to the computer drafting and design revolution, designers created layout drawings as a series of pencil sketches on trash paper, napkins or even cigarette packs. The drafter would then transfer the pencil sketches via construction (reference) lines into scaled working drawings. From this technique, AutoCAD evolved the XLINE and RAY construction line commands.

New users of AutoCAD need not think in terms of construction lines and sketches. However, for initial drawing layout and establishing work points, reference lines can save time when you need to establish angles for lines to meet at a specific location.

XLINE Creates infinite-length construction lines

COMMAND LINE: **xline**

Figure 6-11: The Xline icon from the Line flyout of the Draw toolbar.

To create construction lines of infinite length, choose the Xline icon. XLINE is set to a horizontal default, but lines may also be vertical, angular, bisected and offset. At the prompt Hor/Ver/Ang/Bisect/Offset/<FromPoint>, you may enter one of the following options:

hor (for horizontal) to create horizontal construction lines through picked points, parallel to the current X axis.

ver (for vertical) to create vertical construction lines through picked points, parallel to the Y axis.

ang (for angular) to produce angular lines. At the Ref/enter angle prompt, enter an angle or enter **ref** to specify reference points.

bisect to bisect lines. To bisect lines you must (1) choose an angle vertex point, or point of origin, (2) pick an angle start point and (3) pick the angle end point.

offset to offset an xline by a defined distance. You enter the distance at the keyboard (or at the prompt enter **t** for through and pick two points onscreen).

RAY Creates radiating construction lines of semi-infinite length

COMMAND LINE: **ray**

Figure 6-12: The Ray icon from the Line flyout of the Draw toolbar.

The RAY command produces ray-like construction lines of semi-infinite length. The lines radiate like the spokes of a wheel from a picked point extending to infinity.

To invoke the command, choose the Ray icon. Pick a point onscreen and then pick a second point through which the Ray line should pass. Press Esc to the the command.

Moving on

Learning to draw lines is essential to mastering AutoCAD, but so is erasing them. Chapter 7, "Selecting & Erasing Objects," explains how to remove unwanted lines and other objects from the drawing database.

CHAPTER 7

Selecting & Erasing Objects

Before you can edit or erase objects, you must select them. This chapter explains how to respond to Select Objects prompts, build a selection set of objects and configure object selection. It then tells how to erase objects and undo an erasure.

Answering a Select Objects Prompt

Many editing, inquiry, and dimension commands require that you select an object or objects. Whenever you're prompted to select objects, you can use the following options:

Select one object by clicking on it. You can do this repeatedly.

Select one object by holding down the Ctrl key while clicking on the object. Often when you try to select an object, there are many other objects in the same area, and AutoCAD might select the wrong one. If you hold down the Ctrl key and continue to click in the same location, AutoCAD cycles through all of the objects accessible at that spot. When the desired object is highlighted, release the Ctrl key and continue with normal selection.

You may also use the following keyboard options. After you enter an option, you'll be prompted to continue refining your selection unless you're in single-selection (SI) mode. When you have completed the selection process, press Enter.

Enter **p** (for previous) to reuse the previous selection set (see "Building a Selection Set" below). You may further refine the previous selection set.

Enter **m** (for multiple), select two or more objects with the pointer, and press Enter. Do this when you're working with a very large drawing and want to speed up the process of selecting multiple objects.

Enter **l** (for last) to select the object placed in the drawing most recently.

Enter **w** (for window) to select several items that are completely enclosed in a rectangular window. Then locate two opposite corners of the window.

Enter **wp** (for window polygon) to select several items that are completely enclosed in a polygon-shaped window. Then pick the points that define the corners of the polygon. The polygon can have as many corners as you want, but AutoCAD will not let you enter points that would cause the polygon to cross itself. As you select the third and subsequent corners, the temporary closing line of the polygon appears. After you select the last point in the polygon, press Enter. (If you pull the cursor away from the last point before pressing Enter, the polygon will appear to have an extra leg, but this is only a temporary "rubber band" display. When you press Enter, the polygon closes between the first and last points you picked.)

Enter **c** (for crossing) to select items that are inside or crossing a rectangular window. Then locate two opposite corners of the window. The window is dashed or highlighted to distinguish it from a noncrossing (enclosing) type window.

Enter **cp** (for crossing polygon) to select several items that are inside or crossing a polygon-shaped window. Then pick the points that define the corners of the polygon. Items that are entirely or partially inside the polygon are selected. Like the crossing window, the crossing polygon is shown dashed. Like the window polygon (WP), the crossing polygon can have as many corners as you want. After you select the last point, press Enter to close the polygon.

Enter **f** (for fence) to select several items crossing the "fence." The fence is formed the same way the polygons are formed in the WP and CP options above—you simply pick a series of points. The difference is that the fence is not closed to form a complete polygon, and only items that cross the fence are selected. (Objects are never *inside* a fence in the same sense in which they can be inside a regular or a crossing window.)

Enter **box** to use either an enclosing or a crossing window. If the second corner of the window is to the right of the first, the window is an enclosing window. If it's to the left, the window is a crossing window. (This option has its greatest advantage when used in custom menus.)

Enter **au** (for automatic) to select one object or to use an enclosing or a crossing window. If the pickbox locates an object, that object is selected. If not, that pick location becomes the left corner for an enclosing window or the right corner for a crossing window.

Enter **r** (for remove) to remove an object from the selection set. Because this puts you into Remove mode, all other selection options will remove objects from the selection set until you enter **a** for Add mode (described below). You can also remove objects from the selection set at any time by pressing the Shift key as you select an already-selected object.

Enter **a** to add an item to those already selected (necessary only after using Remove mode).

Enter **u** to undo your last selection.

Enter **si** (for single) to cancel the interactive refinement of the selection set. This forces AutoCAD to accept the first object or group of objects you select. (This option has its greatest advantage when used in custom menus.)

Enter **all** to select all objects in the entire drawing, even on layers that are turned off or locked. Objects can subsequently be removed from this all-inclusive selection set with the R option.

Enter **g** to use a named selection group. (For more information about selection groups, see Chapter 19, "Selection Grouping." Chapter 19 also presents a command for filtering selection sets for specific objects or object properties.)

NOTE: Objects created in Model Space can be selected only in Model Space, and objects created in Paper Space can be selected only in Paper Space. Even though you can select objects by entering coordinates (for pick points or corners of windows), an object must be at least partly onscreen to be selected.

Building a Selection Set

You can also select a set of objects to which editing commands can then be applied.

SELECT OBJECTS Builds a selection set of objects

COMMAND LINE: **select**

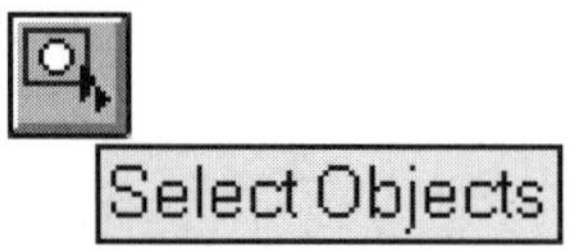

Figure 7-1: The Select Objects icon from the Standard toolbar.

Choose the Select icon to build a selection set of objects for use with other commands.

Use this command to select objects you want to edit later as a group. Select objects for the set using the options explained in "Answering a Select Objects Prompt" above. To use the selection set, type **p** for previous when you are presented with the Select Objects prompt of an edit command.

NOTE: Besides using SELECT, there are two other ways of selecting objects before entering an edit command. One method is to configure AutoCAD to use Noun/Verb Selection as described below in "Configuring Object Selection." The other method is to use the new Release 13 feature of named selection groups. This feature is described in Chapter 19, "Selections—Group 2."

Configuring Object Selection

To configure features related to object selection, choose Selection... from the Options pull-down menu. This displays the Object Selection Settings dialog shown in Figure 7-2.

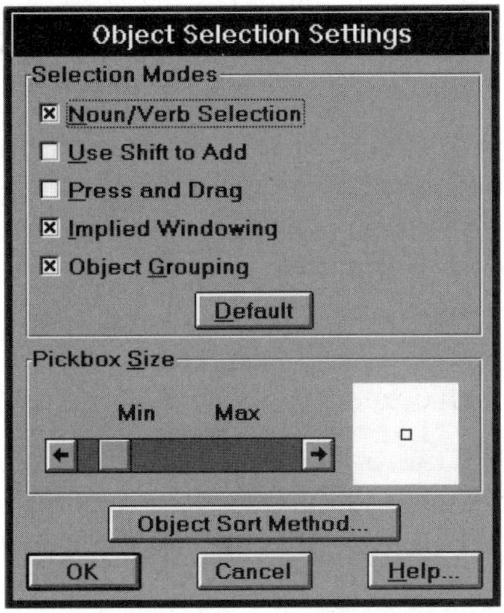

Figure 7-2: Default settings in the Object Selection Settings dialog.

The top half of the dialog presents five check boxes that control the Selection modes:

Noun/Verb Selection
: When this option is checked, you can select objects either before or after entering an editing command. You'll notice that when Noun/Verb Selection is active, the pickbox is always visible at the center of the crosshairs. If you select objects first and then enter an edit command, the objects are immediately passed to the command, and you skip over the regular Select Objects prompt. When Noun/Verb Selection is not checked, you can select objects only at the Select Objects prompt.

Use Shift to Add
: When this option is not checked, you add objects to a selection set simply by selecting them. When this option is checked, you must

hold down the Shift key to add an object to the selection set. If you don't, picking a new object replaces any other objects that were in the selection set.

NOTE: *Remember that if you hold down the Shift key while selecting an already-selected object, it will be removed from the selection set regardless of the Shift to Add setting.*

Press and Drag	This option relates to the manner in which the two corners of a window or crossing are indicated. When checked, you press and hold the pick button at the first corner, drag the cursor to the other corner and then release the pick button. When Press and Drag is not checked, you click at each corner.
Implied Windowing	When this option is checked, AutoCAD activates Box selection (as described under "Answering a Select Objects prompt" above) whenever you click in empty space. If you click on an object, it will be selected as usual; but if you click in empty space, that point becomes the first corner of the Box selection.
Object Grouping	When this item is checked, an entire named group of objects can be selected by clicking on any one object in the group. If it is not checked, the object group can be selected only with the G option described in "Answering a Select Objects Prompt" above.

Just beneath the check boxes is the Default button, which restores the settings to AutoCAD's default configuration as shown in Figure 7-2.

Near the bottom of the dialog is the Pickbox Size slider. The pickbox is the square cursor that appears when you're prompted to select objects. You can click on the arrow buttons or drag the slider to adjust the pickbox size. The new pickbox size is displayed in the icon to the right of the slider.

The Object Sort Method button allows you to select various operations for which you want objects sorted in database order. This is an advanced topic, so for now you can leave the default settings (Plotting and PostScript Output) enabled.

ERASE

Erases selected objects from a drawing

COMMAND LINE: **erase**

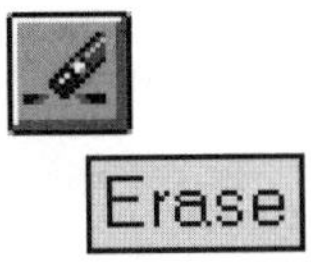

Figure 7-3: The Erase icon from the Modify toolbar.

To erase an object, first click on the Erase icon then select one or more objects as described under "Answering a Select ObjectsPrompt."

OOPS

Lets you restore an erased object

COMMAND LINE: **oops**

Figure 7-4: The Oops icon from the Miscellaneous toolbar.

Often you'll erase objects and immediately regret you did so. Choose the Oops icon (or enter **oops** at the command line) to restore the last object or selection of objects you erased. Remember to do this immediately after the ERASE command.

Moving on

Learning to select objects and erase your mistakes is an important part of learning AutoCAD.

After you erase objects, the screen usually requires refreshing. You can do this either through a redraw or by regenerating your drawing. Chapter 8, "Refreshing the Screen," guides you through the few simple commands for this process.

Refreshing the Screen

Sometimes you'll need to refresh your screen to remove unwanted blips or restore parts of the drawing that seem to be missing as a result of the editing process. This chapter explains how to redraw or regenerate the screen display. It also tells how to turn the marker blips and automatic regeneration options on and off.

REDRAW Redraws the onscreen display

COMMAND LINE: **redraw** or **redrawall**

Figure 8.1: Redraw View and Redraw All icons from the Standard toolbar.

To redraw the objects on your screen, choose Redraw View or Redraw All from the View pull-down menu (or enter **redraw** or **redrawall** at the command line). These commands remove unwanted blips (left from picking points) and restore apparently missing parts of the display resulting from the drawing/editing process.

Redraw View redraws the display of only the current viewport. Redraw All redraws the display of all viewports on your screen. The creation and use of viewports is described in Chapter 31, "Model Space & Paper Space."

*NOTE: As a shortcut, you can enter **r** at the command prompt. This is a command alias in the \ACAD\SUPPORT\ACAD.PGP file. For instructions on creating your own command aliases, see Chapter 40, "Customizing AutoCAD."*

REGEN Regenerates the onscreen display

COMMAND LINE: **regen** or **regenall**

To regenerate the screen display, you can enter **regen** or **regenall** on the command line. The REGEN command rereads the drawing database and performs a more thorough update of the screen than the REDRAW command. Regeneration is also slower than a redraw. Use REGENALL to regenerate all viewports.

Since these commands are slower than redrawing, use them only as a last resort. If you feel that your display is still not correct after a redraw command, then try a regeneration.

REGENAUTO Enables or disables automatic regeneration performed by some commands

COMMAND LINE: **regenauto**

The commands governed by REGENAUTO are ATTEDIT (global editing), BLOCK (redefinition), INSERT (when you use blockname=filename to redefine a block), LAYER (changed linetype or freeze/thaw state) and LTSCALE (linetype-scaling parameter).

When several of the above changes are made back to back, AutoCAD normally regenerates the display after each change. On a complex drawing, this takes considerable time.

Here's a tip to save time. Turn REGENAUTO off, make the series of changes and then turn it back on. AutoCAD will then perform only one regeneration).

The commands ZOOM, PAN, VIEWRES and REGEN aren't affected by REGENAUTO.

Regenauto is initially on when you begin a new drawing, unless the new drawing uses a prototype in which regenauto is off. It's recommended you leave regenauto on for normal drawing. Turn it off when you're using scripts that perform several operations at a time, as they may cause a screen regeneration and slow down or halt the script file.

BLIPMODE Activates marker blips onscreen

COMMAND LINE: **ddrmodes**

When blipmode is on, marker blips are placed on the screen every time you pick a point. To toggle blipmode on and off, choose Drawing Aids from the Options pull-down menu and click on the Blips check box.

Moving on

By now, you know how to redraw the onscreen display and refresh the drawing, and you're more than ready to enter drawing files.

Chapter 9, "Files," will guide you through file management tasks available through AutoCAD.

CHAPTER 9

Files

This chapter describes some of the file management functions available from within AutoCAD. Most file management tasks should be performed using the Windows File Manager. However, some tasks are specific to AutoCAD alone. These tasks are described below.

FILES Lets you list, copy, rename, delete or unlock files

COMMAND LINE: **files**

Windows users of AutoCAD will generally use the Windows File Manager to list, copy, rename and delete files. To switch to the Windows File Manager from AutoCAD, press Alt+Tab or Ctrl+Esc. (For instructions on using the File Manager, see Chapter 1, "Preliminaries.")

As an alternative, the FILES command can be entered at the command line to display the File Utilities dialog, shown in Figure 9-1. You can also display this dialog by choosing Management from the File pull-down menu, then choosing Unlock File.... This dialog is intended mainly for DOS users of AutoCAD, and Windows users will use it primarily to unlock files.

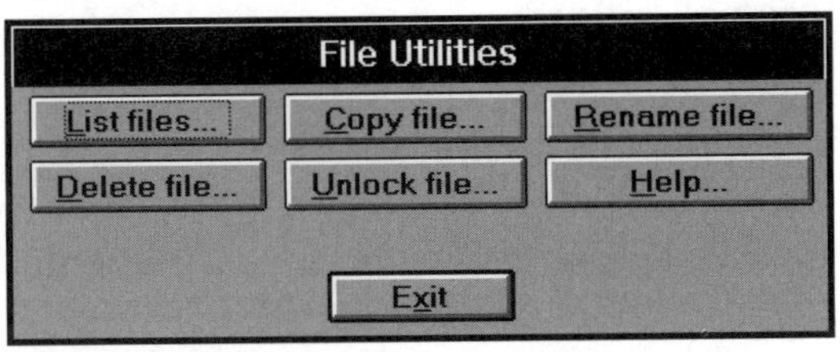

Figure 9-1: The File Utilities dialog.

Click on the Unlock Files button to display the File(s) to Unlock dialog as shown in Figure 9-2.

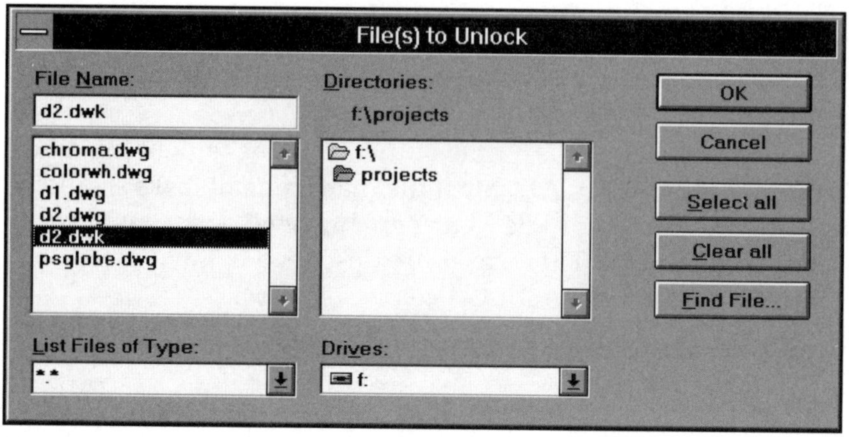

Figure 9-2: The File(s) to Unlock dialog.

If you have file locking enabled (which is the AutoCAD default), AutoCAD prevents other users on a network from loading your drawing file while you are working on it. Sometimes, if you hang your system or otherwise abnormally end AutoCAD, your drawing file may not get unlocked properly.

If you try to access a drawing that AutoCAD reports is locked and you are sure that no one else is currently using that file, you can use the Unlock File command to gain access to it.

Locked files have extensions that end in K (see Chapter 1, "Preliminaries"). For a full discussion of file locking and network drawing access, see the *AutoCAD Reference Manual*.

AUDIT Audits and corrects the current drawing file

COMMAND LINE: **audit**

Choose Management, then Audit from the File pull-down menu to analyze and correct corrupt drawing files.

The AUDIT command examines the integrity of the current drawing file. The prompt asks if you want errors corrected. If you answer **y** for yes, a report is generated onscreen and placed in a file with the same primary name as the current drawing, but with extension .ADT.

RECOVER Corrects a corrupted drawing file as it is loaded from disk.

COMMAND LINE: **recover**

Choose Management, then Recover… from the File pull-down menu to display the Recover Drawing File dialog shown in Figure 9-3. After you select a file to recover, AutoCAD automatically performs an audit as it loads the damaged drawing file.

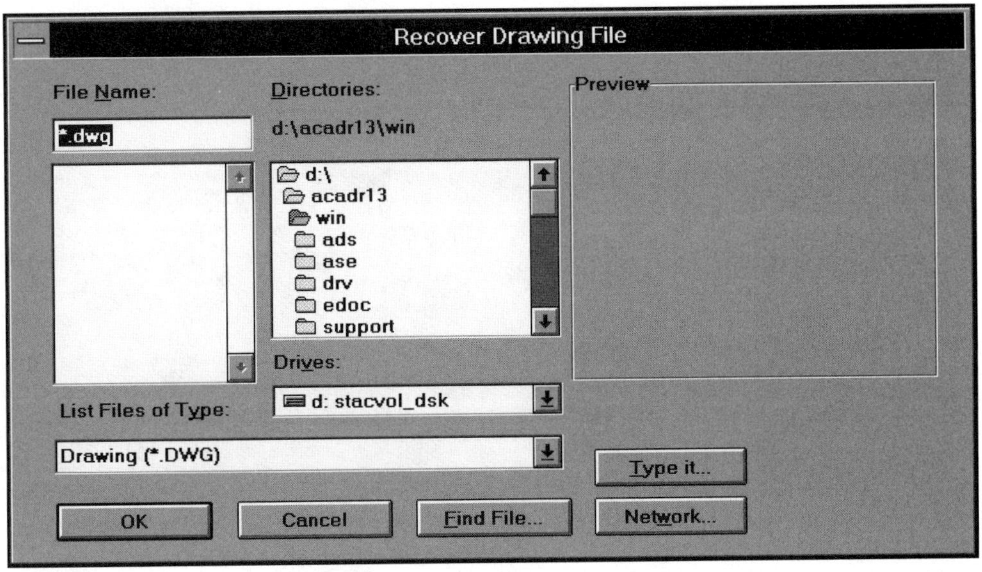

Figure 9-3: The Recover Drawing File dialog.

Occasionally, a drawing file still doesn't load properly, and you must rely on a backup file. The backup file must first be renamed so its extension is changed from .BAK to .DWG.

Moving on

Learning to open, close and save files to the hard drive and floppy disk is fundamental to AutoCAD. Chapter 10, "2D Figures," will introduce you to more fundamentals in the construction of circles, arcs and ellipses.

2D Figures

CIRCLE Places a circle in a drawing

COMMAND LINE: **circle**

Choose the Circle icon to place a circle in a drawing.

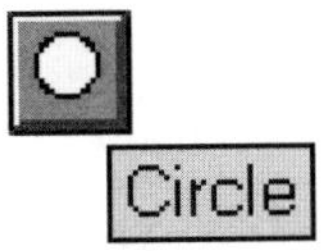

Figure 10-1: The Circle icon from the Draw toolbar.

When prompted for the center point, you have the following options:

Locate the center and then the radius of the circle, using the keyboard or pointer. Also, when you are prompted for the radius, you can enter **d**, and then enter the diameter.

Enter **2p**, then locate the endpoints of any diameter of the circle.

Enter **3p**, then locate three points on the circumference of the circle. You can use the tan (tangent) OSNAP mode to draw a circle tangent to three lines, three circles, two lines and an arc and so on. See "OSNAP" in Chapter 12, "Object Snap."

Enter **ttr** (for tangent-tangent-radius). Select the two lines/arcs/circles that the new circle will be tangent to, and then enter the radius.

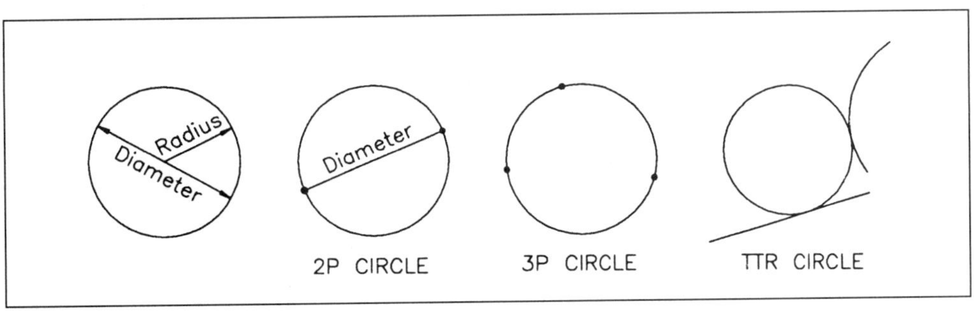

Figure 10-2: Different types of circle entry.

NOTE: *To drag the circle when DRAGMODE is on (see "DRAGMODE" below), you must enter* **drag** *when prompted for the final parameter and then use the pointer to place the circle. When you're dragging an object, a location entered from the keyboard will override the location currently displayed.*

See "Using Point Filters" in Chapter 32, "3D Objects."

DRAGMODE Enables or disables the use of DRAG

COMMAND LINE: **dragmode**

Circles, arcs, blocks and shapes can be dragged dynamically if dragmode is set to on or auto.

When prompted, enter

a (for auto) to enable automatic dragging. Automatic dragging means that you don't have to enter **drag** to activate dragging.

on to enable non-automatic dragging. To activate dragging when you're in a drawing or editing command, enter **drag** when prompted for the final parameter.

off to disable dragging.

By default, dragmode is set to auto, but if a prototype drawing is used, the initial dragmode setting is determined by the prototype. When you save your drawing, the current dragmode setting is saved with it.

ARC Places an arc in a drawing

COMMAND LINE: **arc**

Choose the Arc icon to place an ARC into a drawing.

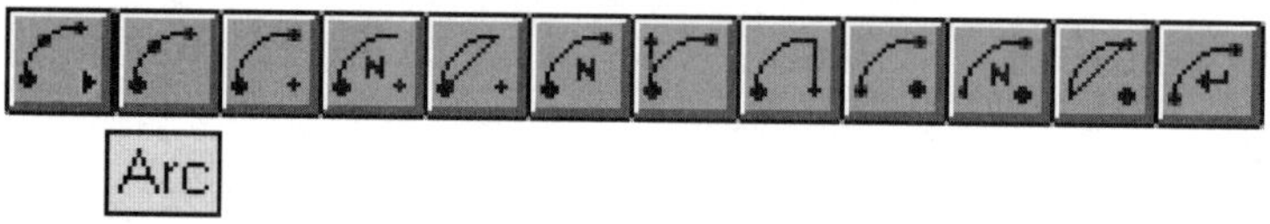

Figure 10-3: The Arc flyout from the Draw toolbar.

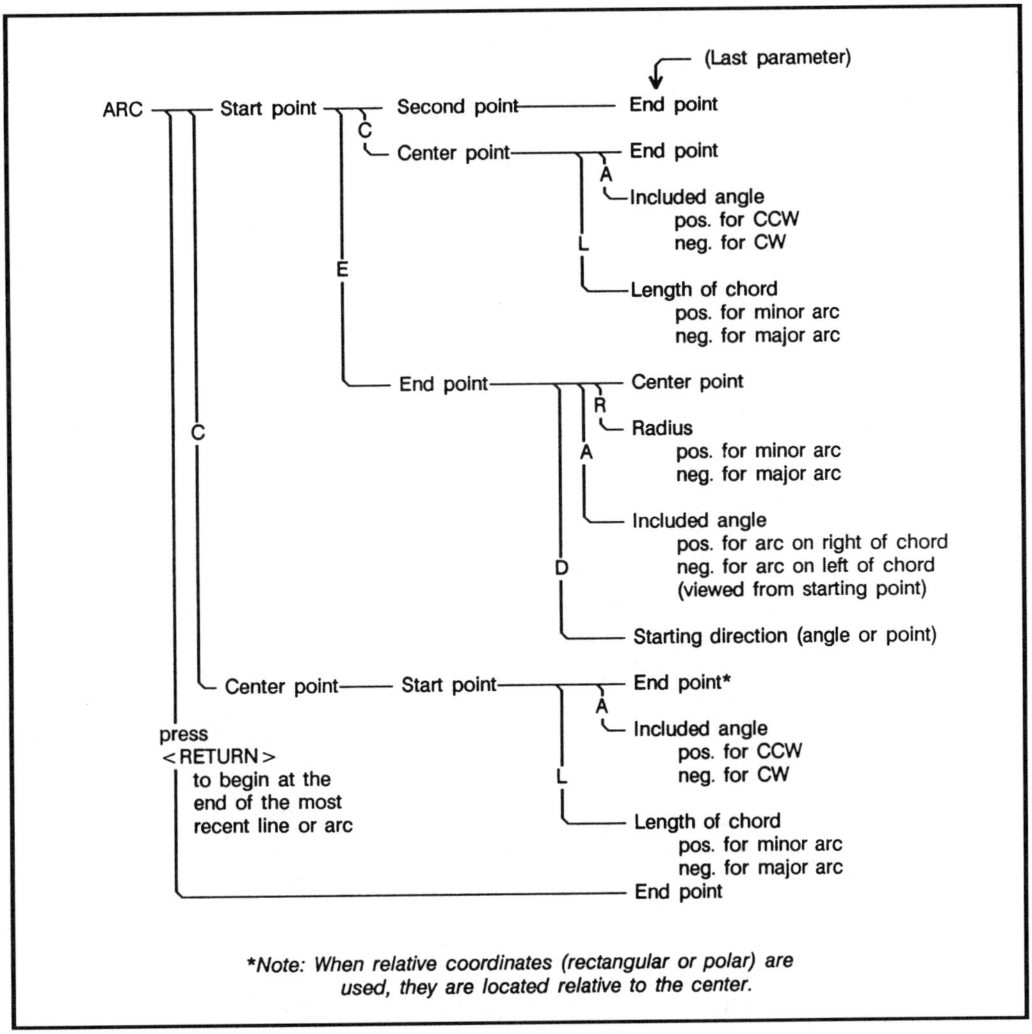

Figure 10-4: Listing of ARC data entry methods.

Figure 10-4 lists the 12 ways to enter the data necessary to define an arc. See Chapter 44, "Hands-on Exercises," for an arc exercise.

NOTE: *When dragmode is on (see "DRAGMODE" above), you can drag the arc by entering* ***drag*** *before entering the last parameter, then use the pointer to place the arc.*

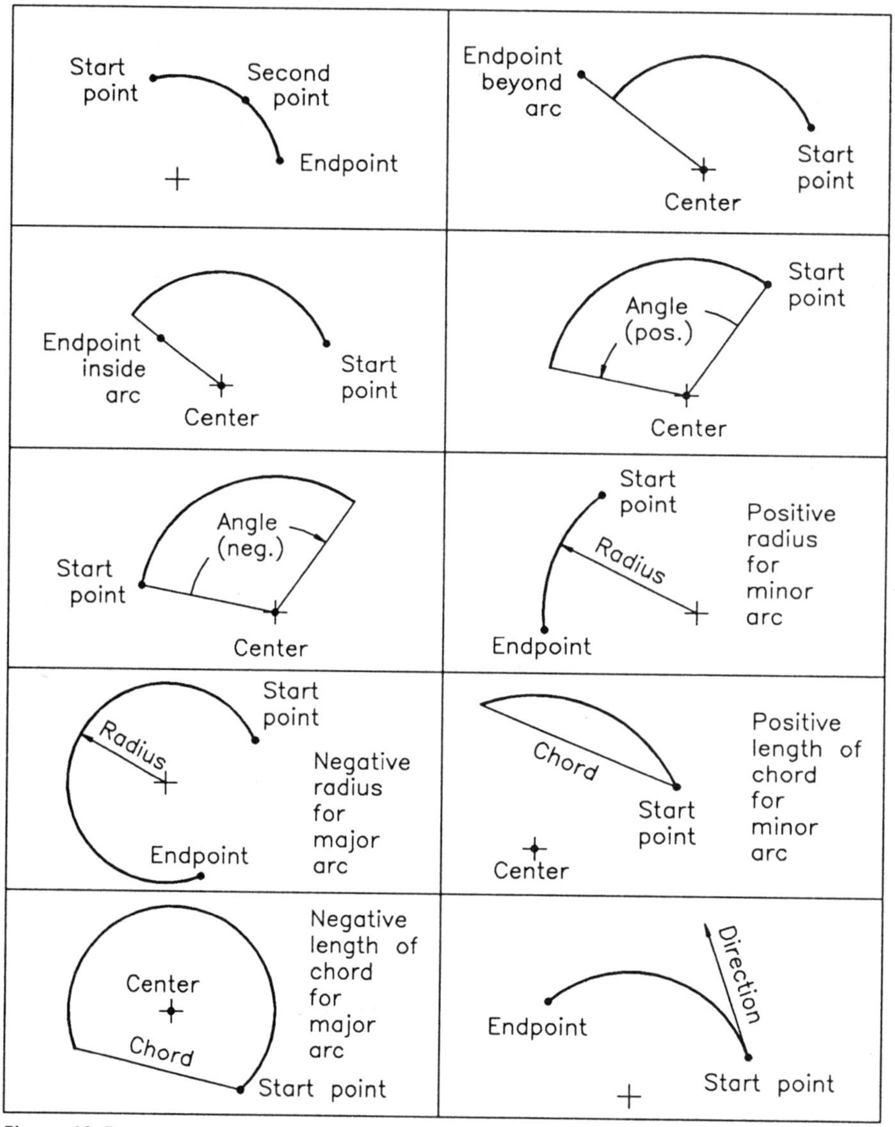

Figure 10-5: Drawings of ARC terminology.

POLYGON Draws a regular polygon

COMMAND LINE: **polygon**

Choose the Polygon icon to draw a regular polygon.

Figure 10-6: The Polygon icon from the Polygon flyout of the Draw toolbar.

When prompted, enter the number of sides. Then locate the center, and enter **i** for a polygon inscribed in a circle or **c** for a polygon circumscribed about a circle. Finally, enter the radius of the circle.

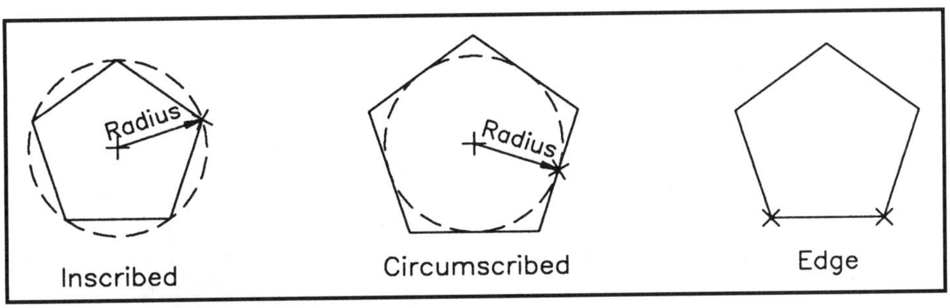

Figure 10-7: Three methods to create a polygon.

Another way to define the polygon is to define one of its edges. After entering the number of sides, enter **e** (for Edge) and then locate the endpoints of one side. The polygon will be drawn counterclockwise from that starting edge.

ELLIPSE Draws an ellipse with specified axes

COMMAND LINE: **ellipse**

Choose the Ellipse icon to draw an ellipse or elliptical arc with specific axes.

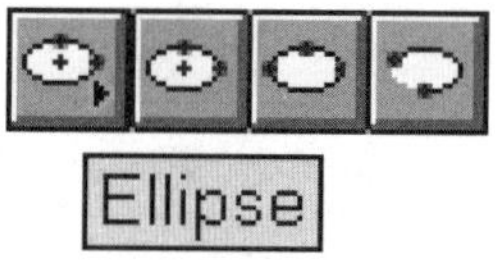

Figure 10-8: The Ellipse flyout from the Ellipse flyout of the Draw toolbar.

Figure 10-9 below shows four methods of creating an ellipse.

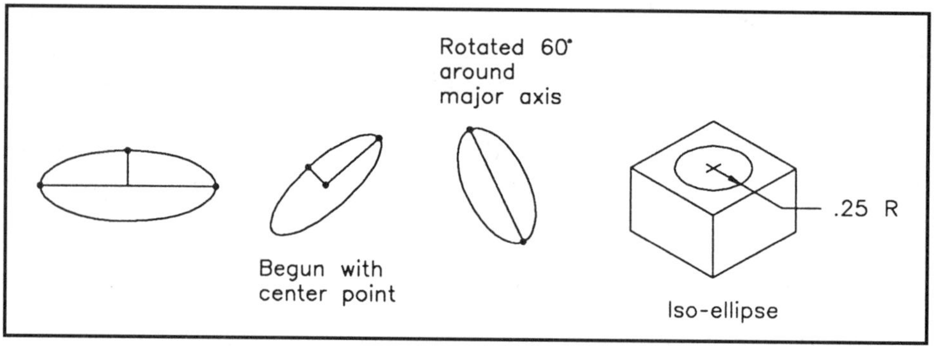

Figure 10-9: Different ways to create an ellipse.

There are four ways to create an ellipse:

1. The default method is to enter three points for the major and minor axis endpoints. The first two points determine the endpoints of one axis, and the third point determines the half-length of the other axis.

2. Another option is to define the center of the ellipse followed by one endpoint for each axis. To do so, choose the Ellipse Center icon or enter **c** at the ellipse prompt.

3. You can also define the ellipse as though it were created by viewing a circle at a certain angle. To do so, enter the first two points to define the major axis (by either method above). Then enter **r**, then the number of degrees that you want the circle rotated around that axis.

A rotation angle of 0 produces a circle, while a rotation angle of near 90 degrees produces an ellipse that's almost flat (nearly an edge view of a circle).

NOTE: *The system won't accept an entry of 90 degrees.*

4. If you're drawing in isometric mode (see Chapter 29, "Isometric Drawing"), one more option appears in the prompt. You can enter **i** for an isometric circle, then locate the center and then set the radius (or enter **d** and set the diameter). AutoCAD will place the ellipse at the proper viewing angle and rotation for whatever isometric plane you are currently on (Left, Top or Right).

If you do not need a full ellipse, you can specify an elliptical arc. Choose the Ellipse Arc icon or enter **a** at the ellipse prompt. You'll define the base ellipse by the same methods described above. The difference is that after defining the base ellipse, you're prompted to define the start and end angles for the elliptical arc.

PELLIPSE A setting variable to control polyline ellipse creation

COMMAND LINE: **pellipse**

AutoCAD Release 13 draws ellipses with a true ellipse object type. If you need to create a polyline approximation of an ellipse for compatibility with older versions of AutoCAD, enter **pellipse** at the command line and set its value to 1.

NOTE. *The system variable PELLIPSE (polyline ellipse) will not be supported in any future release of AutoCAD.*

Moving on

You've learned how to create simple 2D figures, and you're now ready to control views. Chapter 11, "Looking Around," shows you how to manage zoom viewing and adjust magnification of your work.

CHAPTER 11

Looking Around

In this chapter you'll learn about the most commonly used viewing commands. The ability to control views of your work is one of the principal features that sets computer-aided drafting apart from manual drafting. AutoCAD provides a number of commands to adjust the magnification, position and management views of your drawing.

ZOOM Displays a larger or smaller portion of your drawing

COMMAND LINE: **zoom**

Figure 11-1: The Zoom icon image from the Standard toolbar.

The ZOOM command applies only to the current viewport, unless you're in Paper Space, where it applies to the Paper Space view.

When prompted, you may enter a scale factor or a letter option, as described below.

To enter a scale factor, enter a number greater than one to zoom in and magnify part of the drawing. Enter a number smaller than one to zoom out (demagnify) and show more of the drawing. There are several ways to indicate the scale factor.

> Enter the number only to indicate the magnification factor by which the full drawing (limits) will be multiplied, regardless of the magnification of the current display. A magnification factor of 1 displays the drawing at full drawing scale, but centered at the center of the previous display.
>
> Enter the number followed by **x** to indicate the magnification factor by which the current display will be multiplied.

When TILEMODE is 0 and you're in Model Space, enter the number followed by **xp** to scale the current viewport in relation to Paper Space. For example, if you enter **.25xp**, the units in the current viewport will be one-quarter the size of those in Paper Space (both onscreen and in plotmode).

As an alternative, you may enter any of the following letter options:

a to display the full drawing (limits or extents, whichever is greater).

e to display the drawing extents. This fills the screen with all the drawing objects and thus produces the largest-possible magnification of all the objects at once.

c followed by the center point and height of the area you want displayed.

l followed by the lower-left corner and height of the area you want displayed.

p to return to the previous display. The 10 previous displays (whether zooms or pans) are saved in memory for this purpose.

v (for viewmax) to display the entire virtual screen. This zooms out to display the greatest amount of your drawing that can be shown without a regeneration.

w, and then locate opposite corners of the rectangular window you want displayed.

d to zoom and pan dynamically. A special display indicates the current screen as a highlighted (dotted) rectangle; the drawing limits or extents, whichever are larger, as a white rectangle; the high-speed zooming area, as four red corners; and the selection box.

To locate the selection box anywhere onscreen, move the pointer. To adjust the size of the selection box, press the pick button and then move the right edge of the box with the pointer. You can press the pick button as many times as you want to toggle back and forth and refine the location and size of the selection box. After the selection box has been adjusted to the desired location and size, press Enter.

You can zoom while you're in other commands (and if you're being prompted for anything but a text string). To do so, enter **'zoom** (notice the apostrophe). This transparent use of 'ZOOM works only when VIEWRES is set for fast zooms (see "VIEWRES" below) and no regeneration is required. ZOOM All and ZOOM Extents always force a regeneration. But you can give a name to a view that's the equivalent of a ZOOM All, then use 'VIEW transparently to restore that view, assuming a regeneration is not required (see "VIEW" below).

AERIAL VIEW Displays a bird's-eye view for fast panning & zooming

COMMAND LINE: **dsviewer**

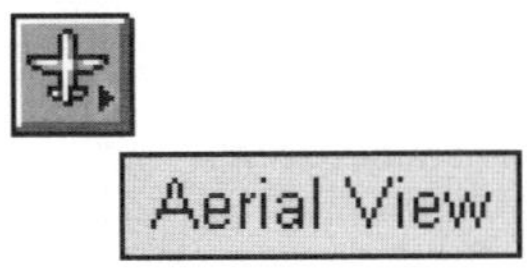

Figure 11-2: Aerial View icon from the Standard toolbar.

Click on the Aerial View icon or choose Aerial View from the Tools pull-down menu. To use the aerial view, AutoCAD must be configured for the Windows Accelerated Display driver with the Display List option turned on. The Aerial View window, shown in Figure 11-3, is similar in some ways to ZOOM DYNAMIC in that it displays your entire drawing and allows you to quickly specify what part to display in the drawing window. The biggest two differences between aerial view and ZOOM DYNAMIC are that the aerial view is displayed in a small window on top of your drawing and that it can be made permanently available.

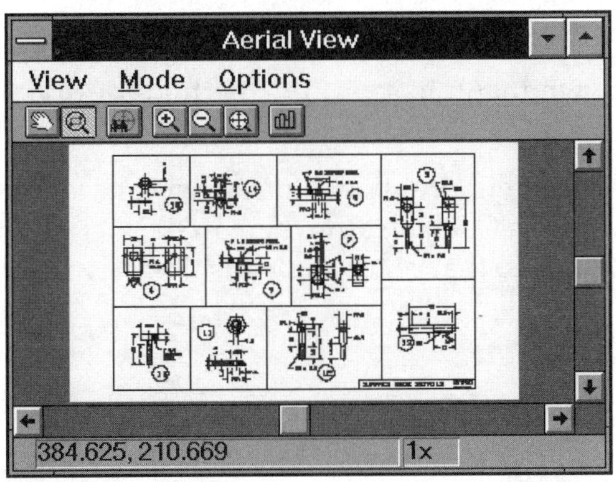

Figure 11-3: The Aerial View window and its icons.

Aerial View Window

Pull down the View menu in the Aerial View window to control the Aerial View. Note that the commands affect the Aerial View only and not the drawing window.

Zoom In Doubles the magnification of the view each time you select it.

Figure 11-4: The Zoom In icon.

Zoom Out halves the magnification of the view.

Figure 11-5: The Zoom Out icon.

Zoom Global displays the entire drawing.

Figure 11-6: The Zoom Global icon.

The scroll bars along the bottom and right side of the Aerial View window allow you to pan around your view. You can drag the scroll box and watch the view pan dynamically, but as soon as you let go, the scroll box centers itself in the bar again. This represents that the aerial view is limitless and that there is no upper or lower boundary to the scroll bar.

Use the Mode pull-down menu to select the method for updating the drawing window:

Pan mode displays the current drawing window view as a dotted rectangle in the Aerial View window. Clicking anywhere in the Aerial View window pans the display rectangle to that point and pans the drawing window.

Figure 11-7: The Pan icon.

Zoom mode displays crosshairs in the Aerial View window. Pick any two points to define a zoom window, which is then displayed in the drawing window.

Figure 11-8: The Zoom icon.

Locator mode is available only from the icon bar. It displays a small target cursor that you drag in the drawing window. As you drag the locator icon, a magnified display of the area appears in the Aerial View window. Release the pick button in the drawing window to zoom in on the located area.

Figure 11-9: The Locator icon.

The Options pull-down menu contains toggles to control the behavior of the Aerial View window. When these options are checked, they set the following actions:

> Auto Viewport sets the aerial view to automatically switch to the active viewport in the drawing window.
>
> Window on Top displays the Aerial View window permanently on top of the drawing window.
>
> Dynamic Update sets the aerial view to track and display every change performed in the drawing window. With large drawings, this option can slow the performance of AutoCAD. When Dynamic Update is off, you must click in the Aerial View title bar to update the view.
>
> Locator Magnification displays a scroll bar to set the magnification value used by the locator mode.
>
> Display Statistics displays various information about the current viewport in the aerial view and the amount of memory being used by the viewer.

Figure 11-10: The Display Statistics icon.

PAN Shifts the displayed part of the drawing without changing the magnification

COMMAND LINE: **pan**

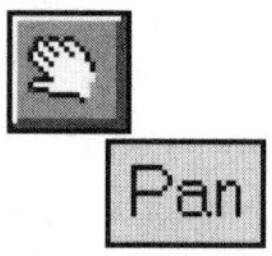

Figure 11-11: The Pan icon from the Standard toolbar.

NOTE: Unless you're in Paper Space, the PAN command applies only to the current viewport.

When prompted for the displacement, enter the following:

1. The coordinates that define the direction (from 0,0) you want the picture to be moved. Press Enter when prompted for the second point.
2. Two points (using keyboard or pointer) that show where you want a point in the picture shifted from and where to place it.

You can also pan by using a dynamic zoom (ZOOM D) and retaining the same size for the selection box.

You can pan while you're in other commands (while you're being prompted for anything but a text string). To do so, click on the Pan icon or enter **'pan** (notice the apostrophe). This transparent use of 'pan works only when VIEWRES is set for fast zooms (see "VIEWRES" below) and no regeneration is required.

VIEW Allows you to save and restore named views

COMMAND LINE: **ddview**

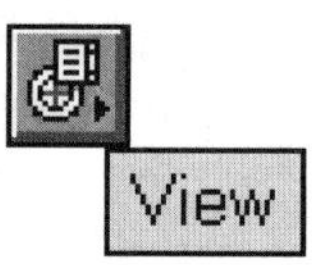

Figure 11-12: The View icon from the Standard toolbar.

Click the View icon or choose Named Views… from the View pull-down menu to display the View Control dialog in Figure 11-13. All the named views are displayed in the Views list box in the top of the dialog. The buttons at the bottom of the dialog activate commands to manipulate the currently highlighted named view.

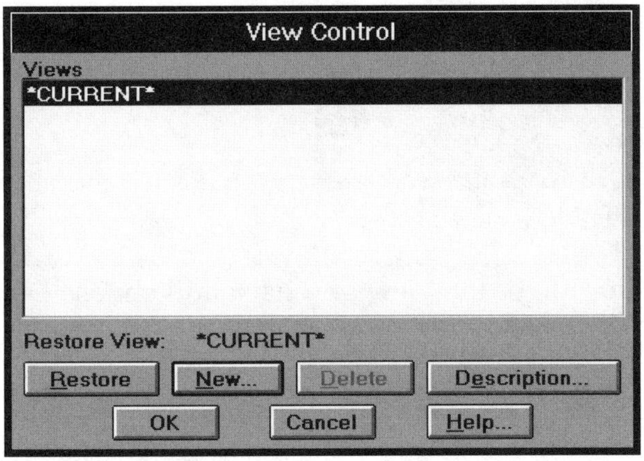

Figure 11-13: The View Control dialog.

To select a view,

1. Highlight the view in the list.
2. Click on Restore to display the highlighted named view in the display window.
3. Click on OK to restore the view.

To name a view,

1. Click on New... to display the Define New View dialog, shown in Figure 11-14.
2. Type the name in the New Name field.
3. The radio buttons let you choose a view save method as follows:

Choose Current Display to save the entire display as the new view. Choose Define Window to activate the Window< button. Then choose Window< and pick two corners of a window.

4. Click on the Save View button to return to the View Control dialog.

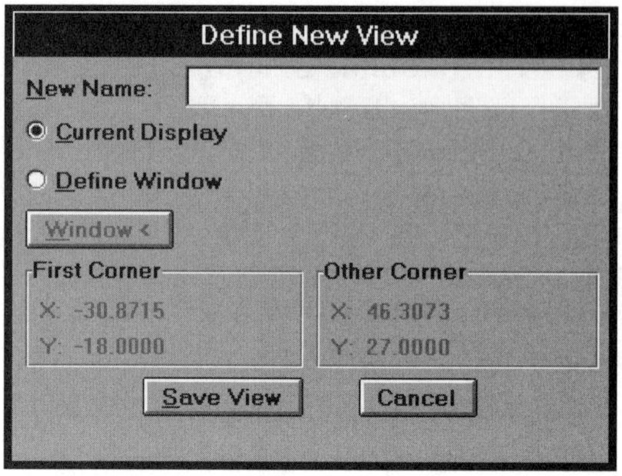

Figure 11-14: The Define New View dialog.

To delete a view, highlight the view in the list and choose Delete.

To display information about the highlighted view, click on the Description button.

NOTE: If you're in Paper Space and select a Model Space view to be restored, you are prompted to select a viewport. AutoCAD then switches you to Model Space and restores the selected view. If you are in Model Space, the Restore button is disabled whenever a Paper Space view is selected.

RENAME Changes the name assigned to an object

COMMAND LINE: **ddrename**

1. Select Rename from the Data pull-down menu to display the Rename dialog, shown in Figure 11-15.
2. Select an object type from the Named Objects list at left; all objects of that type will then be displayed in the Items list at right.

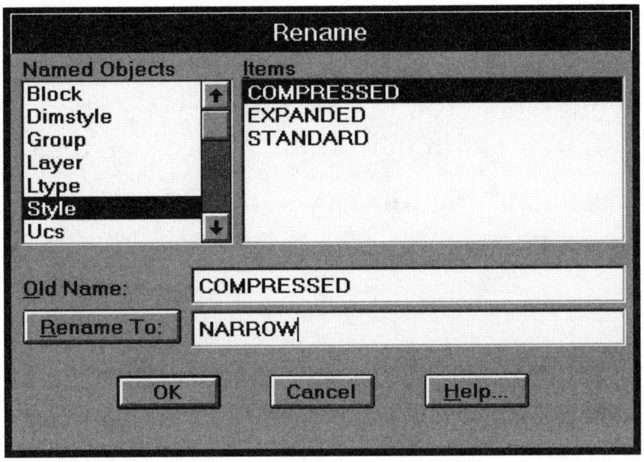

Figure 11-15: The Rename dialog.

3. Select an item from the Items list, and its name appears in the Old Name field.
4. Enter a new name in the Rename To field.
5. Click on the Rename To button to make the change.

NOTE: Certain items cannot be renamed, such as layer 0 or the text style Standard.

VIEWRES Controls the speed of zooms & pans and the resolution of circles & arcs in magnified views

COMMAND LINE: **viewres**

Enter **viewres** at the command line, and then enter **y** if you want faster zooms and pans. If you enter **n**, all zooms and pans will cause a regeneration, which is slower than a redraw.

Then enter the number that defines the circle percent resolution. The higher the number, the rounder the circles and arcs, but the slower the regeneration. The default is 100.

If you have zoomed in and find that the circles and arcs are too crude, do a REGEN to fix the current display, or reset VIEWRES with N or a higher circle percent number.

Moving on

In this chapter you learned common viewing commands and ways to control views of your work. You're now ready to learn how to control the precision of your drawings through AutoCAD's osnap tools.

Chapter 12, "Object Snap," introduces you to object snaps to aid you in the creation of precise drawings.

Object Snap

Every object you design and draw is described by its relationship to other objects in the design drawing. A door, for example, is a certain distance from a wall; a weld is placed at the intersection of two plates; or a belt is tangent to the pulley that drives it. Each of these precise conditions can be located using *object snaps.*

Object snaps locate specific points on existing geometry to assist in the creation of new geometry. They represent the most important concept to master in improving your drawing precision.

OSNAP Snaps new points to points already in the drawing

COMMAND LINE: **ddosnap**

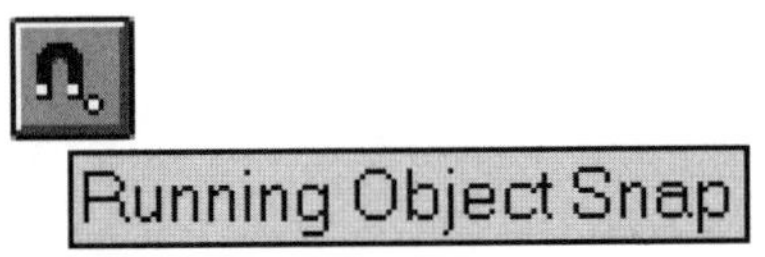

Figure 12-1: The Running Object Snap icon from the Object Snap flyout of the Standard toolbar.

To enter a point with object snap, you must select an object snap mode. You can set a *running osnap,* which then applies the selected mode to all subsequent points until you clear the setting. Or you can select modes on a point-by-point basis using *osnap override.*

Running Osnap

To set a running osnap, select Running Object Snap... from the Options pull-down menu. This command displays the Object Snap dialog shown in Figure 12-2. Click in the check box for the osnap mode you want to activate (as described in "Selecting an Osnap Mode" below), and pick the OK button.

As a general rule, cancel running osnap modes as soon as you finish using them. To cancel a running osnap, display the dialog again and click on the Clear All button beneath the check boxes. The selected osnaps will be evaluated for every point that you pick unless you use an override osnap mode.

No running osnap modes are present when a new drawing is started.

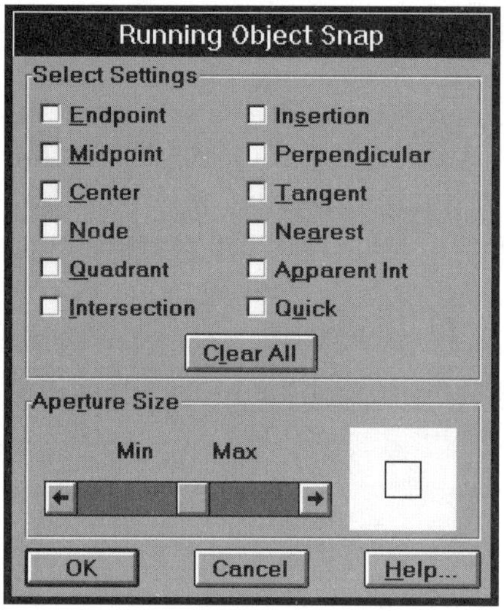

Figure 12-2: The Running Object Snap dialog.

Osnap Override

If you wish to set the osnap mode point by point, or if you wish to depart from the running osnap mode for a particular point, use osnap override. When you are about to enter the point, select a mode as described below under "Selecting an Osnap Mode." The mode you choose works for that point only; then, if you want one, you must select another osnap mode for the next point.

Selecting an Osnap Mode

You can enter any of the following osnap modes from the keyboard or the cursor menu, or you can display the Object Snap toolbar. Choose Toolbars from the Tools pull-down menu and then choose Osnap to display the Object Snap toolbar. To display the cursor menu, shown in Figure 12-3, press Button 3 on your input device or hold down the Shift key while pressing Button 2.

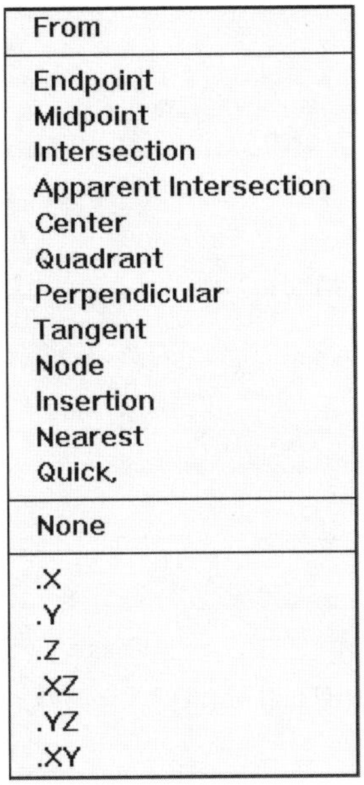

Figure 12-3: The cursor menu.

To use the keyboard, type the first three letters (shown in boldface) of the osnap modes described below:

Figure 12-4: The From osnap icon.

From (**fro**) is not technically an osnap. It allows you to specify a base point followed by a distance to offset from that point. For example, when prompted for the first point of a line segment, you choose the Snap From icon (or enter **fro**). When you are prompted for the base point, you might choose the Snap to Endpoint icon (or enter **end**) to snap to the endpoint of an existing line. When prompted for an offset, you enter **@2,0**. The result is that your line starts 2 units to the right of the selected endpoint.

Figure 12-5: The Nearest osnap icon.

Nearest (**nea**) snaps to the point on a line, circle, arc or point that's nearest to the crosshairs.

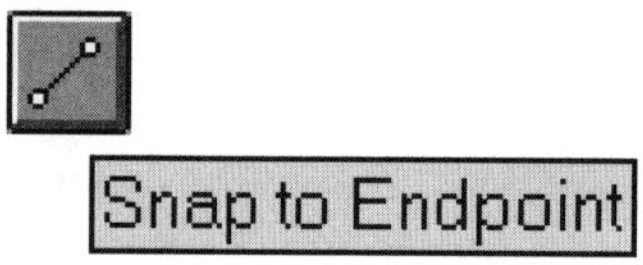

Figure 12-6: The Endpoint osnap icon.

Endpoint (**end**) snaps to the closest endpoint of a line or arc.

Figure 12-7: The Midpoint osnap icon.

Midpoint (**mid**) snaps to the midpoint of a line or arc.

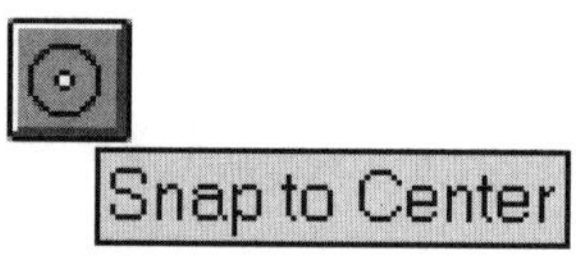

Figure 12-8: The Center osnap icon.

Center (**cen**) snaps to the center of a circle or arc.

Figure 12-9: The Node osnap icon.

Node (**nod**) snaps to a point entity.

Figure 12-10: The Quadrant osnap icon.

Quadrant (**qua**) snaps to a point on a circle or arc. The snap-point is located at 0, 90, 180 or 270 degrees.

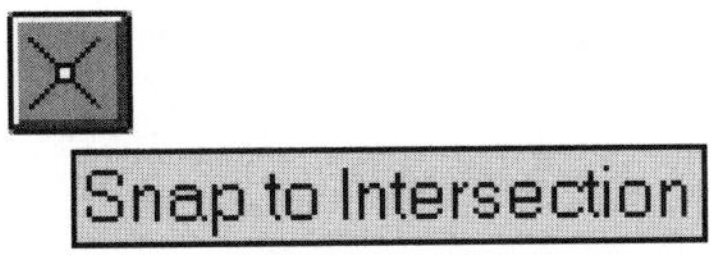

Figure 12-11: The Intersection osnap icon.

Intersection (**int**) snaps to the intersection of two objects such as two lines, arcs or circles.

Figure 12-12: The Apparent osnap icon.

Apparent (**app**) Intersection snaps to the point in the current view where two objects appear to intersect, regardless of whether or not they really intersect in 3D space. The point is placed by calculating a vector from the viewpoint through the apparent intersection and locating where that vector intersects the current User Coordinate System.

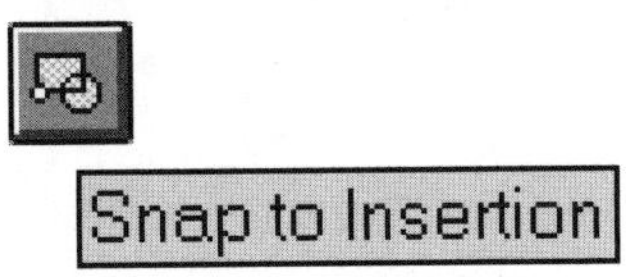

Figure 12-13: The Insert osnap icon.

Insert (**ins**) snaps to the insertion point of text, a block, a shape or an xref.

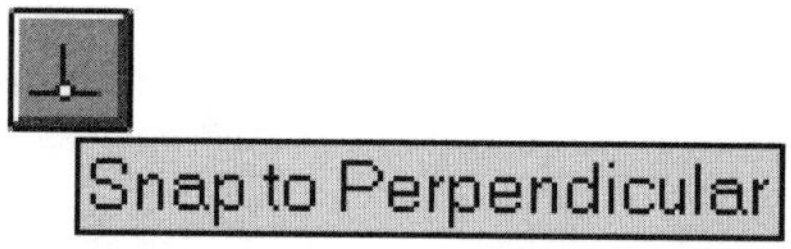

Figure 12-14: The Perpendicular osnap icon.

Perpendicular (**per**) snaps to the point on a line that forms a perpendicular line with the last point entered, or to the point on an arc or circle that forms a line normal to the circle with the last point entered. You can apply perpendicular to both the from and to endpoints of a line.

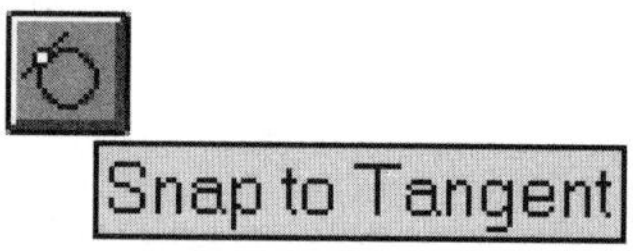

Figure 12-15: The Tangent osnap icon.

Tangent (**tan**) snaps to the point on a circle or arc that forms a tangent with the last point entered. You can apply tangent to both the from and to points of a line and thus draw a line tangent to two circles or arcs. You can also apply tangent to the three points of a three-point circle.

Figure 12-16: The None osnap icon.

None (**non**) temporarily disables any running osnaps for the next point selected.

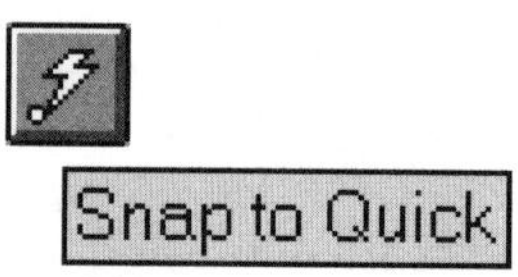

Figure 12-17: The Quick osnap icon.

Quick (**qui**) instructs AutoCAD to accept the first point found that meets the other specified osnap requirements. When AutoCAD finds multiple points that meet the osnap requirements, it selects the point closest to the crosshairs. When quick mode is used with one or more of the above modes, AutoCAD selects the first point it finds that suits the requirements instead of the closest point.

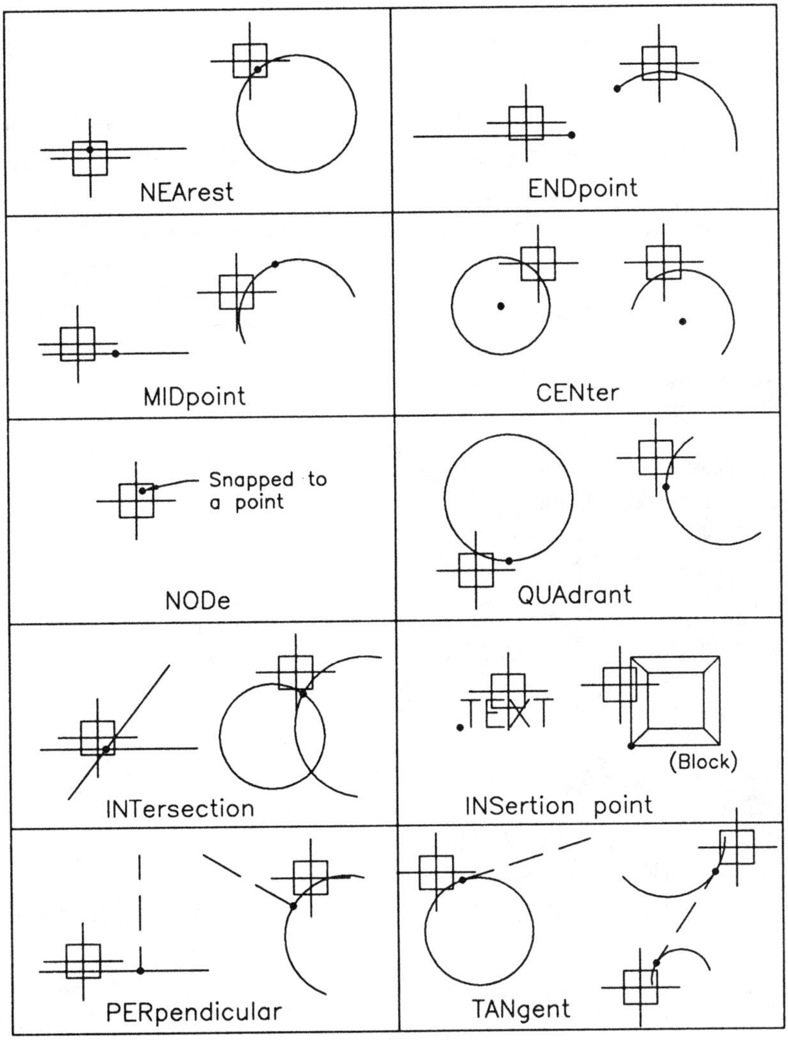

Figure 12-18: Using AutoCAD's object snap modes.

Figure 12-18 illustrates each of the osnap modes. Note that osnap overrides ortho, finds points only on visible layers, and won't snap to endpoints of spaces in hidden lines, center lines and some parts of blocks. Osnap sometimes overrides points entered from the keyboard.

See Chapter 44, "Hands-on Exercises 1," for an osnap exercise.

APERTURE Adjusts the size of the osnap target box

COMMAND LINE: **ddosnap**

The Running Object Snap dialog contains a scroll bar at bottom to adjust the size of the osnap target box. Figure 12-19 shows the scroll bar and the image tile to the right. Drag the scroll box to the left to reduce the aperture size; drag the scroll box to the right to increase the aperture.

You can also type the command **aperture** at the keyboard and, when prompted, enter the desired height in number of pixels (2 through 50).

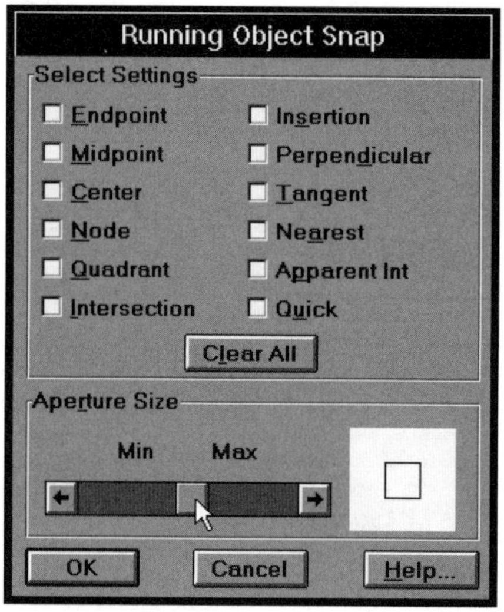

Figure 12-19: The osnap aperture slider bar in the Running Object Snap dialog box.

Moving on

Often, you need to extract information about a drawing. The next chapter, "Inquiry," introduces some of the commands you can use to extract information about drawing geometry.

Nevertheless, the information you extract with the inquiry commands will be useless unless you draw with precision, using coordinates, snap grids and object snaps.

CHAPTER 13

Inquiry

The inquiry commands let you extract information regarding the length, direction and area of the objects that you draw. Most of the commands described below are found under the Inquiry flyout in the Object Properties toolbar.

Figure 13-1: The Inquiry flyout in the Object Properties toolbar.

LOCATE POINT Shows the coordinates or visual location of a point

COMMAND LINE: **id**

Figure 13-2: The Locate Point icon from the Inquiry flyout of the Object Properties toolbar.

Choose the Locate Point icon to show the coordinates or visual location of a point. When prompted, pick a point in the drawing window, and its coordinates will be displayed. Often, it is best to use the osnap tools with the LOCATE POINT command if you need to find the coordinates of a specific point on an object (see "OSNAP" in Chapter 12, "Object Snap").

DISTANCE Displays distances & angles between two points

COMMAND LINE: **dist**

Figure 13-3: The Distance icon from the Inquiry flyout of the Object Properties toolbar.

Choose the Distance icon to display distances and angles between two points. When prompted, pick two points in the drawing window. The order in which you choose the points affects the sign of the rectangular distances and the size of the angle. You may enter 3D locations as X, Y and Z coordinates.

It's best if you use the osnap tools with the DISTANCE command if you are measuring points on an object. See "OSNAP" in Chapter 12, "Object Snap."

AREA Calculates the area of various shapes

COMMAND LINE: **area**

Figure 13-4: The Area icon from the Inquiry flyout of the Object Properties toolbar.

Choose the Area icon, shown in Figure 13-4. When prompted, locate the series of points (corners) defining a polygon. The prompt for the next point reappears until you press Enter. If you have previously initiated the add/subtract mode, you'll then be prompted for further options for adjusting the running total. It's best to use osnap when locating a series of points on an object. See "OSNAP" in Chapter 12, "Object Snap."

Enter **o**, then select an object (that is, a circle or polyline). A polyline's width is ignored; its area is based on its centerline. The prompt for the next circle or polyline reappears until you press Enter. If you have previously initiated the add/subtract mode, you'll be prompted for further options for adjusting the running total:

> Enter **a** to initiate the add mode. The next area(s) are added into a running total.
>
> Enter **s** to initiate the subtract mode. The next area(s) are subtracted from the running total.

Remember that every time you use the AREA command, the running total is reset to 0 (zero).

The internal area surrounded by several overlapping objects can be quickly calculated if you use the BOUNDARY command. See "BOUNDARY" in Chapter 26, "Hatching."

LIST Lists database information & statistics of one or more objects

COMMAND LINE: **list**

Figure 13-5: The List icon from the Inquiry flyout of the Object Properties toolbar.

Choose the List icon. When prompted, select the items you want listed and press Enter. The information is displayed in a scrolling text window. To return to your drawing, click in the drawing window.

DBLIST Lists database information & statistics on all objects in a drawing

COMMAND LINE: **dblist**

DBLIST is an old command that can only be accessed by entering it from the command line. Similar to the LIST command, DBLIST simply provides textual information on every object in your drawing. The information is displayed in a scrolling text window. To return to your drawing, click in the drawing window.

Moving on

Using AutoCAD's internal database, you've learned how to use the inquiry commands and extract drawing information. You'll now learn how to review or edit your drawing, as it's often said that up to 50 percent of computer-aided drafting involves editing.

Chapter 14, "Editing—Group One," will introduce you to the first group of editing commands along with the concept of grip editing. Using these commands, you'll produce basic drafting assignments.

Editing—Group One

The real power of AutoCAD lies not in its drawing commands, but in its editing commands.

When you draw, for example, you create geometry from scratch. When you edit, you reuse the existing geometry to create and/or update new work.

To edit your work is to be more productive and efficient than to draw from scratch. Thus, the more time you spend using editing commands—versus drawing commands—the more productive you'll be.

MOVE Moves one or more objects a specified distance

COMMAND LINE: **move**

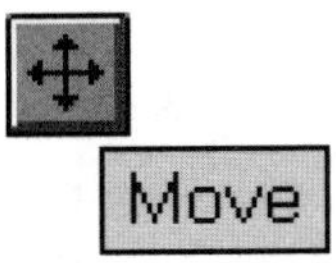

Figure 14-1: The Move icon from the Modify toolbar.

When prompted, select the objects you want to move.

At the prompt for the base point or displacement, enter one of the following, as shown in Figure 14-2:

Method 1 Enter the base point and second point of the displacement vector, using your keyboard or your pointing device.

Method 2 Enter the relative X, Y displacement at the base point prompt. Press Enter when you're prompted for the second point.

Method 3 When prompted for the base point, enter any point (0,0 will do). Then enter any form of relative coordinates when prompted for the second point.

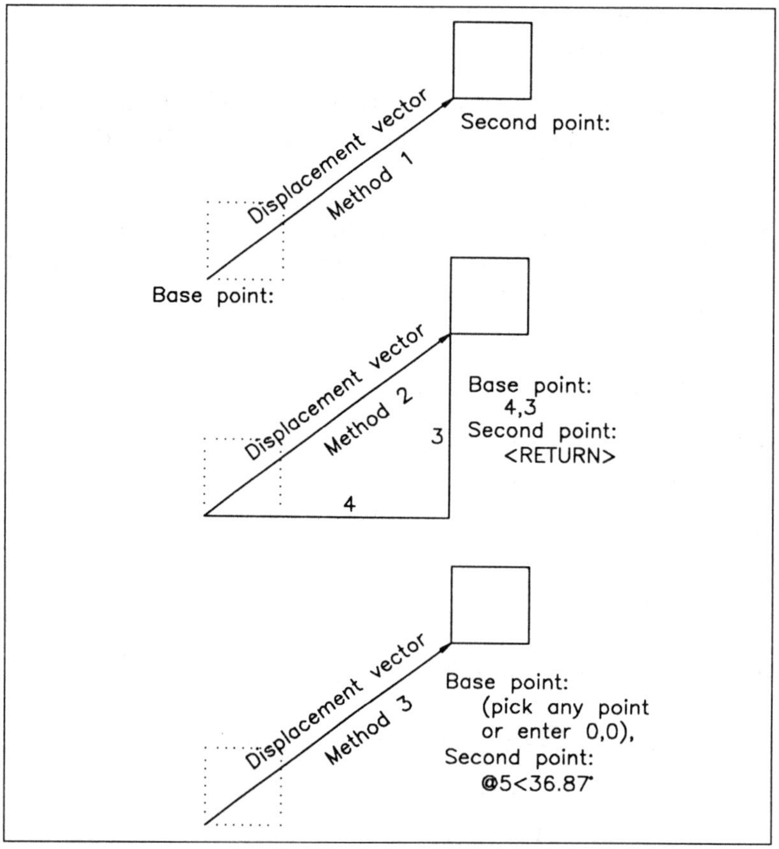

Figure 14-2: Three methods of using the MOVE command.

COPY Places one or more copies of object(s) at a specified displacement from the original objects

COMMAND LINE: **copy**

Figure 14-3: The Copy icon from the Copy flyout of the Modify toolbar.

This command works like the MOVE command, but the original objects remain where they were. You may copy single or multiple objects.

When prompted, select the object(s) you want to copy:

> To make a single copy, locate the base point and a single point of displacement. Press Enter to quit.
>
> To make multiple copies, enter **m** at the base point or displacement prompt, then locate the base point and several points of displacement. Press Enter to quit making copies.

MIRROR Flips one or more objects about a specified axis

COMMAND LINE: **mirror**

Figure 14-4: The Mirror icon from the Copy flyout of the Modify toolbar.

When prompted, select the objects to be flipped. Then locate the endpoints of the flip axis. (You'll usually want to toggle ortho on when locating the second endpoint.) Then enter **y** to delete or **n** to retain the original objects.

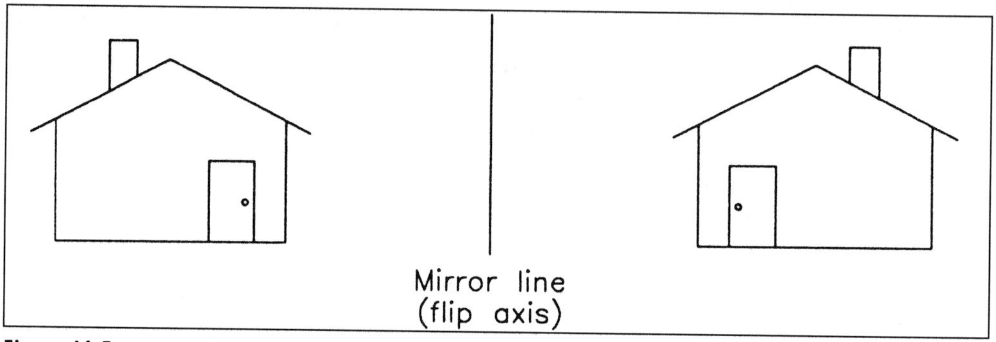

Figure 14-5: Using the MIRROR command.

You can drag the second point of the mirror line.

To keep text from being mirrored, enter **mirrtext** at the command line and set its value to 0.

OFFSET Draws parallel objects at a specified distance from the originals

COMMAND LINE: **offset**

Figure 14-6: The Offset icon from the Copy flyout of the Modify toolbar.

TIP: *For the greatest control, use OFFSET in plan view. When you use editing commands that change the actual geometry of the edited items, you have the most accurate visual control if you're in a plan view of the current UCS. Choose 3D Viewpoint Presets from the View pull-down menu, then choose Plan View, then Current (see Chapter 35, "3D Viewing," for more details). This is already set for you if you're using the AutoCAD default drawing.*

When prompted for the offset distance, you have two options:

Enter the distance for the offset, then select the object and pick a point on the screen to indicate on which side of the original object the new offset object should be placed.

Enter **t**, then select the object and locate a point which the object will pass through.

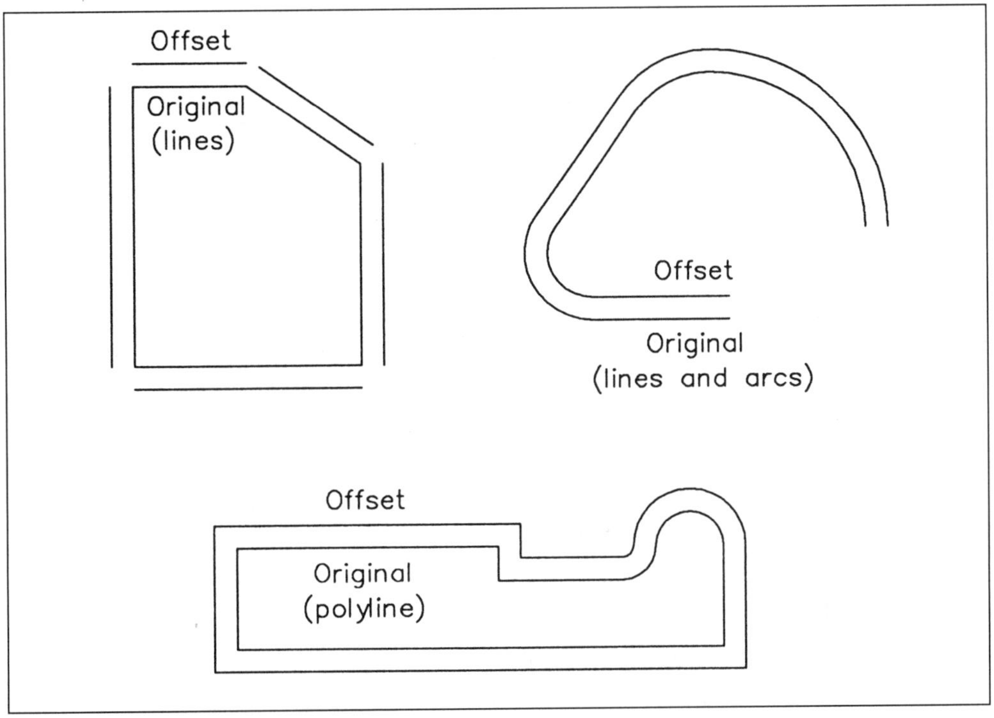

Figure 14-7: Using the OFFSET command.

NOTE: AutoCAD offsets connected lines and arcs differently from polylines, especially at sharp corners. Notice how the lines example in Figure 14-7 allows the offset objects to break apart at the corners while the polyline example preserves corner conditions.

FILLET Fillets objects with a specified radius

COMMAND LINE: **fillet**

Figure 14-8: The Fillet icon from the Feature flyout of the Modify toolbar.

1. Set the radius. When prompted with the fillet options, enter **r** and then enter your desired radius (such as **.25**). To form a sharp corner, you can set the radius to 0. Doing so cleanly connects two lines or arcs and automatically trims them.

This step sets the radius, which is stored in a system variable. Unless you change it, the radius will be the same the next time you use FILLET.

2. Implement the fillet. If the radius has been set, choose the Fillet icon again (or reenter **fillet**), and select the objects you wish to fillet. You can select two lines, two arcs, a line and an arc and so on. Where you select the entity is important. In general, the point that you use to select the object identifies the part of the object that will be retained. The opposite end of the object will be trimmed during the fillet process.

When you fillet a 2D polyline, all corners will fillet at once (see "PLINE" in Chapter 28). 3D polylines cannot be filleted, but 3D solids can (see Chapter 34, "Solid Modeling").

You also have the option of setting the fillet trim mode at the main fillet prompt. Choose the Fillet icon (or enter **fillet**). At the first prompt, enter **t**. You are prompted to choose between the options Trim or No trim. Trim causes the FILLET command to trim the selected objects flush with the fillet arc. No trim leaves the object untouched after placing the fillet arc.

TIP: *For the greatest control, use TRIM in plan view. When you use editing commands that change the actual geometry of the edited items, you have the most accurate visual control if you're in a plan view of the current UCS. Choose 3D Viewpoint Presets from the View pull-down menu, then choose Plan View, then Current (see Chapter 35, "3D Viewing," for more details). This is already set for you if you're using the AutoCAD default drawing.*

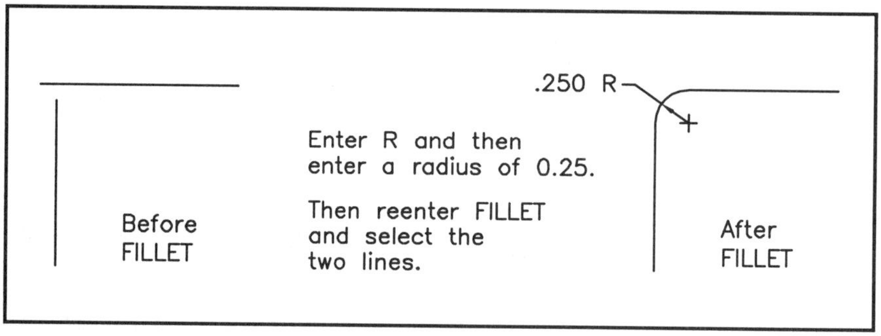

Figure 14-9: Using the FILLET command.

CHAMFER Bevels a corner with specified distances or angles

COMMAND LINE: **chamfer**

Figure 14-10: The Chamfer icon from the Feature flyout of the Modify toolbar.

1. Set the chamfer distances. You can specify a chamfer either by two distances or by a distance and an angle. Use D or A to toggle between the distance or angle mode.

When the CHAMFER prompt (Polyline/Distance/Angle/Trim/Method/<Select first line>) appears, do one of the following:

> To specify two distances, enter **d.** Then enter the first and second chamfer distance. (The default for the second distance is equal to the first distance.) Reenter the CHAMFER command, if necessary, and select the first and second objects. If you set no distances, the command creates a sharp corner—similar to the FILLET command with a radius of 0.
>
> To specify a distance and an angle, enter **a.** Then specify a first distance and an angle from the first line. Reenter the CHAMFER command if necessary, and select the two objects.
>
> The chamfer distances, angle and current mode are stored in a system variable and, unless you change them, will be the same the next time you use the CHAMFER command. This means the next time you enter the command you can simply select the object to chamfer.

NOTE: *Once you've set the chamfer distances and chamfer angle, you can toggle between the two modes by entering **m** at the main CHAMFER prompt. Then enter **d** or **a** to toggle on the distance or angle mode.*

2. Implement the chamfer. If the distances have been set, choose the Chamfer icon again (or reenter **chamfer**) and select the objects you wish to chamfer. You can select two lines, two arcs, a line and an arc and so on.

Where you select the object is important in determining where the chamfer is placed. In general, the point that you use to select the object identifies the part of the object that will be retained. The opposite end of the object will be trimmed during the chamfer process.

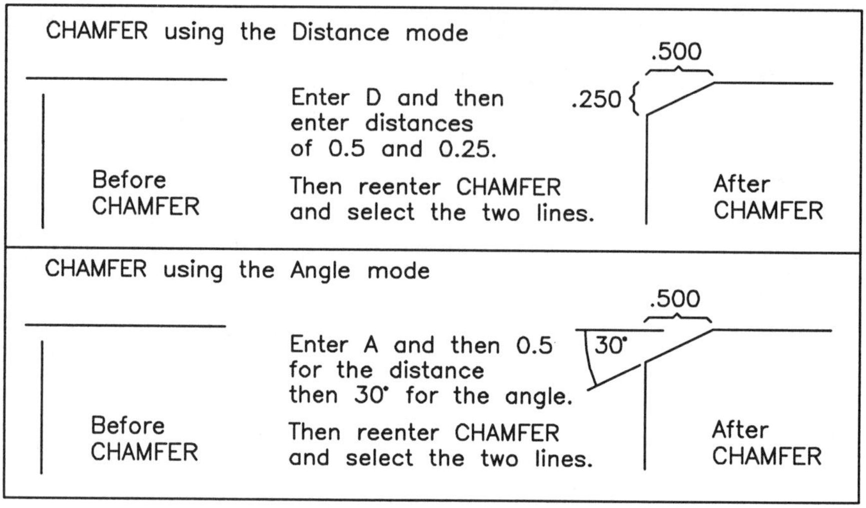

Figure 14-11: Using the CHAMFER command.

When you're using CHAMFER on a 2D polyline, all corners will chamfer at once (see "PLINE" in Chapter 28, "Polylines & Curves"). 3D polylines cannot be chamfered, but you may chamfer 3D solids (see Chapter 34, "Solid Modeling").

TIP: *For the greatest control, use CHAMFER in plan view. When you use editing commands that change the actual geometry of the edited items, you have the most accurate visual control if you're in a plan view of the current UCS. Choose 3D Viewpoint Presets from the View pull-down menu, choose Plan View and then choose Current (see Chapter 35, "3D Viewing," for more details). This is already set for you if you're using the AutoCAD default drawing.*

ROTATE Rotates objects in the X-Y plane about a specified point

COMMAND LINE: **rotate**

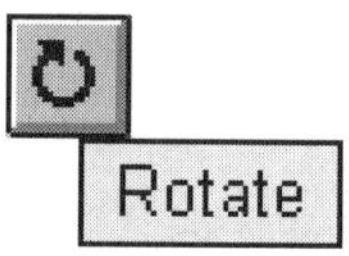

Figure 14-12: The Rotate icon from the Modify toolbar.

When prompted, select the objects. Then enter the base point around which you want the objects rotated. Do one of the following:

Enter the rotation angle (use the keyboard or drag an angle onscreen with the pointer).

Enter the reference angle. Enter **r**, then indicate the reference angle by selecting two features of the objects (such as the endpoints of a line). Then enter a new absolute angle for those two features. All the other selected objects will be rotated by the same amount. You can rotate an entire drawing.

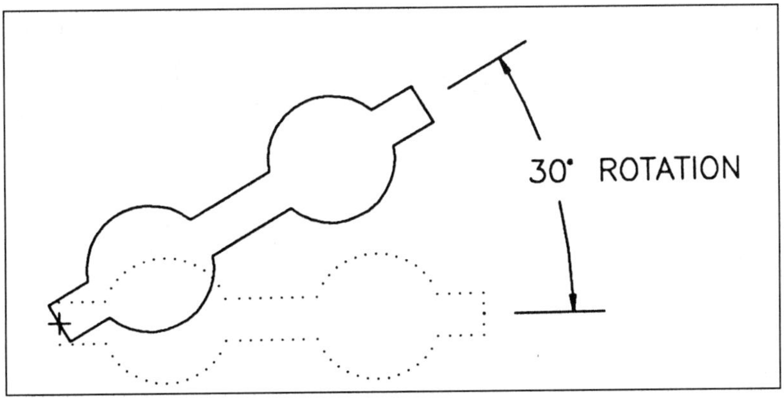

Figure 14-13: Using the ROTATE command.

SCALE Scales the size of objects in relation to a specified point

COMMAND LINE: **scale**

Figure 14-14: The Scale icon image from the Resize flyout of the Modify toolbar.

When prompted, select the object(s). Then enter the base point and the scaling factor, using the keyboard or pointer.

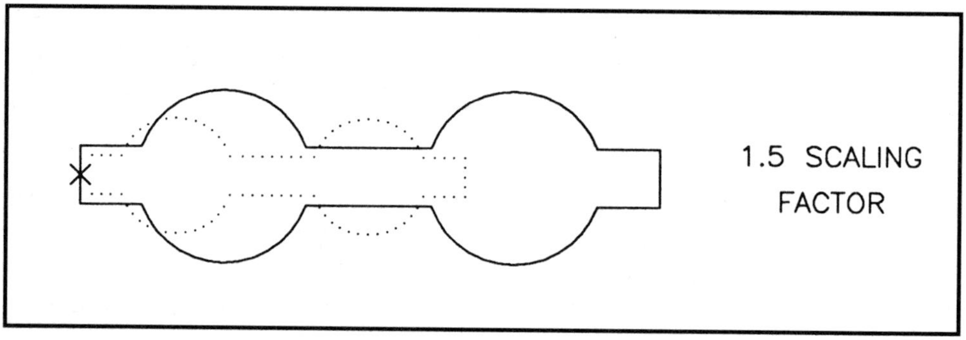

Figure 14-15: Using the SCALE command.

In place of the scaling factor, you may enter **r** and then select a reference distance (such as the endpoints of a line). Then enter a new absolute value for that distance. All the other objects will be scaled by the same amount. You can scale an entire drawing.

STRETCH Moves parts of objects while retaining connections to parts not moved

COMMAND LINE: **stretch**

Figure 14-16: The Stretch icon from the Resize flyout of the Modify toolbar.

How STRETCH affects an object depends on its relationship to the crossing window. Objects that are contained completely within the crossing window are moved. Objects that have one endpoint inside and one endpoint outside the window are stretched.

When prompted, select the objects you want to move and/or stretch using the default crossing method. You can also manually specify either a crossing window or crossing polygon. (If you select this command from the icon, a crossing window is automatically selected.)

Then indicate the displacement, as you do for the MOVE command.

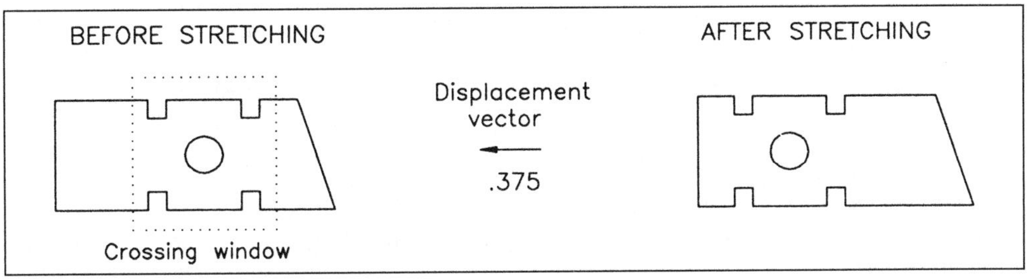

Figure 14-17: Using the STRETCH command.

Dimensions can be stretched (see Chapter 24, "Dimensions," for details on how to do this). Lines and 3D faces can be stretched in any of the three dimensions.

Editing With Grips

Grips are small, square boxes that appear at key locations on existing lines, circles, etc., as in Figure 14-17. Grips let you quickly accomplish certain editing functions (stretch, move, rotate, scale and mirror), each in single- or multiple-copy mode, without using the editing commands.

Even though everything you can do with grips can also be done with the regular editing commands, some people find the grip mode handy because it offers an alternate, intuitive approach to editing. You can toggle grip mode on and off and set the grips' size and color as explained below under "The Grips Dialog Box." AutoCAD's default configuration has grips turned on.

NOTE: *If you've disabled the grip mode, you can reactivate it with the Grips dialog box. Choose Grips... from the Options pull-down menu, click on the Enable Grips check box and then click the OK button.*

For help with grip editing, see the "Grip Exercise" in Chapter 44, "Hands-on Exercises."

Grip Locations

Here are the more common objects and grip locations (for a complete list, see "Grips" in the *AutoCAD Reference Manual*).

Object	AutoCAD grip point locations.
Point	On the point.
Line	Endpoints and midpoint.
Circle	Center and quadrants.
Arc	Endpoints and midpoint.
Polyline	Endpoints of all segments including midpoints of arc segments.
Block	Insertion point. (It is possible to enable grips on all objects within a block, as explained below in "Setting Grips Options.")
Text	Insertion point. (If the text has a second alignment point, a grip is also placed there.)
Paper Space	Viewport corners.

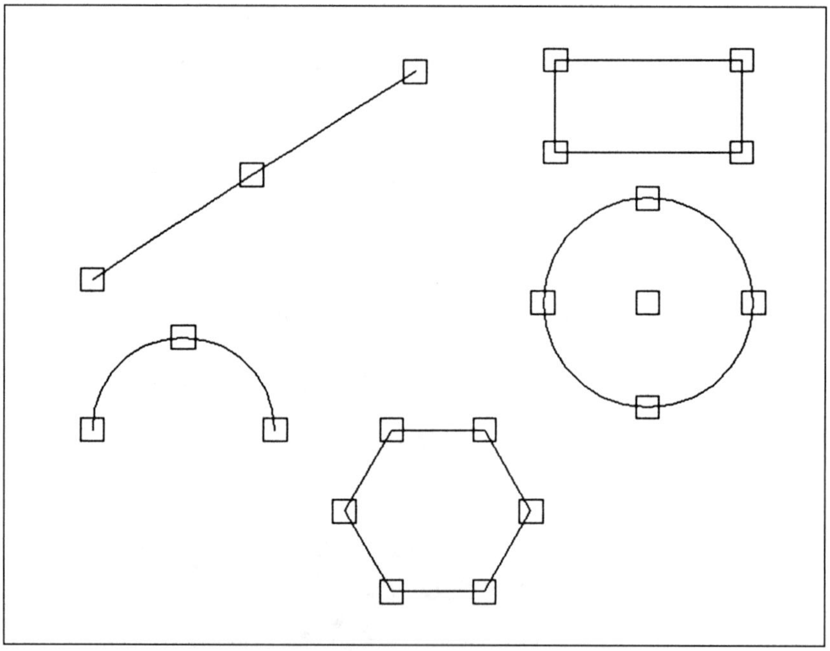

Figure 14-18: The different locator points for grips.

Editing a Single Object

Use grips to edit a single object as follows:

1. Select an object with the pointer. AutoCAD responds by placing grips at key locations.

2. Choose one of the grips.

3. AutoCAD activates stretch mode. You can select the other modes (move, rotate, scale or mirror) by pressing the Spacebar or Enter key one or more times.

4. By choosing a destination point with the pointer or keyboard, you may edit the object and then be returned to the command prompt. The object remains highlighted, and the grips are still available for further editing.

5. To deselect the object, press Esc. To remove the grips, press Esc again.

Editing Multiple Objects

Use grips to edit multiple objects as follows:

1. Select the objects. You can select them individually or, if Implied Windowing is enabled (see Chapter 7), you can use a regular or crossing window to select them. To do this, pick two points onscreen to form a window. If the second point is to the right of the first, then the window is a regular window; objects must be entirely inside it to be selected. If the second point is to the left of the first, then the window is a crossing window; objects must be at least partially inside it to be selected.

AutoCAD responds by placing grips at key locations. When you move the cursor inside the grip, the cursor snaps to the middle of the grip, accomplishing the same objective as if you had activated the corresponding osnap mode (such as endpoint, midpoint or center).

2. Choose one of the grips. This does two things. First, it starts the editing process. Second, it indicates which grip will serve as the base point for editing.

3. AutoCAD activates stretch mode. You can select the other modes (move, rotate, scale or mirror) by pressing the Spacebar or Enter key one or more times. You can move, rotate, scale or mirror the selected objects as a group. If you are in stretch mode, however, only one object will stretch.

NOTE: *You can force the stretch mode to affect more than one object by selecting several objects then holding down the Shift key while you pick grips on each object. Then pick the base point, and all selected objects will be affected.*

4. By choosing a destination point with the pointer or keyboard, you may edit the objects and then be returned to the command prompt. The object remains highlighted, and the grips are still available for further editing.

5. To deselect the object, press Esc. To remove the grips, press Esc again.

You may retain an object's grips but remove it from the selection set by holding down the Shift key and picking the object again. This is handy when, for example, you need to use one of the grips as a location to move or stretch other objects to, or as a target point for rotation.

The Five Modes

Suppose you have picked a line and chosen the end grip. Here is how each of the five modes works. These modes behave in a similar fashion for most objects.

Stretch	As you move the cursor, the line's selected end will stretch while the opposite end remains fixed. (For more on how stretch mode works with lines and other objects, see "Working With Stretch Mode" below.)
Move	As you move the cursor (attached to any grip), the size and orientation of the line remain the same while the line is moved from the base point (grip) to a destination point. The destination point may even be a grip on an object that is not in the current selection set.
Rotate	The selected grip becomes the base point for rotation, while the cursor position determines the amount of rotation.
Scale	The selected grip becomes the base point for scaling, while the cursor position determines the amount of scaling.
Mirror	The selected grip becomes the starting end of the mirror line, while the cursor position determines the other end of the mirror line.

In each of the modes, you may enter any of the following at the prompt:

b to select a different base point (another grip or any other point). Both the base point and the destination point can be entered either by using the pointer or entering coordinates at the keyboard.

c to start multiple-copy mode (described below). You can also enter multiple copy mode by pressing the Shift key while picking the first destination point.

u to undo the last editing operation. You can use U to delete the last copy or copies you placed or to get out of multiple-copy mode.

r (for the Rotate and Scale modes only) to enter a reference angle or scale followed by a new angle or scale. This is similar to the Reference option in the regular ROTATE and SCALE commands.

x to exit editing mode.

Using Stretch Mode With Different Objects

Stretch mode works somewhat differently for different objects. Here are a few examples:

Line	If you pick an end grip, you start in stretch mode and can stretch the line. But if you pick the middle grip, the stretch becomes a move, even though the display still reports that you are in stretch mode.
Circle	If you pick a grip at a quadrant, you start in stretch mode; your next pick determines the radius, while the center remains at the same location. But if you pick the center grip, a stretch becomes a move.
Arc	If you pick an end grip, you can stretch that endpoint, but the arc will continue to pass through its other endpoint and midpoint. If you pick the middle grip, you can stretch the arc so that it passes through the new destination point, but its original endpoints will not move.
Polyline	The stretch affects only the selected vertex. However, after selecting the polyline, you can hold down the Shift key and select several vertices. Then all selected vertices will stretch when you pick a vertex as the base point.

The Multiple-Copy Feature

After you have started the editing process by selecting a grip, you can enable the multiple copy feature. Enter **c** or hold down the Shift key while you pick the first destination point. When this feature is active, the object remains in its original position and a new copy is placed in the stretched, moved, rotated, scaled or mirrored position. You can place as many copies as you wish. If you continue to hold down the Shift key after the first copy is placed, subsequent copies can be placed at similar increments, allowing you to create linear or angular arrays.

Setting Grips Options

When you select Grips... from the Options pull-down menu, the Grips dialog box appears as in Figure 14-19.

Figure 14-19: The Grips dialog box.

The Enable Grips option turns the grip mode on and off.

The Enable Grips Within Blocks feature works as follows: When you turn off the option, a block displays only one grip at its insertion point. When you turn on the option, every object that comprises the block displays its own grip.

Use Grip Colors to set the color for both unselected grips (the initial grips that appear when you select an object) and selected grips (the filled-in grips that appear when you pick a particular grip).

Use the scroll bar at the bottom of the dialog to adjust the size of the grips from 1 to 20 pixels. A graphical representation of the grip size appears in the image tile to the right of the scroll box. (To set a grip size greater than 20 pixels, enter **gripsize** and set its value to the desired number.)

Moving on

Thus far, you've learned ways to edit your work that are more productive and efficient than drawing from scratch. And the more time you spend using editing commands—versus drawing commands—the more productive you'll become.

But sometimes while using drawing or editing commands you'll make a mistake. The following chapter, Chapter 15, "Undo," introduces some commands that allow you to quickly fix your mistakes.

CHAPTER 15

Undo

AutoCAD provides a series of commands that let you undo mistakes. These commands reverse the effect of one or more drawing and editing commands—going back as far as the time you opened the drawing file!

There are two important points to remember about any of the undo commands. First, you cannot undo a command that causes a disk operation. For example, you cannot undo a SAVE command. Second, you cannot undo mistakes made before you opened the drawing in the current editing session. In other words, if you open a drawing file on Tuesday, you cannot undo work performed on Monday.

U Undoes the previous command

COMMAND LINE: **u**

Figure 15-1: The Undo icon from the Standard toolbar.

Clicking the Undo icon—or choosing Undo from the Edit pull-down menu—provides a quick and efficient option to undo one command at a time. If you want to undo an entire command, you must execute the U command at the command prompt. Executing U in the middle of a command usually undoes the previous step or results in an error message.

REDO Reverses an undo command

COMMAND LINE: **redo**

Figure 15-2: The Redo icon from the Standard toolbar.

Redo reverses the last undo command. Redo can only be used immediately following a U or Undo command. Any attempt to execute Redo after a command other than U or Undo results in the message: "Previous command did not undo things."

UNDO Lets you reverse any number of commands, or set up parameters for the U and UNDO commands

COMMAND LINE: **undo**

This command is accessible only from the command line. Undo lets you (1) undo a number of your most recent commands at once, (2) define a group of commands and undo them as a group if needed, and (3) define the scope of the UNDO and U commands

When prompted, you may enter the following:

a number, to undo that number of commands.

a to turn auto-undo on or off. Select this response only when you're using a menu that has macros (groups of commands triggered by one item on the menu). When auto is on, these macros are treated as one command.

m to mark a stopping place in the drawing process. You will be able to undo the drawing from this point on, using the B option, if necessary. ("Marks" are often programmed into LISP file third-party programs to prevent operator error. For more detail, see *AutoLISP in Plain English*, Ventana Press.)

b to undo back to the last marked place in the drawing process. Use this with caution: if there are no marks, entering **b** may undo the entire drawing.

be (for begin) to group the next several commands. This option is mainly for use with custom menus, which are discussed in Chapter 40, "Customizing AutoCAD."

c to select options that control the range of the UNDO and U commands. Then enter one of the following:

a to let UNDO work with all commands

o to limit UNDO to one command (same as the U command)

n (for None) to disable U and UNDO

NOTE: Selecting an O or N option clears the memory space that was holding UNDO information when it was fully active. Thus, after limiting UNDO, you can't return to a fully functioning UNDO for previous parts of the drawing.

Moving on

This chapter introduced you to AutoCAD commands that let you undo or redo your commands.

The placing of notes is an important part of any drawing process, and AutoCAD provides many commands to place and manipulate the text that you create. Chapter 16, "Text," will introduce you to AutoCAD's powerful text-creation and editing abilities.

Text

AutoCAD Release 13 provides many ways to create text. This chapter looks at text creation and editing.

Creating Text

As you choose Text from the Draw pull-down menu, you'll see three menu prompts: Text, Dynamic Text and Single-Line Text.

Choosing Text allows you to create paragraph-style text with the new Multiline Text (MTEXT) command. Choosing Dynamic Text (the DTEXT command) lets you create multiple-line text that is shown dynamically onscreen. Single-Line Text (the TEXT command) allows you to create a single line of text, which is displayed in the command prompt window and then printed to screen as you press Enter.

Editing Text

To edit text, choose Edit Text... from the Modify pull-down menu. (If this menu is not available from the menu bar, enter **menu** at the command line and select Acadfull to display it.) This activates the DDEDIT command, which in turn displays the appropriate dialog box: the Edit Text dialog for single-line editing, or the Edit Mtext dialog for multiline, paragraph-type text editing, complete with an internal spell check.

Setting Font Styles

To set font text styles, use the Text Style command, located under the Data pull-down menu. Included with the many fonts that AutoCAD supplies are TrueType fonts. If you have the Release 13 CD-ROM, you'll find more than 100 font styles to choose from, plus sample font PostScript drawings in the \COMMON\FONTS\PSDWGS directory.

MTEXT Lets you create multiline text (paragraphs)

COMMAND LINE: **-mtext**

Figure 16-1: The Multiline Text icon from the Draw toolbar.

To display the Edit MText dialog, choose the Multiline Text icon or select Text from the Draw pull-down menu. (If this menu is not available from the menu bar, enter **menu** at the command line and select Acadfull to display it.) You can deactivate the dialog box and force all prompts to appear in the command window by entering **-mtext** at the command line.

You're then prompted for two corners of a defining boundary box—that is, a box that determines the width and position of each text line. You may justify the boundary box to be aligned via the top, center or bottom.

As you pick the corners, AutoCAD gives you these options:

Attach	Attach allows you to choose where the paragraph editing is attached, such as: TL/TC/TR/ML/MC/MR/BL/BC/BR, meaning Top Left, Top Center and Top Right, and so forth. Enter a choice from those provided.
Rotation	Rotation sets the rotation angle in degrees. Just enter a number
Style	This option sets the text style. (See "STYLE" later in the chapter.)
Height	Height sets the height of the text. Either enter a number or pick two points onscreen.
Direction	Direction sets the direction in which the text is placed (horizontal/vertical). Enter **h** or **v**.
Width	Enter the object width.
2Points	Select a first point and second point as a width.

The Edit MText dialog then appears.

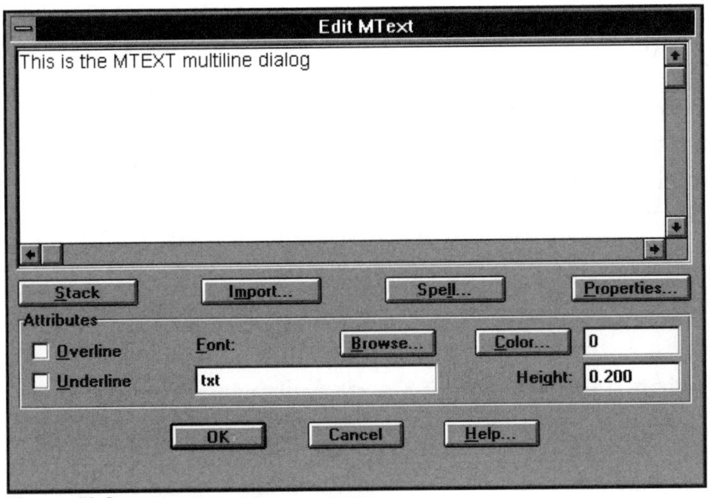

Figure 16-2: The Edit MText dialog.

DTEXT Places text in a drawing dynamically (as it's typed in)

COMMAND LINE: **dtext**

Figure 16-3: The Dynamic Text icon from the Draw toolbar.

Choose the Dynamic Text icon, or choose Dynamic Text from the Draw pull-down menu. (If this menu is not available from the menu bar, enter **menu** at the command line and select Acadfull to display it.)

Although this command is similar to the TEXT command described below, there are some differences. DTEXT places a square cursor on the screen where your text starts. Then, as you type, your text dynamically appears onscreen as it will look in the final drawing.

The DTEXT command assumes that you want to place subsequent lines of text below the present line, so it places the cursor at the beginning of the new line each time you press Enter. You can backspace through one or more lines of text.

To stop entering text, press Enter at the beginning of a line. Note that the temporary text display is always left-justified, even though you may have selected rightjustified, centered, middle and so on (see "Justify Text Options" later in the chapter).

A unique option of this command is that you start a new text line by picking a new location with the pointer at any time while you're entering text.

TEXT Places a single line of text in a drawing

COMMAND LINE: **text**

Figure 16-4: The Text icon from the Draw toolbar.

Choose the Text icon, or choose Single-Line Text from the Draw pull-down menu. (If this menu is not available from the menu bar, enter **menu** at the command line and select Acadfull to display it.)

When prompted, locate the starting point or enter the following:

j to justify the text (explained below).

s to select a text style. Then enter the name of the desired style. One text style, called Standard, is created automatically when you start a new drawing. You must use the STYLE command to create other styles you want to use (see "STYLE" below).

When prompted for height, enter the height of capital letters, using the keyboard or pointer.

When prompted for rotation angle, enter the degrees from horizontal for the baseline of the text, using the keyboard or pointer.

When prompted for text, enter one line of text as you want it to appear in the drawing.

Each time you enter the TEXT command, the most recently entered text is highlighted. To place new text immediately below this highlighted text with the same justification, height and so on, simply press Enter. If you want the new text located somewhere else, pick a new starting point or select the J option.

When you enter **j** to justify the text, you are given possible text insertion points to choose from. The prompt Align/Fit/Center/Middle/Right/TL/TC/R/ML/MC/MR/BL/BC/BR appears. Enter one of the following:

> **a** to align the text between two points, then locate the two points. AutoCAD calculates the appropriate height.
>
> **f** to fit the text between two points, then locate the two points and enter the height. AutoCAD adjusts the width of the text.

Justify Text Options

The following options may be entered directly at the "Justify/Style/<Starting point>" prompt.

TL	Top Left
TC	Top Center
TR	Top Right
ML	Middle Left
M or MC	Middle Center
MR	Middle Right
C	Baseline Center
R	Baseline Right
A	Baseline Aligned
F	Baseline Fit
BL	Bottom Left
BC	Bottom Center
BR	Bottom Right

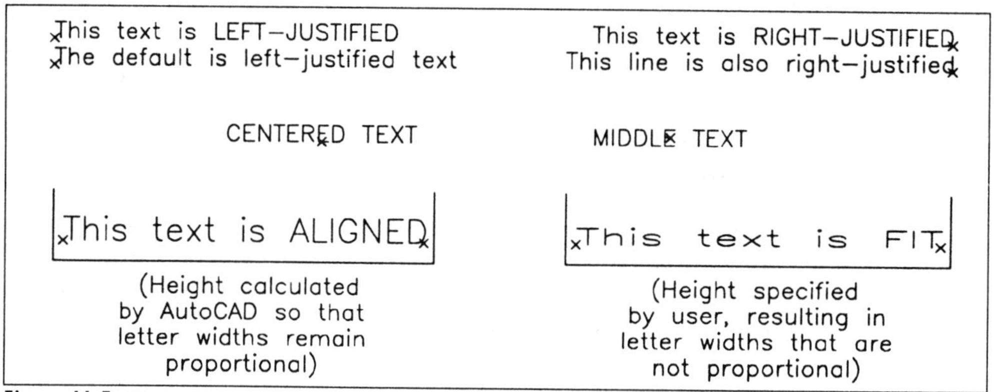

Figure 16-5: Text justification entry methods.

Creating Special Characters With %%

To create special characters in AutoCAD, use the %% (double percent key) and a control code of o, u, d, p, c or nnn. You may create special characters in your text. Special character codes are

%%o	Overscore on/off
%%u	Underscore on/off
%%d	Degree symbol—same as %%127
%%p	Plus-or-minus symbol
%%c	Circle diameter symbol
%%nnn	ASCII character nnn or user-created character (See Special Characters nnn later in the chapter.)

For example, to write overscored and/or underscored text, use the %%o or %%u *before* you enter your text.

Enter the TEXT command, the following, and press Enter:

%%oThis is overscored text

%%uThis is underscored text

Example: To write a degree symbol and a circle diameter symbol as text, use the %%d or %%c *after* you enter your text.

Enter the TEXT command, the following, and press Enter:

This is 112%%dF
(This returns 112 degrees F.)

This circle is 1.0%%c
(This returns 1.0 diameter for the circle.)

NOTE: These special %% characters apply only to the TEXT and DTEXT commands. They do not apply to the MTEXT command below, which has its own control codes.

After the text is placed in the drawing, it can be changed with the CHANGE command or edited in a dialog box with the DDEDIT command, which is described later in this chapter.

Special Text Characters (%%nnn)

There are times when you need to create special ASCII characters.

Look at the top line of your keyboard, at the special ASCII characters such as: ~ ! @ ! # $ % ^ & * ( ) _ + |. These can be entered as three-figure numbers (their ASCII shape numbers).

Let's try creating a few ASCII special shapes.

1. Enter the TEXT command and type as follows:

%%%60 default %%%062:
(This returns <default>:)

2. Try a few more of these special shape numbers. Put in these shape codes: %%%064, %%%127, %%%128, %%%129. You'll get the @ sign, the degree symbol, the plus/minus sign and the circle diameter sign.

Below is a partial list of the (nnn) ASCII character shape numbers and their meanings.

ASCII Number	Meaning
%%%033	!
%%%034	" double quote sign
%%%035	# asterisk sign
%%%036	$ dollar sign
%%%037	% percent sign
%%%038	& ampersand sign
%%%039	' single quote sign
%%%040	(left parenthesis
%%%041	) right parenthesis
%%%042	* wild card or times sign
%%%043	+ plus sign

QTEXT Controls whether text is displayed & plotted as rectangles or full text

COMMAND LINE: **qtext**

Quick Text saves regeneration time when you have a drawing full of text. To activate it, simply enter **qtext** at the command prompt.

When prompted, enter **on** to display text as rectangles, which allows faster redrawing and regeneration of the drawing.

Existing text is displayed as rectangles after qtext is turned on and after a regeneration. (See "REGEN" below.) However, new text is still displayed fully. Rectangles may not be exactly the same length as the actual text.

Enter **off** to display full text (only after a regeneration).

DDEDIT Lets you edit text characters, lines & paragraphs in dialog boxes

COMMAND LINE: **ddedit**

Figure 16-6: The Edit Text icon from the Special Edit flyout of the Modify toolbar.

DDEDIT lets you edit text of attribute tags, prompts and defaults. It also lets you edit single-line text, paragraphs of text and single text characters.

Before you begin, be sure that the Draw, Construct and Modify pull-down menu choices appear in the menu bar at the top of your screen. If they do not, enter **menu** at the command line and then select Acadfull (for "full menu").

To edit text, choose the Edit Text... prompt from the Modify pull-down. This activates the DDEDIT command, which in turn provides one of two dialog boxes depending upon your text entry.

For single-line text editing, it activates the Edit Text dialog, and for multi-line (paragraph type) text editing it activates the Edit Mtext dialog box, complete with an internal spell check option.

Single-Line Text Editing

Choose the Edit Text... prompt from the Modify pull-down menu. If you have created and selected a single line of text to edit, that line is displayed in the Edit Single-Line Text dialog box.

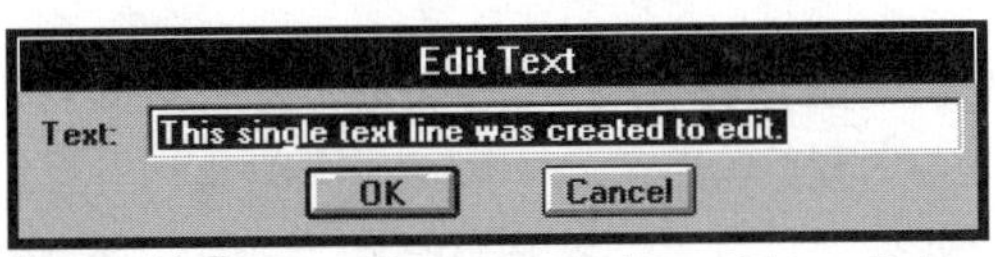

Figure 16-7: The Edit Single-Line Text dialog.

If you select an attribute tag, the dialog box displays the tag, prompt (if any) and default (if any), and allows you to edit them. You may use DDEDIT to edit attribute tags before they are made part of a block, but you cannot use DDEDIT to edit attributes accompanying inserted blocks. To edit the latter, use the ATTEDIT or DDATTE command.

MultiLine Text Editing

Choose the Edit Text... prompt from the Modify pull-down menu. If you have created and selected multiple-line text to edit, the whole selection is displayed in the Edit Mtext dialog box.

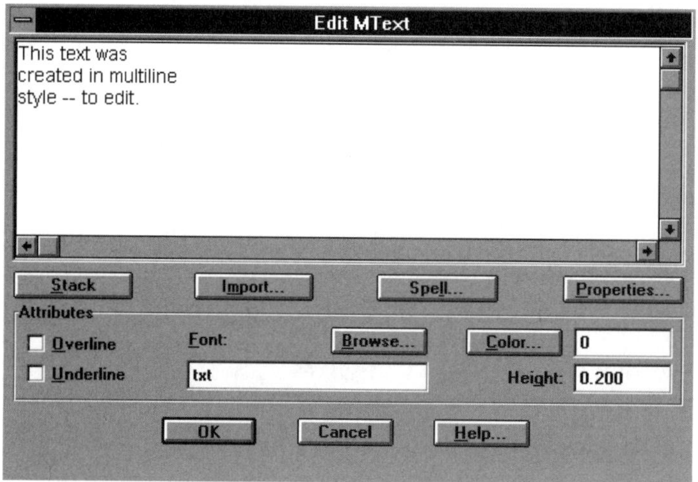

Figure 16-8: The Edit MText (multiline text) dialog.

The Edit Mtext dialog has radio buttons called Stack, Import, Spell, Properties, Browse and Color.

Stack	First, select any text you want to convert. Then choose the Stack button. It converts the selected region into stacked text or stacked fractions.
Import	Activates an Import Text file dialog. Selects an ASCII text file from the list you wish to import into the multiline text editor.

Spell — Either select your paragraph of text to be edited and then choose the Spell... radio button, or choose the button to spell check the whole drawing. It will not check blocks, xrefs or attributes. They must be checked first.

Properties — Activates an MText Properties dialog. This in turn alters Text Style, Text Height, Direction, Attachment, Width and Rotation.

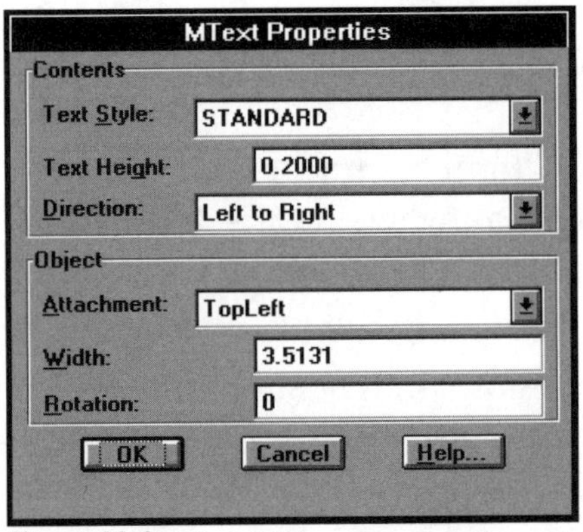

Figure 16-9: The MText Properties dialog.

STYLE Sets a text font according to your style specifications

COMMAND LINE: **style**

All fonts can be chosen through the Select Font File dialog box. To display the dialog, choose Text Style from the Data pull-down menu.

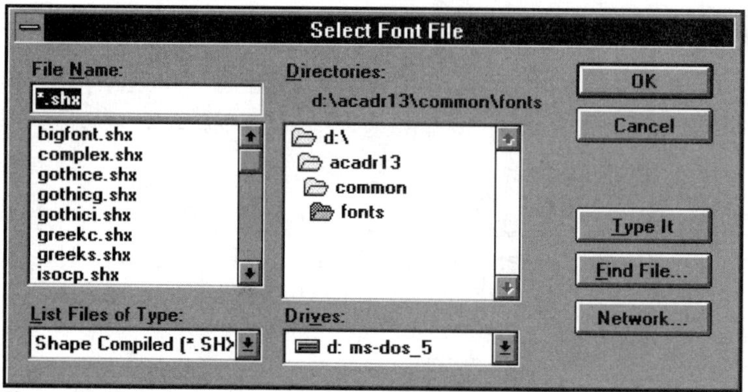

Figure 16-10: The Select Font File dialog.

The STYLE command lets you alter font style, text height, text width and text slant angle in degrees. It also allows text to be backwards, upside down and vertical. Most of the prompts are in the command prompt window.

Choose or type the STYLE command. In the command prompt window you're prompted to enter a style or use the Standard name:

> Text style name or (?) <STANDARD>:

At the text style name prompt, enter a name or a question mark (**?**):

> If you enter **?**, the Graphics window flips to the Text window and lists your text styles. Press F2 to return to the graphics screen.
>
> If you enter a name at the Text style name prompt, it's the name of the new style you want to create or the name of the style you have already created but want to alter. The name can be up to 31 characters long.

You then enter the information necessary to determine the options of font style, text height, text width, text slant angle in degrees and backwards, upside down and vertical text.

> At Font file, provide the name of the font to be styled. (See Figure 16-11.)
>
> The Select Font Style file dialog box helps you find and enter a font name. Scroll through the dialog box and choose a font style.
>
> After you've selected a font file, you're prompted for height. Press Enter to use the <0.0000> (zero) default.

***TIP:** If you want the height to remain as variable text height, use the default of 0.*

The width factor alters the width of each character. 1.0000 is the default. For example, to create wider characters, you could enter **1.5**, or to create narrow characters, you could enter 0.75.

At Obliquing angle, enter the slant in degrees. A positive number slants to the right, and a negative number slants to the left.

At Backward, enter **y** if your text must be backward. Otherwise, press Enter to accept the default (n).

At Upside-down, enter **y** if your text must be upside-down. Otherwise, press Enter to accept the default (right-side up).

If your text must be vertical, enter **y** at Vertical. Otherwise, press Enter to accept the default of horizontal. When you press Enter for the last time, your newly created style automatically becomes the current style used by the TEXT command.

Redefining a Style

You can redefine an existing text style. Most changes you make to an existing style are reflected only in new text added to the drawing using the new style. However, if you redefine a style's text font or vertical/horizontal orientation, all lines of text that are already in the drawing and use the redefined style are affected.

Text Fonts

Alphabet fonts, PostScript fonts, TrueType fonts and Symbol fonts are available in AutoCAD. Twenty-two fonts are illustrated on the following pages. You may choose all fonts through the Select Font Style dialog box described previously.

Some of the fonts are described as serif, some as sans serif. A *serif* is an ending stroke on the arm or tail of a letter. "Sans serif" means "without serif." Your fonts may be created with either horizontal or vertical orientation.

<table>
<tr><th>NAME &
Description</th><th>Sample</th><th>NAME &
Description</th><th>Sample</th></tr>
<tr><td>TXT
simplified letters
for faster
regeneration</td><td>ABC. DEF, GHIJ; KLMN: OPQR' STUV' WXYZ
abc\ def/ ghijl klmn? opqr' stuv~ wxyz
1234567890 !@#$%^&*() _+-=<>[]{}</td><td>SCRIPTC
Script Complex</td><td><i>ABC. DEF, GHIJ; KLMN: OPQR" STUV' WXYZ
abc\ def/ ghij| klmn? opqr' stuv~ wxyz
1234567890 !@#$%~&*() _+-=<>[]{}</td></tr>
<tr><td>MONOTXT
same as TXT but
all characters have
equal spacing</td><td>ABC. DEF, GHIJ; KLMN: OPQR' STUV' WXYZ
abc\ def/ ghijl klmn? opqr' stuv~ wxyz
1234567890 !@#$%^&*() _+-=<>[]{}</td><td>GREEKC
Greek Complex</td><td>ΑΒΧ. ΔΕΦ, ΓΗΙϑ; ΚΛΜΝ: ΟΠΘΡ" ΣΤΥ∇' ΩΞΨΖ
αβχ\ δεφ/ γηιϑ| κλμν? οπϑρ' στυ∈~ ωξψζ
1234567890 !@#$%~&*() _+-=<>[]{}</td></tr>
<tr><td>ROMANS
Roman Simplex
sans serif
single stroke</td><td>ABC. DEF, GHIJ; KLMN: OPQR" STUV' WXYZ
abc\ def/ ghij| klmn? opqr' stuv~ wxyz
1234567890 !@#$%~&*() _+-=<>[]{}</td><td>CYRILLIC
Cyrillic —
alphabetical</td><td>АБВ. ГДЕ, ЖЗИЙ; КЛМН: ОПРС" ТУФХ' ЦЧШЩ
абвЫ где/ жзийы клмн? опрсЯ туфхэ цчшщ
1234567890 !@#$%Э&*() Ю+-=юяЪЬъь</td></tr>
<tr><td>SCRIPTS
Script Simplex</td><td>ABC. DEF, GHIJ; KLMN: OPQR" STUV' WXYZ
abc\ def/ ghij| klmn? opqr' stuv~ wxyz
1234567890 !@#$%~&*() _+-=<>[]{}</td><td>CYRILTLC
Cyrillic —
transliteration</td><td>АБЧ. ДЕФ, ГХИЩ; КЛМН: ОПЦР" СТУВ' ШЖЙЗ
абчЫ деф/ гхищы клмн? опцрЯ стувэ шжйз
1234567890 !@#$%Ю&*() Э+-=юяЬЪьъ</td></tr>
<tr><td>GREEKS
Greek Simplex</td><td>ΑΒΧ. ΔΕΦ, ΓΗΙϑ; ΚΛΜΝ: ΟΠΘΡ" ΣΤΥ∇' ΩΞΨΖ
αβχ\ δεφ/ γηιϑ| κλμν? οπϑρ' στυ∈~ ωξψζ
1234567890 !@#$%~&*() _+-=<>[]{}</td><td>ROMANT
Roman Triplex
serif
triple stroke</td><td><b>ABC. DEF, GHIJ; KLMN: OPQR" STUV' WXYZ
abc\ def/ ghij| klmn? opqr' stuv~ wxyz
1234567890 !@#$%~&*() _+-=<>[]{}</td></tr>
<tr><td>ROMAND
Roman Duplex
sans serif
double stroke</td><td>ABC. DEF, GHIJ; KLMN: OPQR" STUV' WXYZ
abc\ def/ ghij| klmn? opqr' stuv~ wxyz
1234567890 !@#$%~&*() _+-=<>[]{}</b></td><td>ITALICT
Italic Triplex</td><td><b><i>ABC. DEF, GHIJ; KLMN: OPQR" STUV' WXYZ
abc\ def/ ghij| klmn? opqr' stuv~ wxyz
1234567890 !@#$%~&*() _+-=<>[]{}</td></tr>
<tr><td>ROMANC
Roman Complex
serif
double stroke</td><td>ABC. DEF, GHIJ; KLMN: OPQR" STUV' WXYZ
abc\ def/ ghij| klmn? opqr' stuv~ wxyz
1234567890 !@#$%~&*() _+-=<>[]{}</td><td>GOTHICE
Gothic English</td><td><b>ABC. DEF, GHIJ; KLMN: OPQR" STUV' WXYZ
abc\ def/ ghij| klmn? opqr' stuv~ wxyz</b>
1234567890 !@#$%~&*() _+-=<>[]{}</td></tr>
<tr><td>ITALICC
Italic Complex</td><td>ABC. DEF, GHIJ; KLMN: OPQR" STUV' WXYZ
abc\ def/ ghij| klmn? opqr' stuv~ wxyz
1234567890 !@#$%~&*() _+-=<>[]{}</i></td><td>GOTHICG
Gothic German</td><td><b>ABC. DEF, GHIJ; KLMN: OPQR" STUV' WXYZ</b>
abc\ def/ ghij| klmn? opqr' stuv~ wxyz
1234567890 !@#$%~&*() _+-=<>[]{}</td></tr>
</table>

Figure 16-11: AutoCAD text fonts.

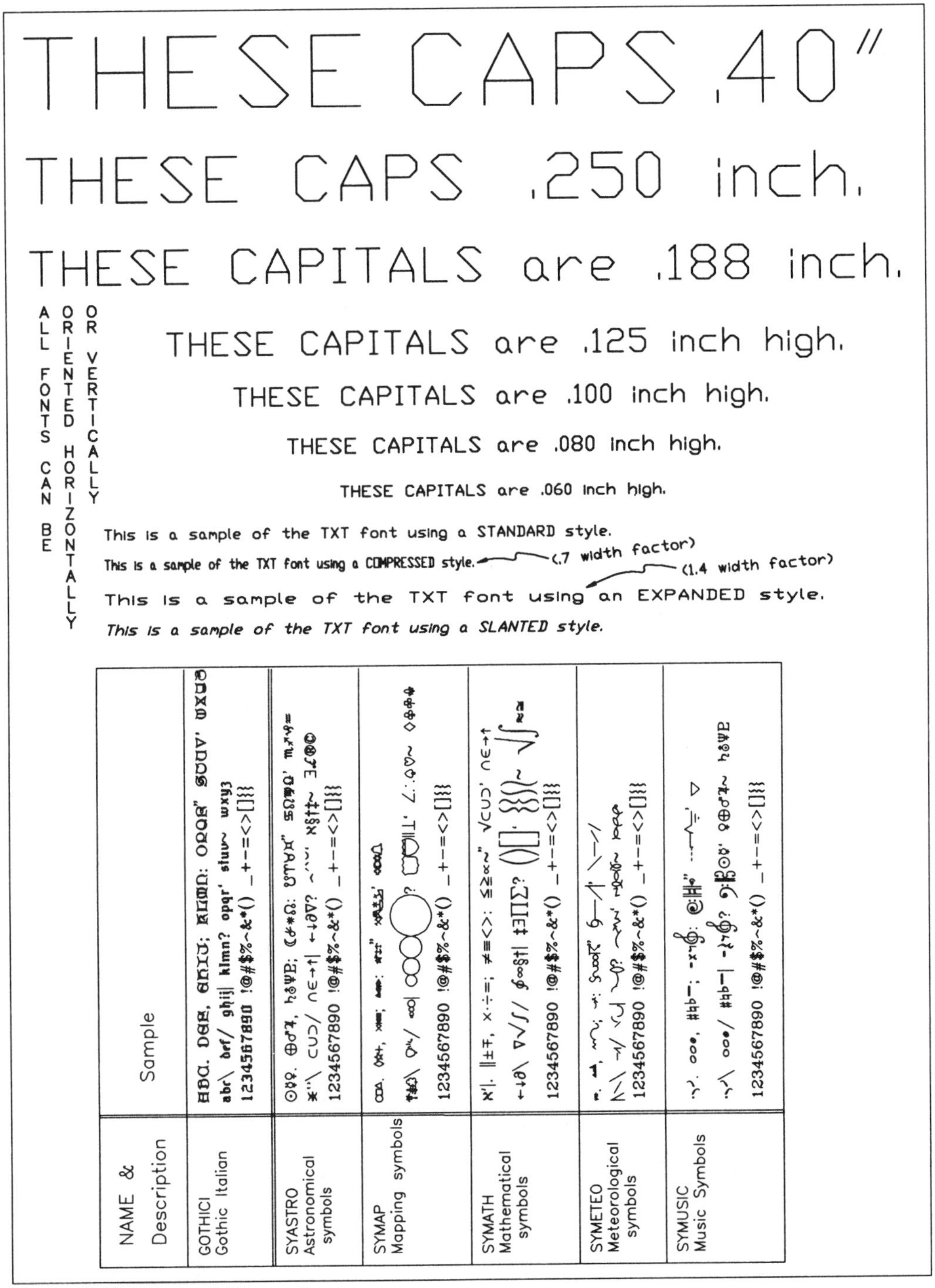

Figure 16-12: AutoCAD text fonts.

Setting the Text Height

You set the text height in one of three ways.

Through the TEXT/DTEXT suboption of Height <...>.

Through the STYLE command, and its suboption of Height<...>.

Through the SETVAR of TEXTSIZE.

Remember, if you use the STYLE command, Height setting<...>, it may lock out all the text height in the drawing, including dimension and leader text heights. It sets everything to the chosen height and may make any text in the drawing appear irregular.

Let's calculate the text height for three different drawing examples. An architectural drawing scaled at 1/8"=1'-0", a full-size drawing scaled at 1=1, and an engineering drawing scaled at 1"=10'.

Example 1: Setting Text Heights for a Scale of 1/8" = 1'-0"

Suppose you want to create an architectural drawing at a scale of

1/8" = 1'-0". Breaking it down, it is .125 = 12". The reciprocal of this is 12 / .125 = 96

The scale factor is therefore 96, which means you are creating a drawing 96 times larger than in its plotted state or when it is plotted to scale.

When the drawing is plotted, you want the text to be (.125) 1/8" high. If your scale factor is 96, calculate the text height as (.125 x 96 = 12); then set the text to a height of 12.

Using the same 1/8" drawing scale and scale factor of 96, you want text to read (.25) 1/4" high when plotted. Your calculation is now (.25 x 96 = 24); therefore, set the text to a height of 24.

Example 2: Using a Scale of Full Size

You create an architectural drawing at a scale of Full size or 1" = 1. (Really, there is no reciprocal.)

The scale factor is 1, which means you are creating a drawing in its true plotted state.

Plotted text you want to be 1/8" (.125) high. Using a scale factor of 1, the calculation is (.125 X 1 = .125). Set it to a true height of .125.

You want the plotted text to be 1/4" (.25). Again, using a scale factor of 1, the calculation is (.25 x 1 = .25). Set it to a true height of .25.

Example 3: Using a Scale of 1" = 10'

You want to create an engineering drawing at a scale of

1" = 10'

Broken down, it is: 1" = (10 x 12).

The reciprocal of this is 120/1, which results in a scale factor of 120.

This means you are creating a drawing 120 times larger than when it is plotted to scale.

If you require text to be 1/8" (.125) high with a scale factor of 120, the calculation is (.125 x 120 = 15). This informs you to set the text to a height of 15.

If you require further text at 1/4" (.25) height, the calculation is (.25 x 120 = 30) to set a text height of 30.

Moving on

The next chapter provides insight into setting up prototype drawings. It also outlines the multiple settings that can be placed in prototype drawings to make you more productive.

CHAPTER 17

Understanding Limits & Prototype Drawings

Prototype drawings let you save time in setting up your drawings. A prototype serves as the basis for new drawings. Think of a prototype drawing as similar to a preprinted title block for manual drafting. Not having to draw a new title block for every sheet saves the manual drafter considerable time and effort, but AutoCAD prototype drawings provide even more advantages than a preprinted sheet. The prototype can preset many options in the drawing such as grid, snap, limits, layer definitions and so on. Anything that you access regularly in the course of creating a drawing should become part of your prototype.

This chapter explains how to create prototype drawings and how to determine the proper limits settings.

Creating Prototype Drawings

When you start a new drawing, AutoCAD normally uses a default prototype drawing (ACAD.DWG) to set limits, snap spacing, grid spacing, layers, blocks and other specifications. A prototype drawing is simply any drawing—it can be blank (no drawing objects), or it can have a border and title block, predrawn blocks and so on. You can edit and then save prototype drawings just like any other drawing. Each time you start a new drawing you have several prototype options (see "Choosing Prototype Drawings" in Chapter 2, "Entering & Exiting AutoCAD").

TIP: *Create a set of drawings that you can use as prototypes, including the various size sheets, borders and formats you'll be using repeatedly. Create some for inches, some for millimeters and some with predefined title blocks. You may also want to include predefined dimension styles and Paper Space viewports in your prototype drawings. See Chapter 44, "Hands-on Exercises," for examples of prototype drawings.*

Setting Limits

Separate limits are maintained for Paper Space and Model Space. In Model Space, always set limits according to the full scale of the object being drawn. In Paper Space, always set limits at the border size of the paper used for plotting, because scaling will be accomplished with the use of Zoom... xp. (See "ZOOM" in Chapter 11, "Looking Around.")

The following discussion of drawing limits applies both to prototype drawings and to any drawing you might create from scratch.

When you create prototype drawings, you must use the LIMITS command to set the limits. Don't use the sheet size for your limits. Rather, use the format, or border, size—the sheet size minus the margins.

The following procedures must be used when you plan to plot from Model Space. If you're drawing at full scale (1=1), it's easy to set the limits for your prototype drawing. In many cases you'll want to set them at the maximum size your plotter will accept for each sheet size it handles.

If you want to end up with a plotted drawing at a scale other than 1=1, then you have to take the scaling process into account when you set your limits. From the plot dialog you can select the Fit option every time you plot, of course, but that can lead to very strange-looking drawings. The notes and dimension text will probably be too big or too small, and the plot probably won't be at one of the customary scales.

It's much better to determine your limits precisely, so that after your drawing is scaled to its final proportions (1) the drawing still fits within the maximum plotting area your plotter will accept, (2) the plot is at a customary scale and (3) your notes and dimension text are the desired size.

You can use the plotting scale chart shown in Figure 17-1 to help determine your drawing limits and final plotting scale. For example, suppose you want to draw a very small machine part (approximately 0.5" x 0.25") and then plot it on an A sheet that's 11" x 8.5" (with a 10" x 7.5" border). If you need two views and also allow extra space for dimensions and notes, you'll probably want a total drawing space of about 2.5" x 2".

11x8.5	12x9	17x11	18x12	22x17	24x18	34x22	36x24	44x34	48x36	Sheet size
.5	.5	.5	.5	.75	.75	1.00	1.00	1.00	1.00	Margins
10x7.5	11x8	16x10	17x11	20.5x15.5	22.5x16.5	32x20	34x22	42x32	46x34	Format (border) size
A	A	B	B	C	C	D	D	E	E	**Plotting Scale Factor**
1.00 x .75	1.10 x .8	1.60 x 1.00	1.70 x 1.10	2.05 x 1.55	2.25 x 1.65	3.20 x 2.00	3.40 x 2.20	4.20 x 3.20	4.60 x 3.40	10 = 1 or 10.00
2.5 x 1.875	2.75 x 2	4 x 2.5	4.25 x 2.75	5.125 x 3.875	5.625 x 4.125	8 x 5	8.5 x 5.5	10.5 x 8	11.5 x 8.5	4 = 1 or 4.00
5 x 3.75	5.5 x 4	8 x 5	8.5 x 5.5	10.25 x 7.75	11.25 x 8.25	16 x 10	17 x 11	21 x 16	23 x 17	2 = 1 or 2.00
10 x 7.5	11 x 8	16 x 10	17 x 11	20.5 x 15.5	22.5 x 16.5	32 x 20	34 x 22	42 x 32	46 x 34	1 = 1 or 1.00
20 x 15	22 x 16	32 x 20	34 x 22	41 x 31	45 x 33	64 x 40	68 x 44	84 x 64	92 x 68	1 = 2 or .50
40 x 30	44 x 32	64 x 40	68 x 44	82 x 62	90 x 66	128 x 80	136 x 88	168 x 128	184 x 136	1 = 4 or .25
80 x 60	88 x 64	128 x 80	136 x 88	164 x 124	180 x 132	256 x 160	272 x 176	336 x 256	368 x 272	1 = 8 or .125
10' x 7'6"	11' x 8'	16' x 10'	17' x 11'	20'6" x 15'6"	22'6" x 16'6"	32' x 20'	34' x 22'	42' x 32'	46' x 34'	1" = 1' or 1/12 or .08333333
20' x 15'	22' x 16'	32' x 20'	34' x 22'	41' x 31'	45' x 33'	64' x 40'	68' x 44'	84' x 64'	92' x 68'	1/2" = 1' or 1/24 or .04166667
40' x 30'	44' x 32'	64' x 40'	68' x 44'	82' x 62'	90' x 66'	128' x 80'	136' x 88'	168' x 128'	184' x 136'	1/4" = 1' or 1/48 or .02083333
80' x 60'	88' x 64'	128' x 80'	136' x 88'	164' x 124'	180' x 132'	256' x 160'	272' x 176'	336' x 256'	368' x 272'	1/8" = 1' or 1/96 or .01041667
160' x 120'	176' x 128'	256' x 160'	272' x 176'	328' x 248'	360' x 264'	512' x 320'	544' x 352'	672' x 512'	736' x 544'	1/16" = 1' or 1/192 or .00520833

DRAWING LIMITS

Figure 17-1: Drawing limits and sheet sizes for Model Space plotting.

Using the Plotting Scale Chart

Use the chart as follows: Look under the first A column (notice the 11" x 8.5" sheet size at the top of the column) and find the 2.5" x 1.875" drawing limits (the closest to your desired total drawing space). Then look across to the Plotting Scale Factor, and you'll see that the plotting scale is 4=1. Of course, you draw and dimension the part at full scale. When you finally plot your drawing at a scale of 4=1 in Model Space, or at 1=1 using properly scaled viewports in Paper Space, your border will be exactly the size you need.

Here's another example. Suppose you want to draw a floor plan of a 500' x 300' building and plot it on an E size sheet that's 48" x 36" (46" x 34" border). Look at the second E column in Figure 17-1. You can see that you need to use a final plotting scale of 1/16" = 1'-0" (or smaller). Set your limits at 736' x 544', DIMSCALE at 192, then draw and dimension the floor plan at full scale as usual. You can then plot the drawing from Model Space at a scale of 1=192 or 1' = 16'. If you use Paper Space, your viewport scale would be 1/192xp.

You can use this information to set up not only your limits but also system variables such as DIMSCALE, LTSCALE and other scale-specific values. (See "Drawing to Various Scales" in Chapter 24, "Dimensions.")

The sheet sizes given in Figure 17-1 are standard. The format sizes, however, are generalized—they were determined by subtracting nominal margins from the sheet sizes. Consult your plotter manual for the maximum plotting sizes available on your plotter for each sheet size. Once you adjust the format sizes accordingly, you can also adjust the drawing limits and thus create a chart that's suited to your particular plotter.

Moving on

In this chapter you've learned that prototype drawings are a useful tool to quickly setting up your drawings without having to create them from scratch. And a great deal of hidden information can be stored in your prototypes.

Next, in Chapter 18, "Plotting," you'll take a look at the plot dialog you'll use to send your drawings for printer or plotter output.

Plotting

Alas, the paperless office has not arrived! For those who will construct your AutoCAD-designed project, you'll still need to share the prints and large plots of your CAD drawings. Using the Plot Configuration dialog, this chapter takes you through the plot settings needed to create accurate plots. In AutoCAD, you can configure up to 32 output devices. The Plot Configuration dialog lets you choose any of the devices you'll use to plot.

PLOT Displays a configuration dialog box that lets you print or plot your drawings

COMMAND LINE: **plot**

Figure 18-1: The Print icon from the Standard toolbar.

A single PLOT command activates the printer and/or plotter you configured. Unlike pre-Release 12 versions of AutoCAD, Release 13 has no separate PRPLOT command. Laserjets, inkjets, pen plotters, color plotters and postscript devices may all be configured in a single dialog—up to a maximum of 32 devices. No more does AutoCAD distinguish between printers and plotters. It's handled by the way you configure the AutoCAD devices. When you choose the Print icon or choose Print from the File pull-down menu, you'll see the Plot Configuration dialog box. (See Figure 18-2.)

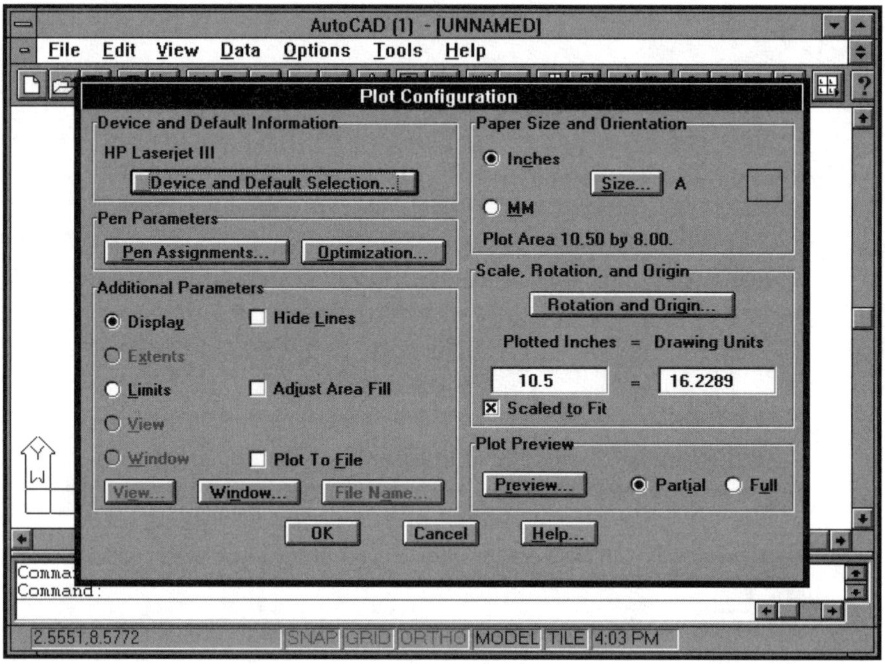

Figure 18-2: The main Plot Configuration dialog box.

The Plot Configuration dialog box has six sections: Device and Default Information: Pen Parameters; Additional Parameters; Paper Size and Orientation; Scale, Rotation, and Origin; and Plot Preview. Each is described below.

Device and Default Information

This section displays the current configured device to which the plot will be sent. The description was entered when the device was originally configured (if no description was entered, the manufacturer's description appears).

TIP: *To add other plotters or change the configuration of the plotter/printer, choose Configure from the Options pull-down menu (or type* ***config*** *at the command prompt window).*

If you pick the Device and Default Selection button, a further dialog box appears that allows you to perform several more tasks (see Figure 18-3):

1. Pick a different device from the list if more than one are configured.
2. Save the current plotter settings to a .PCP file. (See ".PCP file" below.)
3. Get other plotter settings from a different .PCP file.
4. View or change any special plotter requirements in the Device Specific Configuration section of the dialog.

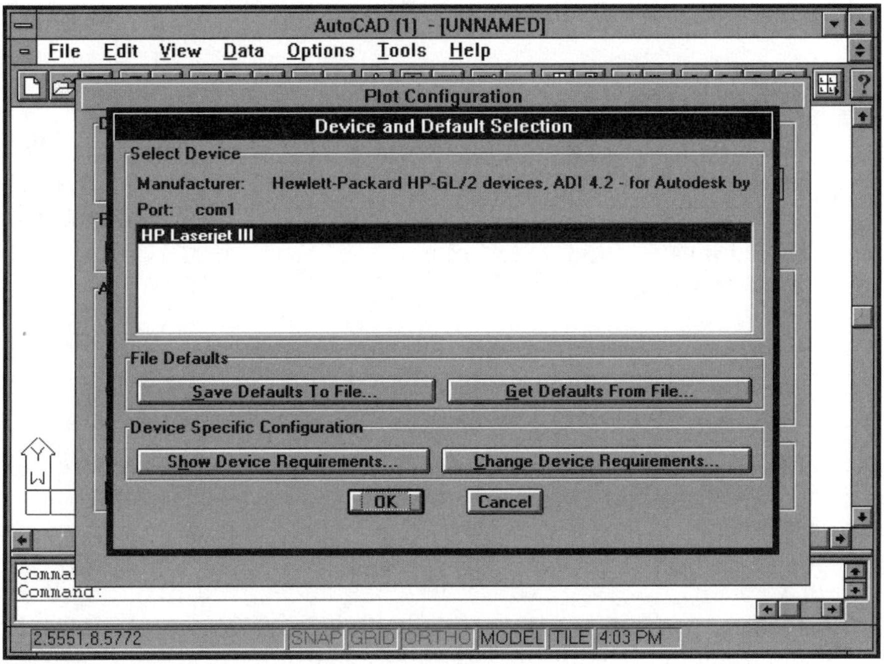

Figure 18-3: Device and Default Selection dialog.

.PCP File

When you pick the Get Defaults From File button, a further dialog box appears to let you choose a saved .PCP file. A .PCP (Plot Configuration Parameters) file holds plot settings a certain way. ***TIP:*** You may have several saved .PCP files and switch back and forth as needed. They're standard ASCII files that you can edit with your DOS text editor.

Pen Parameters

The Pen Parameters section lets you determine pen settings and optimization.

Choose Pen Assignments to set pen colors, pen speeds and in some cases pen widths. *TIP:* Some of these settings also apply to cartridge-type plotters (such as ink-jets), even though they don't use pens.

Optimization refers to the amount of analysis AutoCAD will do to make the plot more efficient. This includes such tasks as plotting all lines assigned to one pen at one time, swapping line endpoints and eliminating redundant lines. *TIP:* In some cases, increasing the amount of optimization will speed up the plot; in others, it can actually slow down the plot.

Additional Parameters

In the Additional Parameters section of the Plot Configuration dialog, you determine the area of the drawing you'll plot. You do this by selecting Display, Extents, Limits, View or Window. You have the further options of Hide Lines, Adjust Area Fill and Plot to File. Let's quickly review the available choices.

Selecting the Display button locks you into the screen display you were in before entering the Plot Configuration dialog. *TIP:* Zoom and pan to the area of drawing you want to plot prior to entering the Plot Configuration dialog.

The Extents button automatically chooses the current drawing extents without regard to your drawing limits in the current drawing session. *TIP:* Make sure you preview your plot before sending out to your print device; you may have unwanted objects you should have erased and haven't seen yet.

The Limits button automatically chooses the latest drawing limits you've set, either at start-up or during your drawing session. *TIP:* Preview the plot to ensure that the limits don't interfere with outside border sizes.

If you select View, a separate View button allows you to pick a view from a list of saved views. *TIP:* This is a good method of plotting because you've already saved specific views. It's also good for plotting with script files.

If you select Window, the Window button allows you to enter or pick onscreen the window's coordinates. *TIP:* Try this method for plotting enlarged details.

The Hide Lines button lets you enable hidden line plotting. *TIP:* This is useful if you're working in 3D and need to remove hidden lines from your plots.

The Adjust Area Fill option adjusts the borders of filled-in areas according to the pen width you allocated in the Pen Assignments option, described above.

Use the Plot to File button when you want to send the plot out as an ASCII plot file. ***TIP:*** When sending the plot to a file, you should first configure the device as a plot file.

NOTE: *Keep in mind that when you plot from Paper Space, all viewports are plotted together as long as they were "on" in the drawing. Whether the objects in the viewports are plotted with hidden lines removed depends on the setting of the Hideplot option in each viewport. The Hide Lines option just mentioned applies only to Paper Space when you plot from Paper Space. Alternatively, it applies to the current viewport being plotted when you plot from Model Space.*

Paper Size and Orientation

This section of the Plot Configuration dialog includes the selection of plotting units—inches or millimeters—as well as the size and orientation of the paper. The orientation is shown graphically at the right edge of this section. When you pick the Size button, you can select from a list of available sizes for the current plotter, including user-designated sizes.

Scale, Rotation and Origin

This section of the Plot Configuration dialog displays the plotting scale. It also lets you set the origin (the distance over and up from the lower-left corner) and rotation of the plot.

Plot Preview

Here, you can request two types of preview for your plots—*Partial* and *Full*. Unless you're sure that your plotting configuration is correct, it's wise to Full preview the plot and be ensured of a correct plot the first time.

A Partial preview shows the rectangular area to be plotted and its orientation on the paper. A small triangle in one corner shows the amount of rotation. (The lower-left corner indicates no rotation.)

A Full preview displays actual drawing geometry and lets you zoom and pan the preview in a manner similar to ZOOM Dynamic.

Moving on

Congratulations! You've completed the Basic section of *AutoCAD: A Concise Guide*. You're now more than ready to proceed into the Intermediate section. Next, in Chapter 19, "Editing—Group Two," you'll learn about more sophisticated methods of selecting objects and specifying points.

Notes:

Notes:

SECTION II

INTERMEDIATE

Selections—Group 2

In Chapter 7, "Selecting & Erasing Objects," you began selecting objects to use with your editing commands. This chapter takes the concept of selection sets even further by showing you how to create permanent selection groups. It also describes how to filter your selections for specific object properties.

We'll take an in-depth look at the main Object Group dialog and its uses. Then we'll move on to using groups and finally take an in-depth look at filters and point filters.

GROUP

Builds a permanent selection set that can be named & recalled at any time

COMMAND LINE: **group**

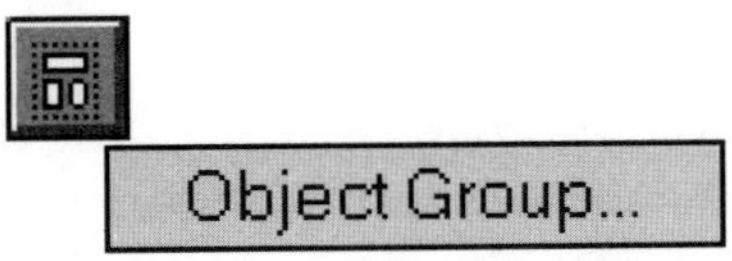

Figure 19-1: The Object Group icon from the Standard toolbar.

Clicking on the Object Group icon displays the Object Grouping dialog as shown in Figure 19-2. This dialog lets you create and modify named selection sets of objects called *groups*. You'll see the dialog divided into four sections: Group Name, Group Identification, Create Group and Change Group.

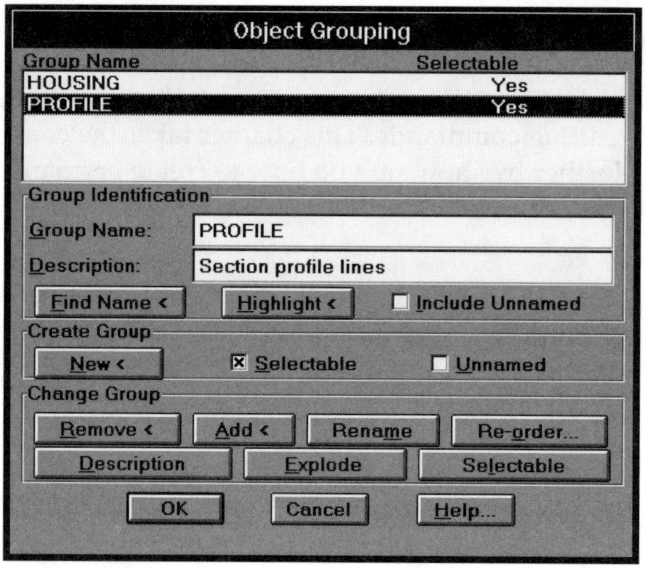

Figure 19-2: The Object Grouping dialog.

Group Name

As you'll see from Figure 19-2, the first item at the top of the dialog is the Group Name list. This lists the names of all groups you've created in your drawing, and it indicates whether or not a group is *selectable*. If a group *is* selectable, you can select the entire group by choosing any single object within the group. A *nonselectable* group may be used only by entering the group name.

To make a group current, click on its name in the Group Name list.

Group Identification

When you choose a group from the Group Name list, its name and description are displayed in the Group Name and Description fields. You may also type in the name and description when you create a new group, as described later.

To identify a group, click the Find Name button. When prompted, pick any single object to display the Group Member List dialog shown in Figure 19-3. This dialog identifies all named groups to which the picked object belongs. Choose the group name you want and then click on OK to return to the Object Grouping dialog.

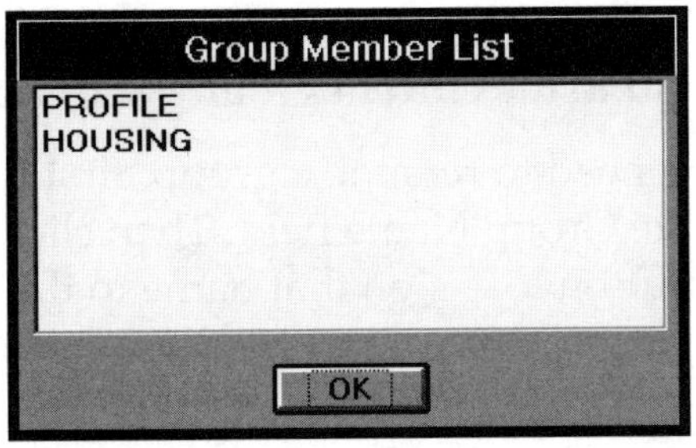

Figure 19-3: The Group Member List dialog.

Clicking the Highlight button temporarily hides the dialog and displays your drawing with all the objects in the current group highlighted. Click on the Continue button to return to the Object Grouping dialog.

The Include Unnamed check box controls the display of unnamed groups in the Group Name list. If the box is checked, unnamed groups will appear in the list preceded by an asterisk. For example, an unnamed group could be *A7.

Create Group

This section of the dialog contains the controls for making new groups. It has three sections: New, Selectable and Unnamed. Unless you're creating an unnamed group, you should first enter a group name and then, optionally, a group description in the Group Identification section of the dialog.

Click the New button to display the drawing window, where you can select objects using any of the standard selection methods.

Check the Selectable check box to make the new group selectable.

Check the Unnamed check box to cause the new group to be unnamed.

Change Group

The Change Group section of the dialog contains buttons for manipulating the groups you create. You'll see from Figure 19-2 that it has seven buttons: Remove, Add, Rename, Re-order, Description, Explode and Selectable. Let's briefly run through the Change Group options:

Remove — Click on Remove, and at the prompt, select objects to remove from the current group. This command is useful if you have selected too many objects.

Add	Click on Add and, at the prompt, select objects you want to add to the current group's selection set.
Rename	When you need to rename a group, first type a new name in the Group Name field. Then click on the Rename button to assign that name to the current group.
Re–order	Click on Re-order to order the group's objects differently. Normally, the objects are stored in the order they were selected (see the *AutoCAD Reference Manual* for details on re-ordering grouped objects).

TIP: *This command is useful if you use AutoCAD with a milling program and need to make sure that certain objects are processed before others.*

Description	To change the group's description, type a new description into the Description field (if necessary delete the old description), then click on the Description button to assign it to the current group.
Explode	Click on Explode to release the objects from the group and delete the group name from the Group Name list.
Selectable	Click on Selectable to toggle the selectable feature on and off for the current group.

Using Groups

Once you have defined groups within your drawing, you can use them whenever a command prompts you to "Select Objects." If your groups are selectable, you can select any object in the group to automatically select the entire group.

If you prefer to select a group by its name, enter **g**, followed by the group's name, at the Select Objects prompt.

If you wish to select a group that is defined as unselectable, your only option is to enter **g** and then the group's name at the Select Objects prompt.

If you need to select a single object that is a member of a selectable group, you must turn off group selection in the Object Selection Settings dialog. You may wish to review Chapter 7, "Selecting & Erasing Objects," for more information.

Filter Constrains object selection based on object properties

COMMAND LINE: **filter**

Figure 19-4: The Selection Filters icon from the Select Object flyout of the Standard toolbar.

Use the FILTER command to constrain the selection of objects based on the object's properties. AutoCAD displays the Object Selection Filters dialog, shown in Figure 19-5. Imagine that you need to select all the circles with a radius of less than 0.5" or all objects with the color Red; these are the kinds of tasks FILTER performs.

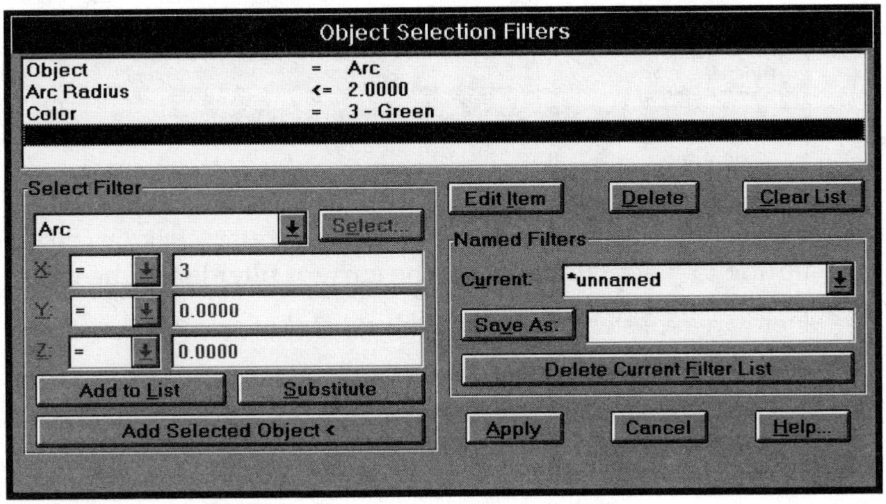

Figure 19-5: The Object Selection Filters dialog.

The top of the dialog contains the current filter list that you create. You can either build the filter list from scratch using the options in the Select Filter section at left, or you can restore a *named filter list* using the options in the Named Filters section at right. Let's take a quick look at both methods.

Select Filter

The heart of the Select Filter section is the pop-up filter list shown in Figure 19-6. This list displays all the available filters. After selecting a filter from the pop-up list, you may be able to further modify the filter with one or more of the fields beneath the pop-up list. Choosing Circle Radius, for example, allows you to specify a radius value in the X field.

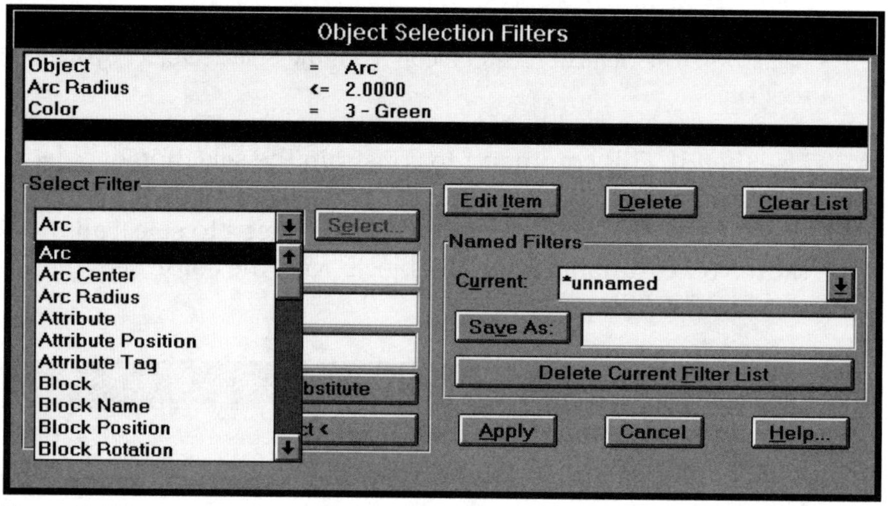

Figure 19-6: Pop-up filter list in the Object Selection Filters dialog.

Once you've set the parameters for your filter, click on the Add to List button to place the filter into the current filter list at the top of the dialog.

Here are five steps to create a filter list that selects all circles with a radius of less than 0.5":

1. First, start the FILTER command by clicking the Filter icon.
2. Click in the filter pop-up list and select the Circle filter.
3. Click on the Add to List button. Click in the filter pop-up list and select the Circle Radius filter.
4. Click on the operand list next to the X field and select <.
5. Finally, enter 0.5" in the field to the right of the operand. Click on the Add to List button.

Do not exit the Object Selection Filters dialog yet. You'll save this as a *named filter list* in the next section.

Named Filters

If you create a filter list that you think will be useful in the future, you can save it as a *named filter list* and call it back at any time—for example, to save the list that you just created:

1. Enter "Small Holes" in the Save As field.
2. Click on the Save As button.

The filter list is now saved in a file called FILTER.NFL in your current working directory. This is a simple text file, so you can edit it and paste in filter lists from other filter lists using any ASCII text editor (such as the EDIT program in DOS).

To call back any named filter list stored in your FILTER.NFL file, click in the Current pop-up list and choose a named filter list.

Using Filters

Once a filter list is defined, click on the Apply button to use it. The Object Selection Filters dialog disappears, and you are prompted to select objects. Use any of the normal selection methods (such as window or crossing), and press Enter. The objects you selected are passed to the filter list, and all objects that do not meet the filter restrictions are removed from the selection set.

If you activated FILTER at the Select Objects prompt of another command, you are returned to that command to continue selecting objects (or even to execute another FILTER, if you wish). If you activated FILTER from the command line, you're returned to the command line. You may then use the objects selected by FILTER by entering **p**, for previous, at the next Select Objects prompt.

Point Filters

Many times you need only partial coordinates from a point. For example, you may need only the X value at the center of a circle or, for 3D work, only the Z value at the end of the line. Point filters force AutoCAD to look at only part of a point's coordinates and ignore the rest. These filters are extremely useful when combined with object snaps.

Point filters can be accessed from the Point Filter flyout of the Standard toolbar or they can be permanently displayed in their own toolbar. Choose Toolbars from the Tools pull-down menu, then choose Point Filters to display the Point Filters toolbar shown in Figure 19-7.

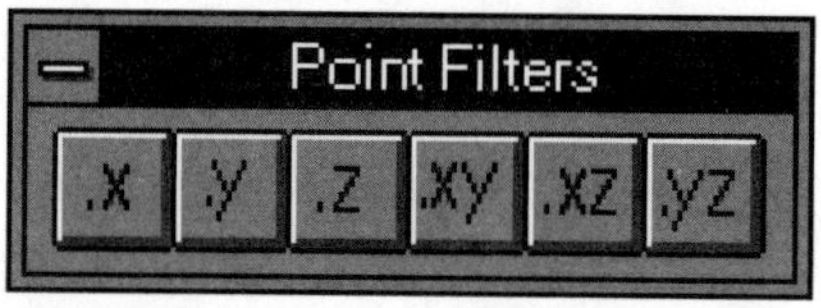

Figure 19-7: The Point Filters toolbar.

Whenever you are prompted for a point, you may use a point filter. At the prompt, take these steps:

1. Enter one of the following or click on the corresponding icon: .X, .Y, .Z, .XY, .XZ, .YZ.

2. At the "of" prompt, pick a point. Only the coordinate components that you specified will be read from that point, and AutoCAD will prompt you for any remaining components needed to complete the command.

Here are the basic steps to use point filters to place a circle at the center of a rectangular box:

1. First, create a rectangular box of any size.
2. Choose the Circle icon.
3. When prompted for a center point, click on the .X icon.
4. When you're prompted with "of," choose the **mid**point osnap and pick the top edge of the box.
5. When you're prompted ("need YZ"), choose the **mid**point osnap again and pick the side of the box.
6. Finally, specify a radius for the circle.

Moving on

The next chapter extends your knowledge of editing commands and explores a couple of powerful commands for changing the properties of the objects you draw.

CHAPTER 20

Editing—Group Two

Chapter 14, "Editing—Group One" introduced some basic commands for manipulating objects in your drawing. This chapter, which opens the Intermediate portion of this book, describes more sophisticated editing commands. Using these commands, you can chop objects apart, rapidly duplicate them within a pattern and change their basic properties.

NOTE: *When you use editing commands that change the actual geometry of the items you're editing, you'll have the most accurate visual control of the editing process if you make sure that you're in a plan view of the current UCS. Choose 3D Viewpoint Presets from the View pull-down menu, then choose Plan View, then Current (see "PLAN" in Chapter 35, "3D Viewing" for more details). This is already set for you if you're using the AutoCAD default drawing*

BREAK Erases part of an object

COMMAND LINE: **break**

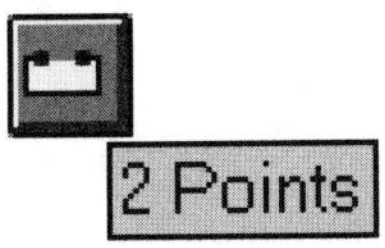

Figure 20-1: The Break 2 Points icon, from the Break flyout of the Modify toolbar.

When prompted, select the object to be broken. If you select the object with the pointer, AutoCAD assumes that the pick-point of the selected object is also the first breakpoint (and endpoint of the portion to be erased). AutoCAD then asks for the second breakpoint. If you want to pick a different first breakpoint, enter **f** and then enter the first breakpoint at this prompt.

Assuming the object has already been selected, the first and second breakpoints need not be on the object. They can be to one side or off the end of the object. AutoCAD selects the nearest point on the object for the actual breakpoint. Remember, when you're breaking a circle or ellipse, the erased portion runs counterclockwise from the first to the second breakpoint.

You can break an object into two portions without a gap by placing the second breakpoint at the same location as the first breakpoint. When prompted for the second breakpoint, enter @.

You can also use the BREAK command to break 2D polylines, as shown in Figure 20-2 .

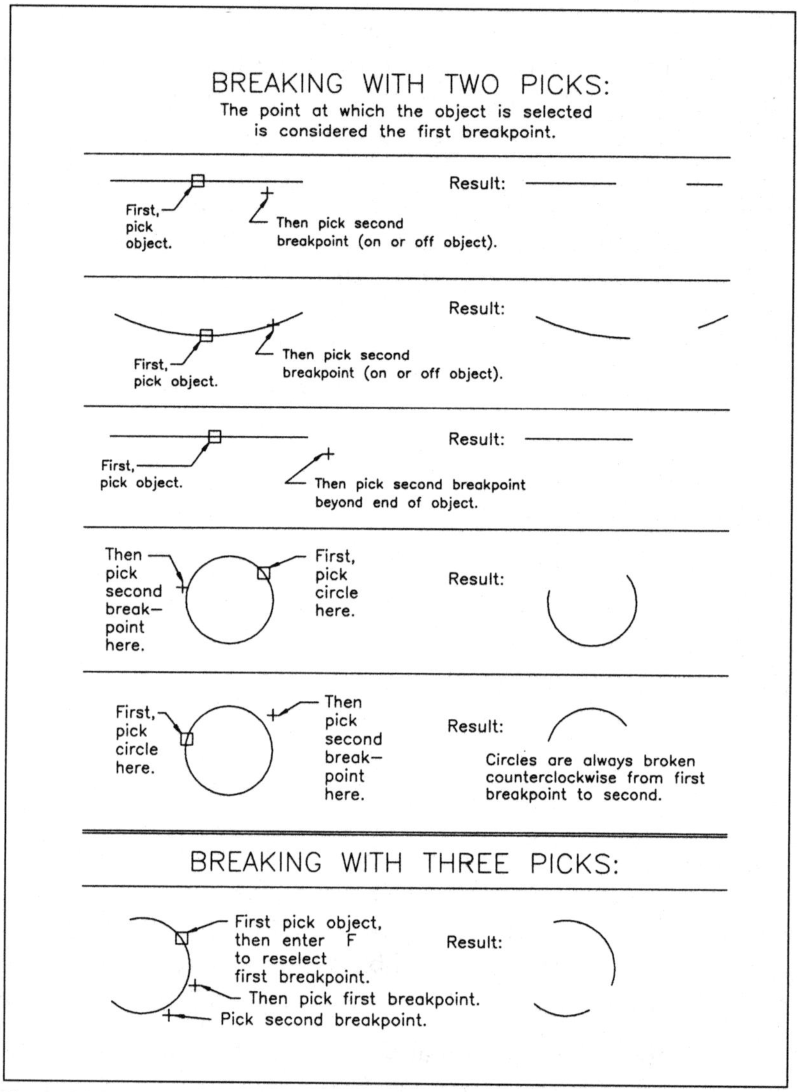

Figure 20-2: Using the BREAK command with two or three picks.

TRIM Cuts away selected parts of an object at the intersection with other selected objects

COMMAND LINE: **trim**

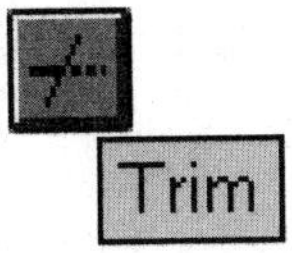

Figure 20-3: The Trim icon, from the Trim flyout of the Modify toolbar.

When prompted, select one or more objects to serve as cutting edges. Press Enter when you've finished selecting the cutting edges. Then select one or more objects you want trimmed. Where you select the object determines which part of it is removed (see Figure 20-4 for examples).

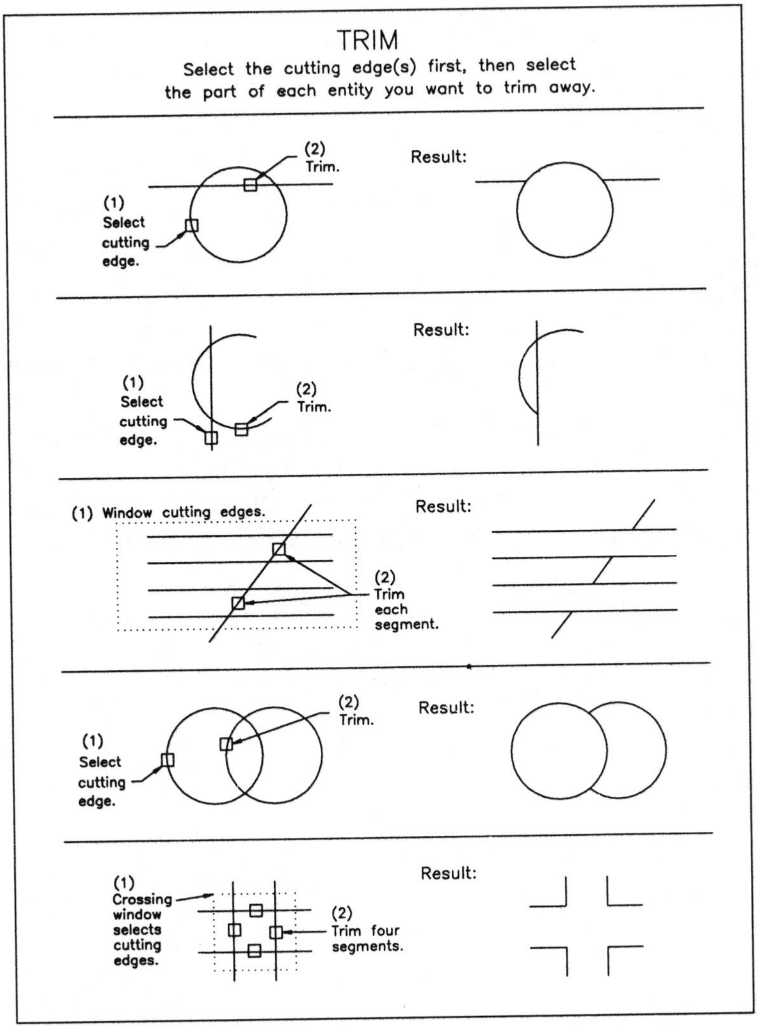

Figure 20-4: Using the TRIM command.

You can modify the way TRIM works by changing the Edge and Projection methods. The default settings work as described above and match the way TRIM works in earlier versions of AutoCAD.

Use the Release 13 TRIM options as follows: After selecting cutting edges, enter **e** to change the Edge condition. If you set the Edge condition to Extend by entering a second **e**, all the selected cutting edges are treated as if they're extended to infinity. Then the objects you select to trim are trimmed wherever they meet or intersect with extended edges. The Projection mode allows you to trim objects that only appear to intersect in three-dimensional space (see Chapter 32, "3D Objects," for more on this new feature).

EXTEND Extends selected objects to meet other selected objects

COMMAND LINE: **extend**

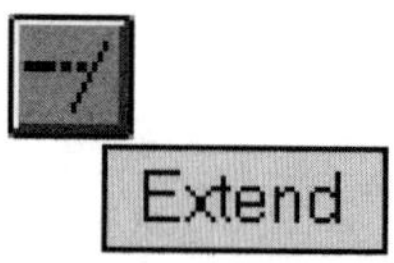

Figure 20-5: The Extend icon from the Trim flyout of the Modify toolbar.

When prompted, select one or more object(s) to serve as boundary edges. Press Enter when you've finished selecting the boundary edges. Then select the objects you want to extend, either using a single pick or a fence. Where you select an object determines which end is extended.

You can reselect an object several times to make it extend to subsequent boundary edges.

You may also specify edge and projection conditions, as described in the TRIM command earlier in this chapter.

LENGTHEN Changes the angles of arcs & lengthens selected objects

COMMAND LINE: **lengthen**

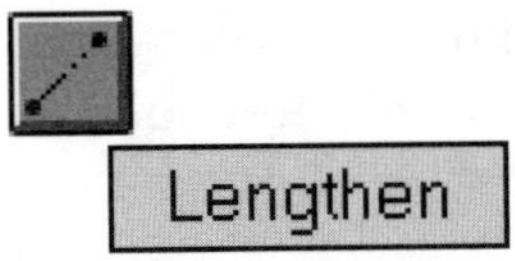

Figure 20-6: The Lengthen icon from the Resize flyout of the Modify toolbar.

When prompted, you should first set the Lengthen mode by entering one of the following options:

de (for delta) — Prompts you to specify the change in length or angle. To change the length, enter the amount of change; to change the angle, enter **a** and then the degree of change. Positive numbers extend the object, while negative numbers reduce it.

percent — Prompts you to set a percent change for the object. Values greater than 100 extend the object, while values less than 100 reduce it.

total — Prompts you to specify the absolute length or absolute angle for the object. To specify the absolute length, enter the length; to specify the absolute angle, enter **a** followed by the angle.

dy (for dynamic) — Prompts you to select an object and then allows you to drag out a new endpoint for the object.

NOTE: All the options allow you to select objects singly or with a fence. Also, where you select the objects determines which end is affected. The end of the object closest to your selection point is the end that will be lengthened.

Changing Objects' Properties

There are two methods to alter the properties of an object, and both are accessed by the Properties icon or by choosing Properties... from the Edit pull-down menu. The DDMODIFY command lets you change all the properties of one selected object. The DDCHPROP command allows you to change the common properties of multiple selected objects. Both commands are described below.

DDMODIFY Changes the properties of a single object

COMMAND LINE: **ddmodify**

Figure 20-7: The Properties icon from the Object Properties toolbar.

When you click on the Properties icon or select Properties... from the Edit pull-down menu, AutoCAD prompts you to select objects. If you select a single object, the DDMODIFY command is executed, and the appropriate Modify dialog appears. Figure 20-8 shows the Modify dialog for a 2D line.

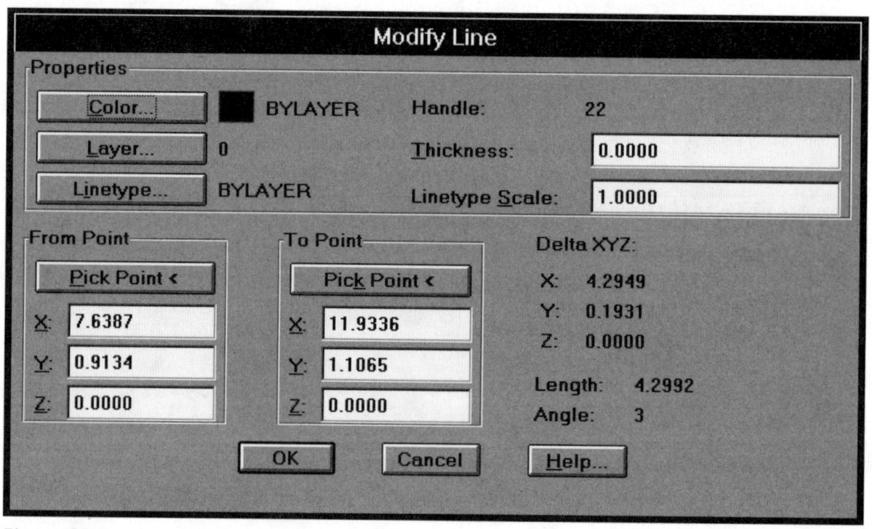

Figure 20-8: The Modify Line dialog.

The top section of the dialog displays properties common to most objects. To change the selected object's properties, you may select

Color...	Displays the Select Color dialog, where you can specify any of AutoCAD's colors.
Layer...	Displays the Select Layer dialog, where you can specify a new layer for an object.
Linetype...	Displays the Select Linetype dialog, where you can specify any loaded linetype.
Thickness	Enter a new number in this field to change the object's Z-axis extrusion thickness.
Linetype Scale	Enter a new number to change the object's linetype scale factor.

Handle cannot be changed. It's displayed for informational purposes only.

The bottom section of the dialog contains buttons, fields and information specific to the selected objects. Figure 20-9 shows the Modify Text dialog with its many fields for modifying text properties.

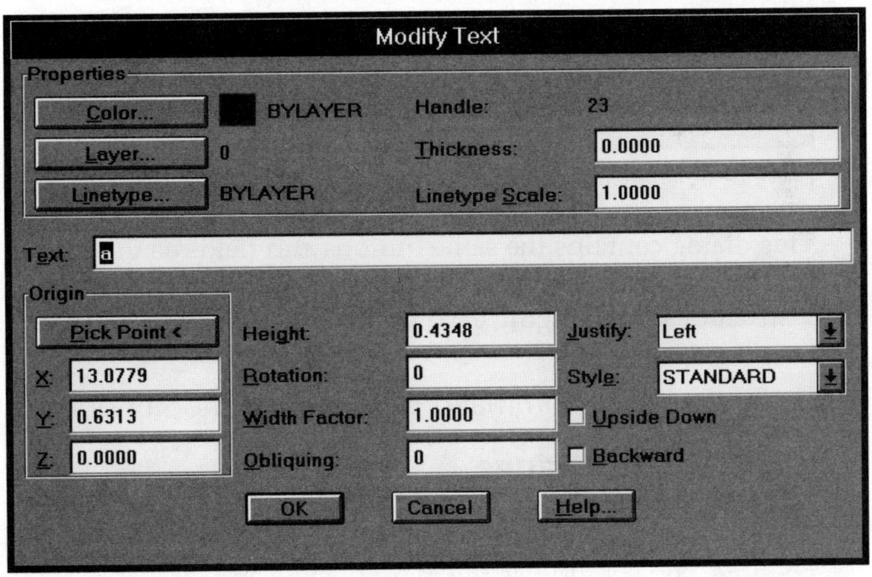

Figure 20-9: The Modify Text dialog.

DDCHPROP Modifies the common properties of selected objects

COMMAND LINE: **ddchprop**

Figure 20-10: The Properties icon from the Object Properties toolbar.

As described above, DDCHPROP and DDMODIFY share the same icon and menu pick. Clicking on the Properties icon will prompt you to select objects. If you select more than one object, the DDCHPROP command is executed and the Change Properties dialog in Figure 20-11 appears.

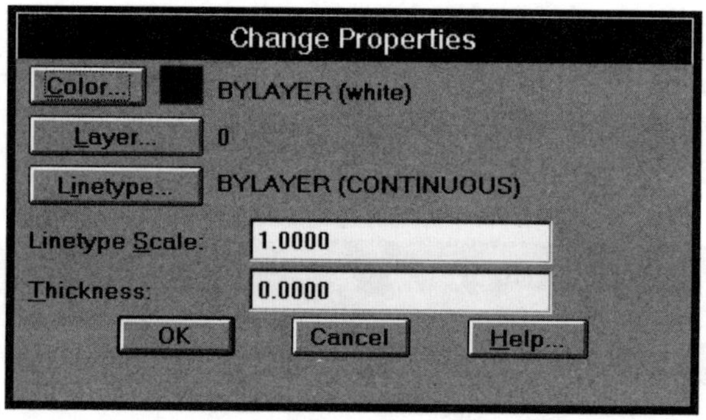

Figure 20-11: The Change Properties dialog.

This dialog contains the same buttons and fields as the top section of the Modify dialog, except that it does not report Handle information. For instructions on changing each property, see "DDMODIFY" above.

CHANGE A text-based command that lets you modify objects

COMMAND LINE: **change**

You may use the CHANGE command to modify objects, but wherever possible, you should use the more flexible and efficient commands of MODIFY and DDCHPROP instead.

Enter **change** at the command line. After selecting the objects you want to change, you'll be prompted for change point or properties. (If the viewing angle isn't perpendicular to the plane of the object being changed, a warning message appears.)

If you are changing properties:

To change properties (rather than the point), enter **p** and then enter one of the following:

c to change color.

la to change layer.

lt to change linetype.

e to change Z-axis elevation.

t to change Z-axis thickness.

If you are changing a line:

The change point becomes the new endpoint of the line. The endpoint nearest the change point will shift to the change point. If ortho is on, the changed line will be orthogonal from its unchanged end. More than one line can be changed at a time, in which case the single change point will apply to all selected lines.

If you are changing a circle:

The change point becomes the new radius of the circle.

If you are changing text:

Enter the information for those aspects of the text you want changed: starting point/endpoint/center/middle, style, height, rotation angle of baseline or the text string (the alphanumeric content). For aspects you want to leave unchanged, simply press Enter.

If you are changing an attribute:

Enter the new tag or text aspects, prompt or default value. (The attribute definition is not part of a block.)

If you are changing a block:

Enter the change point (the new insertion point) and the rotation angle. You can drag the change point for lines, circles and blocks; the rotation angle for blocks; and the starting point, height and rotation angle for text.

ARRAY Creates multiple copies of one or more objects in a rectangular or circular pattern

Figure 20-12: The Rectangular and Polar Array icons from the Copy flyout of the Modify toolbar.

When prompted, select an object or objects to be copied to develop the array.

Then enter **r** for a rectangular array or **p** for a polar (circular) array.

For a rectangular array, you may enter at the prompt

1. The number of horizontal rows.
2. The number of vertical columns.
3. The distance between rows.
4. The distance between columns.

Negative distances generate an array in the negative X and/or Y direction. Instead of entering distances from the keyboard, you can use the pointer to locate opposite corners of a box and thus indicate the spacing between rows and columns. The entire array can be rotated by setting the snap rotation before using the ARRAY command. (See "SNAP" in Chapter 5, "Points.")

There are three ways to define a polar or circular array. After selecting objects, you may enter any of the following:

p, followed by the center, the number of objects and then the angle to fill.

p and then the center, but press Enter when prompted for the number of objects. Enter the angle to fill and then the angle between objects.

c, followed by the center, the angle between objects and then either the number of objects (positive) or the number of degrees to fill (negative).

The last prompt to appear in the polar array sequence asks if you want the objects rotated as they are copied. The default response is **y** (yes) to rotate the objects as they are copied.

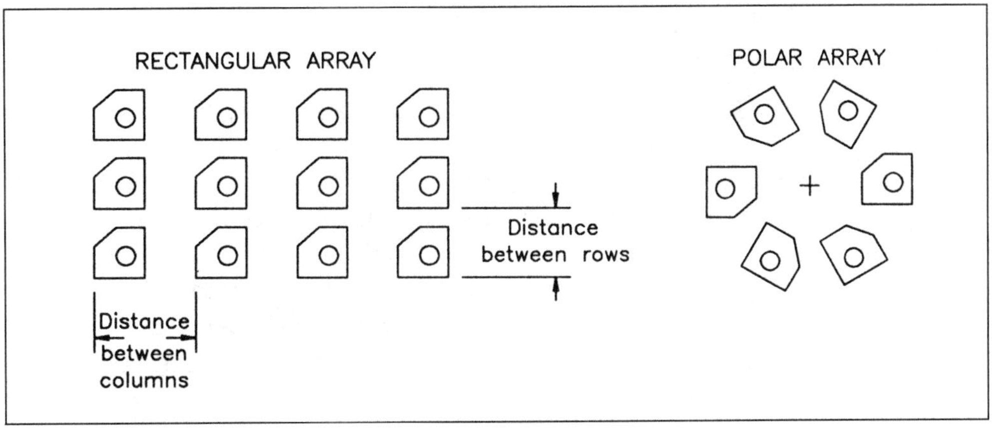

Figure 20-13: Use ARRAY with either rectangular or polar options.

If you choose to make a polar array from a group of objects and you don't rotate the group as it's copied, it may not array properly. (The system will select a reference point on one of the objects in the group. This reference point will be arrayed properly, but the group of objects as a whole may not array as you intended, especially if the reference point isn't centrally located within the group.) To avoid this, create a block out of the group and select an insertion base point in the center of the group. Then make a polar array out of the block. (See "BLOCK" in Chapter 23, "Blocks & External References.")

Objects are arrayed only in an X-Y plane by the regular ARRAY command. However, you may also use the commands 3D Rectangular Array and 3D Polar Array from the Copy flyout. See Chapter 32, "3D Objects," for information about these commands.

DIVIDE Places points or blocks along an object to divide it into a specified number of equal segments

COMMAND LINE: **divide**

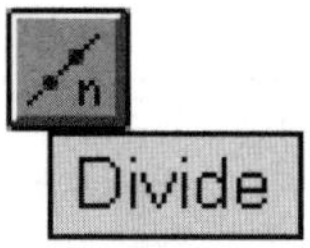

Figure 20-14: The Divide icon from the Point flyout of the Draw toolbar.

When prompted, select the object to be divided. Then enter the desired number of segments. AutoCAD places a point or a block at each location that would divide the object into the specified number of pieces. Note that this command does not actually cut the selected object, it merely places points at the divide locations. If you divide using points, you may want to change the point style to something easier to see. (See "Point Style" in Chapter 5, "Points.")

To mark the divisions with blocks rather than points, enter **b** before entering the number of segments. Then enter the name of the block. Finally, enter **y** to align each block with the object being divided or **n** to leave each block oriented as it was when the block was defined.

MEASURE Places points or blocks along an object to mark a series of measured distances

COMMAND LINE: **measure**

Figure 20-15: The Measure icon from the Point flyout of the Draw toolbar.

When prompted, select the object to be measured. Where you select the object determines from which end the measuring starts. (Circles are always measured counterclockwise from the zero-angle point.)

Then enter the length of the segments you want measured. If the object length is not an even multiple of the measure length, the last segment will be shorter than the rest. AutoCAD then places a point or a block at the specified measure distance along the object. Note that this command does not actually cut the selected object, it merely places points along the object with the specified measure distance. If you measure using Points, you may want to change the point style to something easier to see. (See Chapter 5, "Points.")

To mark the lengths with blocks rather than points, enter **b** before entering the number of segments. Then enter the name of the block. Finally, enter **y** to align each block with the object being divided or **n** to leave each the block oriented as it was when the block was defined.

Moving on

The following chapter introduces a few of the filled-in objects available in AutoCAD. These objects let you create objects that cover parts of your drawing with wide areas of color.

CHAPTER 21

Filled Objects

Solids and donuts form the introduction to filled-in objects. Use these objects whenever you need areas of solid, filled and color.

NOTE: *If you have used earlier versions of AutoCAD, you may wonder why the TRACE command is not covered in this chapter. Polylines, which let you create a line of specified width, have essentially made traces obsolete. TRACE is a memory hog, and it can slow down the system and the regeneration time. For details on polylines, see Chapter 28, "Polylines & Splines." (TRACE is still available, however; just enter* ***trace*** *at the command line or choose the Trace icon from the Miscellaneous toolbar.)*

SOLID Places 2D solid quadrilaterals or triangles in a drawing

COMMAND LINE: **solid**

Figure 21-1: The Solid icon from the Polygon flyout of the Draw toolbar.

This solid is "solid" only in the sense that it is filled in. Do not confuse it with the 3D solid created with the Solid Model commands.

When prompted, enter the four points that define the first quadrilateral, or the three points plus Enter that define the first triangle. (The third and fourth points must be oriented in the same basic direction as the first and second points or you'll get a "bowtie" instead of a quadrilateral.)

To continue the solid, consider the third and fourth points of the last quadrilateral as the first and second points of the next. Then enter the new third and fourth points. To end the solid, press Enter when prompted for the next "third point."

When FILL is off (and the drawing has been regenerated), AutoCAD displays only the outlines of the solid for faster picture regeneration (see "FILL" below).

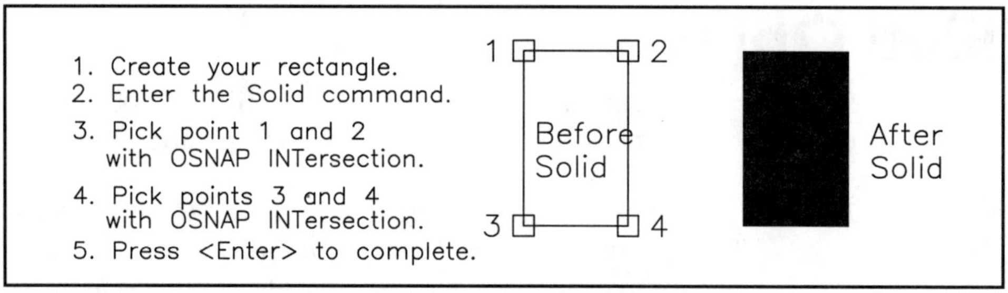

Figure 21-2: How to use the Solid command.

DONUT Creates wide rings & filled circles

COMMAND LINE: **donut**

Figure 21-3: The Donut icon on the Circle flyout of the Draw toolbar.

Donuts, another type of filled object, are a special type of polyline.

When prompted, enter the inside and outside diameters and then locate the center. To draw a filled circle, enter **0** for the inside diameter.

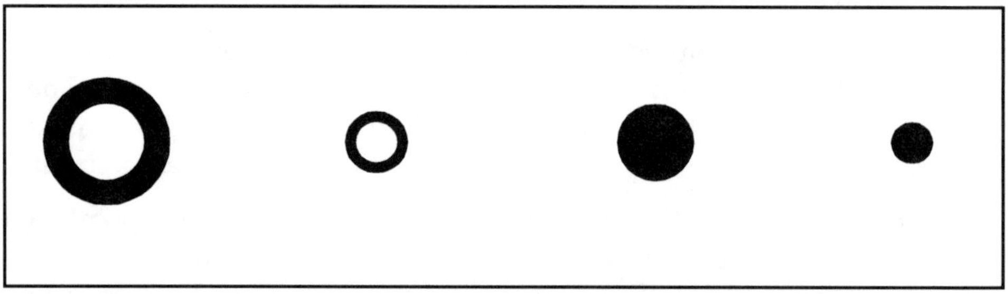

Figure 21-4: Two types of donut—wide rings and filled circles.

To edit a donut, use either the PEDIT or BREAK commands. AutoCAD uses polyline arcs to make donuts, so they can be edited with PEDIT and BREAK.

FILL Governs the way traces, solids & wide polylines are displayed & plotted

COMMAND LINE: **fill**

When prompted, enter **on** to display and plot filled-in outlines. Or enter **off** to display (and plot) their outlines only.

The display doesn't change until after the next regeneration.

Fill is initially on when a new drawing is started.

Moving on

The next chapter deals with layers, one of the most important organizational issues in AutoCAD. The way you set up and manage layers has a great impact on your production efficiency and your ability to share drawings with others.

CHAPTER 22

Layers

Good layering practice is a skill that sets apart a professional CAD user from a beginner. Planning a layering strategy and then using it consistently will make your work easier to edit, plot and share with other professionals. In this chapter, you'll learn how to use the commands to control layers and their associated colors and linetypes. You'll also review wild cards and linetype scaling.

LAYER CONTROL Affects the creation & visibility of layers, colors & linetypes in all viewports

COMMAND LINE: **ddlmodes**

Figure 22-1: The Layer icon from the Object Properties toolbar.

Choose Layers from the Data pull-down menu or click the Layer Control icon to display the Layer Control dialog shown in Figure 22-2.

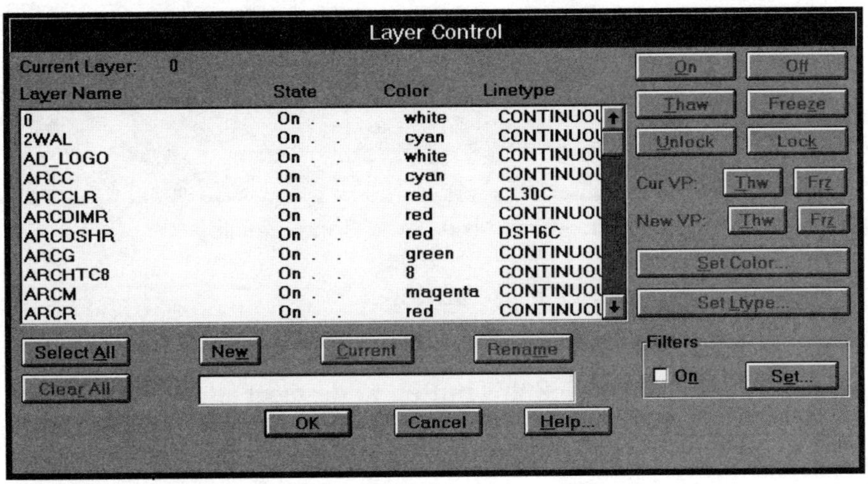

Figure 22-2: The Layer Control dialog.

This imposing dialog is not that hard to understand if you break it into manageable sections. Let's take a look at the various controls that make up the dialog box.

The Current Layer field is for informational purposes only. It indicates which layer you are currently drawing on.

Layer Name, a list of all the layers in your drawing, is the heart of the Layer Control dialog. The list identifies each layer by name and includes information about each layer, such as the State, the Color and the Linetype assigned to that layer. All the other buttons, except New, require you to select one or more layers from this list. If there are more layers in your drawing than can be displayed in the list box, scroll through the list using the scroll bar at right.

Selecting layers is quite easy. Click on a layer's name to select it, and select as many layers as you wish. To deselect a selected layer, click on its name. Some functions require that only one layer be selected; others can work with groups of many layers. Figure 22-3 shows a number of selected layers.

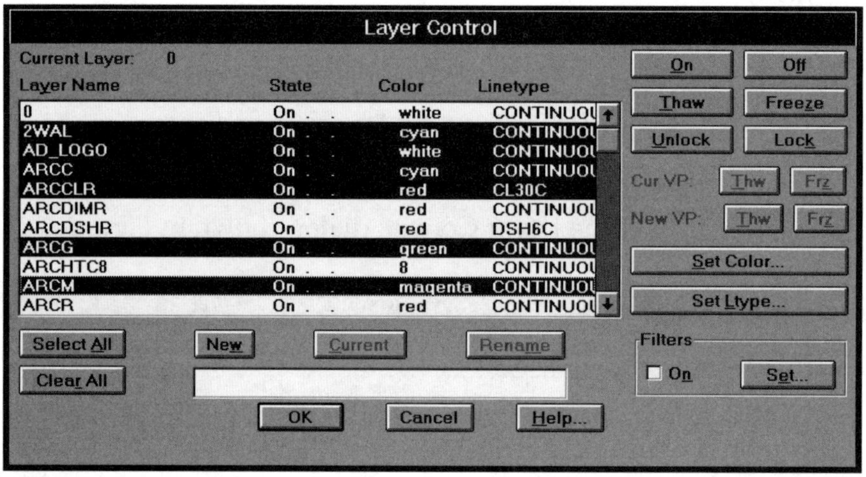

Figure 22-3: Selected layers in the Layer Control dialog.

The dialog provides these buttons:

Select All — Click this button to select all the layers in the layer list.

Clear All — Click this button to deselect all the layers in the layer list. It is good practice to click on the Clear All button as soon as you have finished working with any group of layers. This prevents your accidentally changing the properties of a layer that is selected but not currently visible in the list box.

New — To create one or more layers based on names in the edit box, first type the name of your new layer in the edit box (directly

	beneath the New button). Then click on New. You may create multiple layers at the same time by separating layer names with a comma. The name can have up to 31 characters, but it is good practice to keep the names as short as possible, as many other AutoCAD commands cannot display the full 31 characters of a long layer name.
Current	Click Current to make a single selected layer your current drawing layer. This button cannot be used if more than one layer is selected.
Rename	Rename changes the name of a single selected layer. Select one layer, then type the new name for that layer in the edit box. Then, click on Rename. This button cannot be used if more than one layer is selected.
On/Off	These buttons change the visibility of the selected layers. When On, the layers are visible and can be plotted. Even though a layer is turned off, its objects are still accessible by many commands. Objects on layers that are turned off can still be selected with All or as part of a named group, and they are still taken into consideration by a ZOOM EXTENTS command.
Thaw/ Freeze	These buttons control the active status of the selected layers. When a layer is frozen, it becomes invisible. The main difference between a layer that is frozen and one that is turned off is that entities on the frozen layer cannot be selected and are not checked during zoom extents or drawing regeneration. Because the entities are not checked, freezing unneeded layers can increase performance.
Unlock/ Lock	These buttons determine whether you can edit objects on the selected layers. When a layer is locked, you cannot select objects on that layer for editing commands such as MOVE or ERASE. You can select the locked entities for inquiry commands or as boundaries for commands such as EXTEND or TRIM.
Cur VP New VP	These are Paper Space viewport controls, discussed in depth in Chapter 31, "Model Space & Paper Space."
Set Color	This button controls the color assigned to the selected layers. Click it to display the Select Color dialog box (see Figure 22-4).

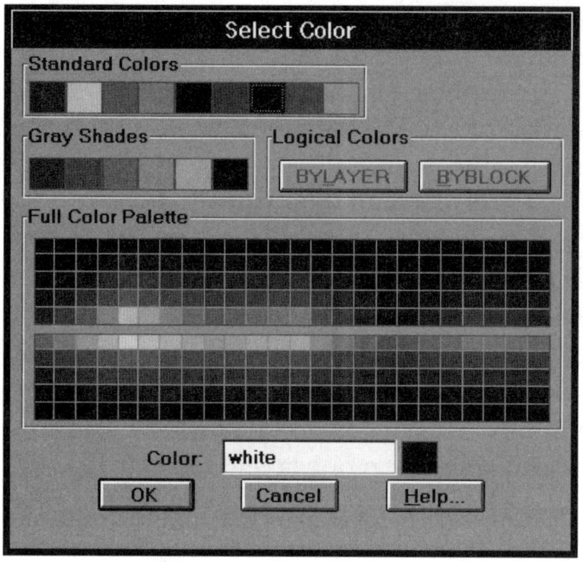

Figure 22-4: The Select Color dialog.

Standard Colors, Gray Shades and Full Color Palette are three areas in this dialog where you can select a color by clicking on a color swatch. The fourth area, Logical Colors, is not available for layer assignment. For more details, see "Object Creation Modes" later in this chapter.

The Standard Colors area contains swatches for the standard colors numbered 1 through 9. Respectively, they are Red, Yellow, Green, Cyan, Blue, Magenta, White, Dark Gray and Light Gray.

NOTE: *Even though there is a color named white, it displays as black. This is to maintain compatibility with the DOS version of AutoCAD, which uses a black background with white lines, whereas the AutoCAD Windows version uses a white background with black lines.*

The Gray Shades area contains six swatches of grays for colors numbered 250 through 255.

The Full Color Palette area contains the remaining colors for numbers 10 through 24.

The Color edit field at the bottom of the dialog displays the name or number of your selected color, or you can type in any valid color name or number.

The Set Linetype... button controls the linetype assigned to the selected layers. Click it to display the Select Linetype dialog, which displays up to eight selected linetypes (see Figure 22-5). Then click on the linetype that you want to assign to the selected layers.

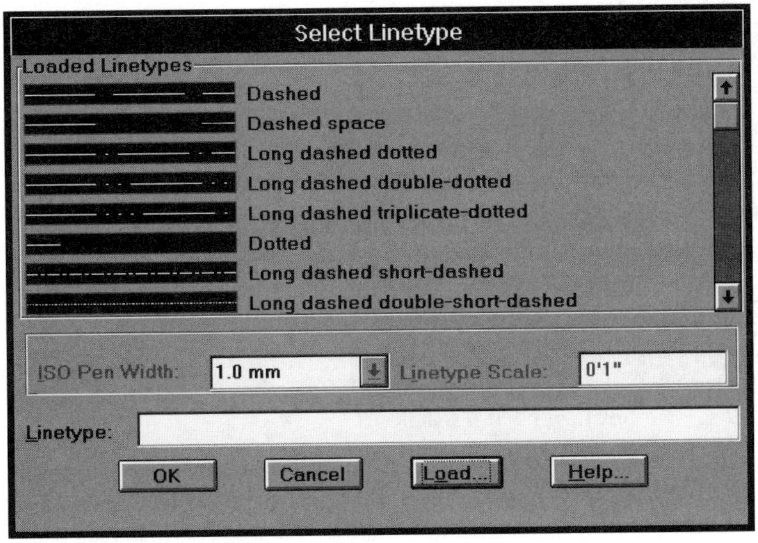

Figure 22-5: The Select Linetype dialog.

If the linetype that you want is not available in the list box, you can click on the Load button to load linetypes from an external file. (The default is the ACAD.LIN file.)

Layer Filters

The filters area of the Layer Control dialog controls the display of layer names in the Layer Names list box. With filters, you can use wild cards and other options to restrict the display to layers with certain properties. Clicking on the Set button in the Filters area displays the Set Layer Filters dialog shown in Figure 22-6.

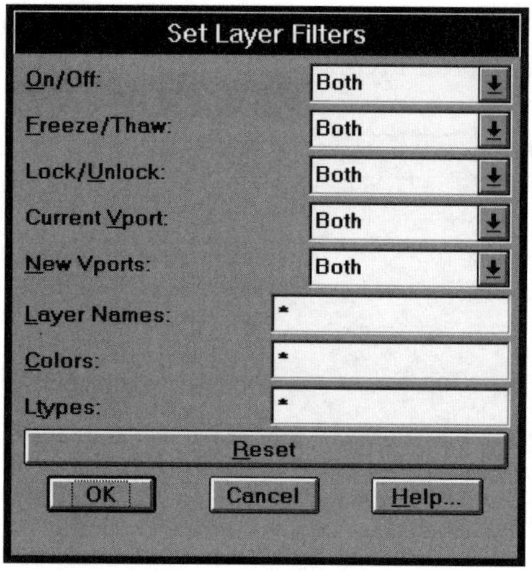

Figure 22-6: The Set Layer Filters dialog.

The first five entry fields (On/Off, Freeze/Thaw, Lock/Unlock, Current Vport and New Vports) restrict layer display based upon visibility and selection properties. Your choices are displayed in a pop-up list when you click on the appropriate field.

The last three fields (Layer Names, Colors and Ltypes) allow you to restrict layer display. All these fields may use wild cards to identify layer and linetype names and to specify ranges of color numbers.

Finally, to restore layer filters to the original AutoCAD standard, you may choose the Reset bar at the bottom. It will restore all your layer filters to the defaults.

Filter Wild Cards

Valid AutoCAD wild cards are defined below:

- # Accepts any single number, 0 to 9.
- @ Accepts any single letter.
- . Accepts any single non-alphanumeric character (for example: $,-,_).
- * Accepts any single character or group of characters. If the * is used by itself, it accepts everything. Unlike the DOS version of this wild card, the * in AutoCAD can be placed at the beginning, middle or end of a search string. It can also stand for "no characters" as well. For example, the search string A*B will accept items named AXB, ATOB, A2B, A_34_B and AB.

? Accepts any single character.

~ The tilde makes the search string negative and accepts anything that does not match the search string. For example, ~A* matches all items that do not begin with the letter *A*.

[ ] Accepts any one of a group of characters or a range of characters separated by a hyphen. For example, [abe-n]* accepts items that begin with the letters *a* or *b* or any letter from *e* to *n*.

Once you specify your filters and click on OK, the Layer Names list box displays only the layers that match your filter restrictions. Clicking the On check box in the filters area enables and disables the filter restrictions. When the box is not checked, all layers are displayed regardless of the filters specified.

OBJECT CREATION MODES Sets the color, current layer, linetype, text style, elevation & thickness for subsequently drawn objects

COMMAND LINE: **ddemodes**

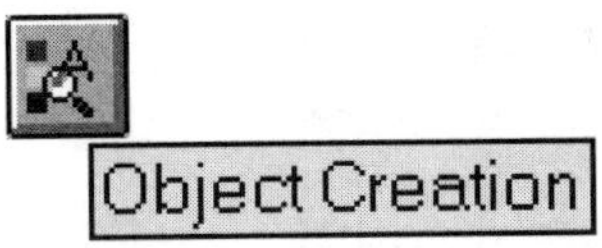

Figure 22-7: The Object Creation icon from the Object Properties toolbar.

Choose Object Creation from the Data pull-down menu or click the Object Creation icon to display the Object Creation Modes dialog box (see Figure 22-8).

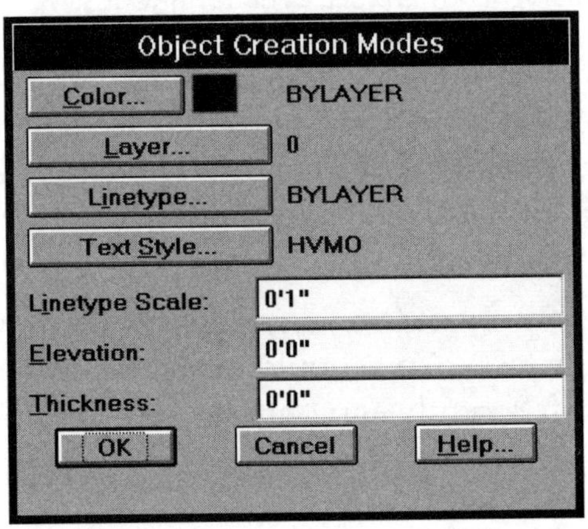

Figure 22-8: The Object Creation Modes dialog.

This dialog reinforces an important advantage of dialog boxes. While there are a number of different commands, both dialog- and command line-based, that allow you to set these parameters individually, the Object Creation Modes dialog groups them in one convenient place. Use this dialog when you want to quickly change one or more creation modes without individually accessing the Layer Control, Color, Linetype and Text Style commands.

Color — This button produces the same Select Color dialog that was described in Layer Control (see Figure 22-9). The only difference is that now you have access to the buttons BYLAYER and BYBLOCK.

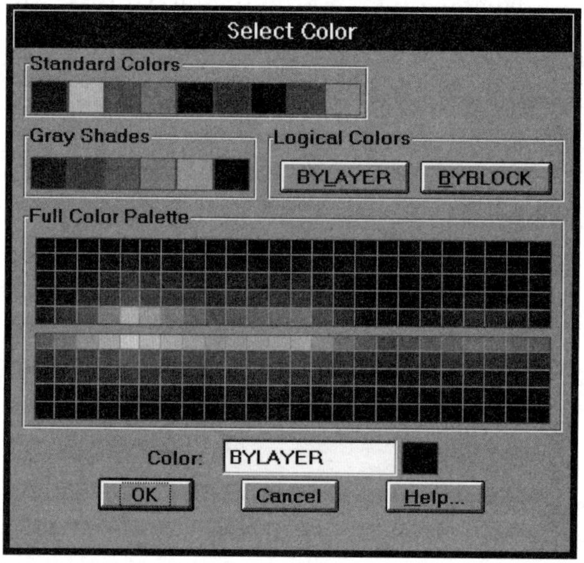

Figure 22-9: The Select Color dialog from Object Creation Modes.

BYLAYER — The BYLAYER color definition tells AutoCAD to respect the color of the current layer when creating objects. Changing the color to anything else will override the current layer color and use whatever color you select.

BYLAYER should be your color choice for most of your drawing tasks. You should override the current layer color infrequently and only for very specific purposes.

BYBLOCK — One of the specific purposes for overriding layer color is the use of BYBLOCK. Choosing BYBLOCK as the object creation color causes newly drawn objects to pick up the block color if they are eventually assigned as part of a block. For more details, see Chapter 23, "Blocks & External References."

Layer... — The Layer... button displays the Layer Control dialog described above. You have full access to all the features of the standard Layer Control command.

Linetype — The Linetype button displays the same Linetype dialog found in the Layer Control dialog. The differences are that you now have access to the BYLAYER and BYBLOCK linetype settings, and you can set the ISO Pen Width and Linetype Scale.

The BYLAYER and BYBLOCK settings have the same meaning for linetypes as they do for colors. The ISO Pen Width field displays a pop-up list that allows you to specify an ISO-based linetype scale based on the selected pen width. The Linetype Scale field lets you enter a scale factor for the current object's linetype scale (see Linetype Scales below).

The fields for Elevation and Thickness are used for 3D drawing. See Chapter 32, "3D Objects," for information on these settings.

Linetype Scaling

There are three system variables that control linetype scales in AutoCAD Release 13: LTSCALE, CELTSCALE and PSLTSCALE. This is what each variable controls:

LTSCALE — Sets the global scale factor applied to all linetypes in the drawing.

CELTSCALE — Sets the Current Entity Line Type scale applied to objects as they are created. The appearance of a linetype in your drawing is a function of LTSCALE multiplied by CELTSCALE.

PSLTSCALE — Sets the Paper Space Line Type scaling based on Paper Space viewports. See Chapter 31, "Model Space & Paper Space," for more information.

If we disregard Paper Space for now, the proper setting for LTSCALE should be based on your intended plotting scale. An easy way to think of this is if you always calculate your plot scale in the form of 1=X. Then your LTSCALE should be equal to X. For example, if you wish to plot at 1" = 4", the plot scale is 1=4 and the LTSCALE is 4.

Likewise, if you wish to plot at 1/16" = 1'-0", the plot scale is 1=192 and LTSCALE is 192. You set the LTSCALE variable by choosing Linetypes from the Options pull-down menu and then choosing Global Linetype Scale.

CELTSCALE is applied to objects as they are created, and it is stored with each object. This allows you to fine-tune the scale of linetypes on an object-by-object basis. Whenever you specify a Linetype scale in a dialog such as Object Creation Modes, Common Properties or Modify Object, you are altering CELTSCALE.

Moving on

The next chapter covers the creation and use of blocks and external references. These objects are important tools for increasing your productivity and sharing drawing components with your colleagues.

CHAPTER 23

Blocks & External References

Blocks and external references provide you with the ability to group, reuse and share multiple objects or even entire drawings. You can think of blocks as being similar to manual drafting templates. When you need a particular symbol in your drawing, you select the appropriate template and add the symbol.

External references are more like manual underlay drawings. You view and reference these drawings while working on your own drawing. The underlay allows you to align your work with the referenced drawing, but you cannot change the referenced drawing.

BLOCK

Combines several objects for repeated insertion anywhere in a drawing

COMMAND LINE: **block**

Figure 23-1: The Block icon from the Block flyout of the Draw toolbar.

When prompted for the block name, enter a descriptive name up to 31 characters long.

When prompted for the insertion base point, enter the point that will best serve as a reference point for future insertions of this block. This will often be the corner of a rectangle or the center of a circle.

When prompted, select the items that will make up the block. When these entities are formed into a block, they're erased. To restore them, enter **oops**.

A block is stored only in the current drawing. To store a block on hard disk or floppy diskette, use the WBLOCK command (see "WBLOCK" below).

Blocks may contain other blocks. But it is not good practice to place blocks within blocks, as this may cause problems if you ever have to recover a drawing.

Redefining a Block

To redefine a block, you must first insert it into your drawing and then make the required changes.

1. Insert the block using the INSERT command (described below) with the Explode option checked.

2. Next, enter **block**, then the name of the block you want to redefine. AutoCAD reminds you that a block by that name has already been defined and asks if you want to redefine it. Enter **y** for yes. Then select the new or altered items that will make up the block.

When a block is redefined, all prior insertions of that block will also change to the redefined configuration upon the next regeneration of the drawing (assuming the blocks were inserted as units; see "INSERT" below).

You can also redefine a block by adopting a block definition from a file, as described under "Revising Blocks From External Files."

INSERT Places a previously defined block in the drawing

COMMAND LINE: **ddinsert**

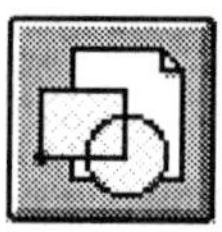

Figure 23-2: The Insert Block icon from the Block flyout of the Draw toolbar.

Clicking the Insert Block icon displays the Insert dialog shown in Figure 23-3. This dialog controls all aspects of inserting a block into your drawing. You can also specify many of the parameters dynamically on screen.

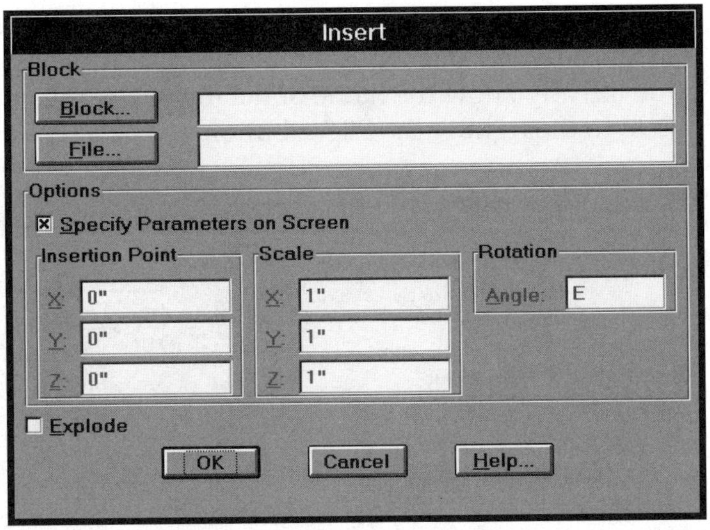

Figure 23-3: The Insert dialog.

Using the Insert Dialog

Click on the Block… button to display the Defined Blocks dialog in Figure 23-4. Choose the desired block from the list of all blocks defined in the drawing. If you already know the name of the block that you want to insert, you can type its name in the edit field to the right of the Block… button.

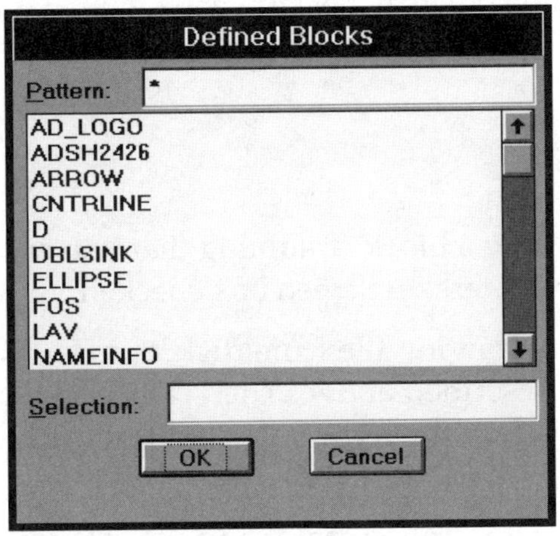

Figure 23-4: The Defined Blocks dialog.

Click on the File... button to display the Select Drawing File dialog in Figure 23-5. Choose a drawing file from any drive or directory to insert as a block. If you already know the name of the file you want, you can type it in the edit field to the right of the File… button.

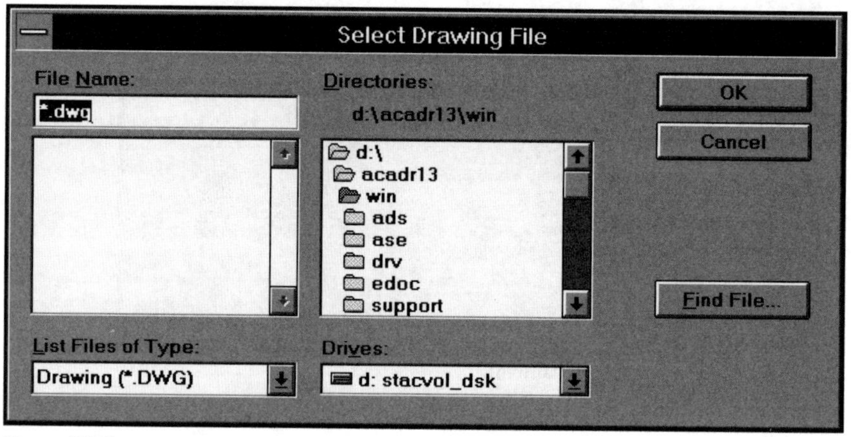

Figure 23-5: The Select Drawing File dialog from Insert.

If Specify Parameters on Screen is checked, AutoCAD will prompt you for the insertion point, scale factors and rotation angle as described below under "Inserting a Block." If it is off, you must enter the information in the appropriate edit fields beneath the check box.

If Explode is checked, the block's contents will be inserted as individual objects rather than as a single block. (Check this box when you want to change and/or redefine a BLOCK, as described above under "BLOCK.")

Inserting a Block

Here are the steps for inserting a block, assuming that you are inserting a block with the Specify Parameters on Screen box checked.

Select a defined block, or a drawing file from disk, to insert using the Block… or File… buttons described above. Then click on OK and specify the insertion point the point at which the base point of the block will be placed. You can enter a 3D location (X,Y,Z).

Enter the X scaling factor, the Y scaling factor and the rotation angle. Use the defaults for these three prompts to insert the block exactly as it was drawn. You can use negative scaling factors to flip the block. Blocks containing 3D elements and 2D objects that have been assigned thickness are scaled in the Z direction the same as in the X direction.

As an alternative, you can indicate the X and Y scaling factors with the pointer. To do so, pick a point when prompted for the X scaling factor. The X and Y distances between the block's insertion point and the point you pick become the X and Y scaling factors.

For dragging, AutoCAD normally assigns a scale factor of 1 and a rotation angle of 0. That is, even if you plan to insert a block at a scale factor of 2 and a rotation angle of -35 degrees, while you're dragging it its scale factor is still 1 and its rotation angle is still 0. However, if you wish to specify a different scale factor or rotation angle, enter one of the following options when AutoCAD prompts you for the insertion point:

s	Overall scaling factor. This specifies the X, Y and Z scale factors of the block to be inserted. For a mirror image, use a negative scale factor.
x	The X-scale factor specifies the X coordinate location of the insertion point.
y	The Y-scale factor specifies the Y coordinate location of the insertion point.
z	The Z-scale factor specifies the Z coordinate location of the insertion point.
r	The Rotation angle specifies a rotation angle at the current UCS.

After entering one of the above options, AutoCAD will prompt you for a value and then return you to the Insertion point prompt. If you want to enter preliminary information for dragging purposes only, but want AutoCAD to prompt you for the final scaling factors and rotation angle, then instead of S, X, Y, Z or R enter **ps**, **px**, **py**, **pz** or **pr**.

AutoCAD then resumes its request for the insertion point, and the image being dragged is scaled and/or rotated according to your instructions. Remaining prompts skip requests for information you've already entered.

By default, inserted blocks are treated as a single object by AutoCAD; that is, the individual objects in the block can't be edited in the usual manner. Blocks inserted with the Explode check box selected aren't treated as a single object, and their individual objects can be edited. However, these blocks cannot be scaled differently in the X direction than in the Y or Z direction.

Objects in a block are inserted on the same layers as when they were originally drawn. However, objects that were originally drawn on layer 0 float to the current layer unless they were inserted with the Explode check box selected as explained above.

Attribute Information

Blocks can contain attribute information (in Chapter 37, see "ATTDEF" and related commands). When such a block is inserted, the attribute values may be entered in response to the prompts in the usual way, or with a dialog box.

Even though a block might contain attributes, it can be inserted without entering any attribute values if you enter the system variable ATTREQ at the command prompt and set its value to 0.

Revising Blocks From External Files

When the block is retrieved from an external drawing file (when it's not already part of the current drawing), that external drawing is unaffected by the insertion. The two drawings are not interactive. That is, changes made to the block in the current drawing do not automatically affect the external drawing, and subsequent changes made to the external drawing do not automatically affect the inserted block.

However, the revised external drawing can be used to redefine the inserted block, as explained below. A more interactive relationship can exist between two drawings using the XREF command (see "External References" at the end of this chapter).

You can use an existing drawing file to redefine a block in the current drawing by specifying both the drawing file name and the block name in the Insert dialog.

First click on the File... button to select the drawing file from the disk, then type the name of an existing block in the edit field to the right of the Block... button. When you click on OK, the Warning dialog in Figure 23-6 will be displayed.

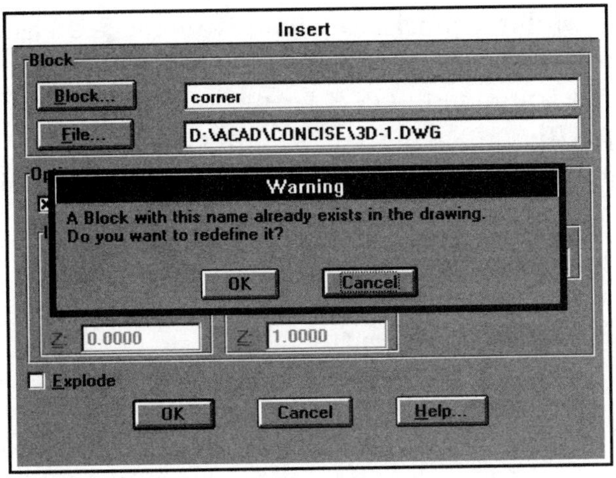

Figure 23-6: The warning dialog.

Click on OK again and then press Esc to cancel the command. For example, suppose you have a block in your drawing called OLDPART, and a drawing file called NEWPART.DWG, and you want to replace OLDPART with NEWPART in your drawing. Select NEWPART.DWG using the File... button and type **oldpart** in the Block edit field. When you click on OK for the warning dialog, all insertions of OLDPART will be replaced with NEWPART.

MINSERT Places multiple insertions of a block in a rectangular array

COMMAND LINE: **minsert**

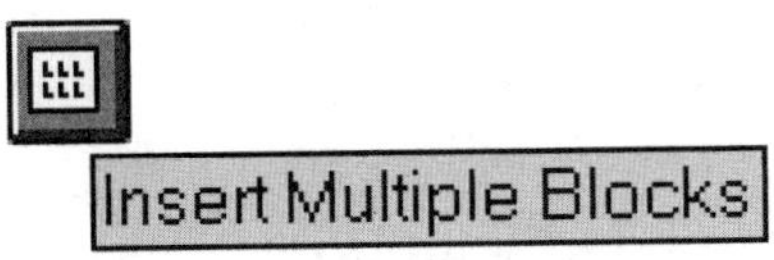

Figure 23-7: The Insert Multiple Blocks icon from the Miscellaneous toolbar.

This is a nearly obsolete command, and it has been banished to the Miscellaneous toolbar with some other obscure commands. To display the Miscellaneous toolbar, choose Toolbars from the Tools pull-down menu and then select Miscellaneous.

Click on the Insert Multiple Blocks icon to activate the text-based MINSERT command. You are first prompted to enter the name of the block that you wish to insert at the command line. After responding to the usual INSERT command prompts (described above), enter the number of rows, number of columns, distance between rows and distance between columns, similar to the ARRAY command.

The entire array is inserted as a unit and cannot be exploded. This makes the MINSERT command of questionable value when compared to the combination of INSERT and ARRAY.

EXPLODE Breaks a complex object into its component parts

COMMAND LINE: **explode**

Figure 23-8: The Explode icon from the Explode flyout of the Modify toolbar.

When you're exploding a block, the block is redrawn as individual objects, which allows them to be edited in the usual way (see "INSERT" earlier in this chapter). This produces the same result as if the block had originally been inserted with the Explode check box selected. Everything should remain the same visually, except that layer-0 (floating) elements may change color or linetype.

Notes on the EXPLODE command:

In Release 13 a block inserted with differing X and Y scaling factors can be exploded. This does not occur with prior releases.

When a polyline is exploded, it's replaced with ordinary, zero-width lines and arcs.

When a mesh is exploded, each facet becomes a separate 3D face.

When an associative dimension is exploded, it no longer functions associatively; and it loses its dimension style reference (see Chapter 24, "Dimensions").

WBLOCK Writes a block to disk as a separate drawing file

COMMAND LINE: **wblock**

Typing **wblock** at the command prompt displays the Create Drawing File dialog shown in Figure 23-9. Navigate to the drive and directory where you want to store the block. Type a file name in the File Name field, then click on OK.

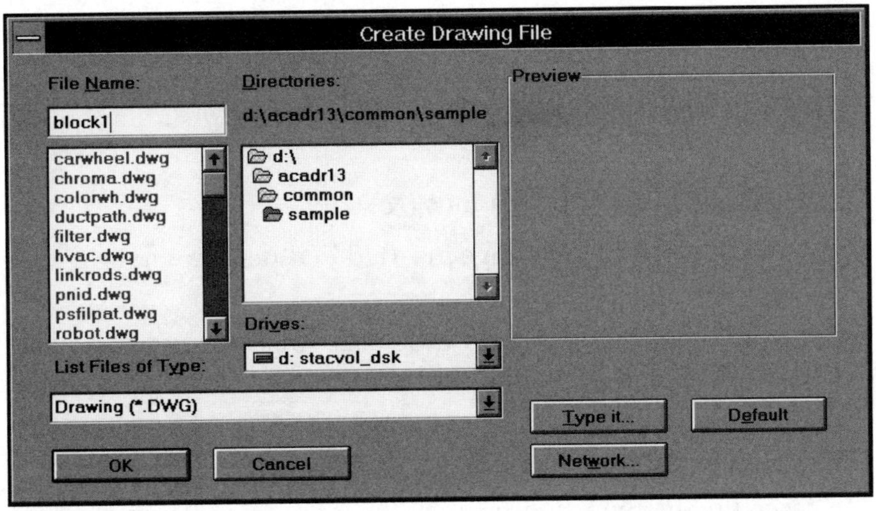

Figure 23-9: The Create Drawing File dialog from the WBLOCK command.

When prompted for the block name, enter the name of the block that you want written to the disk. (You can enter = if the block name and the file name are the same.)

If you have not yet defined the block, press Enter at the block name prompt and you'll be prompted for the insertion point and objects to include in the block.

If you want the entire current drawing written onto disk, enter * for the block name. This does the same as the SAVE command, but unreferenced blocks and layers are not written.

BASE Specifies a base point for future insertion of one drawing into another

COMMAND LINE: **base**

When you create a block using the BLOCK command, you're prompted for an insertion base point. However, when you want to insert an entire drawing into another drawing, the 0,0 point of that drawing is assumed to be the insertion base point *unless* you use the BASE command to specify a different point while you're creating/editing that drawing.

Enter **base** at the command prompted. When prompted for the Base point, enter the point that you want to define as the insertion point for the entire drawing.

BASE will accept 3D locations (X,Y,Z).

BASE also affects drawings inserted in other drawings as xrefs.

PURGE Removes named objects that are not referenced in a drawing

COMMAND LINE: **purge**

Choose Purge from the Data menu to display the list of purge choices in a cascading menu. Choose one of the following to purge unused objects of that type, or choose All to purge all unused objects:

- Layers
- Linetypes
- Multiline Styles
- Text Styles
- Dimension Styles
- Shapes
- Blocks
- All

You will be prompted to confirm purging each object. Layer 0, the Continuous linetype, and the text and dimension styles named Standard can't be purged.

NOTE: *If you are using an earlier release of AutoCAD, you must use this command before the drawing database has been changed with one of the drawing or editing commands (or as soon as you enter a drawing). In Release 13, you may use the command at any time during the editing session.*

Organizing a Block Library

You can save a lot of drawing time by inserting predrawn blocks, especially if you have a well-organized library of blocks. Your block library is most useful when it's fully documented. That includes a sample printout of each block, with the block name/number and insertion point shown.

You'll want to group similar blocks together. This can be done in several ways. One way is to store all related blocks as individual wblocks (drawings) in a separate subdirectory of the hard disk.

Another way is to store all similar blocks in a *library drawing*. All of these block definitions can then be simultaneously called into a different drawing if you insert the library drawing. To do so, use the INSERT command and answer the prompt for the block name with the name of the library drawing. When prompted for the insertion point, press Esc. Although Esc prevents the insertion of the actual library drawing into your present drawing, the block definitions it contains have already been loaded and are now available from within the present drawing.

External References

External reference (or *xref*, for short) is a feature that allows your current drawing to incorporate up-to-date information from external drawings. Xrefs are placed in a drawing with the XREF command. The various options of the XREF command are explained under "XREF" below.

A typical use for XREF is an assembly drawing in which the various components are xrefs.

Xrefs have some similarities to blocks. First, they can be inserted multiple times at different scaling factors and rotation angles. Second, when you list an xref, it's called a *block reference*, although it's also tagged as an xref.

Third, when you use the BLOCK or INSERT command and ask for a listing of blocks presently in the drawing, xrefs will be listed with your regular blocks and identified as xrefs.

However, an xref has one overriding distinction that makes it a very powerful feature: an xref is automatically updated after the external drawing is updated.

Suppose drawing A includes drawing B as an xref. When drawing A is in the drawing editor, the current version of B is added to A. (We'll refer to drawing A as the *referencing drawing,* since it's the drawing in which the reference is made to another (external) drawing. We'll refer to drawing B as *the referenced drawing*.) There is nothing in B to let you know that B is referenced by A; all the reference information is in A. That reference information in A is called the xref. The referenced drawing itself can also be called the xref.

The referenced drawing is attached to the referencing drawing but not a permanent part of it. If B were an external block that had been inserted into A, the block definition would become a permanent part of A. In contrast, since B is used inside A as an xref, the information from B is added to A only for the duration of the editing or plotting session.

The next time drawing A is edited or plotted, information is again read from the B drawing file so that it reflects the current state of drawing B. Whenever B is revised, those revisions appear automatically when they're needed in A.

Nesting Xrefs

Xrefs can be nested. Consider an assembly drawing containing several subassemblies. While A (the main assembly) uses B (a subassembly) as an xref, B might use C and D as xrefs. When you edit B, the information from C and D automatically appears in B. When you edit A, the information from B (including the information from C and D) appears in A.

Although xrefs can be nested, they cannot be circular. In other words, if drawing A includes an xref to drawing B, drawing B cannot include an xref to drawing A. However, you can overcome this limitation by using the overlay option of the XREF command.

Overlaying Xrefs

An xref overlay automatically ignores circular references, but overlays are only one level deep.

Consider the same example as the nested xrefs above. Main assembly A uses B as an overlay xref. It is OK for B to also use A as either an attached or overlaid xref since the circular reference is ignored. If B uses C and D as attached xrefs, they will also appear in A, but if B uses C and D as overlay xrefs they will not appear in A.

Blocks Versus Xrefs

It's important to understand how both blocks and xrefs relate to the current drawing. First, consider blocks. There can be a two-way interaction between blocks in a drawing and their corresponding external drawing files.

While you're in the current drawing, you can revise an external drawing file used as a block. Do this by redefining the block in the drawing and then using that revised block to update the external drawing file with the WBLOCK command.

You can also bring a revision to an external file into the current drawing using a special form of the INSERT command. From the Insert dialog, enter both the external file name in the File field and the block name in the Block field, which updates the internal block definition according to the revised external file. Thus changes to a block can be sent to the file from which the block was originally inserted, and changes to an external file can be brought into the current drawing. The significant point here is that none of this interaction is automatic.

Now consider xrefs. When drawing A includes B as an xref, the relationship between A and B is one-way, but it's automatic. B cannot be changed from within A as long as B remains an xref and isn't converted to a block. However, all changes made to B (by editing B directly) appear automatically in A.

This general rule—that changes in the referenced drawing always appear in the referencing drawing—has an exception. you can enter the system variable **visretain** at the command prompt and set its value to 1 in the referencing drawing. As a reseult, the visibility (on/off or freeze/thaw status) of layers used by xrefs will be determined by the settings in the referencing drawing rather than the settings in the referenced drawing.

Tips for Using Xrefs

An xref can be turned into a block with the Bind option of the XREF command (see "XREF" below).

After you've placed an xref in a drawing, that xref cannot be used as a block; that is, you cannot place it in the drawing with the INSERT command unless you turn it into a block first.

After you've placed a block in a drawing (whether it's originally defined in the current drawing or inserted from a drawing file), that block cannot be used as an xref.

You cannot explode an xref, unless you turn it into a block first.

If you erase an xref, its geometry is removed from the screen, but its definition is still attached to the current drawing.

You can remove an xref entirely from the current drawing with the Detach option of the XREF command. This removes each instance of the xref in the drawing and removes its definition from the drawing database.

Named objects in xrefs are assigned new names in the referencing drawing. This avoids conflicts between similarly named objects. Suppose you have a referenced drawing called FRAME that uses a layer called SOLID. When that drawing is attached as an xref in the referencing drawing, its layer name becomes FRAME|SOLID in the referencing drawing. This change is made so that the xref's color and linetype settings do not interfere with the settings of the SOLID layer (if it exists) in the referencing drawing. This is a temporary layer (not saved with the drawing), so you cannot make it the current layer, nor can you use DDCHPROP to place an existing object on this layer.

Remember that when you want to edit or plot any drawing that includes xrefs, all of its referenced drawings (and all of their referenced drawings, if any) must be available in the same location as when they were originally attached to the referencing drawing. This is because the referencing drawing records only the name and location of the xref and must be able to find that drawing file to include it in the referencing drawing.

Revising Your Xrefs

What happens when you rename a referenced drawing or move it from one directory to another? When you bring the referencing drawing into the drawing editor, a message is displayed that the xref cannot be found. A line of text that says "Xref ..." (followed by the name of the xref) is placed where the xref should be. You must then use the Path option of the XREF command to inform your current drawing database of the external drawing's new name or new location.

You can decide whether you should bring a drawing into the current drawing as a block or an xref based on two considerations—revisions and named objects.

First, if the external drawing is likely to be revised, bring it in as an xref. If it isn't likely to be revised, bring it in as a block.

Second, if the external drawing contains named objects whose definitions would have to be ignored if brought in as a block, bring it in as an xref. For example, suppose you have an external drawing that uses the same layers as your current drawing. However, the color and linetype assignments on those layers are different than they are in the current drawing. If you bring in that drawing as a block, the layer definitions from the external drawing will be ignored; and the block will adopt the color and linetype assignments from the current drawing. But if you bring it in as an xref, it will look just as it does in its external drawing. The layer's color and linetype assignments will be retained (by being renamed) as described above.

As you work with xrefs in your drawing, AutoCAD creates and maintains a file that logs all xref activity. The file has the same name as your drawing (but with the extension .XLG) and is placed on the same directory as your referenced drawing. A lot of xref activity makes this file expand quickly into a rather large file. Unless you need to examine the latest entries in this file, you will probably want to erase it from time to time. Each time you edit a drawing containing xrefs, AutoCAD looks for a corresponding .XLG file to append with the latest xref activity. If it doesn't find this file, it creates one.

Over time, some of your referenced drawings containing xrefs may change. If you may one day need a copy of your drawing as it stands today, archive a copy of your drawing in which you've converted all xrefs to blocks with the XREF Bind command.

XREF Provides controls for external references

COMMAND LINE: **xref**

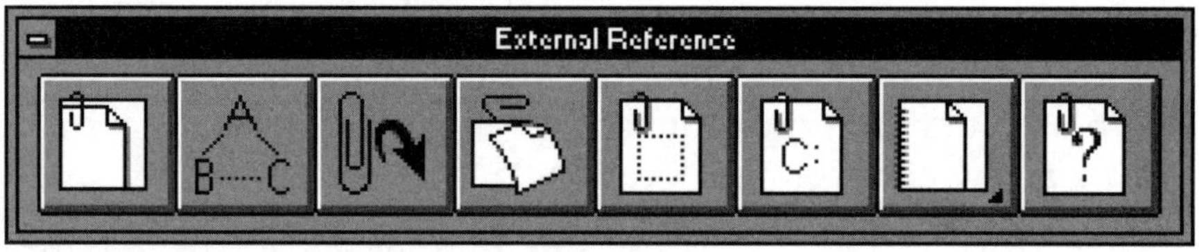

Figure 23-10: The External Reference toolbar.

Although XREF is a single command, Autodesk has provided it with its own toolbar and set of icons to make each XREF option behave as if it were an individual command. To display the External Reference toolbar, choose Toolbars from the Tools pull-down menu, then select External Reference.

From the External Reference toolbar, choose the following options, or type the option letter after entering **xref** at the command line:

Figure 23-11: The XREF Attach icon.

Enter **a** to attach an xref to the current drawing. This option is also used to place another copy of an xref that is already attached. When the Select File to Attach dialog appears, choose the drawing file you want to attach as an xref. At this point, you're prompted for an insertion point, scaling factors and rotation angle just as with the INSERT command.

Only objects from Model Space in the referenced drawing are used. If the xref contains nested attached xrefs, each of those nested xrefs is also attached to the current drawing.

Figure 23-12: The XREF Overlay icon.

Enter **o** to overlay an xref in the current drawing. When the Select File to Overlay dialog appears, select the file you want to overlay and proceed just as you would for attaching an xref. An overlay behaves the same as an attached xref except that circular references and nested overlays are ignored.

Figure 23-13: The XREF Bind All icon from the Bind flyout of the External Reference toolbar.

Enter **b** to bind an xref to the current drawing (to convert an xref to a block). Then enter the name of the xref (wild cards are accepted). If an xref contains nested xrefs, they're also converted to blocks. Any layers or other named objects that were dependent on those xrefs are made a permanent part of the current drawing and renamed. In the new name the vertical bar " | " (called a *pipe*) is replaced with "0". (The number may be higher than 0, if necessary, to create a unique name.)

Figure 23-14: The XREF Detach icon.

Enter **d** to detach an xref from the current drawing. Then enter the name of the xref (wild cards are accepted). When an xref is detached, all instances of the xref are erased and the reference to the external drawing is deleted. A nested xref is also detached, but only if the xref you're detaching is the sole reference to it.

Figure 23-15: The XREF Path icon.

Enter **p** to view or change the path (full file name) associated with an xref. Then enter the name of the xref (wild cards are accepted). You must do this if a referenced file has been moved to a different directory or has been renamed. After you change the path, the xref is reloaded automatically from its new path.

Figure 23-16: The XREF Reload icon.

Enter **r** to reload an xref. Then enter the name of the xref (wild cards are accepted). Nested xrefs are also reloaded. This feature is handy in a network environment when you and someone else are working on referencing and referenced drawings concurrently.

Figure 23-17: The XREF List icon.

Enter **?** for a list of xrefs attached to the current drawing. Press Enter to list all xrefs (to accept the asterisk wild card that appears on the prompt), or use other wild cards to request groups of xrefs.

XBIND Makes named objects from referenced drawings permanent

COMMAND LINE: **bind**

Figure 23-18: The Bind flyout of the XREF toolbar.

As it did with the XREF command, Autodesk has provided each option of the XBIND command with its own icon. These icons are found under the Bind flyout of the External Reference toolbar, as shown in Figure 23-18 above.

The XBIND command lets you convert a named object used by an xref, such as a layer, into a permanent object in the current drawing. This is more selective than converting an entire xref with the Bind option of the XREF command. When you convert an entire xref, you convert everything that the xref uses, including blocks, dimension styles, layers, linetypes and text styles. However, when you use the XBIND command, you can select just one named object to convert.

Click on the icons below to execute the XBIND command with the selected option. Alternatively, you can enter **xbind** at the command prompt and then enter the letter option that you want.

Figure 23-19: The XBIND Block icon.

Enter **b** to bind named blocks.

Figure 23-20: The XBIND Layer icon.

Enter **la** to bind named layers.

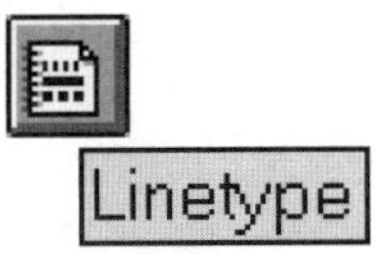

Figure 23-21: The XBIND Linetype icon.

Enter **lt** to bind named linetypes.

Figure 23-22: The XBIND Text Style icon.

Enter **s** to bind named Text Styles.

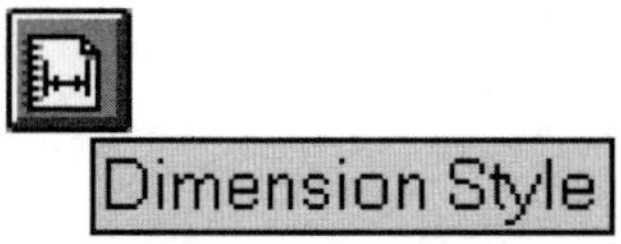

Figure 23-23: The XBIND Dimension Style icon.

Enter **d** to bind named Dimension Styles.

After entering an option, you're prompted for the object's name (wild cards are accepted). Naturally, some named objects include other named objects. For example, a layer will include a linetype. When the layer is converted, AutoCAD also converts the associated linetype.

Moving on

The next chapter looks at the creation of dimensions and dimension styles. Methods for dimensioning your drawings have changed considerably as AutoCAD has developed, and AutoCAD Release 13 again introduces major changes in the dimensioning commands.

CHAPTER 24

Dimensions

A dimension is the most important aspect of a drawing because it shows exact measurements and distances. With mechanical parts, a dimension may show exact X and Y geometric coordinates. In the past, poor or missing dimensions in a drawing were often blamed for the costly mistakes that followed. To alleviate what could be termed "dimension error," AutoCAD has created a new upgraded set of dimension commands.

A dimension is usually made up of two extension lines: a dimension line and the dimension text (see Figure 24-1). Lineal, radial and angular are the regular basic dimensioning types for drawings. AutoCAD provides ways to create them including associative dimensioning, and the more complex ordinate and geometric dimensioning and tolerancing. Later in the chapter we'll review all these topics in depth.

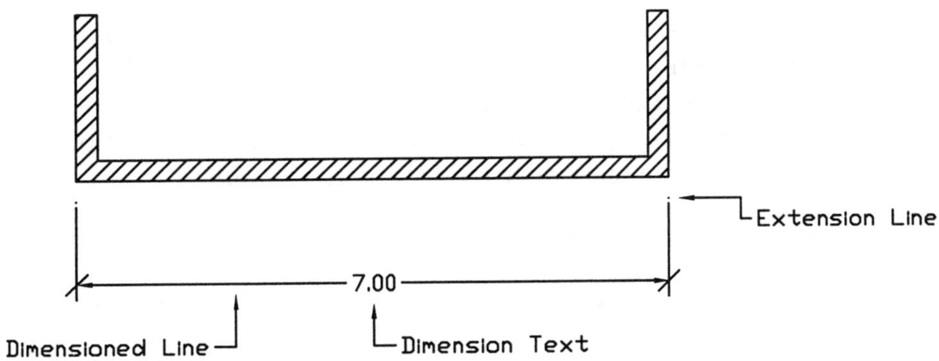

Figure 24-1: Different parts of a dimension line.

AutoCAD's associative dimensions are created in the same way as regular dimensions, but they have several special properties. They are treated as a single object and can be stretched, scaled or rotated at the same time an object is being stretched, scaled or rotated. Thus, the dimension is automatically realigned, and its text is updated to save you time as you revise your drawings.

This chapter is divided into four sections. The first section outlines creation commands. The second section discusses leader, ordinate, geometric dimensioning and tolerancing commands. The third section discusses dimension editing, styles, setup and scaling. The final section covers dimoverride and variable setting commands.

What's New in Release 13

With dimension commands now at your fingertips, you don't have to access the DIM menu. Release 13 provides the following Dimensioning icons: Linear, Aligned, Radial, Angular, Ordinate, Baseline, Continue, Center Mark, Leader, Tolerance, Align Dimension Text and Dimension Style. (There are more than 12 new dimension commands and dialogs in Release 13. They are available from the keyboard, the toolbar icons or the pull-down menu without accessing the old DIM command.)

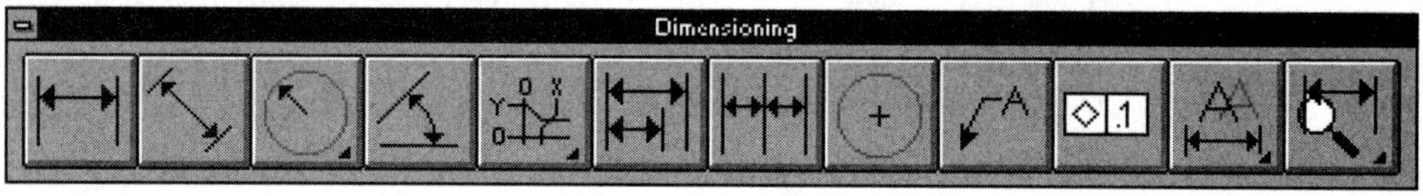

Figure 24-2: The new Dimensioning toolbar.

The Linear icon has been updated to allow to you to create horizontal, vertical and rotated dimensions from a single pick. The Aligned icon allows you to create dimensions at any angle. Radial allows you to create circular radius and diameter dimensions. Angular allows you to create angle degree dimensions for objects. Ordinate allows you to create ordinate style dimensions from a UCS origin point.

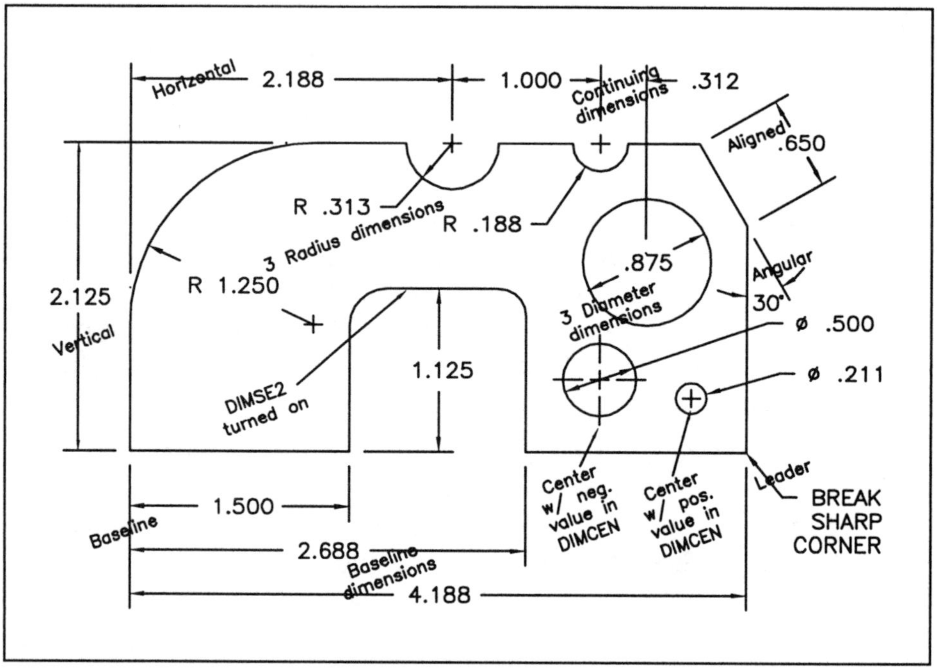

Figure 24-3: AutoCAD's dimensioning features.

Using the Creation Commands

To set up dimensions, use the Dimension Style dialog. It allows you to create, modify and set any dimension style. You may set up dimension families of different styles and make global changes to a drawing or use dimension overrides to suppress singular features to a dimension. To edit your dimensions, use DIMEDIT and DIMTEDIT. You may edit and move dimension text; stretch, extend or trim the extension lines along with the features they are attached to; and much more.

DIMLINEAR Creates a vertical, horizontal or rotated dimension

COMMAND LINE: **dimlinear**

You may create horizontal, vertical and rotated dimensions with this command. Choose an object and then move your cursor left, right, up or down.

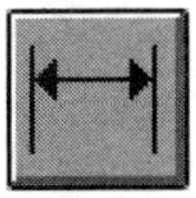

Figure 24-4: The Linear icon from the Dimension toolbar.

Choose the Linear icon, and the following prompt appears: First extension line origin or RETURN to select.

Either press Enter and select an object for automatic dimensioning, or when prompted for first and second extension line origins, you may want to use OSNAP and select specific points. If you press Enter, you select the line, polyline, arc or circle you want to dimension; and AutoCAD finds the extension line origins automatically. This does not work with non-uniformly scaled blocks.

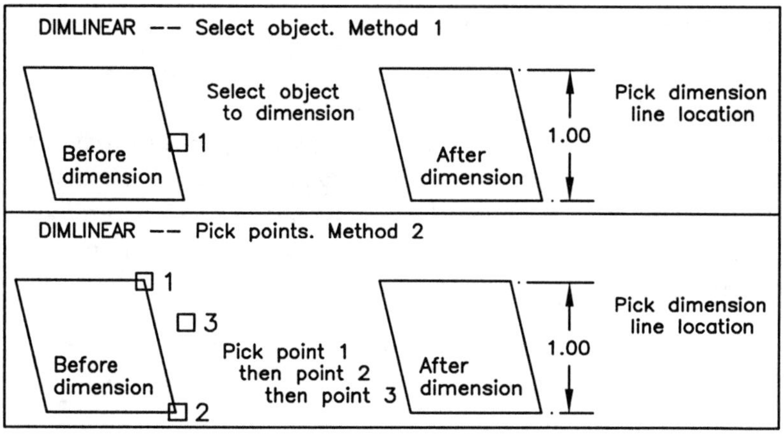

Figure 24-5: Dimlinear point specifications.

After you've chosen the endpoints of the first and second extension line origins, the following prompt appears: Dimension line location (Text/Angle/Horizontal/Vertical/Rotated).

Pick a location for the dimension line, or enter one of the following in the command prompt window:

> **t** for text produces the Edit Mtext dialog, which allows you to customize the dimension text. See "Dimension Text Editing" later in the chapter.
>
> **a** for angle allows you to customize the angle at which the dimension text is displayed. It may be aligned with an angular feature of the object.
>
> **h** for horizontal allows you to create only horizontal dimensions. It immediately moves into horizontal dimensioning mode.
>
> **v** for vertical allows only vertical dimension creation.
>
> **rot** for rotated allows you to customize the angle at which the dimension line is created. The dimension line itself is rotated to a specified angle.

DIMALIGNED Creates an aligned dimension

COMMAND LINE: **dimaligned**

You may automatically create dimension lines aligned with an object.

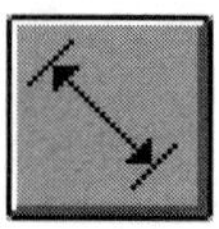

Figure 24-6: The Dimaligned icon from the Dimensioning toolbar.

Choose the Dimaligned icon, and the following prompt appears: First extension line origin or RETURN to select. Either press Enter and select an object for automatic dimensioning, or, when prompted for first and second extension line origins, use OSNAP and select specific points. (If you press Enter, you select the line, polyline, arc or circle you want to dimension, and AutoCAD finds the extension line origins automatically. This does not work with non-uniformly scaled blocks.)

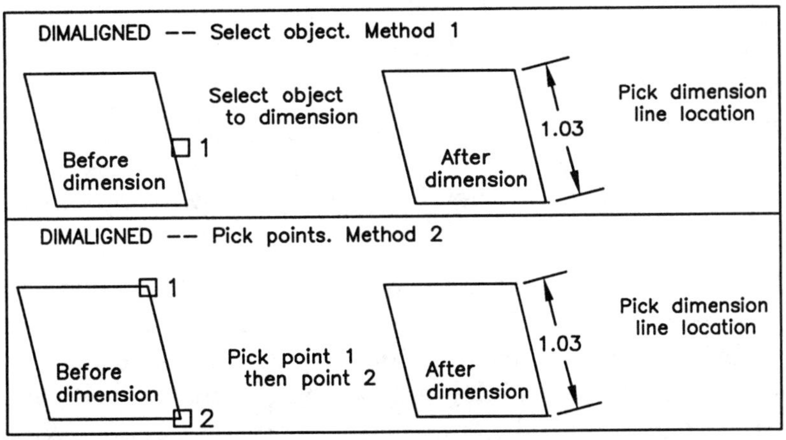

Figure 24-7: Dimaligned point specifications.

After you've chosen the endpoints of the first and second extension line origins, the following prompt appears: Dimension line location (Text/Angle/Horizontal/Vertical/Rotated).

Pick a location for the dimension line, or enter one of the following at the command prompt:

> **t** for text produces the Edit Mtext dialog, which allows you to customize the dimension text. See "Dimension Text Editing" later in the chapter.
>
> **a** for angle allows you to customize the angle at which the dimension text is displayed.
>
> **h** for horizontal allows you to create only horizontal dimensions.
>
> **v** for vertical allows only vertical dimension creation.
>
> **rot** for rotated allows you to customize the angle at which the dimension line is created.

DIMRADIUS Creates radial dimensions for arcs & circles

COMMAND LINE: **dimradius**

You may create internal or external radial dimension lines for arcs and circles. The text displays R and the measured radius. (You may also display a center mark if the DIMCEN variable is nonzero.)

Figure 24-8: The Radial Dimension icon from the Dimensioning toolbar.

Choose the Radial Dimension icon, and the following prompt appears: Select arc or circle.

Select an object for radial dimensioning. To locate the text you may move your cursor around, into or out of the object to be dimensioned. The position of your end-pick point determines the text location. If the radial line angle is less than 15 degrees, it produces the line with text. If greater than 15 degrees it produces an angled leader line connected to a short horizontal line and the text.

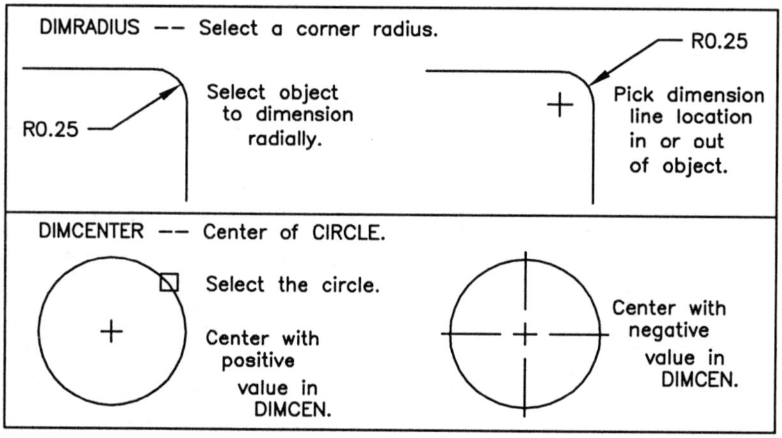

Figure 24-9: Radial point specifications.

After you've chosen the end-pick point of the extension line origin, the following prompt appears: Dimension line location (Text/Angle).

Pick a location for the dimension text, or enter one of the following at the command prompt:

t for text produces the Edit Mtext dialog, which allows you to customize the dimension text. See "Dimension Text Editing" later in the chapter.

a for angle allows you to customize the angle at which the dimension text is displayed.

DIMANGULAR Creates an angular dimension in degrees

COMMAND LINE: **dimangular**

You may create angular degree dimensions between three pick points for two angular lines, two adjacent angular lines, or arcs and circles.

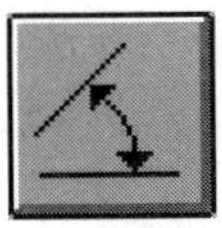

Figure 24-10: The Dimangular icon from the Dimensioning toolbar.

Choose the Dimangular icon, and the following prompt appears: Select arc, circle, line or RETURN.

It allows you to select three pick points to two lines. If you are dimensioning angular lines at this point, press Enter and select three points—Angle vertex, First angle endpoint and Second angle endpoint.

Your first pick point is at the intersection of the angle vertex. (This is the connection joint between the two angular lines.) The second pick point is any point on the first angular line in response to the following prompt: First angle endpoint.

The third pick point is any point on the second chosen angular line in response to the following prompt: Second angle endpoint.

The radial and angular degree dimension lines are then placed in the drawing. See Figure 24-11.

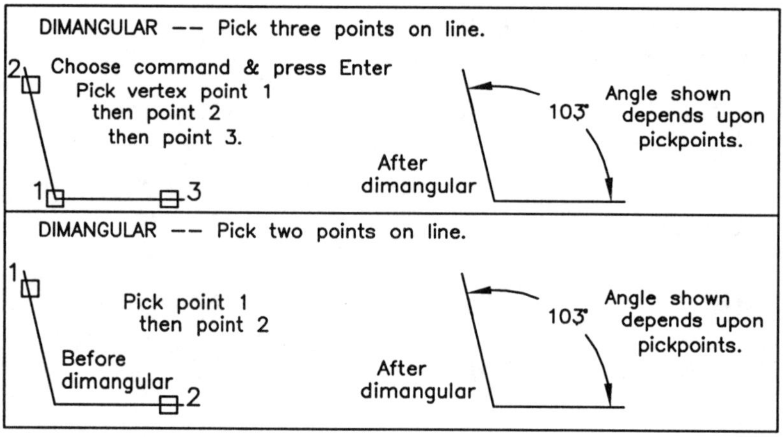

Figure 24-11: Three- and two-pick line methods.

To Select a Line

Choose one of the two lines you want to angular dimension. If you have selected a line, the following prompt appears: Second line.

Select another line, and the location prompt is returned. See Figure 24-11.

To Select an Arc

If you select an arc to angular dimension, AutoCAD automatically defines the arc center and endpoints. A dimension line arc is produced with angular degrees. The location prompt is then returned. See Figure 24-12.

To Select a Circle

If you select a circle to angular dimension, AutoCAD automatically determines the center of the circle as the vertex definition point. The following prompt appears: Second angle endpoint.

Choose a second point, and a dimension line arc is produced with angular degrees. The location prompt is returned. See Figure 24-12.

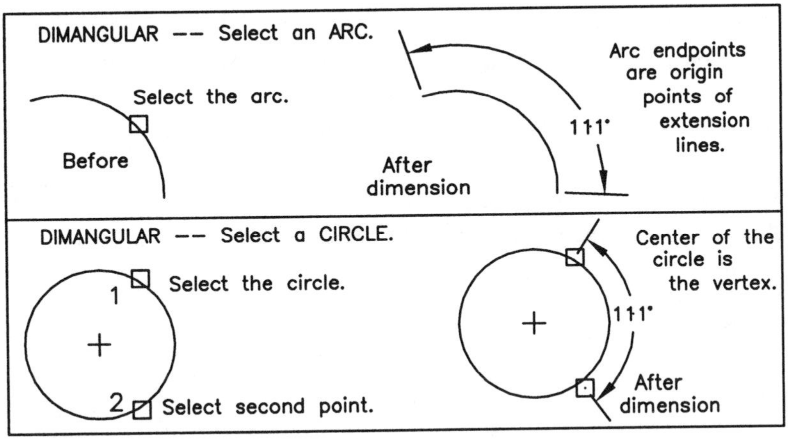

Figure 24-12: Arc and circle entry methods.

After you've chosen the line, arc or circle endpoint origins, the following prompt appears: Dimension line location (Text/Angle).

Pick a location for the dimension line, or enter one of the following at the command prompt:

> **t** for text produces the Edit Mtext dialog, which allows you to customize the dimension text. See "Dimension Text Editing" later in the chapter.
>
> **a** for angle allows you to customize the angle at which the dimension text is displayed.

The radial and angular degree dimension lines are then placed in the drawing.

DIMORDINATE Creates an ordinate style dimension and leader line

COMMAND LINE: **dimordinate**

You may create ordinate dimensions between X and Y datum points of a feature. You must set the UCS to the origin of the part to be dimensioned.

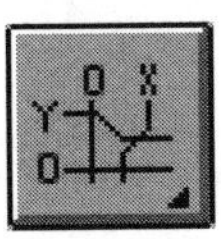

Figure 24-13: The Dimordinate icon from the Dimensioning toolbar.

See "Ordinate Dimensions, Leader Lines, & Geometric Tolerancing" later in the chapter.

DIMBASELINE Continues a horizontal, vertical, angular or ordinate dimension as a baseline or parallel dimension

COMMAND LINE: **dimbaseline**

You may create baseline dimensions between horizontal, vertical, angular and ordinate dimensions. It produces a series of related dimensions—each measured from the same origin point.

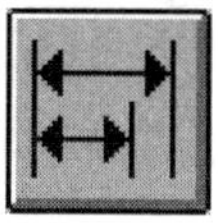

Figure 24-14: The Dimbaseline icon from the Dimensioning toolbar.

Choose the Dimbaseline icon, and the following prompt appears: Second extension line origin or RETURN.

It allows you to select a base dimension if you press Enter or choose a second extension line origin. The previously created dimension must be linear, angular or ordinate. The second extension line prompt is returned to allow you to choose further baselines. Press Esc to end the command. See Figure 24-15.

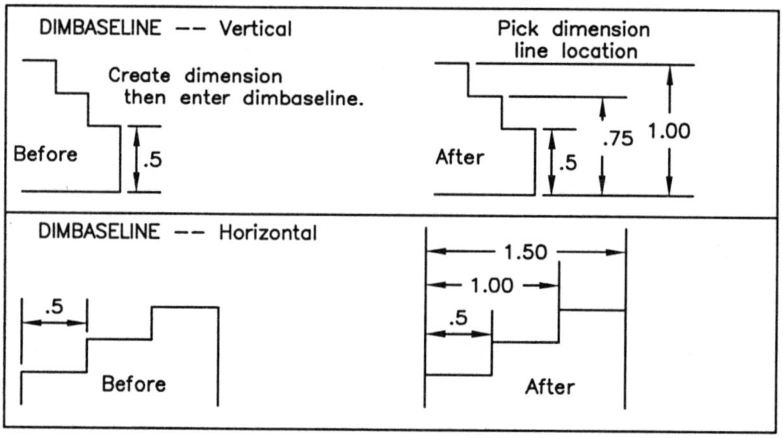

Figure 24-15: Dimbaseline dimensioning.

DIMCONTINUE Continues a horizontal, vertical, angular or ordinate dimension as a sequential chain of dimensions

COMMAND LINE: **dimcontinue**

You may continue dimensions between horizontal, vertical, angular and ordinate dimensions. It produces a series of inter-related dimensions—each measured from the previous origin point.

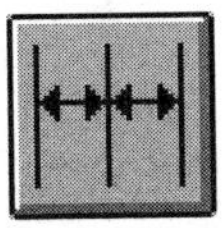

Figure 24-16: The Dimcontinue icon.

Choose the Dimcontinue icon, and the following prompt appears: Select extension line origin or RETURN.

It allows you to select a dimension if you press Enter or choose a second extension line origin. The previously created dimension must be linear, angular or ordinate. The select extension line prompt appears to let you choose further baselines. Press Esc to end the command. See Figure 24-17.

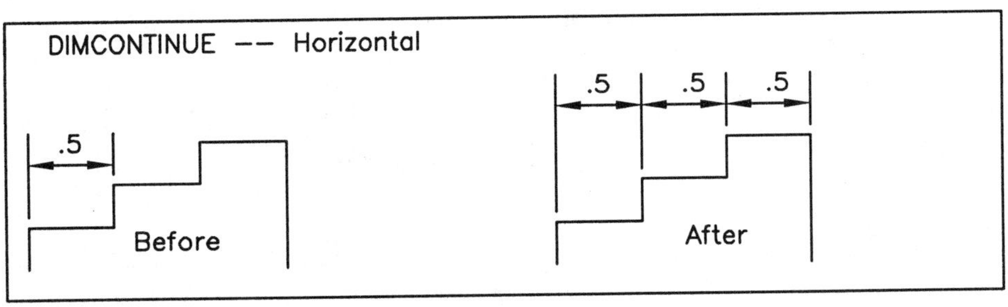

Figure 24-17: Dimcontinue dimensioning.

DIMCENTER Creates a center point or line to an arc or circle

COMMAND LINE: **dimcenter**

You may create center points or center lines for arcs and circles. The Dimension Style dialog controls the settings for center points and lines.

Figure 24-18: The Dimcenter icon from the Dimensioning toolbar.

Choose the Dimcenter icon, and the following prompt appears: Select arc or circle.

It allows you to select an arc or a circle to produce a center mark or a center line.

You should first set up the Dimension Style dialog in the Data pull-down menu. The dialog controls the settings between center points (marks) and center lines. Press Esc to end the command. See Figure 24-19.

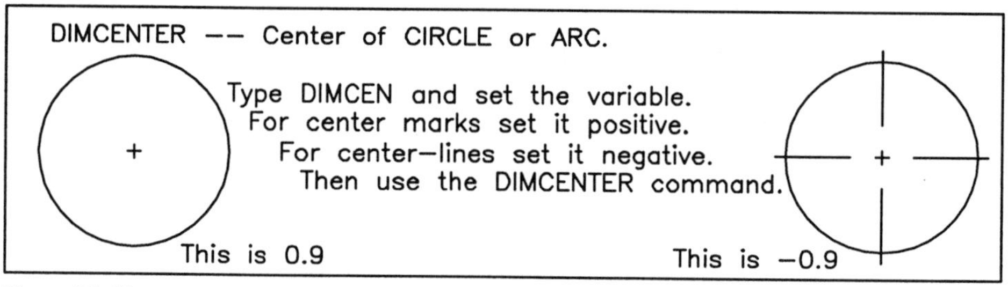

Figure 24-19: Dimcenter dimension mark.

DIMDIAMETER Creates a diameter dimension for an arc or a circle

COMMAND LINE: **dimdiameter**

You may create diameter dimensions between arc and circle objects. The position of the cursor determines the type and placement of the diameter dimension. AutoCAD places a degree symbol in the text automatically.

Figure 24-20: The Radial Dimension icon.

Choose the Radial Dimension icon, and the following prompt appears: Select arc or circle.

Select an object for diameter dimensioning. You may move your cursor around, into or out of the object to be dimensioned to locate the text. The position of your end-pick point determines the text location.

If the diameter line angle is less than 15 degrees, it produces the line with text; if greater than 15 degrees, it produces an angled leader line connected to a short horizontal line with the text. See Figure 24-21.

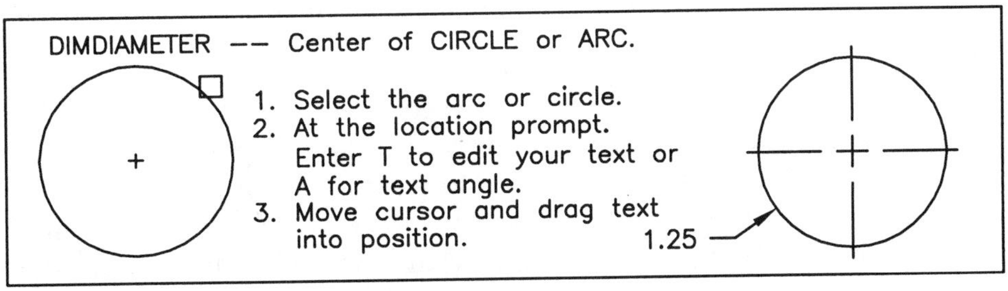

Figure 24-21: Dimdiameter point specifications.

After you've chosen the arc or circle, the following prompt appears: Dimension line location (Text/Angle).

Pick a location for the dimension line, or enter one of the following in the command prompt:

> **t** for text produces the Edit Mtext dialog, which allows you to customize the dimension text. See "Dimension Text Editing" later in the chapter.
>
> **a** for angle allows you to customize the angle at which the dimension text is displayed.

The command is terminated after you place the diameter dimension line.

Ordinate Dimensions, Leader Lines & Geometric Tolerancing

This section reviews the commands that let you work with ordinate dimensioning, leader lines and geometric tolerancing.

Ordinate or datum dimensioning refers to the leader lines that extend from an object in the drawing to the dimension text. Some setup may be required before you create ordinate dimensions, as AutoCAD measures ordinates from the origin point (0,0,0) of the current UCS. Use the Origin option of the UCS command to place the current UCS origin at your desired dimensioning origin. Any text placed is aligned with the leader.

Geometric tolerancing dimensioning refers to a series of geometric tolerance symbols used as a dimension feature.

You may create geometric tolerances to define allowable variations such as profile, location, orientation and runout of an AutoCAD object. AutoCAD has a series of dialog boxes that help you create tolerance symbols and geometry.

A leader line and its text connect to a dimension feature. The LEADER command allows you to create complex leader lines. The annotation attached to the leader line may be edited through Edit Text in the Modify pull-down menu. (If this menu is not available from the menu bar, enter menu at the command line and select Acadfull to display it.) You may choose the LEADER command at any time and create complex leaders.

DIMORDINATE Creates an ordinate style dimension & leader line

COMMAND LINE: **dimordinate**

You may create ordinate dimensions between X and Y datum points of a feature. You must set the UCS to the origin of the part to be dimensioned.

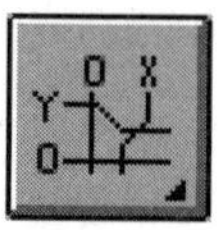

Figure 24-22: The Dimordinate icon from the Dimensioning toolbar.

First, set the UCS origin in the part you wish to dimension. (It may be the lower-left corner of the part, for example.) The UCS is the origin point for the DIMORDINATE command. If you do not set the UCS, the WCS origin is used. See Figure 24-23.

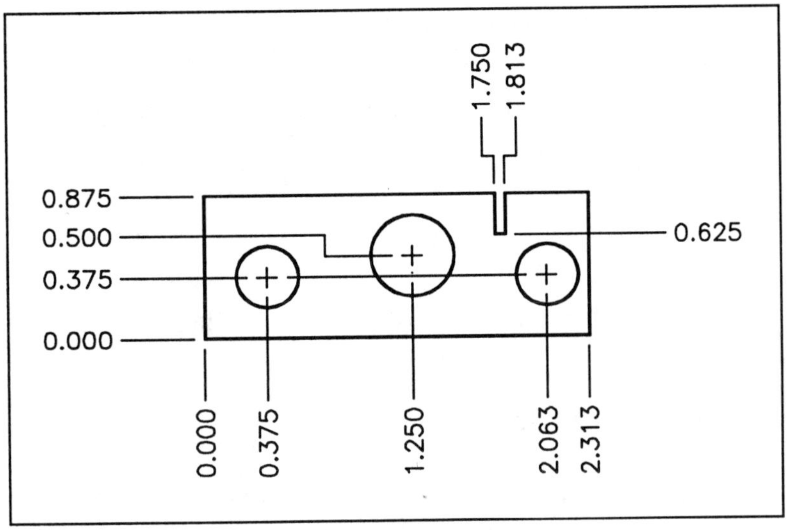

Figure 24-23: Dimordinate point specifications.

You then choose the Ordinate icon, and the following prompt appears: Select feature.

This allows you to select the feature or features you want to dimension. When you choose a feature, the following prompt appears: Leader endpoint (Xdatum/Ydatum/Text).

You may either pick a point, enter **x** and a point, or enter **y** and a point.

Leader Endpoint

Pick an endpoint, and AutoCAD automatically determines between X and Y datum leader points. It draws the dimension.

Xdatum

Entering **x** prompts AutoCAD to use the UCS origin as a start point then automatically measure the distance in the X direction. AutoCAD then prompts you for a leader endpoint.

Ydatum

Entering **y** prompts AutoCAD to use the UCS origin as a start point then automatically measure the distance in the Y direction. AutoCAD then prompts you for a leader endpoint.

After you've chosen the leader endpoint and X or Y origins, the following prompt appears again: Leader endpoint(Xdatum/Ydatum/Text).

Pick a location for the dimension line, or enter **t** for text, which produces the Edit Mtext dialog and allows you to customize the dimension text. See "Dimension Text Editing" later in the chapter.

The ordinate dimension line and text are then placed.

LEADER Creates a leader line with text that connects to a dimension feature

COMMAND LINE: **leader**

You may create leader lines to any type of object or dimension. The LEADER command allows you to create complex leader lines. Annotation attached to the leader line may be edited through Edit Text in the Modify pull-down menu. (If this menu is not available from the menu bar, enter menu at the command line and select Acadfull to display it.) You may choose the LEADER command at any time and provide multiple pick points to create complex leaders. See Figure 24-25.

Figure 24-24: The leader icon image.

Choose the Leader icon, and the following prompt appears: From point.

It allows you to select a series of points for the leader line. Then the next prompt appears: To point(Format/Annotation/Undo).

Format is an arrow head and leader line control feature with multiple subcommands. Format has a further set of options:

Spline	Creates a leader line as a splined (smoothed) curve.
Straight	Creates a leader line in straight segments.
Arrow	Draws a leader line with an arrowhead attached to the start point.
None	Draws a leader line without an arrowhead attached.

Annotation lets you insert text at the end of the leader line. It has the following options:

Tolerance	Provides a control frame and symbol dialog box that contains geometric tolerance options. See "Geometric Tolerance" later in the chapter.
Copy	Is an option to copy text or tolerances.
Block	Lets you insert a block at the end of the leader line.
None	Ends the command.
Mtext	Uses the Edit Mtext dialog box.

Undo undoes up to the last vertex (entry) point, and redisplays the To point prompt.

See "Dimension Text Editing" later in the chapter.

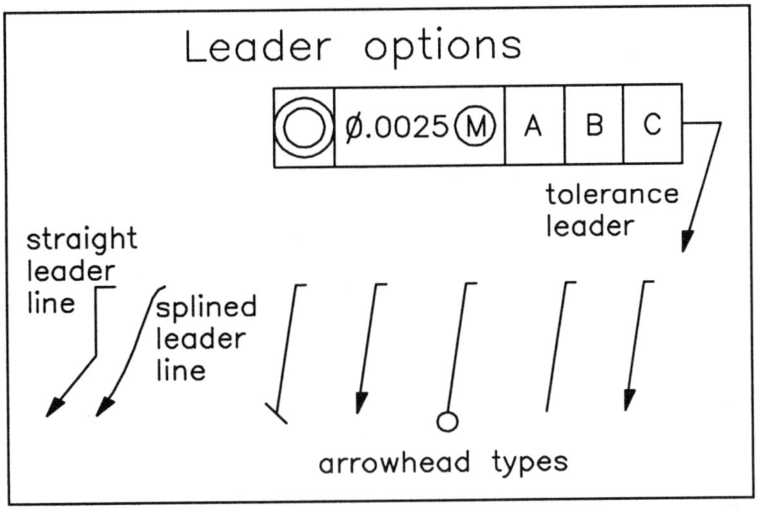

Figure 24-25: Leader options.

TOLERANCE Creates a geometric tolerance as a dimension feature

COMMAND LINE: **tolerance**

You may create geometric tolerances to define the allowable variations of profile, location, orientation and runout of an AutoCAD object. A series of dialog boxes (Symbol, Geometric Tolerance and Material Condition) help you create tolerance symbols and geometry.

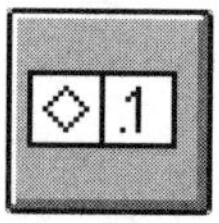

Figure 24-26: The Tolerance icon from the Dimensioning toolbar.

Choose the Tolerance icon, and the Symbol dialog (Figure 24-27) is returned. Figure 24-28 provides an explanation of each of the symbol characteristics. Select the required symbols and pick OK.

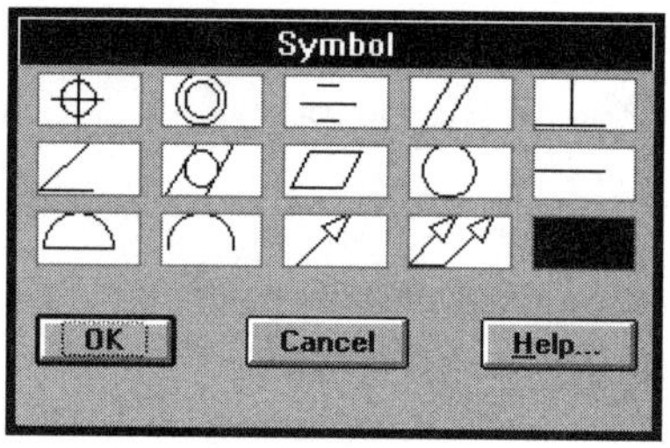

Figure 24-27: The Symbol dialog.

Feature type	Tolerance type	Characteristic	Tolerance Symbol
Individual Feature	Form	Straightness	
		Flatness	
		Circularity	
		Cylindricity	
Individual or Related	Profile	Line Profile	
		Surface Profile	
Related Feature	Orientation	Angularity	
		Perpendicularity	
		Parallelism	
	Location	Position	
		Concentricity	
		Symmetry	
	Runout	Circular Runout	
		Total Runout	

Geometric Attributes of the Symbol Dialog

Figure 24-28: Geometric attributes of the Symbol dialog.

After you've chosen your geometric characteristic symbols and the OK prompt in the Symbols dialog, the Geometric Tolerance dialog appears. This dialog allows you to select and set up geometric tolerances and datums. See Figure 24-29.

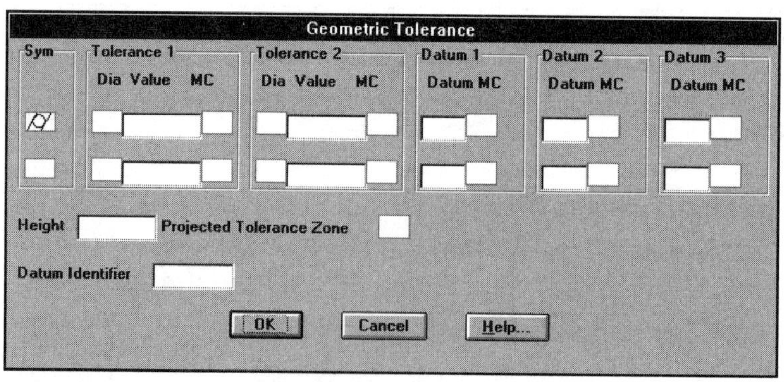

Figure 24-29: The Geometric Tolerance dialog.

The Geometric Tolerance dialog contains the following:

Sym	This section displays the previously selected symbol. If you pick this section, the dialog is redisplayed and you can change the symbol.
Tolerance 1 & 2	Set up the first and second tolerance values to be viewed in the feature control frame. See Figure 24-31.
Dia	Inserts a diameter symbol before the tolerance value.
Value	Is the actual tolerance value.
MC	Displays the Material Condition dialog box in order for you to select a modifying symbol. See Figure 24-30. It has symbol options of M, L and S (Maximum material condition, Least material condition and regardless of feature Size).

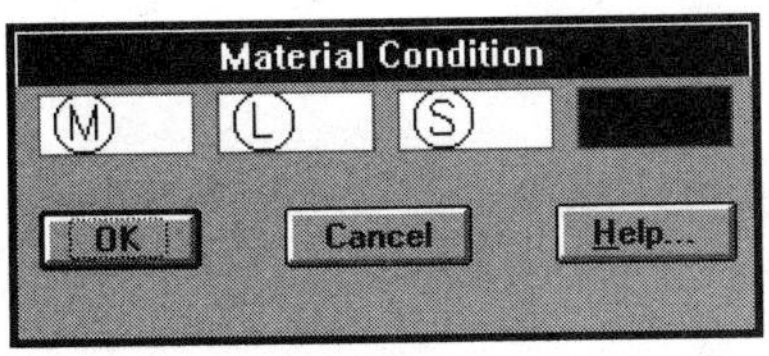

Figure 24-30: The Tolerance Material Condition dialog.

Datum 1, 2 & 3	A datum is an exact geometric reference used to establish the specific tolerance zone for the feature. The three datums create primary, secondary and tertiary datum references in the feature control frame. See Figure 24-31 for a completed frame. Each datum reference consists of a value and a Material Condition (MC) modifying symbol.
Height	Is used in the feature control frame as a projected tolerance zone value. It controls the height of the extended portion of a fixed vertical part. You simply enter the value in the text box.
Projected Tolerance Zone	Is used to insert a projected tolerance zone symbol, P, after a zone value has been entered.
Datum Identifier	Is the reference letter used as a datum identifying symbol. It must have a dash before and after it; as in *-B-*.

Choose OK when all of the geometric tolerance symbols have been inserted into the dialog box. This in turn provides the following response: Enter tolerance location.

You then place the feature control frame reference symbol in the drawing.

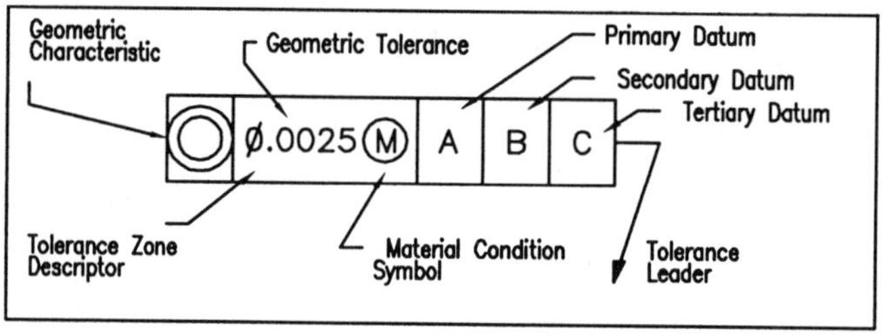

Figure 24-31: Completed tolerance symbol-feature control frame.

Dimension Editing, Styles, Setup & Scaling

Dimension Text Editing

You may edit dimensions in a number of ways: through DIMEDIT to alter text and dimension extension lines, through the DIMTEDIT command to alter text at the keyboard, or through DDEDIT and the Edit Mtext dialog. The DIMSTYLE command allows you to set up dimension styles and families. DDMODIFY also allows you editing functions through the Modify Dimensions dialog box. This dialog box allows you to select a dimension, then change or display its properties, and save the dimension variables altered as overrides.

DIMEDIT Allows you to edit dimension text & dimension features

COMMAND LINE: **dimedit**

The DIMEDIT command allows both dimension text and extension line editing. Its features (on more than one dimension object at a time) allow you to move text left or right or rotate and adjust the obliquing angle of dimension text dimension lines.

In the command prompt window enter **dimedit,** and the following prompt appears: Home/New/Rotate/Oblique.

Select an option, and then pick a dimension object. The options are as follows:

Home	**h**, for home, returns the dimension text to its original location. See Figure 24-32.
New	**n**, for new, allows you to alter the dimension text. If you are in DOS mode, type in the new text and then pick the dimension. If you are in Windows mode, the MTEXT dialog appears, allowing you to change the dimension text onscreen. Change the text and then choose the OK button. A Select objects: prompt then allows you to choose the dimension text to change. See Figure 24-32.
Rotate	**r**, for rotate, allows you to rotate dimension text. (This works the same way as the Angle option of DIMTEDIT below.) The Enter text angle: prompt allows you to specify an angle, such as 0, 45, 90, 135, 180, or -90. See Figure 24-32. Enter an angle and then select a dimension text.

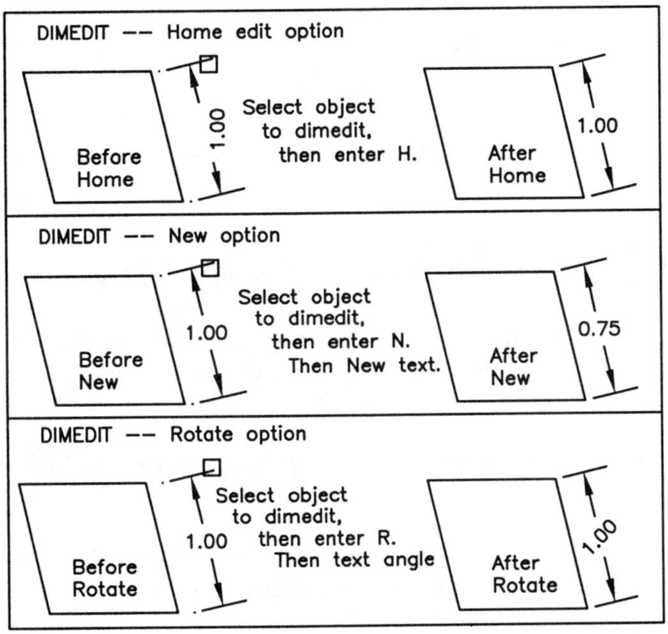

Figure 24-32: The Dimedit Home, New and Rotate options.

Oblique — **o**, for oblique, alters the obliquing angle of the lineal dimension extension line. Use this option when you have feature and extension line conflicts. See Figure 24-33.

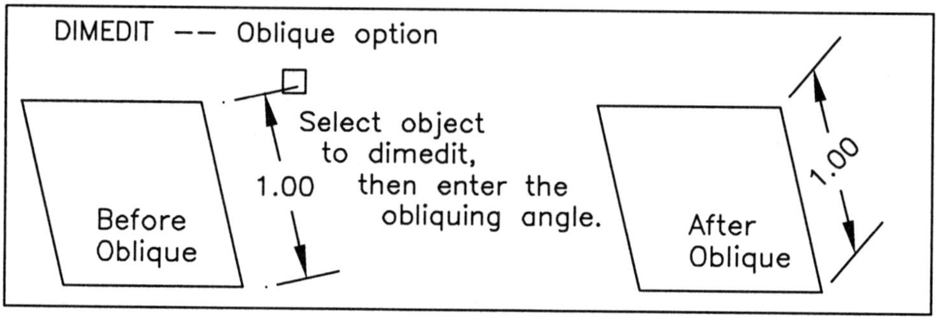

Figure 24-33: The Dimedit Oblique options.

DIMTEDIT Allows you to move & rotate dimension text

COMMAND LINE: **dimtedit**

The DIMTEDIT command allows you to move and rotate dimension text; justify (move) text to the left, right or home; and adjust the angle of the dimension text. The left and right options work only with lineal, radial and diameter style dimensions.

Figure 24-34: The Aligned icon from the Dimensioning toolbar.

Choose Align Text from the Dimensioning pull-down menu or the Aligned icon from the Dimensioning toolbar, and the following prompt appears: Select dimension.

Select a single dimension, and the next prompt appears: Left/Right/Home/Angle.

Enter an option and move your cursor to drag the dimension text to a new location. You can view the new position point as you move the cursor. The options are as follows:

Left	Acts as a justifier and allows you to move the dimension text to the left. See Figure 24-35.
Right	Also acts as a justifier and allows you to move the dimension text to the right. See Figure 24-35.
Home	Returns the dimension text to its original position. See Figure 24-35.
Angle	Alters the angle of the dimension text. The prompt Text angle: is returned. Enter an angle such as 0, 45, 90, 135, 180 or -90 etc. See Figure 24-35.

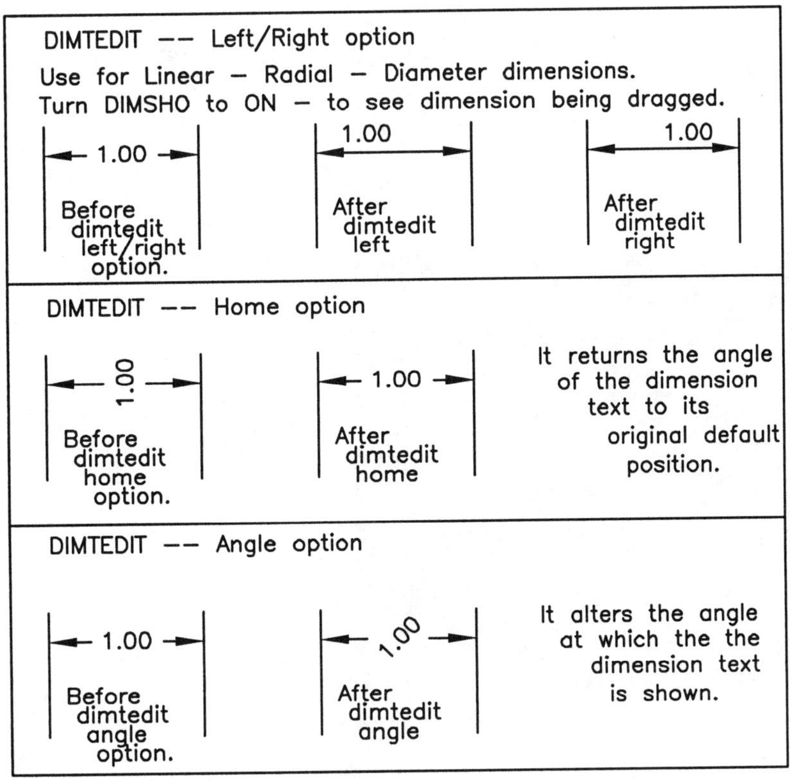

Figure 24-35: Editing with DIMTEDIT.

DDIM Allows you to create & alter dimension styles

COMMAND LINE: **ddim**

There are two commands for dimension styles: DDIM and DIMSTYLE. See "DIMSTYLE" later in the chapter.

The DDIM command allows you to create and modify dimension style groups. A dimension style is a named group of dimension settings that allow you to control the dimensioning standards for a drawing by changing the dimension system variables. The Dimension Styles dialog allows you to modify and create parent dimension styles without having to waste time learning the dimension system variable settings.

Figure 24-36: The Dimension Style icon from the Dimensioning toolbar.

Choose Dimension Style from the Data pull-down menu, or click the Dimension Style icon. The Dimension Styles dialog appears. The main dimension styles dialog (see Figure 24-37) is in three basic parts: Dimension Style, Family and dimension style creation buttons for the Geometry, Format and Annotation dialog boxes.

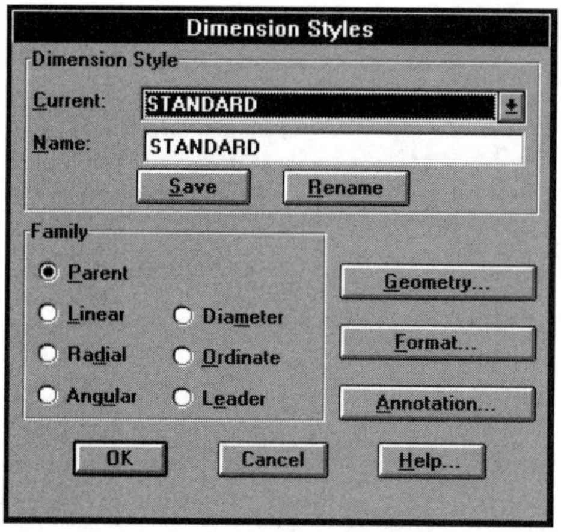

Figure 24-37: The Dimension Styles dialog box.

Creating a Dimension Style in Four Easy Steps

1. From the Dimension Styles dialog (see Figure 24-37) click in the Name bar, enter a dimension style name, then click the Save button. This sets up a name to receive settings. Notice that the Parent toggle is activated by default.

2. To specify and define how your dimension and extension lines, center marks and arrowheads will look, pick the Geometry button. Choose OK to save the geometry and to return to the main Dimension Styles dialog.

3. To specify and define the position of dimension text, pick the Format button. Choose OK to save the format and to return to the main Dimension Styles dialog.

4. To specify and define dimension text style, tolerances, units and gap, pick the Annotation button. Choose OK to save the annotation definitions and to return to the main dialog. Then choose Save in the Dimension Styles dialog again to save the new named dimension style. Finally pick OK to exit the dialog.

When a named (saved) style is current, each associative dimension created has that name attached to it. This means that the dimension keeps its style even when you use STRETCH or SCALE or some other editing command that forces the dimension to be reformed.

The Geometry Dialog

The Dimension Geometry button activates the Geometry dialog. See Figure 24-38. Use this to specify and define how your dimension and extension lines, center marks and arrowheads will look.

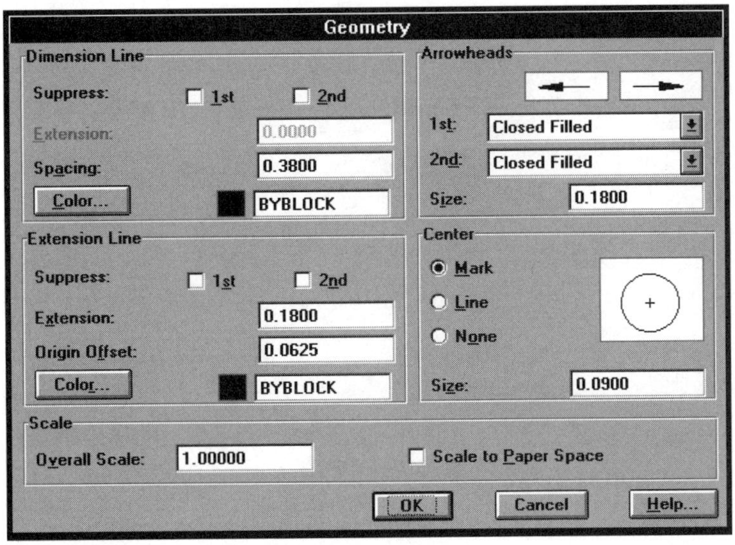

Figure 24-38: The Geometry dialog box.

Notice the principal parts of the dialog box: Dimension Line in the upper-left, Extension Line in the lower-left, Arrowheads in the upper-right and Center in the lower-right. The bottom section provides Scale settings.

Once you have set geometry, choose OK to save and return to the main Dimension Styles dialog.

The Format Dialog

The Dimension Format button activates the Format dialog. See Figure 24-39. Use this to specify your dimension text, leader lines and arrowheads in relation to the extension and dimension lines.

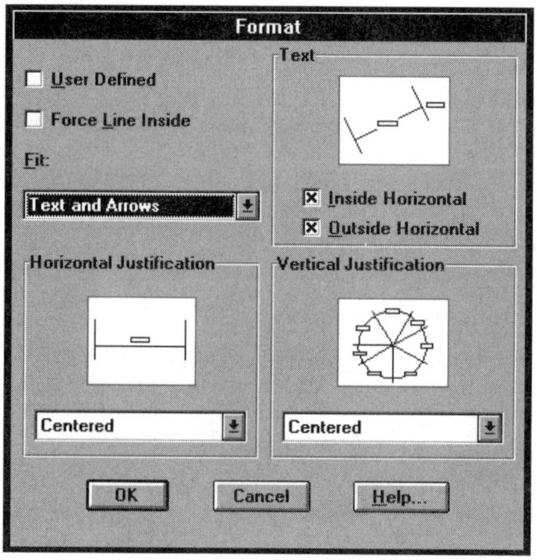

Figure 24-39: The Format dialog box.

Notice the principal locations of the dialog box: The text Fit option in the upper-left, the text Horizontal Justification in the lower-left, Text in the upper-right, and Vertical Justification in the lower-right.

Once you have set the dimension text format, choose OK to save and return to the main Dimension Styles dialog.

The Annotation Dialog

The Dimension Annotation button activates the Annotation dialog. See Figure 24-40. Use this to specify and control your dimension text.

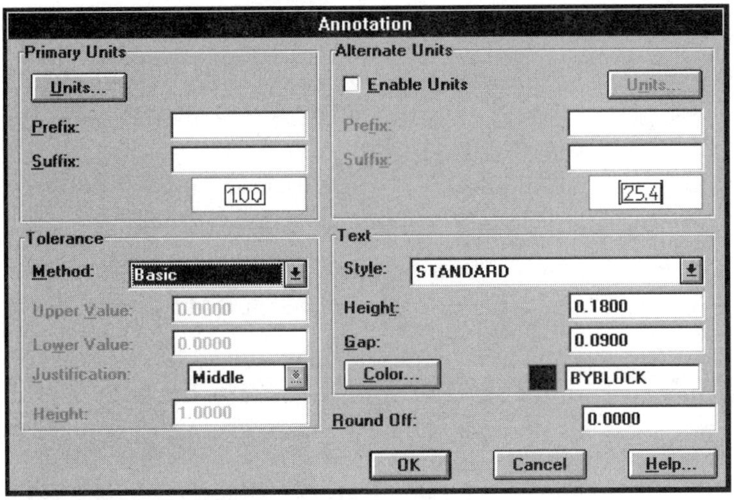

Figure 24-40: The Annotation dialog box.

Notice the principal locations of the dialog box: the Units button in the upper-left, the text Tolerance options in the lower-left, Alternate Units in the upper-right, and Text styles, height and gap in the lower-right.

Once you have set the dimension annotations, choose OK to save and return to the main Dimension Styles dialog.

DIMSTYLE Allows you to create & alter dimension styles

COMMAND LINE: **dimstyle**

There are two commands for dimension styles: DDIM and DIMSTYLE. See "DDIM" earlier in the chapter.

The DIMSTYLE command allows you to create and modify dimension style groups. A dimension style is a named group of dimension settings that allow you to control the dimensioning standards for a drawing by changing the dimension system variables.

In the command prompt window, type **dimstyle**. The following prompt appears: Style Edit (Save/Restore/STatus/Variables/Apply/?<Restore>.

The options are as follows:

Save	Enter **s**, then a name. This option allows you to save the current settings of the dimension system variables to a dimension style name. A further prompt of ?/Name for dimension style is returned. Enter a name or use Enter to choose from a list of saved names.
Restore	Enter **r**, then a name. It restores a named dimension style. Enter a name or enter **?** to choose from a list of saved names.
Status	Enter **st**. This option displays the values of the current dimension system variables and then ends the command.
Variables	Enter **v**. This option lists the settings of the current dimension system variables. Enter **?** to list the dimension styles in the current drawing.
Apply	Enter **a**. Select a single dimension or group of dimensions to update the dimension system variables.
?	Enter **?**. This option lists the named dimension styles in the drawing then ends the command.

DDEDIT Edits single-line text & paragraphs of text

COMMAND LINE: **ddedit**

Figure 24-41: Edit Text icon from the Special Edit flyout of the Modify toolbar.

DDEDIT allows you to edit dimension text. It also lets you edit single line text, paragraphs of text and single text characters. See Chapter 16, "Text," for further use of the DDEDIT command.

To edit text or dimension text, choose the Edit Text... prompt from the Modify pull-down menu. (If this menu is not available from the menu bar, enter menu at the command line and select Acadfull to display it.) This activates the DDEDIT command.

For normal single-line text editing, Edit Text... activates the Edit Text dialog, and for dimension and multiline paragraph type text editing. It activates the Edit Mtext dialog box, complete with an internal spell check option.

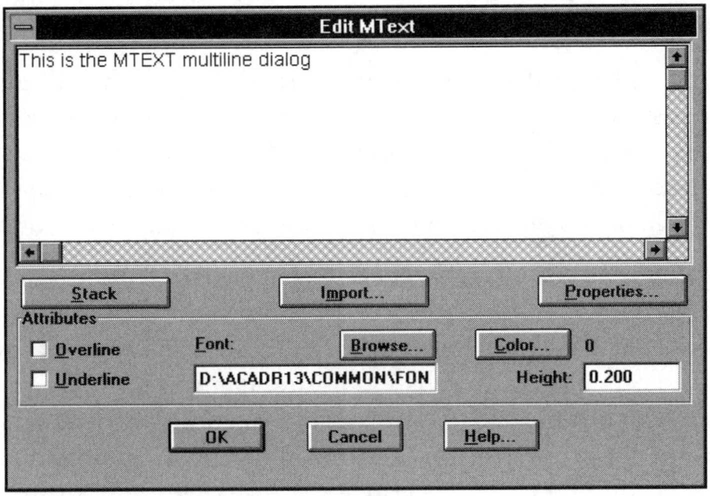

Figure 24-42: The Edit Mtext dialog.

The Edit Mtext dialog has radio buttons called Stack, Import, Spell, Properties, Browse and Color.

Stack	Select any text you want to convert. Then choose the Stack button. It converts the selected region into stacked text or stacked fractions.
Import	Activates an Import Text file dialog. Selects an ASCII text file from the list you wish to import into the multiline text editor.
Spell	Either select the paragraph to be checked and then choose the Spell... radio button, or choose the button to spell check the whole drawing. The spell checker will not check blocks, xrefs or attributes. They must be checked individually.
Properties	Activates an Mtext Properties dialog. This in turn alters text style, text height, direction, attachment, width and rotation.

Dimension Setup

The following setup process applies only when these conditions exist: you plan to plot from Paper Space, you have more than one viewport, and each viewport looks at the same 3D model from a different viewpoint. It doesn't apply when you have extracted separate 2D views from a 3D model.

Even if you use both Paper Space and Model Space, you still place most of your dimensions in Model Space. You should keep in mind several things as you prepare to dimension your drawing. The setup process described below need be used only once to create a prototype drawing. The prototype can become the basis for other prototype drawings or regular drawings.

Let's assume that your viewport configurations in Paper Space are already established. Even though your viewports provide you with several different views of your model, you don't want different views of each dimension. Thus, you need to establish a unique layer in each viewport on which you will place dimensions. This layer is frozen in all other viewports. The linetype and color may be the same on all of these dimension layers, but each layer should be named according to the one viewport in which it is visible. For example, in a typical three-view engineering drawing, you might have layer TDIM for the dimensions in the top viewport, FDIM for the front viewport and RDIM for the right viewport.

The VPLAYER command makes this process easy. While tilemode is 0 and you're in Paper Space, use the Newfrz option of the VPLAYER command to create your layers. (At this point, they're on in the LAYER command's listing of layers, but frozen in the VPLAYER command's listing of layers in all viewports.) Then, use the Thaw option of the VPLAYER command to name your dimension layers one at a time, using the Select option to pick the viewport in which each will be visible.

Using the "xp" suffix with the ZOOM command, make sure your viewport is scaled in the correct proportion to the paper size. Also, make sure that DIMSCALE is 0 to allow AutoCAD to automatically adjust the size of dimension features to compensate for viewport-to-paper-size scaling.

When you're ready to place a dimension in any particular viewport, be sure the X-Y construction plane of the current UCS is perpendicular to the line of sight from the current viewpoint. In most cases, you'll be able to adopt a plan view of one of the UCSes you used to construct your model, or you may want to create and save a UCS with the same name as your dimension layer for each viewport. This would simplify things when you switch from one viewport to another. You could use the LAYER command to make the appropriate layer current and then restore the UCS with the same name.

Associative Dimensioning

Associative dimensions are created in the same way as regular dimensions, but they have several unique properties. They can be stretched, scaled or rotated at the same time an object is also being stretched, scaled or rotated; and the dimension is realigned and its text is automatically corrected and updated. Linear, radial and angular dimensions can be associative dimensions.

Any dimensions created while the dimension variable DIMASO is on are associative (the default). Any dimensions created while DIMASO is off are composed of independent lines, arcs, arrows and text. DIMLEADER and DIMCENTER never produce associative dimensions.

One, several or all associative dimensions can be updated using the Apply option of the DIMSTYLE command so they reflect the current settings of the dimension variables, text style and/or UNITS command. The system variable DIMSTYLE holds the name of the current text style, so you can enter DIMSTYLE to view the current style name. The current style name is also displayed when you use the VAriable and REStore commands.

When you enter the DIMSTYLE command, the following prompt appears: Style Edit (Save/Restore/STatus/Variables/Apply).

When a named (saved) style is current, each associative dimension created has that name attached to it. This means that the dimension keeps its style even when you use STRETCH or SCALE or some other editing command that forces the dimension to be reformed.

And, although associative dimensions behave somewhat like blocks (they're listed, erased and moved as units), the text can be changed with the DIMTEDIT command. They can also be repositioned with DIMEDIT.

Associative dimensions are controlled by special definition points. For example, a DIMLINEAR horizontal dimension has definition points located at the origin points of the witness lines, at the first end of the dimension line and at the midpoint of the text. Two of these definition points lie under object lines, so they should be automatically included in the selection set when an object is stretched with a crossing window.

However, if you scale or rotate some objects and select them individually with the pick box, you won't include the definition points; and the associated dimensions won't be adjusted automatically. As you edit a dimensioned object, notice whether the dimensions are highlighted—to see whether they've been selected.

When you want only one end of a dimension stretched, that end's dimension point must be included in the crossing window.

Definition points are placed on a layer called DEFPOINTS. AutoCAD automatically creates this layer and turns it off the first time you create an associative dimension. As you'd expect, while the DEFPOINTS layer is off, the definition points won't plot. However, the screen visibility of definition points is determined by the on/off status of the layer containing the actual dimensions, not by the DEFPOINTS layer.

Besides STRETCH, SCALE and ROTATE, other editing commands, including TRIM, EXTEND, MIRROR and ARRAY, can affect associative dimensions.

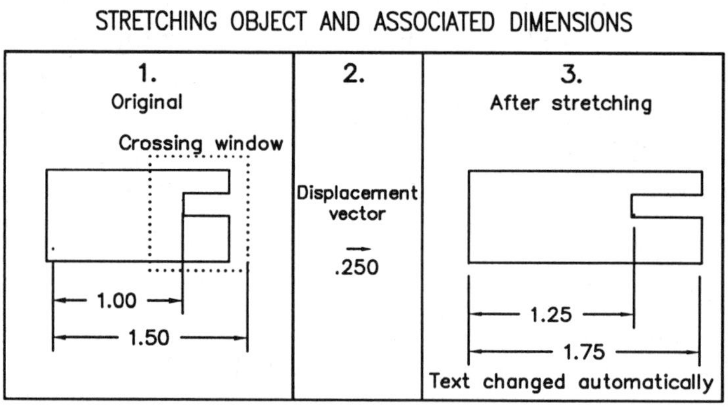

Figure 24-43: Stretching an object with dimensions.

You can stretch a dimension's text to a different place along the dimension line, or even outside the dimension line, and the dimension line adjusts.

When you explode an associative dimension, its elements are placed on layer 0.

Drawing to Various Scales

The following method is only one way of drawing to a scale other than 1:1. It lets you take full advantage of commands such as DIST, LIST and AREA. This procedure applies only when you plan to plot from Model Space.

1. Draw all objects at full scale. Adjust LTSCALE as needed.

2. Dimension with DIMSCALE set to the inverse of the intended final scale.

3. Shrink or enlarge all objects and dimensions to their final size by making the entire dimensioned object into a block and reinserting it as a star block with the appropriate scale factor. (Don't use SCALE, or all the dimensions' texts will also be scaled.)

4. Reset DIMSCALE to 1. (If you were to stretch or update any dimensions after Step 3, your current dimension variables would cause the adjusted dimensions to appear a different size. Resetting DIMSCALE to 1 avoids this problem.) Also, set DIMLFAC to the inverse of the final scale, for the same reason.

5. Reset LTSCALE. (Multiply the adjusted LTSCALE factor from Step 1 by the final scale.)

For example, suppose you want to draw a small machine part at a scale of 4:1.

1. Draw the part at full scale. As you draw, you may need to adjust LTSCALE somewhat.

2. Dimension the part with DIMSCALE set to .25.

3. Make the dimensioned part a block and reinsert it as a star block, using a scaling factor of 4.

4. Reset DIMSCALE to 1. Set DIMLFAC to .25.

5. Reset LTSCALE to approximately four times the adjusted value used in Step 1.

After you shrink or enlarge your drawing, DIST, LIST and AREA won't give true readings. However, automatic dimensioning can be adjusted to give true readings if you set the dimensioning variable DIMLFAC to the inverse of the drawing scale.

A variation of the above procedure would be to follow Steps 1 and 2 as above, but then to keep the drawing at full scale and adjust its scale only on the plotter (see Chapter 18, "Plotting"). This variation has the advantage of keeping the drawing at full scale for later editing. However, it also has some disadvantages, particularly when a large number of drawings are made at various scales. The appropriate scale must be entered each time a drawing is plotted. A different format (border and title block) is required for each scaling as well as for each sheet size. Notes and title block entries must be scaled with the final plotting size in mind.

Dimoverride & Variable Setting Commands

AutoCAD lets you change dimensioning variables when you're in dimensioning mode. To change a variable, you can use the DIMOVERRIDE command to simply enter the variable's name and then its new value.

This section explains how to use DIMOVERRIDE. It also provides a list of variables with descriptions and suggested values.

DIMOVERRIDE Allows you to override dimension system variable settings

COMMAND LINE: **dimoverride**

Any dimension system variable may be altered by the DIMOVERRIDE command. It does not affect the associated dimension style.

In the command prompt window type **dimoverride**, and the following prompt appears: Dimension variable to override (or Clear to remove override).

Enter a system variable name or the letter **c** (Clear). If you enter **c,** it will clear any overrides on dimensions. If you enter a system variable name, an additional prompt appears: Current value <...> New value.

Enter a new value for the dimension system variable, or press Esc to exit. If you enter a value, you'll be prompted to select an object to change. Then press Esc to exit.

Dimension Variables

The dimension variables listed below hold the values that determine how any given dimension will be placed in a drawing. When you're in dimensioning mode, you can change a variable by entering its name, and then entering the appropriate value. You can change these variables either while you're at the Dim prompt, or while you're in the middle of a dimensioning sequence. However, you can't change them while you're being prompted for the dimension text.

The variables can also be changed with SETVAR or entered directly at the command prompt.

The suggested values given in the table below are somewhat different from AutoCAD's default values. The values in this table can be used in dimensioning drawings similar to those in Appendix A. Use them for your first few attempts at dimensioning.

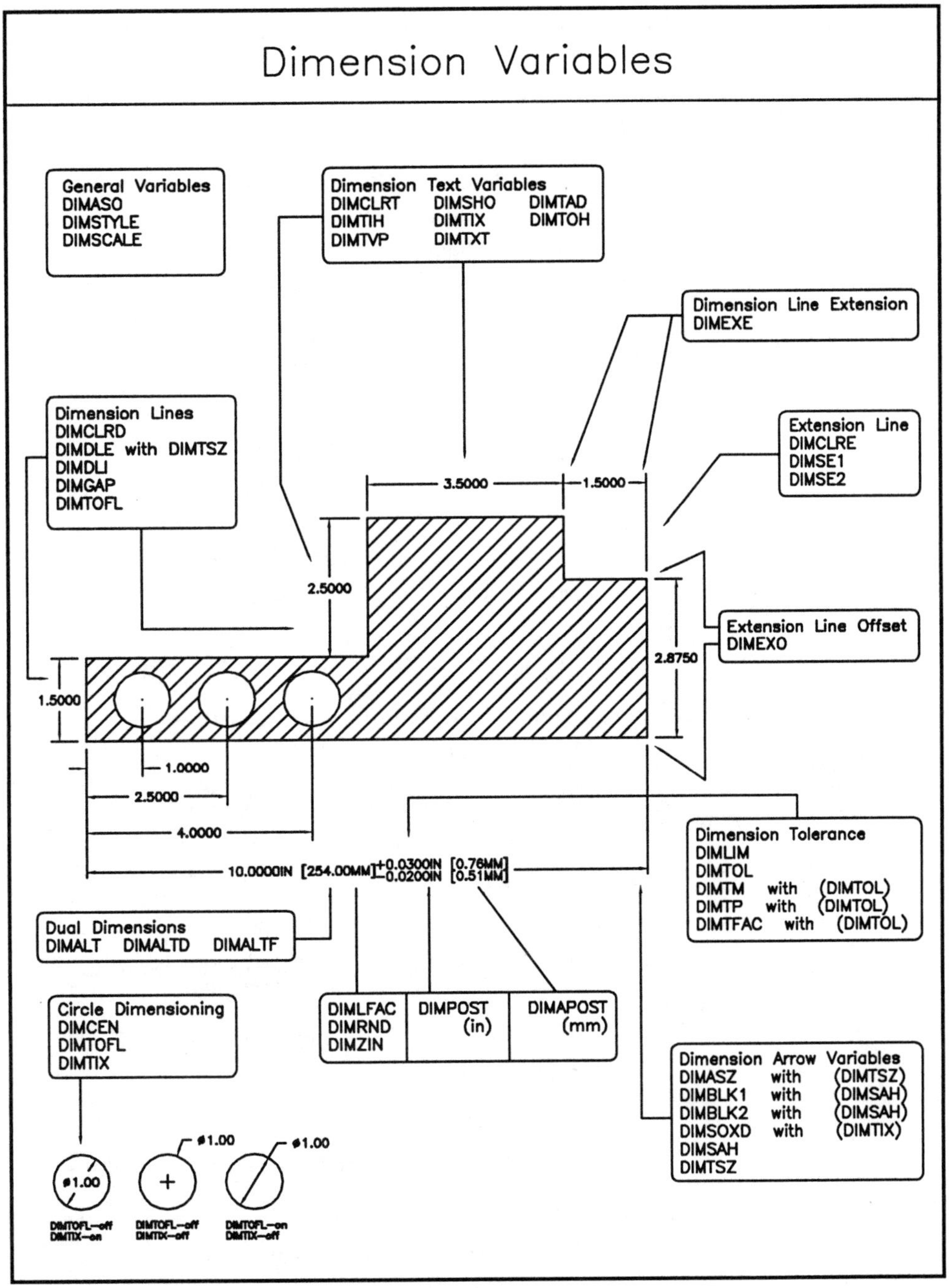

Figure 24-44: Dimension variables explained graphically.

Default Numbers & Text

Variable	Explanation	Suggested Value
DIMLFAC	The factor by which all lengths will be multiplied before being displayed as defaults. A negative value applies to Paper Space, but doesn't affect Model Space.	1.000
DIMRND	Rounds all default dimensions to nearest value (although they're still displayed according to the precision set by the UNITS command).	.001
DIMALT	If on, adds alternate dimension (such as metric), determined by factor in variable DIMALTF	OFF
DIMALTF	Factor for calculating alternate dimensions.	25.4
DIMALTD	Number of decimal places in alternate dimensions.	2
DIMZIN	*Architectural and fractional units— 0 is the default.* If 0, omit zero feet, omit exactly zero inches. If 1, include zero feet, include exactly zero inches. If 2, include zero feet, omit exactly zero inches. If 3, omit zero feet, include exactly zero inches. *Decimal units* 4 suppresses leading zeros. 8 suppresses trailing zeros. 12 suppresses both leading and trailing zeros.	3

DIMPOST	Holds a text string added as a postscript (suffix) to all dimensions except angular.	. (suffix disabled)
DIMAPOST	Same as DIMPOST, but for alternate dimensions.	. (suffix disabled)

Visual Size & Appearance

Variable	Explanation	Suggested Value
DIMSCALE	A scale factor applied to most other dimensioning variables in this group. Set DIMSCALE to 0 when you want the dimension features scaled in each non-tiled viewport to compensate automatically for the scaling ratio between Model Space and Paper Space in that viewport.	1.000, if drawing at full scale (otherwise, use the inverse of the final drawing scale)
DIMTXT	Governs text size (only when the last text style used has a variable height).	.100
DIMASZ	Arrowhead size.	.100
DIMTSZ	Tick size (in place of arrowheads), overrides DIMBLK, DIMBLK1/2 and DIMSAH if nonzero.	0
DIMGAP	Margin around text and minimum lengths for broken dimension lines.	.05
DIMBLK	Name of block that replaces normal arrowheads or ticks. (The block should be created one unit long, pointing to the right, with the insertion base point at the tip of the arrowhead.) A DOT block is built in.	. (none)
DIMBLK1/2	Blocks for first and second ends of dimension line (see DIMSAH below).	. (none)
DIMSAH	If on, allows different arrowheads at each end of dimension line (see DIMBLK1/2 above).	OFF
DIMEXO	Extension line offset (gap).	.100

DIMEXE	Amount extension lines extend past arrowheads/ticks.	.100
DIMDLE	Amount dimension lines extend past extension lines if using ticks.	0
DIMDLI	Spacing increment between dimension lines in successive dimensions from the same baseline.	.300
DIMCEN	Center mark size (use negative value for centerlines instead of centermarks).	.080
DIMCLRD	Color of dimension line and arrows.	BYLAYER
DIMCLRE	Color of extension lines.	BYLAYER
CIMCLRT	Color of text.	BYLAYER
DIMSE1	If on, suppresses first extension line.	OFF
DIMSE2	If on, suppresses second extension line.	OFF

Tolerances

Variable	Explanation	Suggested Value
DIMTP	Tolerance (plus).	0
DIMTM	Tolerance (minus).	0
DIMTOL	If on, the tolerance from DIMTP and DIMTM is automatically added if default text is used.	OFF
DIMLIM	If on, default text is written in limits form.	OFF

Placement of Text

Variable	Explanation	Suggested Value
DIMTIH	If on, text inside extension lines is always horizontal.	OFF
DIMTOH	If on, text outside extension lines is always horizontal.	OFF
DIMTOFL	If on, extra line is placed between arrowheads when text and arrowheads are placed outside extension lines. Also governs placement of arrows in Diameter and Radius dimensions.	OFF

DIMTIX	If on, text is forced inside extension lines (text may conflict with extension lines and arrowheads). Also applies to Diameter and Radius dimensions.	OFF
DIMSOXD	If on, suppresses dimension line; works only when DIMTIX is on.	OFF
DIMTAD	If on, text is placed above dimension line (distance between dimension line and text is one-half text height). See DIMTVP below.	OFF
DIMTVP	Governs distance text is placed above or below dimension line; the value is a factor multiplied by the value in DIMTXT to locate the center of the text; DIMTAD must be off.	0.00

Associative Dimensions

Variable	Explanation	Suggested Value
DIMASO	If on, dimensions are created as associative dimensions (applies to all linear dimensions, plus ANGular, DIAmeter and RADius).	ON
DIMSHO	If on, dimension shape and text is adjusted as it's dragged while using STRETCH.	OFF

Moving on

The next chapter describes the use of the digitizing tablet to copy a drawing or reset the tablet's menu areas. It reviews in depth how to calibrate and configure the tablet for your system and how to digitize a drawing. It provides tips for greater productivity with your digitizer.

It also discusses the SKETCH command.

CHAPTER 25

Tablet & Sketching

AutoCAD Release 13 allows you to configure both a digitizer and a mouse by using the Preferences System dialog box. This chapter reviews the use and setup of digitizing tablets: how to activate the tablet, set it up with a menu and then digitize a drawing.

TABLET

Lets you use the digitizing tablet to copy a drawing or reset the tablet's menu areas

COMMAND LINE: **tablet**

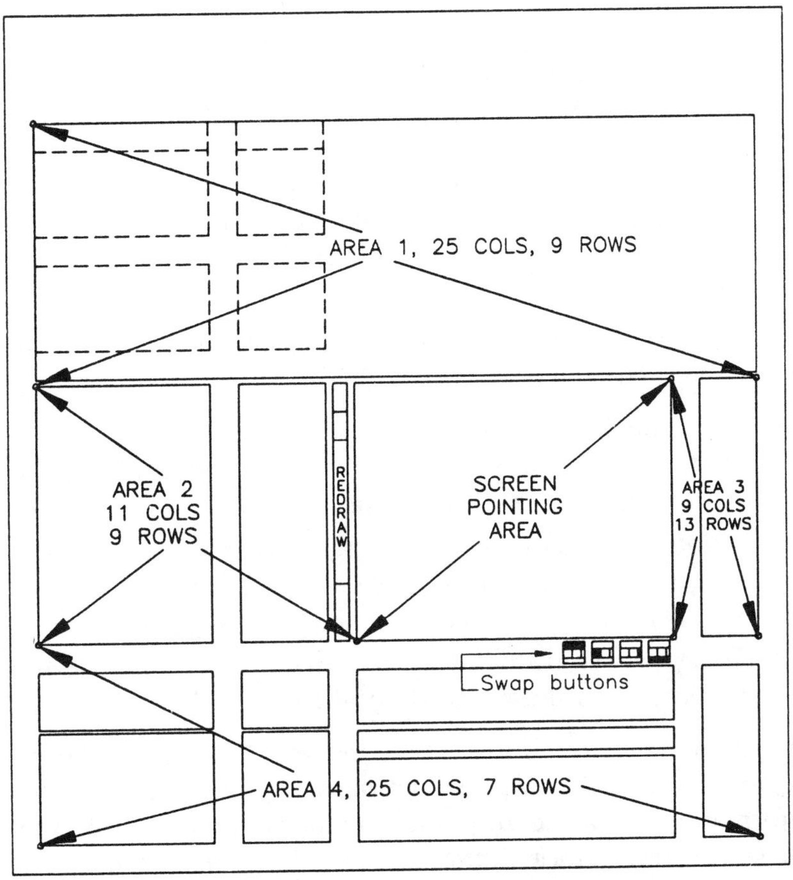

Figure 25-1: Sketch of tablet menu areas for configuration.

Choose Tablet from the Options menu to display a cascading pull-down menu with the following four choices:

On, to turn the tablet mode on (assuming the tablet has been calibrated). Once it is calibrated, you may use the F10 key as an on/off switch while you're digitizing.

Off, to turn the tablet mode off and return to standard pointing device operation.

Calibrate, to match tablet coordinate scaling with a paper drawing.

Configure, to specify and locate up to four tablet menu areas. (See "Tablet Menu Overlays" in Chapter 40, "Customizing AutoCAD.")

Digitizing & Calibrating a Drawing

To calibrate your tablet, you first "tape" the drawing that you want to digitize securely onto your tablet. The drawing doesn't need to be aligned squarely. From the Options pull-down menu, choose Tablet and then Configure. At the command prompt, you're prompted to Digitize Points and then enter their paper coordinates using the keyboard. Enter at least two points.

AutoCAD next displays a table with the following transformation types and asks you to make a choice:

Orthogonal requires only two points. It is accurate for drawings with equal variations applied to each axis (for example, rotation of scaling that is equal about both the X and Y axes).

Affine requires three points and can correct for drawings that have unequal variations applied to each axis.

Projective uses four or more points and can correct variations that change within different parts of the drawing. This method can also correct some minor distortion due to perspective projection.

In general, you should choose the method that reports the smallest RMS Error Value and the smallest Standard Deviation. You can find more information about the different transformation types and the meaning of the report information in the *AutoCAD Reference Manual*.

Digitization Tips

When calibrating, you must enter at least two points, and we suggest two points as optimum. AutoCAD allows multiple points, but entering more than four considerably slows the calculation of the calibration parameters. After digitizing your chosen number of points, press Enter to proceed to the next part of the command.

Tablet calibration done in Model Space works only in Model Space, and tablet calibration done in Paper Space works only in Paper Space.

To digitize a paper drawing that's larger than your tablet, divide the drawing into sections and work on one section at a time. Recalibrate the tablet each time you move the paper. Use ZOOM and PAN to ensure that the area you're digitizing is displayed on the screen.

When tablet mode is on, the pointer's location on the tablet is what's important. In fact, the crosshairs don't need to be on the screen (although we recommend that they be). When tablet mode is off, the location of the crosshairs on the screen and the corresponding coordinate readout are what matter. When you're digitizing a drawing on the tablet, keep tablet mode on while drawing and off while editing.

Snap and ortho still work in tablet mode; use them whenever possible.

SKETCH Allows freehand drawing with lines or polylines

COMMAND LINE: **sketch**

Figure 25-2: The Sketch icon from the Miscellaneous toolbar.

Curves produced by SKETCH are made up of a series of short, straight line segments. Ortho and snap should be off, and your current layer should have a continuous line type.

When prompted, enter the record increment. This determines the length of the line segments that will make up the freehand curves and thus determines the resolution of the sketch. The smaller the record increment, the finer the resolution and the smoother the curve. For experimentation, try a record increment of .1 inch.

While you're in sketch mode, you can enter the following at the command line:

p or the pick button to raise or lower the pen. When the pen is down, a temporary sketch appears on the screen—in a different color—as the pointer is moved. The pen is initially up. (Don't confuse "pen" with "pointer.")

r to record lines already placed on the screen and remain in sketch mode. Or press button 3 on the pointer to record lines. Recorded lines are displayed in the current color and can be edited with the usual editing commands—MOVE, ERASE, etc.

x to record lines already placed on the screen and exit to command mode. Or press Enter.

q to discard temporary lines and exit to command mode.

e to erase part of a temporary sketch not yet recorded. The pen is raised automatically. Move the pointer to the point on the temporary sketch where you want the sketch to end, then enter **p** (or press the pick button). To abort the erase, enter **e** again or enter any other sketch subcommand. Do not confuse this erasing feature with the regular ERASE command.

c to connect to the end of the most recent temporary sketch (the location of the most recent "pen up"). The pen is automatically lowered when the crosshairs come within one record increment. To abort, enter **c** again or enter any other sketch subcommand.

. (period) after raising the pen. This lets you draw a straight line from the end of the most recent temporary sketch to the current pointer location. The pen remains raised. (As an alternative, you can raise the pen and then press the Spacebar or button 2.)

NOTE: *Sketching produces a large number of lines, especially when the record increment is small. A little sketching uses relatively large amounts of memory and disk space. Use an increment that is no smaller than your sketch requires.*

Sketching can also be done in tablet mode (see "TABLET" at the beginning of this chapter).

You can sketch with polylines. Just enter the system variable **skpoly** at the command line and set its value to a positive number other than 0. See "PLINE" in Chapter 28, "Polylines & Splines."

Moving on

The next chapter describes the placement of hatch patterns in your drawing. Using hatch patterns has traditionally been one of the most important methods for indicating materials in a drawing. It has also been one of the most difficult features to implement in a CAD program.

AutoCAD Release 13 now provides you with a number of commands to define, place and edit hatch patterns within your drawings.

CHAPTER 26

Hatching

A feature that sets apart most old manually drafted drawings from modern drawings—both manual and CAD-produced—is the treatment of hatch patterns.

Traditionally, hatch patterns are used to represent changes in material and surface texture on the object being drawn. The problem is that hatch patterns are tedious to produce by hand and, until recently, have not been much easier to produce with CAD systems.

AutoCAD provides commands that help you place detailed hatch patterns into your drawing quickly. More importantly, AutoCAD provides tools that allow you to edit those patterns after they have been placed.

HATCH Fills an area with a cross-hatch pattern

COMMAND LINE: **bhatch**

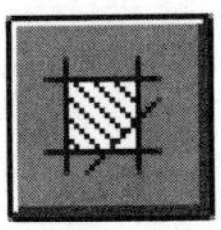

Figure 26-1: The Hatch icon from the Draw toolbar.

Clicking on the Hatch icon displays the Boundary Hatch dialog shown in Figure 26-2. This dialog contains all the options to specify, preview and place a hatch pattern into your drawing.

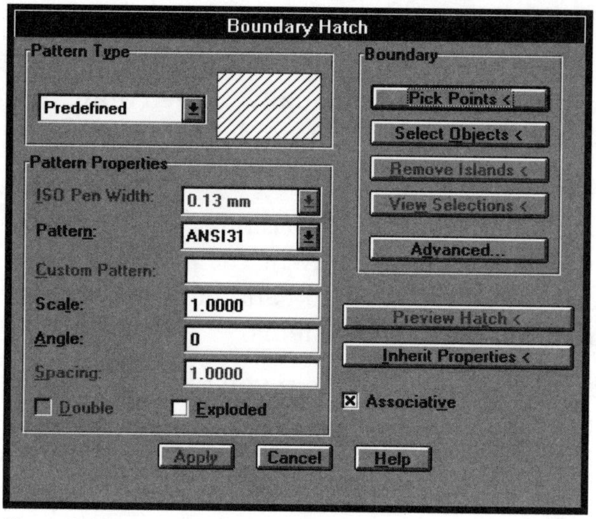

Figure 26-2: The Boundary Hatch dialog.

The Pattern Type area of the dialog contains a pop-up list where you choose whether you want (1) a Predefined pattern from the ACAD.PAT file, (2) a Custom pattern from any .PAT file, or (3) a User-defined pattern created on the fly. Your choice will determine which fields are available in the Pattern Properties area:

ISO Pen Width	This option displays a pop-up list to set pattern scaling based on a selected pen width. This option is available only if you use a Pattern Type of Predefined and choose one of the ISO patterns.
Pattern	This pop-up list presents the predefined patterns in the ACAD.PAT file. The list is unavailable if Predefined is not selected as the Pattern Type.
Custom Pattern	If you select Custom as the Pattern Type, enter the name of your custom hatch pattern in this edit field.
Scale	Sets the size of the hatch pattern. This field is unavailable for User-defined patterns.
Angle	Sets the rotation angle of the hatch pattern.
Spacing	If you select User-defined as the Pattern Type, this field sets the distance in units between the lines that make up the pattern.

Double — If you select User-defined as the Pattern Type, this check box is available. If selected, pattern lines will also be placed at 90 degrees to the angle setting to create a cross-hatch pattern.

Exploded — If this check box is selected, the pattern is placed as a collection of individual objects rather than as a pattern block. Use this option rarely, as it cancels most of the special hatch-editing capabilities for that hatch.

In the Boundary section of the dialog, you specify the hatch pattern's placement. Using the following options, you can have AutoCAD automatically find a boundary that will enclose your hatch pattern, you can manually select the objects to be filled with a hatch, or you can mix the methods:

Pick Points < — This is the automatic method. You are prompted to select an internal point on the screen. After you select a point, AutoCAD searches objects in your drawing to find a closed boundary that surrounds the picked point. Once the boundary is found, it is highlighted and you are prompted to pick another point. Pick as many points and define as many boundaries as you wish. Press Enter to return to the dialog.

Select Objects < — This method prompts you to select objects using the standard selection methods. The selected objects must form an enclosed boundary.

Remove Islands < — The Pick Points method automatically finds other boundaries that are completely enclosed within the selected boundary. These internal boundaries become islands, or holes, within the pattern. Use the Remove Islands button to tell AutoCAD which of these internal boundaries to ignore.

View Selections < — This button highlights the objects you have selected so far.

Advanced... — See the *AutoCAD Reference Manual* for a discussion of advanced hatching options.

The remaining buttons in the dialog perform the following functions:

Preview Hatch <	Hides the dialog and displays how the hatch pattern will appear using the current boundaries and pattern properties. Click on the Continue button to restore the Boundary Hatch dialog and make changes.
Inherit Properties <	Prompts you to select an existing hatch pattern in the drawing and then sets the pattern properties to match the existing hatch. This does not work with exploded hatch patterns.
Associative	If this check box is selected, the boundaries of the hatch pattern can be edited after the pattern is placed. You almost always want this option selected.
Apply	This button completes the command by actually placing the defined hatch pattern in your drawing.

BOUNDARY Creates a boundary object defined by the edges of one or more objects in the drawing

COMMAND LINE: **boundary**

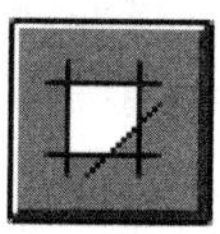

Figure 26-3: The Boundary icon from the Polygon flyout of the Draw toolbar.

Click on the Boundary icon to display the Boundary Creation dialog shown in Figure 26-4. This command creates a polyline or 2D Region representing the internal boundary of several objects—the same perimeter created for hatch patterns with the HATCH command described above.

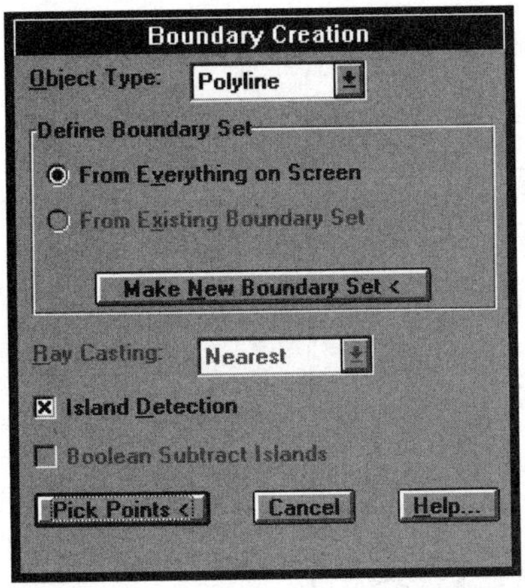

Figure 26-4: The Boundary Creation dialog.

This dialog is similar to the Advanced Options dialog under the HATCH command. You can find detailed descriptions of these options in the *AutoCAD Reference Manual*. Normally, you can just click on the Pick Points < button and proceed the same way that you pick points for boundary hatching. Creating a boundary and then using the AREA command to compute the enclosed area can be a very handy technique (see "AREA" in Chapter 13, "Inquiry").

HATCHEDIT Lets you edit hatch patterns after they have been placed in the drawing

COMMAND LINE: **hatchedit**

Figure 26-5: The Edit Hatch icon from the Modify toolbar.

Clicking on the Edit Hatch icon prompts you to select a hatch pattern that you want to replace the current pattern with and then displays the Hatchedit dialog shown in Figure 26-6. The options in this dialog work the same as those in the Boundary Hatch dialog except that now you are editing the selected hatch pattern rather than defining a new pattern.

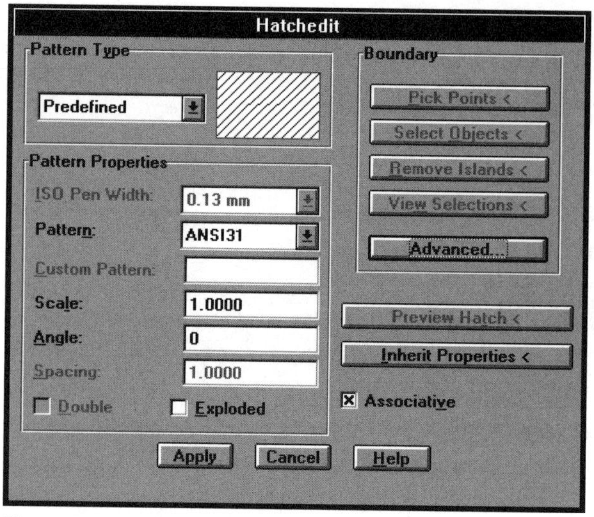

Figure 26-6: The Hatchedit dialog.

If the Associative check box is selected, you can edit the boundary objects directly, using normal edit commands; and the hatch pattern will automatically adjust to the new boundary.

Moving on

The next chapter introduces commands that control the capture and display of images on your screen. These images do not become part of your drawing, but they are a handy way to present your work without having to close your current drawing.

CHAPTER 27

Images

Many times you need to display your work on the computer screen, but you don't want to exit the current drawing or pan around in other drawings. The solution is to display images of your work in a slide-show fashion.

AutoCAD supports this technique in two ways: first, through the slide commands that create and display AutoCAD's own slide format and, second, through the image commands that create and display images in many standard file formats.

This chapter describes the slide and image commands.

Slide Commands

A slide is a file of a particular display. You can't edit a slide, but you can view a slide even when you're working with a different drawing.

Use slides to quickly reference other drawings, charts or tables. Or produce a slide show that automatically displays any number of slides by means of a script (see "SCRIPT" in Chapter 39, "Text Editing & Scripts").

MSLIDE Makes a slide file

COMMAND LINE: **mslide**

Before using the MSLIDE command, set up the display exactly as you want it to appear in the slide, using commands such as ZOOM, PAN and LAYER.

From the Tools pull-down menu, choose Slide and then choose Save. This displays the Create Slide File dialog shown in Figure 27-1.

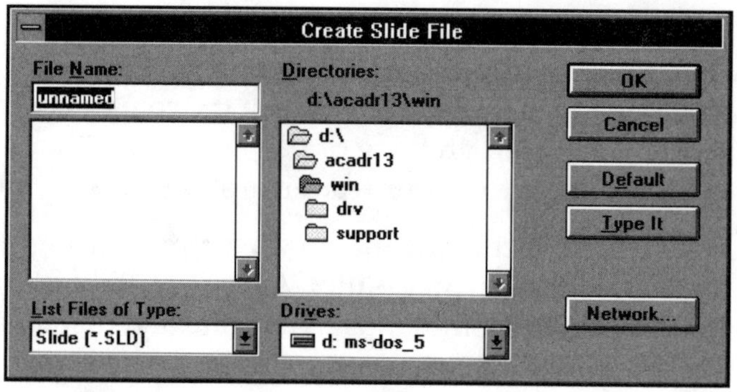

Figure 27-1: The Create Slide File dialog.

Navigate to the desired directory and enter an eight-character name in the File Name field. AutoCAD creates a slide file with the extension .SLD.

A slide created in Model Space makes a slide of only the current viewport (which may be the entire graphics screen). A slide created in Paper Space always includes the entire graphics screen.

VSLIDE Displays a slide

COMMAND LINE: **vslide**

From the Tools pull-down menu, choose Slide and then View. The Select Slide File dialog shown in Figure 27-2 appears. Navigate to the desired directory and select a slide file.

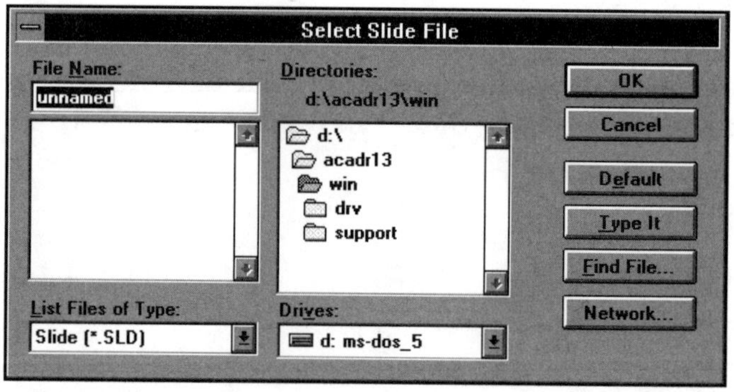

Figure 27-2: The Select Slide File dialog.

AutoCAD displays the selected slide in the graphics screen, replacing the view of your current drawing. You cannot edit the slide. Choose Redraw View from the View pull-down menu to view your current drawing.

NOTE: *To display a series of slides from different drawings, use the VSLIDE command in a script file.*

Slide Libraries

You can place a group of individual slide files into a larger file called a *slide library*. Storing a large number of slides in slide libraries uses disk space more efficiently than storing each slide separately.

The program that constructs a slide library is called SLIDELIB.EXE and is found on the AutoCAD support disk. (We assume here that this program resides in the \ACAD\SUPPORT directory under your AutoCAD program files.)

Before you can use the SLIDELIB program, you must create a text file containing the names of the slides you want included in the larger file. Enter the names one per line, with or without the .SLD extension.

This file becomes the input for the SLIDELIB program. You must redirect the input for the SLIDELIB program using the DOS redirection symbol <. For example, if your file of slide names is called SLIST.TXT, and the name of your new library file is LIBRARY1, you'd use this command line at the DOS prompt:

```
SLIDELIB LIBRARY1 <SLIST1.TXT
```

The SLIDELIB program produces a file with an extension .SLB.

When you want to add slides to a library file or remove slides from it, you must revise the text file that contains the slide names and then rerun the SLIDELIB program, making sure that all the original slides are present.

NOTE: *The icon selections that are available through the pull-down portion of AutoCAD's standard menu are in the slide library file called ACAD.SLB. Never create an ACAD.SLB slide library file, as you'll overwrite the original AutoCAD version.*

Image Commands

AutoCAD also provides a SAVEIMAGE command that lets you save images for use by other programs.

The REPLAY command displays image files.

SAVEIMAGE Saves an image in a standard graphics format

COMMAND LINE: **saveimg**

AutoCAD can also save an image of your screen, or the results of a RENDER command, to a standard graphics format that can be used by other programs. These formats include .TGA, .TIF and .GIF (for detailed information on the properties and uses of these file types, see the *AutoCAD Reference Manual*).

From the Tools pull-down menu, choose Image and then Save.... This displays the Save Image dialog shown in Figure 27-3.

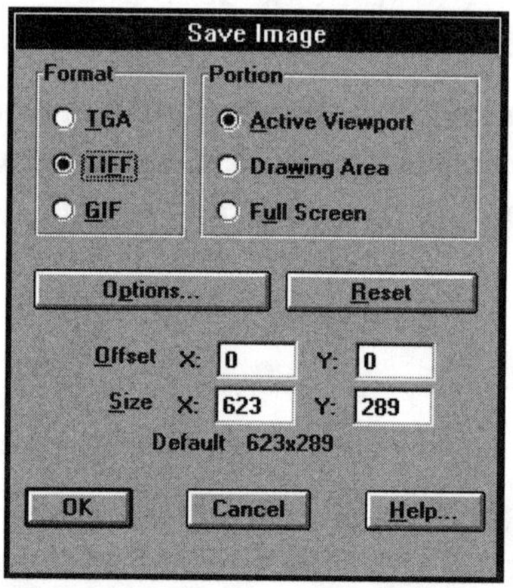

Figure 27-3: The Save Image dialog.

Choose the file format you desire from the left side of the dialog, and choose the screen portion you want to save from the right side. As a default, AutoCAD saves the image at the same resolution as the selected portion of the screen.

To increase your control of the file format and image size, use the Options button and the Offset and Size fields (see the *AutoCAD Reference Manual* for details).

When you click on OK, the Image File dialog appears. Navigate to the directory where you wish to store the image file and enter a name in the File Name field.

REPLAY Displays an image file

COMMAND LINE: **replay**

From the Tools pull-down menu, choose Image and then View. This displays the Replay dialog shown in Figure 27-4.

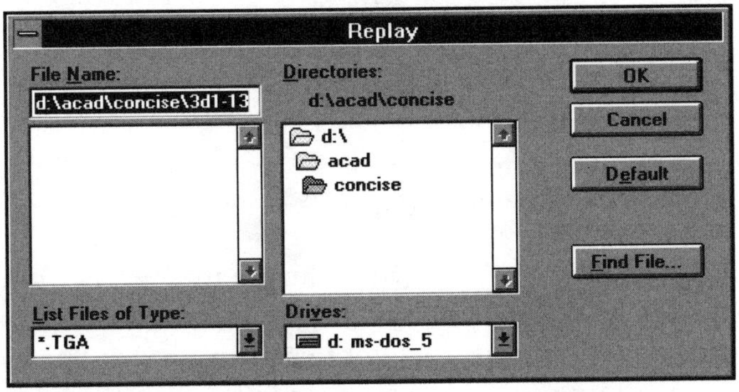

Figure 27-4: The Replay dialog.

Choose the file format you wish to display by making a selection from the List Files of Type pop-up list at the lower-left corner of the dialog. Then navigate to the directory where the desired file is located.

When you click on OK, the Image Specifications dialog, shown in Figure 27-5, appears.

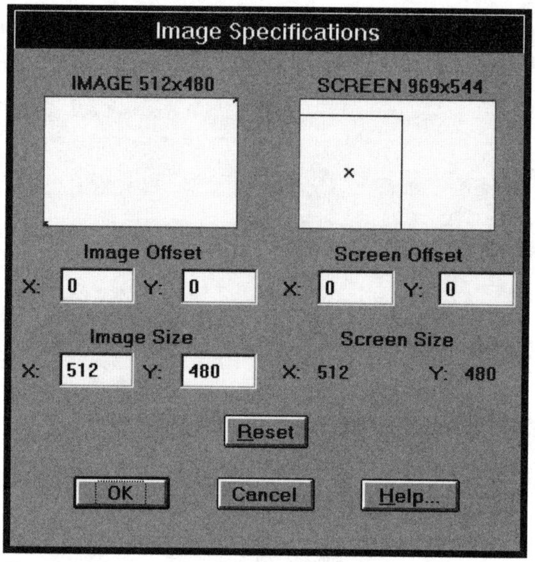

Figure 27-5: The Image Specifications dialog.

The Image tile displays the size of the selected image. As a default, it displays the entire image. You can clip out a portion of the image to display by picking two points; this defines a clipping rectangle in the Image tile. As an alternative, you can specify the points by typing coordinates in the Image Offset and Image Size fields.

The Screen tile displays the size of the current viewport and places a rectangle where the image will be displayed. The default is to place the lower-left corner of the image in the lower-left corner of the viewport. To specify the placement of the image, pick the image center point in the Screen tile or enter an offset distance in the Screen Offset fields.

Click on OK to display the image in the current viewport. Choose Redraw View from the View pull-down menu to return to your drawing.

Using the REPLAY command in a script file is not as easy as using VSLIDE, since it requires the use of AutoLISP. However, REPLAY is the only way to view images created with other graphics programs or to view rendered images created by the RENDER command.

Moving on

The next chapter introduces you to polylines and splines. These commands create complex objects that contain straight line and arc segments as well as smooth-flowing spline curves.

CHAPTER 28

Polylines & Splines

Polylines and splines are complex objects used to define boundaries, contours and complex curves. Polylines may consist of both straight line segments and arcs or be curved as a bezier spline. Splines are always curved and provide more control over their definition than do polylines.

PLINE Creates a polyline

COMMAND LINE: **pline**

Figure 28-1: The Pline icon from the Polyline flyout of the Draw toolbar.

PLINE draws a polyline, a sequence of lines or arcs with special properties, on the current X-Y construction plane. In contrast to a series of regular lines and arcs, a polyline is treated as one object by AutoCAD. Its various segments can have varying widths.

When prompted, enter the endpoint of a line. This is the default response, and if you're starting a polyline this is your only choice. Or enter the following:

> **w**, then enter the starting and ending widths for the next segment. The default width is 0. The ending width is retained for the beginning and ending widths of subsequent segments unless you change them.
>
> **h**, then enter the starting and ending half-widths. This choice is especially suitable if you use the pointer to indicate the half-width.
>
> **l**, then enter the length to draw a line from the end of the most recent line or arc. The direction is already determined by the most recent line or arc.
>
> **c** to close the polyline (draw a line back to its origin).
>
> **u** to undo the most recent line or arc. You can use U repeatedly.
>
> **a** to draw an arc.

When you enter **a** for arc, a new prompt will appear with several options unique to arcs. However, the Undo, Width and Half-width options operate just as they do when you're drawing straight segments. The options are

> **l** to return to line mode.
>
> **ce**, then locate the center of the arc. The remaining prompts are self-explanatory.
>
> **r**, then enter the arc's radius. The remaining prompts are self-explanatory.
>
> **a**, then enter included angle (positive for counterclockwise, negative for clockwise). The remaining prompts are self-explanatory.
>
> **s**, then enter the second point of the arc. The remaining prompts are self-explanatory.
>
> **cl** to close a polyline with an arc.
>
> **d** to set a starting direction other than the direction of the most recent line or arc.

You can find the area inside a closed polyline by using the LIST command or the AREA command. See Chapter 13, "Inquiry" for information on using LIST and AREA.

See Chapter 45, "Hands-on Exercises," for a polyline exercise.

PEDIT Edits a 2D polyline or 3D mesh

COMMAND LINE: **pedit**

Figure 28-2: The Edit Polyline icon from the Special Edit flyout of the Modify toolbar.

PEDIT can be used to edit 2D polylines, 3D polylines and 3D meshes, as well as other objects created from polylines, such as donuts and polygons. This section focuses on editing 2D polylines.

When prompted, select the 2D polyline. If the line or arc you select isn't a polyline, AutoCAD says so and gives you the option of turning it into a one-segment polyline. After selecting the polyline, you are prompted to enter one of the following options:

s to exit from PEDIT.

c to close an open polyline (adds a closing line if necessary).

o to open a closed polyline (removes the closing line or arc if it was created by entering **C**).

j to join a line or arc that already meets the end of an open polyline (2D polylines only). Several lines or arcs can be selected at once. If a spline has been fitted to a polyline that is joined, it's automatically straightened.

w to specify a new uniform width for the entire polyline (2D polylines only).

f to fit a curve to a series of straight line segments (2D polylines only). This curve is made up of pairs of arcs, and it passes through all vertices.

s to apply a B-spline to the polyline based on the frame that connects its present vertices. This spline passes through only the first and last vertices of an open polyline. The more vertices a polyline has, the more closely the spline will conform to the shape of the frame. Three system variables control the shape and appearance of the spline, as explained below.

Enter the system variable **splinetype** at the command prompt and set its value to 5 for a quadratic B-spline, or to 6 for a cubic B-spline. The quadratic B-spline conforms more closely to the spline frame, while the cubic B-spline is more generalized or smoother.

To display the frame, enter the system variable **splframe** at the command prompt and set its value to nonzero, then regenerate the screen by entering **regen**.

The splined polyline is composed of short, straight line segments. The number of segments employed is governed by the variable SPLINESEGS (default = 8). If the polyline is a 2D polyline, a negative value for SPLINESEGS creates a spline that's both "splined" and then automatically fitted (see F above). Changing SPLINESEGS affects only newly splined or resplined polylines. Enter **splinesegs** at the command prompt and set its value to any integer.

d to decurve a polyline (cancels the effect of F or S).

u to undo the effect of the most recent PEDIT operation. You can enter **u** more than once within a single PEDIT command to undo several operations.

e to edit a vertex or segment(s) between two vertices.

2D Versus 3D PEDIT

If you're editing a regular 2D polyline, all the options listed below will appear in the prompt. But if you're editing a 3D polyline, the prompt won't include Width or Tangent. AutoCAD marks the vertex to be edited with an X, beginning with the first vertex. To edit the vertex, enter one of the following:

x to exit vertex editing (return to PEDIT).

n to move the marker to the next vertex.

p to move the marker to the previous vertex.

b to break between the current vertex and another selected vertex. Then enter **n** (next) or **p** (previous) to move the marker to another vertex. Then enter **g** (go) to effect the break, or enter **x** to exit the break procedure. If you enter **g** without moving the marker, the polyline is broken into two segments with no visible gap.

NOTE: Breaking a closed polyline converts it to an open polyline with the closing segment removed (if the closing segment was created with the C option).

i to insert a new vertex after the marker, then locate the new vertex.

m to move the marked vertex, then locate the new position.

w to change beginning and/or ending widths for the single segment following the marker (2D polylines only). New widths aren't displayed until the display is regenerated.

r to regenerate the display.

s to place a straight line segment between the current vertex and another selected vertex. Then enter **n** (next) or **p** (previous) to move the marker to another vertex. Then enter **g** (go) to effect the straight line. Or enter **x** to exit the straightening procedure. If you enter **g** without moving the marker, the next segment (if it's an arc) is straightened.

t to indicate a tangent direction (using keyboard or pointer) for later curve fitting (2D polylines only). This option does not affect a spline.

NOTE: The BREAK command can be used on a 2D polylines. The EXPLODE command, when applied to a polyline, converts the polyline into individual lines and arcs with a width of 0.

SPLINE Creates a spline curve

COMMAND LINE: **spline**

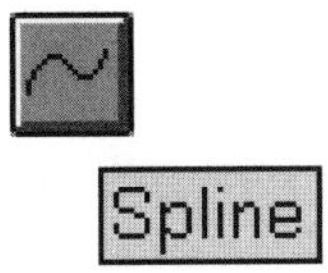

Figure 28-3: The Spline icon from the Polyline flyout of the Draw toolbar.

Unlike polylines, splines are always curved and always have a width of 0. The first prompt has the following two options:

1. Object, to convert a spline fit polyline into a true spline. True spline curves are more efficient and use less memory than spline fit polylines. Enter **o** for object and select the polyline to convert.
2. <Enter first point>, the default to begin entering points to define a new spline object. After entering the first point, you may define more points on the spline or enter the following options:

    Close, to place the end vertex of the spline coincident to the first vertex and make the points tangent to each other. After choosing Close, you must also specify a tangent direction for the closed points. You can pick a point to set the tangent direction or press Enter to let AutoCAD calculate a default direction. The command is then completed, and you return to the command prompt.

    Fit Tolerance to specify how close the spline curve must come to the points. A fit tolerance of 0 forces the spline to pass through the points. Larger values create splines that pass within the tolerance distance of the points. Changing the fit tolerance affects all points on the spline curve.

    Undo, to remove the last point entered.

Press Enter to complete the specification of points. You are next prompted to specify the Start and End Tangents for the spline. You can either pick a point to set the tangent direction or press Enter to let AutoCAD calculate a default tangent.

SPLINEDIT Edits a spline

COMMAND LINE: **splinedit**

Figure 28-4: The Splinedit icon from the Special Edit flyout of the Modify toolbar.

When prompted, select the spline object. The spline is highlighted, and grips appear at all the spline's fit points and control points. (The fit points are the points that you picked when you created the spline.) The spline passes through, or near, the fit points based on the fit tolerance setting.

The control points only touch the spline at its first and last point, and they define the spline control frame. You can view the spline frame by entering **splframe** at the command line and setting its value to 1. Regenerate the drawing to display the frame. Set **splframe** back to 0 and regenerate again to hide the frame. Figure 28-5 shows a spline with its fit points, control points and spline control frame visible.

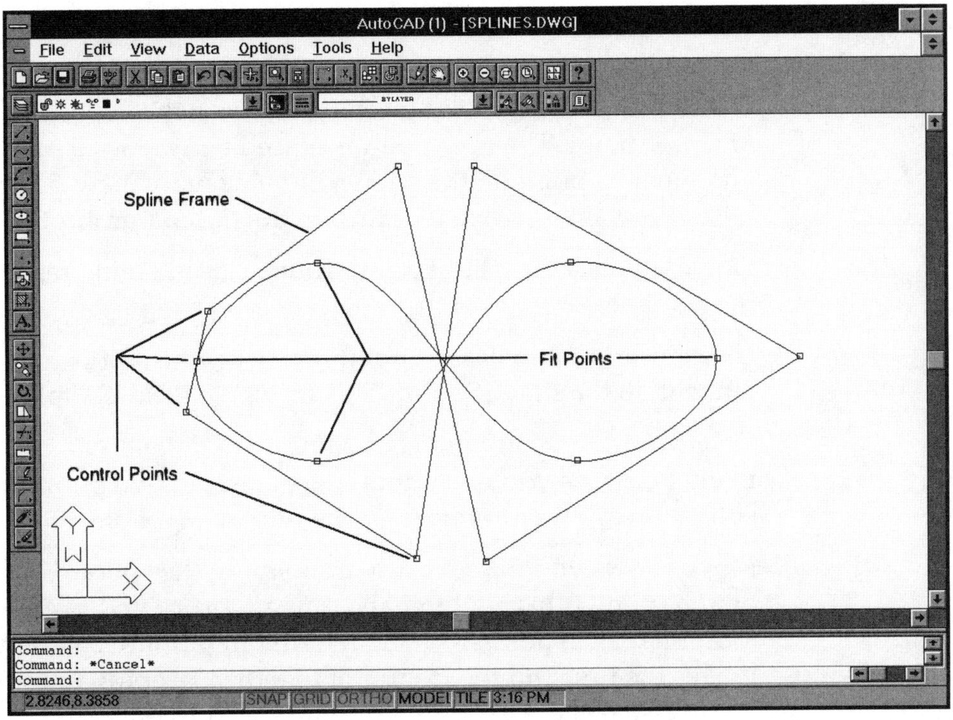

Figure 28-5: A selected spline curve and its control frame.

You can edit splines through either the spline frame control points or the fit tolerance fit points. After selecting the spline, you are then presented with the following options:

Fit Data is used to adjust the fit points of the spline. Not all splines contain fit tolerance data. Polylines converted to splines have no fit data, and splines edited without the fit data option will also lose their fit data. Using fit data provides global control over the entire spline. Changes made at one point with fit data cause profound changes to the spline at all other points on the spline.

Splines without fit data can only be edited by the spline frame control points, which provide more local control of the spline. Changes made at one control point on a spline without fit data will only affect the spline curve near the changed point.

NOTE: *Once a spline loses its fit data, there is no way to get it back unless you undo the SPLINEDIT command.*

The following options are available under Fit Data:

The Add option adds a new fit point to the spline. You are prompted to select an existing point on the spline and then specify the location of a new point. The new point is placed between the selected point and the next point on the spline. Enter as many new points as you wish. Press Enter twice to return to the fit data prompt.

Open removes the last fit point from a closed spline resulting in an open spline.

Close inserts a new last fit point for the spline that is coincident, and tangent, to the first fit point. This results in a closed spline curve.

Delete prompts you to select a fit point to delete. You can delete as many points as you wish until there are only two points left on the spline. Press Enter to return to the fit data prompt.

Move allows you to move any fit point on the spline. The first fit point on the spline is highlighted and you are prompted to enter a new location for the point. Moving the first fit point of a closed spline moves the first and the last point together, keeping the spline closed. Move also has the following options: Next to select the next point on the spline; Previous to select the previous point on the spline; Select Point to manually select any point on the spline; and eXit to return to the fit data prompt.

Purge removes all fit data information from the spline and exits the fit data option of SPLINEDIT. The spline doesn't change appearance after a purge, but the fit data options are no longer available when the spline is edited.

Tangents allows you to adjust the tangent directions for the two end points. If the spline is closed, specify only one tangent for both points.

toLerance prompts you to enter a new fit tolerance for the entire spline.

eXit returns to the standard SPLINEDIT prompt.

Open removes both the first and the last control points of a closed spline, resulting in an open spline curve. This command also removes any fit data associated with the spline.

Close inserts a new last control point coincident and tangent to the first control point, creating a closed spline. This command also removes any fit data.

Move Vertex allows you to move any control point. The first control point on the spline is highlighted, and you are prompted to enter a new location for the point. Move Vertex has the same suboptions as Move under the Fit Data option described above. Moving the first control point of a closed spline does not affect the location of the last point and results in an open spline. Moving any control point on a spline with a fit tolerance greater than zero removes all fit data from the spline.

Refine allows you to change the properties of the control points. Refine always removes fit data and has the following options:

> Add control point allows you to add new control points to the spline without changing its shape. You are prompted to select a point on the spline. After entering the point, a new control point is added near that position; and the control points to either side are automatically adjusted to maintain the spline curve's shape. You can add as many points as you wish. Press Enter to return to the Refine prompt.
>
> Elevate Order changes the mathematical description of the curve to a higher order. Default splines are cubic and are described as a fourth order curve. You are prompted to enter a new order for the curve that must be equal to or higher than its current order and no greater than 26. The end result is that more control points appear on the spline. Increasing the order of a spline provides more localized control at each point, but it also slows the calculation of the curve.
>
> Weight highlights the first control point and prompts you to enter a new weight value that must be greater than zero. The higher the weight value, the more the spline is pulled to the control point's location. Weight has the same suboptions as the Move command under the Fit Data option.
>
> eXit returns you to the SPLINEDIT prompt.

rEverse flips the order of the control points and fit points. The first point becomes the last and the last point becomes the first. This option does not remove fit data.

Undo reverses the effect of the previous SPLINEDIT option.

eXit ends the SPLINEDIT command and returns to the command prompt.

Moving on

The next chapter examines techniques for creating 2D isometric drawings. While creating true 3D models and generating an isometric view is becoming the preferred method, you may often need to create this traditional type of drawing.

CHAPTER 29

Isometric Drawing

Isometric drawings are a mainstay of traditional drafting. They produce a three-dimensional view of an object, yet make true measurements of the object along all three axes.

While the development of new and powerful 3D modeling tools may one day make isometric drawings obsolete, they are not dead yet. AutoCAD still includes a number of tools to assist you in the creation of isometric drawings.

Setting an Isometric Snap Grid

The Drawing Aids dialog was discussed in Chapter 4, "Setup," and Chapter 5, "Points." This same dialog also activates AutoCAD's isometric grid and snap functions. Choose Drawing Aids from the Options pull-down menu to display the Drawing Aids dialog in Figure 29-1. The isometric snap/grid controls are in the lower-right corner.

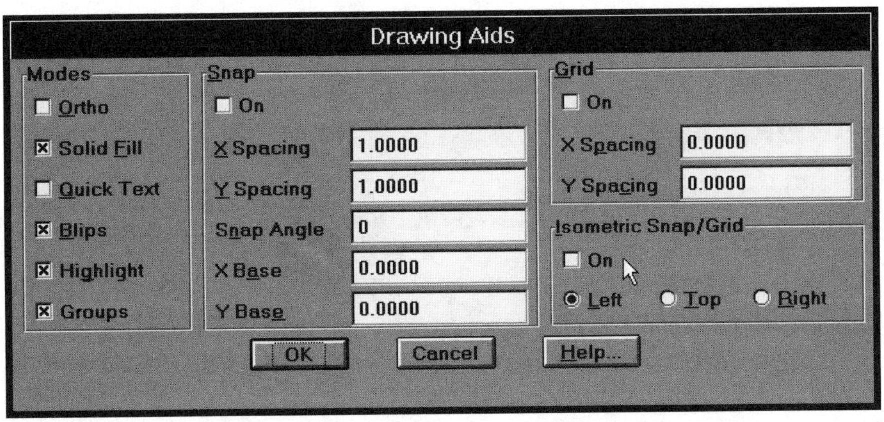

Figure 29-1: The isometric functions of the Drawing Aids dialog.

There are two controls in this section:

The On check box controls whether the isometric snap/grid functions are used instead of the standard orthogonal snap/grid functions.

The Left, Top and Right radio buttons control the orientation of the isometric plane to represent a drawing on the specified isometric surface.

In the Drawing Aids dialog box, the settings in the standard snap and grid fields are also used by the isometric snap and grid. However, the X Spacing field is inaccessible, and the Y Spacing field controls spacing for all three axes (both of the horizontal axes and the vertical axis).

Be cautious about setting the snap angle to anything other than zero. While it is possible to rotate the isometric snap/grid, it is confusing in appearance and does not fit any standard drafting projection. You should leave the snap angle at zero.

ISOPLANE Selects the left, top or right isometric plane

COMMAND LINE: **isoplane**

After entering this command using the keyboard, you select the left, top or right isometric plane by entering **l**, **t** or **r**, respectively.

It's much easier to use Ctrl+E to switch from one isometric plane to the next (left, then top, then right, etc.). This can be done while you're in the middle of another command, without having to enter the ISOPLANE command.

Isometric Drawings

In isometric drawings, the two receding axes are at 30 degrees to horizontal. Distances are measured on the vertical and on the receding axes.

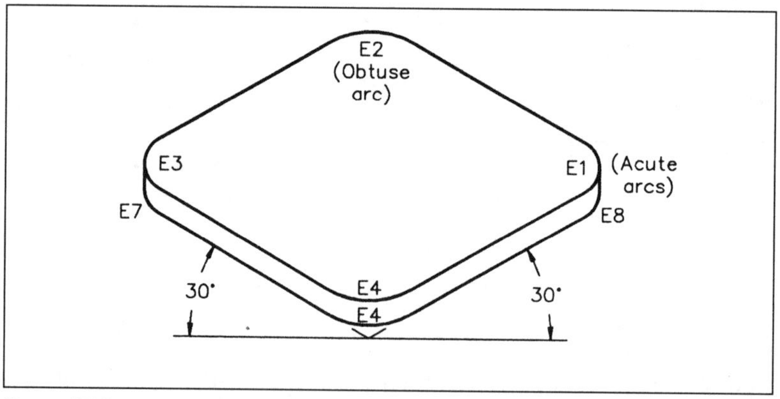

Figure 29-2: An isometric drawn with axes at 30 degrees.

When circular objects are drawn in isometric, they're most accurately represented by ellipses. The ELLIPSE command and its isometric option were presented in Chapter 10, "2D Figures." The next two sections review the process of creating isometric ellipses and elliptical arcs in an isometric drawing.

Method 1: Using ELLIPSE to Draw Isometric Circles

Use Ctrl+E to place the crosshairs on the desired isometric plane. Then click on the Ellipse Axis End icon. When prompted, enter **i** for isocircle, then locate the center and enter the radius (or enter **d** and then the diameter). A full ellipse will be placed on the current isometric plane. The ellipse is a true ellipse (rather than a polyline approximation, as in earlier versions of AutoCAD), and can easily be edited with commands such as TRIM and BREAK.

Method 2: Using ELLIPSE to Draw Isometric Arcs

When you need only a segment of an ellipse, you can trim a full ellipse or you can use the Arc option of the ELLIPSE command. Click on the Ellipse Arc icon, then enter **i** for isocircle. After specifying a center and a radius (or diameter), just as with the full ellipse command, you are prompted for the start angle and end angle for the arc. AutoCAD then draws a segment of an ellipse counterclockwise between the specified angles.

Moving on

The next chapter takes you into the Advanced section of this book, beginning with a discussion of Coordinate Systems.

SECTION III

ADVANCED

CHAPTER 30

Coordinate Systems

This chapter describes User Coordinate Systems (UCS) and X-Y construction planes. A UCS involves two commands (UCS and UCSICON) and several system variables that are described in further detail in separate sections below. There's a UCS exercise in Chapter 45, "Hands-on Exercises 2."

NOTE: *Be careful not to confuse User Coordinate Systems and their construction planes with viewpoints.*

World Coordinate System & User Coordinate Systems

The standard (default) coordinate system is called the World Coordinate System (WCS) to distinguish it from coordinate systems established by the user. AutoCAD adopts the WCS at the beginning of a new drawing, assuming that it hasn't been replaced by a different UCS in your prototype drawing. You'll notice the UCS icon in the lower left corner of your screen (with a W in it to indicate it's in WCS default mode).

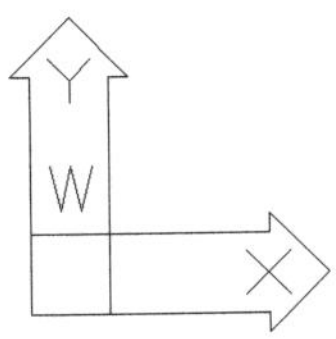

Figure 30-1: The UCS icon.

The WCS and its X-Y construction plane were described in Chapter 3 under "Cartesian Coordinates & Angles." That basic coordinate system is adequate for most 2D drawings. However, for many 3D drawings you'll want to establish one or more User Coordinate Systems with the 0,0,0 origin located in different places and/or the axes pointing in different directions. You can set up as many different UCSes as you need.

Complex 3D geometry would be difficult to construct if all objects had to be located from an X-Y construction plane in the WCS. AutoCAD allows you to place an X-Y construction plane anywhere in space and orient it at any angle. This lets you place various objects in a complex configuration using simple X-Y distances in the new X-Y plane.

Once you've defined a new UCS, all coordinates that you enter and all coordinates that are displayed are based on it. If you enter coordinates preceded by an asterisk (such as ***2,4,6** or **@*5<<30**), they are interpreted as WCS coordinates. You can easily switch between various coordinate systems at any time during the drawing process.

The UCS is independent of the current viewpoint, although the viewpoint can be automatically tied into the current UCS. Only one UCS is active at any given time, even though you may have various viewports displayed. The view from 0,0,1 toward 0,0,0 is called the *plan view*.

Since the UCS and the viewpoint don't necessarily coincide, you'll want to pay close attention to the UCS icon to help you see the current orientation of the three axes. (See "UCSICON" later in this chapter.)

When you save a drawing, the current UCS is saved with it and automatically becomes the initial coordinate system when you begin to edit that drawing the next time.

Right-Hand Rules

The X-Y-Z axes will always be oriented in relation to one another according to a right-hand rule. When your right hand is positioned as shown below, with the thumb representing the positive X axis and the first finger representing the positive Y axis, the positive Z axis will point in the direction of the second finger.

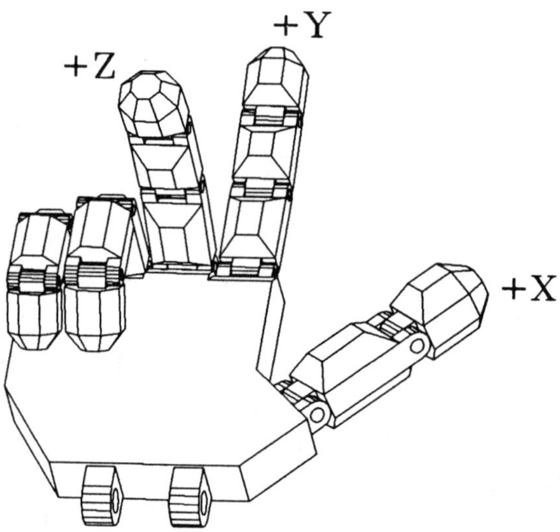

Figure 30-2: The first right-hand rule, showing X, Y, Z on the right hand.

Rotation around any given axis follows another right-hand rule. When the thumb of the right hand points along the positive direction of any given axis as shown below, then positive rotation around that axis follows the direction of the curled fingers.

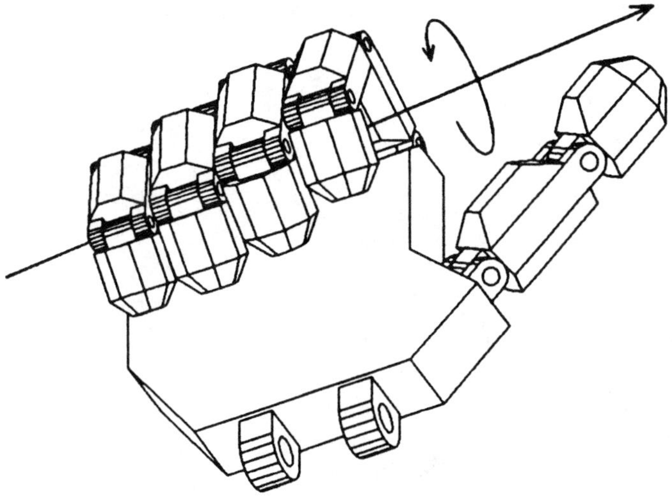

Figure 30-3: Second right-hand rule, showing positive rotation about an axis.

Grid & Pointer

The grid always appears on the construction plane, which is the X-Y plane at the current elevation in the current UCS.

Remember that whenever you place objects in your drawing with the pointer, all locations will be on the X-Y construction plane (at the current elevation). This is true even when the current viewpoint or your current UCS makes the crosshairs appear to be somewhere above the construction plane.

UCS Establishes, saves or recalls a User Coordinate System

COMMAND LINE: **ucs**

You can access the many options of the UCS command by choosing Set UCS from the View pull-down menu. This displays the cascade menu shown in Figure 30-4.

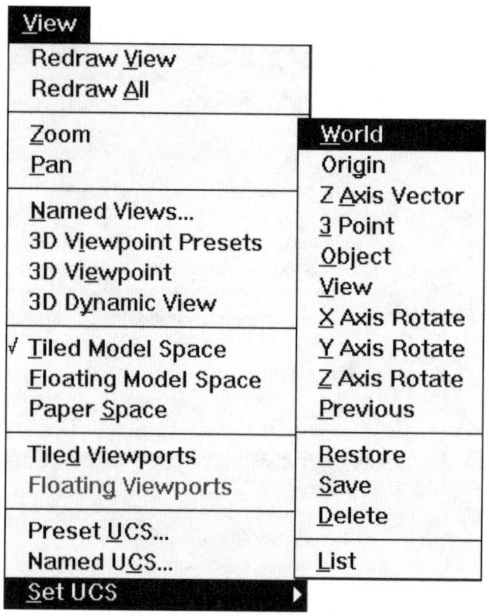

Figure 30-4: The Set UCS cascade menu.

You can also access these options from the UCS flyout of the Standard toolbar, or by displaying all of the UCS options in their own toolbar. Choose Toolbars from the Tools menu, then select UCS to display the UCS toolbar shown in Figure 30-5.

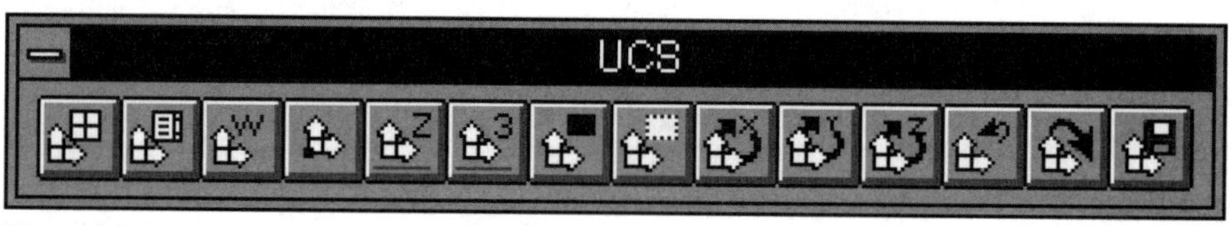

Figure 30-5: The UCS toolbar.

You may choose the following Set UCS options:

Figure 30-6: The World UCS icon.

Choose World to make the World Coordinate System the current system.

Figure 30-7: The UCS Origin icon.

Choose Origin to enter coordinates of the origin of a new UCS. This new coordinate system will have an origin that is shifted from the current system, but its X, Y and Z will point in the same direction as the current system.

Figure 30-8: The UCS Z Axis Vector icon.

Choose Z Axis Vector to enter coordinates of the origin of the new UCS (if different from the origin of the current system), and then a point through which the positive Z axis will pass. This option is handy if you merely want to designate a Z direction to extrude an object but don't care where the X and Y axes are pointing.

Figure 30-9: The UCS 3 Point icon.

Choose 3 Point to enter three points to define the new UCS: (1) the origin, (2) a point on the positive X axis and (3) a point on the positive Y half of the X-Y plane. Once the X and Y axes are so determined, the Z axis is determined by the right-hand rule. The defaults for these three points are as follows:

First point	The origin of the current system.
Second point	The direction of the positive X axis in the current system.
Third point	A direction parallel to the current X-Y plane. This option is useful if you want to attach the new coordinate system to certain features of an object using various osnap modes.

Figure 30-10: The UCS Object icon.

Choose Object to define the new UCS by using an object already in the drawing. Whenever you use this option, the positive Z axis is oriented in the same direction as it was when the object was created. This, in turn, forces the X-Y plane to be parallel to the X-Y plane that was current when the object was created; however, the direction of the X and Y axes may differ.

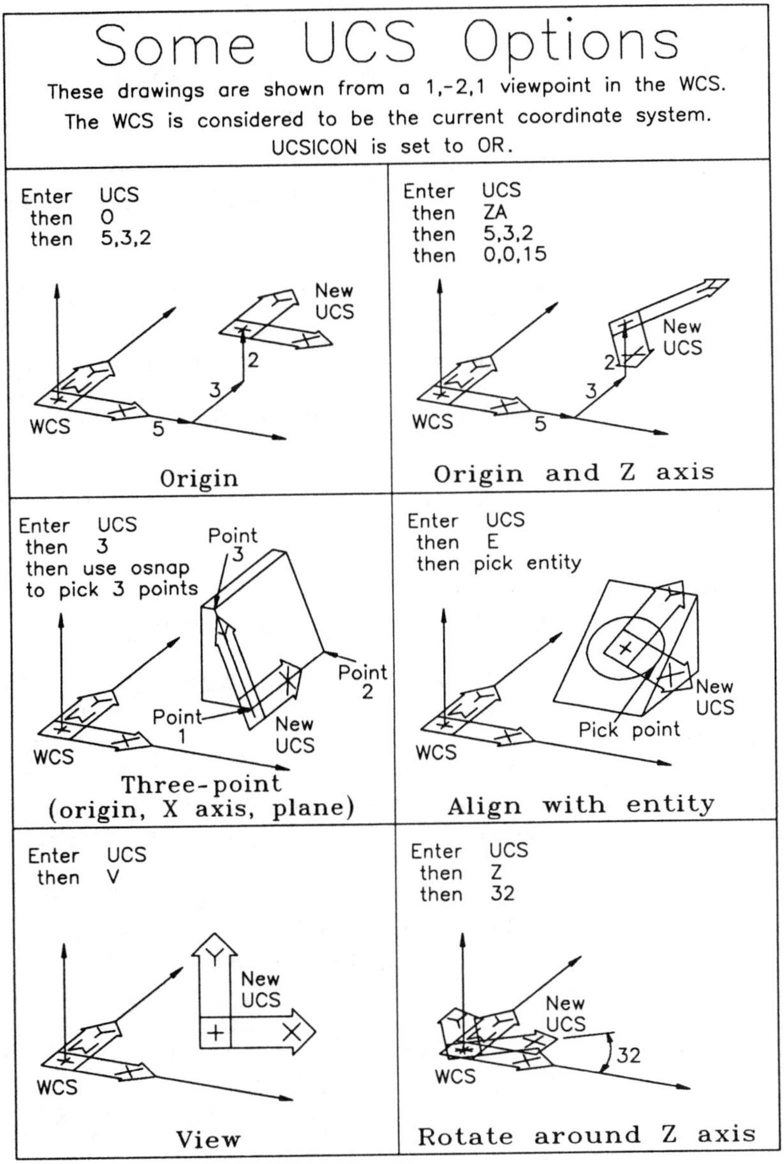

Figure 30-11: User Coordinate System options.

Various objects determine the new coordinate system in varying ways:

Circle	Its center becomes the new origin, and the X axis runs through the pick point.
Arc	Its center becomes the new origin, and the positive X axis runs through the end of the arc that's visually nearest the pick point.
Line	The end visually nearest the pick point becomes the new origin, and the positive X axis usually runs through the other end of the line.
Point	Its location becomes the new origin, and AutoCAD determines the rest.
2D polyline	Its start point becomes the new origin, and the positive X axis runs through the next vertex.
Trace	Its start point becomes the new origin, and the positive X axis runs through its next endpoint.
Solid	Its first point becomes the new origin, and the positive X axis runs through its second point.
3D face	Its first point becomes the new origin, the positive X axis runs through the second point. The fourth point lies on the positive half of the X-Y plane.
Dimension	The middle point of the text becomes the new origin, and the positive X axis runs the same direction as the positive X axis that was in effect when the dimension was drawn.
Inserted Object	For an inserted shape, text, block, attribute tag or value, the insertion point becomes the new origin, and its rotation angle will be 0 in the new UCS.

Figure 30-12: The UCS View icon.

Choose View to adopt the current viewing direction as the direction of the negative Z axis (the origin remains unchanged). This option is handy when you want to plot a drawing from a particular viewpoint and still want to place text in the drawing so that it will appear straight on when plotted.

Figure 30-13: The UCS X Axis Rotate icon.

Choose X Axis Rotate, Y Axis Rotate or Z Axis Rotate to enter an angle (from the keyboard or by picking two points) by which to rotate the new coordinate system around the X (or Y or Z) axis. The origin will remain unchanged. The right-hand rule determines the direction of rotation.

NOTE: Whenever you create a new UCS, you can establish a plan view by using the VPOINT command and entering ***0,0,1****. Alternatively, you can use the PLAN command. Or you can activate the system variable UCSFOLLOW (see "UCSFOLLOW" later in this chapter), and AutoCAD will automatically establish the plan view each time you change to a new UCS.*

Figure 30-14: The UCS Previous icon.

Choose Previous to return to the previous coordinate system. AutoCAD remembers the 10 previous coordinate systems that you have used (named or unnamed).

Saved UCS Prompts

The remaining choices apply to the manipulation of saved, or named, UCSes. With the exception of Save, these options are handled better by the Named UCS dialog, described later in this chapter under "Named UCS." This option does not have an icon in the toolbar.

Choose List to get a listing of the names and orientations of all the saved coordinate systems. The World Coordinate System is listed first. The current coordinate system is also listed and called *NO NAME* unless you've given it a name. Remember that each coordinate system is listed according to the current coordinate system. If you change coordinate systems and then look at the same listing, the numbers will be different. The prompt reappears after the listing. Since W is always the default in the prompt, be careful not to press Enter to return to Command mode unless you intend to change to the WCS at the same time. Instead, use Esc to exit the listing and return to Command mode.

Figure 30-15: The UCS Save icon.

Choose Save to save the current coordinate system. Then enter a name (up to 31 characters). When you save a coordinate system, you do not save the current viewpoint.

Figure 30-16: The UCS Restore icon.

Choose Restore to enter the name of the coordinate system you want to restore. The viewpoint will remain the same unless the system variable UCSFOLLOW is active (see "UCSFOLLOW" later in this chapter).

Choose Delete to delete the name of a saved coordinate system. You can list several names separated by commas, or use wild cards.

NAMED UCS Provides functions to manage the use of Named User Coordinate Systems

COMMAND LINE: **ducs**

Figure 30-17: The Named UCS icon from the UCS toolbar.

To manage named UCS systems, click the Named UCS icon or choose Named UCS from the View pull-down menu. AutoCAD displays the UCS Control dialog shown in Figure 30-18.

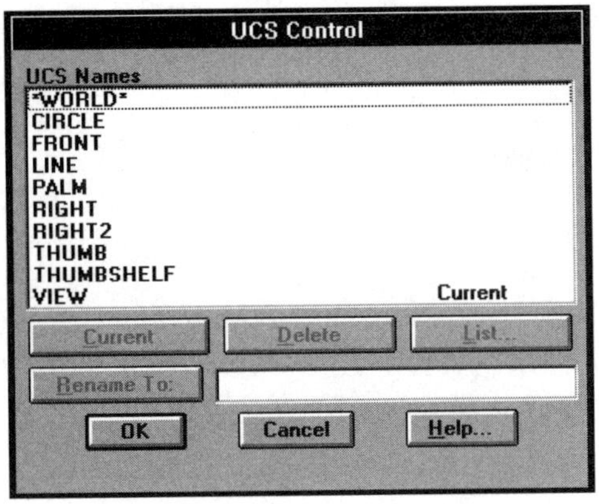

Figure 30-18: The UCS Control dialog.

This dialog displays the names of all saved UCSes in the UCS Names list box and provides four buttons to manipulate them. The reserved UCS names of *WORLD*, *NO NAME*, and *PREVIOUS* are also included in the list. The buttons are as follows:

Current makes the selected UCS the current UCS.

Delete deletes the selected UCS.

List displays the origin and axes information for the selected UCS in the UCS dialog (see Figure 30-19).

The selected name is displayed in the edit field to the right of the Rename To button. First type a new name in the edit field and then click on the button to change the name of the selected UCS.

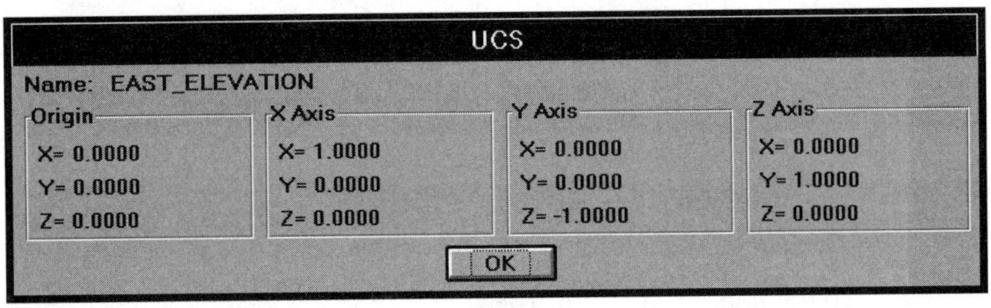

Figure 30-19: The UCS List.

PRESET UCS To quickly change the User Coordinate System to one of nine preset definitions

COMMAND LINE: **ddusp**

Figure 30-20: The Preset UCS icon.

This command can be accessed by clicking on the Preset UCS icon or by choosing Preset UCS... from the View pull-down menu. This displays the UCS Orientation dialog shown in Figure 30-21.

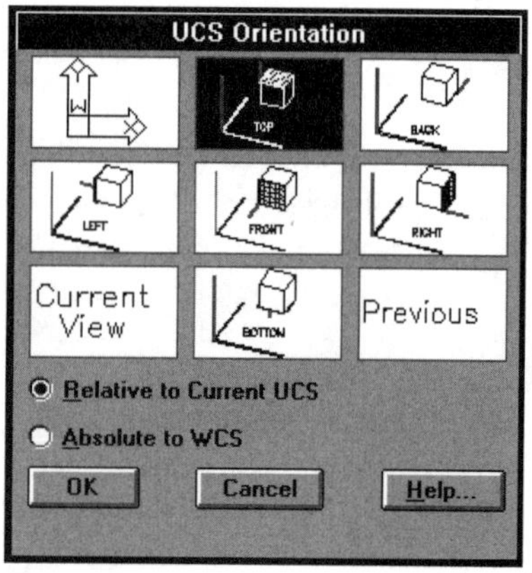

Figure 30-21: The UCS Orientation dialog.

The radio buttons at the bottom of the dialog determine whether the preset coordinate systems are based on the current coordinate system or the World Coordinate System.

Starting in the upper-left corner of the dialog, the presets are as follows:

World returns to the World Coordinate System. This choice ignores the setting of the World UCS versus Current UCS radio buttons.

Top sets the UCS to a top orthogonal view. If the Relative to Current UCS radio button is active, the Top view is the same as the current view.

Back sets the UCS to the back view.

Left sets the UCS to the left view.

Front sets the UCS to the front view.

Right sets the UCS to the right view.

Current View aligns the UCS with the current viewport (same as the View option under the Set UCS option of the View pull-down).

Bottom sets the UCS to the bottom view.

Previous returns to the previous UCS.

NOTE: If the Relative to Current UCS radio button is active, all these presets are calculated as if the current UCS is equal to the Top view. This can lead to some confusion. If you need a selection of standard orthogonal UCS settings, it is better to save them as named UCSes and then restore them with the NAMED UCS command.

UCSICON Controls display of the UCS icon

COMMAND LINE: **ucsicon**

The UCS icon is displayed in the drawing window and provides information about the current coordinate system (see Figure 30-22). The settings for the UCSICON command affect only the current viewport unless you use the A option explained below.

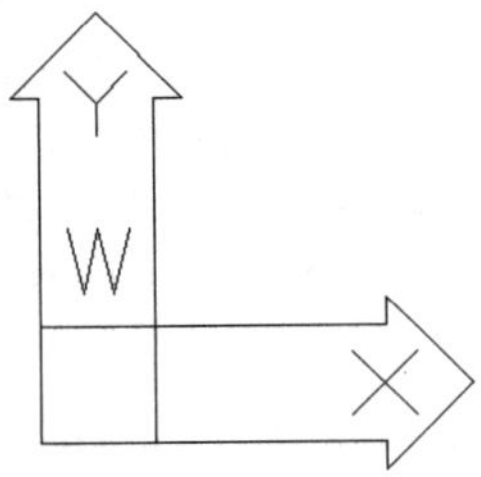

Figure 30-22: User Coordinate System reference icon, displayed in the drawing window.

If the current coordinate system is the WCS, a *W* appears in the Y-arm of the icon. If the icon is positioned at the origin of the current coordinate system, a plus appears in the icon. If the current viewpoint looks at the object from the underside (originates from a negative Z location), the box at the elbow of the icon will be missing.

Most of the options for the UCS icon are found in the cascade menu after you choose UCS from the Options pull-down menu (see Figure 30-23).

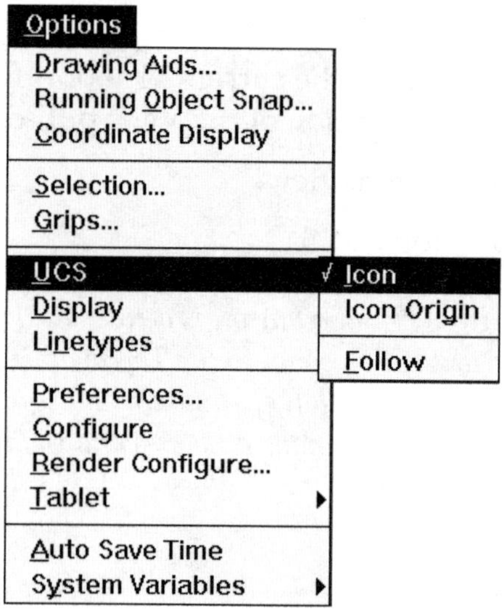

Figure 30-23: The UCS icon menu choices.

The Icon option toggles display of the UCS icon on and off in the current viewport.

Icon Origin toggles on and off the placement of the icon at the origin of the current coordinate system. If this would move the icon off or too near the edge of the viewport, it is displayed in the lower-left corner of the viewport.

Another option that is not on the menu is A for All. This option copies the current settings for the UCS icon to all other viewports. To use this option, first activate the viewport with the UCS icon settings that you want to use, then enter **ucsicon** at the command prompt. When prompted, type **a** and press Enter.

The UCS icon also appears in two other forms, shown in Figure 30-24. When your viewing direction is parallel to the X-Y construction plane of the current UCS, the icon appears as a broken pencil in a box. When this icon appears, change your viewing direction before trying to indicate locations with the pointer. When you're using perspective (see "DVIEW" in Chapter 35, "3D Viewing"), the icon appears as a cube.

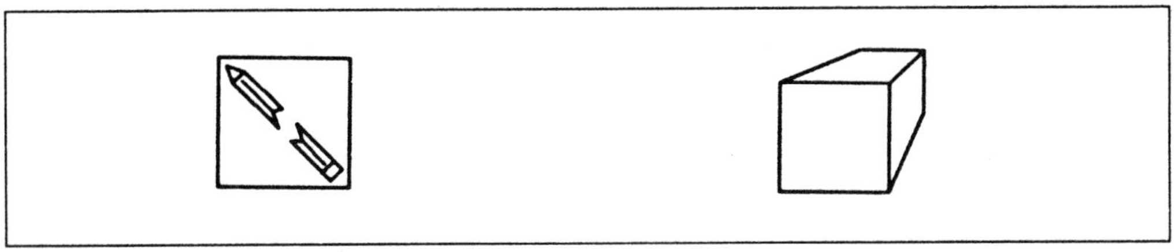

Figure 30-24: Alternate User Coordinate System icons.

The icon shown in Figure 30-25 indicates Paper Space. The "+" and "W" and box operate as described above.

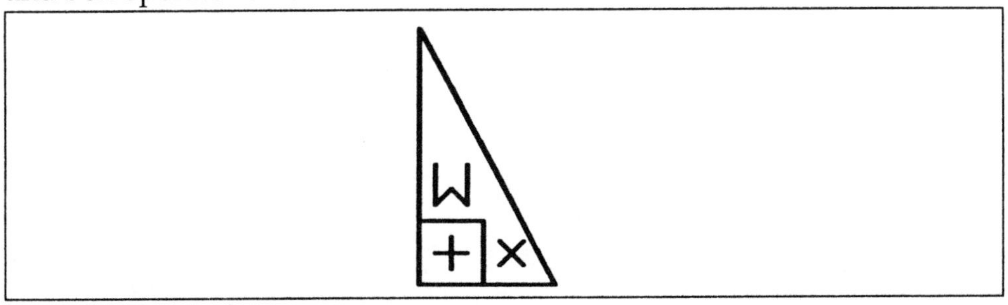

Figure 30-25: User Coordinate System icon for Paper Space.

UCSFOLLOW Enables or disables automatic display of the plan view each time you change coordinate systems

COMMAND LINE: **ucsfollow**

Choose UCS from the Options menu. Then choose Follow to toggle the on/off status of this option. A check next to this menu item indicates that AutoCAD will make plan view the initial viewpoint each time you select a different coordinate system. You can change to any other viewpoint thereafter as you wish. This option is meaningless in Paper Space.

Moving on

Now that you understand how to manipulate User Coordinate Systems, we'll look at the use of Model Space and Paper Space in Release 13.

CHAPTER 31

Model Space & Paper Space

AutoCAD maintains two distinct spaces—Model Space and Paper Space. You create your drawing in real world units and at true full-size scale, but you switch to Paper Space when ready to plot. This chapter explains how to use Model Space, Paper Space and related commands before sending a drawing to the plotter.

Model Space

You construct your 2D drawing or 3D model in Model Space. In the ACAD.DWG prototype drawing supplied with AutoCAD, Model Space is the default. To distinguish Model Space, AutoCAD displays the Model Space icon in the lower-left corner of your screen.

You have two options for creating viewports. You can create them from Model Space or you can create them from Paper Space.

As you create drawing geometry in Model Space, you may create viewports through the VPORTS command. Or choose the Tiled Vports dialog from the View pull-down menu and choose a Tiled set of viewports from the icon menu list, shown in Figure 31-2. Just double-click on the Tiled Vport icon of your choice.

To configure your viewports, use the VPOINT command. Then save the entire tiled configuration by choosing Save. The saved configuration may then be used in Paper Space through the MVIEW command, described below.

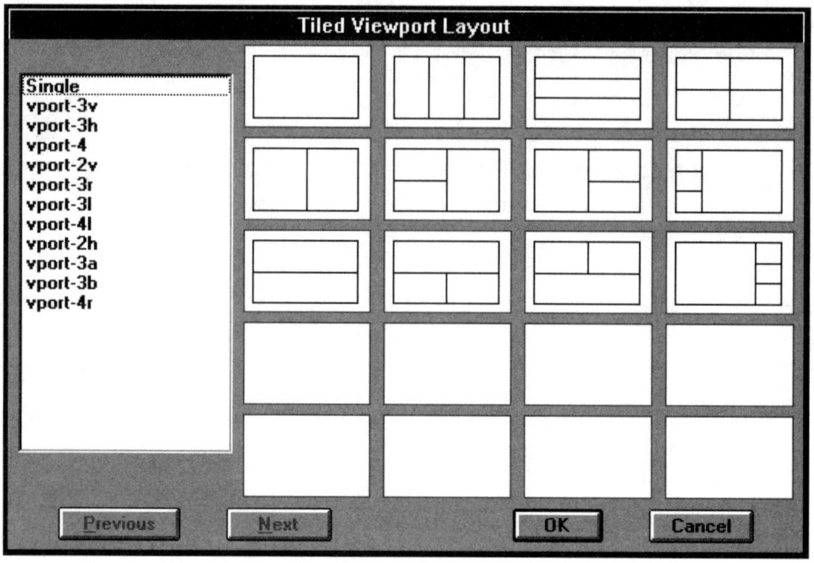

Figure 31-1: The Tiled Vports dialog.

Paper Space

Paper Space allows you to construct viewports and plot drawings. In Paper Space you organize multiple views of your 3D model and add annotations for plotting. Paper Space is primarily two-dimensional, and its limits should be set to the dimensions of the border on the sheet on which it will be plotted. (Remember to leave a margin for the pinch wheels if you are using a pen plotter.)

To denote Paper Space, AutoCAD displays the Paper Space icon in the lower-left corner of the screen. You'll also see the PAPER label in the status bar.

Switching to Paper Space

To switch to Paper Space, you may either (1) choose Paper Space from the View pull-down menu or (2) enter **tilemode** and then **0** (zero) at the command prompt. (For more details on the TILEMODE command, see the next section.)

When you first switch to Paper Space, no viewports are visible. Using the MVIEW command, you must either create the viewports in Paper Space or insert viewports that you created in Model Space. When you switch to your drawing geometry in Model Space and then return to Paper Space, your viewports will be displayed in the same placement and size as you left them.

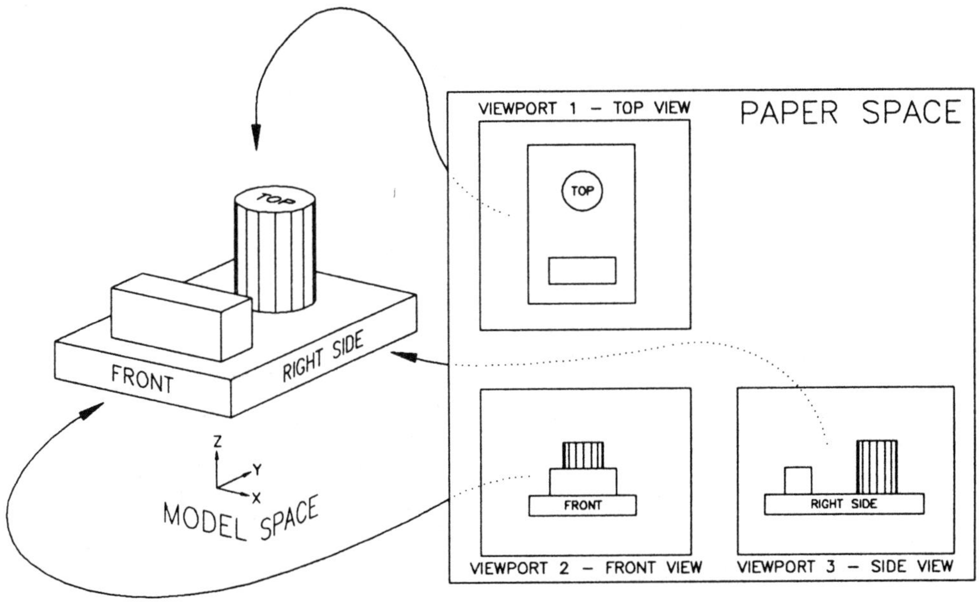

Figure 31-3: Paper Space, with three viewports opened into Model Space.

TILEMODE Switches between Paper Space & Model Space

COMMAND LINE: **tilemode**

TILEMODE is simply an internal switch that flips a user from Model Space to Paper Space and vice-versa. It's set to either 0 (Paper Space off) or 1 (Paper Space on). Let's try it.

1. First, notice the check mark next to Tiled Model Space in the View pull-down menu. Notice also that the selections for Floating Model Space, Paper Space and Floating Viewports are grayed out. Finally, look at your status bar at the bottom of the screen to see the MODEL label toggled on.

2. At the command prompt, type **tilemode**, and enter **0**. You'll get this prompt: Entering Paper space. Use MVIEW to insert Model Space viewports. Take another look at your status bar. It now displays the PAPER

label. Pull down the View menu and notice that Tiled Model Space is now grayed out, and the check mark is gone. Finally, look at the icon in the lower-left screen corner; you'll see it's changed to a triangle.

That's how simple it is to switch to Paper Space. You may now use MVIEW, described below, to create viewports or use viewports that you created in Model Space. To return to Model Space, reset tilemode to 1, and the last viewport configuration (tiled) is displayed.

NOTE: *TILEMODE is saved with your drawing. This means that each time you open a drawing into the drawing editor you'll be in the same space as when you last ended the drawing.*

Model Space vs. Paper Space

Before we explore MVIEW and related commands, let's quickly compare the characteristics of Model Space and Paper Space.

Model Space: Tilemode is set to 1.
Paper Space: Tilemode is set to 0.

Model Space: Viewports are tiled; that is, they do not overlap and are always directly adjacent to each other.
Paper Space: Viewports are not tiled; that is, you can overlap, separate or arrange them any way you like.

Model Space: You are in Model Space only. The MVIEW command automatically switches to Paper Space to create a viewport, then switches back to Model Space.
Paper Space: You can switch between Model Space and Paper Space with the MSPACE and PSPACE commands.

Model Space: Your construction of 3D models and 2D drawings is done here, at full scale, with dimensions.
Paper Space: Your drawing's border, title block, parts list, revision history and similar annotations reside in Paper Space.

Model Space: The MSPACE, PSPACE and VPLAYER commands are disabled.
Paper Space: The MSPACE, PSPACE and VPLAYER commands are enabled. The VPORTS command is disabled, as are VPOINT, DVIEW and PLAN.

Model Space: Only one viewport is current. The cursor crosshairs appear only in the current viewport (although moving the cursor-arrow to a different viewport allows you to pick that viewport and make it current).

Paper Space: Viewports can be turned on and off with the MVIEW command. By default, they're on when first created. Turning some viewports off will speed up regeneration time. The cursor crosshairs extend across the entire graphics screen, independent of viewports.

Model Space: Zooming and panning occur only within the current viewport.

Paper Space: You can zoom and pan around your Paper Space, resulting in some viewports being partially or fully off-screen.

Model Space: The number of viewports is limited by your operating system. You can plot only the current viewport.

Paper Space: As far as plotting is concerned, there's no limit to the number of viewports you can have in Paper Space. But the number of viewports that can be active onscreen is limited by the system variable MAXACTVP. To set the number, enter **maxactvp** at the command line and set its value.

More Notes on Paper Space . . .

Viewports are created with the MVIEW command.

Each viewport contains a view of your object in Model Space. The viewpoint and magnification can be different in each viewport.

Viewports behave like other objects. They can be moved, scaled, erased, stretched and placed on layers.

Each viewport resides on the layer on which it was created. The viewport border adopts its color from its layer, but the border linetype is always continuous. Different layers can be frozen and thawed from viewport to viewport with the VPLAYER command.

You can PLOT all your viewports at once.

MVIEW Creates viewports in Paper Space

COMMAND LINE: **mview**

Select Floating Viewports from the View pull-down menu (or enter **mview** at the command prompt.) When prompted, pick the first point and opposite corner of the viewport. This new viewport will be the current viewport.

Enter **on** and then select the borders of the viewports you want turned on. To change the number of viewports that can be turned on at once, enter **maxactvp** at the command line and set its value to the number of viewports you want to activate.

Enter **off** and then select the borders of viewports you want turned off.

Enter **h** (for hideplot) to designate a viewport for hidden line removal during plotting. When prompted, enter **on** to turn hideplot on or **off** to turn it off. Then select the viewports you want turned on or off. This doesn't affect the viewport's appearance on the screen. To see hidden line removal on screen, use the HIDE command.

Enter **f** (for fit) to create a new viewport that fits in the entire graphics area.

Enter **2, 3** or **4** to create that number of viewports in one operation. You are prompted to choose either (1) the Fit option, which makes new viewports fit the entire graphics screen, or (2) the First point option, in which a window determines the boundaries of the new set of viewports. Then you're prompted for the number of viewports. If you enter

2, they can be divided horizontally or vertically

3, you may choose to have three equal-size viewports divided vertically or horizontally, or one large and two small viewports with the large viewport located above, below, to the left or to the right of the others.

4, four equal-size viewports are created.

Enter **r** (for restore) to use a viewport configuration previously saved in Model Space. Then enter its name. Pick the opposite corners of the window it will fit in, or enter **f** (for fit) to fill the entire graphic area with the viewport configuration.

MSPACE Switches to a Model Space viewport while in a Paper Space view

COMMAND LINE: **ms**

While you are in Paper Space, enter **ms** to switch to Model Space.

PSPACE Switches back to Paper Space from a Model Space viewport

COMMAND LINE: **ps**

While you're in Model Space, enter **ps** at the command line to switch to Paper Space.

VPLAYER Provides independent layer control

COMMAND LINE: **vplayer**

While you're in Paper Space, you can control the status of layers in a viewport independent of other viewports. The layers you want to control must already be thawed and on globally. If they're not, use the LAYER command to thaw them or turn them on.

Choose Viewport Layer Control from the Data pull-down menu.

When prompted,

> Enter **?** to list layer status in one viewport, and then select the viewport.
>
> Enter **f** to freeze one or more layers. Then enter the name(s) of the layers to freeze. At the prompt, choose All (all viewports), Select (then pick one or more viewports) or Current (for the current viewport).
>
> Enter **t** to thaw one or more layers. Then enter the name(s) of the layers to thaw. At the prompt, choose All (all viewports), Select (then pick one or more viewports) or Current (for the current viewport).
>
> Enter **r** to reset the default status of layers. Then enter the name(s) of the layers to reset. At the prompt, choose All (all viewports), Select (then pick one or more viewports) or Current (for the current viewport). See the V option below for changing defaults.

> Enter **n** (for newfrz) to create new, frozen layers in all viewports. Then enter the name(s) of the new layers. Of course, you'll next want to thaw the layer in at least one viewport so you can use it. To do so, use VPLAYER Thaw.
>
> Enter **v** (for vpvisdflt) to establish a layer's default status in subsequently created viewports. Then enter the layer name(s). Then enter **t** to set the indicated layer(s) default at thawed, or **f** to set the default to frozen.

Each time you select one of the above options, the main prompt reappears. Press Enter to return to the command prompt.

VPOINT Lets you set a 3D view within the drawing

COMMAND LINE: **vpoint**

The VPOINT command lets you set up a drawing from a 0,0,0 origin and any point specified in space. You set up your viewports with this command, which can be used only in Model Space.

At the command line, enter **vpoint**. At the Rotate/<view point> prompt, enter one of the following:

> Press Enter to use a globe compass and axis tripod to pick and rotate your drawing.
>
> Enter **r** for rotate. At the prompt for an angle, specify an angle to set up the X axis. The prompt is repeated; this time, specify an angle for the up or down view of the X-Y axis.

Moving on

Every AutoCAD user wants to draw in 3D, and the next chapter helps you get started. If you are a true 3D fanatic, you may want to look at *The AutoCAD 3D Companion* (Ventana Press). It goes into much more detail.

CHAPTER 32

3D Objects

This chapter covers a few drawing commands AutoCAD uses to generate three-dimensional objects, as well as display commands needed to view the objects from various angles and perspectives.

3D Drawing

Now let's try a sample 3D drawing. We'll also look at point filters (which are very handy in 3D drawing) and two simple 3D commands, ELEV and 3DFACE.

NOTE: *Certain 3D shapes can be constructed using built-in AutoLISP commands. These commands are available from the Surfaces toolbar.*

3D drawing makes use of the X, Y and Z axes according to the right-hand rule (see Chapter 30, "Coordinate Systems"). On the screen, when positive X extends to the right and when positive Y extends up, positive Z extends toward you.

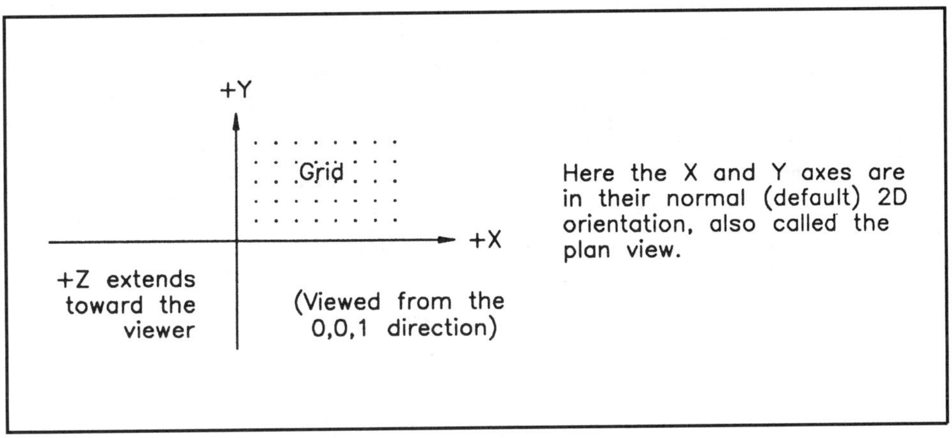

Figure 32-1: The X and Y axes in their default 2D orientation.

If a normal 2D drawing were placed flat on a table with positive X to the right of the table and positive Y to the far side, positive Z would extend above the table. When such a drawing is viewed from a +X, Y, +Z quadrant, it appears as in the following illustrations.

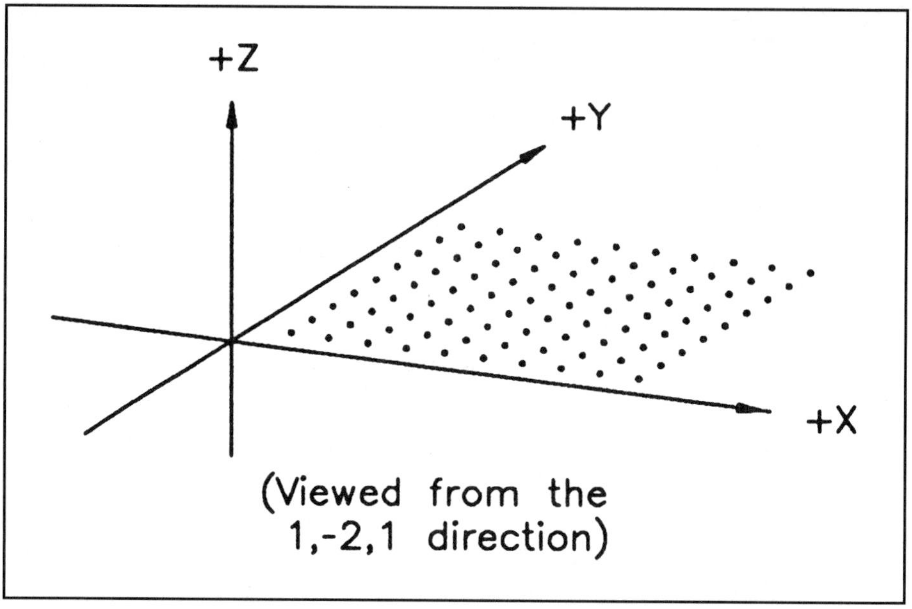

Figure 32-2: Drawing from VPOINT 1,-2,1 showing X, Y and Z axes.

A new drawing normally begins on the X-Y construction plane (at an elevation of 0) in the current UCS, unless your prototype drawing is set up differently. You view the drawing straight on from a positive Z direction. When you use regular 2D drawing commands such as CIRCLE, ARC, TRACE, SOLID and PLINE, all drawing is on an X-Y plane at a certain Z elevation in the current UCS (Z locations will all be the same). To give these objects depth in the Z direction, you must use the ELEV or CHANGE command to assign a thickness that's figured from the elevation, as illustrated in Figure 32-3.

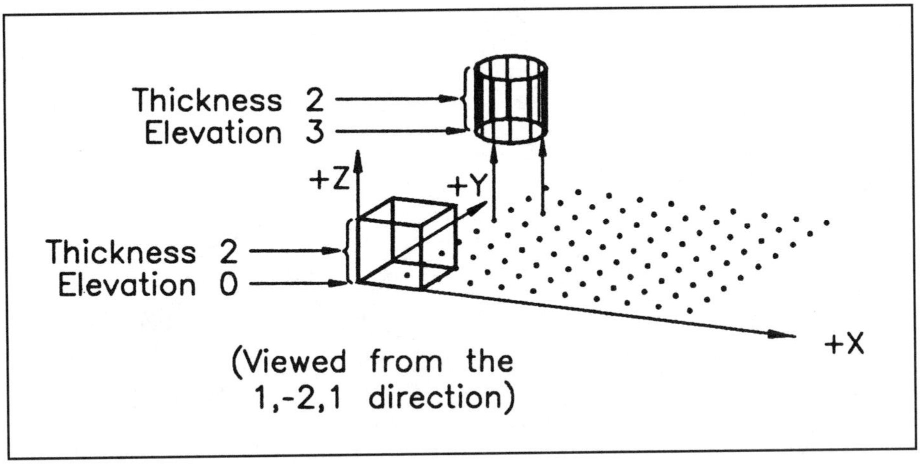

Figure 32-3: Drawing from VPOINT 1,-2,1 showing an object's thickness and elevation.

Example

Here are the steps for drawing the above picture:

1. First use ELEV (see "ELEV" below) to set the elevation at 0 and the thickness at 2, then draw a 2-unit square with its lower-left corner at 0,0.

2. Use ELEV to set the elevation at 3. Keep the thickness at 2. Then draw a 2-unit-diameter circle centered at 1,7.

3. Use VPOINT to set the viewpoint at 1,-2,1. The grid will appear at the current elevation of 3. To move the grid back to its original location so the display looks like the picture above, use ELEV to set the elevation back to 0.

NOTE: *These extruded 2D objects give a visual appearance of surfaces, but they are different from the true surfaces created with, for example, the 3DFACE command.*

A number of 3D commands—including LINE, 3DFACE, 3DPOLY and the meshes—also accept X,Y,Z coordinates. A command that expects a 3D point (three coordinates) will accept just the X and Y coordinates from the keyboard or pointer and adopt the current elevation as the Z coordinate.

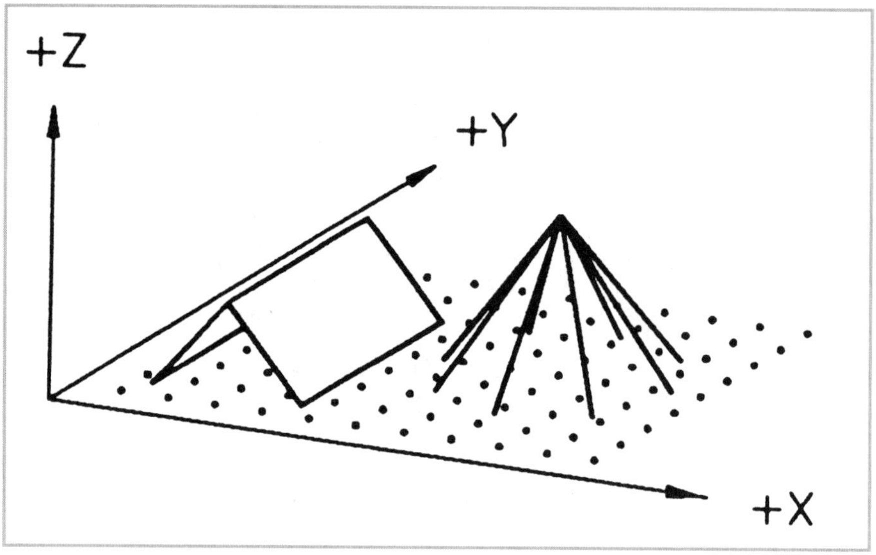

Figure 32-4: Drawing from VPOINT 1,-2,1 showing 3DPOLY and 3DFACE commands with X, Y and Z coordinates.

When you use one of these 3D drawing commands, all drawing is done in relation to the current X-Y construction plane; but various parts of a single object can have Z locations that differ from one another. As illustrated below, these commands can produce lines/edges/surfaces that are slanted with respect to the X-Y construction plane. (They intersect an X-Y plane instead of lying completely within it.)

Using Point Filters

Partial coordinates can be extracted from various kinds of 3D locations. For example, you can extract one or two coordinates from the endpoint or midpoint of a line or 3D polygon, the corner of a 3D face or the midpoint of the edge of a 3D face. To do so, enter **.x, .y, .z, .xy, .xz** or **.yz** when prompted for a point. (To activate the cursor menu filters, hold down the Shift key and click your right mouse button.)

For example, suppose you have a line that ends at 4,5,8. To begin another line at the same Y and Z coordinates, enter **.yz** when prompted for the From point of the new line. AutoCAD responds with "of." Then osnap to the end of the line. AutoCAD next prompts you for the missing X coordinate.

Point filters can also be used with 2D objects to extract one of the two needed coordinates.

ELEV Sets Z elevation & thickness for subsequent objects

COMMAND LINE: **elev**

When prompted, enter the new elevation and new extrusion thickness. The elevation can be positive, negative or 0. The thickness can also be positive, negative or 0.

You can osnap to the extruded portion of an object if (1) your viewpoint is something other than 0,0,1 (plan view) in the current UCS and (2) your current command will accept a Z coordinate.

To change the elevation or thickness of an existing object, use the CHANGE command described later in this chapter.

NOTE: *To check the current elevation and thickness, use the STATUS command.*

AutoCAD maintains separate elevation and thickness settings for Model Space and Paper Space. You'll probably want to keep elevation at 0 and control the Z-height of the X-Y construction plane with the UCS command.

3DFACE Creates a surface bounded by three or four edges

COMMAND LINE: **3dface**

From the menu bar, pull down the Draw menu (if this option is not displayed, enter **menu** at the command line, and then select Acadfull). Then choose Surfaces.

3DFACE works much like SOLID, except that the third and fourth points should continue around the perimeter. The third and fourth corner points should face opposite directions from the first and second corner points.

To create a 3D face that has only three edges instead of four, press Enter when prompted for the fourth corner.

Only the edges of 3D faces are displayed; 3D faces never have thickness. However, they will hide other objects. To make an edge invisible, enter **i** before entering the coordinates of the corner preceding the edge (and before entering osnap modes or point filters), as illustrated below. This lets you combine several 3D faces into complex shapes with only the outer edges visible. You can accomplish the same thing with the PFACE command described in Chapter 33, "3D Meshes."

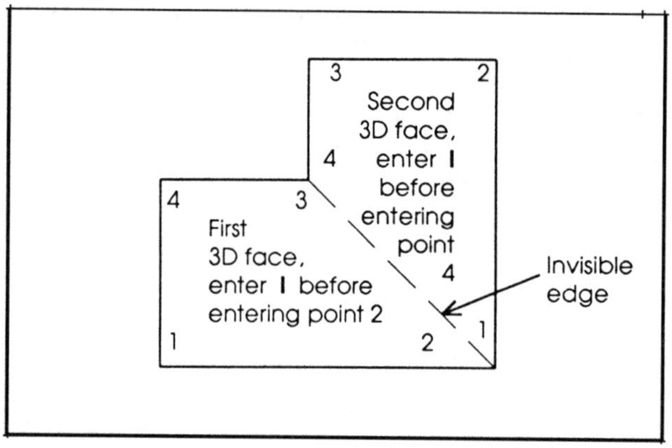

Figure 32-5: When creating a 3D face with an invisible edge, enter **i** before you enter the coordinates.

If you create a 3D face with all edges invisible, you won't be able to list or edit it while the edges remain invisible. However, you can display hidden edges by entering **splframe** at the command line, setting its value to 1, and then regenerating the screen display (REGEN). Also, an AutoLISP program called EDGE (found in the \ACADR13\....\SAMPLE directory, under your AutoCAD program files) lets you turn selected visible edges into invisible ones and vice versa. The program also lets you highlight invisible edges so they can be selected.

Regarding relative coordinates, the OSNAP command, the construction of 3D and 2D elements, and editing, the same limitations that apply to LINE apply to 3DFACE.

Moving on

In Chapter 33, we'll pick up where we've just left off by exploring 3D meshes. A mesh is a network of 3D surface elements. Like a net, 3D meshes can curve in any direction in space. AutoCAD uses meshes to approximate different kinds of 3D surface shapes.

For hands-on exercises, see Chapter 45.

CHAPTER 33

3D Meshes

A *mesh* is a network of 3D surface elements. Like a net, it can curve in any direction in space. AutoCAD uses meshes to approximate different kinds of 3D surface shapes, as illustrated on the next several pages. Each of a mesh's surface elements has four sides and four vertices, or corners. Each also has up to four edges in common with adjoining surface elements. You can imagine a mesh as a rectangular matrix of surface elements with columns (running in the M direction) and rows (running in the N direction). Even though each element acts somewhat like a small 3D face, the entire mesh is one object. Meshes never have thickness.

This chapter describes the five commands AutoCAD uses to create meshes. They can be executed from the Surfaces toolbar.

Four of the commands (TABSURF, RULESURF, REVSURF and EDGESURF) create a large number of surface elements automatically when you select certain objects that define the mesh. The fifth command (3DMESH) lets you define an irregular mesh by entering the location of every vertex, one by one. This command is designed mainly for use in AutoLISP programming.

The chapter also discusses the system variables SURFTAB1 and SURFTAB2, which determine the density or resolution of meshes (the number of surface elements in each direction).

Mesh Characteristics

A mesh is said to be open or closed in the M and/or N direction. It's open in a given direction if the last surface elements in that direction are separate from the first ones; it's closed if the last surface elements are joined to the first.

A mesh can be edited as a unit with the usual editing commands. Also, a mesh is listed as a polyline; and you can use the PEDIT command to move individual vertices and fit a smooth surface to the mesh.

When you explode a mesh, the elements become individual 3D faces.

When you use the HIDE command, the surface elements of the mesh hide other objects and other mesh surfaces behind them.

A variety of standard shapes constructed from meshes are available in the Draw-3D Construction icon menu.

3DMESH Creates a mesh, one vertex at a time

COMMAND LINE: **3dmesh**

Figure 33-1: The 3D mesh icon on the Surfaces toolbar.

Locate the command on the surfaces toolbar or under the Draw pull-down menu (if this menu is not available, enter **menu** and select Acadfull). When prompted, enter the number of vertices in the M direction, then the number in the N direction. The number in either direction can range from 2 through 256.

AutoCAD then prompts for the X-Y-Z coordinates of each vertex. The vertices are identified by their M and N positions, so you're prompted for vertex 0,0, then vertex 0,1, and so on. You're asked for all the vertices in the N direction before proceeding in the M direction.

As with regular points, you can enter either 2D points or 3D points (the Z coordinate is optional). If the vertices are entered in the order illustrated below, the M and N directions are as shown. After you've located all the vertices, AutoCAD draws the mesh. 3DMESH always produces an open mesh, but you can close it, in one or both directions, with the PEDIT command.

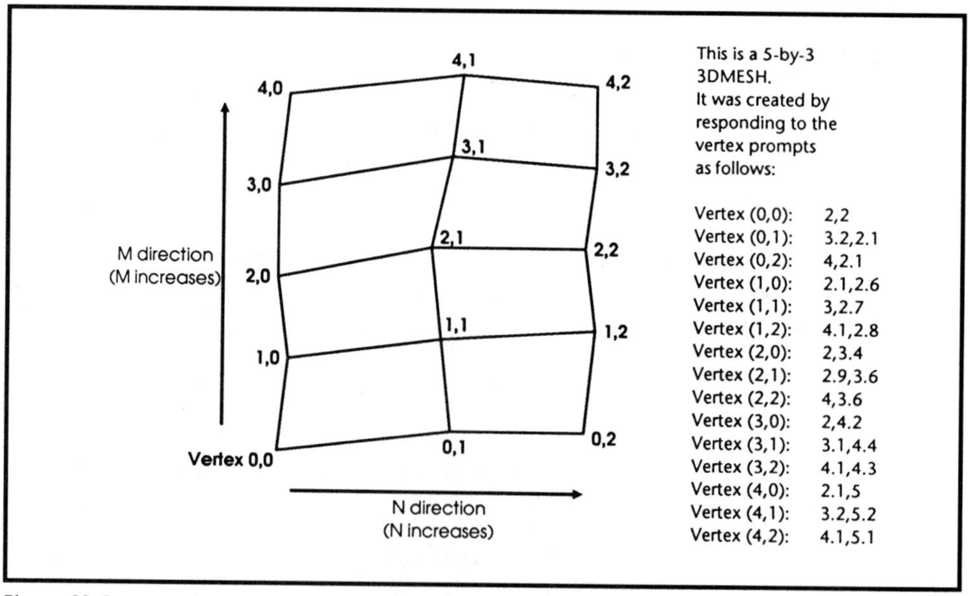

Figure 33-2: 3DMESH allows you to create mesh vertices.

When the M and N directions are oriented as illustrated above, and you're using the PEDIT command to edit vertices, the Left/Right/Up/Down portion of the prompt works correctly and the vertex marker moves in the indicated direction.

When the M and N directions are oriented differently, you can still move from vertex to vertex successfully with Left/Right/Up/Down if you remember that Up always moves in the direction of increasing M, and Right always moves in the direction of increasing N.

The above mesh isn't a typical 3D mesh, because it's flat (all the Z coordinates are 0 by default). It's intended only to illustrate the relationship between the order of the vertices (as they appear in the prompts of the 3DMESH command), the M and N directions, and the Left/Right/Up/Down directions in the PEDIT command. A more typical mesh, with vertices at varying Z locations, is shown below from a viewpoint of 1,-2,1.

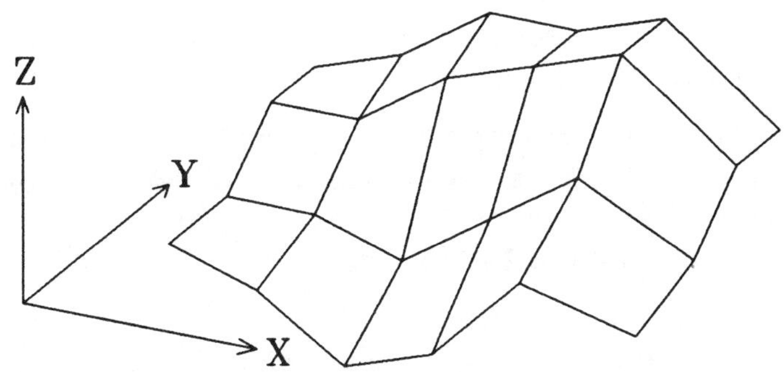

Figure 33-3: 3DMESH is used with X, Y and Z values.

PFACE Creates a polyface mesh

COMMAND LINE: **pface**

The PFACE command produces a polyface mesh vertex by vertex.

In general, polyface meshes, like 3D meshes, are best applied to irregular surfaces. When you need to mesh a regular surface, use TABSURF, RULESURF, REVSURF or EDGESURF.

Like the 3DMESH command, PFACE produces the mesh one vertex at a time. This means that very irregular surface shapes can be represented by both a 3D mesh and a polyface mesh. Creating a very complex mesh vertex by vertex would be a tedious operation, which is why both commands are intended primarily for use by AutoLISP or other programs.

However, the polyface mesh differs from a 3D mesh in some important ways. First, each element in a 3D mesh is made up of either three or four vertices and thus three or four edges. In contrast, a polyface mesh can have many vertices and thus many edges assigned to one face. Second, a 3D mesh cannot have invisible edges without being exploded into individual 3D faces (whose edges are then made invisible with the EDGE AutoLISP program). In contrast, the polyface mesh can be assigned invisible edges. Third, while a 3D mesh can be edited with the PEDIT command, a polyface mesh cannot. A polyface mesh can be moved, scaled, and so on, as a unit, but cannot be edited internally.

When a polyface mesh is exploded, it breaks down into a number of 3D faces whose "internal" edges are invisible.

The procedure for creating a polyface is divided into two parts. First, all the vertices are located, then each face is defined by assigning as many vertices as are needed to that face.

First, you're prompted for vertex 1, then vertex 2, and so on. The vertices can be located from the keyboard or with the pointer with possible osnap modes. Be sure to make note of the vertex numbers corresponding to each location. When you are finished locating vertices, press Enter.

Next you're prompted for the vertices that will be assigned to face 1. Enter these by vertex number. When you have assigned all the vertices belonging to face 1, press Enter. Then you're prompted for the vertices that will be assigned to face 2, and so on. When you're done creating faces, press Enter when prompted for the first vertex of the next face.

To make an edge invisible, place a minus sign in front of the vertex number as you assign it to a face. The edge between that vertex and the next vertex will be invisible. If you place a minus sign in front of the last vertex assigned to a face, the edge between the last and the first vertex will be invisible.

Although the overall polyface mesh is created on the current layer and the current color, you can assign each face a layer or color independent of the current layer and color. To do so, enter **layer** or **color** when prompted for the first vertex of any face. Then enter the desired layer or color when prompted. You're next asked again for the first and subsequent vertices for that face. Press Enter as indicated below.

Figure 33-4 shows a simple polyface, viewed from -1,-2,1, and hidden with the HIDE command.

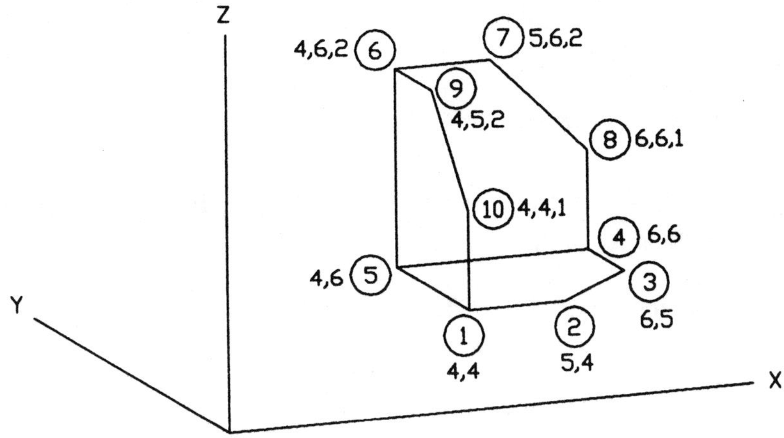

Figure 33-4: PFACE can be used with X, Y and Z values.

Enter **pface**, then respond to the prompts as follows:

```
Vertex 1: 4,4
Vertex 2: 5,4
Vertex 3: 6,5
Vertex 4: 6,6
Vertex 5: 4,6
Vertex 6: 4,6,2
Vertex 7: 5,6,2
Vertex 8: 6,6,1
Vertex 9: 4,5,2
Vertex 10: 4,4,1
Vertex 11: :(Press Enter)
Face 1, vertex 1: 1
Face 1, vertex 2: 2
Face 1, vertex 3: 3
Face 1, vertex 4: 4
Face 1, vertex 5: 5
Face 1, vertex 6 (Press Enter)
Face 2, vertex 1: 4
Face 2, vertex 2: 5
Face 2, vertex 3: 6
Face 2, vertex 4: 7
Face 2, vertex 5: 8
Face 2, vertex 6:(Press Enter)
```

```
Face 3, vertex 1: 1
Face 3, vertex 2: 5
Face 3, vertex 3: 6
Face 3, vertex 4: 9
Face 3, vertex 5: 10
Face 3, vertex 6: (Press Enter)
Face 4, vertex 1:(Press Enter)
```

TABSURF Creates a tabulated surface mesh from a path curve & a direction vector

COMMAND LINE: **tabsurf**

Figure 33-5: The Tabsurf icon on the Surfaces toolbar.

Choose the Tabsurf icon or select Tabulated Surface from the Draw pull-down menu. (If this menu is not available from the menu bar, enter **menu** at the command line and select Acadfull to display it.) When prompted, select the path curve and then the direction vector. The path curve, which can be a line, circle, arc or polyline, actually traces out the surface and is traditionally known as the *generatrix*. The direction vector determines the direction and distance the path curve will move as it traces out the surface; it is traditionally known as the *directrix*.

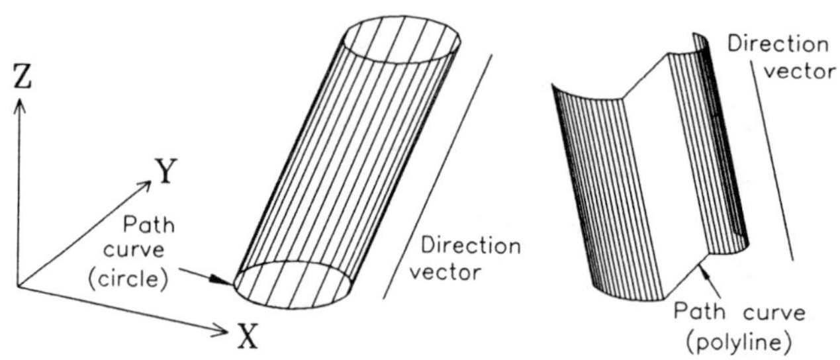

Figure 33-6: TABSURF lets you create a profile surface mesh by using a direction vector.

Although the direction vector can be either a line or an open polyline, only its endpoints are important. The beginnings of both the path curve and the direction vector are nearest the points at which they are selected, except for a circle (whose beginning is at its zero angle) or a closed polyline (whose beginning is at its first endpoint). Thus, the 0,0 vertex is located at the corner of the mesh that corresponds to the beginning of the path curve and the beginning of the direction vector.

In a tabulated surface mesh, M is always 2 and increases in the direction of the direction vector.

N increases in the direction of the path curve and is determined by system variable SURFTAB1. If SURFTAB1 is set at 12 and the path curve is a line, arc, circle or spline-fit polyline, there are 12 equally spaced vertices in the N direction. If SURFTAB1 is set at 12 and the path curve is a 2D polyline with both line segments and arc segments, vertices occur at the ends of each line segment; and each arc segment is divided into 12 equally spaced vertices.

RULESURF Creates a ruled surface mesh between two objects

COMMAND LINE: **rulesurf**

Figure 33-7: The Rulesurf icon on the Surfaces toolbar.

Choose the Ruled Surface icon or select Ruled Surface from the Draw pull-down menu. (If this menu is not available from the menu bar, enter **menu** at the command line and select Acadfull to display it.)

When prompted, select the two objects that will define the mesh. The objects can be points, lines, circles, arcs or polylines. If one of the objects (a circle or a closed polyline) is closed, then the other object must also be closed. A point can be used with either an open or closed object, but not with another point.

The 0,0 vertex is located at the beginning of the object you select first. The M direction increases from the first object to the second, and therefore is always 2. The N direction increases from the beginning to the end of the first object if it's an open object; it is determined by system variable SURFTAB1.

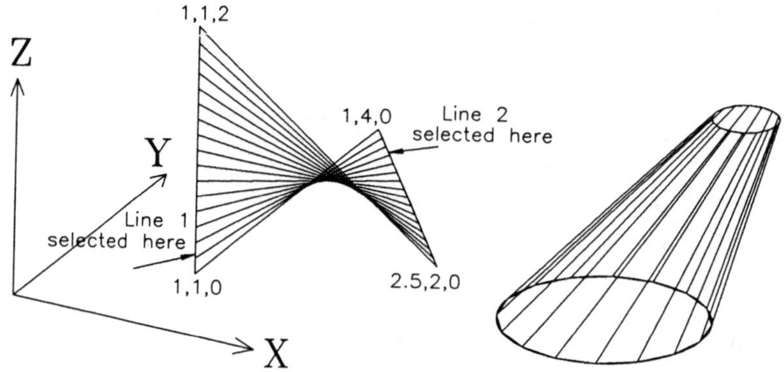

Figure 33-8: RULESURF lets you create a ruled surface mesh between surface objects.

For circles, the N direction starts at the circle's zero-angle point. If a ruled surface is created between two circles, the edge lines joining vertices will usually not cross each other as long as the construction plane for one circle is parallel to the construction plane for the other. However, if the second circle is drawn on a construction plane that is tilted or rotated in relation to the first construction plane, the edge lines may cross each other or give an hourglass effect.

For closed polylines, the N direction starts at the polyline's last vertex. Suppose your two objects are a circle and a polyline and the ruled surface crosses over itself. To correct this, you may need to reconstruct the polyline in reverse order, or use two polyarcs in place of the circle, or reconstruct the circle in the same location but on a flipped construction plane.

REVSURF Creates a surface-of-revolution mesh from a path curve & an axis of revolution

COMMAND LINE: **REVSURF**

Choose the Revolved Surface icon, or select Revolved Surface from the Draw pull-down menu. (If this menu is not available from the menu bar, enter **menu** at the command line and select Acadfull to display it.)

Figure 33-9: The Revolved Surface icon on the Surfaces toolbar.

When prompted, select the path curve (generatrix), and then the axis of revolution; enter the start angle, then the included angle. The direction of the axis of revolution runs from the end nearest its pick point to the opposite end. In turn, this direction and the right-hand rule determine the direction of rotation for the two angles, as illustrated below.

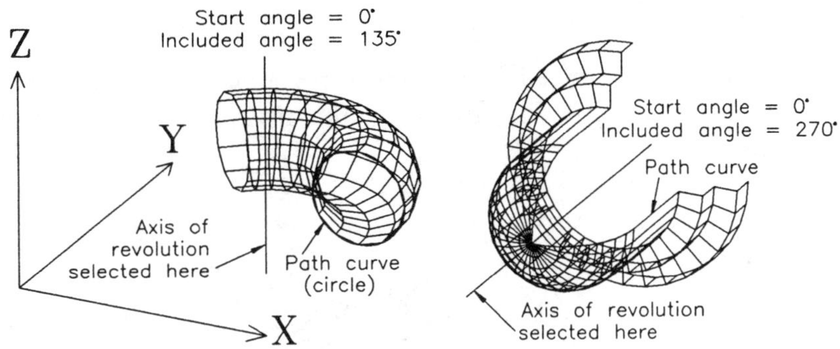

Figure 33-10: REVSURF lets you create a surface mesh from a path curve and axis point for the REVolution.

The path curve can be a line, circle, arc or polyline. The axis of revolution can be a line or an open polyline (in which case only the endpoints are important). The path curve doesn't need to lie in the same plane as the axis of revolution. The M direction revolves around the axis of revolution, and the number of vertices is determined by system variable SURFTAB1. The N direction runs along the path curve, and the number of vertices is determined by system variable SURFTAB2 in a manner similar to the TABSURF command.

EDGESURF Creates a Coons surface mesh with four connected objects as defining edges

COMMAND LINE: **edgesurf**

Figure 33-11: The Edge Surface icon from the Surfaces toolbar.

Choose the Edge Surface icon, or choose Edge Surface from the Draw pull-down. (If this menu is not available from the menu bar, enter **menu** at the command line and select Acadfull to display it.) When prompted, select the objects that will be the four defining edges. These objects can be any combination of lines, arcs or open polylines. The endpoint of each object must coincide with the start point of the next object, forming a complete circuit. The first edge you select will determine the M direction, running from the endpoint nearest the pick point to the opposite end.

The variable SURFTAB1 determines the number of vertices in the M direction, while SURFTAB2 determines the number in the N direction.

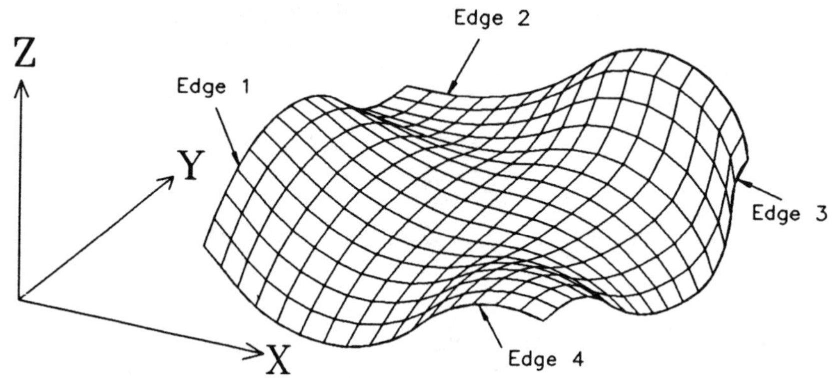

Figure 33-12: EDGESURF lets you create a Coons surface mesh from four connected objects. You must set SURFTAB 1 & 2.

System Variables

The system variables SURFTAB1 and SURFTAB2 control the number of surface elements in the M and N directions of a mesh.

In the TABSURF and RULESURF commands, SURFTAB1 determines the number of surface elements in the N direction. (M is always 2 for these types of meshes.)

In the REVSURF and EDGESURF commands, SURFTAB1 determines the number of surface elements in the M direction, while SURFTAB2 determines the number in the N direction. Enter SURFTAB1 and SURFTAB2 at the command line.

When a mesh is closed in a given direction, the number of surface elements and the number of vertices in that direction are equal. When a mesh is open in a given direction, the number of vertices is one more than the number of surface elements. The smallest possible value for either variable is 2.

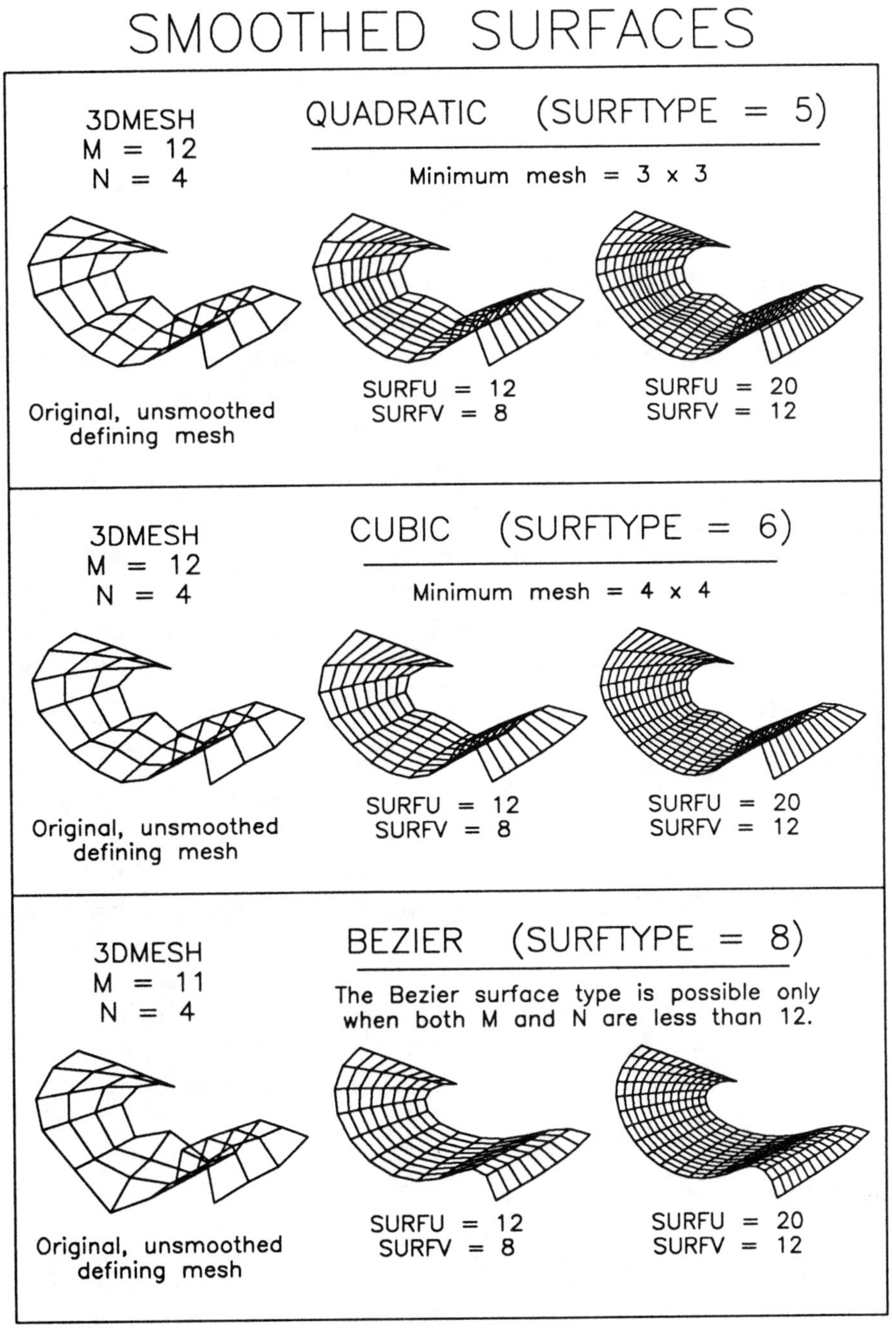

Figure 33-13: With the variable SURFTYPE and PEDIT you can set smooth 3DMESH surfaces to be Quadratic, Cubic or Bezier.

PEDIT Lets you edit polylines & 3D polygon meshes

COMMAND LINE: **pedit**

Figure 33-14: The Edit Polyline icon from the Special Edit flyout of the Modify toolbar.

Choose the Edit Polyline icon, or select Edit Polyline from the Modify pull-down. (If this menu is not available from the menu bar, enter **menu** at the command line and select Acadfull to display it.) You can smooth a mesh by editing it with the PEDIT command and selecting the S option (see "PEDIT" in Chapter 28, "Polylines & Splines").

System variable SURFTYPE controls the level of smoothness. A setting of 5 produces a quadratic surface with a low level of smoothness, 6 produces a cubic surface with a medium level of smoothness, and 8 produces a Bezier surface with a high level of smoothness (see the illustrations in Figure 33-13). Notice that smoothness and conformity are inversely related—the smoother the surface, the less it conforms to the defining mesh.

When system variable SPLFRAME = 0, the smoothed surface is displayed. When SPLFRAME is nonzero, only the defining mesh is displayed.

System variables SURFU and SURFV control the number of elements in the smoothed surface. SURFU controls the number of elements in the M direction of the mesh, SURFV in the N direction. High values in SURFU and SURFV produce a fine, smoothed mesh, but they also take longer to regenerate on the screen.

NOTE: Don't confuse SURFU and SURFV with SURFTAB1 and SURFTAB2, which control the number of vertices in the original (unsmoothed) mesh. SURFU and SUFRV apply only to smoothed surfaces.

Moving on

Now that you've learned about 3D, you're ready for solid modeling. The next chapter introduces you to Release 13's ACIS Solid Modeler.

CHAPTER 34

Solid Modeling

AutoCAD has had the ability to create solid models for quite some time through the purchase of an add-on program called AME. AutoCAD Release 13 adds solid modeling as a core capability for all AutoCAD users. This chapter introduces the solid model creation and editing commands available in Release 13. For more detailed explanations and examples, see *Solid Modeling With AutoCAD*, published by Ventana Press.

What Is a Solid Model?

Solid models go one step beyond wireframe and surface models. The advantages of solid models will become clear if we consider wireframe and surface models first.

In a wireframe model, the "wires" (lines, circles, arcs and ellipses) represent the edges of an object. Wireframe models are useful in certain circumstances but have disadvantages. Since wireframe models represent only an object's edges, you can't extract much more information from a wireframe model than you can get from a 2D, multiview drawing. Wireframe models are often difficult to visualize because they have so many confusing edges.

A surface model is more complete than a wireframe model. It can be created with 3D faces and meshes that represent both edges and surfaces. It can be displayed as a wireframe, but it can also be displayed as a set of surfaces, which gives it a more realistic look and makes it easier to visualize. A surface model can also be shaded, and you can use the RENDER command to create realistic images with multiple light sources and varying surface reflectivity.

Nevertheless, a surface model is still just an empty shell—only the skin of the object. The most complete way to represent an object is with a solid model. Solid models have all the usefulness of wireframe and surface models, and more. They're relatively easy to construct and can be displayed as wireframes or as surfaces. Or they can be "cut" to reveal a section view. A solid model can also be used to calculate volume, center of gravity, moment of inertia and more.

The Mental Process

In the traditional design setting, the designer thinks in 3D but sketches or draws in 2D. Unconsciously, much energy is devoted to the process of translating 3D ideas into 2D format.

When working with a solid model, the designer doesn't have to waste energy translating between 3D and 2D. The designer can focus on developing and refining the 3D model. With solid modeling, the designer sketches or draws directly in 3D. Two-dimensional drawings, when needed, can be produced from the solid model. And since the software can easily produce any views, including primary and secondary auxiliary views and section views, this part of the task is largely automated.

Solid Modeling in AutoCAD

The ACIS solid modeler built into AutoCAD Release 13 does not require any extra loading or unloading. A complete solid model is created by putting pieces together. The pieces, called primitives, include Box, Wedge, Cylinder, Cone, Sphere and Torus. You may also create solids through special commands such as Revolve and Extrude. The pieces are combined into composite solids by using the Boolean operations of Union, Subtraction and Intersection. This allows you to create a realistic model in much less time than a wireframe or surface model. You can view and render a solid model from any angle, or from multiple angles, to obtain a realistic picture of the object. You also can perform mass property calculations to determine such things as volume and center of gravity.

When the solid model is complete, you may dimension and plot several views of the object. Solid models make good use of the Paper Space features described earlier. Or you may extract 2D views from the solid model to create standard engineering detail drawings.

Thus, solid modeling is an efficient way to design. Although the 2D engineering drawing is well established and will undoubtedly last a long time, designers would do well to explore the potential of solid modeling.

Solids Creation

The following commands let you create solids using AutoCAD Release 13's internal solid modeler. Be careful not to confuse solid models with their 3D mesh objects.

For example, you can use the SPHERE command to create a solid sphere, or you can use the 3D command with its sphere option to create a surface model with a similar appearance. If you have any doubt about whether an object is a solid or a mesh, use the LIST command. LIST always identifies a solid object as a 3D solid, while a mesh object is identified as a type of polyline.

All of these commands, with the exception of REGION, are found under the Solids toolbar. Select Toolbars from the Tools pull-down menu, and then select Solids to display the Solids toolbar.

REGION Converts closed polylines, splines or selected objects forming a closed area into a single solid region

COMMAND LINE: **region**

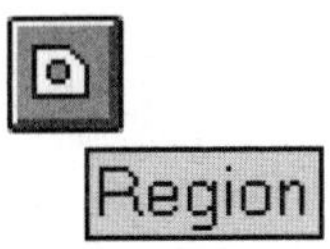

Figure 34-1: The Region icon from the Polygon flyout of the Draw toolbar.

Click on the Region icon from the Polygon flyout. When prompted, select objects that form one or more closed areas. Each closed area is converted into a separate region.

Areas made up of intersecting lines or overlapping objects will not form regions. Areas must consist of closed objects such as closed splines and polylines, or the selection of objects must match end vertex to end vertex to form the closed area.

BOX Constructs a solid box

COMMAND LINE: **box**

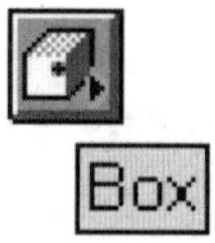

Figure 34-2: The Box icon from the Solids toolbar.

Click on the Box icon. When prompted, pick a point on the screen to locate one corner of the box, or enter **c** for center. You then have three options:

1. Pick another point for the diagonal corner of the base of the box and then enter the height to the top of the box.
2. Enter **l** and specify the length, width and height.
3. Enter **c** for cube and specify the length of one edge.

WEDGE Creates a wedge-shaped solid

COMMAND LINE: **wedge**

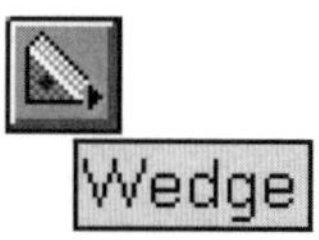

Figure 34-3: The Wedge icon from the Solids toolbar.

The process for creating a wedge is the same as for creating a box. The only difference is that the top inclines to meet the base.

CYLINDER Creates a cylindrical solid

COMMAND LINE: **cylinder**

Figure 34-4: The Cylinder icon from the Solids toolbar.

Click on the Cylinder icon. You are prompted to define the base of the cylinder. Pick a center point for a circular cylinder, or enter **e** to specify an elliptical cylinder.

If you are creating a circular cylinder, pick a center point followed by a radius or diameter. If you are creating an elliptical cylinder, you are prompted for three axis endpoints, or you can enter **c** to specify a center and two axis endpoints.

After specifying the base, you are prompted to enter a height for a vertical cylinder, or you can pick a point to specify a cylinder that slants at an angle.

CONE Creates a conical solid

COMMAND LINE: **cone**

Figure 34-5: The Cone icon from the Solids toolbar.

The CONE command is similar to the CYLINDER command. You first specify a circular or elliptical base, and then enter a height or pick a point (the apex). Entering a height gives you a vertical cone. The apex option creates a slanted cone.

SPHERE Creates a spherical solid

COMMAND LINE: **sphere**

Figure 34-6: The Sphere icon from the Solids toolbar.

Click on the Sphere icon, and then locate the center of the sphere. Then enter a radius for the sphere, or enter **d** to specify a diameter for the sphere.

TORUS Creates a torus (3D donut or ring) solid

COMMAND LINE: **torus**

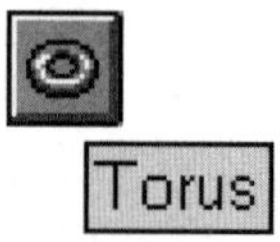

Figure 34-7: The Torus icon from the Solids toolbar.

Click on the Torus icon, and then locate the center point of the torus. Then enter the radius, or enter **d** to specify the diameter of the torus. Next, enter the radius or diameter of the circular cross section.

EXTRUDE Creates a solid by projecting a closed object along a straight line or sweeping it along a path

COMMAND LINE: **extrude**

Figure 34-8: The Extrude icon from the Solids toolbar.

Click on the Extrude icon. When prompted, select the object that you want to extrude. You can select multiple objects, but each object must be a closed shape such as a region, circle, or closed polyline or spline.

You now have two options: either extrude the objects along the Z-axis of the current UCS, or sweep the objects along a path object.

The default is to enter the height of the extrusion along the Z-axis. Then enter the taper angle for the extrusion. Positive angles cause the object to taper toward its center. Negative angles cause the object to taper out. An angle of zero creates a straight extrusion with no taper.

Enter **p** for extrusion along a path. When prompted, select a line, arc, circle, elliptical arc, ellipse, polyline or spline as the extrusion path. If necessary, the path is relocated to the center of your selected extrusion object, and the object is passed along the path to generate a 3D solid.

The path option does not allow for an extrusion taper angle. Figure 34-9 shows an example of a Z-axis extrusion with taper and an example of an extrusion along a path.

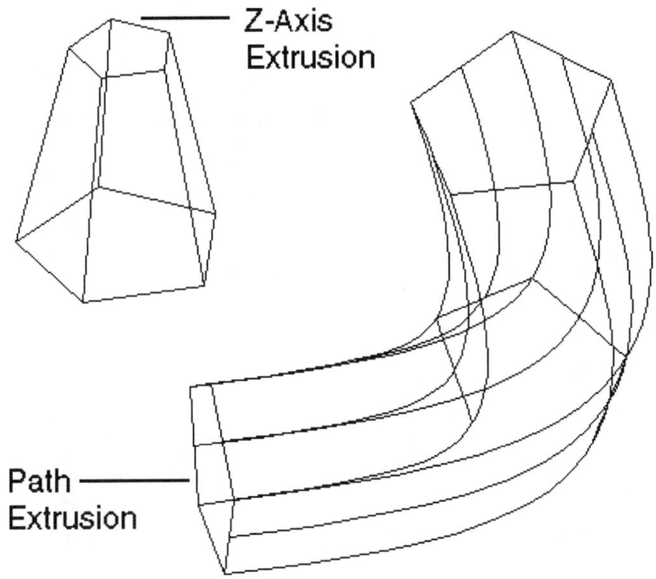

Figure 34-9: Two types of extruded objects.

REVOLVE Creates a solid by revolving a closed object around an axis

COMMAND LINE: **revolve**

Figure 34-10: The Revolve icon from the Solids toolbar.

Click on the Revolve icon and select the objects that you wish to revolve. You may select more than one object, but each object must be closed and each object will become a separate solid.

After selecting the objects to revolve, you have four methods for defining the axis of revolution:

1. Locate Endpoints is the default method. You locate any two points on the screen, and the line between those points becomes the axis of revolution.
2. Object revolves the object around a selected line or single-segment polyline.
3. X revolves the object around the X-axis of the current UCS.
4. Y Revolves the object around the Y-axis of the current UCS.

The final prompt is to specify the angle of revolution. Enter the desired angle or press Enter to accept the default of 360 degrees (a full circle).

Booleans

A useful modeling technique for solids involves Boolean operations. These operations allow you to create composite solid objects by combining objects and cutting objects away from one other. These operations are named Union, Subtraction and Intersection.

The Boolean operations are found under the Explode flyout of the Modify toolbar.

UNION Creates a new solid by blending together two or more solids

COMMAND LINE: **union**

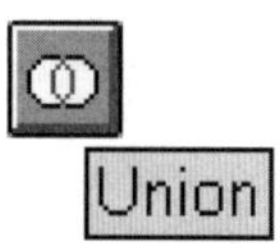

Figure 34-11: The Union icon from the Explode flyout of the Modify toolbar.

Click on the Union icon. When prompted, select two or more solid objects. The objects merge into a single composite object.

SUBTRACT Creates a new solid by cutting one selection of solids from another selection of solids

COMMAND LINE: **subtract**

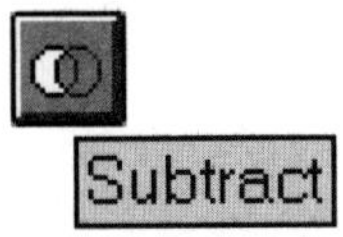

Figure 34-12: The Subtract icon from the Explode flyout of the Modify toolbar.

Click on the Subtract icon. When prompted, select the solids that will have parts subtracted. You can think of this as the *keeper* selection. Then select the solids that you will cut from the first selection. Think of these as the *cutting* objects.

The result is a single new solid that is the union of the keeper objects after the cutting objects have been removed.

INTERSECT Creates a new solid from the volume where two or more solids overlap

COMMAND LINE: **intersect**

Figure 34-13: The Intersection icon from the Explode flyout of the Modify toolbar.

Click on the Intersection icon. When prompted, select two or more overlapping solids. The new solid is the volume that was shared by all of the selected solids.

INTERFERE Identifies the area where two selections of solids overlap & provides the option to create a new solid from the overlap volumes

COMMAND LINE: **interfere**

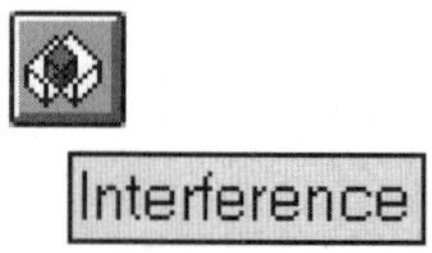

Figure 34-14: The Interference icon from the Solids toolbar.

This command is different from the previous Boolean commands in that it does not alter the selected objects. After clicking on the Interference icon, pick the first set of solids. Press Enter, and then pick the second set of solids. AutoCAD calculates the volumes where the objects in the first selection overlap the objects in the second selection. The text window reports how many objects from the first selection set overlap or interfere with objects from the second selection set.

You are then asked if you want to create new interference solids from the overlapping volumes. The default response is **n** for No. If you enter **y** AutoCAD creates multiple new solids based on the interference volumes.

AutoCAD then asks if you want to highlight pairs of solids that interfere with each other. Entering **y** highlights one solid from each group to show which pairs of solids will interfere with each other.

CHAMFER Chamfers the edges of solid objects

COMMAND LINE: **chamfer**

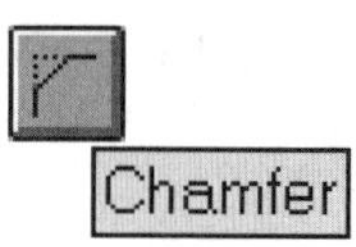

Figure 34-15: The Chamfer icon from Feature flyout of the Modify toolbar.

If necessary, review Chapter 14, "Editing—Group One" for a general discussion of the CHAMFER command.

Click on the Chamfer icon. When prompted to select the first line, select a solid instead. You are then prompted to identify the base surface. The base surface defines which edges of the object are valid for chamfering since only the edges that surround the base surface can be chamfered.

After selecting the base surface, you are prompted to enter the base surface distance (similar to distance 1 on a 2D chamfer) and the other surface distance (similar to distance 2). The angle method of chamfering is not available for solids.

Once you specify the distances, you have two options for selecting edges to chamfer:

1. Select edges one at a time and then press Enter to chamfer only the selected edges.
2. Enter **l** (for loop), and then select a single edge to select all the connected edges that surround the base surface.

FILLET Fillets the edges of solid objects

COMMAND LINE: **fillet**

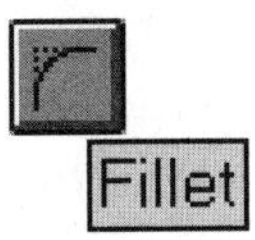

Figure 34-16: The Fillet icon from the Feature flyout of the Modify toolbar.

If necessary, review Chapter 14, "Editing—Group One" for a general discussion of the FILLET command.

Click on the Fillet icon. When prompted to select the first object, select a solid. You are then prompted to enter a fillet radius. After entering a radius, you have two options:

1. Select individual edges and press Enter to fillet the selected edges.
2. Enter **c** to select an edge chain. If you select a single edge in chain mode, AutoCAD will find and select all edges that are tangent to the selected edge.

SLICE Cuts a selection of solids along a specified plane

COMMAND LINE: **slice**

Figure 34-17: The Slice icon from the Solids toolbar.

Click on the Slice icon. When prompted, select one or more solid objects.

The selected objects are cut by a plane that you specify with one of the following options, which appear on the command line:

3 Points	This is the default method. Pick three points on the screen that explicitly define the desired cutting plane.
Object	Aligns the cutting plane with a 2D object such as a circle, arc, ellipse or polyline. You are then prompted to select the alignment object.
Z-axis	Pick two points that define the Z-axis that is perpendicular to the cutting plane. The first point locates the origin of the axis and the cutting plane.
View	Aligns the cutting plane with the current viewport. You then pick a point to locate the position of the cutting plane.
XY/YZ/ZX	Aligns the cutting plane with the selected axes of the current UCS. You then pick a point to locate the position of the cutting plane.

After specifying the cutting plane, pick which part of the selected objects to keep, or enter **b** to retain both sides of the objects after cutting.

SECTION Creates a 2D region based on a section plane passing through a 3D solid

COMMAND LINE: **section**

Figure 34-18: The Section icon from the Solids toolbar.

SECTION uses the same prompts as SLICE, described above. The difference between SLICE and SECTION is that SECTION does not alter the original selected solids. Instead, it creates a 2D region to represent the cut surface of the objects.

Moving on

The next chapter demonstrates various commands that assist you in viewing 3D models you create. These commands allow you to quickly set up any number of orthographic, isometric or perspective views.

CHAPTER 35

3D Viewing

Once you have constructed your 3D model, AutoCAD allows you to view it from multiple vantage points. Even though you may view your model from any point in three-dimensional model space, there are only two types of views: parallel projection and perspective viewing.

Using the Commands

Parallel projection views represent the traditional drafting views. Orthographic and isometric views are types of parallel projections.

Perspective views simulate real human vision, or the type of view that you get from a camera.

This chapter discusses the 3D viewing commands used to create parallel and perspective views.

3D VIEWPOINT Sets up a 3D parallel projection view

COMMAND LINE: **ddvpoint** or **vpoint**

Choose 3D Viewpoint from the View pull-down menu to see the three viewpoint options shown in Figure 35-1. The options—Rotate, Tripod and Vector—are described below.

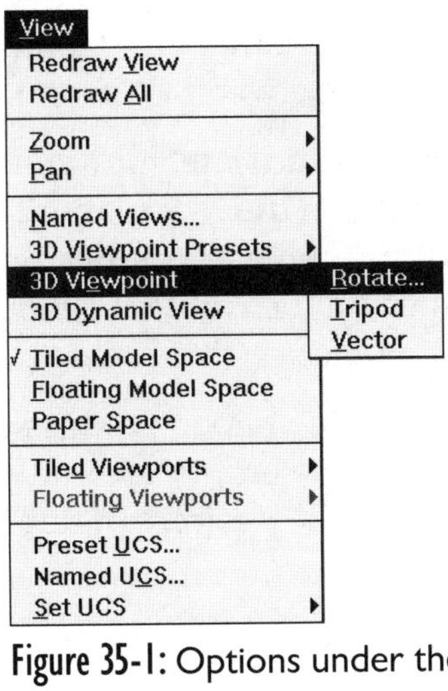

Figure 35-1: Options under the 3D Viewpoint menu pick.

Rotate

Rotate activates the DDVPOINT command, which displays the Viewpoint Presets dialog shown in Figure 35-2. Use this dialog to set your viewing angle from the origin point in the X-Y plane and your elevation angle above the X-Y plane.

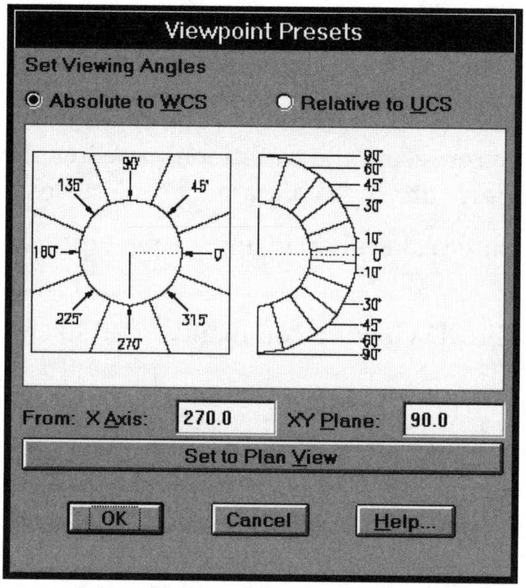

Figure 35-2: The Viewpoint Presets dialog.

The two radio buttons at the top of the dialog determine whether the angle that you specify will be measured from the World Coordinate System (absolute) or the current UCS (relative). See Chapter 30, "Coordinate Systems," if you need to review the differences between WCS and UCS.

Below the radio buttons are two charts that indicate your viewing angles. The chart on the left represents your angle in the X-Y plane. The center of the chart is the coordinate origin 0,0,0, and the black indicator line points toward your viewing location. The chart on the right represents your angle above or below the ground (X-Y plane).

To specify the desired angles, click in the pie-shaped wedges to choose one of the standard angles, or click within the empty area near the indicator to specify any angle. You can also type the desired angles in the edit fields below the charts.

A view similar to the standard isometric views is created when you set the From X Axis field to 45, 135, 225 or 315 degrees and set the XY Plane field to 35.3 degrees.

Standard plan view occurs any time that you set your elevation above the X-Y plane to 90 degrees. A shortcut for specifying the plan view is clicking on the Set to Plan View button.

Tripod

Choosing this option activates the VPOINT tripod mode, which allows you to set the viewpoint using the compass and axis tripod shown in Figure 35-3.

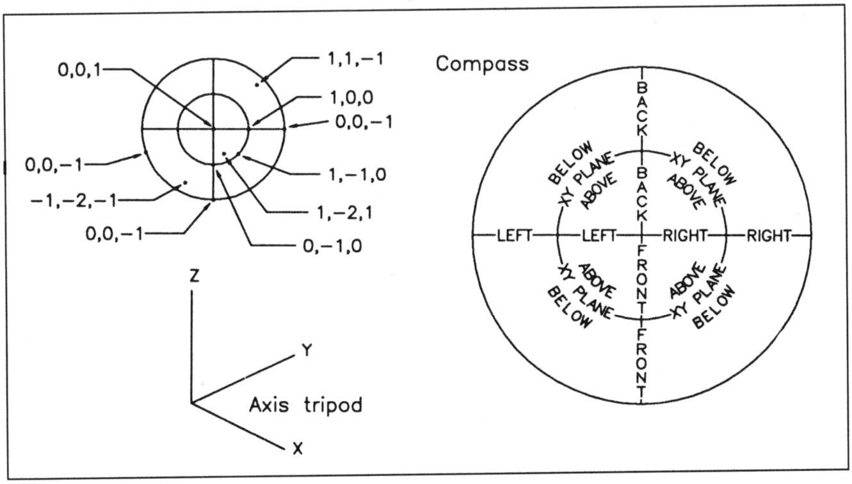

Figure 35-3: Setting viewpoint with the compass and axis tripod.

To use the compass, imagine yourself above the surface of a globe at the North Pole, looking toward the center of the globe. Think of the compass as a flattened globe with the center as the North Pole, the outer circle as the South Pole and the inner circle as the equator.

As you move the pointer around the compass, the tripod shows the relative positions of the positive X, Y and Z axes. Select your viewpoint by locating the appropriate point on the compass. The vector from that point to the center of the (round) globe defines the line of sight.

Vector

Choose this option to activate the VPOINT vector mode and specify the viewpoint with X,Y,Z coordinates. When prompted, enter the X, Y and Z coordinates, separated by commas. The line of sight is a vector from the entered coordinates to the origin 0,0,0. The distance from the coordinates isn't important, only the direction. Thus, a viewpoint location of 1,-2,2 is identical to 5,-10,10.

A view similar to the standard isometric views is created when you specify a vector where the X and Y coordinates are 1 or -1 and the Z coordinate is always 1. The ZOOM and PAN commands work as usual, no matter what viewpoint you've selected.

3D VIEWPOINT PRESETS Quickly displays a predefined viewpoint

Choosing 3D Viewpoint Presets from the View pull-down menu displays a cascading menu with options for the standard orthographic and isometric views. Choosing one of these options activates the VPOINT command in vector mode as described above and enters the proper coordinates to generate the selected view.

If you choose Plan from the cascading menu, you are presented three more options:

Current, for a plan view of the current UCS.

World, for a plan view of the World Coordinate System.

Named, for a planed view of a previously saved UCS. You are prompted to enter the name of the desired UCS.

Dynamic Viewing

Dynamic viewing includes a wide variety of viewing options especially designed for 3D drawing. The regular ZOOM and PAN commands are adequate for 2D drawing, but 3D drawing demands more.

When you're drawing a 3D item, it's helpful to be able to see the following:

The item from all sides and all angles.

The item being dragged; that is, changing dynamically on the screen as you select your desired view.

The item either in parallel projection or in perspective.

Inside the item, by clipping objects near the observer.

The DVIEW command lets you do these and more.

Parallel Projection & Perspective

Every view you select can be seen in either parallel projection or perspective.

Parallel projection is the standard projection used in engineering drawings. The theoretical viewpoint is an infinite distance from the item being viewed, so the projectors (projection rays) from the item to the projection plane (the sheet of paper or the display screen) are always parallel.

An item that's far away from the viewer will appear the same size on the projection plane as one that's closer. A typical engineering drawing shows how to manufacture a certain item, so precise alignment and dimensioning are important. Parallel projection helps make alignment and dimensioning precise.

Perspective, which has been used since the 1400s, shows items differently. The projectors converge at the theoretical viewpoint, which is a certain distance from the item being viewed rather than at infinity. This makes the item appear differently on the projection plane than it does in parallel projection.

In perspective, an item that's far away from you appears smaller on the projection plane than one that's closer. Edges that would be parallel on the actual item appear to meet at a distant vanishing point. This type of projection makes items look more like they do in the real world, especially if the real viewer's location is close to the theoretical viewpoint established when the projection was made.

If the real location and the theoretical location are very different, distortions can occur. One such distortion mentioned below (DVIEW command, Zoom option) occurs when the focal length of the camera is too short.

Terms

Here are some terms you may need to know:

Camera	The viewer or viewpoint.
Target	The point near or within the item at which the camera aims.
Line of sight	The line from the camera to the target.
Field of vision (field of view)	The amount of the item that's visible when you're looking in any one direction.
Lens focal length	In photography, the distance between the lens and the focal point of the lens (the point where parallel rays of light converge after passing through the lens). A lens with a lot of curvature (small diameter and thick) has a short focal length and a wide field of vision. One with less curvature has a longer focal length and a narrower field of vision. In AutoCAD, changing the focal length changes the field of vision. A short focal length gives a wide field of vision and, if too short, produces a distorted image. A long focal length gives a narrow field of vision and, if too long, produces a perspective image that's difficult to distinguish from a parallel projection.
Clipping	Removing items or parts of an item from the display. Items closer than the front clipping plane won't be seen. Items farther than the back clipping plane won't be displayed. Clipping planes are always perpendicular to the line of sight.

DVIEW Dynamically sets the 3D display

COMMAND LINE: **dview**

Choose 3D Dynamic View from the View pull-down menu to activate the DVIEW command. (It is disabled when you're in Paper Space.)

You're prompted to select objects. These are the preview objects that AutoCAD drags dynamically if you select your desired view with the pointer. You'll need to select the right number of objects—not too few and not too many. If you select too few, the preview may not provide enough information for you to select your view wisely. If you select too many objects, AutoCAD won't be able to generate all of the preview objects quickly enough and, to compensate, you'll have to move the pointer very slowly. After you select your desired view, all of the objects are redisplayed in the new view.

For several of the options described below, you can use slider bars that appear on the screen to indicate your choice of angle, magnification, etc. As you move the pointer, the preview objects change and a diamond moves in the slider bar indicating the amount of the change. A rubber band connects the diamond to the old value, which is also the default value. To accept the default value, press Enter.

After selecting the preview objects, you use the following options.

CAmera

Use CAmera to rotate the camera (your viewpoint) around the target. Then enter the angle up or down from the current X-Y construction plane, using the keyboard or slider bar. Then enter the angle around the Z axis in the current construction plane, using the keyboard or slider bar.

TArget

Use TArget to rotate the target (the point you're looking at) around the camera. This is like turning your head. Then enter the angle up or down, then the angle left or right, using the keyboard or slider bar.

Distance

Use Distance to change your distance from the objects. Since distance makes no sense in parallel projection (the theoretical viewpoint is always at infinity), this option automatically turns on perspective viewing; and a perspective icon replaces the usual UCS icon. You can enter the distance with the keyboard or slider bar. If you want to view more, or less, of the object without turning perspective on, use the Z option instead of this option.

POint

Use POint to enter point coordinates for the target, then the camera. Object snap and point filters apply. If you're in perspective when you select this option, you're temporarily returned to parallel projection until the points have been selected.

PAn

Use PAn to pan the display in any direction. You can use the keyboard or the pointer if you're in parallel projection. If you're in perspective, you must use the pointer.

Zoom to zoom in or out or change your field of vision. If you're in parallel projection, this works much like the regular ZOOM command. Just enter the zoom scale factor to apply to the current display. However, if you're in perspective, this option lets you change the focal length of the camera lens.

The default focal length when you first enter perspective is 50mm, which is similar to the focal length of the human eye. If you use a very short focal length, you'll get a very wide view but you'll also get more distortion, like the distortion you get with a fish-eye lens on a camera. If you use a long focal length, you'll get a narrow view similar to a telephoto lens on a camera.

When the focal length is very long, the screen image appears almost identical to parallel projection. (The projectors from object to camera are close to parallel.)

TWIst

Use TWIst to twist (rotate) the view around the line of sight from camera to target. Enter the twist angle with the keyboard or pointer.

CLip

The CLip option is used to clip the drawing. Then enter **b** to set the distance of the back clipping plane, or turn it on or off. Or enter **f** to set the distance of the front clipping plane (**e** sets it at the camera "eye"), or turn it on or off. The default position for the front clipping plane is at the camera "eye."

Distances for the front and back clipping planes are measured along the line of sight with the zero distance located at the target. Positive distances are measured toward the camera: negative distances away from the camera. Distances can be entered with the keyboard or the slider bar. Front clipping is always on when you're in perspective.

Hide

Use Hide to remove hidden lines in the preview objects.

Off

Use Off to turn perspective off. To turn it back on, enter **d**.

Undo

Use Undo to undo the previous DVIEW operation. You can undo as often as necessary while you remain in the DVIEW command.

Exiting DVIEW

Each time you use one of the above options, you're returned to the same DVIEW prompt. To exit the DVIEW command, enter **x** or press Enter. When you exit the DVIEW command, the entire drawing will be regenerated, with the same options as in the last setting.

NOTE: After you use DVIEW Distance to turn perspective on, ZOOM, PAN and SKETCH won't work.

Moving on

The final step in 3D modeling is generating images from your 3D views. The commands described in this chapter allow you to set up 3D views from any point in Model Space, yet your models are still shown in wireframe. Most people have a difficult time relating to 3D models in wireframe because wireframe views are often cluttered and hard to read.

The next chapter shows you how to use the various commands under the Render toolbar. Using the commands in the next chapter, you can create images of your models starting with traditional hidden line views and progressing to fully shaded renderings.

CHAPTER 36

Rendering

Standard orthographic drawings and wireframe models have a meaning and beauty that only the trained technician, drafter or engineer can understand and appreciate. Most people need more training before they can grasp what the drawing or model represents. This is where rendering comes in. Rendering takes a technical drawing and makes it look more like a photograph of the finished item.

The rendering capabilities are in an ADS application that is loaded into AutoCAD whenever you use one of the rendering commands. Like other ADS applications, it can be loaded from the menus or with the (xload) AutoLISP function. Don't confuse this ADS application with Autodesk's RenderMan, which is an entirely separate software package.

Using the Commands

Most of the commands in this chapter are located in the Render toolbar.

To display the Render toolbar, choose Toolbars from the Tools pull-down menu and then choose Render.

HIDE Produces a hidden line image of objects in the current viewport

COMMAND LINE: **hide**

Figure 36-1: The Hide icon from the Render toolbar.

Click on the Hide icon to produce a hidden line image of the current viewport. The results of a HIDE command remain visible only until the next time the display is regenerated.

Solids, circles and wide polyline segments have tops and bottoms when assigned a thickness, so HIDE treats them accordingly.

Objects on layers that have been turned off may still obscure objects on visible layers. To avoid this problem, freeze the layers that were turned off.

Here are a few things to consider when using HIDE with a complex drawing. (Also, see "Hide" in the *AutoCAD Reference Manual*.)

Text and attribute definitions are always created with a thickness of zero and don't normally respond to HIDE. You can change the thickness of text with the Properties icon from the Object Properties toolbar.

The insertion point assigned to a block and the base assigned to a drawing adopt the current elevation as their Z coordinate, unless you explicitly assign a Z coordinate.

HIDE often does not properly represent edges where objects intersect.

SHADE Produces a flat shaded view of the objects in the current viewport

COMMAND LINE: **shade**

Figure 36-2: The Shade icon from the Render toolbar.

Click on the Shade icon to produce a flat shaded image of the current viewport. The SHADE command functions the same as the HIDE command except that the 3D surfaces are filled in with a shade color rather than being represented by their edges. SHADE produces a more realistic view of the objects than HIDE.

To produce the shaded effect, AutoCAD assumes that there is a light source shining along the line of sight for the current viewport. This is the same line of sight that you specify when using the Viewpoint or Dynamic View commands described in Chapter 35, "3D Viewing."

The SHADE command is also controlled by two system variables called SHADEDGE and SHADEDIF.

SHADEDGE

Entering SHADEDGE at the command prompt allows you to set the variable's value to a number between 0 and 3. The meaning of each value is described below:

0	Shades the surfaces of the objects without highlighting the edges.
1	Shades the surfaces of the objects and draws the edges using the background color.
2	Does not shade the surfaces but fills them with the background color and draws the edges using the object color. This option simulates the HIDE command.
3	Fills the surfaces with the object color and draws the edges with the background color. This is the default setting.

Options 0 and 1 produce the most realistic images, while options 2 and 3 work best on systems that are not capable of displaying the full 256-color palette.

SHADEDIF

Entering **shadedif** at the command prompt allows you to set the variables' value to a number between 1 and 100. The higher the value, the more contrast you will see in the shaded image. Generally, medium-high contrast shaded images look best. The default value is 70.

Rendering a Drawing in Seven Steps

Creating a rendering is fairly straightforward and can be summarized in seven steps.

1. Create the model. It can be a surface model—created with 3D faces, pfaces and meshes—or a solid model.
2. Set up a view of the object. For large objects you often need a perspective view.
3. Create lights and place them in the drawing. You often use a combination of ambient lights and point lights. Spotlights and distant lights can be added for more dramatic effects.
4. Save the view and lights in a scene so it can be recalled later if needed.

5. Create or import material definitions and apply them to your objects.
6. Set up your rendering preferences such as Gouraud or Phong shading and the smoothing parameters.
7. Render the object. The view, lighting and finish can be adjusted and rendered again to improve the appearance. When you are satisfied with the rendering, it can be saved in various file formats.

The easiest method for accessing rendering commands is to make the Render toolbar visible. Choose Toolbars from the Tools pull-down menu and then choose Render.

Rendering Terminology

In order to use the rendering commands wisely, you need to understand the terminology of rendering—especially the terminology for lights, reflection and other concepts, such as frame buffers, shading and scenes.

Light Sources

AutoCAD uses four different light sources: ambient, point, distant and spotlight. All of these lights can be adjusted for color and intensity. None of the light sources can cast shadows.

Ambient light represents general background illumination that is always present in any scene. Ambient light illuminates all surfaces with equal intensity from all directions. Most scenes require only a small amount of ambient light.

Point light is similar to a light bulb. The rays of light spread out in all directions from a single source. Light from a real light bulb diminishes as it gets further from its source. AutoCAD allows you to control this effect by setting attenuation for point light sources.

The Distant light source is like the sun. The sun is really a point light source, but it is so far away that its rays of light are parallel and come from a single direction. Distant lights can be aimed at objects, and the light does not diminish no matter how far it travels.

Spotlight is like a theatrical light. Spotlights can be aimed at an object like a distant light, but they diminish over distance like point lights. They can also be focused and limited to a certain area by adjusting the hotspot and falloff settings.

Types of Reflection

A surface that produces *diffuse* reflection (a rough or matte surface) scatters the light in all directions. No matter where the viewer is located in relation to the light source, the surface appears to have the same amount of brightness.

A shiny surface produces a *specular* reflection. On a shiny surface, light rays follow the rule that the angle of reflection equals the angle of incidence. This means that light coming from a point source is reflected in one particular direction. If the viewer is located in that direction, the place where the light hits the surface appears very bright. In the extreme case, specular reflection behaves just like light bouncing off a mirror. Specular reflection is most noticeable with convex surfaces. Only a very small portion of a convex surface reflects light directly to the viewer, causing a bright highlight.

Screen Palette

Rendered images require many colors to represent the effects of light and shade on the surface of an object. When rendering on systems that only support 256 colors, you have to instruct AutoCAD how you want to manipulate the limited color palette. The fewer colors available on your system, the less realistic your rendered images are. If you have a system that supports 16-bit or 24-bit color, you do not have to worry about this.

Smooth Shading

All 3D objects in your drawing are converted into face meshes for rendering. Since face meshes consist of many small, flat faces, their edges show at render time and make the object appear to be made of small tiles or facets. The smoothing controls in AutoCAD allow you to determine when the edges of faces should be blended into a smooth surface.

Face Normals

Rendering speed depends on the number of faces to be rendered. AutoCAD tries to figure out which faces are on the back sides of your objects and tries not to render them. AutoCAD determines this by checking face normals. For 3D solids and 3D mesh objects, AutoCAD automatically orients the face normals to point from the center of the object. If a face normal is pointing away from the viewport, it is on the back side of an object and does not need to be rendered.

3D objects that you construct from 2D objects with thickness may not have their face normals oriented properly. The same is true of manually drawn 3D faces. Because of this, AutoCAD lets you disable face normal calculations. The rendering is slower but all faces render.

Scenes

Each view can be accompanied by any number of light sources. A view can have no light sources, one specific light source or several light sources of either type. When a view is saved (usually with several light sources), it is called a scene.

AutoCAD's Rendering Commands

The following commands make up AutoCAD's rendering capability. The first time you use any of these commands, the rendering module is loaded into memory. Before you make your first rendering, you are prompted to configure the rendering module. You can configure the renderer at any time with the Reconfigure button from the Rendering Preferences dialog described below.

The rendering commands are described roughly in the order you use them. These are brief explanations intended to introduce you to the commands. For complete explanations see the *AutoCAD Reference Manual.*

LIGHT Creates & positions lights

COMMAND LINE: **light**

Figure 36-3: The Lights icon from the Render toolbar.

Click on the Lights icon to display the Lights dialog shown in Figure 36-4. Using this dialog, you can adjust the ambient light settings and create or modify the other three light types: point, distant and spot.

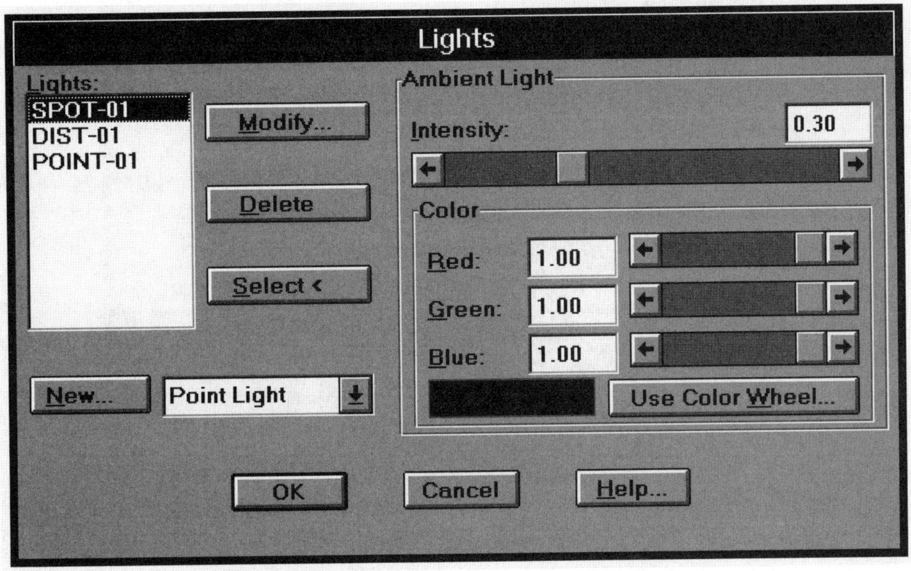

Figure 36-4: The Lights dialog.

The right side of the dialog controls the intensity and color of ambient light. The intensity slider controls how bright the light is. An intensity of 0 means the light is turned off. The color slider controls the color of the light by allowing you to adjust the amounts of red, green and blue that are mixed into the light. When red, green and blue are all equal you have a shade of gray.

The left side of the dialog contains the controls for point, distant and spotlight lights. These controls allow you to delete, modify and create new lights. To select a light, click on its name in the Lights list or click on the Select< button and select the light object from the screen using the standard selection methods.

To delete a light, select the light and click on the Delete button.

To adjust a light, select the light and click on the Modify button.

To create a new light, select the type of light from the pop-up list and click on the New button. A dialog for creating the type of light selected will appear on the screen. These dialogs are described below.

Point Lights

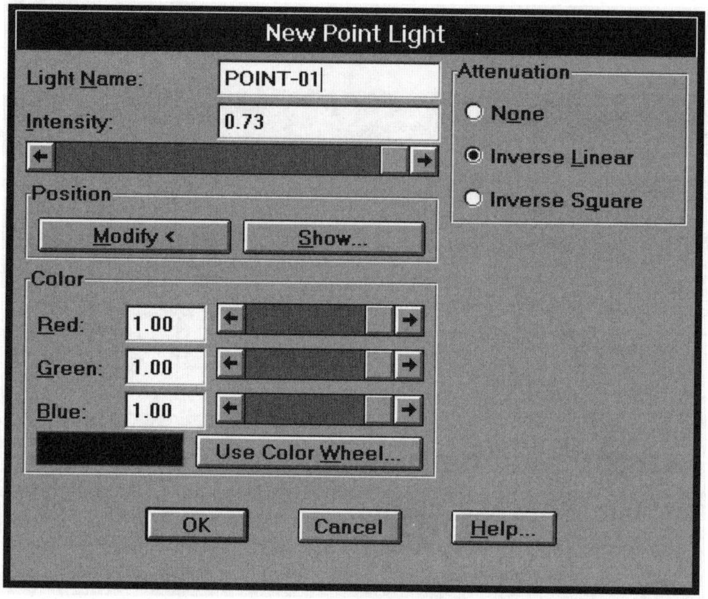

Figure 36-5: The New Point Light dialog.

With the exception of ambient light, all lights need a name. Enter a name for the new point light in the Light Name field.

Adjust the intensity and color sliders as described for ambient light.

The three options for attenuation are represented by radio buttons on the top right corner of the dialog. None means the light has no attenuation and projects with even intensity to infinity.

Inverse Linear means the intensity of the light fades to 0 as a straight-line function of the distance from the light source. The farther from the source, the dimmer the light. This is the standard choice for most rendering.

Inverse Square means the intensity of the light fades to 0 as a function of the distance from the light source squared. This is the way light really behaves but it usually produces images that are too dark.

Click on the Modify< button to temporarily hide the dialog and pick points for placing the light. Click on the Show button to display the current coordinates for the light.

When you have specified the settings for your light, click on OK.

Distant Lights

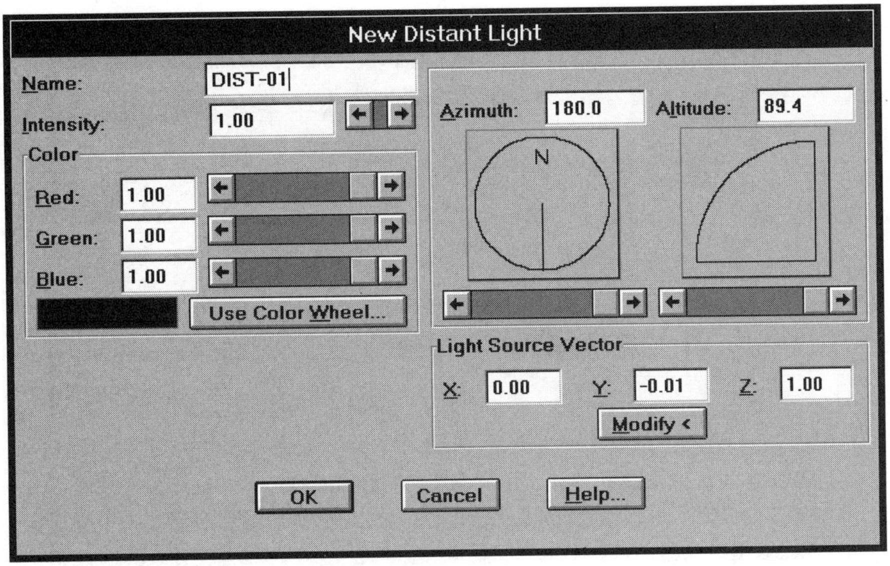

Figure 36-6: The New Distant Light dialog.

The name, intensity and color settings for a distant light are similar to those for point lights.

Distant lights have no attenuation and are located with a light source vector rather than with a specific coordinate location. There are two ways to specify the light source vector:

1. Azimuth and altitude angles. This method is similar to specifying a viewpoint with the Viewpoint Presets dialog described in Chapter 35, "3D Viewing." Click in the azimuth image to set the compass direction of your light where North is aligned with the Y-axis of the World Coordinate System. Click in the altitude image to set the angle of elevation for the light.
2. Light Source Vector. Click on the Modify< button to pick two points on the screen identifying a line parallel with the rays from the distant light. The first point that you are prompted for is the target that the light is shining toward. The second point is the light source.

Spotlights

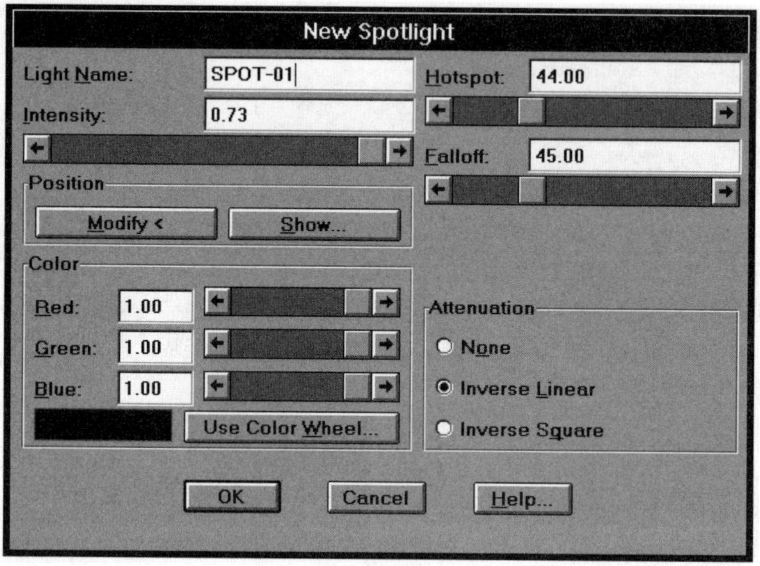

Figure 36-7: The New Spotlight dialog.

The name, intensity, color and attenuation settings all function similarly to the settings used with point lights. The Modify< and Show buttons also work similarly to those used with point lights, except that now you have two points to locate. The first is the target that the light is shining toward, and the second is the light source.

The hotspot and falloff sliders control how wide an area the spotlight illuminates. Think of the spotlight as a cone of light with its apex at the light source and its base at the light target.

The hotspot and falloff angles define the width of the cone as the angle from the cone's center to its surface. The hotspot defines a cone of light at the full intensity set by the intensity slider. The falloff defines a cone of light that must always be larger than the hotspot, and it represents the area where the light diminishes from the full intensity of the hotspot to 0 at the edge of the falloff.

SCENE Creates & recalls named sets of lights associated with views

COMMAND LINE: **scene**

Figure 36-8: The Scene icon from the Render toolbar.

Click on the Scene icon to display the Scenes dialog in Figure 36-9. Named scenes are listed on the left side of the dialog.

To delete a scene definition, select a scene name and click on the Delete button.

To modify a scene definition, select a scene name and click on the Modify button. The Modify Scene dialog is the same as the New Scene dialog described below.

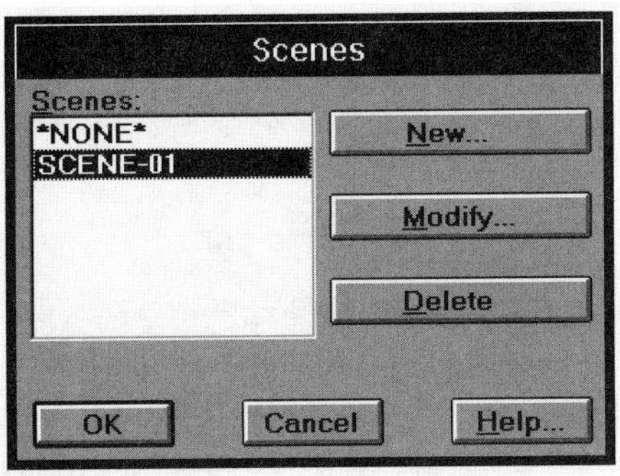

Figure 36-9: The Scenes dialog.

To create a new scene, click on the New button to display the dialog in Figure 36-10. First, enter a scene name in the name field. Then select one view from the Views list and any number of lights from the Lights list to complete the scene definition.

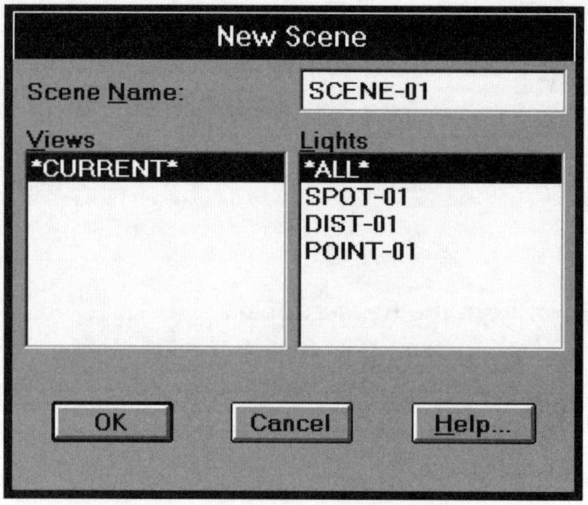

Figure 36-10: The New Scene dialog.

MATERIAL Creates and applies materials to selected objects

COMMAND LINE: **rmat**

Figure 36-11: The Materials icon from the Render toolbar.

Click on the Materials icon to display the Materials dialog in Figure 36-12. This dialog contains a list of all materials defined in the current drawing, controls for creating and modifying materials, and controls for assigning materials to the objects in your drawing. You can check what a material looks like by selecting its name from the Materials list and clicking the Preview button.

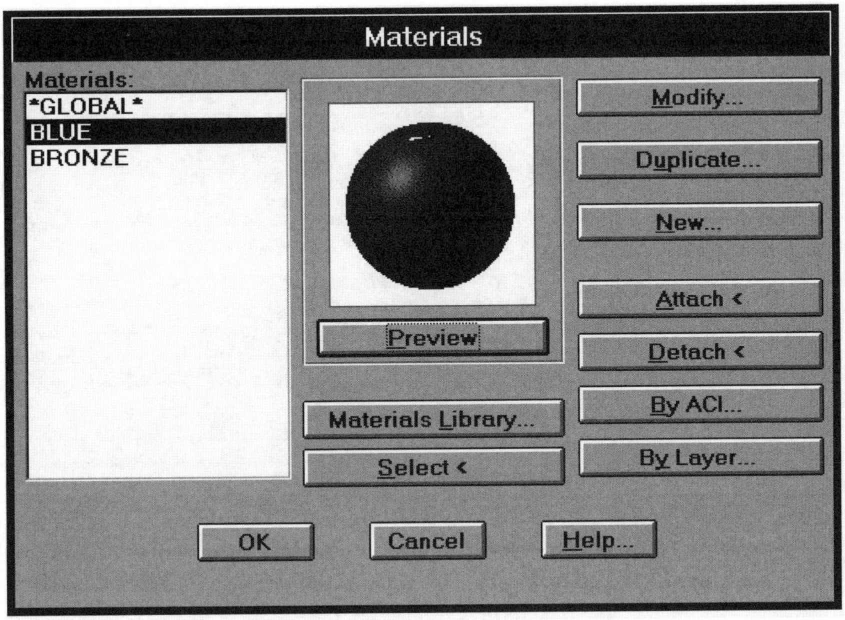

Figure 36-12: The Materials dialog.

Under the Preview button are two general purpose buttons: Materials Library... and Select<.

Creating /Modifying Materials

The top three buttons on the right side of the Materials dialog allow you to create and modify materials. They all use a dialog similar to the New Standard Material dialog described below.

New...

To create a new material, click on the New button to display the New Standard Material dialog shown in Figure 36-13.

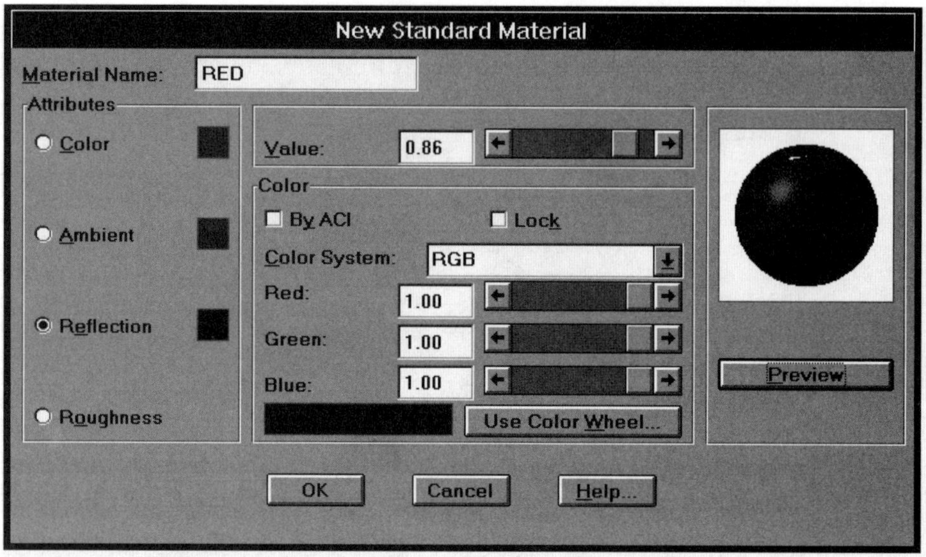

Figure 36-13: The New Standard Material dialog.

First, enter a name for the new material in the Material Name field in the upper left corner of the dialog.

Adjust the controls to set the base color, ambient color, reflective color and surface roughness of the material. Details on manipulating these sliders can be found in the *AutoCAD Reference Manual.*

As you adjust the settings you can check the appearance of your material by clicking on the preview button.

Modify...
To modify an existing material, select a material name from the Materials list and click on the Modify button. The dialog that appears is similar to the New Standard Material dialog described above.

Duplicate...
To create a new material based on the properties of an existing material, select a material name from the Materials list and click on the Duplicate button. The dialog that appears is similar to the New Standard Material dialog described above. Your first step is to enter a name for the duplicated material.

Assigning Materials

The buttons at bottom-right of the Materials dialog control how you assign materials to the objects in your drawing. First, select a material from the list as the current material. Then click on the appropriate button to perform the following functions:

Click the Attach< button to hide the Materials dialog and select objects in your drawing using the standard selection methods. The current material is assigned to the selected objects.

Click the Detach < button to hide the Materials dialog and select objects in your drawing using the standard selection methods. All materials are removed from the selected objects. When an object does not have a material assigned to it, it renders as its current object color.

Click the By ACI... button to display the dialog shown in Figure 36-14. (ACI refers to the AutoCAD Color Index.) Using this dialog, you can assign a material to one or more color numbers from the standard AutoCAD color palette. All objects using the selected object colors render with the assigned material.

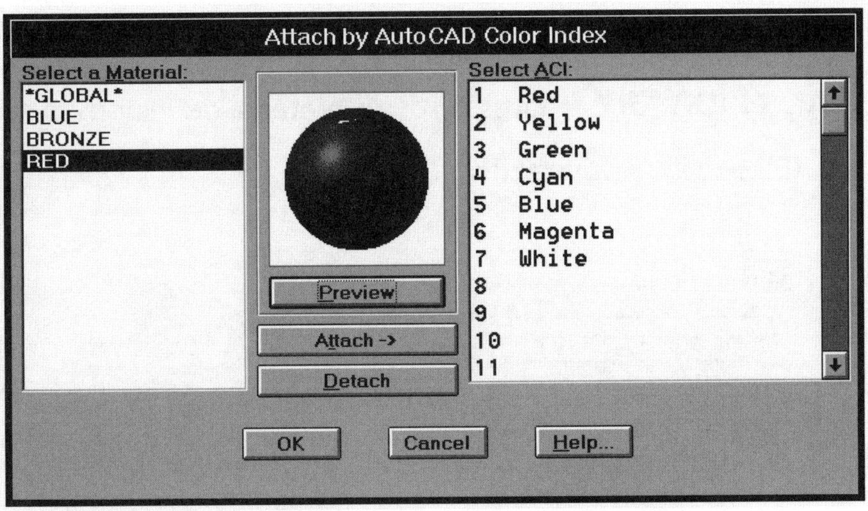

Figure 36-14: The Attach by AutoCAD Color Index dialog.

Click the By Layer... button to display the dialog shown in Figure 36-15. Using this dialog, you can assign a material to one or more layers. All objects on the selected layers render with the assigned material.

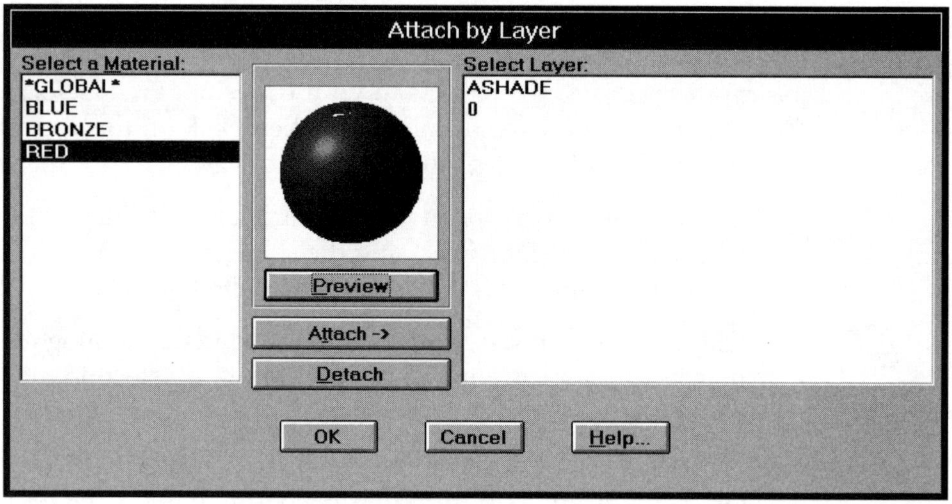

Figure 36-15: The Attach by Layer dialog.

NOTE: Assigning materials by ACI or by layer does not override materials assigned directly to an object with the Attach< button. If you want a object that was previously assigned a material to use the assigned ACI or layer material, you first have to detach the original material from the object.

MATERIALS LIBRARY Saves & recalls material definitions in separate files

COMMAND LINE: **matlib**

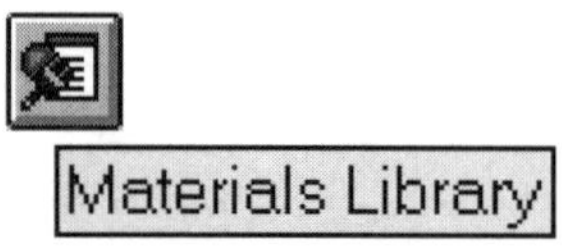

Figure 36-16: The Materials Library icon from the Render toolbar.

Click on the Materials Library icon to display the dialog in Figure 36-17. This dialog provides functions for managing, saving, and transferring material definition between files. The dialog can be divided into three parts: the materials controls, the library controls and the transfer controls.

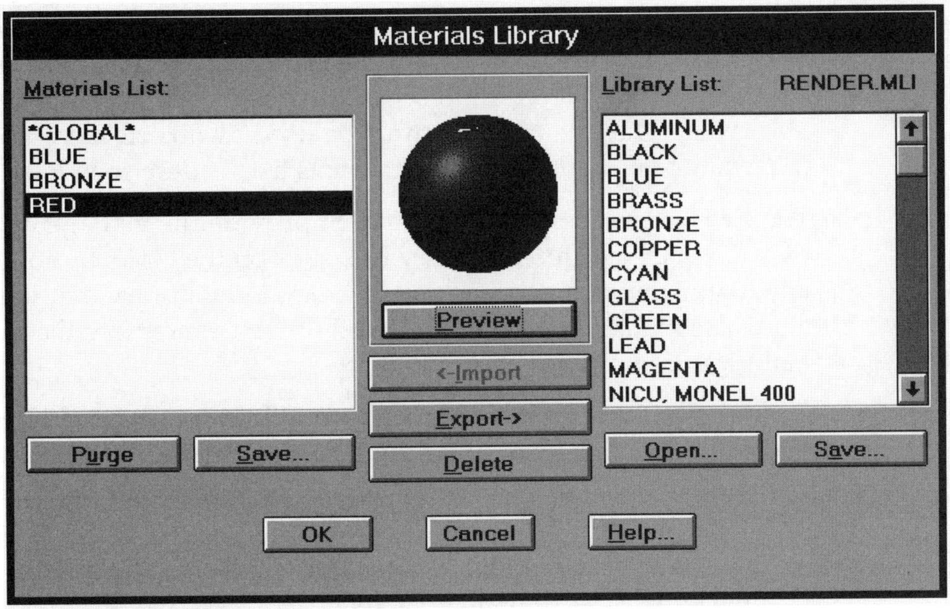

Figure 36-17: The Materials Library dialog.

The Materials List

The left side of the dialog contains the materials list and its related controls. As you design materials using the Materials command described above, the new materials name and definitions are placed in the materials list. These materials are stored as part of your drawing file and are not available to objects in other drawings.

The two buttons beneath the materials list allow you to purge unused materials and save the material definitions to an external file.

To remove unused materials, click on the Purge button. A dialog appears asking if you are sure that you want to delete all unused materials. Click on OK to delete materials that have not been assigned to either an object, an ACI value or a layer name.

To save the current material definitions to an external library file, click on the Save button. The library file dialog appears and you specify the drive, directory and name for the new material library. Material library files have an extension of .MLI. Materials stored in libraries can be loaded and used by other drawing files.

The Library List

The right side of the dialog contains the library list and its related controls. All the materials stored in the currently loaded library appear in the library list. These materials cannot be used by objects in your drawing until they are imported to the materials list, as described later.

The two buttons below the library list provide file management for library files. To open a different library file, click on the Open button. The Library File dialog appears and you select the material library that you want to load. The materials from the selected library file replace the previous materials in the library list.

To save any changes made to the current library, click on the Save button. It is possible to delete materials and to export materials from your drawing into the current library. When you do this, you will probably want to save those changes in the library file. Clicking on the Save button causes the Library File dialog to appear again so that you can save the library to its original name or give it a new name.

Material Transfer Controls

The buttons in the middle of the Materials Library dialog provide controls for moving between your drawing and the current materials library. The functions of these buttons are described below:

Preview	Click on this button to display a single selected material from either list. If more than one material is selected, this button is not available.
<Import	If materials are selected in the library list, the <Import button is available. Click on <Import to copy the selected materials into the drawing's materials list. Once the materials are in the materials list, they are saved with the drawing whether or not they are actually used.
Export>	If materials are selected in the materials list, the Export> button is available. Click on Export> to copy the selected materials into the library list. Once the materials are copied into the library list, you must save the library if you want them permanently saved on disk.
Delete	If materials are selected in either list, you can click on the Delete button to remove them from that list.

RENDER PREFERENCES Sets up rendering preferences

COMMAND LINE: **rpref**

Figure 36-18: The Render Preferences icon from the Render toolbar.

Click on the Render Preferences icon to display the dialog box in Figure 36-19. Using this dialog you can

- Select the rendering type. Third-party rendering programs can be loaded from this pop-up list.
- Set the screen palette parameters based upon your current screen driver.
- Determine the rendering procedure such as rendering the entire scene or only selected objects.
- Set rendering options for smoothing and materials application.
- Determine where the rendered image is sent—either to the current viewport, a separate rendering window or a standard graphics file on disk.
- Adjust the display size of the icon block in the drawing to make it easier to see.

You can also click on the Reconfigure< button to change the configured rendering display driver.

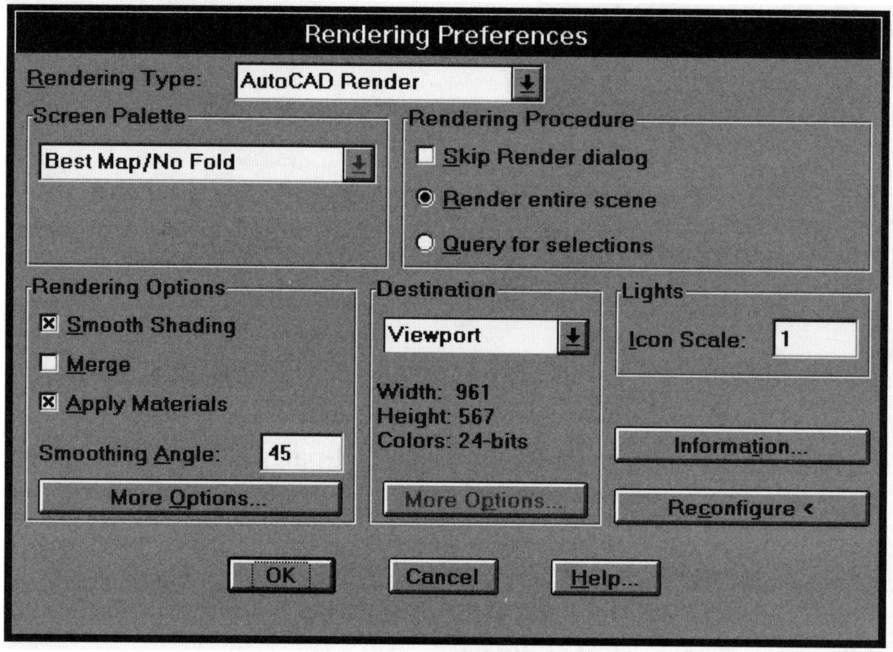

Figure 36-19: The Rendering Preferences dialog.

See the *AutoCAD Reference Manual* for details on the Rendering Preferences options.

RENDER Creates a rendered image

COMMAND LINE: **render**

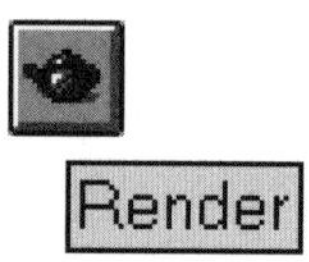

Figure 36-20: The Render icon from the Render toolbar.

Clicking on the Render icon displays the Render dialog in Figure 36-21. Using this dialog, you can select which of your named scenes to render and you can override many of the rendering preferences described above.

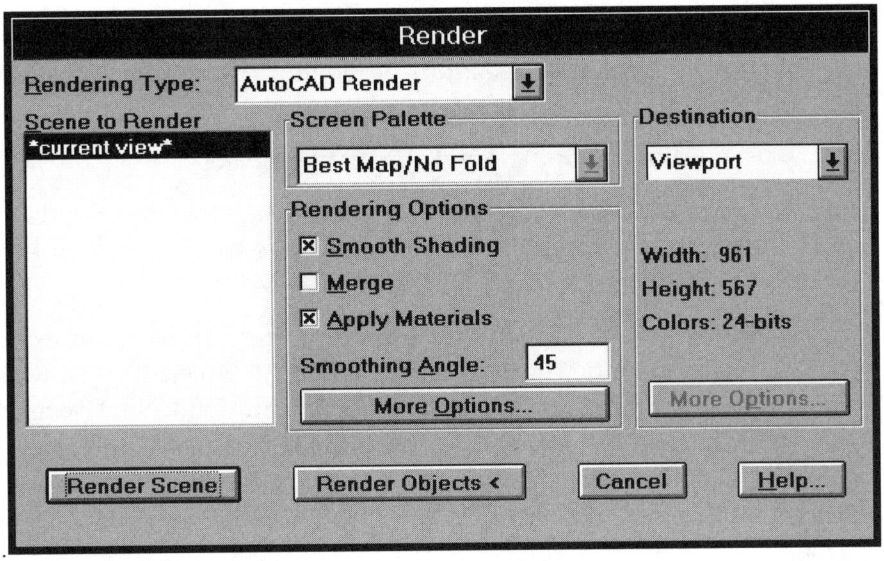

Figure 36-21: The Render dialog.

Click on the Render Scene button to render the selected scene.

Click on the Render Objects< button to hide the dialog and select individual objects for rendering.

STATISTICS Display information about the last image rendered

COMMAND LINE: **stats**

Figure 36-22: The Statistics icon from the Render toolbar.

Clicking on the Statistics icon displays a dialog with the following information:

Name of the last scene rendered.

Type of last rendering.

Time to produce the last rendering.

Total faces and triangles rendered.

You also have the option to save the information to a text file.

Rendering Tips

If you follow these suggestions while you're creating AutoCAD models, your renderings will be faster and better:

Avoid overlapping and intersecting objects.

Use the 3D construction tools in the Surfaces and Solids toolbars whenever possible. These objects have their surface normals aligned for faster rendering.

Avoid a high density of faces on planar surfaces. For example, a flat surface can be represented by a 3DFACE (one face), a RULESURF (several faces) or an EDGESURF (multiple faces). For rendering purposes, the fewer faces used the better.

Moving on

The next chapter introduces the use of attributes as a method of storing non-graphic data in your drawings.

CHAPTER 37

Attributes

This chapter shows you how to *create, use* and *extract* text attributes. An Attribute is a variable text field within a block. Put simply, it is a block with text information data attached.

To use attributes, you first define them, placing as many different attributes in a block as needed. Second, use the INSERT command and insert the attributes into a drawing, anwering the onscreen prompts. Third, edit the Attributes to update the drawing as required. Finally, extract the Attributes with the ATTEXT command.

Choose Tools, and then choose Toolbar and activate the Attribute icons (see Figure 37-1 below). The four icons are Define Attribute, Redefine Attribute, Edit Attribute and Edit Attribute Globally.

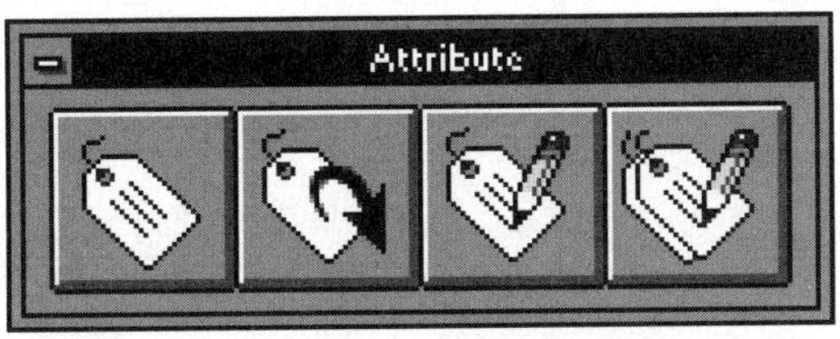

Figure 37-1: The four Attribute icons.

The Define Attribute icon displays the Attribute Definition dialog (see DDATTDEF later in this chapter). The three remaining icons—Redefine Attribute (ATTREDEF), Edit Attribute (DDATTE) and Edit Attribute Globally (ATTEDIT)—allow you to edit Attributes. See "Editing Attributes" later in the chapter.

Attribute Uses

Several different attributes are usually included in one block. An attribute can also be the only object in a block.

Attributes can be used in dimensions and notations as well as with actual parts of the drawing's geometry. For example, you could define a block called TOL (for tolerance) with two attributes; one called PLUS and the other called MINUS. As the block was inserted, it would display prompts for plus and minus tolerances. The text's height would be smaller than usual so that when you placed the attribute in the drawing, the dimension with its tolerance would be proportional to a typical hand-lettered dimension.

Or you could create a block called FR (for fraction) with two attributes and tags of NUMERATOR and DENOMINATOR. After prompting for numerator and denominator, this block would place a true fraction in the drawing with the numerator above, rather than in line with the denominator.

Attribute Commands & Their Meanings

There are two commands to create attributes with onscreen tags and user prompts. Each has the same end result, but the method of input is different—one is input at the command line, the other within a dialog. Choose the Define Attribute icon from the Attribute toolbar to display a dialog box. Alternatively, at the command line type **attdef** and follow the onscreen prompts. ATTDEF uses the same prompts as DDATTDEF, explained below.

DDATTDEF Creates attributes through an onscreen dialog box

COMMAND LINE: **ddattdef** or **attdef**

An attribute is simply information in the form of text assigned to a block. The text can either be predetermined or entered at the same time a block is inserted.

Figure 37-2: The Define Attribute icon from the Attribute toolbar.

To display the dialog, choose the Define Attribute icon.

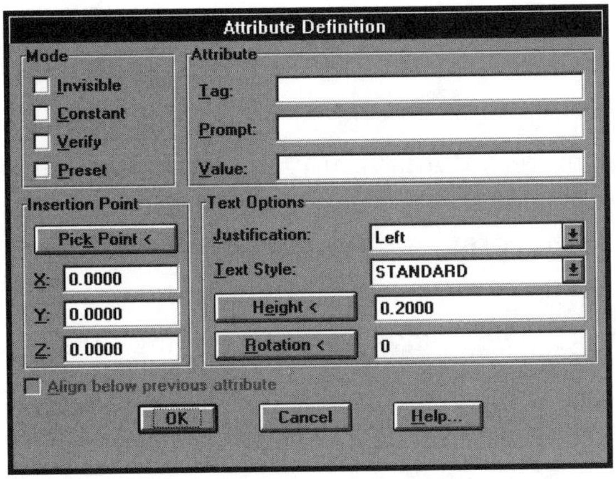

Figure 37-3: The Attribute Definition dialog box.

The Attribute Definition dialog displays four modes which are, by default, turned off. To turn a mode on, click in the appropriate check box.

Invisible	By default, attributes appear onscreen and are plotted. Check this option to make attributes invisible.
Constant	The default is N. You're prompted to enter a value each time you insert the block with this attribute active. (If Constant is changed to Y, each insertion of the block has the same value, which cannot be edited later.)
Verify	The default is N; there is no opportunity to verify a constant value.
Preset	The default is N. The value is requested during insertion of the block. If Preset is changed to Y, AutoCAD does not request the value, but assigns the default value (or assigns null if there is no default value). Dialog boxes used to assign attribute values operate the same, whether Preset is N or Y.

In the Tag field, enter the attribute tag (the name of the attribute). It must be a single name with no spaces.

In the Prompt field of the dialog, enter the prompt that you want to appear when the block is inserted and the default value in response to that prompt, if any. Phrase your response in this field in question format, as it is aimed at the operator who will eventually insert the attribute.

NOTE: *If you checked the Constant mode, you're asked for the value instead of the default value.*

Choose Pick points> in the dialog to locate the starting point of the text (or A for aligned, C for centered, R for right-justified or S for style), then enter the height and angle, similar to the TEXT command. To place an attribute tag immediately below the previous tag, press Enter when asked for a starting point.

Then choose OK. AutoCAD displays the attribute tag (in all caps) on the drawing.

To make this attribute part of a block, you select it with the other attributes and objects that make up the block.

When the block is subsequently inserted, the prompt you entered earlier asks you for the value (text) to be associated with this attribute. The value you enter is displayed in place of the tag (assuming Invisible mode is N).

Editing Attributes

The three remaining icons within the Attribute toolbar are as follows:

The Redefine Attribute icon uses the ATTREDEF command and allows you to redefine an attribute or insertion base point onscreen. The Edit Attribute icon uses the DDATTE command to activate the Attribute Editing dialog for single-attribute edits. And the Edit Attribute Globally icon uses the ATTEDIT command to allow you to edit multiple attributes throughout the whole drawing at the keyboard.

ATTREDEF Redefines an attribute block & updates its attributes

COMMAND LINE: **attredef**

Use the ATTREDEF (redefine attribute) command to modify and update an existing attribute within a block. Choose the Redefine Attribute icon.

Figure 37-4: The Redefine Attribute icon from the Attribute toolbar.

As you activate the command, you'll enter the responses in the floating command window. Answer the prompts as follows:

1. Name of block you wish to redefine: Type in a block name at this response.

2. Select objects for new block: Pick any new and existing objects onscreen you wish to place into your existing block. If you wish to include old attributes associated with the block, do so. Otherwise they are deleted.

3. Insertion base point of new block: Either choose the original insertion base point, or choose a new location. Your block will then be updated.

DDATTE Edits the individual variable attributes of a block already placed in a drawing

COMMAND LINE: **ddatte**

Use the DDATTE command to update text information in your attribute block. You can edit individual variable attributes onscreen through the Edit Attributes dialog.

Choose the Edit Attribute icon from the Attribute toolbar.

Figure 37-5: The Edit Attribute icon from the Attribute toolbar.

At the select Block prompt, select the attribute block to be edited. Your attributes are then displayed in the Edit Attributes dialog. Simply edit the attributes you need to update, then pick OK.

You cannot edit an attribute's properties (location, height and style) with this command. You must use the next command, ATTEDIT.

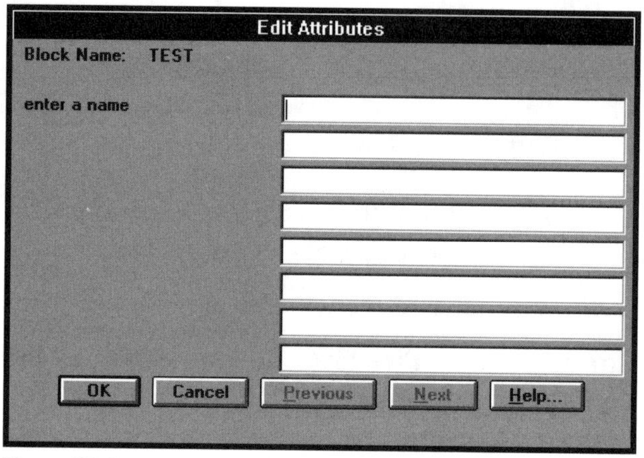

Figure 37-6: The Edit Attributes dialog.

ATTEDIT Edits attributes associated with inserted blocks

COMMAND LINE: **attedit**

With this command, you can edit an attribute's properties such as location, height and style, globally or singly. A global attribute edit limits you to replacing a single text string with an updated text string. A single attribute edit allows you to make multiple changes to a single attribute.

Figure 37-7: The Edit Attribute icon from the Attribute toolbar.

Choose the Edit Attribute Globally icon or type the command at the command window prompt. Then enter

y to edit attributes individually.

n to edit attributes globally (replacing one specified text string with another in a specified group of attributes).

You're then prompted for block name, tag and value specifications. You can limit the group of attributes selected for editing by entering specific block names, tag names or values in response to the above prompts. Or you can use the wild card default to edit all blocks, tags and values.

Then indicate whether you want your editing limited to onscreen attributes. Onscreen editing can be further limited to a window.

If you're doing global editing, enter the old text string and the new text string.

If you're doing individual editing, the first attribute is marked with an X.

Now enter

n to select the next attribute.

v to change the value of the marked attribute. Then enter **c** to change a few characters, or enter **r** to replace the entire value.

p to change the position of the marked attribute.

h to change the height of the marked attribute.

a to change the angle of the marked attribute.

s to change the text style of the marked attribute.

l to change the layer of the marked attribute.

You may also edit attribute values with a dialog box. To call up the dialog box, enter **ddatte**.

ATTDISP Determines visibility of attributes (use it to hide the attributes before plotting)

COMMAND LINE: **attdisp**

If you have placed attributes within a drawing and wish to plot the drawing file, you can use ATTDISP to turn off the attributes before plotting and later turn them back on.

Enter **attdisp** at the command line. When prompted, enter

> **n** for normal display mode. Whether attributes are displayed depends on whether invisible mode was N or Y when the attribute was created with the ATTDEF command.
>
> **on** to display all attributes.
>
> **off** to suppress all attributes.

DDATTEXT Extracts attributes to an ASCII text file for use by other programs

COMMAND LINE: **ddattext** or **attext**

To access the Attribute Extraction dialog, enter **ddattext** in the command window. Before you can use DDATTEXT to extract a CDF or SDF file, you must create a Template File. See "Creating a Template File" below. You may also type **attext** at the command line.

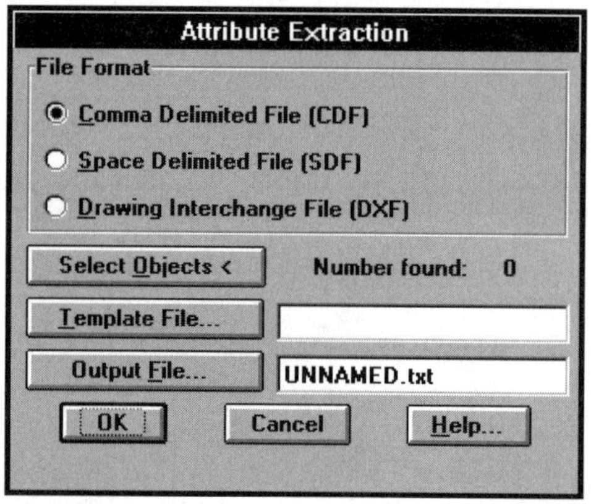

Figure 37-8: The Attribute Extraction dialog.

The dialog box shown in Figure 37-8 offers three file formats that you may choose:

> **CDF** (**C**omma **D**elimited **F**ormat) file. This is a sequential file that can be processed by another program.
>
> **SDF** (standard data, or **S**pace **D**elimited **F**ormat) file. This is a random access file that can be processed by another program.

DXF (**D**rawing e**X**change **F**ormat) file. This is similar in format to AutoCAD's drawing interchange files.

Choosing the Select Objects < button flips you to the graphics screen and lets you select objects from which you want to extract attribute information. You may select individual blocks or simply type **all**.

Choosing the Template File... button activates the dialog shown in Figure 37-9 to let you select the template text file. It informs the system how to extract attribute information. See "Creating a Template File" below.

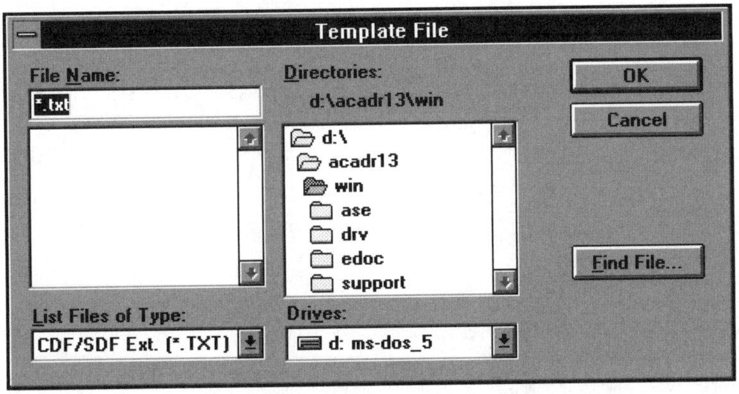

Figure 37-9: The Attribute Extraction Template File dialog.

Choose the Output File... button to activate the dialog shown in Figure 37-10 to let you select the output text file. It informs the system where to extract your attribute information and what to name it.

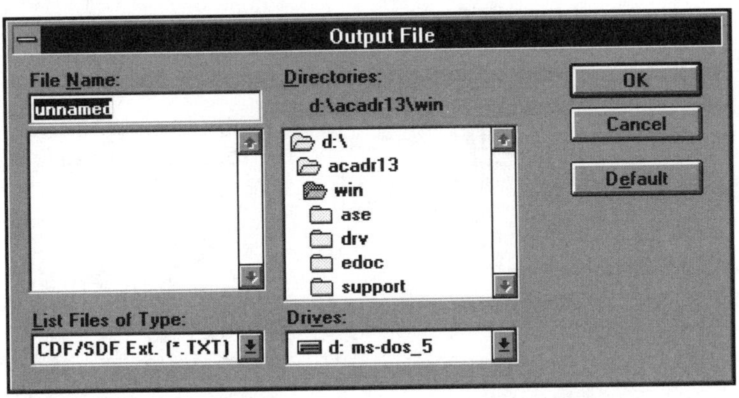

Figure 37-10: The Attribute Extraction Output File dialog.

Creating a Template File

Template files determine the structure of CDF and SDF extract files. They have the extension .TXT and are created with a text editor. Each line in the template file specifies one type of column to be included in the extract file. The number of lines of values under these headings in the extract file is determined by the number of blocks from which the attribute values are extracted.

The sample template file below would produce an extract file having the headings NAME, X(coordinate), Y(coordinate), Z(coordinate), PART_NO and VENDOR. A heading name such as VENDOR in the template file must be exactly the same as the tag name for the attribute in the drawing. The headings below that start with BL will pick up the indicated information from the various blocks.

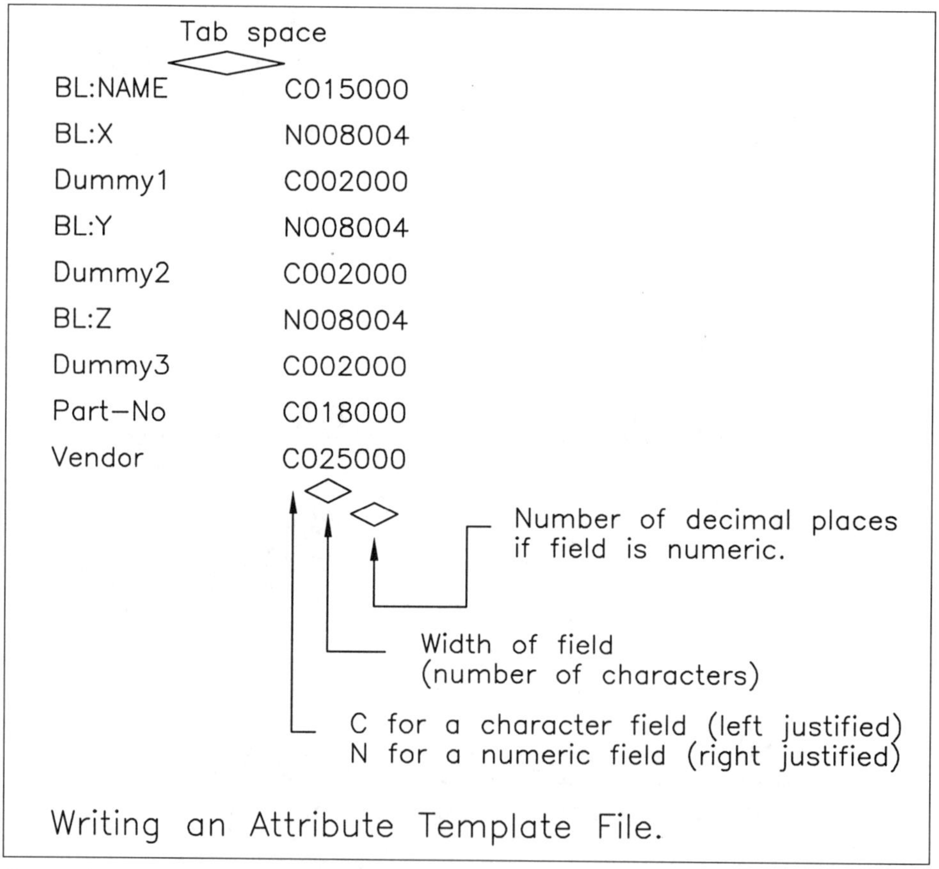

Figure 37-11: Writing an attribute template file. It must be set into fields as shown.

Besides using BL:NAME to extract the block's name and BL:X, BL:Y, and BL:Z to extract the block's location, you can also extract the block's nesting level, number, handle, layer of insertion, rotation, scaling factors and extrusion. See the *AutoCAD Reference Manual*.

The AutoCAD program files include some sample BASIC programs that post-process these files. See Appendix B for a sample extract file and post-process file.

Moving on

If you've worked through this chapter, you've now got a good grounding in attributes. The next chapter, "Shapes," reviews creating shapes and text font files.

CHAPTER 38

Shapes

Shapes are a type of drawing object in many ways similar to a block. A shape is a complex graphic inserted into your drawing by placing a single point. A shape may also be scaled and rotated as it is inserted. That is where the similarity to blocks ends.

Unlike blocks, shapes are read from an external file every time AutoCAD loads a drawing. If you use shapes in your drawing, you must keep the external shape file available or AutoCAD will post an error message the next time it tries to load the drawing. Also, unlike blocks, shapes cannot be created in the drawing editor. You must define a shape by writing its description with an ASCII text editor.

Because of these limitations, few people create shapes for their own use. Most purchase shapes from third-party programmers or use the shapes shipped with AutoCAD. Shapes are popular with programmers because they are compact and efficient, and can be compiled for speed and security.

Shape files mostly define text fonts, but you can also use shape files for other types of drawing components. This chapter shows you how to use, load and create shape files.

LOAD Loads a shape file into memory

COMMAND LINE: **load**

Choose Shape File from the Data pull-down menu to display the Select Shape File dialog shown in Figure 38-1. Select the shape file that you want to load and click on OK. Before you can use a shape, you must load the external shape file into memory.

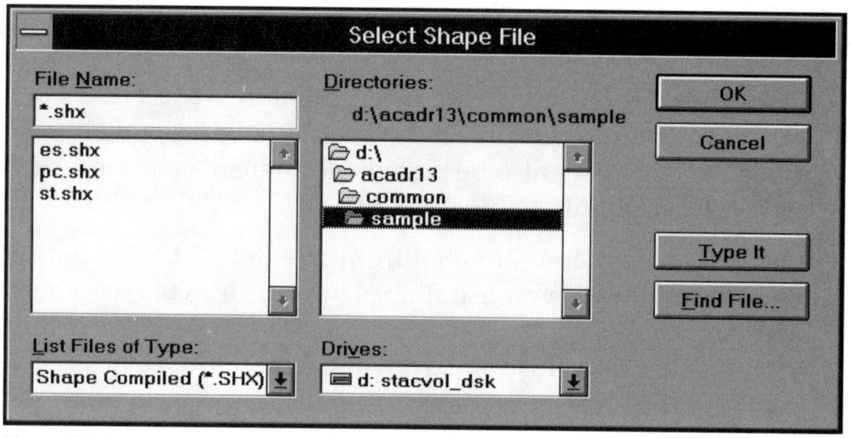

Figure 38-1: The Select Shape File dialog.

NOTE: Although text fonts are also shape files, they are loaded automatically when you define a text style. See Chapter 16, "Text."

SHAPE

Places a predefined shape in a drawing

COMMAND LINE: **shape**

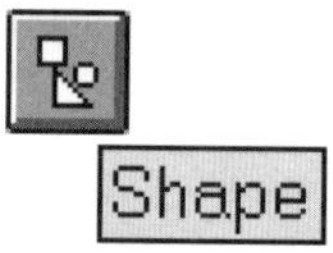

Figure 38-2: The Shape icon from the Miscellaneous toolbar.

When you click on the Shape icon, you are prompted to enter the shape name. You have two options:

1. Enter the desired shape name.

2. Enter **?** to display a list of the available shapes, then restart the shape command and enter the desired shape name. Next, you are prompted for a starting point, shape height and rotation angle. This procedure is similar to inserting blocks.

Creating Shape and Text Font Files

This section describes how to create shape files and text font files. These files are similar in many ways, but text font files have certain unique features, which are mentioned where appropriate.

Shape files and text font files are created as regular text files with the extension .SHP. They can be created using a text editor.

For AutoCAD's use, these files are then compiled using the COMPILE command. When they are compiled, a new file is created and given the same name but with extension .SHX. To edit a shape file, edit the .SHP file, then recompile it.

Sample shape files ES.SHP, PC.SHP and ST.SHP are supplied with AutoCAD on the \ACADR13\COMMON\SAMPLE directory under the AutoCAD program files. PC.SHX is for printed circuit layout. ES.SHX is for electronics schematics. ST.SHX is for surface texture files.

The ST.SHP (Surface Texture File)

The shape definitions in this file may be loaded into AutoCAD and then used to annotate mechanical part drawings that specify surface texture.

NOTE: AutoCAD provides the shapes as examples of shape definition only.

Examine the .SHP files with the TYPE command or use the text editor. Remember to make copies of the files before editing them.

Each shape in a file is assigned a number from 1 to 255. The shapes (letters, etc.) in a text font file are assigned their ASCII numbers (for example, A is ASCII #65, a is #97, 1 is #49, etc.).

Each shape is created in two lines in the file (see the sample below). The first line (the identifying line) contains an asterisk, then the assigned number, then the number of bytes used in the second line to define the shape, then the name of the shape (in uppercase letters for shape files, preferably in lowercase letters for text font files).

When a text font file that has the shape names in lowercase is compiled, the names are not loaded, which saves space in memory. (AutoCAD doesn't need the names of text font shapes because the shapes are accessed by ASCII number instead of name.)

The second line (the defining line) contains a series of numbers. Some of these numbers define vectors in the shape; other numbers are special codes, which are explained later.

Some of the numbers in the defining line are hexadecimal numbers (base 16) rather than decimal numbers (base 10).

Decimal notation:	0	1	2	3	4	5	6	7	8	9	10	11	12	13	14	15
Hexadecimal notation:	0	1	2	3	4	5	6	7	8	9	A	B	C	D	E	F

Sample: These two lines define the uppercase A pictured in Figure 38-3.

(Identifying line) `*65,12,uca`

(Defining line) `063,2,04B,1,040,2,045,1,06D,2,020,0`

Each three-digit number is a hexadecimal number. The leading zero identifies the next two digits as hexadecimal digits. In these three-digit numbers, the middle digit gives the length of the vector, while the final digit gives the direction of the vector. Notice that the number of bytes in the identifying line (12) includes the terminating zero.

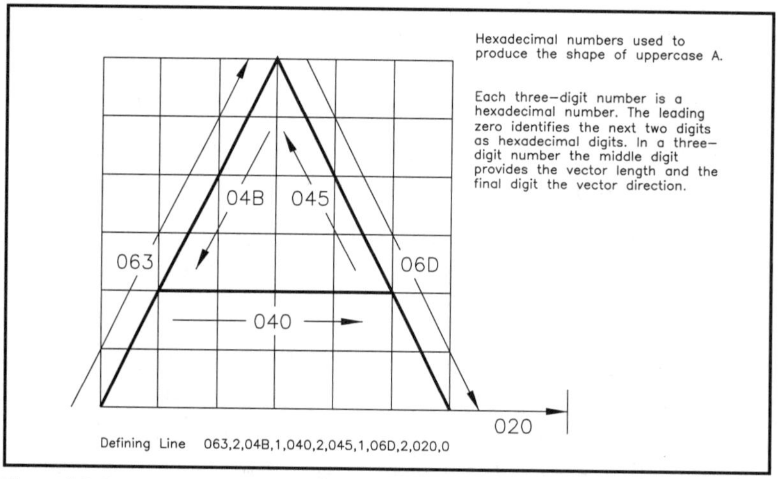

Figure 38-3: Hexadecimal numbers to create shape of uppercase A.

Vector directions are given in the diagram below. Even though the vectors have slightly different lengths, they are all considered one vector-length long for purposes of defining shapes.

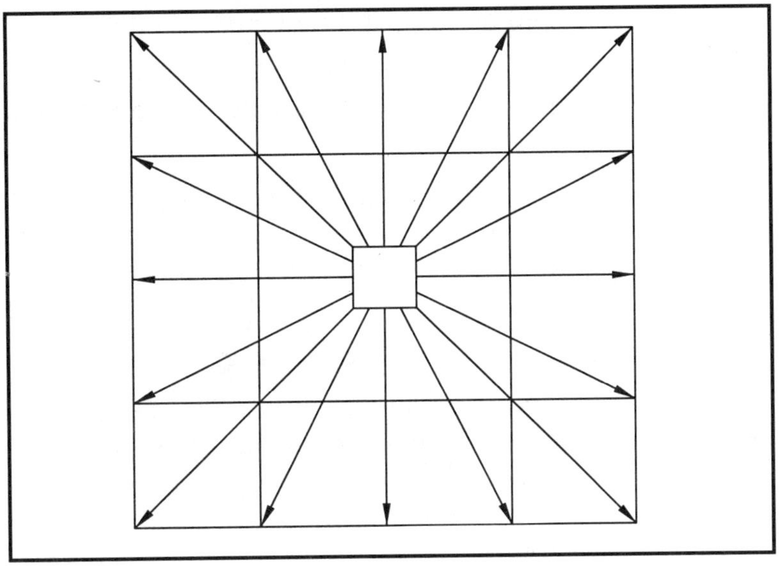

Figure 38-4: Vector directions used for defining a shape.

Shape and font definitions can include nonstandard vectors, which are simply X,Y displacements if codes 8 and/or 9 are used (see codes below). You can also use octant arcs and bulge arcs. For more information, see the *AutoCAD Reference Manual.*

Besides the three-digit numbers in the defining line that give the length and direction of vectors, one- and two-digit numbers are used to encode special instructions, as follows:

0	End of shape definition
1	Pen down
2	Pen up
3	Divide vector lengths by next byte
4	Multiply vector lengths by next byte
5	Push current location onto stack
6	Pop current location from stack
7	Draw sub-shape number given by next byte
8	X,Y displacement given in next two bytes
9	Multiple X,Y displacements, terminated by (0,0)
10	Octant arc defined by next two bytes
11	Fractional arc defined by next five bytes

12 Arc defined by X,Y displacement and bulge
13 Multiple bulge-specified arcs
14 Process next command only if vertical text style (used in dual-orientation fonts)

Although it isn't necessary, readability is improved if these code numbers are in decimal notation (without leading zeros) and vector indicators are in hexadecimal notation (with leading zeros); as illustrated in the earlier sample.

The pen is assumed to be down at the start of each shape.

For several lines of text to be written by a text font file, that file must also contain a pair of lines that will allow for a line feed (ASCII #10).

Line feed: `*10,3,lf`
`2,0AC,0`

In the illustration given earlier, capital letters are six vector-lengths high, so a suitable line feed is 10 vector-lengths down. Thus, the defining line for the line feed gives the following instructions: Raise the pen, move A vector-lengths, move in direction C.

One more pair of lines is needed to complete a text font file. These two lines must be the very first lines in the text font file, since they contain the name of the font and certain governing statistics about the font, as shown below.

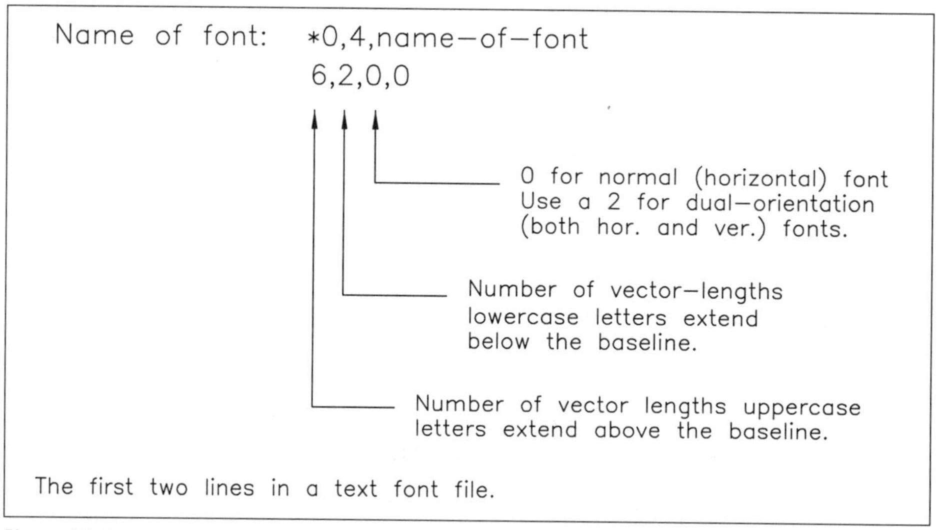

Figure 38-5: The first two lines in a text font file.

COMPILE Compiles a shape or text font file

COMMAND LINE: **compile**

A compiled shape or font file is more proficient and faster to load. Besides normal shape and font compilation, Release 13 also allows you to compile and use PostScript and TrueType font files.

Choose Compile from the Tools pull-down menu to display the Select Shape File dialog shown in Figure 38-6. Standard AutoCAD shape and font files have an extension of .SHP but you can also compile PostScript fonts, which have an extension of .PFB. Compiling a PostScript font file will create an .SHX file the same as compiling a standard shape file.

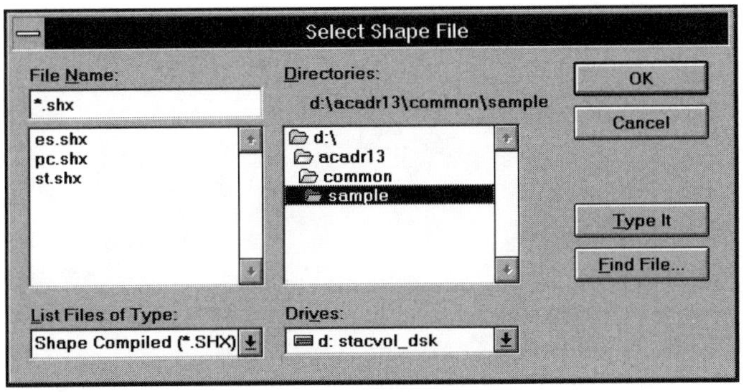

Figure 38-6: The Select Shape File dialog.

Moving on

The next chapter discusses the creation of AutoCAD script files for creating slide shows and automating repetitive tasks. The next chapter also provides some general tips for using the Windows Notepad ASCII text editor.

CHAPTER 39

Text Editing & Scripts

If you'd like to adjust AutoCAD features, you'll be glad to know that AutoCAD is wide open to customization. In fact, one of its greatest strengths is that you can adapt so many of its features and automate almost any sequence of steps. To customize AutoCAD, however, you must use an ASCII text editor.

Customized text files add efficiency and power to AutoCAD. Among the many types of text files that AutoCAD uses, particularly for customization, are script files, linetype files, shape and font files, menu files, dialog control files and AutoLISP programs.

Using a Text Editor

It's worth your while to master a good text editor that produces straight ASCII files, especially if you plan to advance to the point of customizing AutoCAD. Windows has a suitable text editor in the Notepad program, and DOS has its own EDIT.

This chapter uses the Windows Notepad for creating a sample script. A number of other text editors cater to the needs of programmers. The alternative to a text editor is to use a word processor, but be careful. Most word processors add formatting symbols to your files or save the text in a non-ASCII format. If you use a word processor, you need to check its documentation for a way to save as ASCII or print to a DOS text file.

NOTE: *Some text editors can erase or overwrite your drawing backup files, particularly if they create backup files with a .BAK extension. For example, if your text file has the same primary name as one of your drawings, that drawing backup file is lost when you exit the ASCII editor. One solution is to avoid giving any text file the same name as a drawing file. A second but easier solution is to create and edit your text files in a directory that contains no drawing backup files.*

SCRIPT

Executes a series of commands & responses from an external script file

COMMAND LINE: **script**

Choose Run Script from the Tools pull-down menu to display the Select Script File dialog. Select a script file and click on OK to run the script.

A script file, which is created using a text editor, must have an extension of .SCR and consists of a series of AutoCAD commands and responses to command prompts. AutoCAD executes the commands and responses stored in the script file as though you had typed them from the keyboard.

Note that the script command was developed early in the AutoCAD life cycle. Scripts only work with commands that can be executed entirely from the keyboard. You must always use the older, command line-based version of a command when you include it in a script, and you must know exactly the order and format of every prompt that the command presents.

This is not a problem with commands that support both methods. An example of this is the creation and managing of layers. DDLMODES is the dialog-based version of layer control, and LAYER is the older, command line-based version. However, some commands such as GROUP, MTEXT and FILTER always display a dialog and are unusable within script files.

NOTE: *Many dialog-based commands can be used by accessing their LISP-based equivalent functions within a script. This is a very advanced technique. See the book* AutoLISP in Plain English *for details of LISP programming.*

Script files are useful for setting up such drawing configurations as units, limits, snap and grid, and for establishing several layers with associated colors and linetypes. Prototype drawings do the same thing, but you use those only when a new drawing is started. In contrast, scripts can be run at any time from the beginning to the end of a drawing.

You can also use script files to

1. Add predetermined sets of layers to a drawing.
2. Convert system variables, dimension styles and text style to adjust for changes in a drawing's plotting scale.
3. Run presentations and slide shows. See Chapter 27, "Images," for details of the VSLIDE command.

To stop a running script, press the Backspace key. Restart a script that has been stopped by entering **resume** at the command line.

A Sample Script With the Windows Notepad

The following script file manipulates layers in a drawing by changing the colors of some layers, turning some layers off and turning other layers on. Perhaps you have a site plan of a hospital complex used for facilities management. This plan contains many layers showing drainage flow, soil properties, building outlines and paving areas. As a technician in the facilities department, you use this drawing to make plots of various site conditions. This script shows how you could set up the layers for plotting a presentation landscape plan.

1. Minimize the AutoCAD window by clicking on the minimize button.
2. Launch the Notepad program by double-clicking the Notepad icon.
3. Enter the following, pressing Enter at the end of each line:

```
; Beginning of Script
LAYER
S 0
OFF * Y
ON
BUILDINGS,PAVING,PARKING,TREES,PLANTING,P-NOTES
C RED
BUILDINGS,TREES,PLANTING
C YELLOW
PAVING,PARKING
C GREEN
P-NOTES
   This is a blank space for return
; End of Script
```

4. Choose Save from Notepad's File pull-down menu and save the file as SITE-P.SCR in your projects directory.
5. Minimize Notepad and restore AutoCAD by double-clicking on the AutoCAD icon.
6. Choose Run Script from the Tools pull-down menu and select SITE-P.SCR in the dialog.

This script executes the command line-based version of the LAYER command, sets layer 0 as the current layer and turns off all other layers. It then turns on the layers needed for the presentation site plan and assigns the layers the proper colors for that type of plot. You could create a number of scripts that would set up this drawing for many different types of plots.

Tips on Writing Script Files

1. Lines beginning with a semicolon are considered comments and are ignored by AutoCAD.

2. Everything in the script is treated exactly the same as if you typed it at the command line. Spaces are treated the same as pressing Enter. In a script file

```
ERASE ALL
```

is the same as:

```
ERASE
ALL
```

3. Because of number two above, you should not end any line of a script file with spaces. Extra spaces at the end of a line are treated as returns. Even if you need an extra return (as with the last executable line of the sample script above), it is best to use a blank line rather than extra spaces.

There are two reasons not to use spaces at the end of a line. First, some text editors automatically remove spaces from the ends of lines while others do not. This leads to problems if you share scripts with people who use different text editors. Second, spaces do not show up well at the end of a line, and this makes it difficult (if not impossible) to go back and edit your scripts later.

4. Any time that you find yourself repeating a sequence of several commands over and over, you should consider writing a script to accomplish the same task. Once a script is written and saved in an .SCR file, it can be used repeatedly and with many different files.

Scripts have one advantage over AutoLISP programming—they're easier to write since you don't have to learn a programming language and you already know the AutoCAD commands. However, scripts also have a major drawback—they aren't interactive. You can't write a script that asks for information in the middle of the script. However, AutoLISP programs are interactive. They can also make complex calculations, work with files and access the drawing's database, which makes AutoLISP a far more powerful and flexible tool. Nevertheless, scripts are just right for repetitive tasks.

RESUME Restarts a script that's been stopped

COMMAND LINE: **resume**

Scripts stop when they come to an invalid response to a prompt or command. You can stop a running script by pressing the Backspace key.

In either case, enter **resume** to restart the script at the next command in the script file.

DELAY Delays execution of the next command for a specified period

COMMAND LINE: **delay**

To delay the execution of the next command in a script file, use the DELAY command, followed by a space, followed by a number to indicate the length of the delay. Computer models vary; experiment with DELAY 1000 or DELAY 5000 to see how your computer reacts to the delay timer. On most models, DELAY 1000 is usually one second (the 1000 refers to micro-second time units).

RSCRIPT Causes the current script to repeat from the beginning

COMMAND LINE: **rscript**

Entering **rscript** at the command line reruns the previous script. Include the command RSCRIPT as the last line of a script file to cause that script to repeat continuously. You must then exit the script by pressing Esc or Backspace.

TEXTSCR Displays the text window within a script

COMMAND LINE: **textscr**

Using TEXTSCR in a script file causes the text window to appear, the same as pressing F2 when the drawing window is active.

GRAPHSCR Displays the drawing window (hides the text window) with a script

COMMAND LINE: **graphscr**

Using GRAPHSCR in a script file will cause the text window to disappear, the same as pressing F2 when the text window is active.

You can use the TEXTSCR and GRAPHSCR commands in single-screen systems to do what F2 does. Like F2, you can use them in the middle of another command by placing an apostrophe in front of them.

Moving on

The next chapter delves even deeper into customizing AutoCAD to meet your particular needs. Chapter 40, "Customizing AutoCAD," explores the creation of linetypes and menus and the customization of icons.

CHAPTER 40

Customizing AutoCAD

By customizing AutoCAD files, you can become more productive and efficient. AutoCAD's great adaptability makes file customization uncomplicated. You can quickly automate a sequence of CAD steps or adapt certain files and features. By the end of this chapter, you'll be able to adapt your toolbars, write menus and create AutoLISP files to increase your productivity.

The chapter begins with simple customization techniques you can perform from the Preferences dialog and the Configuration menus. It then moves on to the creation of linetypes, hatch patterns and on-line help. Later it explains some more complex types of customization, including customization of shape and font files, the status bar, menu files, tablet and button menus, and finally AutoLISP programs and toolbars.

In our examples throughout, we use the Windows Notepad as a text editing tool. You may prefer the DOS EDIT program or one of the other text editors that professional programmers use.

Customizing System Environment

The Preferences dialog lets you customize system and environment settings. Its settings simply inform AutoCAD where to find certain files and directories. Any changes you make in the Preferences dialog are saved to the ACAD.INI and ACADENV.INI files.

Think of Preferences as the equivalent of the Windows Control Panel, where you set the environment for Windows. But in this instance you configure system and environment settings for AutoCAD to run optimally in Windows. AutoCAD normally configures its own operating environment automatically, and you will not need to alter many settings. If you do make changes, you have to reactivate AutoCAD for them to take effect.

PREFERENCES Lets the user choose system & environment settings

COMMAND LINE: **preferences**

Choose Preferences... from the Options pull-down menu (or from the history cursor menu in the floating command window) to display the Preferences dialog. Five subdialog boxes are then available: System, Environment, Render, International and Misc. To display a different subdialog, pick the tab showing its name.

Preferences System Dialog

Use the Preferences System dialog box to access and alter simple screen type settings. For example, you can activate the Screen menu or the scroll bars. Activating digitizer and mouse input and setting up keystroke commands are others. You have these options:

Screen Menu	Turn on this option to display the screen (side screen) menu. The default is off.
Window Repair	Select this option to repair overlay graphic images as they are removed from the Windows program. The default setting is Bitmap, which means that it uses the standard display driver from AutoCAD. You may have more options.
Digitizer	Toggle here to select a radio button to activate either mouse and digitizer or digitizer only. If you turn on Digitizer, AutoCAD uses the configured digitizer device. If you turn it off, the mouse is used as an input device.
Keystrokes	Toggle here to control how AutoCAD interprets keystrokes. If you toggle the AutoCAD Classic radio button, it allows mode toggle keys to function regardless of the accelerator definition. The Menu File toggle will allow accelerator keys to take precedence.
Automatic Save	If this option is on, AutoCAD automatically saves your current drawing periodically, at the interval you specify here (the default is 120). To change the interval, click in the minutes number box and enter the new number.

Font	Choose Font to display the Font dialog, which shows the current font used to display text in graphics and text windows.
Color	Choose Color to display the Color dialog, which shows the current color settings for elements in the application window.

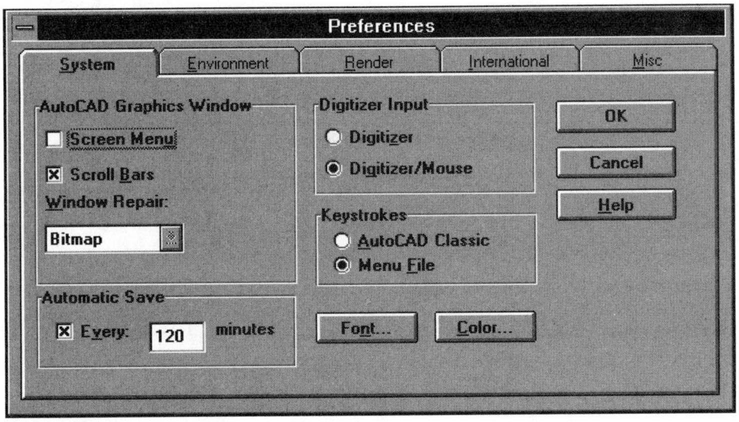

Figure 40-1: Preferences System dialog.

Preferences Environment Dialog

Use the Preferences Environment dialog box shown in Figure 40-2 to update environment settings in your system—that is, to tell AutoCAD where to find the files needed to perform particular tasks. When you install AutoCAD, standard paths and settings are established. However, you may want to change the settings for a variety of reasons.

For example, if you are using a network with a hardware lock, use this dialog to set up and provide access to a directory of temporary files and swap files (\ACAD_TMP). You follow the same procedure for a configuration file, but with a directory of \ACAD_CFG.

At Support, you must also enter the directory of the editor you wish to use for entering paragraph text (using the MTEXT, or multiline text, command). See "Misc. Dialog" later in this chapter.

For files from this book's Companion Disk, you may create a C:\CONCISE directory on your hard-drive before coming to the Environment dialog. Then enter the directory name at Support in the Environment dialog.

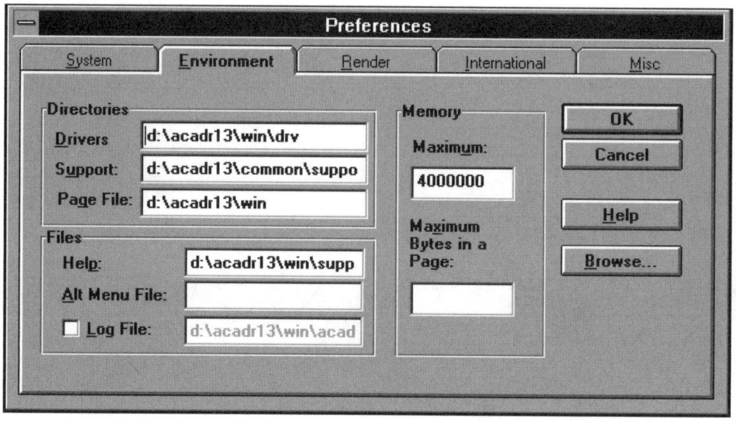

Figure 40-2: Preferences Environment dialog.

Preferences Render Dialog

In the Render dialog, you inform AutoCAD where to find the render environment files and directories. By default, AutoCAD uses the \ACADR13 directory. If you have only a small amount of remaining space in the directory and disk drive, you may wish to use a different disk drive and directory with more space. Set up the rendering environment, configuration, face and page fields to a new directory and drive.

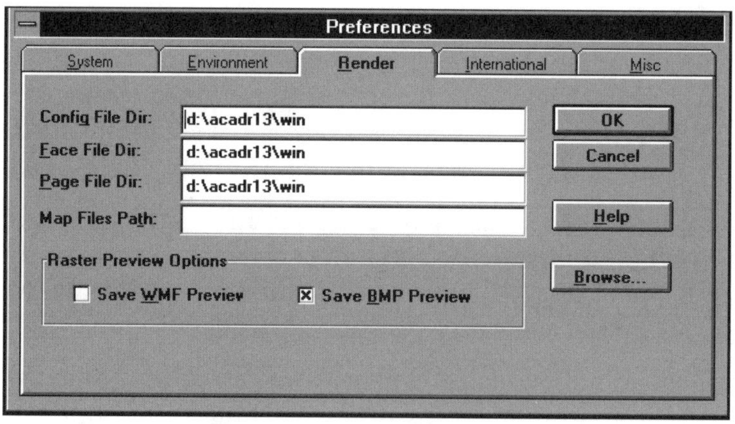

Figure 40-3: Preferences Render dialog.

Preferences International Dialog

The Preferences International dialog box lets you choose English or metric settings and identify the type of prototype drawing to use. The dialog in Figure 40-4 indicates that the English measurement system is in use. It also indicates the Drawing Type as Standard Imperial and the name of the Prototype Drawing as ACAD.DWG. If you wish to use a new or favorite prototype drawing, you'll see its name in the drawing name box. To set the prototype permanently, see the next section on the Configuration menus.

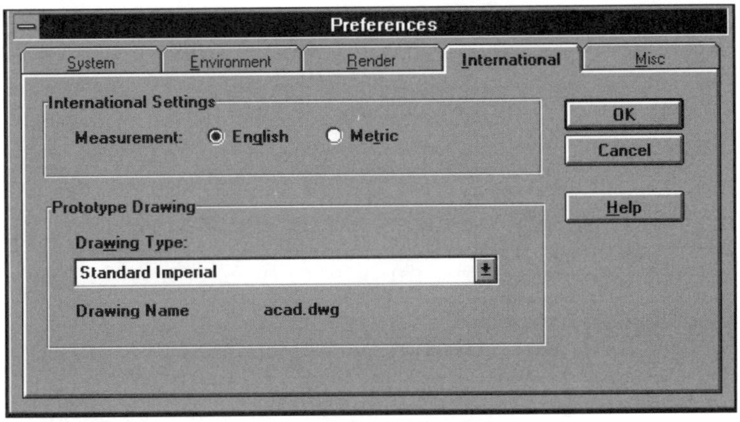

Figure 40-4: Preferences International dialog.

Preferences Misc. Dialog

The Preferences Misc. dialog box is the final settings dialog. It includes miscellaneous items that tell AutoCAD your preferences concerning the text editor, font mapping files and plot spooling.

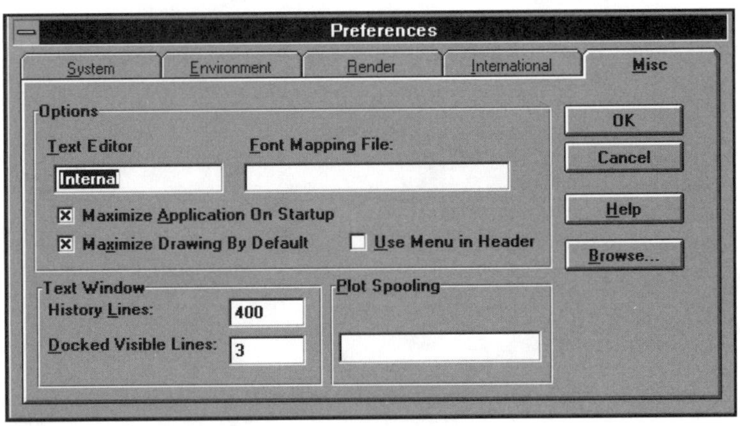

Figure 40-5: Preferences Misc. dialog.

You have these options:

Text Editor	Enter the name of the text editor used by the MTEXT command. The directory where the editor is stored must be specified in Support in the Preferences Environment dialog.
Font Mapping File	The MTEXT command uses this as a naming field to specify its font mapping file.
Maximize	The two maximize toggles control the size of the application window and the AutoCAD drawing window on startup.
Menu in Header	If you toggle this on, the AutoCAD menu file uses this to load the menu file associated with the drawing in the drawing header. Otherwise, AutoCAD uses the loaded menu file for every drawing.
Text Window	Enter the number of lines you wish AutoCAD to show at a time in the floating command window. The History Line option is the number of lines above the command line. The Docked Visible Lines option specifies the number of lines that show as you move the floating command prompt window.
Plot Spooling	If you use a plot spooler to plot in the background as you continue to draw, set up your plot spooler third-party application in this box. (This option sets up the variable ACADPLCMD.)

Configuration Menus

You can do some further customization of the system using the Configuration menu and its submenu, the Configure Operating Parameters menu.

To display the Configuration menu, choose Config from the File pull-down menu (or enter **config** at the command line). To display the submenu, choose Configure Operating Parameters.

Some items on the menus are predetermined by your system's hardware, but there are others you may set up to suit your needs. A few possibilities are mentioned below.

Reassigning Ports

By default, AutoCAD uses the first serial port (COM1) for digitizer input and the first parallel port (LPT1) for output to a printer-plotter or other raster-based printer (such as a dot matrix or laser printer).

If you have more than one serial or parallel port, and especially if you use software that favors a particular port, you may want to choose Allow detailed configuration from the Configuration menu. After you've indicated that you want to configure the I/O ports, AutoCAD lets you select the desired I/O port while you're configuring digitizer, plotter or printer.

Warning Beep

You may want AutoCAD to beep at you when you make an input mistake. Or you may want it to let you make your mistakes in silence. Alarm on Error, on the Configure Operating Parameters menu, lets you decide.

Assigning a Default Prototype

You can install any drawing as the default prototype. To do so, select Initial drawing setup from the Configure Operating Parameters menu and enter the name of the desired drawing.

Customizing the ACAD.PGP File

The ACAD.PGP file lets you access other programs or DOS commands directly from the command prompt. Part of the generic file supplied with AutoCAD is listed below. You will find the ACAD.PGP file on the \ACADR13\COMMON\SUPPORT directory under the directory holding your AutoCAD program files.

```
CATALOG,DIR /W,    0,File specification: ,0
DEL,DEL,           0,File to delete: ,4
DIR,DIR,           0,File specification: ,0
EDIT,EDIT,         0,File to edit: ,4
SH,,               0,*OS Command: ,4
SHELL,,            0,*OS Command: ,4
TYPE,TYPE,         0,File to list: ,0
```

In each line, the first field is the command you would enter while in command mode. The second field is the command sent to the other program or operating system. The third field specifies the amount of memory that must be released in order to execute the command or program. (AutoCAD manages this, so your file can include 0 here.) The fourth field is an optional prompt. If this field begins with an asterisk, the user may include spaces in his/her response. Otherwise, a space "enters" the response. The optional fifth field specifies special codes for specific software. Notice that it's either a 0 (zero) or a 4. The code 0 returns you to a monotext screen, and a 4 returns you to the graphics screen if that's where you started.

If you decide that you want to use a text editor as a function from inside AutoCAD, you may change the ACAD.PGP file accordingly. To add the ability to access WordPerfect from the command prompt, for example, use a text editor to add this line to the ACAD.PGP file:

```
EDIT,WP,        0,*File to edit: ,0
```

Assuming your path is set up appropriately, this would let you move directly from the drawing editor to the WordPerfect editor and back to the drawing editor again. Remember, if you use WordPerfect in AutoCAD, you must save the file as DOS text using Ctrl +F5 (Text In/Out). No matter what text editor you set up, remember to save your files as DOS text.

Command Aliases

AutoCAD already includes several command aliases. You can modify these abbreviations, replace them or create your own by using your text editor to modify the ACAD.PGP file (located in the \ACADR13\COMMON\SUPPORT directory).

The part of the ACAD.PGP file that creates abbreviations is listed below.

```
A,      *ARC
C,      *CIRCLE
CP,     *COPY
DV,     *DVIEW
E,      *ERASE
L,      *LINE
LA,     *DDLMODES
LT,     *DDLTYPE
M,      *MOVE
MS,     *MSPACE
P,      *PAN
PS,     *PSPACE
PL,     *PLINE
R,      *REDRAW
T,      *MTEXT
Z,      *ZOOM
```

Notice the format of each line. When you add your own abbreviations, be careful to duplicate the exact format illustrated above. Each line has this format: the abbreviation, comma, tab space, asterisk, full command name. (The tab space between the comma and the asterisk is ignored.)

Each alias uses a small amount of memory, so if your system is operating with a minimal amount of memory, you'll want to limit your abbreviations to those you use most often. See "Using AutoLISP" at the end of this chapter, for more in-depth alias commands.

Let's add a few abbreviated commands to the file, after the Z, *ZOOM entry.

1. Minimize the AutoCAD window by clicking on the minimize button.
2. Launch the Notepad program by double-clicking the Notepad icon.
3. In the Notepad, navigate to the ACAD.PGP file and open it.
4. Now add the following command aliases:

```
B,      *BREAK
CH,     *CHPROP
F,      *FILLET
Q,      *QUIT
RE,     *REGENALL
T,      *TRIM
V,      *DDVPOINT
```

5. Save and exit the file.

6. Reenter AutoCAD.

7. At the command line, enter **reinit** to reactivate the ACAD.PGP file. (See "REINIT" next in this chapter.) Choose ACAD.PGP in the Re-initialization dialog and choose OK. Then test your new alias commands.

Don't try to create abbreviations that duplicate some of the shorter built-in commands or external commands in the ACAD.PGP file, such as U, SH, ID, ARC, PAN, DEL, and DIR. Also avoid names of any machine driver commands, display driver commands, AutoLISP programs and ADS programs. If you try to use one of these names as an abbreviation, it won't work. That's because AutoCAD checks its list of built-in commands, then machine and display driver commands, then external commands in ACAD.PGP, then ADS and AutoLISP programs before it checks its list of abbreviations in ACAD.PGP. AutoCAD executes what it finds first.

Reactivating ACAD.PGP After Editing

If you've changed the ACAD.PGP file from within the drawing editor (using the SHELL command or the Windows Program Manager), you must use the REINIT command for the new file to take effect. Here's how it's done: After you've changed the ACAD.PGP file, save and exit the editor in which you changed it. Then enter **exit** to return to the AutoCAD drawing editor. At the command line, enter **reinit**, which activates the Re-initialization dialog box. Then check in the ACAD.PGP box area and pick OK. Your changes to the ACAD.PGP file immediately take effect.

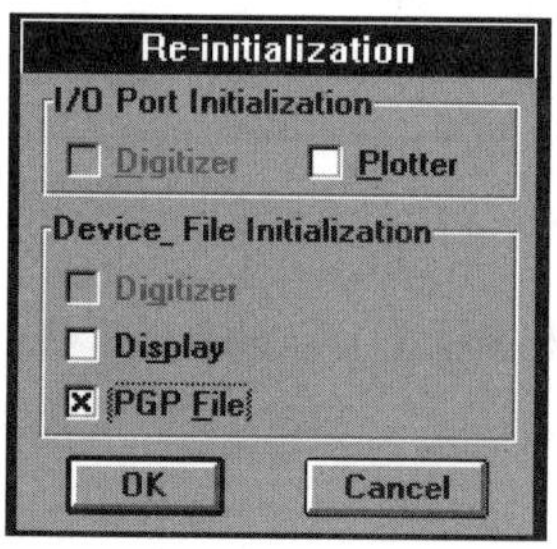

Figure 40-6: The Re-initialization dialog.

Substituting AutoLISP Commands

Using the UNDEFINE command, you can "undefine" AutoCAD commands and replace them with AutoLISP commands of the same name. Naturally, they can also be REDEFINEd to recapture their original definitions.

To undefine a command, enter **undefine**. At the prompt, enter the name of the command you wish to change. To restore a command, enter **redefine**.

Customizing Linetypes

Linetypes are stored in a linetype file, which is simply a text file with the extension .LIN. For each linetype, the file contains a pair of lines (an identifying line and a defining line). AutoCAD's default linetype file is ACAD.LIN, and when you create a linetype it is stored there (unless you are using a customized linetype file with another name).

There are two ways to create linetypes. One is to use the LINETYPE command described below. Using this command, you can create simple linetypes composed of dots, lines, and spaces, like these:

```
        . . __ . . __ . .
or      - . - . - . - . - . - .
```

In Release 13, you can also create complex linetypes that include shapes and/or text strings in the pattern, like these:

```
        — XOX — XOX — XOX
or      — Boundary — Boundary —
```

To create a complex linetype, you must edit the ACAD.LIN file using the Windows Notepad, the DOS Editor or another text editor. For instructions, see "Complex Linetypes: Editing ACAD.LIN" below.

When you create a linetype, it's merely written to a file on disk. It isn't associated with the current drawing until it's loaded in the drawing, as described below under "LINETYPE."

LINETYPE Loads or defines linetypes

COMMAND LINE: **linetype**

Using the LINETYPE command, you can list or load existing linetypes, and you can create or revise simple linetypes.

To use the command, first enter **linetype** at the command prompt. You then have these options:

List Linetypes	Enter **?**. Then enter the name of the linetype file (usually **acad.lin**) to list available linetypes.
Load Linetypes	Enter **l** (for load). Enter the linetype name (or * for all linetypes). Then enter the name of the linetype file. After you load a linetype, you can assign it to a layer using the LAYER command. (If the linetype is in the ACAD.LIN file, AutoCAD loads it automatically when it is needed by the LAYER command or the LINETYPE Set command.)
Create Linetypes	Enter **c**, and then define the linetype as described below under "Creating a Simple Linetype."
Revise Linetypes	Enter **r** to revise an existing simple linetype. Then revise the linetype as described below under "Revising a Simple Linetype."

Creating a Simple Linetype

1. Enter **linetype** at the command line.

2. At the prompt, enter **c**. Then enter the name of the file that will contain the linetype definition (for example, **acad.lin**).

3. Enter the descriptive text (up to 47 characters). As an alternative, you can type in a visual representation of the new line using a series of underlines, spaces and periods.

4. When A (for alignment) appears onscreen, define the linetype by entering the pen-lift pattern—a series of numbers that defines the linetype through the lengths of pen-down and pen-up segments. Enter the lengths of the pen-down segments (positive numbers, or zero to create a dot) and pen-up segments (negative numbers). Enter only one pattern. Begin the pattern with the longest pen-down segment and end it with a pen-up segment.

```
_______ __ __ __ ________ __ __ __ ________
```

would be defined as

```
A,1,-.12,.1,-.05,.1,-.05,.1,-.12
```

Here are the standard code numbers for the segments of pen-lift pattern:

0 (zero) produces a dot.

.5 produces a standard dash.

-.25 produces a standard space.

Revising a Simple Linetype

1. Enter **linetype** at the command line.

2. At the prompt, enter **r**. Then enter the name of the linetype you wish to revise. AutoCAD displays the linetype's current definition and gives you the opportunity to redefine it.

If the linetype defined above were called Trace, it would look like this in a text file created with DOS EDIT or Windows Notepad (see "Complex Linetypes: Editing ACAD.LIN.").

```
(Identifying line) *TRACE, ____________ __ __ ___
(Defining line)   A,1,-.12,.1,-.05,.1,-.05,.1,-.12
```

If you wish to add a shape or text string to a simple linetype pattern, you must edit the linetype file as described below under "Complex Linetypes: Editing ACAD.LIN."

Complex Linetypes: Editing ACAD.LIN

You may create and edit simple or complex linetypes in the ACAD.LIN file. You may examine the file in the Windows Notepad. Remember to make a copy of the file before you edit it. (Copy it as ACADLIN.BAK.) Then if you corrupt the original file, you can replace it with the backup.

To define a complex linetype, you enclose the different fields of shapes or strings with square brackets.

For example, the code for new shapes is written as follows:

```
Shapes [Shape Name, Shape File, Scale, Rotation, Xoffset,
Yoffset]
```

In the line above, Shape Name is the name of a created shape, and Shape File is a compiled (.shx) shape file. Scale is a number whose value is the height of the shape. The rotational value has two options: A (absolute) and R (relative) to refer to the origin of the shape. The rotational value is given in (d) degrees, (r) radians or (g) gradians. Xoffset and Yoffset define the X-Y axis distance the shape is to be moved from the end of the last line segment; zero signifies no offset.

For new text Strings the code is written as

```
Strings ["String", Text Style, Scale, Rotation, Xoffset,
Yoffset]
```

Here, "String" is the actual text you want placed within the line. Be sure to enclose all text in quote marks (""). Text Style is the name of the text font (if you don't include it, AutoCAD uses the current style). The rest of the String code is the same as that for Shapes above.

Other linetype modifiers you may use in the patterns include the following:

Linetype Scale, a scaling variable. A positive value affects both the spacing and scale of the shape you create. A negative value affects the spacing of the line but not the shape you create.

Linetype Elaboration Offset, a shape offset value. It affects the X-Y axes of the shape's offset position in the linetype pattern. A negative or positive value moves the shape in the X-Y axes. The default offset is 0 (zero).

Linetype Text Scale, a text modifier. Allows you to size text within the linetype. It does not affect the linetype scale.

Linetype Rotation, a text angle modifier. Allows you to rotate the angle of the text or shape within the linetype pattern.

Creating a Complex Linetype

Here are the basic steps for creating a complex line type in the ACAD.LIN file.

1. Minimize the AutoCAD window by clicking on the minimize button.
2. Launch the Notepad program by double-clicking the Notepad icon.
3. In the Notepad, navigate to the ACAD.LIN file and open it. Move to the very end of the file.

4. Add the following:

```
*Boundary, Boundary Line
A,2,-.25,["BOUNDARY",Bold,S=.25,A=0,X=0.05,Y=-0.1],-1.5,1.5
```

In this example, the complex linetype named Boundary draws a dashed line interspersed with the word "BOUNDARY." The linetype uses Bold as the text style. It's scaled at factor .25 and offset in the X-Y axis from other elements.

Creating Hatch Patterns

Creating a hatch pattern is slightly harder and more complex than creating a linetype. It cannot be accomplished from the graphics editor.

Instead, you must use an ASCII text editor such as the Windows Notepad to access the ACAD.PAT file, which stores hatch patterns. Hatch patterns are similar to the pen-lift patterns above but have the added features of angle, X,Y origin and Offset-X, Offset-Y.

A hatch pattern comprises four parts to every line:

```
Angle
X,Y Origin
Offset-X, Offset-Y
Pen-lift pattern
```

Create a new hatch pattern as shown in the example below:

```
*Spacer, Double line and double dot.
0, 0,0, 0,.5, .5,-.25,.5,-.25,0,-.25,0,-.25
```

This breaks down as follows:

```
Angle  0,
X,Y Origin 0,0
Offset-X, Offset-Y  0,.5,
Penlift pattern .5,-.25,.5,-.25,0,-.25,0,-.25
```

Here are the basic steps to start customizing the ACAD.PAT file:

1. Minimize the AutoCAD window by clicking on the minimize button.
2. Launch the Notepad program by double-clicking the Notepad icon.

3. In the Notepad, navigate to and open the ACAD.PAT file, then move to the very end of the file.

4. Add the following new Hatch pattern:

```
*Spacer, Double line and double dot.
0,  0,0,  0,.5,
0,  .5,-.25,.5,-.25,0,-.25,0,-.25
```

To run your new Hatch pattern, simply load and use it.

Customization With Scripts

You can save time in doing repetitive tasks by writing scripts that execute a series of commands. Chapter 39 explained how to create and use scripts. Here are some ideas for the kinds of tasks scripts can simplify.

Run slides and show slide images. With the use of the RSCRIPT command, they will loop indefinitely.

Set up your drawing environment, including the following:

Borders	Create drawing titles and borders.
Dimensions	Set dimension styles and variables.
Grid control	Set up and activate grid size.
Limits	Set up drawing limits.
Layer control	Name layers and set layer colors.
Linetypes	Set up and load linetypes.
SETVAR	Automate drawing setting variables.
Snap control	Set up and activate snap size.
Symbols	Create symbols libraries.
Text control	Create and set up text style.
Toggle modes	Toggle osnap, ortho, coords and snap modes.
Units control	Set up and activate units.
Viewports	Set up viewports in Paper and Model Space.
Zoom control	Zoom to set window sizes in a drawing.

Customizing On-line Help

You can write your own on-line help messages. Two files provide help information windows. First, the On-line Help file is activated when you pick the HELP ? icon or press the F1 key. Second, the About AutoCAD... file shows a message text. You may customize this last file with, for example, your company logo and message. Let's start by customizing the ABOUT file.

Changing the About AutoCAD File

Choose the Help pull-down menu and select About AutoCAD (as an alternative, you may enter **about** at the command line). The brief message you see onscreen is located in the ACADR13\COMMON\SUPPORT directory in a file named ACAD.MSG.

You might wish to place simple company information in this file and/or a set of instructions to new users of the system.

Here are the basic steps to start customizing the ACAD.MSG file.

1. Minimize the AutoCAD window by clicking on the minimize button.

2. Launch the Notepad program by double-clicking the Notepad image.

3. In the Notepad, navigate to the ACAD.MSG file in the \COMMON\SUPPORT directory, and open the file.

4. Make the desired changes and save the file.

Changing the On-line Help

To change the on-line help, you must modify the standard ACAD.AHP file. This file activates the Help window and in turn creates and maintains an index file of ACAD.HDX. As you enter HELP, a Help information window appears which allows you to enter the name of a specific command or pick a command from a scrolling index. Of course, you create Help text in a similar format using the Help viewer.

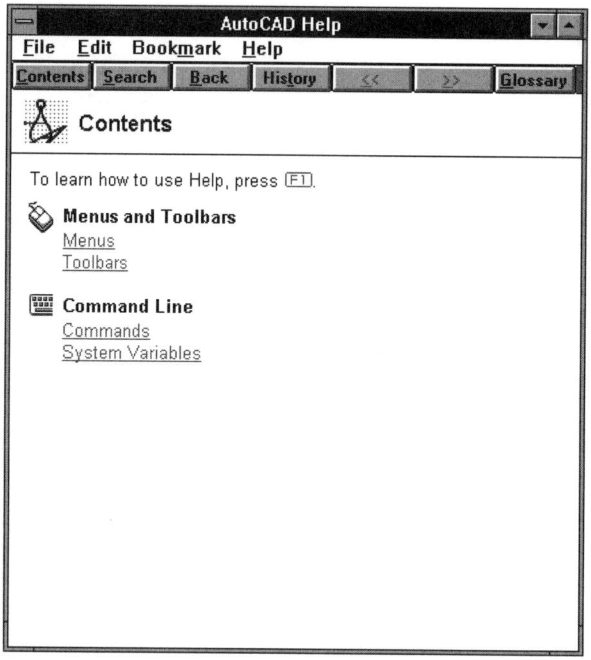

Figure 40-7: The AutoCAD HELP window dialog.

AutoCAD provides a Help viewer feature to let you review and edit topic text. You should follow specific Help directives. Here are some general rules:

\# is used internally as a topic ID. Every new topic you create must have a topic ID (context string). You end the topic when you enter any new directive such as: \$, \K and \E.

\$ is a title for history and search topic lists.

\K is a key word search list. Use ; to separate key words.

\E is end of the Help file.

\space is a comment in the Help file.

Customizing the Status Bar

You may customize the status bar at the bottom of the screen.

In Release 13, the status bar displays help two ways. First, it displays help text on the use of each image or menu item as your cursor passes over it.

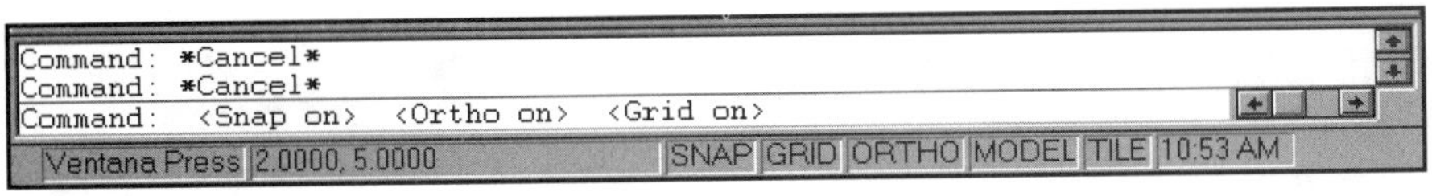

Figure 40-8: The status bar.

In separate horizontal label areas it displays the time of day, coordinate data and on/off toggles for snap, grid, ortho, model/paper space and tilemode status. To customize the status bar, first enter **modemacro** at the command line and then enter **$(getvar,Layer: $(getvar, clayer) $(getvar, dwgname)**.

This causes the layer and drawing names to appear instead of the standard status bar. Or you could just enter your company name.

It's more difficult, but you can also use AutoLISP to customize the status bar. To do this, you have to create an AutoLISP file and include DIESEL expressions in it. Create the file below called MODE.LSP as follows:

1. Minimize the AutoCAD window by clicking on the minimize button.

2. Launch the Notepad program by double-clicking the Notepad icon.

3. Create MODE.LSP in the \COMMON\SUPPORT directory by entering the following:

```
(defun C:MODE ( )
   (setvar “modemacro” (strcat
   Snap:$(substr,$(getvar,snapunit) $(fix,$(*,
   $(getvar,snapang),$(/,180,3.14159),1,8)”)
   “$(if,$(getvar,orthomode), Ortho)”
   “$(if,$(getvar,snapmode), Snap)”
   “$(if,$(getvar,tabmode), Tablet)”
   “$(if,$(=,$,(getvar,tilemode), 0),”
   “$(if,$(=,$,(getvar,cvport), 1), P”
   “$(if,$(getvar,date),DDD”, “D MON YYYY)”
 “)”
)))
```

Customizing the Cursor Menu

The cursor menu appears where your cursor is located when you press your right mouse button or Shift-Button 2, or the middle button (depending on your pointing device). The cursor menu can be customized to provide all your favorite commands right at your cursor crosshairs.

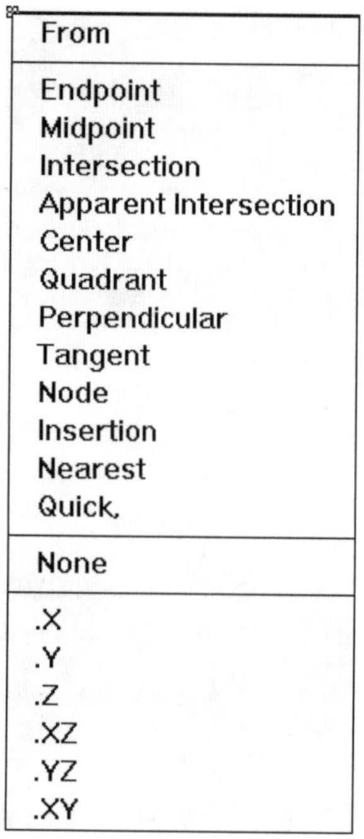

Figure 40-9: The cursor menu.

Cursor menus, assigned to your pick button instead of the pull-down menu bar, are a special type of cursor pull-down menu. Easily accessible, they also offer the option of cascading menus (see "Creating Custom Menus" later in the chapter for an explanation of the main screen and tablet menus).

Note the following basics for customizing the cursor menu:

1. Name the cursor menu as ***POP0.

2. Assign the cursor menu to a button. It's more efficient if the menu appears at the cursor.

3. You should have one existing pull-down menu before you create an extra cursor menu. Number and overall content don't matter.

Let's create CURSOR.MNU to demonstrate how easy it is to combine a pull-down menu with a cursor menu. To do this, you will alter the ***POP0 section in the menu file. Before you begin, copy the ACAD.MNU file to a new file named CURSOR.MNU. The new file will be your working file for this example (never work in the ACAD.MNU file!).

1. Minimize the AutoCAD window by clicking on the minimize button.

2. Launch the Notepad program by double-clicking the Notepad icon.

3. In the Notepad, navigate to CURSOR.MNU in the \SUPPORT directory. Alter the ***POP0 section only. Do not alter any other part of the menu. The listing is as follows:

```
***POP0
[Cursor Menu]
[->Osnap Tools]
[From]_from
[--]
[Endpoint]_endp
[Midpoint]_mid
[Intersection]_int
[Apparent Int]_appint
[Center]_center
[Quadrant]_qua
[Perpendicular]_per
[Tangent]_tan
[Node]_nod
[Insertion]_ins
[Nearest]_nea
[Quick,]_qui^Z
[--]
[<-None]_non
[--]
[->Filters .xy]
[.X].X
[.Y].Y
[.Z].Z
[.XZ].XZ
[.YZ].YZ
[<-.XY].XY
[--]
```

```
[->Draw Objects]
 [->Lines]
  [Multi-lines]^c^cmline
  [Single lines]^c^cline
  [<-Const. Lines]^c^cxline
 [Edit Mline]^c^cmedit
 [Copy]^c^ccopy
 [<-Erase]^c^cerase
[--]
[->Edit Objects]
 [->Change]
  [Group Properties...]^c^cddchprop
  [<-Single Entity...]^c^cddmodify
 [Text Edit...]^c^cddedit
 [<-Rename...]^c^cddrename
[--]
[->Data]
 [Object Creation...]^c^cddemodes
 [Selection...]^c^cddselect
 [Grips...]^c^cddgrips
 [Layers...]^c^cddlmodes
 [Object Snaps...]^c^cddosnap
 [Points Style...]^c^cddptype
 [Units...]^c^cddunits
 [<-Drawing Aids...]^c^cddrmodes
[--]
[->View]
 [Views...]^c^cddview
 [->UCS Options]
  [Preset UCS...]^c^cdducs
  [<-UCS Right Angle...]^c^cdducsp
 [<-Viewpoints...]^c^cddvpoint
[--]
[->Attribute]
 [Define...]^c^cddattdef
 [Edit...]^c^cddatte
 [Extract...]^c^cddattext
 [Block objects]^c^cblock
 [Insert objects...]^c^cddinsert
 [<-Explode]^c^cexplode
```

```
[--]
[->Plot-Save-Quit]
 [Plot]^c^cplot
 [SAVE]^c^cQsave
 [<-Quit]^c^cquit
[--]
[Preferences...]^c^cpreferences
```

When you have altered the CURSOR.MNU, save it. Then reenter AutoCAD. Enter **menu** at the command line and pick the CURSOR.MNU; AutoCAD compiles it. Then activate the cursor pull-down. Notice that a simplified cursor pull-down menu with built-in cascading menus has been created.

Creating Custom Menus

This is only a brief introduction to full-menu customization. See the *AutoCAD Customization Manual* for full details. In this book, see Appendix B for a sample custom menu.

A menu file is a text file that contains AutoCAD commands and/or command strings. (Command strings include both commands and responses to prompts.) A template menu file has the extension .MNU. The standard AutoCAD menu files are called ACAD.MNU (source file) and ACAD.MNX (DOS-compiled) or ACAD.MNC (Windows-compiled files). ACAD.MNU is found in the \ACADR13\...\SUPPORT directory under the AutoCAD program files.

Using your text editor, you can create a custom menu file.

AutoCAD can use many sections in one menu file:

Screen menu—One section, SCREEN.

Pointer button menu—Four sections, BUTTONS1 through BUTTONS4.

Digitizer tablet areas—Eight sections, TABLET1 through TABLET4 and TABLET1ALT through TABLET4ALT.

Auxiliary function box menu—Four sections, AUX1 through AUX4.

Pull-down menus—Sixteen sections, POP0 through POP16.

Image menus—One section, Image (this used to be ICON section).

Each section must be headed with a section label. The section label includes the section name preceded by three asterisks, such as ***SCREEN, or ***TABLET1 or ***POP7.

For the screen menu, only eight or fewer characters can be displayed. The onscreen portion is placed in square brackets ([ ]) with the actual command or command string immediately following the closing bracket.

On some monitors, only 21 lines of a screen menu may be displayed at once.

Sample Menu File

Figure 40-10 illustrates a short sample menu file. It has only two sections: a screen root menu and a tablet menu.

```
***SCREEN
[STATUS]status
[LOCATION]id
[DISTANCE]dist
[DESCRIBE]list
[ZOOM IN] zoom 1.3333x
[ZOOM OUT] zoom .75x
[ZOOM ALL] zoom a
[SAVE]save ;
[END]end
[QUIT]quit
[*CANCEL*]^C^C
***TABLET1
line
circle
arc
text
layer s \;
```

On-screen portion (can be upper- or lowercase).

Command portion (can be upper- or lowercase).

A semicolon causes a carriage return.

(= CTRL-C CTRL-C)

A backslash allows for user input, either from the keyboard or from the pointer.

Figure 40-10: Example of screen menu.

Notice the semicolons in lines 9 and 18. In a menu file, AutoCAD interprets a semicolon as a carriage return (<RETURN>). Since AutoCAD also interprets a space as a carriage return, lines 9 and 18 function as follows:

Line 9	Keys in SAVE. The space acts as a carriage return and enters the command. (AutoCAD responds by displaying the drawing name as the default response.) Then the semicolon causes a carriage return, which accepts the default response.

Line 18 Keys in LAYER. The first space acts like a carriage return and enters the command. (AutoCAD responds with its usual LAYER prompt.) Keys in S. The second space acts as a carriage return and enters the S. (This selects "Set" from the LAYER prompt.) AutoCAD responds by asking for the layer number or name. Then the backslash lets you key in and enter the number or name of the desired layer. AutoCAD responds by redisplaying the usual LAYER prompt. Then the semicolon causes a carriage return, which exits the LAYER command and returns to command mode.

If you tried to use the above sample menu, you discovered that the pointer buttons (all but the pick button) had adopted new functions from the screen menu. Button 2 adopts the STATUS command, 3 adopts the ID command, etc. If any one of the seven sections of a menu file is missing, the commands from the first section are automatically assigned to that section.

The following section of a menu file will assign <RETURN> to the second button and REDRAW to the third button. (The first button is always the pick button; it cannot be reassigned.)

```
***BUTTONS
;
redraw
```

A screen menu can have submenus and sub-submenus, etc. Any submenu has a heading in the following form, with up to 33 characters, and no spaces:

```
**NAME-OF-SUBMENU
```

To display a submenu from an item in the root menu (or parent menu), the command portion should have the following form:

```
$S=NAME-OF-SUBMENU
```

Let's suppose that we want to expand the three zoom commands in the sample screen menu given earlier, and we want to set up a submenu with six zoom options. We'd replace the three zoom commands in the root menu with the following line:

```
[ZOOM]$S=ZOOM-OPTIONS
```

Then we would add the following lines at the end of the screen section of the menu file:

```
**ZOOM-OPTIONS
   [1/2 size]zoom .5
   [2X size]zoom 2
   [ZOOM IN]zoom 1.3333x
   [ZOOM OUT]zoom .75x
   [ZOOM ALL]zoom a
   [ZOOM #]zoom
   [--root--]$S=SCREEN
```

Notice that the last line lets you return to the root section of the screen menu. If you had created the above six zoom options as a sub-submenu, and you wanted to be able to return to the submenu from which these options were called, then the last line would read as follows:

```
[--root--]$S=
```

The above examples assume that AutoCAD is in command mode when each command is entered. However, it's better to make sure that AutoCAD is in command mode by placing two Ctrl+Cs at the beginning of the command portion, as follows:

```
[STATUS]^C^Cstatus
```

Type a Ctrl+C into a menu file by typing a caret (above the 6) and a C rather than using a regular Ctrl+C.

If you place an asterisk in front of the two Ctrl+Cs (*^C^C) in the command portion, the command with its options is repeated automatically until you use Ctrl+C to cancel the repetition.

Pull-down menu sections (POP0 through POP16) should have as their first line just the onscreen portion; that is, just the text that will appear in the menu bar at the top of the screen—up to 14 characters. (This is because some displays support not more than 80 characters in the whole menu bar at the top of the screen.) Each following line has both an onscreen portion and a command portion. For example:

```
***POP0
[DISPLAY]
[ZOOM IN]^C^Czoom 1.3333x
[ZOOM OUT]^C^Czoom .75x
```

Items in pull-down menus can call submenus just like submenus in the screen section. For example, the line below would install a submenu called P3B in place of the present POP3 menu.

```
$P3=P3B $P3=*
```

The last part, $P3=*, forces the newly installed P3B submenu to be displayed.

If a submenu is shorter than the one it's replacing, use a single blank line at the end of the shorter menu to make it overwrite the longer menu entirely.

The Image tile menu section of the menu displays slides that represent certain choices. It can be divided into any number of subsections. This allows image displays to be called from any other menu item. It also permits image nesting or branching. See "Creating Slide Libraries & Image Tile Menus" later in the chapter. It tells you how to compile slides into images.

The first line of any image menu section is centered at the top of the image page as a title. Each of the following lines in the section includes a slide portion and a command portion. You can use up to 20 image slides in any one image group.

```
***Image
**IPATTERNS
[PATTERN OPTIONS]
[slide1(patt1)]
[slide2(patt2)]
[slide3(patt3)]
```

When the above subsection (**IPATTERNS) is called from another menu item, AutoCAD assembles an image slide menu on the screen with the heading PATTERN OPTIONS as the title. It displays each of the slides. Each line that displays an image slide also includes a command that calls an AutoLISP function.

Suppose you want a menu to access a certain subdirectory. For example, the menu item might call for a certain linetype to be loaded from the C:\LINETYPES\SET3.LIN file. Since menu items use the backslash for user input, you must specify the file path with forward slashes like so: C:/LINETYPES/SET3.LIN.

See Appendix B for a sample menu that includes an image section as well as tablet, button and pull-down sections.

Tablet Menu Overlays

To create and install a tablet menu overlay, you must:

1. Design and draw the tablet areas for the overlay.
2. Write a custom menu file that includes the commands that will correspond to each box in the overlay.

The Summagraphics 1201 digitizing tablet takes an overlay with an active area of up to 11" x 11." The tablet overlay can have up to four areas. The blank overlay shown in Figure 40-11 illustrates only one of many ways to arrange these areas.

Within each tablet area, the individual boxes are numbered from left to right, then from top to bottom, to correspond to the commands or command strings in that section of the menu file.

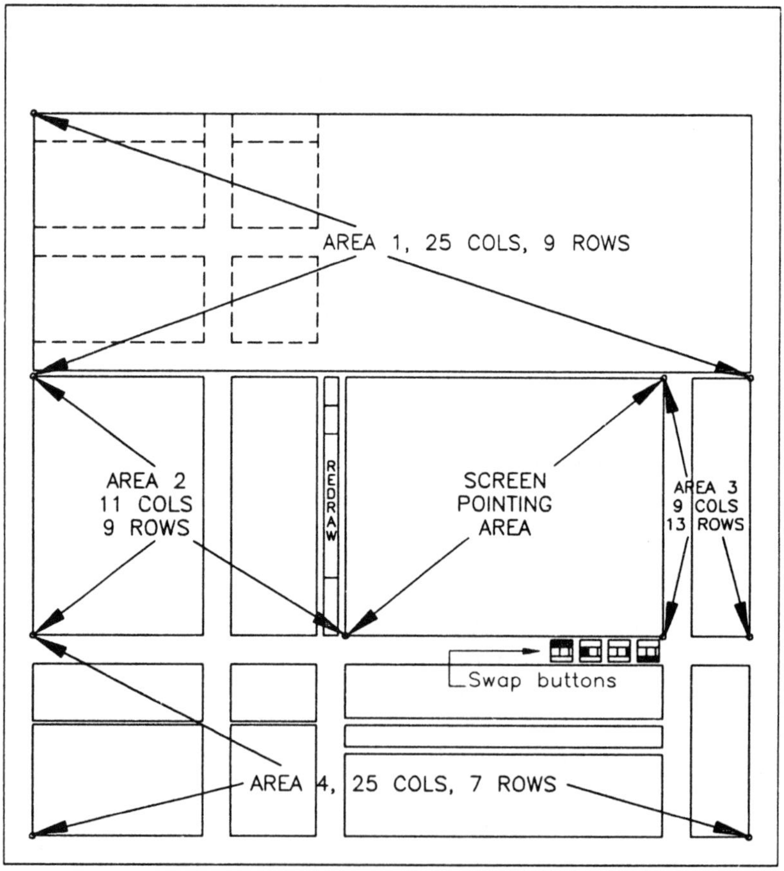

Figure 40-11: Example of tablet menu areas 1 through 4.

After you have created both the overlay and the menu file, you must install them and configure AutoCAD accordingly. Follow these steps:

1. If you want to use the tablet menu overlay exclusively and eliminate the screen menu area, go to AutoCAD's configuration menu, select "configure video display," and enter **n** when asked if you want a screen menu area.

2. Start a new drawing. When you're in the drawing editor, enter **menu**, and then choose the name of your menu file (without the extension) in the Menu dialog box. AutoCAD activates and automatically compiles the file if it has not been used.

3. Place your tablet overlay on the digitizing tablet. Then enter **tablet**. (Or choose Tablet from the Options pull-down menu.) When prompted, enter **cfg** to configure menu areas on the tablet, and then enter the number of tablet areas. See Figure 40-10 for an example of tablet menu areas 1 through 4 and the number of columns and rows you have to enter.

For each tablet area, locate the upper-left, lower-left and lower-right corners. Enter the number of columns and rows within that tablet area.

Then enter the lower-left and upper-right corners of the screen pointing area.

Once the tablet is configured, AutoCAD assumes this configuration for the tablet every time you start AutoCAD. The drawings edited with the menu written for this tablet configuration will automatically call the same menu when they are edited again. This menu must reside in the current directory or in the directory with the AutoCAD program files.

See the sample custom tablet overlay and menu in Appendix A.

Using Two Menu Configurations

You can switch between two or more configurations of AutoCAD without having to repeat all the steps to set up each configuration.

When AutoCAD starts, it uses the ACAD.CFG file and other configuration files (in the same directory where its other program files reside) to determine its present configuration. However, you can instruct AutoCAD to use different configuration files.

Suppose that you want to use two different configurations at different times, as follows:

Configuration 1	The standard screen menu and the standard tablet overlay supplied by AutoCAD.
Configuration 2	A custom tablet menu overlay and no screen menu.

Configuration 1 can be used in the normal way (assuming AutoCAD was initially configured using the standard screen menu and standard tablet overlay). When you start AutoCAD, follow the same steps as usual.

To establish Configuration 2, take these steps:

1. Create a subdirectory under the root directory called TMO (for tablet menu overlay).

2. Establish this subdirectory in the environment by using the SET command as follows:

```
set acadcfg=\tmo
```

(When AutoCAD starts, it checks for any value that has been assigned to ACADCFG. When it finds \TMO, it searches for configuration files in that subdirectory instead of defaulting to its usual configuration files.)

3. Copy the ACAD.CFG file, which resides with the AutoCAD program files, into the \TMO subdirectory

4. Start a new drawing. When you're in the drawing editor, use the TABLET command to configure the tablet. Now all the necessary configuration files should be present in subdirectory \TMO.

Configuration 2 can now be used by entering **set acadcfg=\tmo** as an environment variable into either the Program Manager or the AutoCAD Preferences Environment dialog box.

Each time you start a new drawing under this configuration, use the MENU command to load your custom menu if needed. It will be loaded automatically if you use a prototype drawing that was created or edited with your custom menu.

Creating Slide Libraries & Image Tile Menus

A slide image menu in pictorial/graphic symbol mode is easy to use. It saves you time in choice selection.

When you use image tile menus as part of customization, you have to create a library text list in order to access the image slide files. The slide files become part of the image menu(s.) AutoCAD provides a command called SLIDELIB.EXE, invoked at the DOS or SYSTEM prompt. To create it correctly, you must be very careful when you compile the slide library file routine.

Steps to Create an Image Tile Set

1. Write the menu file and list the image slides you wish to use.

2. Create the slides for the library. Keep the images simple and make them fill the entire center of the screen before you use the MSLIDE command.

3. Make a text file listing the names of the individual slides. Remember, it must be one slide per line. See the example below. To create the four image slides of plus, minus, times and divide, you would create the drawings, make slides of them and create a text file called CALC.TXT. In it would be the list of the four slides without the extension, as follows:

```
Plus
Minus
Times
Divide
```

In your menu you would create a small image section as the following listing:

```
***image                   (An AutoCAD prompt for the menu)
**image1                   (User defined to invoke Image1)
[AutoLISP CALC]            (Heading in pop-down)
[Calc(Plus)]^c^c(+ \);     (First slide – with built-in macro)
[Calc(Minus)]^c^c(- \);    (Second slide etc.)
[Calc(Times)]^c^c(* \);    (Third slide etc.)
[Calc(Divide)]^c^c(/ \);   (Fourth slide etc.)
```

4. Finally, to compile the slides into images, you then run the Slidelib from the system prompt. The syntax of the slidelib command is as follows:

```
C:>Slidelib CALC <Calc.txt  (See below for explanation.)
```

CALC is the library and name of the slides you wish to create.

Calc.txt is the name of the text file which lists the names and paths of the slides you want in the library.

Creating Single-Keystroke Commands

You can use AutoLISP to create single-keystroke commands.

The AutoLISP file below can be copied from the Companion Disk into your AutoCAD\SUPPORT directory. Each line has a short explanation attached after the semicolon. (Any text after a semicolon in AutoLISP is ignored.)

```
;;; Key.lsp created November 22nd 1994
;;; Brian Matthews
;;; Ventana Press.
(Defun C:A   ( ) (Command "Arc")) ;; Arc
(Defun C:BF  ( ) (Command "Break" )) ;; Break
(Defun C:C   ( ) (Command "Circle")) ;; Circle
(Defun C:CH  ( ) (Command "Change")) ;; Change
(Defun C:CL  ( ) (Command "Color")) ;; Color
(Defun C:CP  ( ) (Command "Chprop")) ;; Change Properties
(Defun C:D   ( ) (Command "Dim")) ;; Dim menu
(Defun C:DV  ( ) (Command "Dim" "Ver")) ;; Dimension - vertical
(Defun C:DH  ( ) (Command "Dim" "Hor")) ;; Dimension - horizontal
(Defun C:DS  ( ) (Command "Dist")) ;; Distance
(Defun C:DI  ( ) (Command "Divide")) ;; Divide
(Defun C:E   ( ) (Command "Erase")) ;; Erase
(Defun C:EL  ( ) (Command "Erase" "L")) ;; Erase - Last
(Defun C:EX  ( ) (Command "Extend")) ;; Extend
(Defun C:F   ( ) (Command "Fillet")) ;; Fillet
(Defun C:FO  ( ) (Command "Fillet" "R" 0)) ;; Fillet 0 Radius
(Defun C:G   ( ) (Command "Grid")) ;; Grid
(Defun C:H   ( ) (Command "Hatch")) ;; Hatch
(Defun C:HA  ( ) (Command "DDhatch")) ;; Hatch dialog
(Defun C:I   ( ) (Command "Insert")) ;; Insert
(Defun C:IN  ( ) (Command "DDinsert")) ;; Insert dialog
(Defun C:CP  ( ) (Command "Copy")) ;; Copy
(Defun C:L   ( ) (Command "Line")) ;; Line
(Defun C:LA  ( ) (Command "DDlmodes")) ;; Layer dialog
(Defun C:LS  ( ) (Command "Layer" "Set")) ;; Layer-set option
(Defun C:LN  ( ) (Command "Linetype")) ;; Linetype
(Defun C:LI  ( ) (Command "List")) ;; List
(Defun C:M   ( ) (Command "Move")) ;; Move
```

```
(Defun C:ME   ( ) (Command “Medit”)) Medit
(Defun C:ML   ( ) (Command “Mline”) ;; Multi-line
(Defun C:MR   ( ) (Command “Mirror”)) ;; Mirror
(Defun C:MS   ( ) (Command “Measure”)) ;; Measure
(Defun C:MI   ( ) (Command “Minsert”)) ;; Multiple Insert
(Defun C:N    ( ) (Command “OSNAP” “None”)) ;; Osnap - none
(Defun C:O    ( ) (Command “Offset”)) ;; Offset
(Defun C:P    ( ) (Command “Pline”)) ;; Polyline
(Defun C:PE   ( ) (Command “Pedit”)) ;; Polyline Edit
(Defun C:Q    ( ) (Command “Quit”)) ;; Quit
(Defun C:QS   ( ) (Command “Qsave”)) ;; Quick save
(Defun C:R    ( ) (Command “Rotate”)) ;; Rotate
(Defun C:S    ( ) (Command “Snap”)) ;; Snap
(Defun C:SC   ( ) (Command “Scale”)) ;; Scale
(Defun C:SA   ( ) (Command “Saveas”)) ;; Saveas
(Defun C:T    ( ) (Command “Trim”)) ;; Trim
(Defun C:TX   ( ) (Command “Dtext”)) ;; Text
(Defun C:V    ( ) (Command “View”)) ;; View
(Defun C:VR   ( ) (Command “View” “R”)) ;; View Restore
(Defun C:VS   ( ) (Command “View” “S”)) ;; View Save
(Defun C:VA   ( ) (Command “View” “A”)) ;; View All
(Defun C:VP   ( ) (Command “Vplayer”)) ;; Viewport layer control
(Defun C:WB   ( ) (Command “Wblock”)) ;; Wblock
(Defun C:X    ( ) (Command “Explode”)) ;; Explode
(Defun C:ZE   ( ) (Command “Zoom” “E”)) ;; Zoom Extents
(Defun C:ZP   ( ) (Command “Zoom” “P”)) ;; Zoom Previous
(Defun C:ZW   ( ) (Command “Zoom” “W”)) ;;Zoom Window
(Defun C:ZV   ( ) (Command “Zoom” “V”) ;;Zoom Vmax
(Princ) ;;clears the screen
```

To load Key.lsp, use the Applications... dialog from the Tools pull-down menu. Pick the Key.lsp file and then the Load button. Then start using your single-keystroke commands.

Feel free to add other single keystrokes to customize your menu system further.

Customizing Toolbars

AutoCAD introduced fifty toolbars into Release 13 for Windows. You need not be a programmer to customize icons—it's all a matter of point-and-click.

Choose Toolbars from the Tools pull-down menu and choose any of the Toolbars. Then pick an icon using the right button of the mouse. The Toolbars dialog appears so you can customize the toolbars (see Figure 40-12). The purpose of the Toolbars dialog box and its subdialogs is to let you alter icons, change commands to your icons, add flyouts to icons or add icons to other icon groups. You may drag-and-drop icons from one toolbar into another.

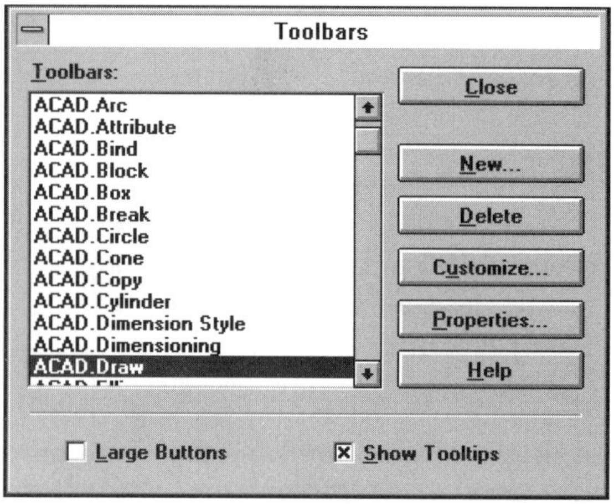

Figure 40-12: The Toolbars Access dialog box.

In Figure 40-12, notice the five radio buttons situated under the Close button. If Large Buttons is checked, you may have 32 x 32 pixel icons instead of the standard 16 x 16 pixel size. If you toggle on Show Tooltips, AutoCAD activates the naming text for each icon. The naming text appears just below each icon as you hold your pointing device over it. By default, this toggle is on. The radio buttons work as follows:

New	Choose this button to create a new toolbar, by naming it in the dialog. See Figure 40-13. Simply enter a new name in the blank name area and pick OK. The menu group is a string of 32 characters as a menu name tag.

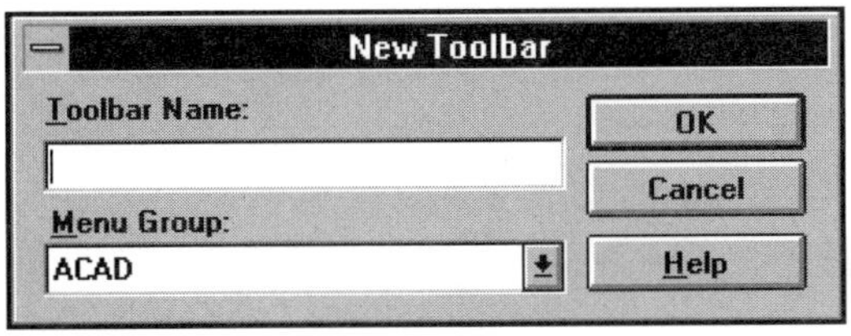

Figure 40-13: The New Toolbar naming dialog.

Delete — Choose this button to remove an unwanted toolbar. It will question your sanity by providing a ? response. So if you inadvertently pick Delete, you will have time to correct the error by choosing No. See Figure 40-14.

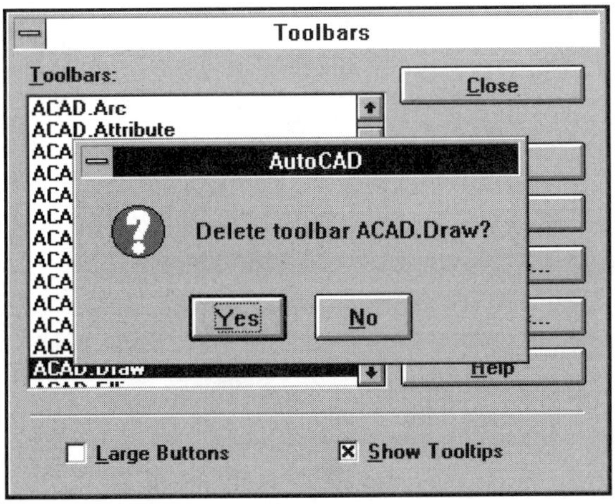

Figure 40-14: The Delete Toolbar response.

Customize — Choosing this button activates the Customize Toolbars dialog, which allows you to set up tool, osnap and other command configurations for your icons. See Figure 40-15. You can drag-and-drop tools from the Customize Toolbar dialog onto a new toolbar. Press the Ctrl key and then use drag-and-drop to copy a tool from an adjacent toolbar onto a new toolbar. To list the organization of the toolbars, choose the Categories scroll device. AutoCAD organizes commands into groups based on their common use.

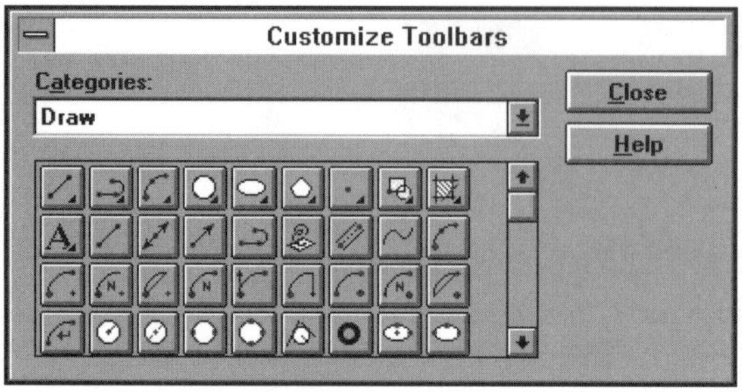

Figure 40-15: The Customize Toolbar dialog.

Properties — Choosing the Properties button activates the Toolbar Properties dialog. See Figure 40-16. The dialog is a multiple control feature. The Hide toggle is an off/on switch for the toolbar named in the display. The Alias bar shows the alias prompt of your icon and the Toolbar name. It includes a prefix of the toolbar's menu group. The Help bar displays help text as it appears in your onscreen status bar.

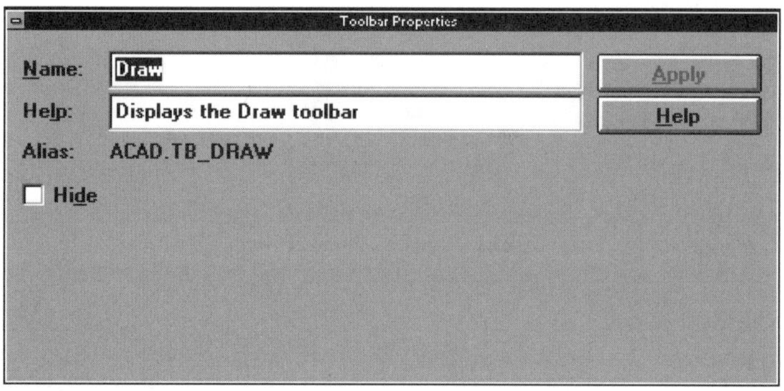

Figure 40-16: The Toolbar Properties dialog.

Help — The Help button of the Toolbars dialog produces a Help Window. See Figure 40-17.

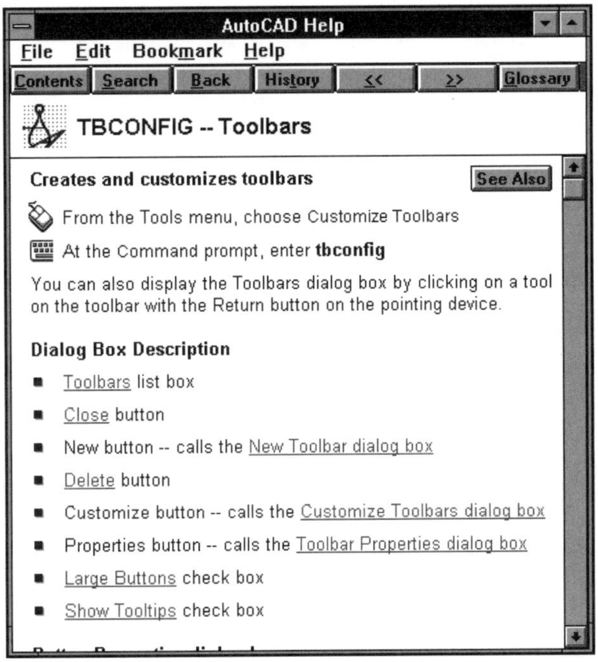

Figure 40-17: The Toolbar TBCONFIG help window.

Moving on

AutoCAD customization can be a complex subject. Yet if you've gotten this far, you're now able to adapt your system using more complex menu writing and LISP files.

Chapter 41, "Importing & Exporting," reviews the multiple ways to import and export files in AutoCAD.

Importing & Exporting Files

In this chapter you'll learn how both vector and raster files can be imported and exported in AutoCAD. You'll use IMPORT and EXPORT commands located under the File pull-down menu.

You also may "post-process" AutoCAD files. "Post-processing" refers to files created from or extracted from a drawing file outside of AutoCAD. (See "Post-processing" later in this chapter.)

NOTE: *You cannot import or export IGES files in Release 13. The IGESOUT and IGESIN commands are discontinued.*

IMPORT Allows you to import various file types into AutoCAD

COMMAND LINE: **import**

To produce the Import File dialog, choose Import from the File pull-down menu. The dialog lets you import the following types of files:

Extension	File Type
.WMF	Metafiles
.SAT	ACIS Solid Modeler
.EPS	Encapsulated PostScript
.PCX	Paint
.TIF	TIFF (compressed 32-bit RGBA tagged image file)
.GIF	GIF (bitmapped picture format used by the CompuServe Information Network)
.3DS	3D Studio

You can also use the PSIN command to import and scale a PostScript (.EPS) file as a block (see "PSIN" later in this chapter).

And you can use the DXFIN command to import files in Drawing eXchange Format (see "DXFIN" later in this chapter).

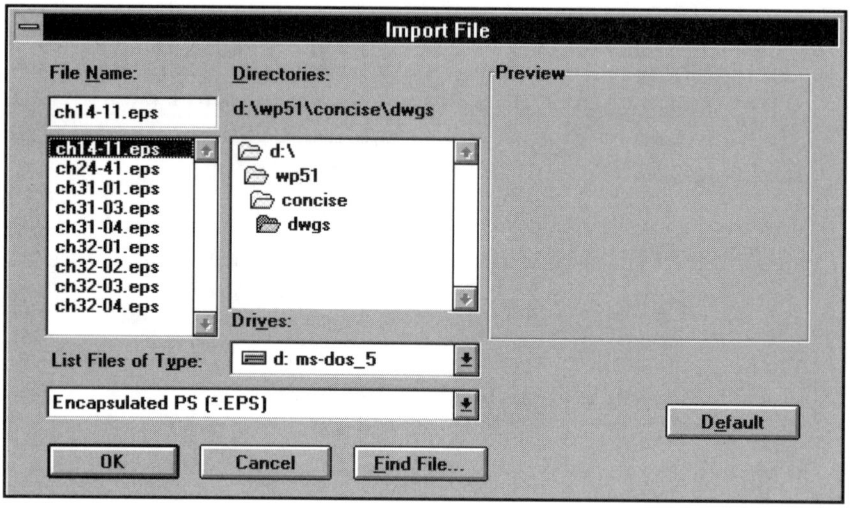

Figure 41-1: The Import File dialog.

When prompted in the dialog box, you enter the name of the intended interchange file (without the extension). Choose the file extension and either pick OK or press Enter to accept the default (the drawing name) as the interchange file name.

EXPORT Allows you to export various file formats out of AutoCAD

COMMAND LINE: **export**

Under the File pull-down menu, choose Export. The Export Data dialog lets you export the following types of files:

Extension	File Type
.WMF	Metafiles
.SAT	ACIS Solid Modeler
.PFB	PostScript font
.3DS	3D Studio

Using ATTEXT, you may export CDF/SDF (*.TXT) or DXF (*.DXF). You also may also export Lithography files (*.STL), Bitmap files (*.BMP) and drawings (*.DWG).

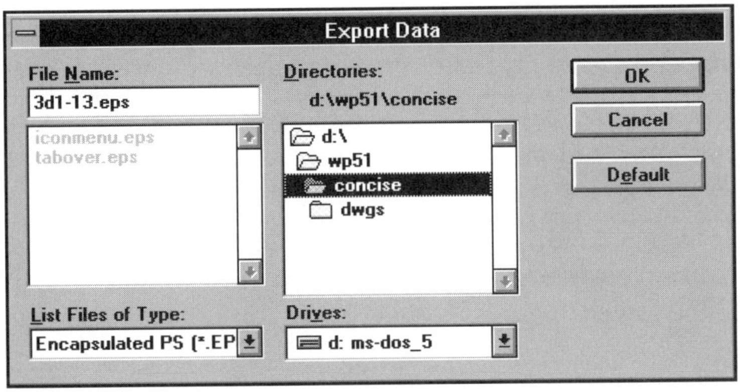

Figure 41-2: The Export Data dialog.

When prompted in the dialog box, you'll enter the name of the intended interchange file (without the extension). Choose the file extension and either pick OK or press Enter to accept the default (the drawing name) as the interchange file name.

Post-processing

"Post-processing" is a general term referring to any use of an AutoCAD drawing file or files created from or extracted from a drawing file outside AutoCAD.

Various types of post-processing include:

Material lists generated from attribute extract files.

Area and energy calculations for architectural drawings.

Cost-estimate calculations for architectural drawings.

Generation of tool-path programs for CAD/CAM applications.

Conversions to files usable by mainframe systems.

Finite element analysis.

Post-processing can be performed on drawing interchange files created with the DXFOUT command or on CDF, SDF or DXF format extract files created with the ATTEXT command.

Further Post-processing References

The *AutoCAD Customization Manual* includes a detailed description of the structure of a drawing interchange file.

See Appendix B in this guide for sample BASIC and AutoLISP programs that post-process attribute files.

See Appendix C in this guide on how to write a .DXF file from AutoCAD 13 to a lower release, how to DXFIX it and how to then import that DXF file into the lower release.

Using Handles

What is a handle? A handle is a hexadecimal number assigned to an object in a drawing. The handles feature, included since Release 10, is a transparent pointer that connects to the database. It uses both the drawing name and code number to create a unique code for each database record.

To see an object's handle, simply list the object while the handles are enabled. Since handles are output to DXF files and are available to AutoLISP, you can use them in both internal and external programs, including database programs.

Each object in a drawing keeps its handle for the life of the drawing. That is, handles are saved with the drawing so that any given object has the same handle during all editing sessions. If you're using handles to link your drawing objects to an external database, it's important for each object to retain its original handle.

Commands Affecting Handles

All of the drawing commands affect handles as they create objects. The following editing commands also affect handles because they too create objects: ARRAY, CHAMFER, FILLET, MIRROR and OFFSET.

The following editing commands do not affect handles: MOVE, MIRROR, SCALE, ROTATE, CHANGE, EXTEND and STRETCH. BREAK and TRIM affect handles only when they create new objects by separating one object into two.

When an object is erased, its handle is discarded and not reused. When a block is exploded, the block's handle is discarded and the individual parts of the block are assigned new handles.

The WBLOCK command discards handles and sets the HANDLES system variable to 0 in the WBLOCK output file. If you use the INSERT command or the DXFIN command to add objects to your drawing, those objects are assigned new handles in the present drawing.

The handle is associated with group code 5 both in a DXF file and in the association list obtained from the AutoLISP entget function. You can't use the AutoLISP entmod function to change an object handle. For more on this subject, see *AutoLISP in Plain English* by Ventana Press.

DXFOUT Creates a drawing interchange file (ASCII text file) from an existing drawing

COMMAND LINE: **dxfout**

Drawing interchange files can be used by other post-processing programs for a wide range of applications. (See "Post-processing" at the beginning of this chapter.)

Files created by the DXFOUT command have the extension .DXF.

When prompted, enter the name of the intended interchange file (without the .DXF extension). Or press Enter to accept the default (the drawing name) as the interchange file name.

Then enter the precision (0 to 16) for floating point numbers. Or enter **e** to select objects to be written to the DXF file. When you finish selecting objects, you're prompted again to enter the precision. Keep the precision default of 6 if you are sending the DXF file to a lower release of AutoCAD. See Appendix C of this guide on how to use DXFIX, DXFOUT and DXFIN in an earlier AutoCAD release.

DXFIN Creates an AutoCAD drawing file from a drawing interchange file

COMMAND LINE: **dxfin**

If you use the DXFIN command as the first command in the drawing editor, the drawing interchange file is converted into an AutoCAD drawing. If you use the DXFIN command after you've already created part of a drawing, only the objects section from the drawing interchange file is added to the drawing.

When prompted, enter the name of the drawing interchange file (without the .DXF extension).

PostScript

AutoCAD can import and export PostScript fonts, fill patterns and files. You can output a drawing as an Encapsulated PostScript (.EPS) file and then print on a PostScript device or import it into desktop publishing software. You can also import and scale an .EPS file as a block.

PSOUT Creates an (.EPS) Encapsulated PostScript (.EPS) file from an existing drawing

COMMAND LINE: **psout**

The PSOUT command lets you output your drawing as an Encapsulated PostScript (.EPS) file, which can be printed on a PostScript device or imported into desktop publishing software. PSOUT does not produce HIDE and SHADE output. Files created by PSOUT have the extension .EPS.

Figure 41-3: The Create PostScript File dialog.

The sequence is very similar to plotting. It lets you choose a specific portion of your drawing, such as display, extents, limits, view or window.

Display	Allows you to export a view from the current viewport, and the current display, if you are in Model Space, or the current view, if you are in Paper Space.

Extents	Allows you to export the equivalent of the ZOOM extents view command, within the current display. What you see depends on whether you are in Model Space or Paper Space.
Limits	If you are in plan view (VPOINT 0,0,1), it allows you to export the entire drawing limits.
View	To use this option, you must have previously saved and named a view. (Use the VIEW command with the Save option. Do not confuse this with the drawing SAVE command.)
Window	Simply pick two opposing corner points for this option.

PSOUT creates a preview image of 128 x 128, 256 x 256, or 512 x 512 pixels. You may create TIFF or EPSI viewing headers. Use two types of units (inch or mm). You can also scale and set the output size.

Seven Easy Steps to Using PSOUT

1. In the Create PostScript File dialog, enter the name and directory of the file.

2. At the "What to plot" prompt, choose Display, Extents, Limits, View or Window (enter the appropriate letter for your choice).

3. You can preview your drawing onscreen if you wish. To do so, enter **epsi** (for Encapsulated PostScript format) or **tiff** (for desktop publishing use) as appropriate. If you do not wish to preview the drawing, press Enter to accept the default of None.

4. The screen preview image size of 128 x 128 is the default. You can accept the default by pressing Enter, or you can make another selection.

5. Choose the size units (the default, inches, or millimeters).

6. Specify output scale by entering one of the following:

   The default, Fit, to accept the current overall screen size as the output scale.

   The desired scale, in the format *inches=drawing units*. For example, enter **1=96** to specify 1/8" = 1'.

7. Finally, from the displayed list of standard sheet sizes, enter the letter that represents the size you want. Or press Enter to accept the default of User, which sets the size to that of a standard A size sheet of paper.

PSIN Imports an .EPS file into AutoCAD

COMMAND LINE: **psin**

The PSIN command imports and scales an .EPS file as a block.

The system variables PSDRAG and PSQUALITY also control PostScript input and output.

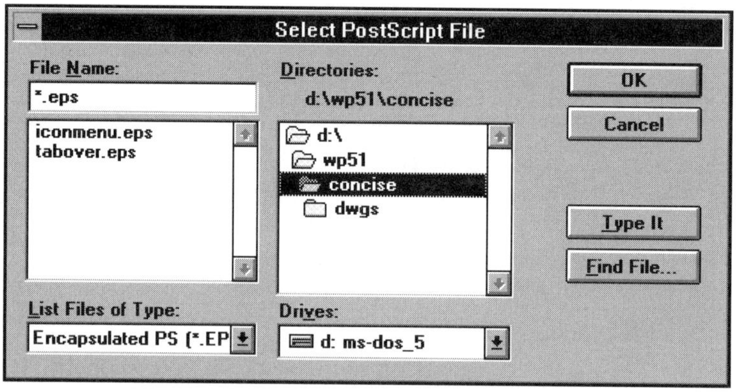

Figure 41-4: The Select PostScript File dialog.

Four Steps to Using PSIN

1. At the command prompt window, enter the name of the file you wish to import into AutoCAD (without the .EPS extension). Then wait.
2. A line of dots appears onscreen to show the command is working.
3. Enter the insertion point, or press Enter to accept the default (0,0,0).
4. Pick a point onscreen or enter a scale factor.

PostScript Variables

PSDRAG	When using the PSIN command and the system variable PSDRAG is 0, only the image's border is dragged. When PSDRAG is 1, the full image is dragged.
PSQUALITY	When you use the PSIN command and the system variable PSQUALITY is 0, only the border is displayed. If PSQUALITY is a positive number, that number determines the number of pixels per drawing unit. When PSQUALITY is a negative number, the image is displayed in outline form.

PostScript Fonts

PostScript fonts are provided with AutoCAD. To use these fonts, assign them to a text style created with the STYLE command.

The FONTS directory is included in the ACADR13\COMMON\FONTS environment variable. Filled-in fonts appear in outline form in a drawing and on a vector plotter but are filled in when output to a PostScript device.

Seven-bit fonts include the following:

1. CIBT	City blueprint
2. COBT	Country blueprint
3. ROM	Romantic
4. ROMB	Romantic-bold
5. SAS	Sans Serif, Helvetica style
6. SASB	Sans Serif bold, Helvetica style
7. SASO	Sans Serif oblique, Helvetica style
8. SASBO	Sans Serif bold oblique, Helvetica style
9. TE	Technic, Leroy style
10. TEL	Technic light, Leroy style
11. TEB	Technic bold, Leroy style

Eight-bit (extended character) fonts include:

1. EUR — EuroRoman
2. EURO — EuroRoman-oblique
3. PAN — PanRoman
4. SUF — SuperFrench

The PAN and SUF fonts each include all of the characters for 130 languages. PAN is designed for single-character typing of French, German and Spanish accents. SUF is also designed for single-character typing and for translation from languages that do not use the Roman character set. Character mapping for these fonts is shown in the sample drawings in the FONTS directory.

Fill Patterns

The PSFILL command lets you fill a closed polyline with one of the following PostScript fill patterns: Grayscale, Ailogo, Lineargray, Radialgray, Square, Waffle, Zigzag, Stars, Brick or Specks. These patterns are shown in the *AutoCAD Reference Manual*. While AutoCAD does not attempt to produce these patterns in your drawing, they are included in the output from the PSOUT command.

Moving on

AutoLISP, a command language, drives AutoCAD's many third-party applications. Chapter 42, "AutoLISP ADS/ARX," looks at some program files provided with your system.

AutoLISP & ADS/ARX

The first programming language supported by AutoCAD was the very flexible AutoLISP, which allows you to write programs with an ASCII text editor and run them from the command line. AutoLISP programs are known as *interpreted programs*. This means that the program is always run from the ASCII file and AutoCAD reads and executes each line of code one at a time.

Interpreted programs are easy to test and debug because you can directly edit and then run your programs without first going through a compiling process. The drawback is that AutoLISP programs are usually slower than compiled programs.

AutoLISP opened the door to sophisticated third-party, add-on programs. Beginning with AutoCAD Release 11, developers could write their programs using the C programming language and compile their code into executable ADS programs. Compiled ADS programs have the advantages of security, tighter integration with AutoCAD, and in some instances, faster execution. AutoCAD Release 13 introduces the new ARX programming environment, which expands the abilities of add-on programs.

APPLOAD Loads AutoLISP, ADS & ARX programs

COMMAND LINE: **appload**

Choose Applications from the Tools pull-down menu to display the dialog shown in Figure 42-1. You use the dialog by placing your most frequently used LISP and ADS programs in the Files to Load list. Once the programs are in the list, you can load and unload them from memory.

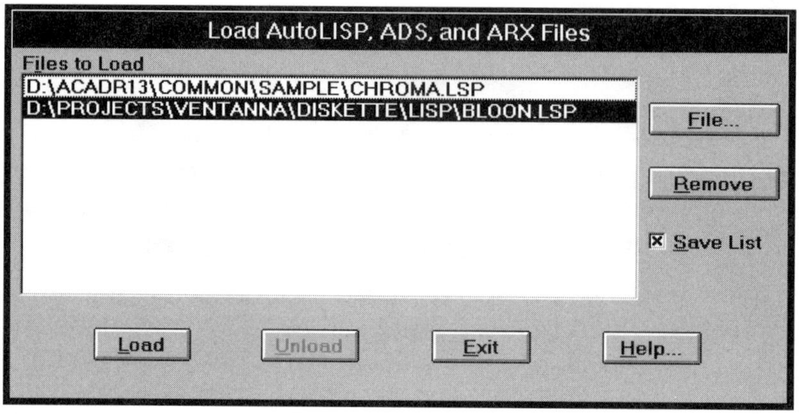

Figure 42-1: The Load AutoLISP, ADS, and ARX Files dialog.

The following buttons allow you to manage the files in your list:

File... — Displays the familiar select file dialog, which allows you to search your drives and directories for the programs that you want to load. Selecting a file places the file name and its path in the Files to Load list but does not load it into memory.

Remove — Takes a file out of the list. Use this button to weed out programs that you no longer use, or when you want to reduce the number of files in your list.

Save List — When this box is checked, AutoCAD saves your program selection list in an ASCII text file named APPLOAD.DFS. The next time that you enter AutoCAD your selected files are immediately available in the dialog.

The Load and Unload buttons move programs in and out of memory.

Load — To use this button, first select one or more programs from the list, then click on Load. The program can then be run from the command line.

Unload — Your AutoLISP programs cannot be unloaded. Only ADS and ARX programs can be unloaded to make room in memory for more programs. To use this button, first select the ADS or ARX programs that you want to remove from memory and then click the Unload button. If you have selected only LISP programs, the Unload button is not available.

AutoLISP Programs

Several AutoLISP program files are supplied in the SUPPORT and SAMPLE directories under the main AutoCAD directory, and more AutoLISP programs are available on the diskette included with this book. These programs are useful enhancements to the regular drawing and editing commands.

First, load these programs into memory with the APPLOAD command described above, and then execute the program from the command line. The convention with many LISP programs is that you execute the program with the same name as the file name. For example, a LISP program for drawing balloon leaders is provided on the bonus diskette with this book. After loading BLOON.LSP with APPLOAD, you run the program by entering **bloon** at the command line.

Not all AutoLISP programs are executed with the same name as their file name. You should always check the documentation provided with an AutoLISP routine for information on its use.

ADS and ARX Programs

Because they require more expensive compilers, ADS and ARX applications are not as plentiful as AutoLISP programs. A few sample ADS applications are provided with AutoCAD, and some of the core commands described previously in this book are actually ADS/ARX programs. For example, the commands described under "Rendering" in Chapter 36 are part of an ARX application.

As stated before, you load ADS and ARX programs with APPLOAD and then execute them from the command line.

Automatic Loading

A file named ACAD.ADS lets you automatically load ADS files. To make a file load automatically, use your text editor to add the file name into the ACAD.ADS file. Alternatively, if you have a specific directory with your favorite ADS applications listed, you can copy the edited ACAD.ADS file into it, then start AutoCAD from within the directory.

Moving on

Most of the commands and techniques discussed in this book have focused on the Windows version of AutoCAD Release 13, but they also apply to the DOS version of AutoCAD as well. The next chapter looks at commands and techniques that are unique to running AutoCAD under Windows.

CHAPTER 43

Special Windows Functions

One of the major advantages to running AutoCAD under Windows is the ability to share data among multiple applications. For example, you can easily place an AutoCAD drawing in a word processor document, or you can place a spreadsheet containing component prices into your AutoCAD drawing.

The tool used to share this data is the Windows Clipboard. AutoCAD provides great flexibility in how the contents of the Clipboard are interpreted. This chapter introduces the use of the Windows Clipboard in AutoCAD.

Understanding the Windows Clipboard

The Windows Clipboard is like a holding bin for documents and other data that you are working with. If you want to take some data from one place and put it into another you use the following steps:

1. First, select the data using the selection commands in your application.

2. Place the data into the Clipboard using the commands CUT or COPY. The difference between the commands is that CUT removes the data from its original location, while COPY leaves the original data in place.

3. Go to the place where you want to place the Clipboard data. This can mean either moving to a different place in the same document or launching a different application with another document.

4. Place the data into the document using the PASTE command.

Even though you have pasted the data into a document, you still have a copy of it stored in the Clipboard. You can paste the same data as many times as you want until you place something else in the Clipboard or empty the Clipboard with the CLEAR command.

Copying & Pasting at the Command Line

As mentioned earlier in this book, AutoCAD provides you with a scrolling text window containing all of the command line inputs entered since you opened the current drawing. The command history is useful for looking back to see what you have done, but AutoCAD also allows you to copy and paste commands from the text window to the command line. You can then execute a command that you have pasted to the command line.

The process of copying and pasting from the text window follows standard Windows conventions.

Copy

You can repeat any command in the text window by copying it to the Clipboard and pasting it on the command line. To copy a command, perform the following steps:

1. Position the cursor in front of the command that you wish to copy in the scrolling command window, or in the text window (press F2 to display the text window).

2. Press and drag the cursor across the command to highlight it. Make sure that you do not include the command prompt or any other text in you selection.

3. With the cursor in the command or text window, right-click (button 2) to display the command menu as seen in Figure 43-1.

4. Choose Copy from the command menu.

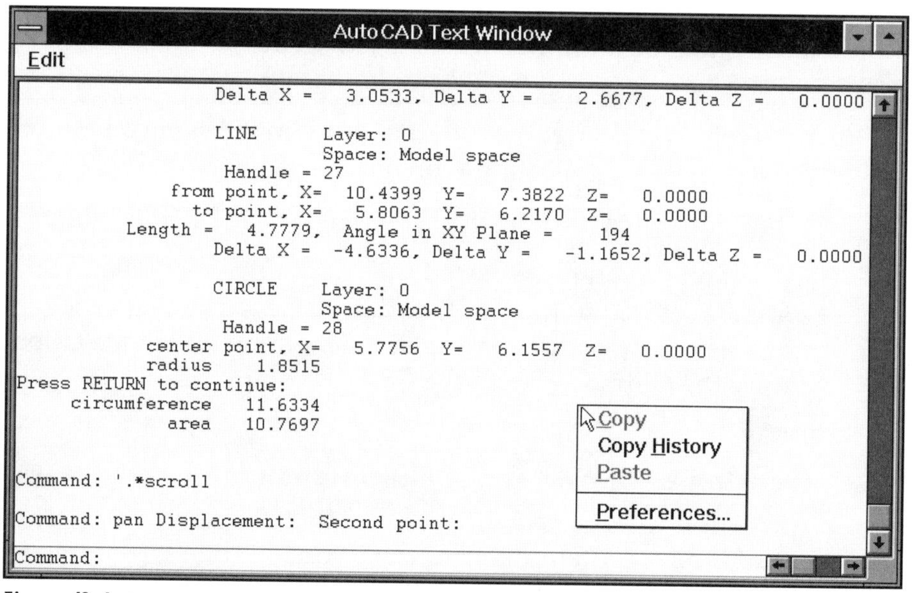

Figure 43-1: The command menu in the text window.

Your selected command is now in the Windows Clipboard.

Paste

Once a command is in the Clipboard, you can paste it to the command line.

1. Position the cursor anywhere in the command window or text window.

2. Right-click to display the command menu again.

3. Choose Paste from the command menu, and the command in the Clipboard appears on the command line.

4. Press Enter to execute the command.

If you select and copy multiple lines in the text window, AutoCAD ignores all but the first line.

COPY HISTORY Places the contents of the text window into the Clipboard

COMMAND LINE: **copyhist**

You can use the Copy History command to place the entire contents of the text window into the Clipboard. This is useful if you want to paste the commands that you have executed into a word processing document.

Choose Copy History from the command menu, or type **copyhist** at the command line. All text in the text window will be copied to the Clipboard.

Copying and Pasting Objects

Far more useful than copying and pasting commands to the command line, is the ability to cut, copy and paste objects to and from your AutoCAD drawings.

CUT TO CLIPBOARD Deletes objects from the drawing and places them in the Clipboard

COMMAND LINE: **cutclip**

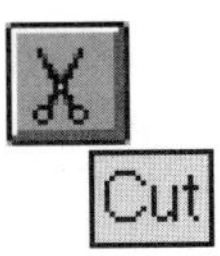

Figure 43-2: The Cut icon from the Standard toolbar.

Choosing Cut from the Edit pull-down menu, or clicking on the Cut icon, prompts you to select objects. Use normal selection methods to select the object to cut and press Enter. The selected objects are deleted from the drawing and placed in the Clipboard.

Once the objects are in the Clipboard they can be pasted into other AutoCAD drawings, or into documents created by other Windows programs.

COPY TO CLIPBOARD Copies objects to the Clipboard

COMMAND LINE: **copyclip**

Figure 43-3: The Copy icon from the Standard toolbar.

Choosing Copy from the Edit pull-down menu, or clicking on the Copy icon, works exactly like Cut (described above) except that the selected objects are not deleted from your drawing.

PASTE FROM CLIPBOARD Places the contents of the Clipboard into the current drawing

COMMAND LINE: **pasteclip**

Figure 43-4: The Paste icon from the Standard toolbar.

Choosing Paste from the Edit pull-down menu, or clicking on the Paste icon, places the contents of the Clipboard into your current drawing. The behavior of the Paste command varies based on the type of objects in the Clipboard.

AutoCAD objects are pasted as anonymous blocks with each block's insertion point defined as 0,0,0 at the time it was copied or cut to the Clipboard. The remaining prompts are the same as those for the INSERT command. See "Insert" in Chapter 23, "Blocks & External References."

ASCII Text, such as text created with the Windows Notepad or another text editor, is pasted as an AutoCAD MTEXT object. See "MTEXT" in Chapter 16, "Text."

Other text, such as that from word processing or desktop publishing programs, is embedded in your drawing using the format of the program that created it. See "Object Linking & Embedding" below. The text is pasted into the upper-left corner of the drawing window.

Graphics and formats from other programs are also embedded in the upper-left corner of the drawing window. See "Object Linking & Embedding" below.

Object Linking & Embedding

Object Linking and Embedding (OLE) is a special form of Paste supported by most Windows programs. When you link or embed an object into a document, the object retains the format of the program that created it. You can also edit that object using the program that created it, even though the object is now part of some other program's document. For example, if you embed a spreadsheet into an AutoCAD drawing, you can still edit that spreadsheet with its native program from within AutoCAD.

The difference between embedding and linking is similar to the difference between blocks and xrefs.

If you embed an object in an AutoCAD drawing, that object is copied into the drawing and it retains no connection to the document that it originally came from. If you embed a spreadsheet into an AutoCAD drawing, you can later edit or delete the spreadsheet file without affecting the copy embedded in your drawing.

If you link the spreadsheet into your drawing, then the spreadsheet maintains a connection to its original document and any changes made to the original document will show up in the linked object in the AutoCAD drawing.

NOTE: *If you link or embed objects into your AutoCAD drawing, they are only accessible when the drawing is loaded into AutoCAD for Windows. Linked and embedded objects do not appear when a drawing is loaded into AutoCAD for DOS. Also, linked and embedded objects will plot only to the Windows system printer. Standard AutoCAD plotter drivers do not know how to deal with linked and embedded objects.*

COPY VIEW Copies the current view to the Clipboard

COMMAND LINE: **copylink**

Choosing Copy View from the Edit pull-down menu copies the current view to the Clipboard so that it can be linked into another application's document (such as a word processing file). The difference between Copy View and Copy Clip is that Copy View quickly puts the current viewport with all of its visible obejcts into the Clipboard while Copy Clip requires you to manually select objects.

PASTE SPECIAL Lets you control the format of an object that is pasted into a drawing

COMMAND LINE: **pastespec**

Choosing Paste Special from the Edit pull-down menu displays the Paste Special dialog. The options in this dialog give you control over the format of an object that is pasted into your AutoCAD drawing, and whether that object is embedded or linked. Before you can use Paste Special, you must have copied something from another application to the Windows Clipboard. Figure 43-5 shows the Paste Special dialog with text and graphics from a Microsoft Word document in the Clipboard.

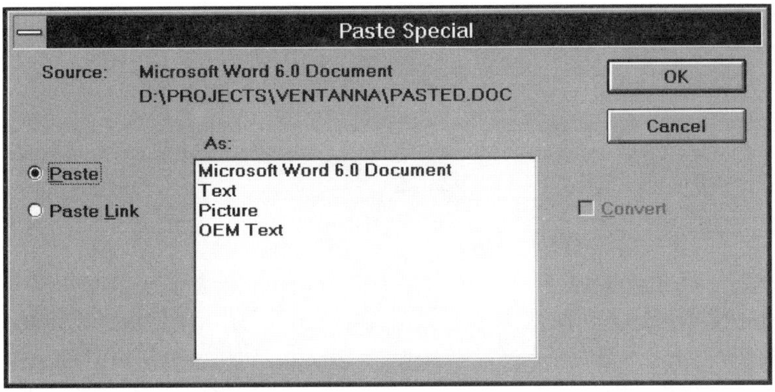

Figure 43-5: The Paste Special dialog.

The options of the Paste Special dialog are as follows:

Paste causes the Clipboard object to be embedded into your AutoCAD drawing using the format selected in the As: list. Embedded objects can be edited by programs outside of AutoCAD, but they do not retain any connection with their original file of origin.

Paste Link causes the Clipboard object to be linked into your AutoCAD drawing using the format selected. Linked objects retain a connection to their external file of origin and can be edited by programs outside of AutoCAD.

As: displays a list of the valid formats supported for the objects in the Clipboard. The item at the top of the list is the native format of the application that created the objects, if that information is available. Otherwise, the first item in the list is named Unknown. The other formats may or may not support all of the features of linking and embedding.

For example, choosing Text in the As: list of Figure 43-5 would ignore the graphics in the Clipboard and insert only the text as an AutoCAD MTEXT object. Since the Clipboard objects are converted into true AutoCAD objects, they lose all connection with their file and application of origin and are neither embedded nor linked regardless of the setting of the Paste or Paste Link buttons.

Convert is available only for formats other than text that are capable of being converted into true AutoCAD objects. For example, in Figure 43-5, if Picture were selected as the format and the Convert box were checked, the objects pasted from the Clipboard would be converted into AutoCAD objects (such as polylines and circles) rather than being pasted as a Word Picture object. Converting objects always cancels embedding or linking.

OLE LINKS Displays the Links dialog

COMMAND LINE: **olelinks**

Choosing Links... from the Edit pull-down menu displays the Links dialog only if there are linked objects in your drawing. Otherwise the command does nothing. Figure 43-6 shows the Links dialog after a Microsoft Word document has been linked into the drawing.

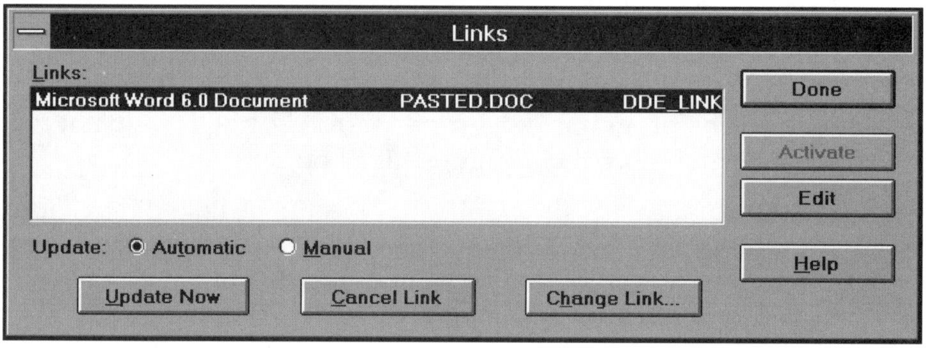

Figure 43-6: The Links dialog.

The options of the Link dialog are explained below:

Links: displays a list of all the active links in your drawing. The list shows the object format on the left, followed by the linked document name and the link ID. You can select one or more links from the list to be affected by the other dialog options.

Update: sets the update method of the selected links with two radio buttons. Automatic sets the selected links to update immediately whenever the linked document changes. Manual prompts you to update any changed links only when you first open the drawing.

Update Now updates all selected links to the current status of the linked document.

Cancel Link severs the selected links and converts them into embedded objects.

Change Link... displays a file selector dialog that allows you to respecify the linked document name. Use this command to re-establish a link with a document that has been renamed or moved to another directory.

Activate runs executable links. For example, if you linked an AVI movie file to your drawing, selecting the movie's link and clicking on Activate would play the movie.

Edit launches the parent application of the linked document and loads the document for editing. Exiting the application returns you to AutoCAD and updates the link based upon its update setting (automatic or manual).

Done closes the dialog and returns you to the drawing window.

INSERT OBJECT Provides access to applications that can create objects for linking and embedding

COMMAND LINE: **insertobj**

This command does not really insert an object into your AutoCAD drawing, rather, it provides quick access to those applications on your system that are capable of creating objects for linking and embedding. Choosing Insert Object from the Edit pull-down menu displays the Insert New Object dialog (Figure 43-7) with a list of all the applications on your system that support linking and embedding.

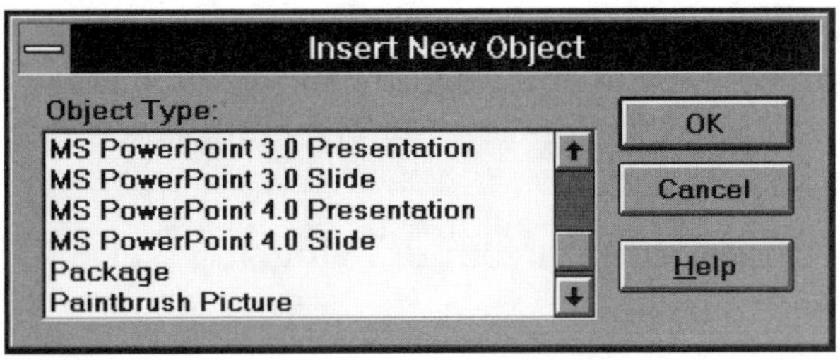

Figure 43-7: The Insert New Object dialog.

Selecting an application from the list, and clicking on OK, launches that application. You then create new objects, copy them to the Clipboard and paste them into your drawing using the commands described above.

Editing Linked & Embedded Objects

Linked and embedded objects do not respond to normal AutoCAD editing commands. Using special features of OLE you can resize and move these objects within AutoCAD, or launch their parent application to edit the objects themselves.

These are the methods available for manipulating linked and embedded objects within AutoCAD:

1. Clicking inside an object displays the object's frame. The cursor changes to a move cursor as shown in Figure 43-8. You can then drag the object to a new location in the drawing.

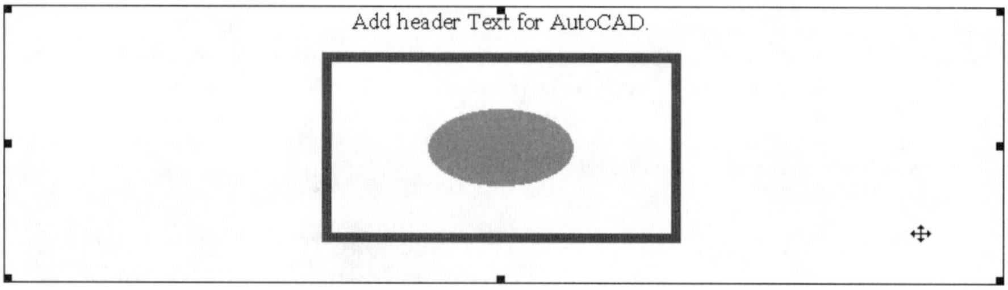

Figure 43-8: A linked object and its frame.

2. When the frame is visible you can see grips at the frame's corners and midpoints. You can drag a corner grip to scale the width and height of the object simultaneously. You can also drag a midpoint grip to stretch the object along a single axis, either horizontally or vertically.

3. When the cursor is over the object , you can right-click to display the command menu as shown in Figure 43-9. The commands in the command menu have the following functions:

Cut removes the object from your drawing and places it in the Clipboard.

Copy places a copy of the object in the Clipboard.

Clear removes the object from your drawing. This is how you erase a linked or embedded object.

Edit launches the application that created the object and opens the object for editing. Saving the object from its parent application updates the embedded or linked object in your drawing.

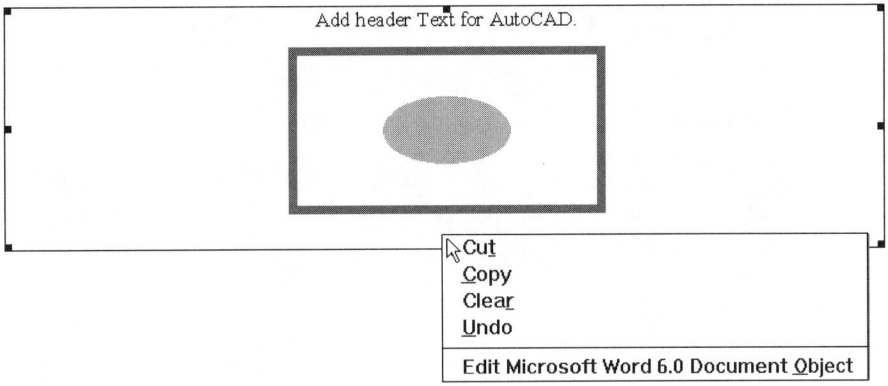

Figure 43-9: The command menu for linked and embedded objects.

Drag & Drop

If you launch the Windows File Manager while you are working in AutoCAD, you can take advantage of another Windows feature known as *drag-and-drop*. Just as the name implies, you can drag a file over to the AutoCAD window and drop it into your drawing. The result of a drag-and-drop is dependent upon what type of file was dropped into your drawing. Below is a list of the most common file types and what AutoCAD does with them:

ASCII text files with an extension of .TXT are placed into your drawing as AutoCAD MTEXT objects using the current text style. The initial location of the object is the upper-left corner of the drawing window.

For Font files with an extension of .SHX, .PFB or .TTF, AutoCAD creates a text style using the same name as the font file and makes the new style current.

Drawings are inserted as blocks just as with the INSERT command. After dropping the file, you must click in the AutoCAD window to proceed with the standard insertion prompts. The block will have the same name as the drawing file.

Slides display just as with the VSLIDE command.

Scripts run as if they had been executed with the SCRIPT command.

For linetype files, AutoCAD loads all of the linetype definitions stored in the file.

Menu files are loaded as they are with the MENU command.

LISP files are loaded as if they had been selected with Appload.

ADS programs are Xloaded as if they had been selected with Appload.

If AutoCAD does not understand a particular file type it displays an alert dialog that states "No Association *filename*" where filename is the file that you dropped into the AutoCAD window. Clicking OK returns you to AutoCAD.

Moving on

You have reached the end of the Advanced section of *AutoCAD: A Concise Guide*. The remaining sections of the book provide hands-on exercises and appendices with helpful information.

CHAPTER 44

Hands-on Exercises I

The next two chapters present a variety of exercises concerning drawing and editing with AutoCAD. To learn AutoCAD, you must use AutoCAD—so here's your chance.

Exercises are grouped in the same general order as the topics in the earliest chapters of *the Concise Guide*. As you read each chapter in the first part of the book, you can find the related exercises here and try out the procedures you're studying.

Some of the exercises (mostly the earlier ones) include step-by-step instructions; others are sample drawings for you to reproduce—with a few suggestions on how to set up a drawing or complete certain features. Simple drawing and editing exercises follow, with more advanced exercises in Chapter 45.

As you work through these two final chapters, keep in mind the following tips:

> Learn the fundamental concepts and skills well, as everything else builds on the basics. This includes methods of point entry, creation of objects (lines, circles and arcs) and basic editing procedures.
>
> From the outset, draw accurately. Use snap, osnap and keyboard entry to construct an exact "skeleton" of your drawing outline. Everything you build on that skeleton falls into place more easily.
>
> Check your work often with the inquiry commands (ID, DIST and LIST) to make sure your drawing is accurate.
>
> Remember, if you take the time to master the fundamentals, you'll be prepared to master the more advanced AutoCAD procedures involving polyline editing, UCS and 3D construction.

General & Specific Instructions

Many of the exercises in this chapter are organized into two columns: general instructions and specific instructions. If possible, try to do as much of each exercise as you can by following the general instructions only. If you get stymied, or if you want to see another way to carry out the general instructions, then look at the specific instructions.

Specific instructions guide you in entering every command and locating every point from the keyboard. You may find it easier to activate the commands by using the icons, the pull-down menus or the tablet overlay. Also, since you'll usually set snap to an appropriate spacing, you may want to enter most locations with the pointer. As usual, unless you pick an icon or enter AutoCAD commands from the keyboard, you need to press Enter after typing each command or each pair of coordinates.

Prototype Drawings

This exercise sets up several prototype drawings for use in Model Space. Drawing setup in AutoCAD can be simple or complex. The simplest setup involves using the default sheet that appears when you first enter the drawing editor. This sheet is 12 x 9 inches, and it uses decimal units with grid and snap both set to 1. It has one layer and one text style. Naturally, this setup is only suitable for a certain type of drawing.

In this exercise, you'll use LIMITS, GRID, SNAP and other commands, and in the process you'll create four separate drawings to use as prototypes. Three of the drawings use inches; the fourth uses millimeters. Each one has a simple border around the edge of the limits.

Specifications of the four drawings:

Sheet	Size	Format size	Orientation
SHEET-A.DWG	Size A	10 x 7.5 inches	Horizontal
SHEET-V.DWG	Size A	7.5 x 10 inches	Vertical
SHEET-B.DWG	Size B	16 x 10 inches	Horizontal
SHEET-BM.DWG	Size B	406 x 254 mm	Horizontal

These four sheets are useful as prototype drawings for many drawing exercises in this guide. For example, when you're starting a new drawing and want to use one of the prototype drawings, choose the name of the prototype file in the Prototype drawing dialog box or, if you're using a prior release, place the name of the prototype drawing after an equals sign when you enter the name of the new drawing, using the format XXXX=SHEET-A. See "Starting a New Drawing" in Chapter 2, "Entering & Exiting AutoCAD."

To set up prototype drawings for scales other than 1=1, see the chart in "Setting Limits" in Chapter 17, "Understanding Limits & Prototype Drawings."

Prototype drawings let you avoid repeating the setup procedure every time you begin a new drawing. A prototype drawing might include the settings listed below. All the settings, which you normally establish at the beginning of a drawing, can be changed any time during the drawing/editing process. You may also edit a prototype drawing at any time.

A full prototype drawing can include the following settings:

1. Types of linear and/or angular units with accuracy of readout, direction of zero angle and positive rotation.
2. Limits—lower-left corner and upper-right corner.
3. Grid spacing.
4. Snap style and spacing.
5. Layers and associated linetypes and colors.
6. Linetype scales as determined by the final plotting scale.
7. Default text height as determined by the final plotting scale.
8. Text styles as needed.
9. Multiline styles.
10. Predefined blocks as needed.
11. Dimension styles—including dimensioning variables as determined by the final plotting scale.
12. System variable settings such as FILEDIA and CMDDIA.

Since this is a beginning exercise, we're assuming that you haven't yet learned to use layers, dimensioning variables, text styles or blocks. Thus, the prototype drawings created here won't include any of these items. Later, when you learn to use them, you can edit your prototype drawing to suit your needs.

Our approach is as follows: We start a "temporary" drawing and establish various settings for Sheet-A, then save the drawing under the name SHEET-A. Then we change the settings for each of the next sheets and save the drawing under the appropriate name.

Plotters and printers are different. If your plotter or printer has maximum drawing limits that differ from the format sizes listed, substitute the appropriate numbers as you work through this exercise.

This exercise is organized into general and specific instructions.

Before you begin, be sure that the Draw, Construct and Modify menu choices appear in the menu bar at the top of your screen. If they do not, enter **menu** at the command line and then select Acadfull (for "full menu").

SHEET-A Prototype—Setup (Size A, horizontal orientation, inches)

General instructions:	Specific instructions:
1. Start a new drawing and name it Temp.	From the File pull-down menu pick New... and name it TEMP. Check the No Prototype box.
2. Set your Units to Decimal with four places of precision.	You may type the command UNITS or choose Units... from the Data pull-down menu. Notice the dialog box is split vertically into Units and Angles (left and right) columns. Pick Decimal as your Lineal Units and choose (0.0000) for four places of precision. Choose Decimal Degrees in the Angles column, again with a four-place precision readout.
	To activate the Direction Control box, choose the Direction button and set it to Zero angle direction—East (0.0), with positive angles and counter-clockwise rotation. Choose OK to save the settings and exit the dialog box.
3. Set the Drawing Limits to 10 x 7.5.	You may type the command LIMITS or choose Drawing Limits... from the Data pull-down menu. Accept the default. Leaving the lower-left corner at 0,0, set the upper-right corner to 10,7.5.
4. Do a ZOOM All.	Pick the Zoom-All icon. Or choose Zoom from the View pull-down menu and choose Zoom-All.

5. Set the grid to 0.5 and the snap to 0.0625.	Activate the Drawing Aids… dialog from the Options pull-down and set your grid to 0.5 and the snap to 0.0625. Toggle them both on and choose OK to save the settings and exit the box.
6. Toggle on the Coordinates.	Move the cursor around the screen, and notice the coordinate readout in the status line jumps in increments of .0625. Press F6 if your coordinate readout is frozen.
7. Draw a line around the limits.	Activate the Draw Toolbar, choose the Polygon flyout and pick the Rectangle icon. Create a rectangle from the lower-left of 0,0 to the upper-right of 10,7.5.
8. Save the drawing as SHEET-A.	From the File pull-down choose Save As… and save this drawing with a name of SHEET-A.

SHEET-V Prototype—Setup (Size A, vertical orientation, inches)

9. Erase the rectangular border line.	Choose Erase from the Modify pull-down menu and pick the rectangular border you created earlier.
10. Change the limits to 7.5 x 10 and then ZOOM All.	Choose Drawing Limits… from the Data pull-down. Press Enter to accept the default of the lower-left corner at 0,0 and set the upper-right corner at 7.5,10. Then ZOOM All.
11. Draw a line around the border.	Activate the Draw pull-down menu, choose Polygon, then choose Rectangle. Create a rectangular box from 0,0 to 7.5,10.
12. Save this drawing under the name SHEET-V.	From the File pull-down choose Save As… and Save this drawing with a name of SHEET-V.

SHEET-B Prototype—Setup (Size B, horizontal orientation, inches)

13. Erase the border line.	Choose Erase from the Modify pull-down menu and pick the rectangular border you created earlier.
14. Change the drawing limits to 16,10 and do a ZOOM All.	Choose Drawing Limits... from the Data pull-down. Press Enter to accept the lower-left corner at 0,0 and set the upper-right corner at 16,10. Then ZOOM All.
15. Change the grid to 1 and the snap to 0.125.	In the Drawing Aids... dialog set your grid to 1 and the snap to 0.125. Turn them both on and choose OK.
16. Draw a line around the border.	Activate the Draw pull-down menu, choose Polygon, then choose Rectangle. Create a rectangular box from 0,0 to 16,10.
17. Save this drawing under the name SHEET-B.	From the File pull-down menu choose Save As... and save this drawing with a name of SHEET-B.

SHEET-BM Prototype—Setup (horizontal orientation, millimeters)

18. Erase the border line.	Choose Erase from the Modify pull-down menu and pick the rectangular border you created earlier.
19. Change grid to 10, snap to 1.	In the Drawing Aids... dialog set your grid to 10 and the snap TO 1. Turn them both on and choose OK .
20. Change limits to 406 x 254 and do a ZOOM All.	Choose Drawing Limits... from the Data pull-down menu. Press Enter to accept the lower-left corner at 0,0 and set the upper-right corner at 406,254. Then ZOOM All.

21. Change units to three-place readout for linear units.	From the Data pull-down menu choose Units… Notice the dialog box is split vertically into Units and Angles (left and right) columns. Pick Decimal as your Lineal Units, and choose (0.000) for three places of precision. Choose Decimal Degrees in the Angles column, again with a three-place precision readout.
22. Draw a line around the border.	Activate the Draw pull-down menu, choose Polygon, then choose Rectangle. Create a rectangular box from 0,0 to 406,254.
23. Save this drawing under the name SHEET-BM.	From the File pull-down choose Save as… and save this drawing with a name of SHEET-BM.
24. End AutoCAD.	From the File pull-down menu, choose Exit.

Lines, Circles & Arcs

Line Exercise I

This exercise is organized into general instructions and specific instructions. You draw the two picture frames shown below. The exercise uses two methods of point entry—absolute and relative (both relative rectangular and relative polar). To pick commands, you either choose the pull-down menu or your icons. Type in any coordinates at the keyboard.

Before you begin, be sure that the Draw, Construct and Modify menu choices appear in the menu bar at the top of your screen. If they do not, enter **menu** at the command line and then select Acadfull (for "full menu").

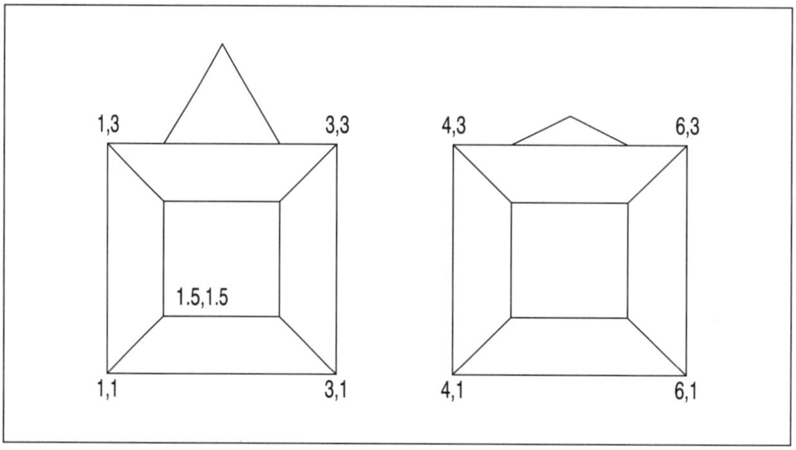

Figure 44-1: Completed picture frames for Line Exercise 1.

1. Start a NEW drawing and name it LINEX1. Do not use a prototype.

From the File pull-down menu choose New. In the "Create New Drawing" dialog pick the No Prototype button and enter **linex-1**.
Or just enter **linex=** in the drawing name prompt line and pick OK. The = sign automatically chooses *no prototype* for you. (If you are using a prior release, add the equals sign when prompted for the name. The option of =*blank* indicates no prototype.)

2. Turn the UCS icon off.

Type **ucsicon** at the keyboard and press Enter. Then type **off** and press Enter.

3. Draw a 2-inch square for the outside of the left frame, with lower-left corner at 1,1. Use absolute coordinates.

Choose Line from the Draw pull-down menu or click the Line icon. Enter the absolute coordinates as follows:

```
LINE <Enter>
1,1 <Enter>
3,1 <Enter>
3,3 <Enter>
1,3 <Enter>
1,1 <Enter> <Enter>
```

4. Draw a 1-inch square for

Choose Line from the Draw pull-down

the inside of the left frame, with the lower-left corner at 1.5,1.5. Again, use absolute coordinates.

menu or click the Line icon. Enter the absolute coordinates as follows:

```
LINE <Enter>
1.5,1.5 <Enter>
2.5,1.5 <Enter>
2.5,2.5 <Enter>
1.5,2.5 <Enter>
C <Enter>
```

5. Redraw the screen.

Choose Redraw View from the View pull-down menu, click the Redraw icon, or press F7 twice.

6. Draw a 2-inch square for the outside of the right frame, with the lower-left corner at 4,1. Use relative rectangular coordinates.

Choose Line from the Draw pull-down menu or click the Line icon. Enter the relative rectangular coordinates as follows:

```
4,1 <Enter>
@2,0 <Enter>
@0,2 <Enter>
@-2,0 <Enter>
@0,-2 <Enter> <Enter>
```

7. Draw a 1-inch square for the inside of the right frame, with the lower-left corner at 4.5,1.5. Use relative rectangular coordinates.

Choose Line from the Draw pull-down menu or click the Line icon. Enter the relative rectangular coordinates as follows:

```
4.5,1.5 <Enter>
@1,0 <Enter>
@0,1 <Enter>
@-1,0 <Enter>
C <Enter>
```

8. Redraw the screen.

Choose Redraw View from the View pull-down menu, click the Redraw icon, or press F7 twice.

9. On the left frame, draw the four diagonal lines connecting the corners of the larger square to the corners of the smaller square. Use relative rectangular

Choose Line from the Draw pull-down menu or click the Line icon. Enter the relative rectangular coordinates as follows:

```
1,1 <Enter>
```

coordinates. Each line extends .5 inch in both the X and the Y directions.

@.5,.5 <Enter><Enter>
Choose Line again or press Enter to reactivate it.
3,1 <Enter>
@-5,.5 <Enter><Enter>

Choose Line again or press the Spacebar to reactivate it.
3,3 <Enter>
@-5,-5 <Enter><Enter>

Press the right pick on the mouse to reactivate Line.
1,3 <Enter>
@.5,-5 <Enter><Enter>

10. On the right frame, draw the four diagonal lines connecting the corners of the larger square to the corners of the smaller square. Use relative polar coordinates. The length of each line is .7071.

Choose Line from the Draw pull-down menu or click the Line icon. Enter the relative polar coordinates as follows:
4,1 <Enter>
@.7071<45 <Enter><Enter>
Choose Line again.
6,1 <Enter>
@.7071<135 <Enter><Enter>

Choose Line again.
6,3 <Enter>
@.7071<-135 <Enter><Enter>

Choose Line again.
4,3 <Enter>
@.7071<-45 <Enter><Enter>

11. Redraw the screen.

Choose Redraw View from the View pull-down menu, click the Redraw icon, or press F7 twice.

12. Draw the string holding the left frame. Both sides of the string meet the top of the frame .5 inch from the edge, are one inch long, and are 60 degrees from horizontal. Use relative polar coordinates.

Choose Line from the Draw pull-down menu or click the Line icon. Enter the relative polar coordinates as follows:
1.5,3 <Enter>
@1<60 <Enter>
@1<-60 <Enter><Enter>

13. Draw the string holding the

Choose Line from the Draw pull-down

right frame. Both sides of the string meet the top of the frame .5 inch from the edge and extend .25 inch above the frame. Use relative rectangular coordinates.

menu or click the Line icon. Enter the relative coordinates as follows:

```
4.5,3 <Enter>
@.5,.25 <Enter>
@.5,-25 <Enter><Enter>
```

14. Redraw the screen.

Choose Redraw View from the View pull-down menu, click the Redraw icon, or press F7 twice.

15. Save your drawing.

From the File pull-down menu, choose Save.

Line Exercise 2

This exercise emphasizes the use of the pointer, along with three drawing aids—snap, ortho, and the coordinate readout on the status line. Use the default limits of 0,0 (lower-left corner) to 12,9 (upper-right corner).

Start a new drawing called LINEX-2 that again uses no prototype. (Use the same procedures you used in "Line Exercise 1.")

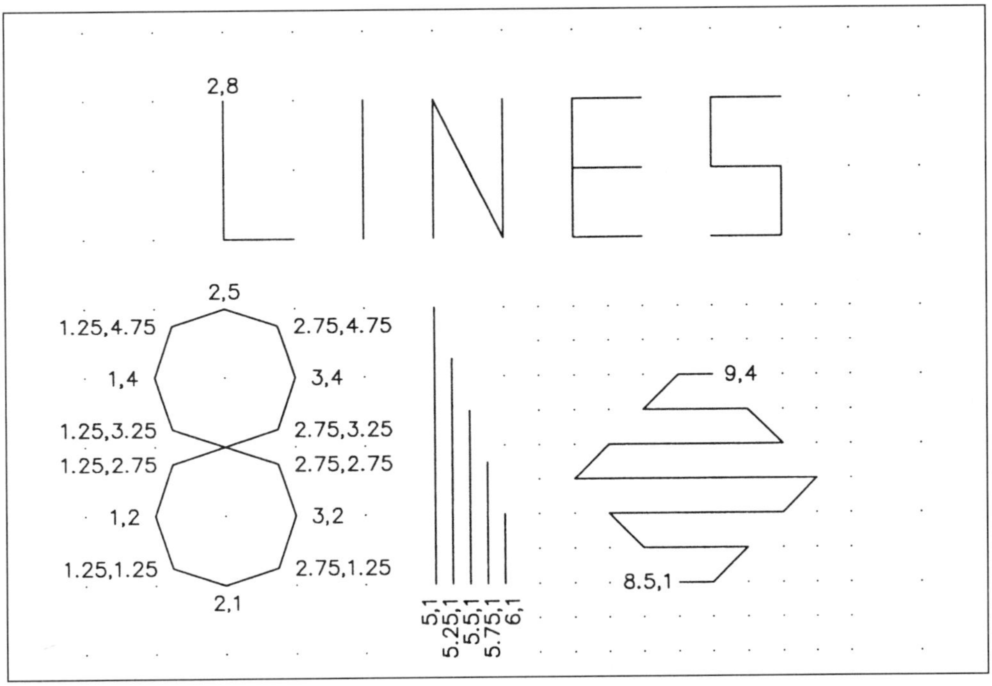

Figure 44-2: Completed graphics for Line Exercise 2.

Drawing the Lines

Set both the grid and snap to 1.

From the Options pull-down menu, choose Drawing Aids. Set both the grid and snap to 1. The grid appears on the screen only if you turn it on in the dialog box. Choose OK to activate and save the settings.

Ortho (F8) can be on or off.

Start by entering the LINE command, then move the pointer to the appropriate location so the coordinate readout displays 2.0000,8.0000. You may need to press F6 once or twice to get the coordinate readout to display absolute coordinates. As you draw the lines, use the grid points to guide you in locating each endpoint.

Drawing the Figure Eight

Keep the grid at 1 and turned on. Reset the snap to .25 and turn it on. Turn ortho (F8) off.

As you draw the lines that make up the figure eight, watch the coordinate readout in the status line to make sure your pointer is at the right location.

Drawing the Vertical Lines

The lengths of the lines are 4, 3.25, 2.5, 1.75 and 1.

Keep grid at 1. Keep snap at .25. Use F8 to turn ortho on.

Start at the bottom of each line and watch the coordinate readout to see when your line is the proper length. You may need to press F6 once or twice to get the coordinate readout to display distance and angle. As you move the pointer up, the vertical distance must be exact, but the pointer (crosshairs) can be somewhat left or right of the desired endpoint since you have ortho turned on.

Drawing the Zig-zag

Set grid and snap to .5. Turn ortho (F8) on and off as needed.

SHEET-A — Model Space Exercise

This exercise creates a prototype drawing to use in Model Space.

Before you begin, be sure that the Draw, Construct and Modify menu choices appear in the menu bar at the top of your screen. If they do not, enter **menu** at the command line and then select Acadfull (for "full menu").

If you've already made the SHEET-A prototype drawing in the setup exercise under "Prototype Drawings," open that drawing. Then skip to the section "Draw the Left & Top Edges of the Title Block" below.

If you're starting from scratch, begin at "Setup."

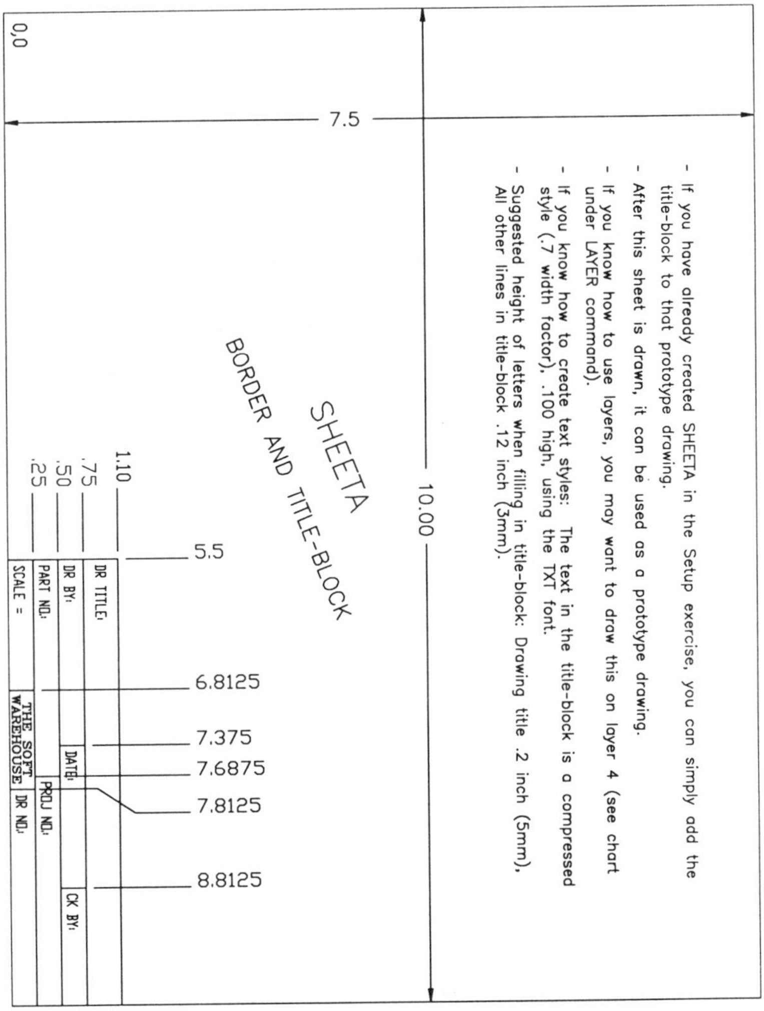

Figure 44-3: Sheet-A prototype with title block added.

Setup

Start a new drawing and name it SHEET-A.

Set grid at .5.

Set snap at .0625. This will let you snap to most of the endpoints.

Set limits with the lower-left corner at 0,0 and the upper-right corner at 10,7.5.

Do a ZOOM All.

Drawing the Border

Use F8 to turn ortho on. Choose the LINE command and use the pointer to draw the bottom border line from 0,0 to 10,0. (You can press F6 once or twice so the status line displays absolute coordinates.) Stay in the LINE command and draw the right and top lines. Watch the coordinate readout in the status line as you draw. Then enter **c** to close the border. Redraw the screen (press F7 twice).

Draw the Left & Top Edges of the Title Block

Leave ortho on. Enter the LINE command and use the pointer to locate 5.5,0. Then enter relative coordinates **@0,1.1**. Then use the pointer to draw the top edge of the title block extending to the right border. Then exit the LINE command. Redraw the screen.

Draw the Remaining Lines

With ortho and snap still on, use the pointer to draw the three remaining horizontal lines and the short vertical lines in the title block. Redraw the screen.

Save your drawing.

Line Exercise 3

Draw each of the objects on your own using the explanation text as needed. For the octagon, hexagon and pentagon figures, you may wish to use the Polygon option from the Draw pull-down menu.

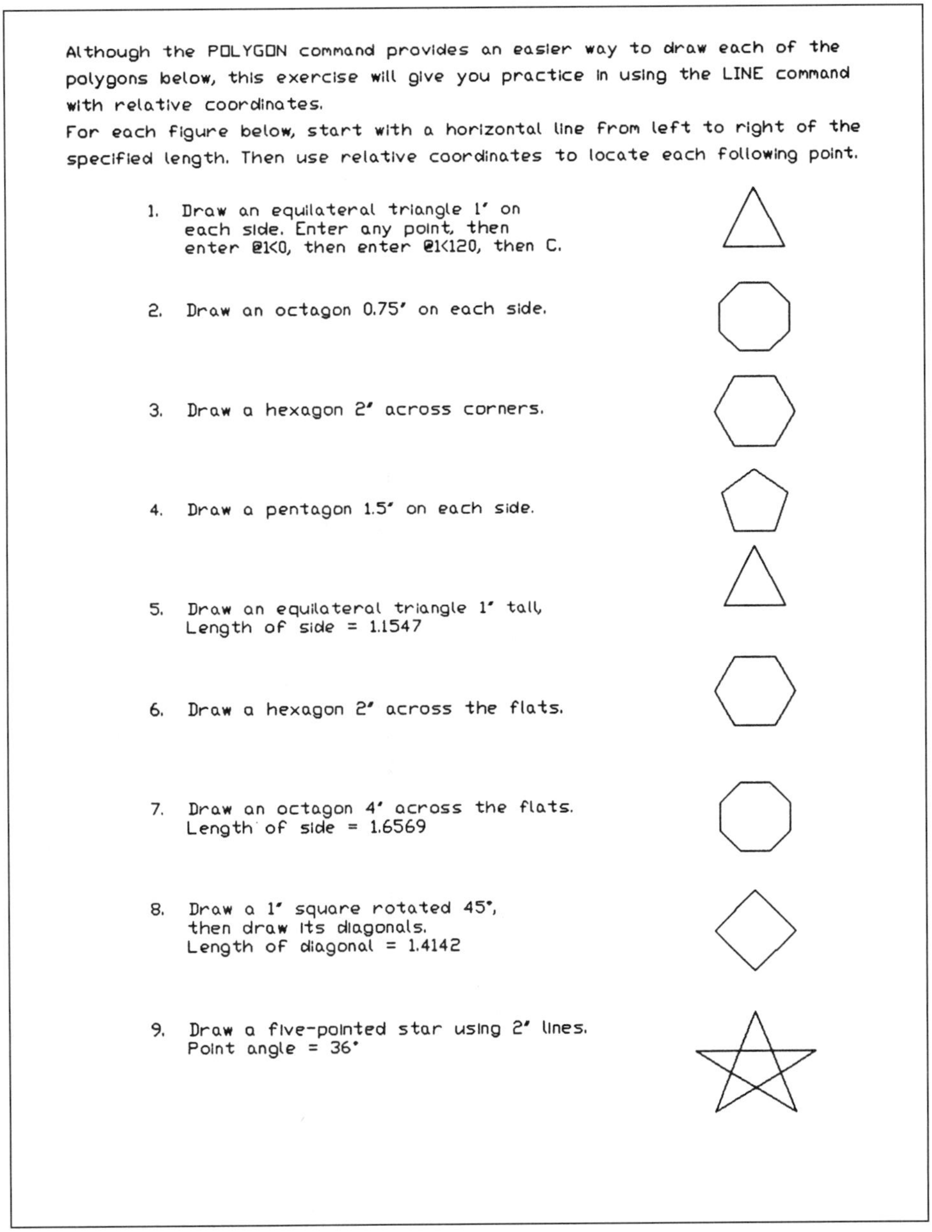

Figure 44-4: Line Exercise 3.

Circle Exercise

Draw each of the circles on your own using the explanation text as needed.

Draw a line from 2,2 to 6,2 to 6,6 to 2,6 then close.

Draw the following circles:

1. Center at 4,4 Radius = 2
2. Center at 4,3.5 Dia. = 3
3. 2P circle: 3,3 and 5,3
4. 3P circle: 4,3 3.5,2.5 4.5,2.5
5. 2P circle: 3.5,3.5 4.5,3.5
6. Center at 4,4.5 Dia. = 1
7. Center at 4,5.5 Radius = .5

8 & 9. Use TTR with a radius of .25 to place the two circles in the top corners.

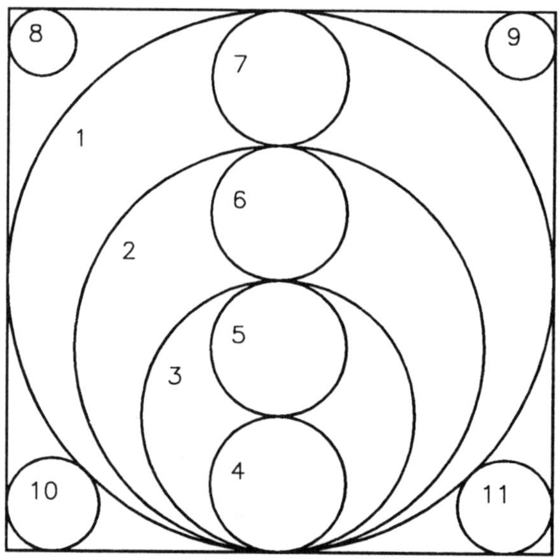

10 & 11. If you know how to use immediate osnap modes, use 3P with tan, tan, tan to place the two circles in the bottom corners.

Figure 44-5: Circle Exercise.

Plate Profile

Draw the plate profile using the plate profile setup explanation on the next page and the notes in Figure 44-6.

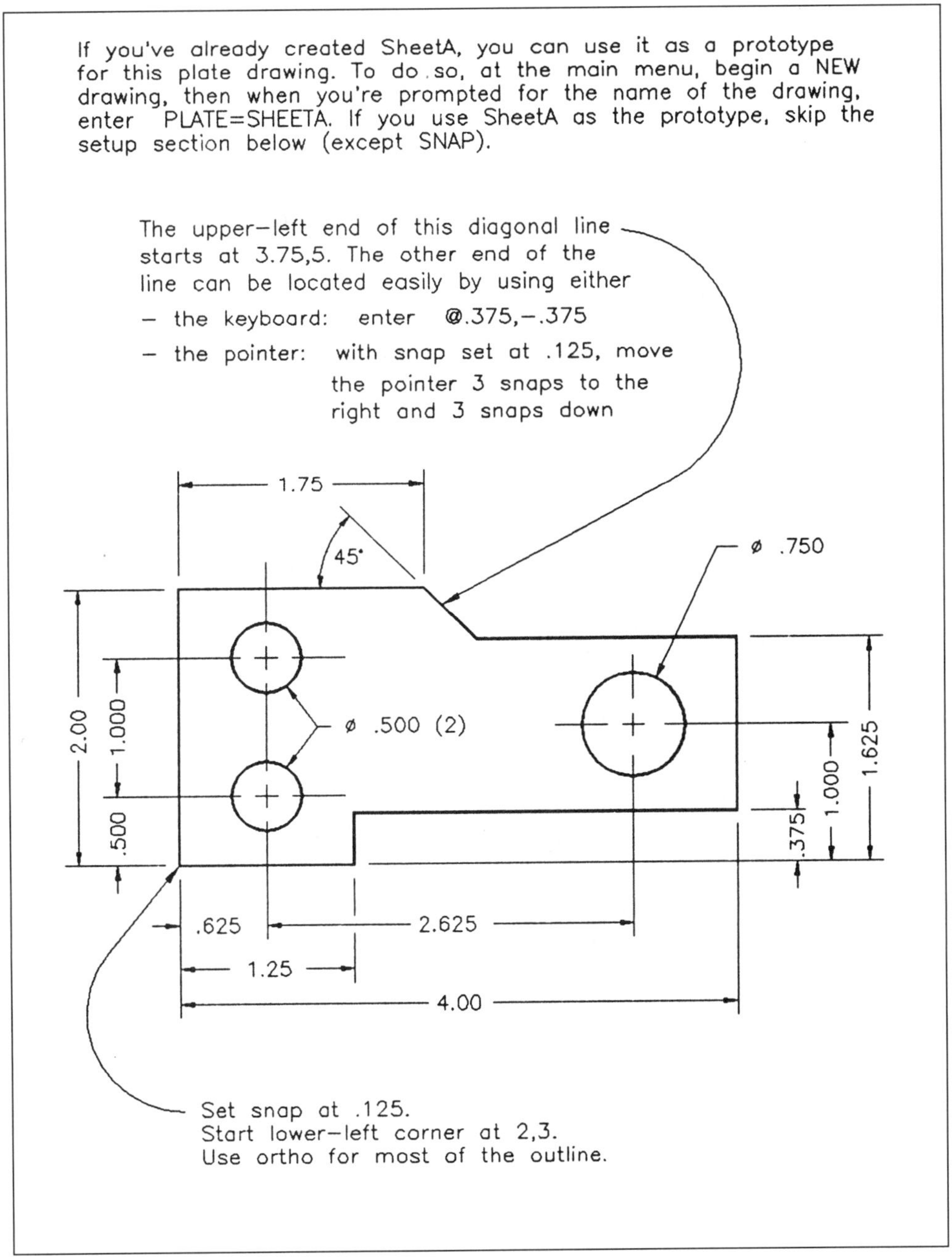

Figure 44-6: Plate profile.

Plate Profile Setup

Set grid at .5.

Set snap at .125. This lets you snap to all points.

Set the limits with the lower-left corner at 0,0 and the upper-right corner at 10,7.5.

Do a ZOOM All.

Drawing the Outline

Start a line at 2,3. Ortho and snap should be on.

Press F6 to place the coordinate readout in polar mode (displaying distance and angle).

From 2,3 draw a line 1.25 to the right, then .375 up, then 2.75 to the right, then 1.25 up, then exit the LINE command.

Start another line at 2,3 that goes 2.00 up, then 1.75 to the right.

Stay in the LINE command, but turn ortho off (use F8) so you can draw the line at the 45-degree angle. (This line moves .375 vertically, and since it's at 45 degrees, moves .375 horizontally as well.)

Since snap is set at .125, you can draw this line easily by moving your crosshairs 3 snaps down and 3 snaps over. Or you can use relative rectangular coordinates: @.375, -.375. Redraw the screen.

Drawing the Circles

Draw the lower-left circle first.

Start the CIRCLE command. With snap on, use the pointer to locate the center of the circle. Use the grid to help you find the point that's .625 over and .500 up from the lower-left corner of the plate. After you pick the center, enter **d**, then enter the diameter (**.5**). Use the grid to help you locate the next circle 1 inch above this circle.

To locate the center of the large circle, place the crosshairs at 5.25,4. After you've drawn this circle, redraw the screen. Then save your drawing.

Arc Exercise

Enter the coordinates given below by using the keyboard or by setting the snap to .25 and using the pointer.

You can enter the coordinates given below by using the keyboard or by setting SNAP at 0.25 and using the pointer.

1	(3 POINT)	Start point 4.25,4	Second point 4,4.25	End point 3.75,4
2	SCE	Start point 3.75,4	Center 4.25,4	End point 8,4
3	SCA	Start point 4.75,4	Center 4,4	Angle 180
4	SCL	Start point 3.25,4	Center 4.25,4	Length of chord 2
5	SEC*	Start point 5.25,4	End point 2.75,4	Center 4,4
6	SER	Start point 2.75,4	End point 5.75,4	Radius 1.5
7	SEA	Start point 5.75,4	End point 2.25,4	Included angle 180
8	SED	Start point 2.25,4	End point 6.25,4	Direction 270
9	CSE	Center 4,4	Start point 6.25,4	End point 0,4
10	CSA	Center 4.25,4	Start point 1.75,4	Included angle 180
11	CSL	Center 4,4	Start point 6.75,4	Length of chord 5.5
12	Continue	End point 7.25,4		

* Not on screen menu

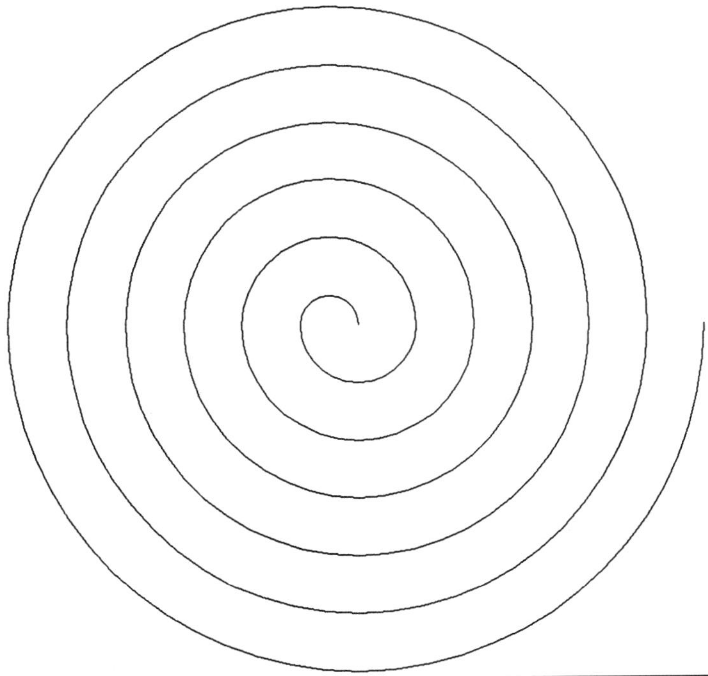

Figure 44-7: Completed arc exercise.

Quarter-panel Drawing

Draw the quarter-panel using the dimensions and text as shown in Figure 44-8. Set the snap to .125. Start at 2,3. Create a 3.00 x 3.00 square as a rough outline. Start drawing the first arc at a center of 2,3. Place the remaining outer arcs and trim them from the rectangle. Then draw the inside arcs or circles and lines. Use TRIM to clean up the exercise.

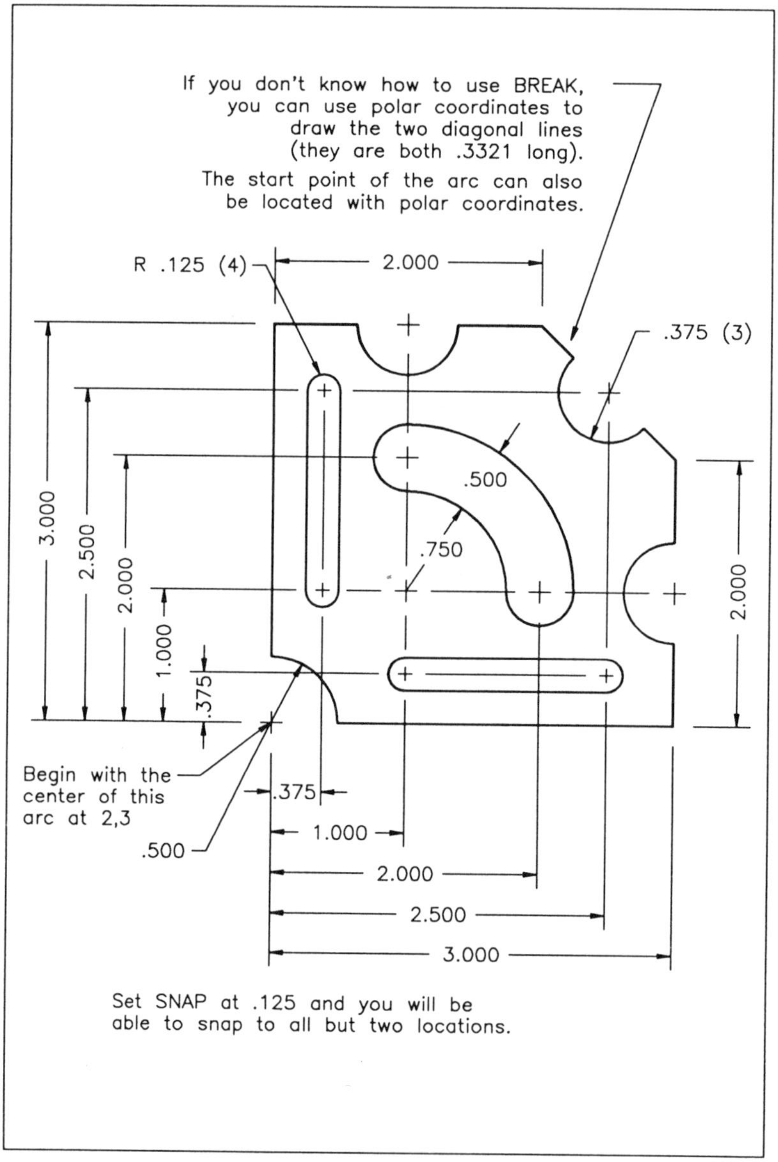

Figure 44-8: Quarter-panel drawing exercise.

Plat Drawing

Draw the plat using the dimensions and notes in Figure 44-9.

Set your lineal units to decimal with two places of precision. Set the angular measure to surveyor's units with four places of precision. Set the direction for angles to East, measured counterclockwise.

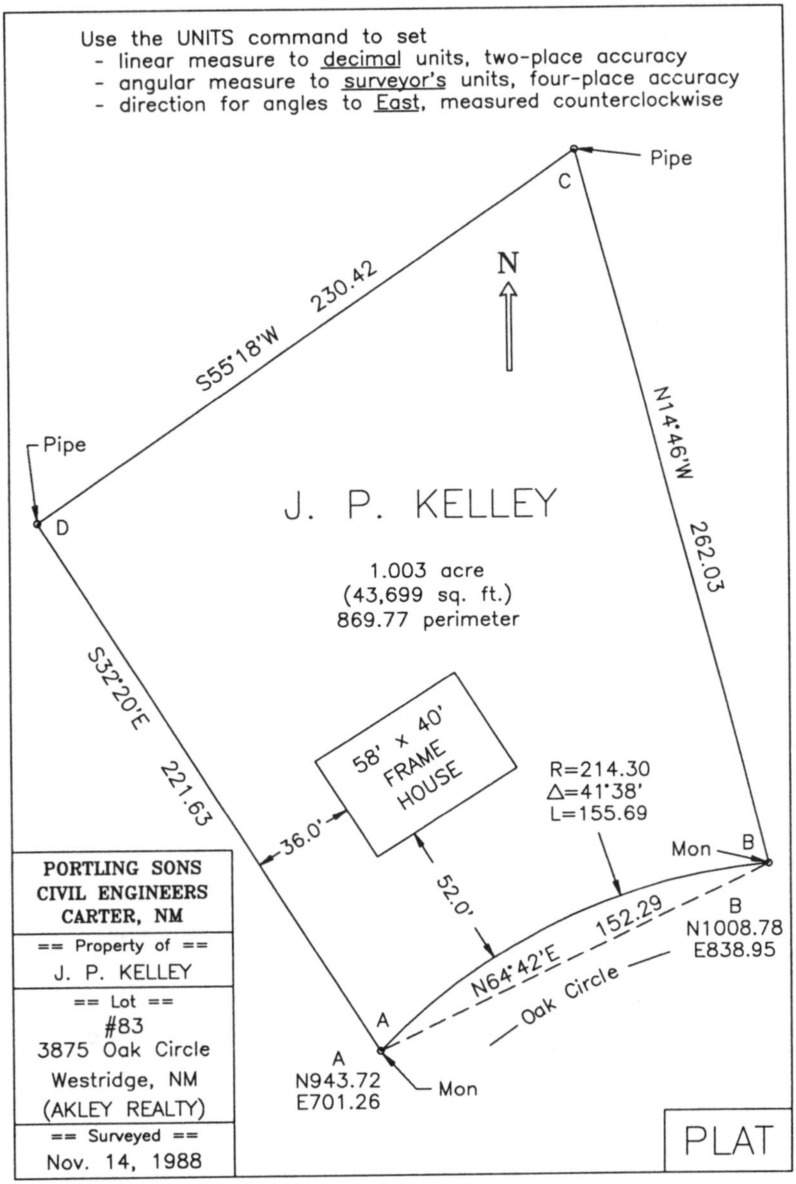

Figure 44-9: Plat drawing exercise.

Display Exercise

This exercise uses several commands related to the display, including ZOOM, PAN, VIEW, RENAME, VIEWRES and REGEN. Like previous exercises it is organized into general and specific instructions. See Figure 44-10 for the simple objects you will draw.

Setup

General instructions:	Specific instructions:
1. Start a new drawing. Name it DISPLAY.	Use AutoCAD's default drawing area of 12 x 9, or use the SHEET-A prototype drawing you created in the Setup exercise under "Prototype Drawings." (If you change the limits, do a ZOOM All.)
2. Set grid at 1 and snap at .25.	In the Drawing Aids... dialog, set the grid to 1 and the snap to .25. Turn them both on and choose OK.
3. Draw the circles, lines and square as shown below. When you're done, leave the grid on the screen. Turn snap off.	

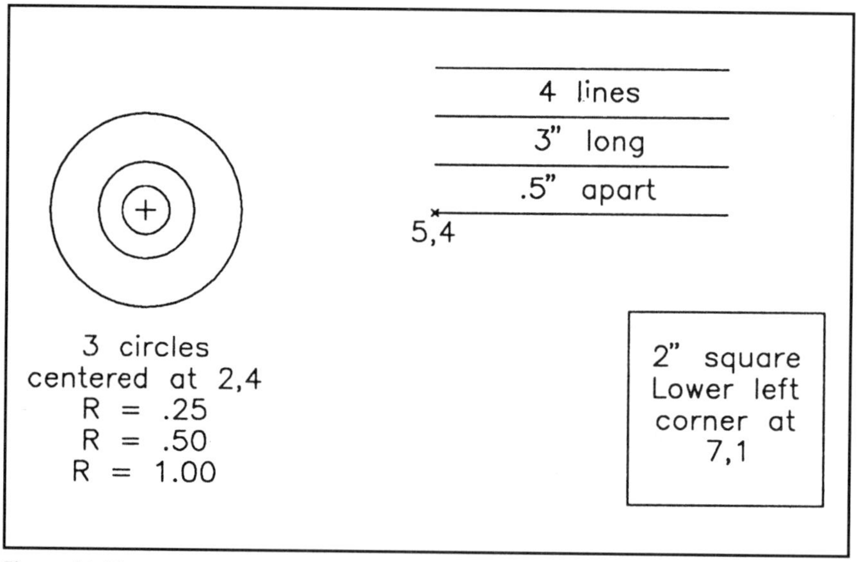

Figure 44-10: Objects for the display exercise.

Using ZOOM & PAN

4. Zoom out by a factor of 3.	To make the objects on the screen appear one-third their original size, pick Zoom and at the response type in **.33**.
5. Return to the previous screen.	To return to the previous screen, you'll choose Zoom Previous.
6. Zoom in by a factor of 2.	To make the objects appear twice as large on the screen, pick Zoom and then enter **2** at the response.
7. Zoom in again by a factor of 2.	Your objects should be twice the size of the current display. To do so, pick Zoom and enter **2x**.
8. Zoom out to the limits.	Enter the ZOOM command and select the option of All.
9. Zoom in on the circles.	Enter the ZOOM command and pick two opposite corners forming a window around the circles, approximately .5" larger than the circles on all sides.
10. Pan over to the lines.	You may need to pan twice to get a full view of the lines. (Make sure ortho is off.) Choose Pan and pick a point near the right edge of the screen, then a point near the left edge. If needed, do another pan.
11. Pan down to the square.	You may need to pan twice to get a full view of the square. (Make sure ortho is off.) Choose Pan and pick a point near the bottom of the screen, then a point near the top. If needed, do another pan.
12. Return to a view of the lines.	Choose the ZOOM command and use the Previous option. If needed, repeat the command with the Previous option until you get to the view you need.

13. Zoom out to the limits.	Enter the ZOOM command, then use the All option.
14. Zoom in tightly on the lower-left corner of the square.	Reactivate ZOOM and pick two opposite corners forming a small window around the lower-left corner of the square.
15. Zoom out to the full display.	In order to have the largest possible display of all the objects in the drawing, you'll do a ZOOM Extents. Reenter the ZOOM command and choose the E option.
16. Zoom out the display to 0.9 of the full display by using .9x.	To view this current display so you have a small blank area around the objects, you'll enter ZOOM, then **.9x**.
17. Zoom in on the lines.	Reactivate the ZOOM command and pick two opposite corners forming a window around the lines.

Dynamic ZOOM

18. Use ZOOM Dynamic to zoom in on the square.	Choose Zoom and use the Dynamic option. Move the cursor so the window surrounds the square.
19. Use ZOOM Dynamic to zoom in on the circles.	Pick Zoom and the Dynamic option again. Move the cursor so the window surrounds the circles.
20. Use ZOOM Dynamic to include both the lines and the square.	Pick Zoom and the Dynamic option. Move the cursor so the left edge of the window is just to the left of the lines. Press the pick button, then move the cursor to the right so the window surrounds both the lines and the square. You can also move the cursor up and down.

21. Use ZOOM Dynamic to zoom in on the smallest circle.	If the smallest circle isn't visible after you do a ZOOM Dynamic, you may have to approximate its location, then do a second ZOOM Dynamic. Choose Zoom and Dynamic. Move the cursor so the left edge of the window is just to the left of the smallest circle. Press the pick button, then move the cursor to the left so the window surrounds just the smallest circle.
22. Zoom out to the limits.	Reactivate the ZOOM command and enter All.

Using View Names

23. Save a window view of the circles under the name C.	Enter the VIEW command and at the ?/Delete/Restore/Save/Window prompt enter **w** to form a window. Then at the View name to Save: prompt save the view with the name C. Finally, pick the opposite corners forming a window around the circles.
24. Save a window view of the lines under the name L.	Again enter VIEW and the **w** option. Then save the view with name L. Pick the opposite corners forming a window around the lines.
25. Zoom in on the square.	Choose the ZOOM command. Pick the opposite corners forming a window around the square.
26. Save the current display under the name SQ.	Enter the VIEW command and use the **s** option. Then save the view with the name SQ.
27. List the views you've saved. Return to the graphics window.	To list the views, pick the VIEW command and enter **?**. Return to the graphics window by pressing F2.

28. Restore the view (L) of the lines.	To restore a view, enter the VIEW command. Use the **r** for restore option. Enter **l** to restore the lines view.
29. Restore the view (C) of the circles.	To restore a view, enter the VIEW command. Use the **r** for restore option. Enter **c** to restore the circles view.
30. Delete the name of the square from the saved views list.	To delete a view, enter the VIEW command. Use the **d** for delete option. Enter **sq** to delete the square view.
31. Change the name of the view of the lines from L to LINES.	To rename a view, enter the RENAME command. At the prompt of Block/ Dimstyle/LAyer/LType/Style/Ucs/ VIew/VPort: enter **vi** for view. At the Old (object) name: prompt, enter **l**. Then at the New (object) name: prompt enter **lines**.
32. Change the name of the view of the circles from C to CIRCLES.	To rename a view, enter the RENAME command. At the prompt of Block/ Dimstyle/LAyer/LType/Style/Ucs/ VIew/VPort: enter **vi** for view. At the Old (object) name: prompt, enter **c**. Then at the New (object) name: prompt enter **circles**.
33. List the views saved and return to the graphics window.	Re-activate the VIEW command. Enter **?** to list the saved views. Return to the graphics window by pressing F2.

Changing the View Resolution (VIEWRES)

34. Zoom out to the limits.	Pick the ZOOM command and enter All.
35. Zoom in tight on the smallest circle.	Use the ZOOM command and pick opposite corners forming a small window surrounding just the smallest circle. Notice the polygon appearance of the circle. This is a result of AutoCAD's use of its virtual screen.

36. Regenerate the screen.	Enter the REGEN command. Notice the effect on the shape of the circle.
37. Zoom out to the limits.	Reenter the ZOOM command. Use the All option.
38. Turn fast zooms off.	Enter the VIEWRES command and then enter **n**. Press Enter to return to the command prompt.
39. Zoom in tight on the smallest circle.	Notice its appearance. When you turn fast zooms off, AutoCAD doesn't use its virtual screen but regenerates the display for each zoom. Enter the ZOOM command and pick opposite corners forming a small window surrounding just the smallest circle.
40. Zoom out to the limits.	Use the ZOOM command and enter All.
41. Turn fast zooms on and set the view resolution at 10000.	Enter the VIEWRES command and **y** for yes at the response. Then enter **10000** as a zoom percent.
42. Zoom tight on the smallest circle.	Notice the higher resolution setting produces a round circle even though AutoCAD is using its virtual screen. This greater accuracy of the screen representation of circles and arcs takes more time to generate. Use ZOOM and pick opposite corners forming a small window surrounding just the smallest circle.
43. Zoom out to the limits.	Pick the ZOOM command and enter All.
44. Leave fast zooms on and reset view resolution to 10.	Use VIEWRES and enter **y**, then **10**. Notice that even without zooming in, circles look like polygons because of the low resolution setting. These approximations of circles generate

	very quickly. Despite their appearance on the screen, the circles are still round in the database and in a plot.
45. Save the drawing.	From the File pull-down menu, choose Save.

Keep in mind that all of these display operations have been within a single viewport. Each of the operations works the same (within a single viewport) when several viewports are active. When you use more than one viewport, you won't need to use ZOOM and PAN quite so often, even though each viewport covers a smaller area on the screen.

Object Snap & Inquiry

Object Snap & Inquiry Exercise

To draw the objects, enter the coordinates given below by using the keyboard or by setting the snap to .5 and using the pointer. Then turn snap off and start the osnap exercise.

Before you begin, be sure that the Draw, Construct and Modify menu choices appear in the menu bar at the top of your screen. If they do not, enter **menu** at the command line and then select Acadfull (for "full menu").

Draw a 4" square with lower left corner at 1.5,2.5.
Draw a 1" radius circle with center at 3.5,4.5.
Draw four 90° arcs centered at 2,3 5,3 5,6 and 2,6 with .5 radius.
Draw a point at 6,4.5.

Turn snap off and use osnap to draw line segments through the 15 points with the following immediate osnap modes:

1 cen	5 endp	9 per	13 int
2 qua	6 mid	10 tan	14 nod
3 mid	7 tan	11 mid	15 nea
4 endp	8 cen	12 cen	

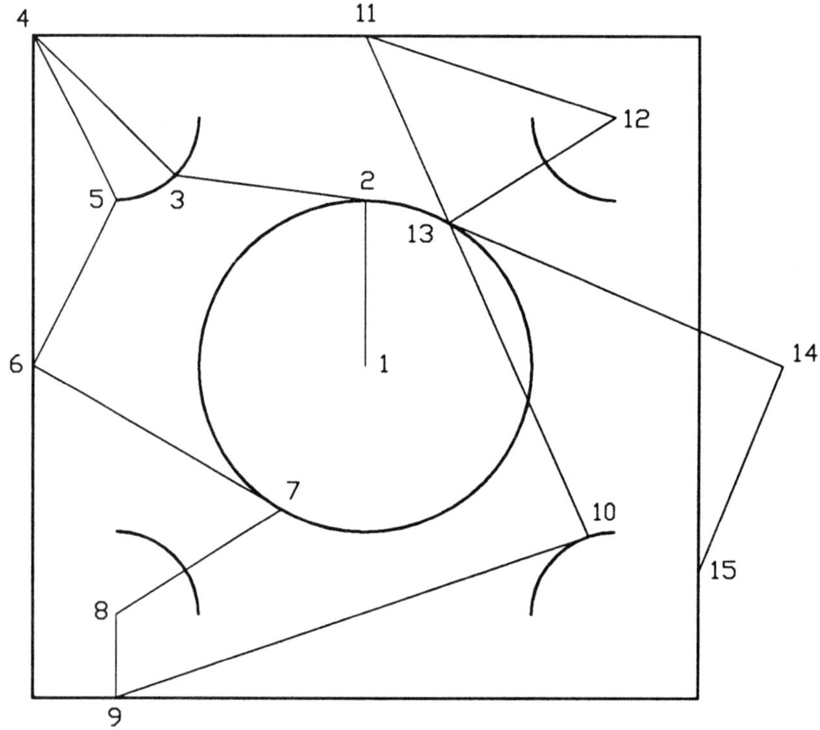

Use LIST to get the length, angle, delta-X and delta-Y for lines 1-2 and 3-4.
Use DIST to measure the distance, etc. from point 7 to point 2.
Use ID to get the coordinates of point 7.
Use AREA to find the area of triangle 11-12-13.

OSNAP & INQUIRY EXERCISE

Figure 44-II: Object snap/inquiry exercise.

Area Exercise

To draw the objects, enter the coordinates given below by using the keyboard or by setting the snap to .25 and using the pointer. Then turn snap off and start the area exercise.

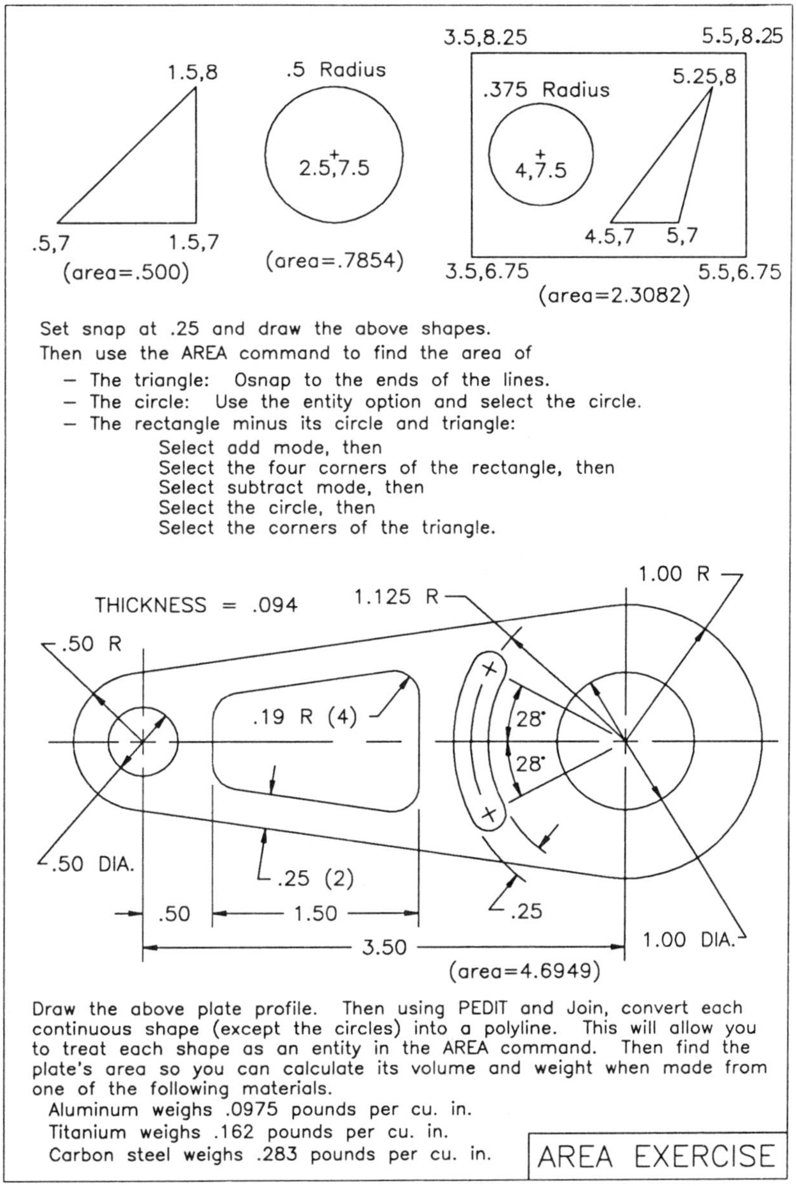

Figure 44-12: Area exercise.

Editing—Group One

Editing Exercise

This fun exercise involves the editing commands MOVE, COPY, MIRROR, ROTATE and SCALE.

The exercise doesn't show you the most efficient way to produce this drawing. Instead, it illustrates some of the options for each of the editing commands. The exercise is organized into general and specific instructions.

Setup

General Instructions:	Specific Instructions:
1. Start a new drawing. Name it EDIT-EX.	Check if the limits are set at 0,0 (lower left) and the upper-right corner at 12,9. Then use ZOOM All. Set the grid to 1 and the snap to .25.

Drawing the Border Lines

2. Draw a horizontal line from 0,3 to 12,3.	Choose Line from the Draw menu or toolbar. Enter the first coordinate of 0,3, then the second coordinate of 12,3.
3. Copy the line 6 units up. Move the original line 3 units down.	Enter the COPY command and use the **l** for Last option. At the Base point prompt pick any point on the line. At the Second point displacement prompt enter **0,6**. Activate the MOVE command. Pick the lower line and move it 0,-3.
4. Draw a vertical line from 2,0 to 2,9.	Choose Line from the Draw menu or toolbar. Enter the first coordinate of **2,0** and the second coordinate of **2,9**.
5. Copy this line 10 units to the right. Move the original line 2 units to the left.	Enter the COPY command and use the **l** for Last option. At the Base point prompt pick any point on the line. At the Second point displacement prompt enter **10,0**. Activate the MOVE command. Pick the original vertical line and move it -2,0.

6. Draw four arcs with a radius of 0.75, running from 0 to 90 degrees. The first arc should have its center at 4,5. After drawing one arc, use the Multiple option in the COPY command to create the other three arcs. Place the center of the second arc at 5,5, the third at 6,5 and the fourth at 7,5.

From the Draw toolbar or pull-down menu choose the ARC command. Type **c** for center and enter **4,5** as the center. Enter **@.75,0** as the start point. At the prompt for Angle/Length of chord/End point, enter **a** for Angle. Then at the Included angle prompt enter **90** to finish the arc. To multiple copy, in the Edit pull-down menu choose Copy, then enter **l** for Last and press Enter twice. Then enter **m** for Multiple and press Enter. Enter the points of displacement as follows:

```
4,5 <Enter>
5,5 <Enter>
6,5 <Enter>
7,5 <Enter><Enter>
```

Finally, press F7 twice to clean up the screen.

Figure 44-13: Editing exercise after step 6.

7. Move the first arc from 4,5 to 11,8.

To move the first arc choose the Move icon or type the MOVE command. Pick the first arc and press Enter. Type **4,5** and press Enter, and then type **11,8** and press Enter again.

8. Move the second arc from 5,5 to 1,8. Rotate it 90 degrees counterclockwise around its own center.

To move the second arc choose the Move icon or type the MOVE command. Pick the second arc and press Enter. Type **5,5** and press Enter, and then type **1,8** and press Enter again. To rotate it 90 degrees, choose the ROTATE command from the Modify pull-down menu. Pick the arc you just moved. At the first displacement enter **1,8** and press Enter. Then type **90** and press Enter.

9. Rotate the third arc 180 degrees around its own center. Then move it 5 units to the left and 4 units down.

To rotate the third arc choose the ROTATE command from the Modify pull-down menu. Pick the third arc. At the first displacement enter **6,5** and press Enter. Then enter **180** and press Enter. To move it, choose the Move icon or type the MOVE command. Pick the second arc and press Enter. Type **0,0** and press Enter, and then type **-5,-4** and press Enter.

10. Move the fourth arc 4 units right and 4 units down. Rotate it 90 degrees clockwise around its own center.

To move the fourth arc, activate the MOVE command. Pick the fourth arc and press Enter>. Then pick any point, press Enter, type **@4,-4** and press Enter. To rotate it 90 degrees, choose the ROTATE command from the Modify pull-down menu. Pick the arc you just moved. The DISPLACEMENT point is 11,1, and the amount of rotation is -90 degrees.

11. Draw a line starting at .25,1 and extending 7 units up. Copy this line 11.5 units to the right.

Activate the LINE command. Start from 0.25,1 and press Enter; then move to @0,7 and press Enter until you return to the command prompt. To copy the line, activate the COPY command. Enter **l** for Last and press Enter twice. Then enter **11.5,0** and press Enter until you return to the command prompt.

12. Draw a line that starts at 1,8.75 and extends 10 units to the right. Then copy this line 8.5 units down.

Choose Line from the Draw menu or toolbar. Enter the first coordinate of **1,8.75**, then the second coordinate of **@10,0**. Enter the COPY command and use the **l** for Last option. At the Base point: prompt pick any point on the line. At the Second point displacement: prompt enter **@8.5<-90**. Finally, press F7 twice to clean up the screen.

Figure 44-14: Editing exercise after step 12.

Drawing the Face

13. Draw a circle centered at 6,5 with a radius of 3 units.

Choose the CIRCLE command from the Draw menu or toolbar. Set the center of the circle to 6,5 and the radius to 3.

14. Draw a circle centered at 6,8.5 with a radius of .5 units.

Choose the CIRCLE command from the Draw menu or toolbar. Set the center to 6,8.5 and the radius to .5.

15. Scale the small circle (at its own center) by a factor of 1.5.

From the Modify pull-down menu, choose Scale. Enter **l** for Last and press Enter twice. Use the center of the circle as the base point, which is 6,8.5. Press Enter. Finally, enter **1.5** as the scale factor.

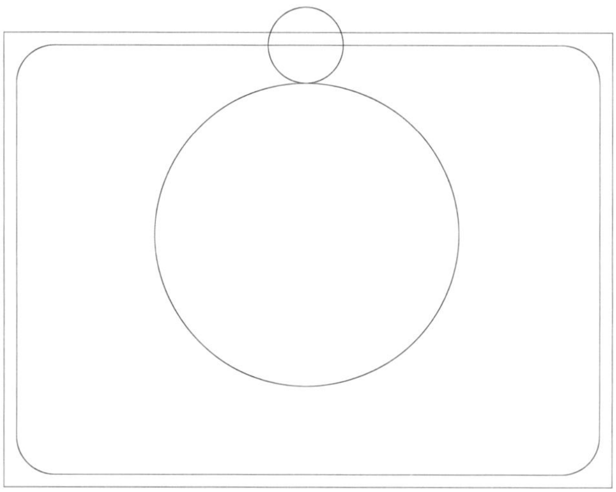

Figure 44-15: Editing exercise after step 16.

16. Move the small circle up .25.

To move the small circle, activate the MOVE command. Pick the circle and press Enter. Pick any point as a base, type **0.25** and press Enter.

17. Rotate the small circle 90 degrees clockwise around the center of the large circle.

Activate ROTATE, enter **l** for Last, and press Enter twice. Then enter **6,5** as the central rotation point, and **-90** for clockwise rotation around the center of the large circle.

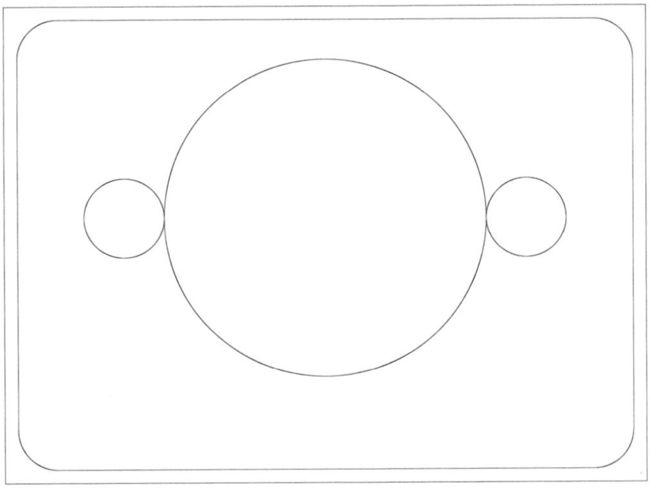

Figure 44-16: Editing exercise after step 18.

18. Copy the small circle 7.5 units to the left.

Activate the COPY command. Choose the small circle or enter **l** for Last, and press Enter twice. Then enter **-7.5,0** and press Enter twice.

19. Draw an arc through three points: 6.5,6 7.1,6.25 and 7.7,6.

Enter the ARC command. In turn, enter the coordinates of **6.5,6**, then **7.1,6.25**, then **7.7,6**.

20. Mirror the last arc about a mirror line from 6,6 to 8,6 and retain the original arc.

Activate the MIRROR command. Select the arc or enter **l** for Last and press Enter twice. Mirror the arc about the coordinates of 6,6 and 8,6. Do not delete the original arc.

21. Now flip (mirror and delete original) the upper arc about a mirror line from 6,6 to 6,8.

Activate the MIRROR command. Select the upper arc and press Enter. Mirror the arc about the coordinates of 6,6 and 8,6. Delete the original arc.

22. Flip (mirror and delete original) the left arc around a mirror line from 4,6 to 6,6.

Activate the MIRROR command. Select the left arc and press Enter. Mirror the arc about the coordinates of 4,6 and 6,6. Delete the original arc.

Figure 44-17: Editing exercise after step 22.

23. Copy the left arc 2.6 units at an angle of -65 degrees.

Activate the COPY command. Choose the left arc. Pick any point as a base point and enter a displacement of **@2.6<-65**.

24. Mirror this lower arc around a mirror line from 5,4.25 to 7,4.25 and retain the original arc.

Activate the MIRROR command. Select the lower arc and press Enter. Mirror the arc about the coordinates of 5,4.25 and 7,4.25. Do not delete the original arc.

25. Scale this last arc around the center of the large circle so that the distance between the ends of the arc becomes .65 (use the Reference option).

From the Modify pull-down menu choose Scale. Enter **l** for Last and press Enter twice. Use the center of the large circle as the base point, which is 6,5. Enter **ref** for reference. Using the Shift-right button of your mouse, activate the cursor menu and choose Endpoint. Then osnap to one end of the arc. Then reactivate the cursor menu for Endpoint and osnap to the other end of the arc.
Finally, enter **.65** as the scale factor.

Figure 44-18: Editing exercise after step 25.

26. Rotate the entire face around the center of the large circle so that the center of the arc representing the eye on the right side of the picture is directly above the center of the arc representing the mouth (use the Reference option).

Activate ROTATE and enter **w** for Window; then press Enter. Pick one corner of the window. Pick the other corner. Then enter **6,5** as the central rotation point. Enter **r** for reference. Choose Center from the cursor menu and pick right arc. Choose Center again from the cursor menu and pick the bottom arc. Enter **270**.

27. Flip (mirror and delete original) both eyes around a diagonal mirror line joining the corners of the eyes.

Activate the MIRROR command. Select both eyes and press Enter. Mirror the arc about the corner of each eye. Activate the cursor menu and choose Endpoint, then pick the corner of one eye. Reactivate the cursor menu and choose Endpoint. Pick the corner of the other eye. Finally, enter **y** to delete the original eyes.

28. Scale the entire face at base point 1,8 so that the distance between the centers of the eyes becomes 1.7. (Use the Reference option.)

From the Modify pull-down menu choose Scale. Enter the subcommand ALL for all the objects and press Enter. Use the base point, which is 1,8. Enter **ref** for reference. Using the Shift-right button of your mouse, activate the cursor menu and choose CENter. Osnap to one eye. Then reactivate the cursor menu for CENter and osnap to the other eye. Finally, enter **1.7** as the scale factor.

Figure 44-19: Editing exercise after step 28.

29. Rotate the entire face around base point 1,1 so that the face is upright again (use the Reference option).

Activate ROTATE, enter **p** for point; and press Enter. Pick one corner of the window. Pick the other corner. Then enter **1,1** as the central rotation point. Enter **r** for reference. Choose CENter from the cursor menu and pick the left ear. Choose CENter again from the cursor menu and pick the other ear. Enter **0**.

30. Move the entire face so that it's centered in the drawing (the center of large circle is at 6,4.5).

To move the entire face, activate the MOVE command. Enter the subcommand ALL or use **p** for previous selection set. Pick the CENter of the large circle as a base point. Then move it by entering **6,4.5**.

Figure 44-20: Completed exercise.

CHAPTER 45

Hands-on Exercises 2

This chapter presents a variety of applications for drawing and editing with AutoCAD. It is divided into intermediate and advanced exercises.

Exercises are grouped in the same order as topics in the *Concise Guide*. As you read each chapter in the final part of the book, you will find related exercises here.

Some of the exercises include complete step-by-step instructions, while others are sample drawings for you to reproduce—with a few suggestions on how to set up a drawing or how to complete certain tasks or features.

If you have mastered the fundamentals of Chapter 44, you now have a solid foundation for mastering the more advanced AutoCAD procedures that involve polyline editing, UCS and 3D construction.

Intermediate Exercises

Fork Profile

If you already created the SHEET-A prototype drawing, use it as a prototype for this fork drawing. To do so, start a new drawing and choose SHEET-A in the prototype drawing part of the dialog.

The general objective is to draw the top half of the fork first, then use the MIRROR command to create the bottom half.

Set the grid at .5.

Set the snap at .125. This lets you snap to most points.

Set drawing limits with lower-left corner at 0,0 and upper-right corner at 10,7.5.

Do a ZOOM All.

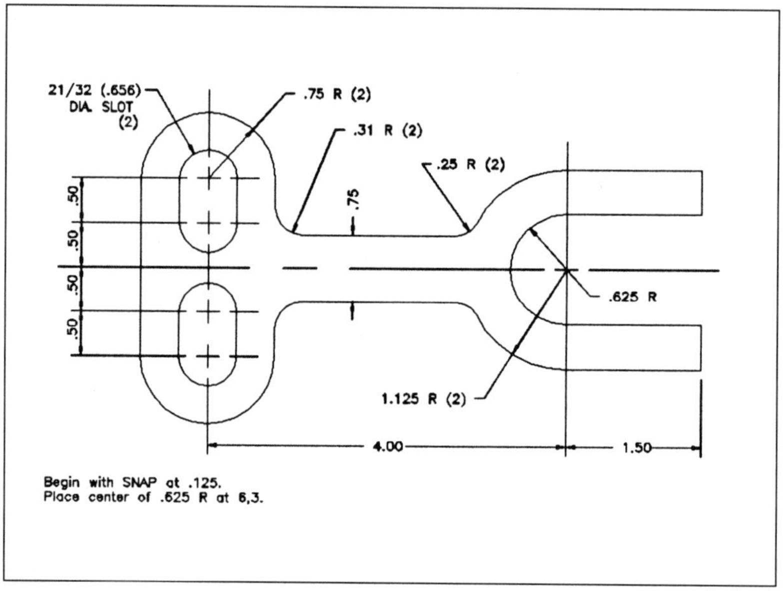

Figure 45-1: Fork profile drawing.

Drawing the Upper-right End

Make sure snap and grid are on. Use the pointer to locate all your points.

Draw the small arc first using the Center-Start-Angle option. Place the center at 6,3. Place the start point 0.625 above the center and use 90°.

Then draw the large arc. Place the start point 1.125 above the center and use 60°. The exact number of degrees is unimportant because this large arc will be filleted later.

Draw the three remaining lines that are to the right of these arcs. Redraw the screen.

Drawing the Upper-left End

Draw the large arc first, using the Center-Start-Angle option. Place the center at 2,4. Place the start point 0.75 to the right of the center and use 180°.

Next draw the small arc at the top of the 21/32 dia. slot. After locating the center, use relative coordinates to locate the start point of the arc (@.328,0 or @.328<0). Draw the lower arc in a similar manner.

You can connect vertical lines to the ends of these arcs with immediate osnap. Turn snap off. Enter the LINE command. When prompted for the From point: (1) enter **endp** from the keyboard or select Endpoint from the osnap options in the screen menu or pull-down menu, then (2) attach the line to the right end of one of the arcs (to do this, capture the right half of the arc in the aperture that appears on the crosshairs). Repeat (1) and (2) to attach the other end of the line to the right end of the other arc. Use a similar procedure to connect the left ends of the arcs with a vertical line. Redraw the screen.

Completing the Top Half

Turn snap and ortho on. Start a line at the right end of the R .75 arc, .625 down and 2.00 to the right. Fillet these two lines with a radius of .31.

Fillet the horizontal line and the 1.125 arc with a radius of .25.

Creating the Bottom Half

Start the MIRROR command, use a window to select everything, then (with ortho on) indicate a mirror line extending to the right or left of 6,3. Add the vertical line at the extreme left end of the fork. Redraw the screen and save your drawing.

Hanger

The objective of this exercise is to create and edit lines, arcs and circles. See Figure 45-2.

Draw the hanger at full scale (do not use a prototype drawing). Place the center of the 1.50 hole at a coordinate of 0,0,0 in your WCS (World Coordinate System).

For extra practice, dimension and add notes to the hanger when you have finished drawing.

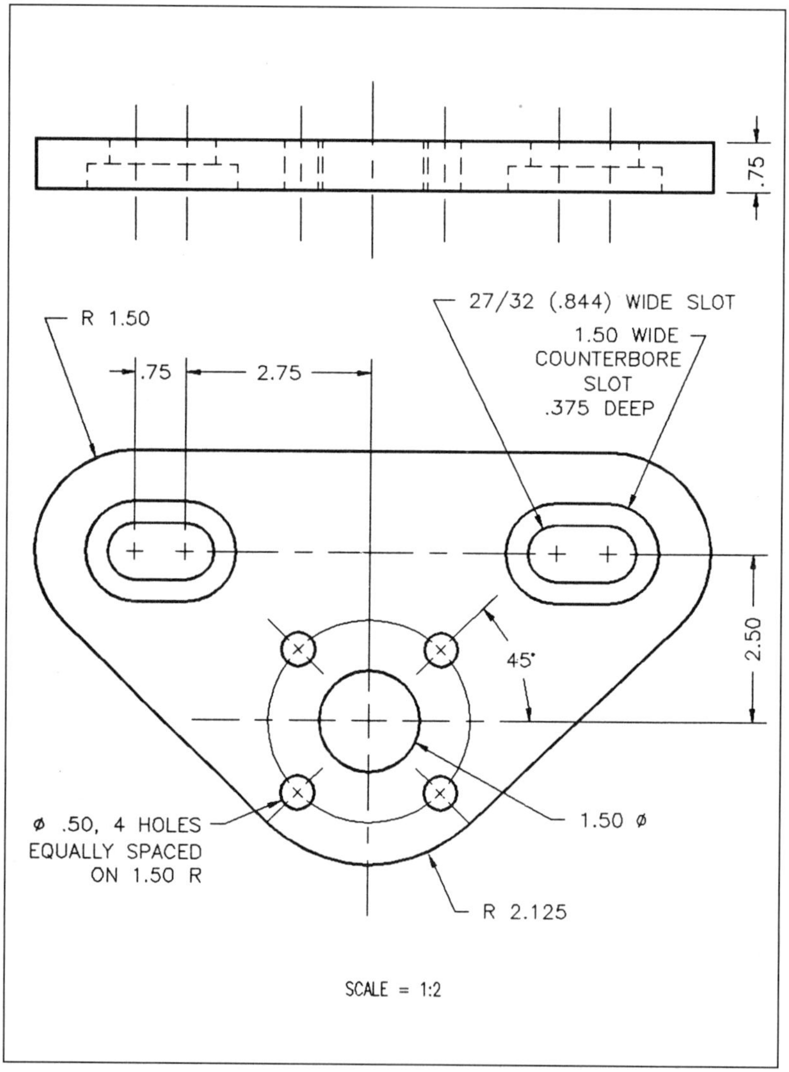

Figure 45-2: Hanger drawing.

Clip

This exercise has three objectives: to use PLINE, to use MLINE and to use OFFSET—all with polar coordinate entry.

(1) Use the PLINE command set to a width of 0.062. Proceed one section at a time toward lower left, making full use of osnap and polar coordinates.

(2) Use the MLINE command with top justification. Proceed one section at a time toward lower left, making full use of osnap and polar coordinates. Remember to set up the multiline style with an offset of 0.062 for the two lines. Toggle the display joints off and set the end caps at 90 degrees.

(3) Construct one side of the clip first, then use the OFFSET command to offset the lines and fillet arcs by 0.062.

In any of these methods, start the drawing at the upper-right end of 6,6,0. Then proceed a section at a time toward the lower-left end of the clip. Remember, for accuracy, use osnap and relative polar coordinates.

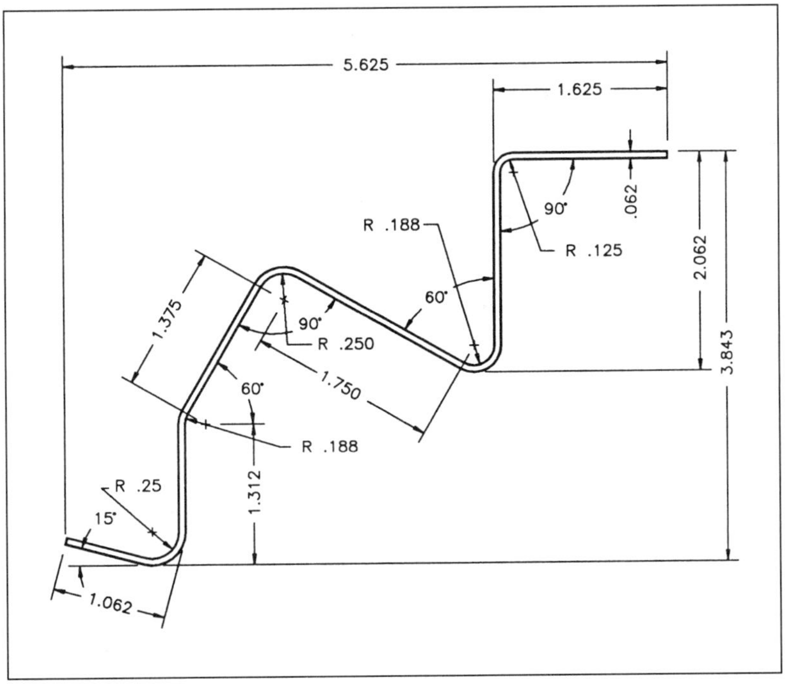

Figure 45-3: Clip drawing.

Strip Layout

The objective of this exercise is to create arcs, circles and lines. It also provides practice with the MIRROR, COPY, ROTATE and HATCH commands.

Draw the strip at full scale. Create the arcs and circles and mirror them as needed. Copy the part, then rotate and hatch it. Finally, place dimensions and notes and save the drawing.

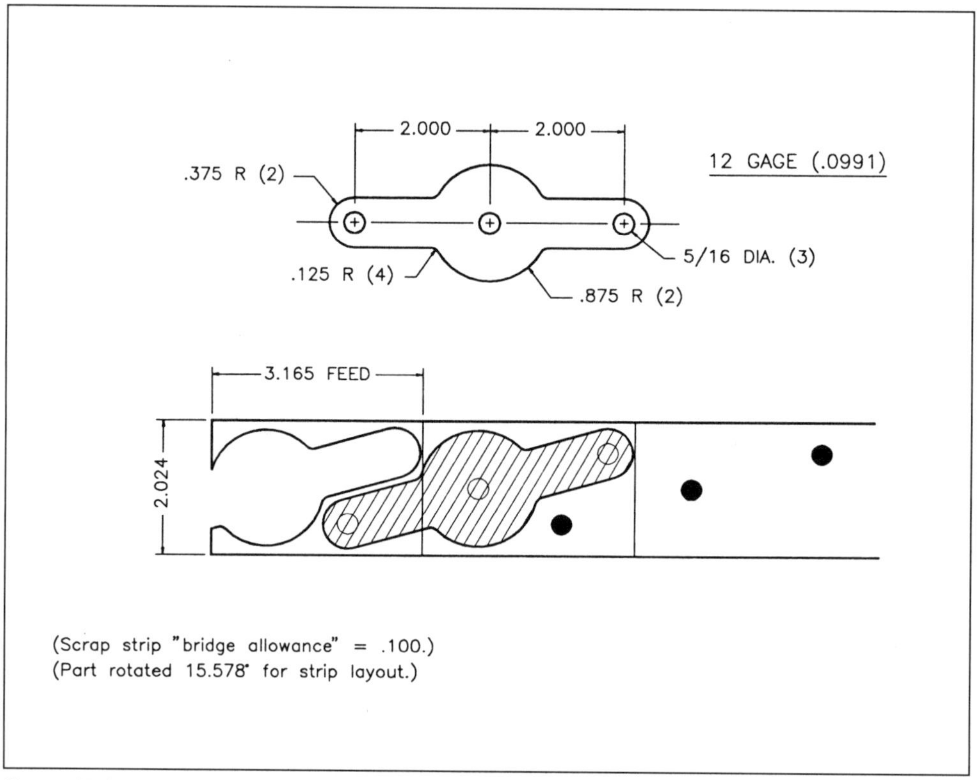

Figure 45-4: Strip layout drawing.

Grip Exercise

The objective of this exercise is simple grip editing. This exercise starts with three objects (a line, an arc and a circle) and produces the following brace (see Figure 45-5) entirely by the use of grips. Most of the exercise can be done with the pointer and very little use of the keyboard.

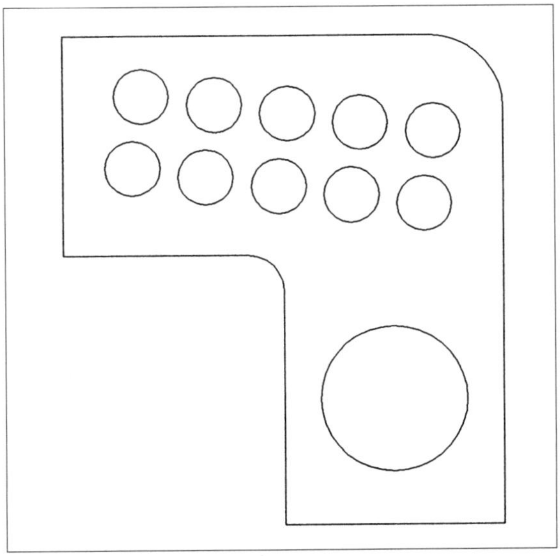

Figure 45-5: Grip exercise drawing.

You will create the array of 10 circles horizontally first, then rotate it into the position shown.

While the exercise does not necessarily illustrate the most efficient way to create this drawing, it shows most of the options available when you use grips for editing.

Before you begin, be sure that the Draw, Construct and Modify menu choices appear in the menu bar at the top of your screen. If they do not, enter menu at the command line and then select Acadfull (for "full menu").

Grip Exercise—Setup

1. Start a new drawing called GRIP-EX. Do not use a prototype drawing.

From the File pull-down menu pick New to activate the New Drawing dialog and enter **grip-ex** in the name box; then toggle the button labeled

No Prototype. Or, type **grip-ex=** as the new drawing name without choosing prototype and pick OK. (The = sign after the name automatically chooses no prototype.)

2. Enter the following settings:

Set the grid to 1 and the snap to 0.25.

Set grips to 1 and gripsize to 6.

Set pickauto to 1 and pickbox to 5.

Activate the Drawing Aids... dialog from the Options pull-down menu and set your grid to 1 and the snap to 0.25. Toggle them both on. Choose OK to save the settings and exit the box.

Activate the Grips dialog from the Options pull-down menu, toggle on the Enable Grips button, move the grips slider bar at the bottom of the dialog about halfway to enlarge the gripsize and pick OK to exit the box.

From the Options pull-down menu pick Selection to activate the Object Selection Settings dialog. Click the Default button and make sure the Noun/Verb and Implied Windowing toggles are on, then move the Pickbox Size slider bar to about halfway. Pick OK to save the settings.

3. Create three starting objects: a line, an arc and a circle.

Choose the Line command from the Draw pull-down menu or the Draw toolbar. Draw the line from 2,2 to 2,3.

Choose the Circle command from the Draw pull-down menu or the Draw toolbar. Draw the circle with its center at 2,5 and a radius of 0.5.

Choose the Arc command from the Draw pull-down menu or the Draw toolbar. Type **c** for center, and enter **2,7** as the center point. Then enter **@.5,0** as the start point. At the response prompts for Angle/Length of chord/End point, enter **a** for Angle. Then at the Included angle prompt enter **90** to finish the arc.

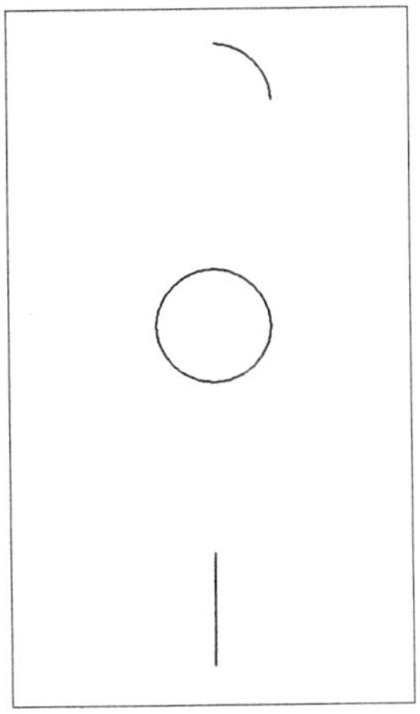

Figure 45-6: Grip exercise after step 3.

4. Move the line into position.

Pick the line to display its three grips. Choose the bottom grip. The cursor should snap to the center of the grip before you press the pick button. Press Enter (or the Spacebar) once or enter **mo** to select move mode. Press F9, if needed, to turn snap on and F6 once or twice if needed to set the coordinate for absolute readout. Move the cursor to 4,4 and press the pick button.

5. Scale the line by a factor of 3.

Pick the bottom grip of the line. Press Enter or the Spacebar three times, or enter **sc** to select scale mode. Then enter **3** as the scale factor.

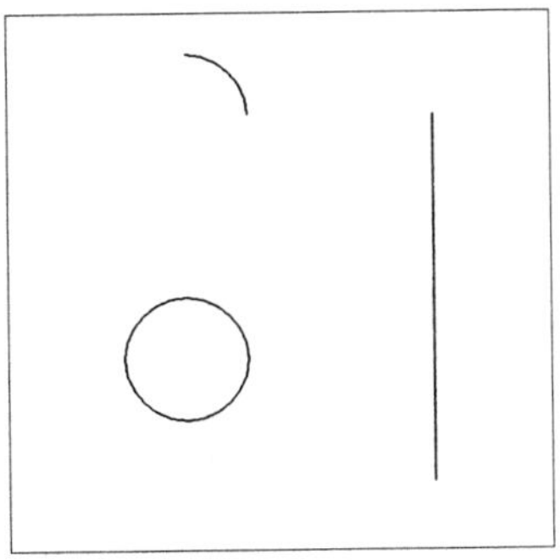

Figure 45-7: Grip exercise after step 5.

6. Stretch a copy of the vertical line to form the top horizontal line.

Pick the bottom grip. Type **c** and press Enter. (This puts you in copy mode. You may also hold down the Shift key while you pick the next point to copy the line.) Pick a point six units to the right of the top of the line. Then press Enter to exit multiple mode.

7. Rotate the vertical line to form the bottom line of the top section.

Pick the bottom grip of the vertical line. Press Enter once or the Spacebar twice or enter **ro** to select rotate mode. Then type **c** and press Enter. Then type **90** and press Enter, or swing the line down by picking any snap point directly below the line. Finally, press Enter to exit multiple mode.

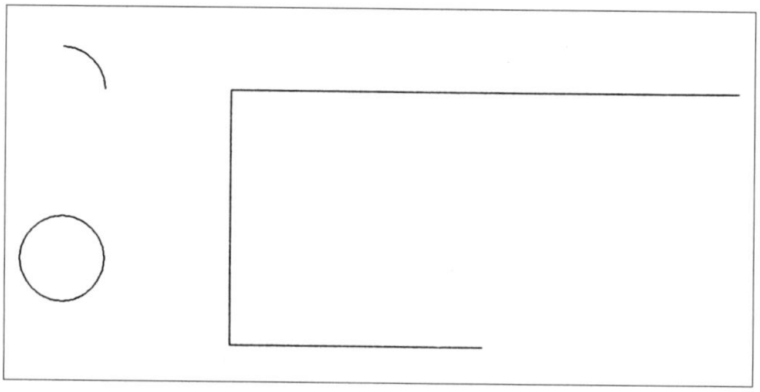

Figure 45-8: Grip exercise after step 7.

8. Mirror all three lines to form the bottom section.

Use a regular or crossing window to pick all three lines to display the grips. Hold down the Shift key and pick the middle grip on each line, then release the Shift key. (This selects these lines to be edited as a group.)

Pick the right grip on the top line. This will be the start point of the mirror line. Press Enter once or the Spacebar four times or enter **mi** to select mirror mode. Type **c** and press Enter. Pick the right grip on the bottom line as the other end of the mirror line. Then press Enter to exit multiple mode.

Press Esc to deselect the lines and then Esc again to remove the grips.

9. Stretch the bottom section down 0.72 units.

Using a crossing window (the second corner of window must be to the left of the first corner), pick the bottom three lines to display the grips.

Hold down the Shift key and pick the middle grip on the bottom line and the bottom grips on the vertical lines, then release the Shift key. Pick the middle grip on the bottom line as the base point.

Type **@0,-.72** and press Enter. Then press Esc until you return to the command prompt.

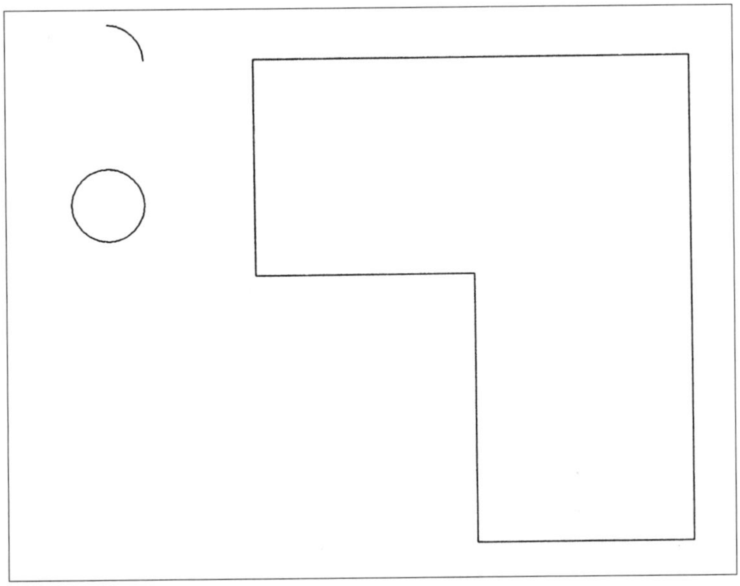

Figure 45-9: Grip exercise after step 9.

10. Move the circle into position.

Pick the circle to display the grips. Pick the center grip. Move the cursor to 5,6 and press the pick button.

11. Scale the circle by a factor of 0.75.

Pick the center grip. Press Enter once or the Spacebar three times or enter **sc** to select scale mode. Then type **0.75** and press Enter.

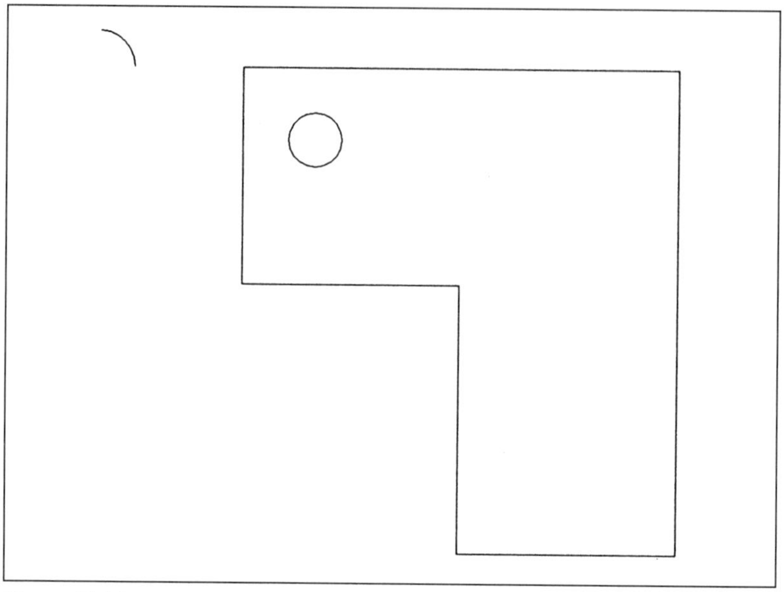

Figure 45-10: Grip exercise after step 11.

12. Copy the circle down one inch.

Pick the circle and its center grip. Type **c** and press Enter. Move the cursor down one unit and press the pick button. Press Enter again. Press Esc to exit multiple mode.

13. Make four additional copies of this pair of circles, spaced one inch between centers.

Use a crossing window to pick both circles to display the grips. Hold down the Shift key and pick the center grip on each circle, then release the Shift key. Pick the center grip on one of the circles. With snap on and with the Shift key held down, pick a point one inch to the right.

Continue to hold the Shift key down while you place the third, fourth and fifth pairs of circles (they will snap into position at one-inch increments), then release the Shift key. Press Enter. Then press Esc to exit multiple mode.

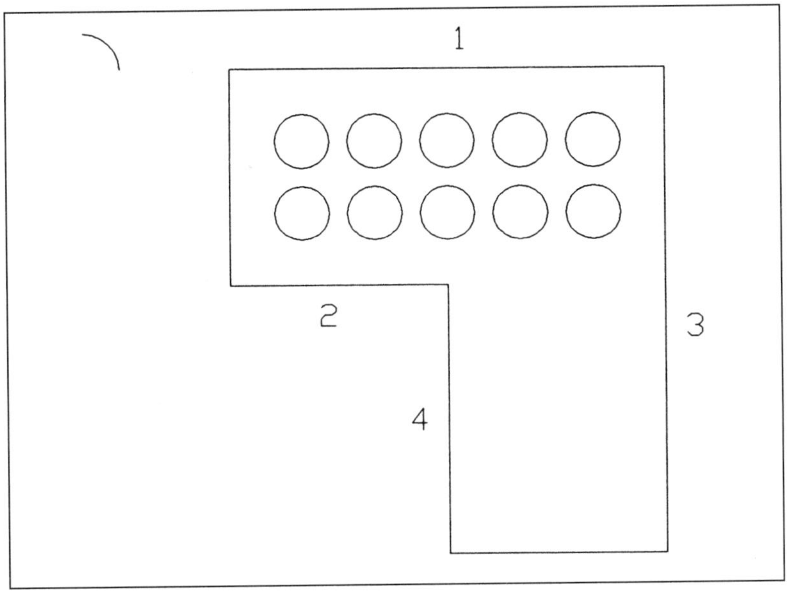

Figure 45-11: Grip exercise after step 13.

14. Stretch the lines as shown to make room for the rounded corners.

Pick line 1 to display the grips. Pick the right grip. With snap on, move the cursor one inch to the left and press the pick button. Use a similar procedure to stretch line 3 down one inch. Use a similar procedure to stretch line 2, then line 4, each 0.5 inch. Press Esc twice to return to the command prompt.

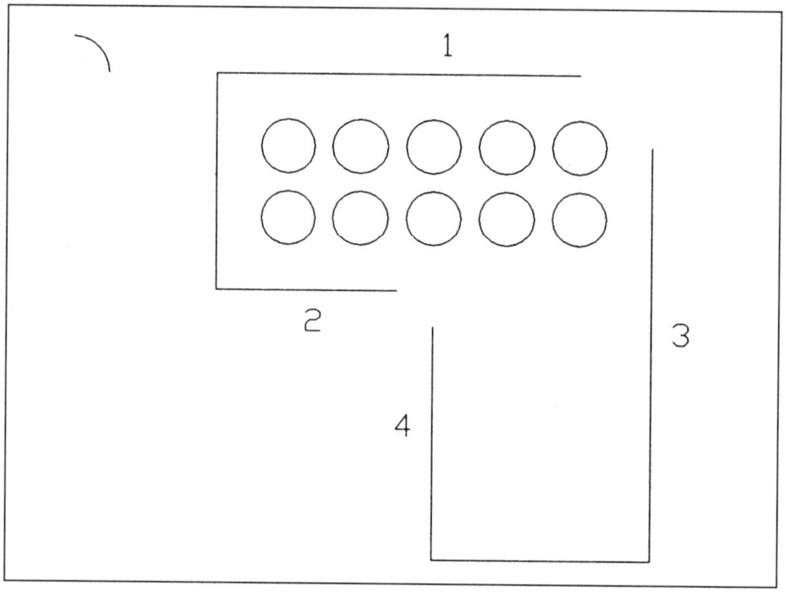

Figure 45-12: Grip exercise after step 14.

15. Turn snap off, then move the arc into position between lines 2 and 4.

Press F9 to turn the snap off. Pick line 2 to display the grips. Hold down the Shift key and pick line 2 again to deselect it. The grips will remain. Pick the arc to display the grips. Pick the left grip on the arc. Press Enter to select move mode. Move the cursor to the grip on the right end of line 2 and press the pick button.

16. Copy this arc to the outer corner.

Pick line 3 to display the grips. Hold down the Shift key and pick line 3 again to deselect it. Pick the bottom grip on the arc. Press Enter to select move mode. Type **c** and press Enter. Move the cursor to the top grip on line 3 and press the pick button. Press Enter. Use the Esc key to return to the command prompt.

17. Scale this outer arc by a factor of 2.

Pick the outer arc to display the grips. Pick the bottom grip. Press Enter once or the Spacebar three times or enter **sc** to select scale mode. Type **2** and press Enter. Press Esc to return to the command prompt.

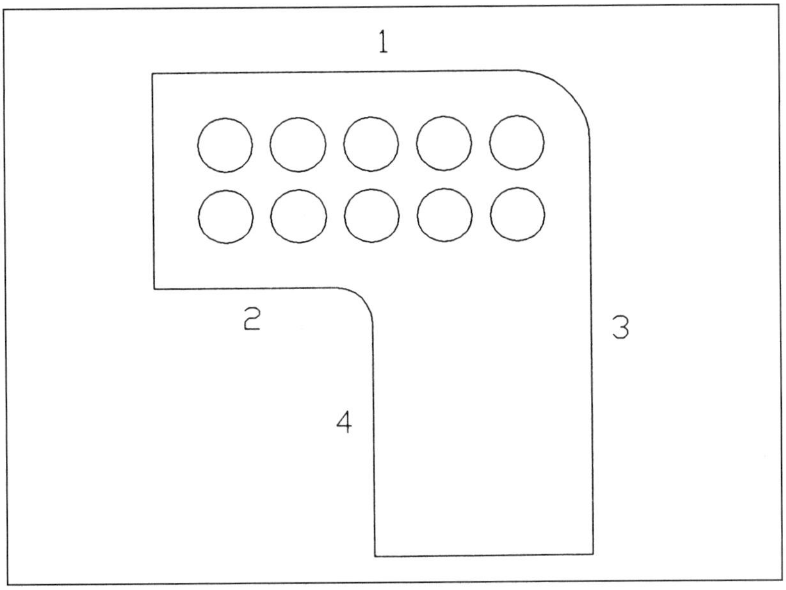

Figure 45-13: Grip exercise after step 17.

18. Rotate the 10 circles.

Use a crossing window to select all 10 circles. Hold down the Shift key and select the center grip on each circle. Pick any grip. Press Enter once or the Spacebar twice or enter **ro** to select rotate mode. Type the letter **b** and press Enter. Then enter **6.5,5.5** and press Enter. Then enter **-7** and press Enter again. Press Esc to return to the command prompt.

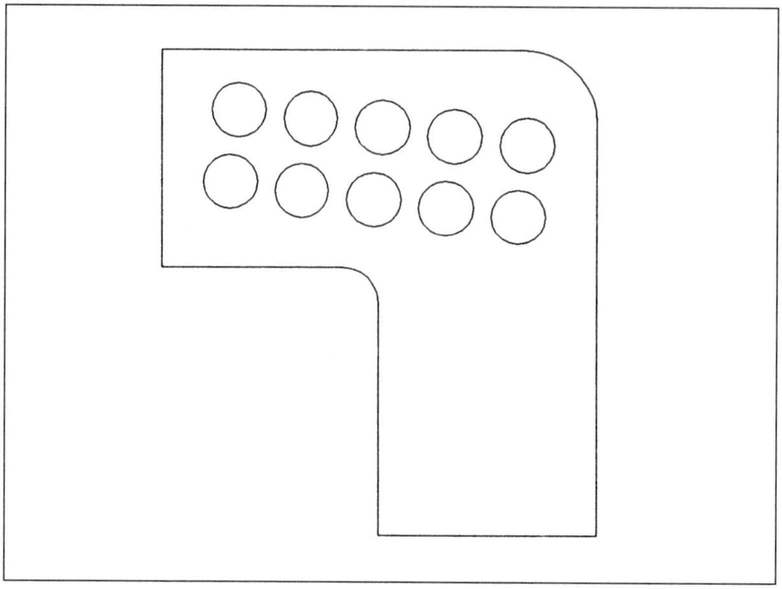

Figure 45-14: Grip exercise after step 18.

19. Copy any circle to 8.5,2 in the bottom section.

Pick a circle to display the grips. Pick the center grip. Hold down the Shift key and move the cursor to 8.5,2, then press the pick button. Press Enter to exit multiple mode. Press Esc to return to the command prompt.

20. Finally, stretch the bottom circle to a 1-inch radius.

Pick the bottom circle to display the grips. Pick the right grip. Move the cursor to 9.5,2.0 and press the pick button. Press Esc to return to the command prompt.

Text Exercise

In this exercise you create simple text using different text justifications.

Using the DTEXT command, reconstruct the half-page of text below according to the specifications in each block of text.

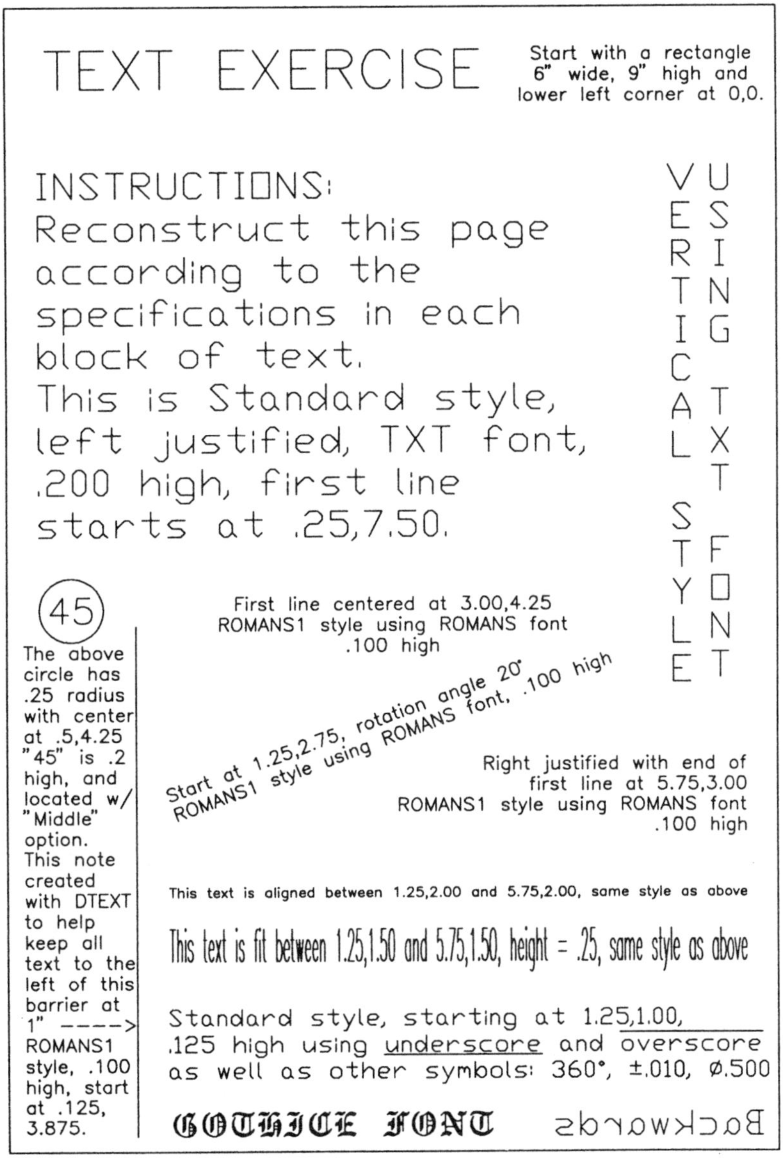

MTEXT Exercise

In this exercise you use the MTEXT command and edit text.

Using the MTEXT command, create the half-page of text shown and edit the styles for different fonts.

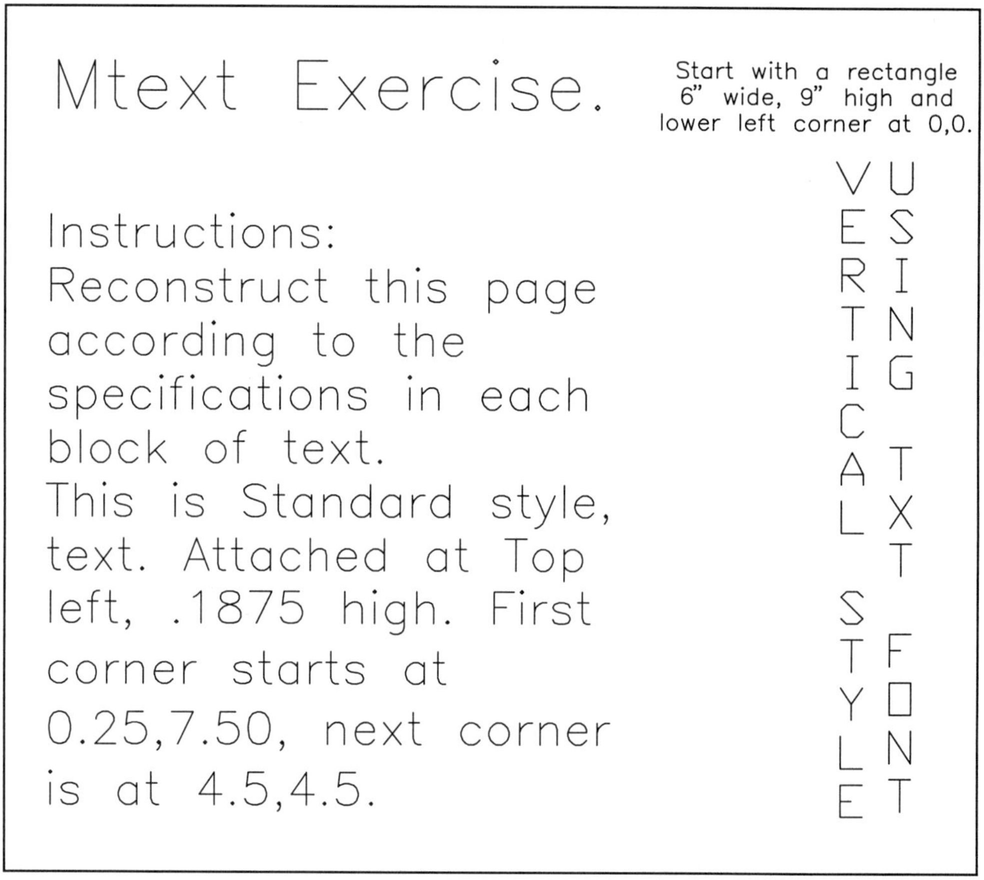

Figure 45-16: Creating and editing multitext.

Filters Exercise

In this exercise you create a simple rectangle and then place a circle in its exact center using filters. See Figure 45-17.

Before you begin, be sure that the Draw, Construct and Modify menu choices appear in the menu bar at the top of your screen. If they do not, enter menu at the command line and then select Acadfull (for "full menu").

1. Create a rectangle from 2,2 to coordinate 7,7.

Choose the Rectangle command from the Draw pull-down menu, icon or toolbar. The first corner is at 2,2; the other corner is at 7,7.

2. Using filters, draw a circle in the exact center of the rectangle.

Choose the Circle command from the Draw pull-down menu, icon or toolbar. At the Center point: prompt, type **.X**.

An of prompt appears. Choose the MIDpoint osnap option from the cursor menu, and pick a point anywhere along the top edge of the rectangular box.

The following prompt appears: need .YZ. Choose the MIDpoint osnap option again from the cursor menu. Then choose a left or right edge of the box. The circle prompt then prompts for Diameter/Radius. Choose the PERpendicular option from the Cursor menu and choose the nearest side of the box.

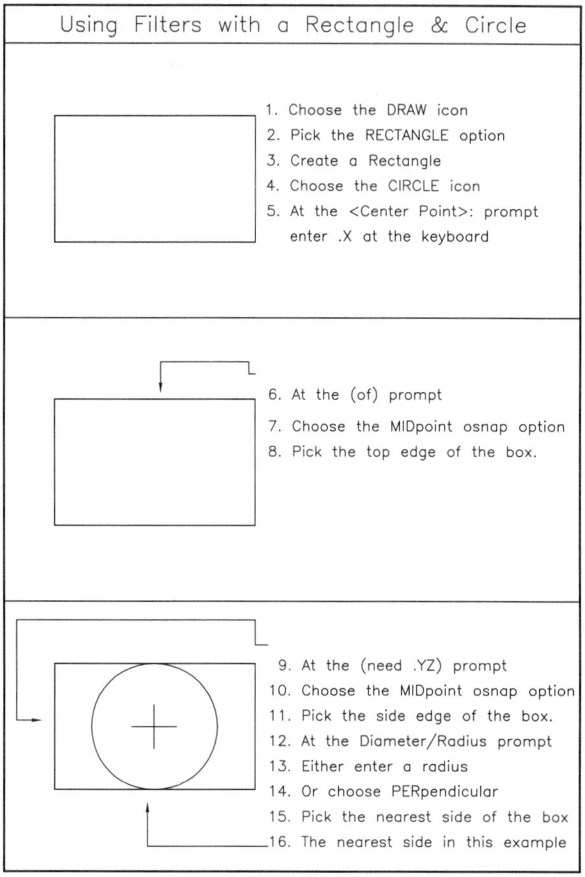

Figure 45-17: Using filters with a rectangle and circle.

Editing—Group Two

Stencil Drawing

In this exercise you create a stencil of the letters A and B and place ordinate dimensions as shown. See Figure 45-18.

Set your Snap to 0.0625. Create the shapes using rectangles and parallelograms. Use the BREAK, TRIM, EXTEND, FILLET and CHAMFER commands. Using the POINT command, draw a node point at 0,0,0. Set the UCS to 0,0,0 as the origin. Activate the UCSICON command and set it to origin. Then create the ordinate dimensions with DIMORDINATE. Figure 45-18 shows full dimensions.

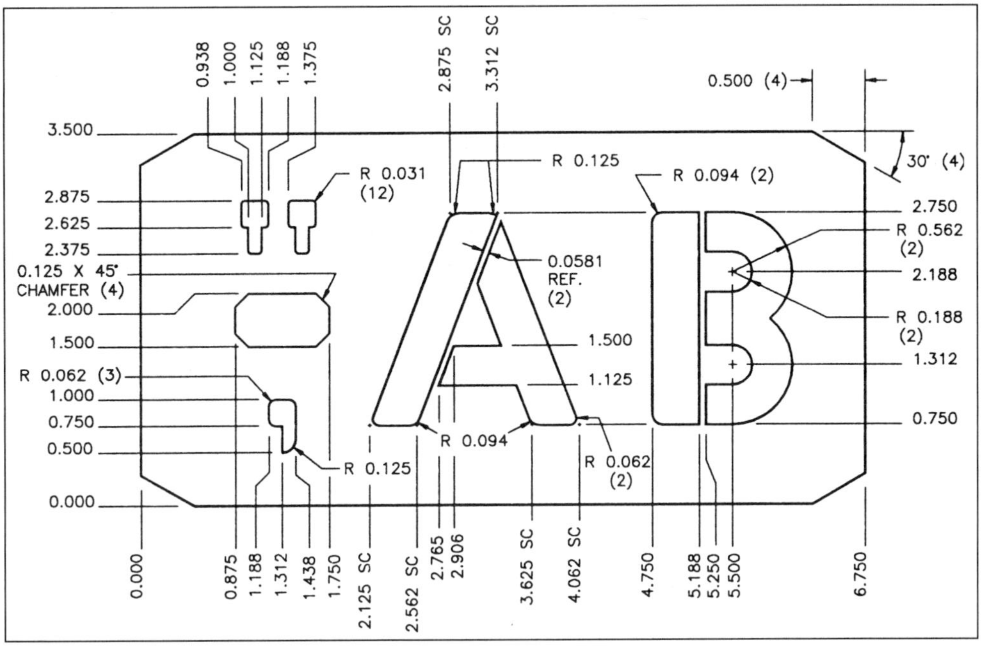

Figure 45-18: Stencil exercise.

Leaf Spring Profile

In this exercise you create a leaf spring profile and place radial dimensions as shown. See Figure 45-19.

Construct the center lobe first with both circles. Then use the ARRAY command to array first to the left then the right. Set the FILLET command to a radius of 0.188 and fillet the four inner locations. Complete and clean up the drawing. Finally, radial dimension the leaf spring profile as shown in the sketch.

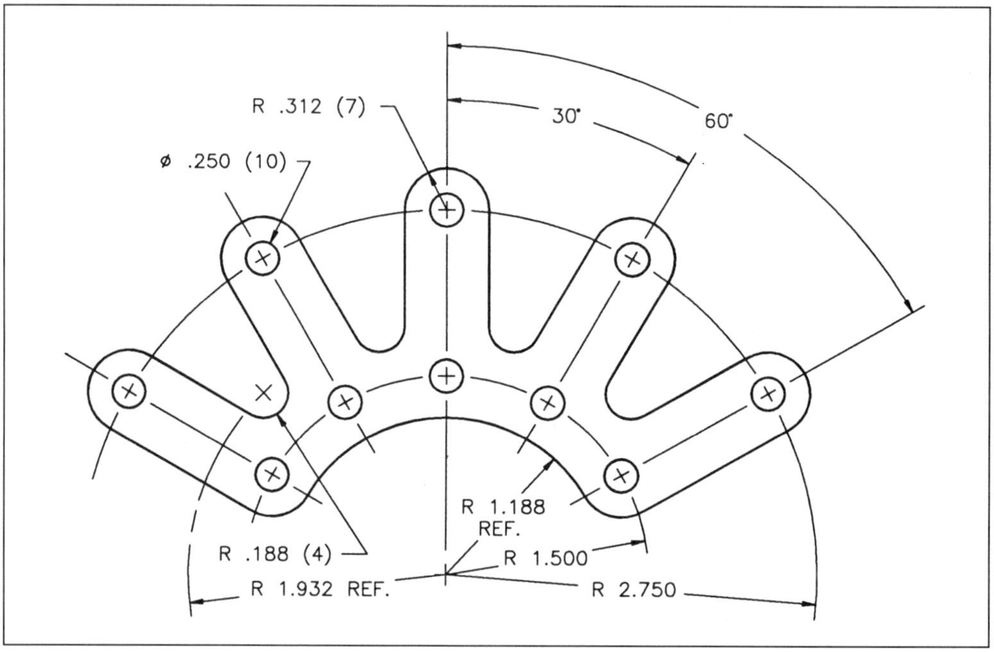

Figure 45-19: Leaf spring profile.

Pivot Arm Profile

In this exercise you create a pivot arm profile and place vertical and angular dimensions as shown. See Figure 45-20.

Use the ELLIPSE and TRIM commands as needed and clean up.

Place the dimensions as shown in the sketch.

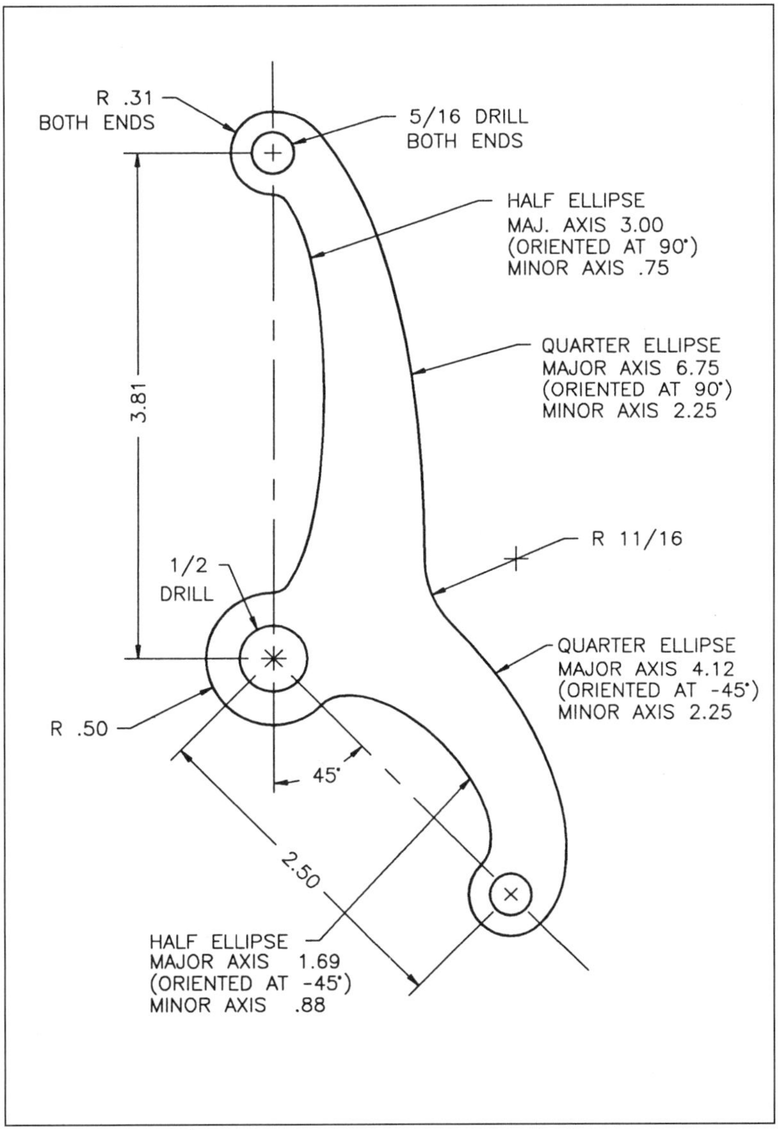

Figure 45-20: Pivot arm profile.

Blocks

In this exercise you create a series of blocks as shown. See Figure 45-21.

Do not dimension the sketch.

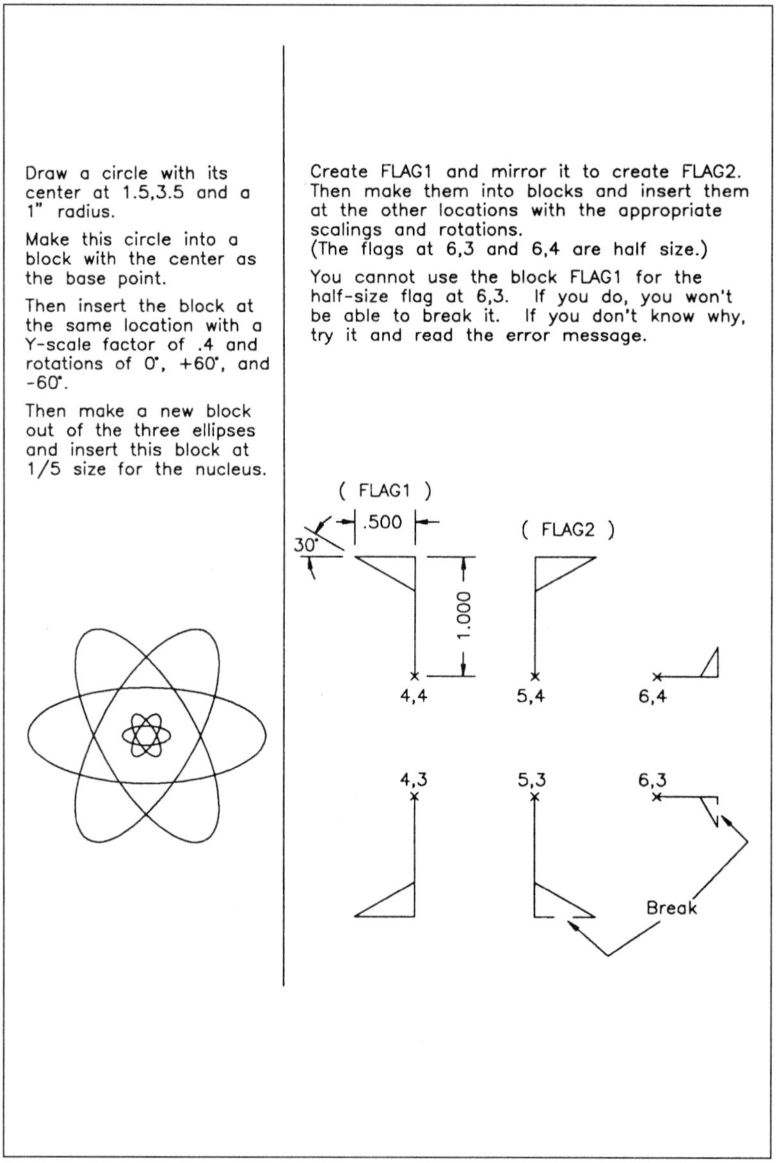

Figure 45-21: Blocks exercise.

Cylinder

In this exercise you create a cylinder and place its dimensions as shown. See Figure 45-22. (You may wish to try the new ACIS solid modeler with its cylinder command.)

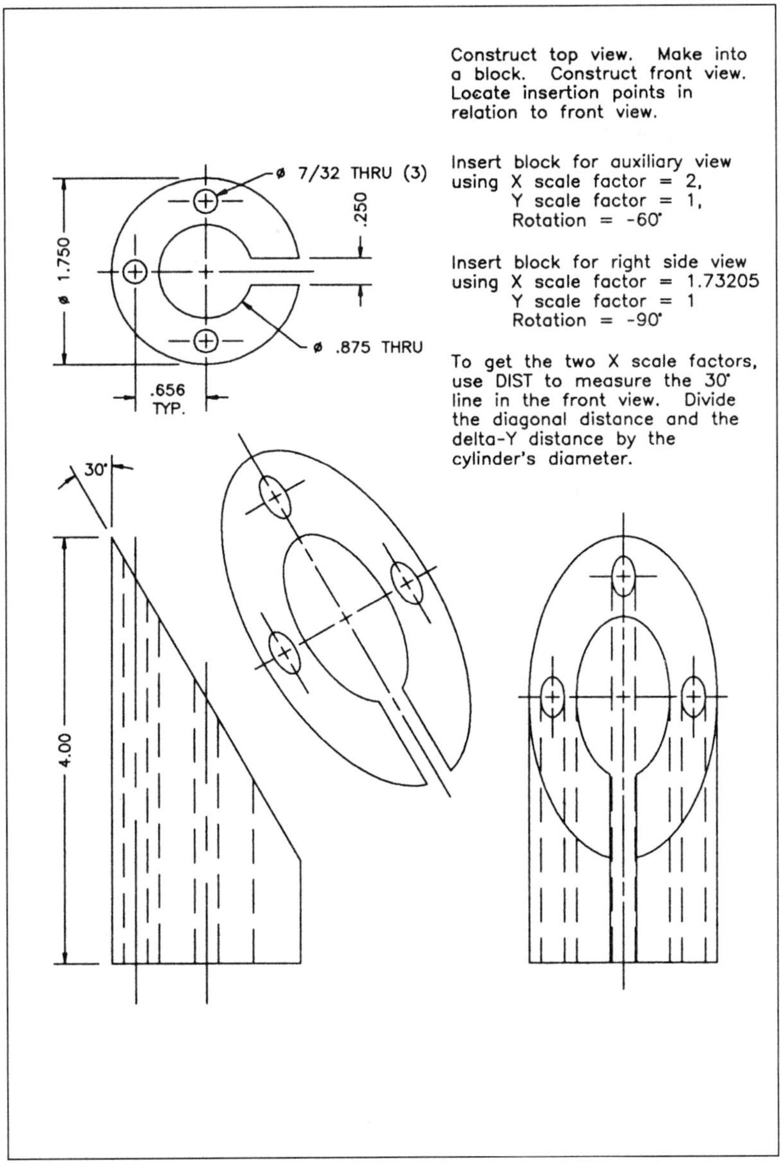

Figure 45-22: Cylinder exercise.

Advanced Exercises

XREF Exercise

The objective of this exercise is to XREF external files into a drawing, then edit the files.

You create an assembly drawing that contains referenced drawings. An external referenced drawing is known as an "xref." See Chapter 23, "Blocks & External References," for an explanation of external references and the XREF command.

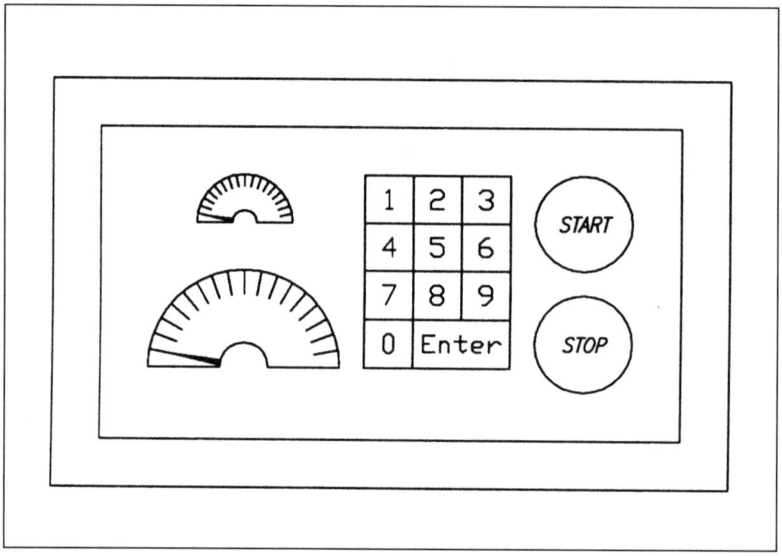

Figure 45-23: Control box assembly with Xrefs.

The assembly drawing is a control box. The control master drawing references two other drawings, a frame drawing and a panel subassembly drawing. The panel drawing then references a meter drawing. The relationship between these drawings is shown in the diagram below.

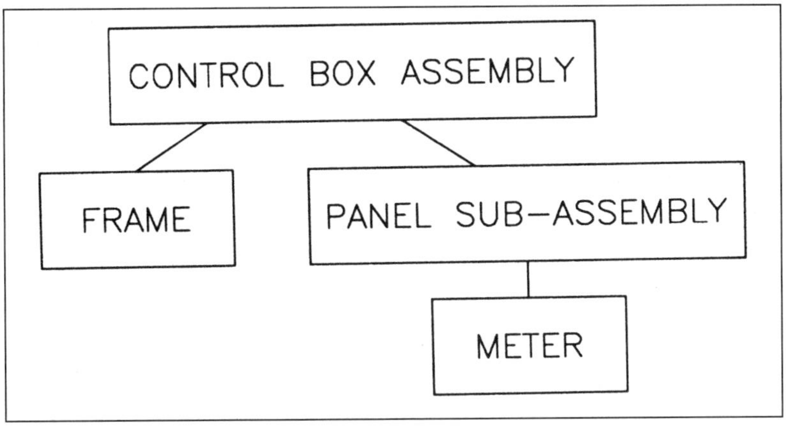

Figure 45-24: Relationship of Xref drawings.

Our approach is to create a prototype drawing first, then the meter drawing, then the panel subassembly, then the frame drawing, and finally the control box assembly. For ease of reference, be sure to create all the drawings in the same directory.

As you create these drawings, keep in mind that this exercise illustrates how the XREF command creates interactive relationships between referencing drawings and referenced drawings. With this in mind, you may want to omit some details from the drawings in order to complete the exercise faster. You could easily omit the text on the numeric keypad and the increment marks on the meter.

Part I: Creating the XPROTO Drawing

1. Start a new drawing. Name it XPROTO.

2. From the Data pull-down menu, select Units. In the Units dialog, select decimal units. Set to three places of accuracy. Choose OK to save the settings and exit the dialog.

3. Type the command **limits**. Press Enter to accept the default setting for the lower-left corner at 0,0. Type in **10,7** to set the upper-right corner at 10,7. Then use ZOOM All.

4. Set the snap to .125, the grid to 1 and the dimscale to 0.7.

5. Under the Data pull-down menu or toolbar use Layer to create three new layers: OBJECT, OBJ- and DIM-. Assign green to layer OBJECT.

Assign red to OBJ-. Assign magenta to layer DIM-. Make OBJECT the current layer.

The OBJECT layer contains the objects you want to have visible when one drawing is referenced in another drawing. The layers OBJ- and DIM-, whose names end with a minus sign (hyphen) contain objects and dimensions you want to have subtracted (invisible) when one drawing is referenced in another drawing. OBJECT is the current layer.

6. Save the drawing.

Part 2: Creating the Meter Drawing

7. Create a new drawing called METER using the XPROTO prototype drawing. Assign green to the OBJECT layer. Make sure OBJECT is the current layer when you create the meter geometry pictured below.

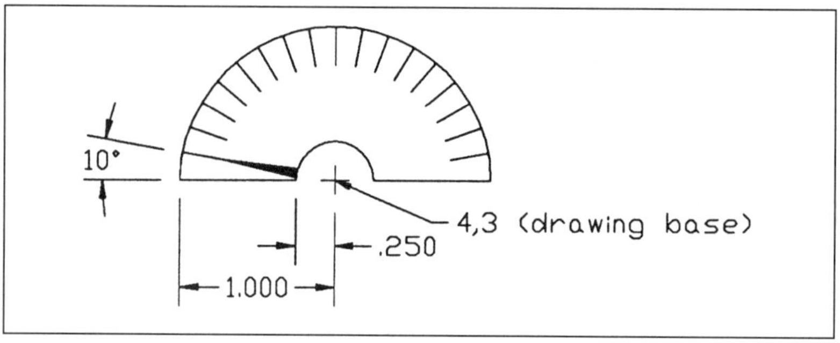

Figure 45-25: The meter.

8. Place the centers of both arcs at 4,3. See Figure 45-25. Make the pointer from a polyline. Start the pointer with a width of 0.125 and end with a width of 0 (zero). This pointer is altered later.

9. Use BASE to locate the base insertion point at 4,3. (The center of the arcs.)

10. Make DIM- the current layer, then add one or two dimensions to the drawing.

11. Save the drawing.

Part 3: Creating the Panel Drawing

12. Start a new drawing, naming it PANEL. Use XPROTO as a prototype drawing.

13. Make OBJ- the current layer.

14. Create the panel's outer edges. See Figure 45-26. These edges are created on layer OBJ- so the layer can be frozen later in the control assembly drawing to make the panel edges invisible.

15. Make OBJECT the current layer.

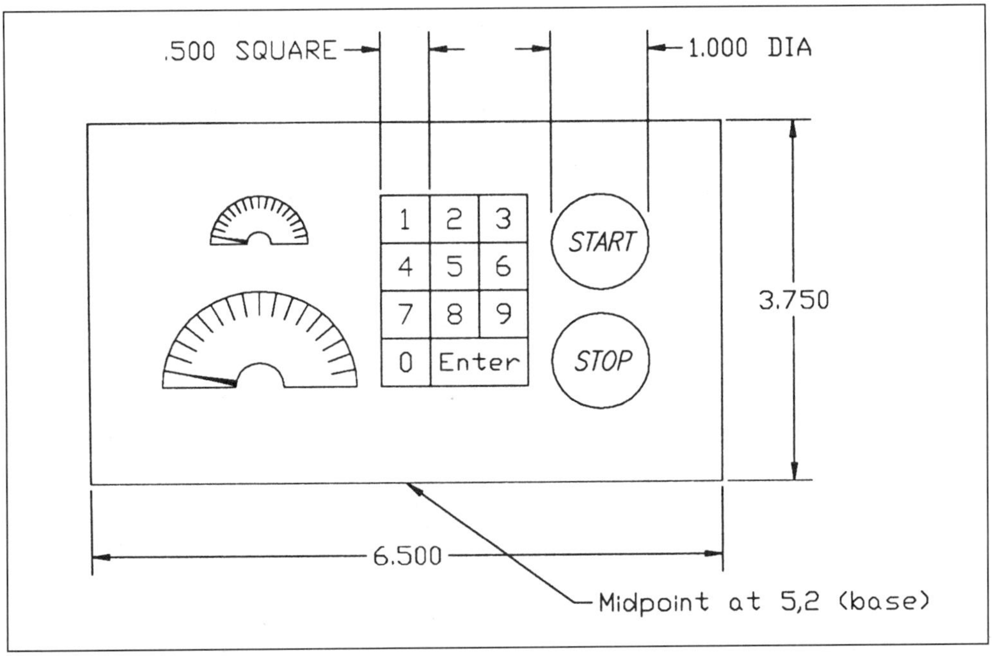

Figure 45-26: The panel.

16. Use the Attach option of the XREF command to attach METER to this drawing. You will attach the meter twice, once at full scale, and once at half scale. See Figure 45-26. Attach the full-scale meter at 1.625,1 and the half-scale meter at 1.625,3.

17. Activate the Layers dialog from the Data pull-down menu or from the Layer icon to display all the names of the layers. Notice that all the layers from the meter drawing have a "METER | " prefix in this drawing to keep them independent from the layers in the current panel drawing.

18. Notice also that the dimensions from the meter drawing are visible. Activate the Layers dialog. The layer that these dimensions are on in the meter drawing has been renamed METER | DIM in the current drawing.

Freeze layer METER | DIM and choose OK. The dimensions disappear from the screen.

19. Use LIST to display information about both instances of METER. Notice that the listing is very similar to listings of regular blocks, but these are identified as external references.

20. Use the XREF command and request a listing of external references by entering **?**. METER is cited as an external reference.

21. Use the BLOCK command and request a listing of blocks by entering **?**. Notice that external references are listed under blocks.

22. Draw the numeric keypad and the start and stop buttons roughly as shown above. See Figure 45-26.

23. Before you place the text in the start and stop buttons, use the STYLE command to create a new text style, called Slanted, that uses the Romans font, height 0.00, width factor .8, obliquing angle 15 degrees. Later, you bind this text style to the Control drawing. After you place the text in the start and stop buttons, restore Standard as the current text style.

24. Make DIM the current layer and add one or two dimensions to the drawing. See Figure 45-26.

25. Use BASE to locate the base insertion point at 5,2 (the midpoint of the bottom edge of the panel).

26. Save the drawing.

Part 4: Creating the Frame Drawing

27. Create a new drawing named FRAME. Use the XPROTO prototype drawing.

28. Assign blue to layer OBJECT and make sure OBJECT is the current layer.

29. Create FRAME using the RECTANGLE command. See Figure 45-27.

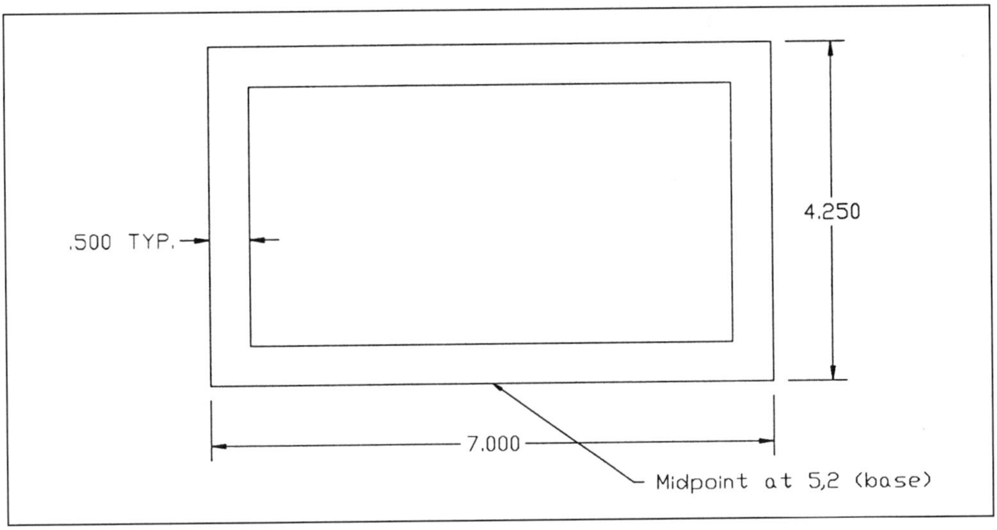

Figure 45-27: The frame.

30. Make DIM the current layer and add one or two dimensions to the drawing.

31. Use BASE to locate the base insertion point at 5,2 (the midpoint of the bottom edge of the panel).

32. Save the drawing.

Part 5: Creating the Control Assembly Drawing

33. Start a new drawing named CONTROL. Use the XPROTO prototype drawing.

34. Make sure OBJECT is the current layer.

35. Using the XREF command, attach FRAME at 5,1.5 (full scale) and attach PANEL at 5,1.75 (full scale).

36. Activate the Layers dialog and freeze all layers ending with the minus sign. Your drawing should look like the assembly shown at the beginning of this exercise except for the words "CONTROL BOX ASSEMBLY," which you'll add later.

37. Use the LAYER, LIST, XREF and BLOCK commands to examine the contents of this drawing. Notice that attaching the panel automatically includes both occurrences of METER since they're attached to the PANEL drawing.

38. Save the drawing.

You've now finished XREFerencing the drawing. Obviously, the unique purpose of an XREFerence, as opposed to inserting a block, is its convenience in updating drawings. This next part of the exercise reviews how to revise referenced drawings. The last part of the exercise reviews the XREF detach and bind options.

Part 6: Modifying a Referenced Drawing

39. Open and edit the FRAME drawing as follows: Fillet the outer corners of the frame with a .5 radius and the inner corners with a .125 radius. Remember that the frame is constructed from polylines. Save the drawing.

40. Open the CONTROL drawing and notice that the changes made to the frame appear automatically. Save the drawing.

Part 7: Binding an XREF

41. Open and edit the PANEL drawing as follows: Use the XREF command with the Bind option to make the two METERs a permanent part of PANEL. (This converts the METERs into regular blocks in the PANEL drawing.)

42. Use the RENAME command to change the name of block METER to METER1.

43. Erase the small METER1.

44. Make sure you are on the OBJECT layer, then re-attach the small meter (half-scale) with the XREF command. Activate the Layer dialog and freeze layer METER | DIM.

45. List METER1 and METER. METER1 lists as a regular block and METER lists as an external reference. Save the drawing.

46. Open and edit the METER drawing. Modify the meter by changing the color of the pointer to cyan with the CHPROP command. Save the drawing.

47. Open the PANEL drawing once more and notice that the change you made to the meter appears automatically only on the small METER since it is an XREF. The large METER1 is bound to the PANEL drawing as a regular block defined within the PANEL drawing, so the change made to METER does not affect it.

48. Use the Detach option of the XREF command to eliminate the meter.

Notice that the small METER (the xref) is removed from the drawing while the large METER1, which is a regular block, remains in the drawing. To place the small METER back in the drawing, use the Attach option of the XREF command, not the Reload option. (Reload is used when a referenced drawing has been revised while you're working on the referencing drawing and you want to update your drawing according to the latest version of the referenced drawing without exiting the drawing editor.) Save the drawing.

49. Make sure all your files that hold your CONTROL, FRAME, PANEL and METER drawings are in the same directory. If you're in Windows, press Ctrl+Esc and double-click on the Program Manager. Go to the Main Window and click on the DOS Prompt icon.

Use the DIR command as follows to get a directory listing. Type **dir**, then at the prompt type ***.xlg** and notice there are several files with the extension .XLG that AutoCAD has been maintaining. You may use the TYPE command or a text editor to examine the contents of these .XLG files. These files may be erased without affecting the contents of any of the drawings.

Part 8: Relocating Referenced Drawings

50. While you're still at the DOS prompt in the directory holding your drawings, create a directory called XR under the current directory by entering **md xr**. Copy the FRAME drawing to this new directory and erase it from the current directory. Use the DIR command to check both the current directory and the XR directory and make sure that FRAME.DWG is in XR, not the current directory.

51. To return to AutoCAD, type **exit**. When you return to the graphics screen, open the CONTROL drawing. Notice that AutoCAD is unable to find FRAME. In its place in the drawing, you see the words "Xref frame."

52. With the Path option of the XREF command, change the path of the FRAME drawing from FRAME to its new path; and AutoCAD is then able to load the FRAME.

Part 9: Using the XBIND Command

53. Use the STYLE command and display a list of available text styles. The styles from the referenced drawings are then listed. One of these styles is PANEL | SLANTED.

54. Open the CONTROL drawing. Use the Style option of the TEXT command to attempt to assign PANEL | SLANTED as the current text style. AutoCAD does not let you use this style since it's defined in an external drawing.

55. Use the Style option of the XBIND command to bind the style to the CONTROL drawing. When prompted for the style name, enter: PANEL | SLANTED.

56. Again, use the STYLE command to display the styles and you will see that PANEL | SLANTED has been renamed PANEL0SLANTED.

57. You can now use the Style option of the TEXT command to establish PANEL SLANTED as the current style. Place the words "CONTROL BOX ASSEMBLY" at the bottom of the CONTROL drawing, and your assembly is complete.

XREF Reinforcement

Finally, to reinforce the XREF skills you've learned, you use the drawings supplied on the disk. (See the back cover of the book.) If you have already installed the disk, it has unpacked the drawings and installed them into a directory named \CONCISE. In the next two exercises, you'll XREF drawings into a title sheet, complete the dimensions and notes, and then plot the finished drawings.

Dimensions & Hatching

Wheel Puller

The wheel puller drawings are on the Companion Disk. Your objective is to XREF four drawings into a fifth title sheet drawing, then plot.

Open the WP-TITLE drawing. Then XREF these drawings from the disk: WP-ARM, WP-PLAN, WP-SCREW and WP-BRACK. Complete the dimensions as shown in Figure 45-28 and plot the drawing.

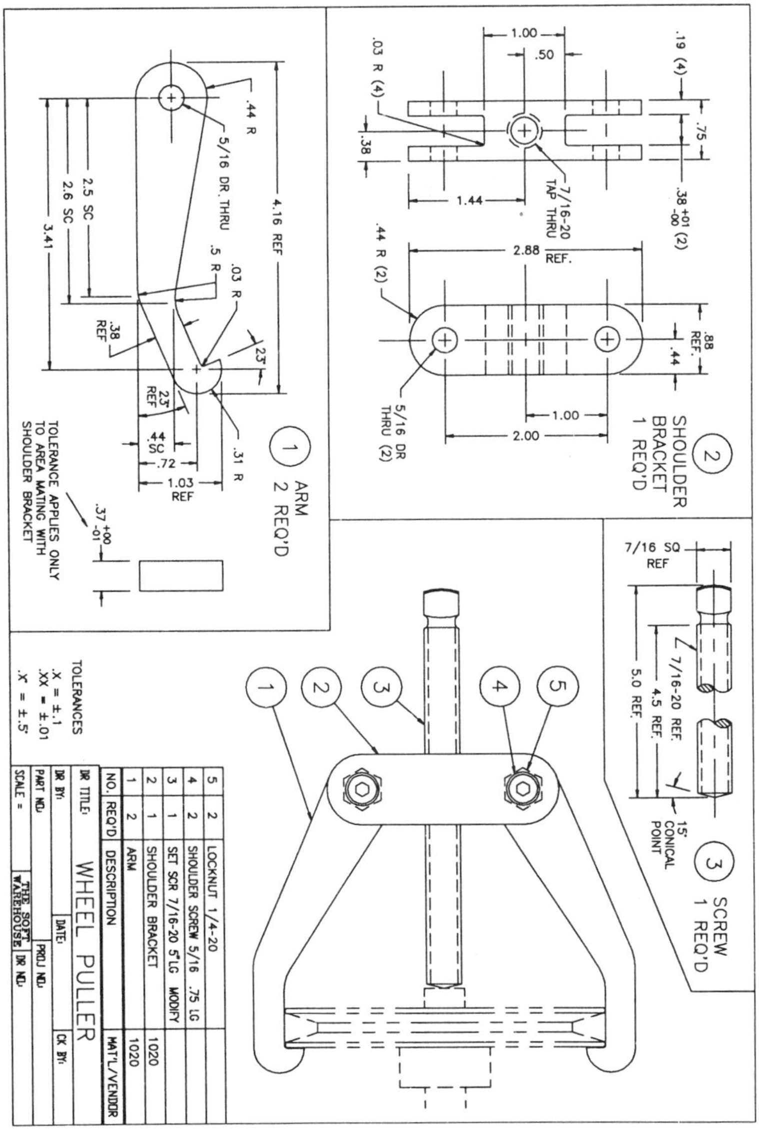

Figure 45-28: Completed wheel puller.

Surface Gage

The six surface gage drawings are on the Companion Disk. Again, your objective in this exercise is to XREF five detail drawings into a sixth title sheet drawing, then plot. Figure 45-29 shows the master list for all the details. You will only use the first five details in this exercise.

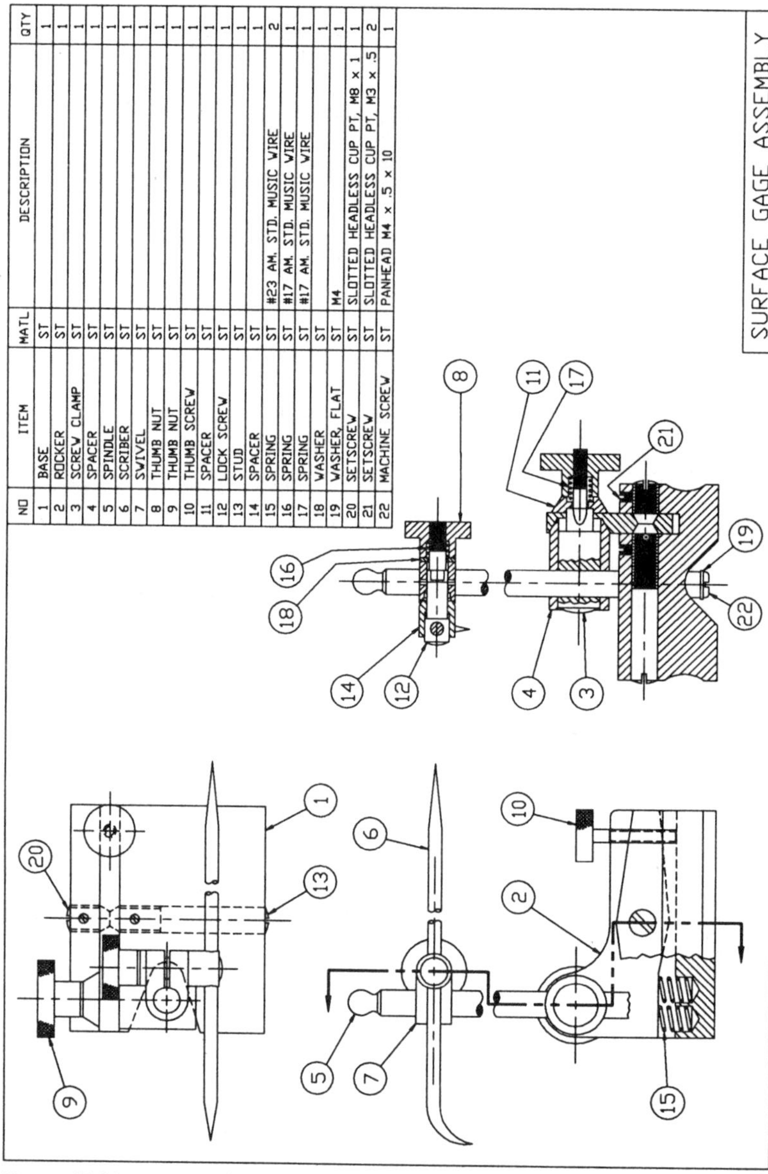

Figure 45-29: Completed surface gage assembly.

First, open the SG-TITLE drawing. Then XREF the five remaining drawings from the disk. They are named: SG-ONE, SG-TWO, SG-THREE, SG-FOUR and SG-FIVE. Complete the dimensions as shown in Figure 45-30 and plot the drawing.

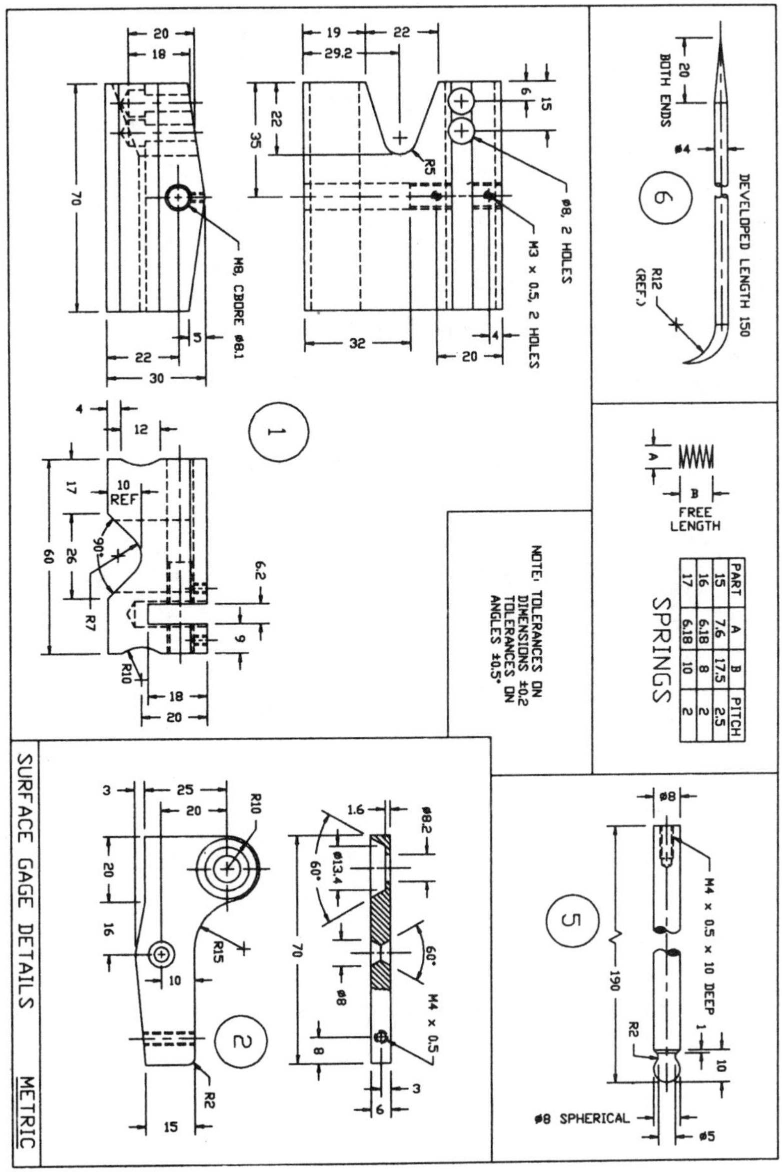

PART	A	B	PITCH
15	7.6	17.5	2.5
16	6.18	8	2
17	6.18	10	2

Figure 45-30: Completed surface gage detail sheet 1.

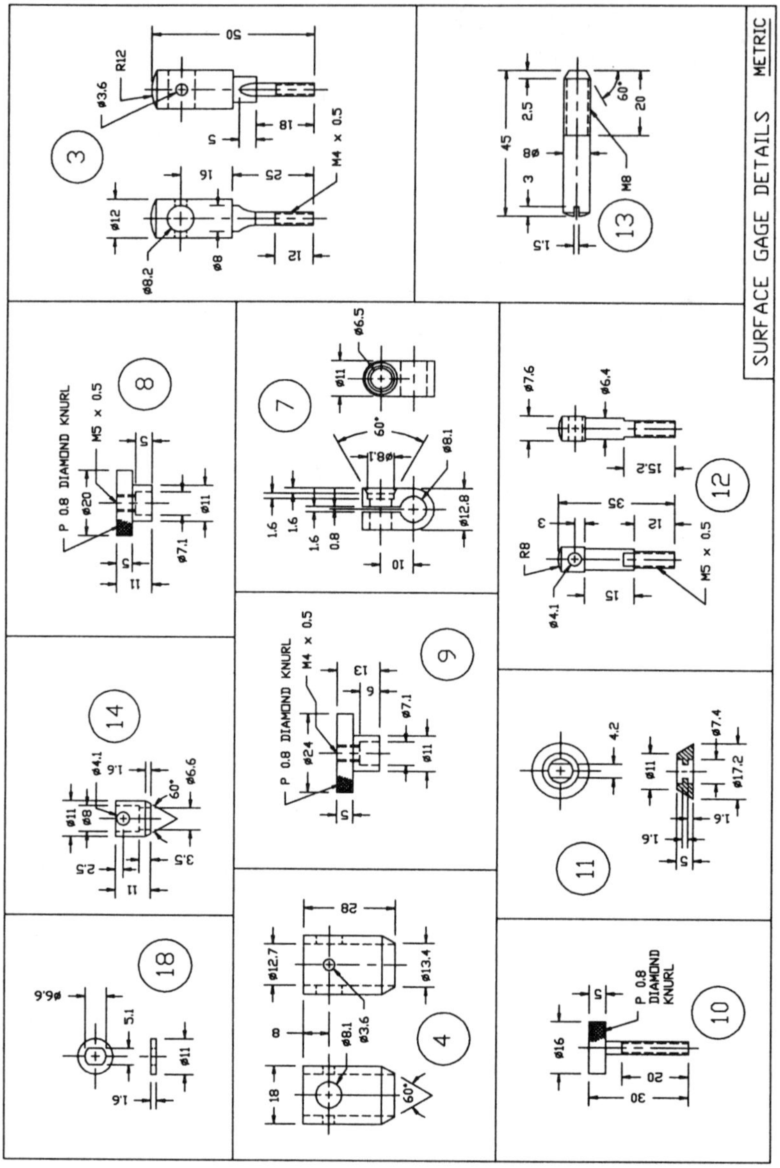

Figure 45-31: Completed surface gage detail sheet 2.

Polyline Exercise

Using the PLINE command, create the simple figures in the exercise. See Figure 45-32. You may create the figures at the top of the sheet, and then determine area. For example, if you close the Pline with the drawings you can use the AREA command to find the area. You may also try using the Width option for two of the figures. The command FILL should be on.

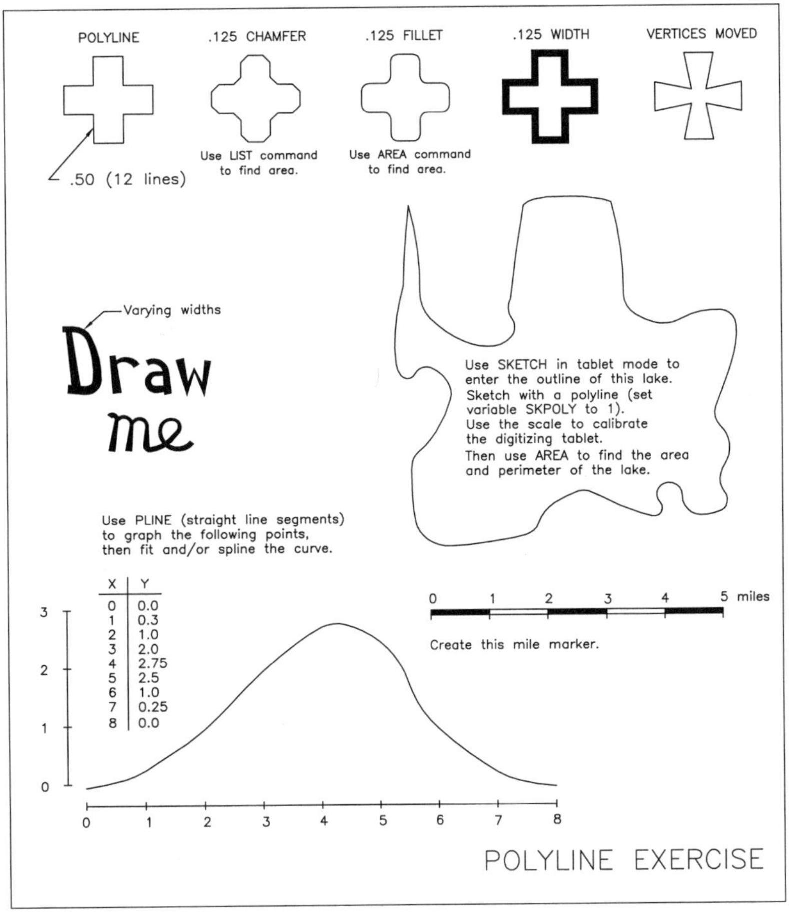

Figure 45-32: Polyline exercise.

Isometric Drawings

Channel Block

Create the channel block in an isometric drawing. The block is symmetrical about the center on all its axes. See Figure 45-33.

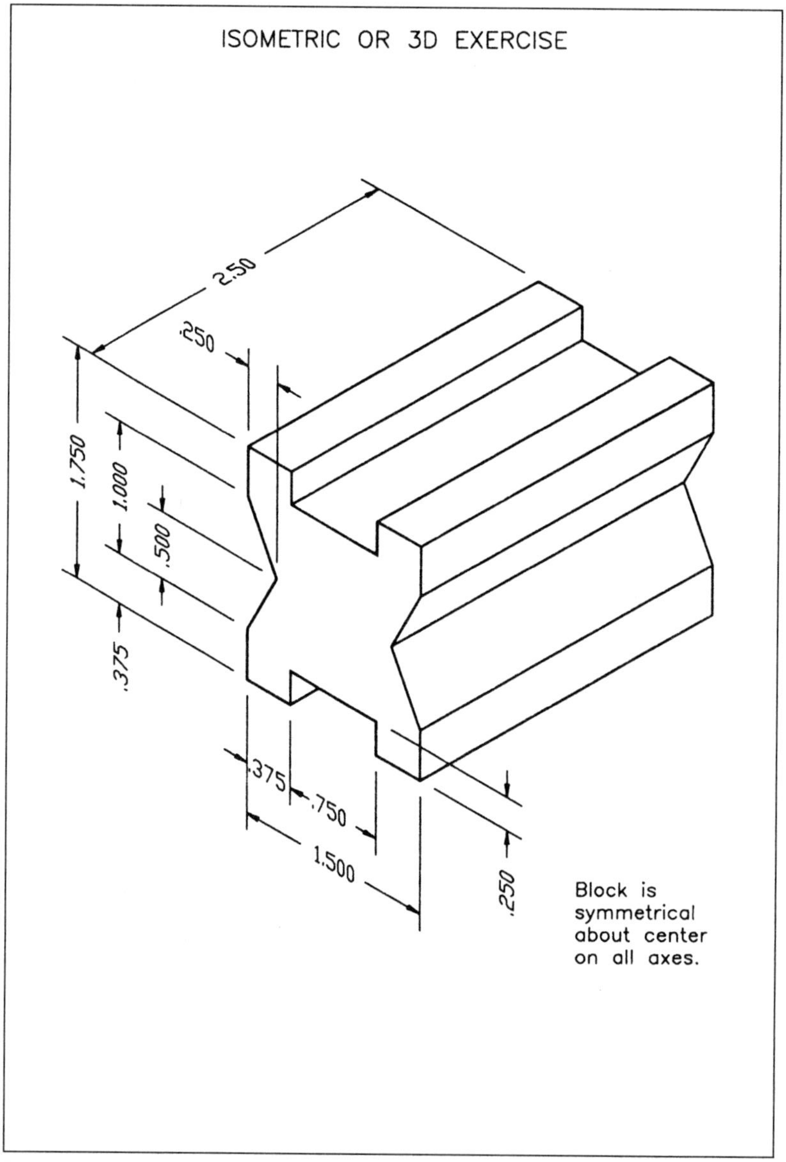

Figure 45-33: Channel block exercise.

Iso-Ellipse Comparison

Figure 45-34 shows three iso-ellipses created with different techniques, each of which provides the same result. The first iso-ellipse is constructed with the ELLIPSE command. The second is made with blocks formed from reinserted circles and arcs. The final iso-ellipse is constructed with blocks and arcs formed and edited with the FILLET command.

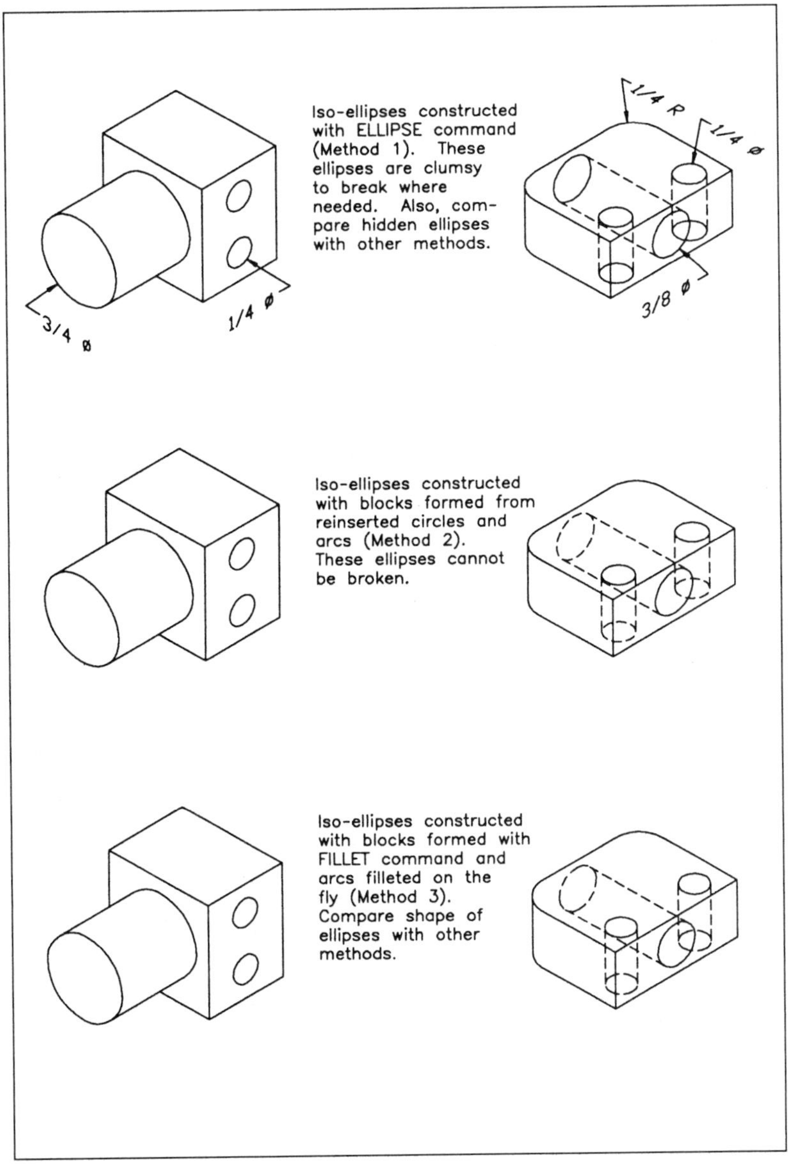

Figure 45-34: Iso-ellipse exercise.

Linkage Base

Create the Linkage Base drawing (see Figure 45-35) using the new ACIS solid modeler. You create two rectangular solids first, then create and place three cylinders. Then use the FILLET command to fillet the three corners and finally union the part as a whole.

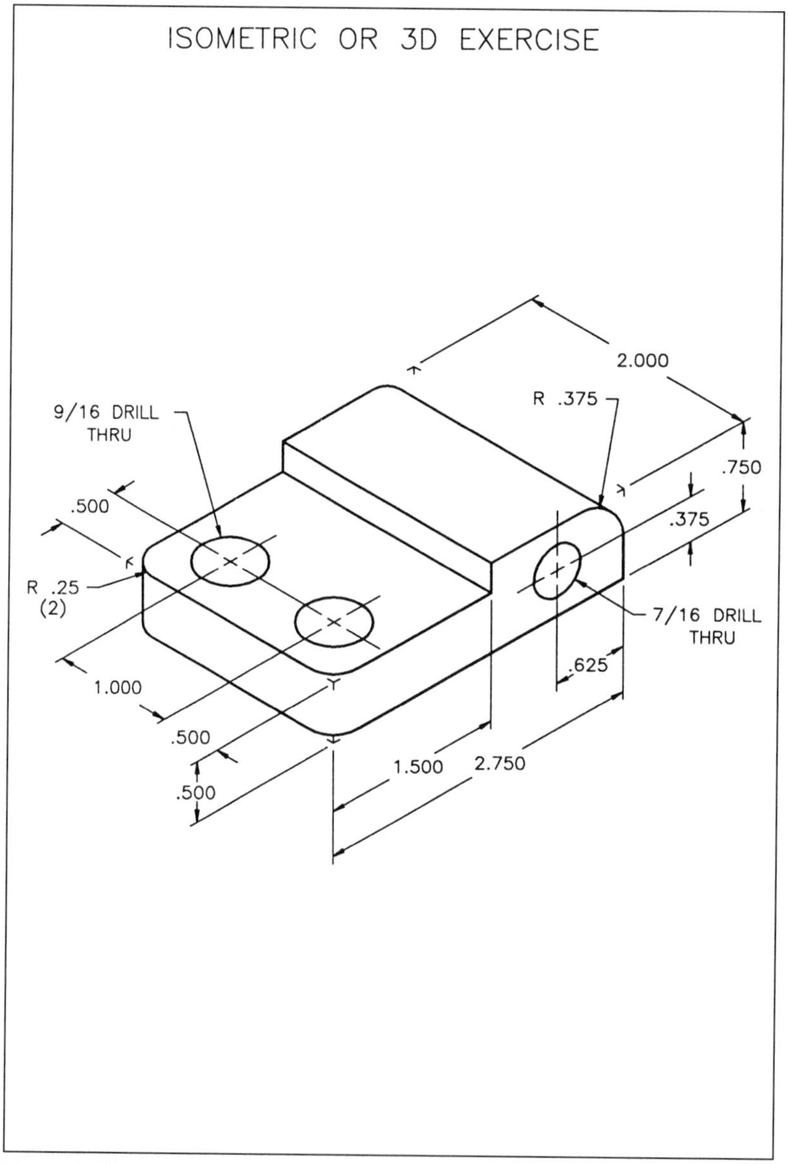

Figure 45-35: Linkage base exercise.

Swivel Bracket

Again create the swivel bracket drawing (see Figure 45-36) using the new ACIS solid modeler. You create four rectangular solids first, then create five cylindrical holes, one of which is a horizontal through hole. Use the FILLET command to fillet the three corners and the CHAMFER command for the top two chamfers. Then finally union the part as a whole.

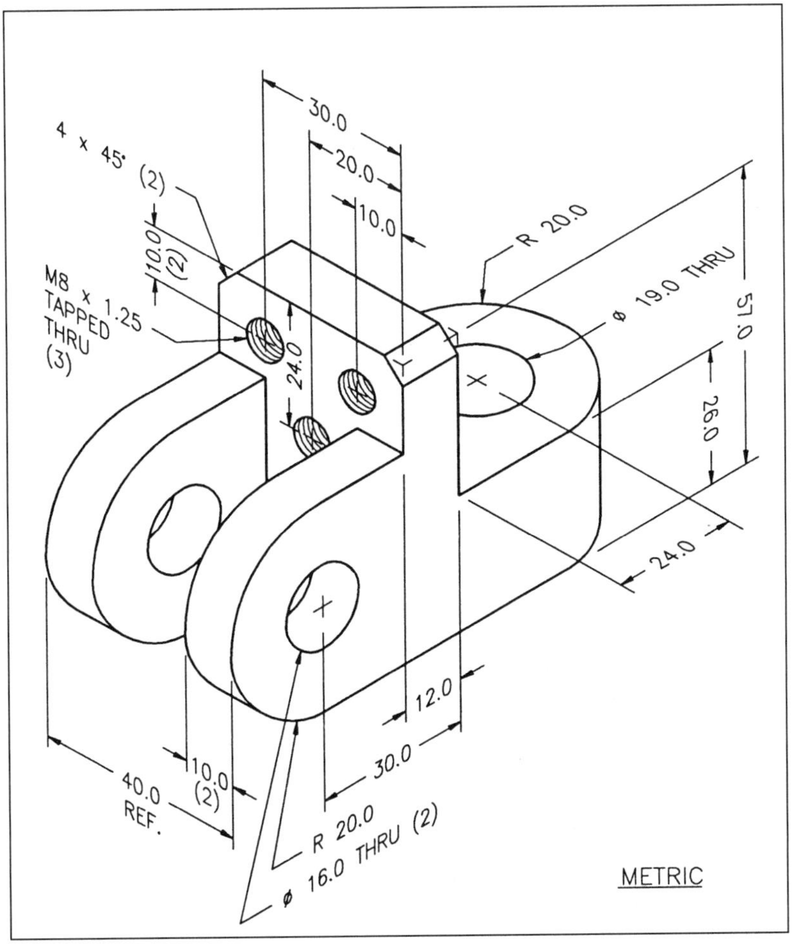

Figure 45-36: Swivel bracket exercise.

UCS Exercise—Dodecahedron

This exercise gives you practice in establishing, saving and restoring various X-Y construction planes (User Coordinate Systems) as well as combining 3D faces with invisible edges. The exercise refers to the face numbers and corner numbers shown in the drawing below.

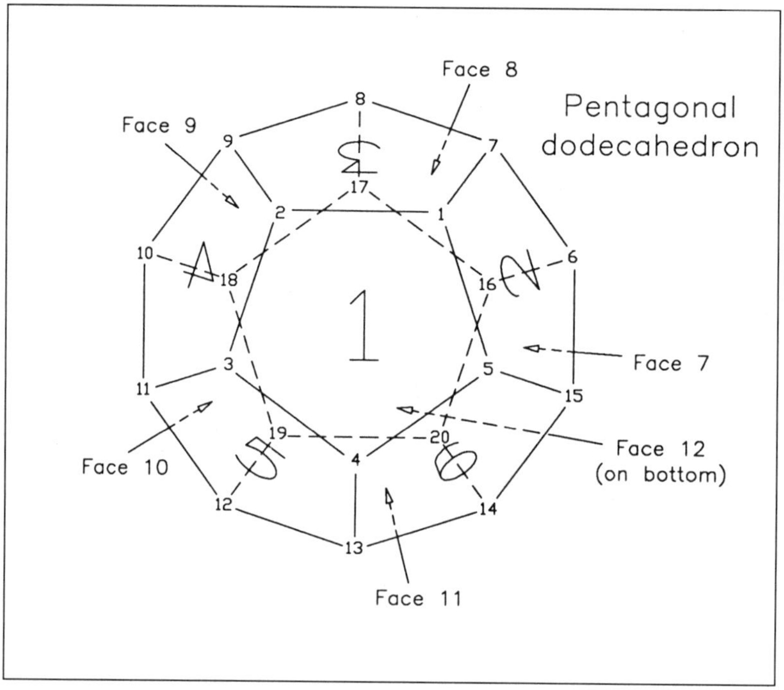

Figure 45-37: Dodecahedron exercise.

The overall strategy for drawing the dodecahedron is as follows: First, construct a pentagonal face from two 3D faces and make it into a block. Then, for each face of the dodecahedron, create an X-Y construction plane (UCS), insert the pentagonal face and draw the appropriate number.

Be sure to include the numbers on the faces. If you don't, you'll find the dodecahedron much harder to construct.

Before you begin, be sure that the Draw, Construct and Modify menu choices appear in the menu bar at the top of your screen. If they do not, enter menu at the command line and then select Acadfull (for "full menu").

Constructing Face 12

1. Start a new drawing. Name it DODECA.

Face 12 (the bottom face) is created first, then used as a pattern to construct the other 11 faces.

2. Set the lower-left corner of the limits at -3,-3 and the upper-right corner at 3,3. Then do a ZOOM All.

3. Hint: If you need to, use the UCSICON command to make the UCS icon visible. Refer to this icon often.

4. Use the POLYGON command (located under the Draw toolbar and pull-down menu) to create a five-sided polygon, centered at 0,0,0, inscribed, with a radius of 1. Enter the radius from the keyboard so the bottom of the polygon is horizontal. This polygon is temporary. It serves only to establish points 16, 17, 18, 19 and 20.

5. Make a 3dface located under Surfaces in the Draw toolbar and pull-down menu using points 18, 19, 20 and 16, with the edge between points 16 and 18 invisible. Osnap to the corners of the polygon. Then make another 3dface using points 16, 17 and 18, again with the edge between points 16 and 18 invisible.

6. Make a block called PENTA that includes these two 3dfaces, with the insertion point at 19. When you select the 3dfaces for the block, select them with the pick box rather than with a window, because you don't want the original polygon in the block. After the block disappears, redraw the screen so the original polygon reappears. Draw a reference line from point 19 to anywhere, then erase the polygon.

7. Reinsert PENTA at its original location and size (using the end of the reference line for the insertion point). Do not use oops. Then erase the reference line.

The rest of the dodecahedron is constructed on top of this face, in the positive Z direction (toward the viewer according to the present viewpoint). You're now looking at what will become the inside of face 12.

8. To place the number 12 on this surface so it appears correct from the outside of the dodecahedron, create an X-Y construction plane on the flip side of the current construction plane. Use the UCS command and the three-point option, as follows:

When prompted for the 0,0,0 point, select point 20.

When prompted for a point on the positive X axis, select point 19.

When prompted for the point on the positive Y plane, select point 17.

9. Use PLAN to switch to a plan view in this current UCS. Use the UCS command again to save this UCS under the name 12.

10. Place 12 in the middle of the surface. Use lines and arcs to create the numbers for each surface; text may not hide properly. Also, the lines and arcs forming the numbers may occasionally hide as though they were just behind the surface they were drawn on. Solution: Move these lines and arcs a short distance, perhaps .001, in the positive Z direction.

11. Return to the World Coordinate System (WCS) and establish a vpoint of 3,-5,2.

Constructing Face 11

12. To construct face 11, you must create a new UCS that forms the proper dihedral angle with face 12. We'll do this in two steps:

Shift the origin. Use UCS, select 0, then osnap to point 19 (the leftmost point on the screen).

Rotate the X-Y construction plane around the X axis of this present construction plane. Use UCS, select X, and enter an angle of **116.56505118**.

13. Use the UCS command again to save this UCS under the name 11.

14. Insert PENTA at 0,0,0, full scale, unrotated.

15. Draw number 11 on this face.

To help visualize the objects, use HIDE frequently throughout the rest of this exercise.

Constructing Faces 7, 8, 9 and 10

16. Return to WCS. If needed, establish a vpoint of 3,5,2.

17. Make a polar array of face 11 around 0,0 (five items, filling 360°, rotating the objects as they are copied).

18. If needed, do a ZOOM All, then use HIDE. Then use REGEN to prepare for the next step.

19. Establish and save a UCS for each of these four new faces. Then switch to the plan view of each of these UCSs and draw the appropriate numbers on each face.

Constructing the Top Half

20. In WCS, establish a viewpoint of 3,5,2. Use HIDE.

21. Begin with face 6. Create a UCS using points 13, 14 and 15.

22. Insert PENTA in this new UCS at 0,0,0, full scale, unrotated.

23. Switch to WCS and array the new surface around 0,0,0 to form surfaces 2, 3, 4 and 5.

24. Do a ZOOM All.

25. Finally, create a UCS on the very top and insert PENTA one more time for face 1.

26. Establish and save a UCS for each of these five new faces. Then draw the appropriate numbers on each face.

27. Return to WCS and view the dodecahedron from various viewpoints.

3D Objects

3D Surface Exercise

The object of this exercise is to use the Surface commands. They're located under the Draw toolbar and pull-down menu.

Before you begin, be sure that the Draw, Construct and Modify menu choices appear in the menu bar at the top of your screen. If they do not, enter menu at the command line and then select Acadfull (for "full menu").

Figure 45-38 shows a wedge, five cylinders and a hexagonal shape. Create the objects using the commands suggested in the figure.

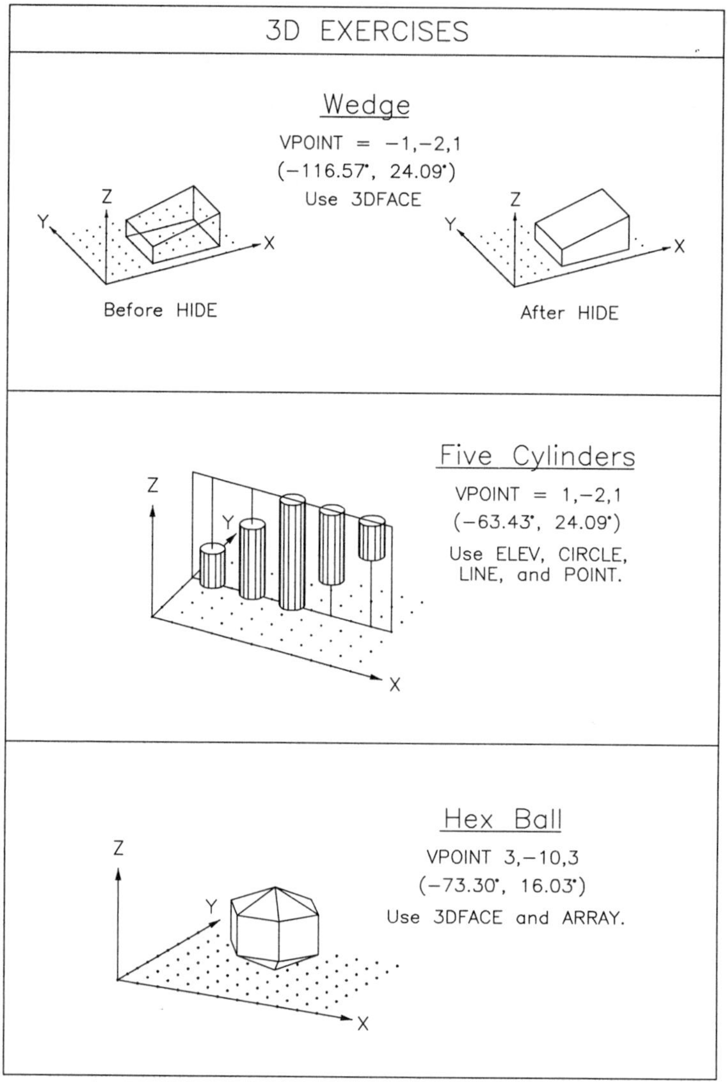

Figure 45-38: Surface modeling exercise.

3D Exercise

The object of this final exercise is to create 3D objects. You may use the Surface commands as needed.

Figure 45-39 shows a tree, a tepee and two pencils as 3D objects. Create the objects using the commands suggested in the figure.

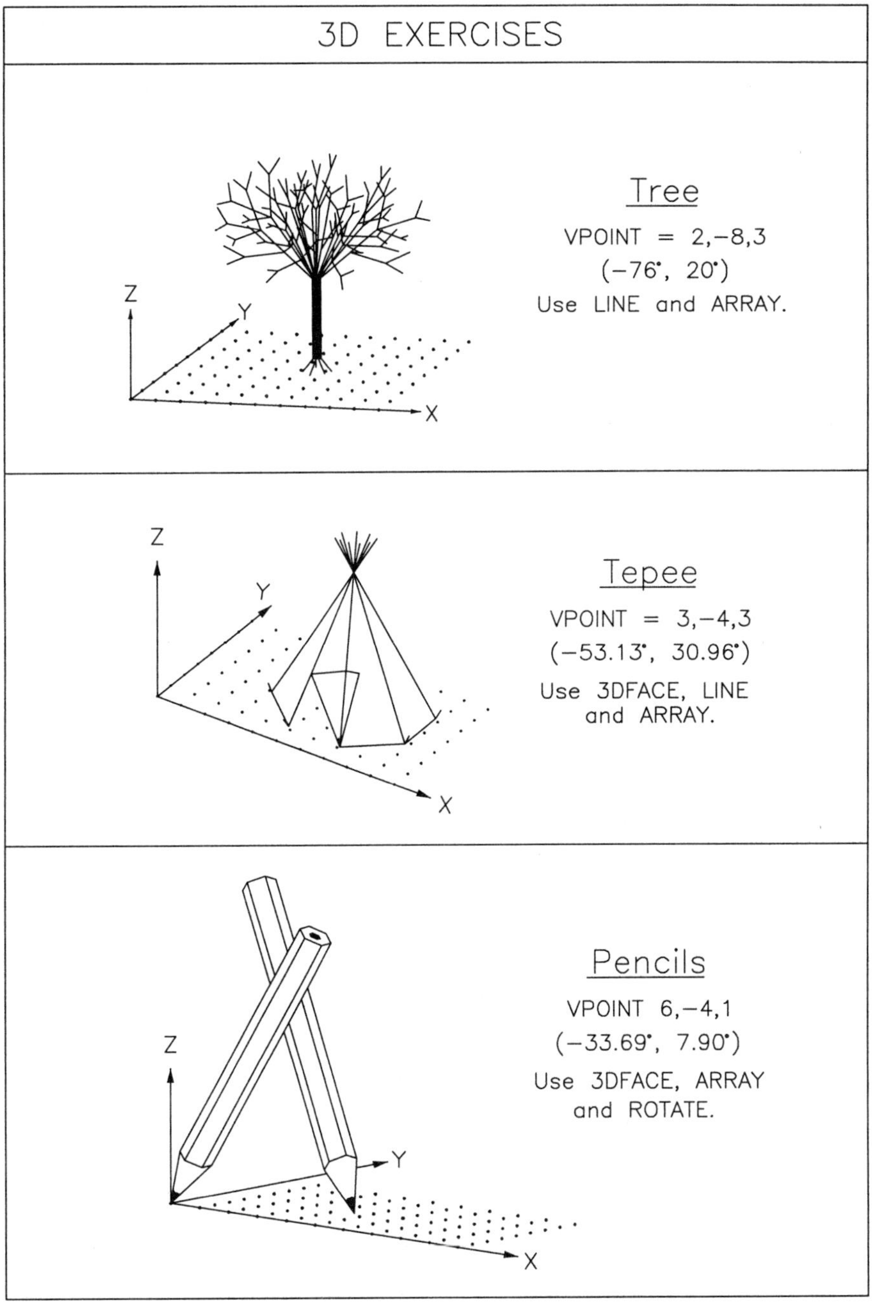

Figure 45-39: Surface modeling exercise.

SECTION IV

APPENDICES

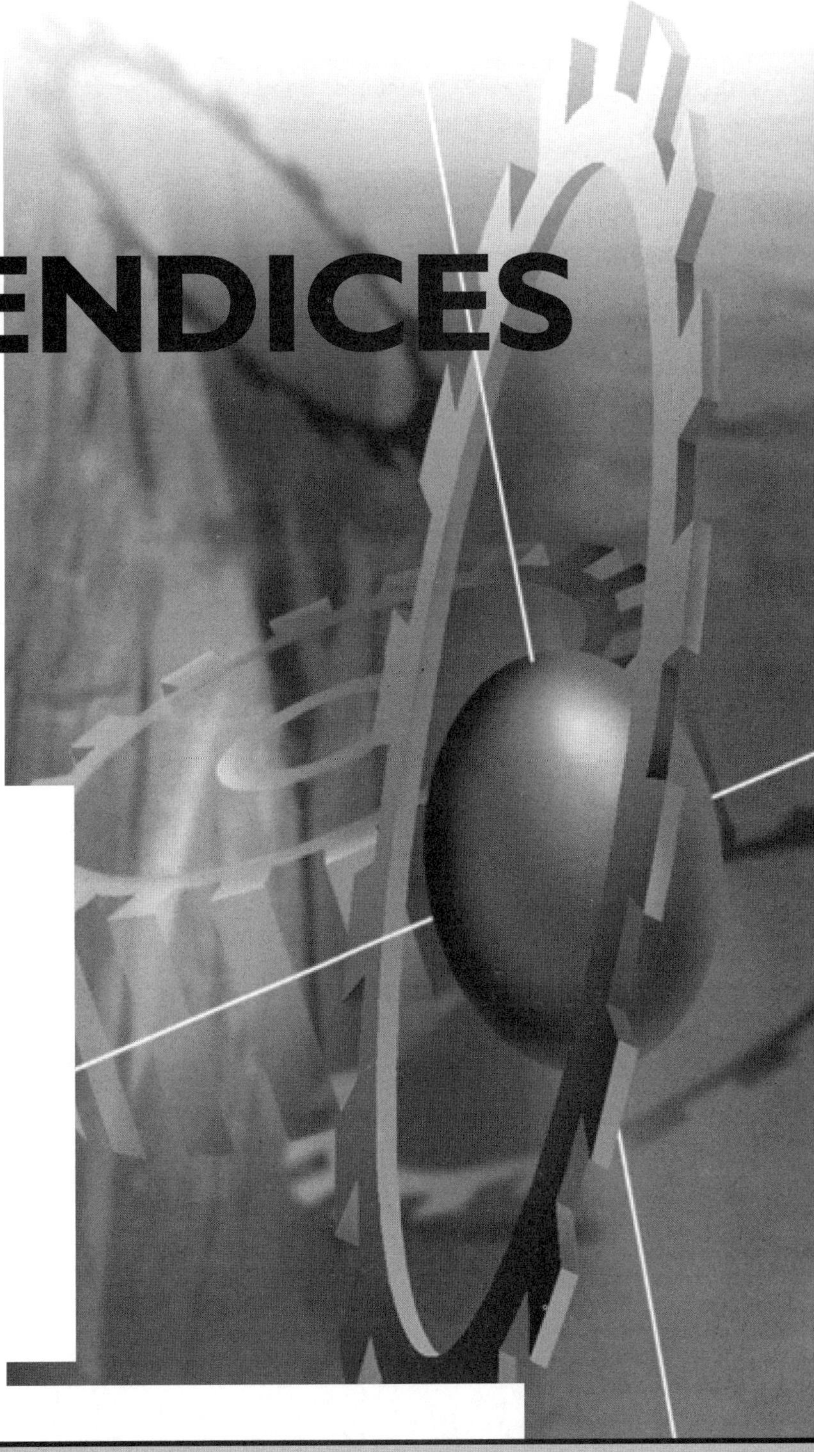

Custom Menu & Tablet Overlay

The sample menu and tablet overlay in this appendix are intended for use with a digitizing tablet that has an 11-inch-square active area and a four-button pointer. The menu is at the end of the appendix.

The menu is designed for use without a screen menu area. If you have displayed the screen menu, you can remove the screen menu area by using Configure Video Display on the Configuration menu.

The tablet overlay that corresponds to the ***TABLET sections of the menu is illustrated below. The overlay is purposely kept simple and limited to those commands used most frequently. By keeping the overlay uncluttered, you can easily spot the command you want and quickly memorize where commands are.

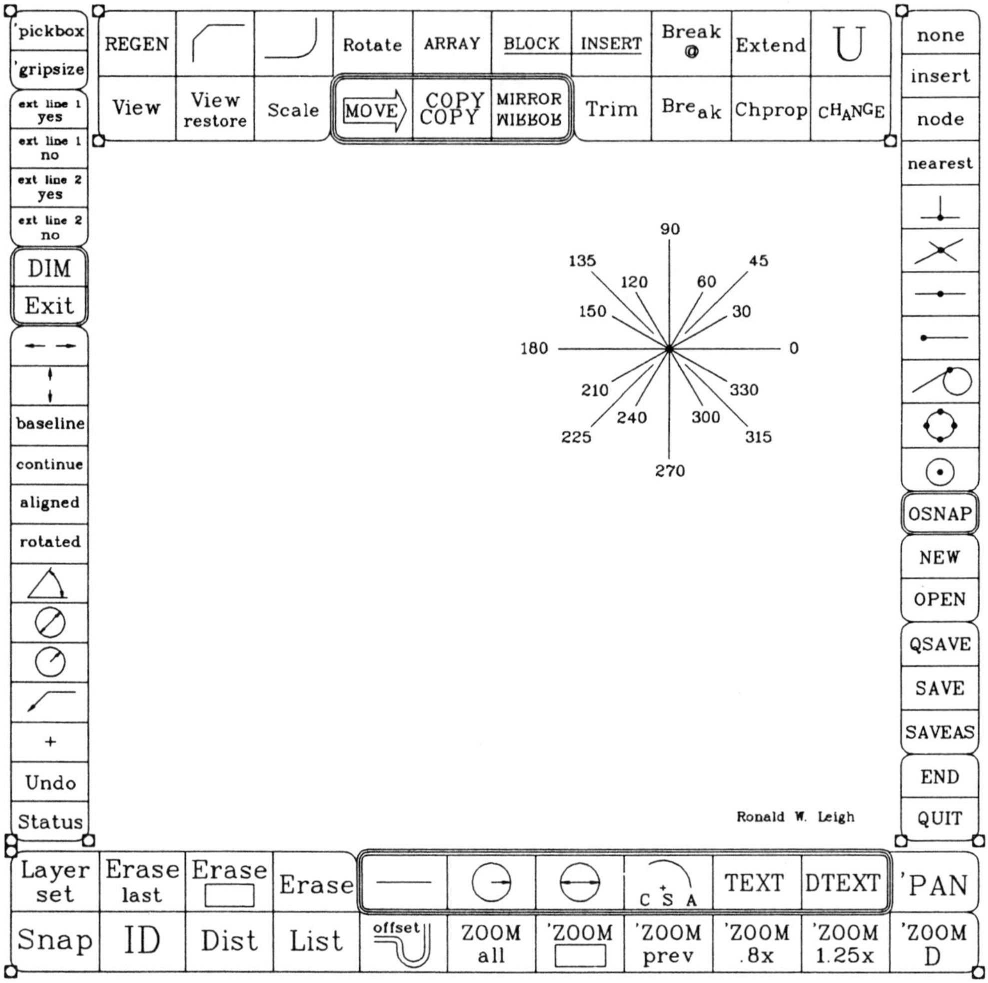

Figure A-1: Tablet overlay drawing.

Most AutoCAD commands are included, in alphabetical order, within the ***POP (pull-down) sections of the menu. The pull-down menus are illustrated in Figure A-2.

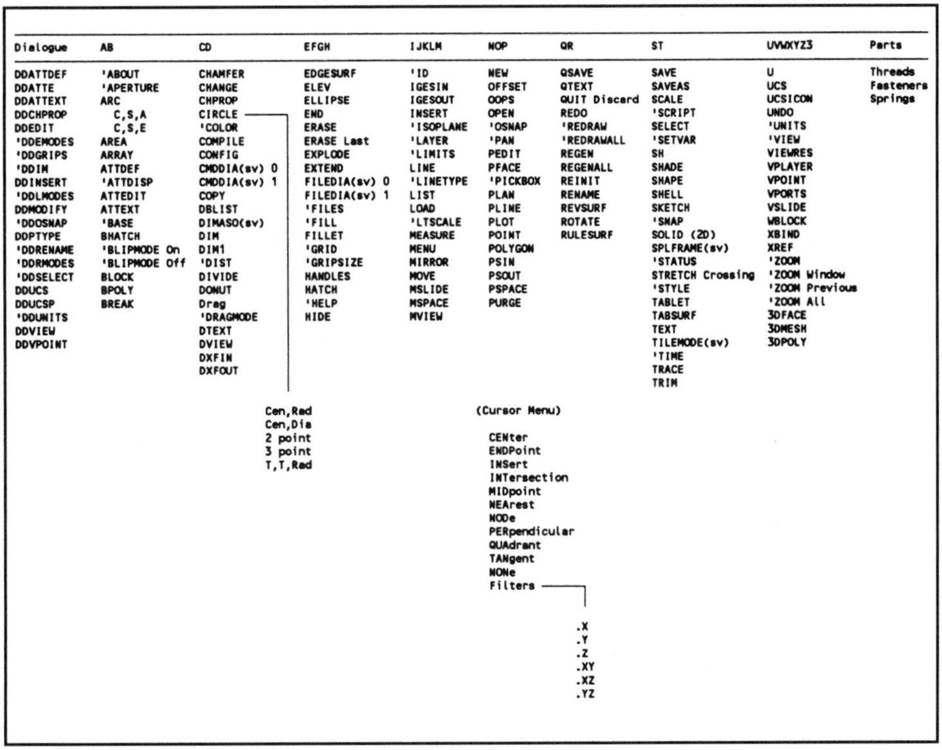

Figure A-2: Custom POP menu.

By comparing the above display with the menu listing at the end of this appendix, you'll notice that the ***POP sections of the menu illustrate the following features:

First, the ***POP1 section illustrates the use of dialog boxes, called by the 'dd commands.

Second, the ***POP0 section and the ***POP3 section illustrate cascading menus.

Third, the ***POP10 and ***ICON sections illustrate the use of icon menus. In ***POP10, only the Threads item is functional (no command portions are included for Fasteners or Springs). The Threads item makes THREADS the current icon menu and displays the icon menu shown below. In the **THREADS portion of the menu, thdsld1, thdsld2, etc., call slides for display in the icon menu, while (thd1), (thd2), etc., call various AutoLISP functions.

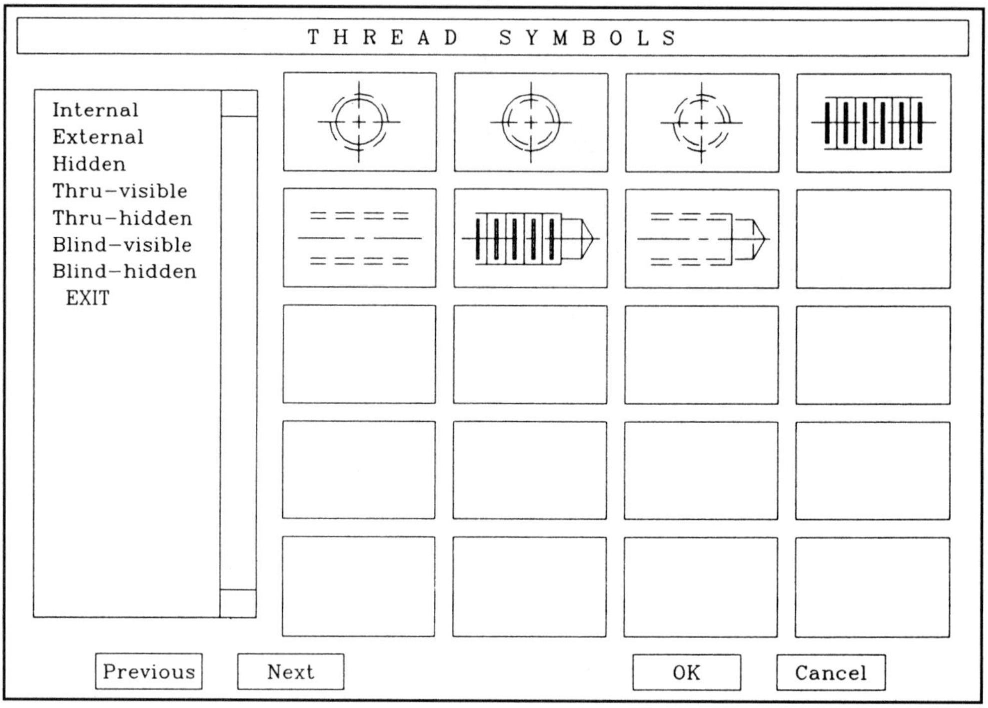

Figure A-3: Icon menu drawing.

The new custom POP menu file is listed below.

```
***BUTTONS
;
$P0=*
'redraw

***TABLET1
^C^Cregen
^C^Cchamfer
^C^Cfillet
^C^Crotate
^C^Carray
^C^Cblock
^C^Cinsert
^C^Cbreak \f \@
^C^Cextend
^C^Cu
^C^Cview
'view r
^C^Cscale
^C^Cmove
^C^Ccopy
^C^Cmirror
^C^Ctrim
^C^Cbreak
^C^Cchprop
^C^Cchange

***TABLET2
'pickbox
'gripsize
dimse1 off
dimse1 on
dimse2 off
dimse2 on
```

```
^C^Cdim
exit
hor
ver
bas
con
ali
rot
ang
dia
rad
lea
cen
und
sta

***TABLET3
non
ins
nod
nea
per
int
mid
endp
tan
qua
cen
^C^Cosnap
^C^Cnew
^C^Copen
^C^Cqsave
^C^Csave
^C^Csaveas
^C^Cend
^C^Cquit

***TABLET4
^C^Clayer s \;
^C^Cerase L ;
^C^Cerase box
^C^Cerase
^C^Cline
^C^Ccircle
^C^Ccircle \d
^C^Carc c \\a
^C^Ctext
^C^Cdtext
'pan
^C^Csnap
^C^Cid
^C^Cdist
^C^Clist
^C^Coffset
^C^Czoom a
'zoom w
'zoom p
'zoom .8x
'zoom 1.25x
'zoom d

***POP0
[Osnap]
[CENter]cen
[ENDPoint]endp
[INSert]ins
[INTersection]int
[MIDpoint]mid
[NEArest]nea
[NODe]nod
[PERpendicular]per
[QUAdrant]qua
[TANgent]tan
[NONe]non
[->Filters]
  [.X].X
  [.Y].Y
  [.Z].Z
  [.XY].XY
  [.XZ].XZ
  [<-.YZ].YZ

***POP1
[Dialogues]
[Attribute Define]^C^Cddattdef
[Attribute  Edit]^C^Cddatte
[Attribute Extract]^C^Cddattext
[Change Properties]^C^Cddchprop
```

```
[Text  Edit]^C^Cddedit
[Object Creation]'ddemodes
[Grip Modes]'ddgrips
[Dim Style]'ddim
[Insert Blocks]^C^Cddinsert
[Layer Control]'ddlmodes
[Linetypes]^C^Cddltype
[Modify]^C^Cddmodify
[OSNAP Tools]'ddosnap
[Point Type]^C^Cddptype
[Rename]'ddrename
[Drawing Aids]'ddrmodes
[Select]'ddselect
[UCS]^C^Cdducs
[UCS Presets]^C^Cdducsp
[UNITS]'ddunits
[Views]^C^Cddview
[View Points]^C^Cddvpoint

***POP2
[AB]
['ABOUT]'about
[ACISin]^C^Cacisin
[Align]^C^CAlign
[Aperture]'aperture
[Appload]^C^Cappload
[->Arcs]
   [Arc]^C^Carc
   [  C,S,A]^C^Carc c \\a
   [<-  C,S,E]^C^Carc c
[AREA]^C^Carea
[ARRAY]^C^Carray
[ASEadmin]^C^Caseadmin
[ASEexport]^C^Caseexport
[ASElinks]^C^Caselinks
[ATTDEF]^C^Cattdef
['ATTDISP]'attdisp
[ATTEDIT]^C^Cattedit
[ATTEXT]^C^Cattext
[AUDIT]^C^Caudit
['BASE]'base
[BHATCH]^C^Cbhatch
['BLIPMODE On]'blipmode on
['BLIPMODE Off]'blipmode off
[BLOCK]^C^Cblock
[BOUNDARY]^C^Cboundary
[BOX]^C^Cbox
[BPOLY]^C^Cbpoly
[BREAK]^C^Cbreak

***POP3
[CD]
[CALCULATOR]^C^C'cal
[CHAMFER]^C^Cchamfer
[CHANGE]^C^Cchange
[CHPROP]^C^Cchprop
[->CIRCLE]$P3=P3B $P3=*
  [Cen,Rad]^C^Ccircle $P3=P3A
  [Cen,Dia]^C^Ccircle \d $P3=P3A
  [2 point]^C^Ccircle 2p $P3=P3A
  [3 point]^C^Ccircle 3p $P3=P3A
  [<-T,T,Rad]^C^Ccircle ttr
$P3=P3A
['COLOR]'color
[COMPILE]^C^Ccompile
[CONFIG]^C^Cconfig
[CMDDIA(sv) 0]^C^Ccmddia 0
[CMDDIA(sv) 1]^C^Ccmddia 1
[COPY]^C^Ccopy
[CONE]^c^CCone
[CUBE^c^CCube
[CYLINDER]^C^CCylinder
[DBLIST]^C^Cdblist
[DISH]^c^cdish
[DIMASO(sv)]^C^Cdimaso
[->Dimensions]
   [DimAligned]^C^Cdimaligned
   [DimAngular]^C^Cdimangular
   [DimBaseline]^C^Cdimbaseline
   [DimCenter]^C^Cdimcenter
   [DimContinue]^C^Cdimcontinue
   [DimDiameter]^C^Cdimcontinue
   [DimEdit]^C^Cdimedit
   [DimLinear]^C^Cdimlinear
   [DimOrdinate]^C^Cdimordinate
   [DimOverride]^C^Cdimoverride
   [DimRadius]^C^Cdimradius
   [DimStyle]^C^Cdimstyle
```

```
   [<-DimTedit]^C^Cdimtedit
[’DIST]’dist
[DIVIDE]^C^Cdivide
[DOME^C^Cdome
[DONUT]^C^Cdonut
[Drag]drag
[’DRAGMODE]’dragmode
[DSVIEWER]^C^Cdsviewer
[DTEXT]^C^Cdtext
[DVIEW]^C^Cdview
[DXFIN]^C^Cdxfin
[DXFOUT]^C^Cdxfout

***POP4
[EFGH]
[EDGE]^C^Cedge
[EDGESURF]^C^Cedgesurf
[ELEV]^C^Celev
[ELLIPSE]^C^Cellipse
[END]^C^Cend
[ERASE]^C^Cerase
[ERASE Last]^C^Cerase L ;
[EXPLODE]^C^Cexplode
[EXTEND]^C^Cextend
[FILEDIA(sv) 0]^C^CFILEDIA 0
[FILEDIA(sv) 1]^C^CFILEDIA 1
[’FILES]’files
[’FILL]’fill
[FILLET]^C^Cfillet
[FILTER]^C^Cfilter
[’GRID]’grid
[’GRIPSIZE]’gripsize
[GROUP]^C^Cgroup
[HANDLES]^C^Chandles
[HATCH]^C^Chatch
[’HELP]’help
[HIDE]^C^Chide

***POP5
[IJKLM]
[’ID]’id
[INSERT]^C^Cinsert
[INSERTOBJ]^C^Cinsertobj
[INTERFERE]^C^Cinterfere
[INTERSECT]^C^Cintersect
[’ISOPLANE]’isoplane
[’LAYER]’layer
[LEADER]^C^Cleader
[LENGTHEN]^C^Clengthen
[LIGHT]^C^Clight
[’LIMITS]’limits
[LINE]^C^Cline
[’LINETYPE]’linetype
[LIST]^C^Clist
[LOAD]^C^Cload
[’LTSCALE]’ltscale
[MATLIB]^C^Cmatlib
[MEASURE]^C^Cmeasure
[MENU]^C^Cmenu
[MESH]^C^Cmesh
[MINSERT]^C^Cminsert
[->Multi-Lines]
   [MLEDIT]^C^Cmledit
   [MLINE]^C^Cmline
   [<-MLSTYLE]^C^Cmlstyle
[MIRROR]^C^Cmirror
[MOVE]^C^Cmove
[MSLIDE]^C^Cmslide
[MSPACE]^C^Cmspace
[->Multi-Text]
   [MTEXT]^C^Cmtext
   [<-MTPROP]^C^Cmtprop
[MVIEW]^C^Cmview
[MVSETUP]^C^Cmvsetup

***POP6
[NOP]
[NEW]^C^Cnew
[OFFSET]^C^Coffset
[OLElinks]^C^Colelinks
[OOPS]^C^Coops
[OPEN]^C^Copen
[’OSNAP]’osnap
[’PAN]’pan
[PEDIT]^C^Cpedit
[PFACE]^C^Cpface
[’PICKBOX]’pickbox
[PLAN]^C^Cplan
```

```
[PLINE]^C^Cpline
[PLOT]^C^Cplot
[POINT]^C^Cpoint
[POLYGON]^C^Cpolygon
[PREFERENCES]^C^Cpreferences
[PSFILL]^C^Cpsfill
[PSIN]^C^Cpsin
[PSOUT]^C^Cpsout
[PSPACE]^C^Cpspace
[PURGE]^C^Cpurge
[PYRAMID]^C^Cpyramid

***POP7
[QR]
[QSAVE]^C^Cqsave
[QTEXT]^C^Cqtext
[QUIT Discard]^C^Cquit d
[RAY]^C^Cray
[RCONFIG]^C^Crconfig
[REDO]^C^Credo
['REDRAW]'redraw
['REDRAWALL]'redrawall
[REGEN]^C^Cregen
[REGENALL]^C^Cregenall
[REGION]^C^Cregion
[REINIT]^C^Creinit
[RENAME]^C^Crename
[->RENDER]
   [RENDER]^c^crender
   [RENDSCR]^C^Crendscr
   [<-REPLAY]^C^Creplay
[REVSURF]^C^Crevsurf
[REVOLVE]^C^Crevolve
[RMAT]^C^Crmat
[ROTATE]^C^Crotate
[RPREF]^C^Crpref
[RULESURF]^C^Crulesurf

***POP8
[ST]
[SAVE]^C^Csave
[SAVEAS]^C^Csaveas
[SAVEIMG]^C^Csaveimg
[SCALE]^C^Cscale
[SCENE]^C^Cscene
['SCRIPT]'script
[SELECT]^C^Cselect
[SECTION]^C^Csection
['SETVAR]'setvar
[SHADE]^C^Cshade
[SHAPE]^C^Cshape
[SHELL]^C^Cshell
[SKETCH]^C^Csketch
[SLICE]^c^cslice
['SNAP]'snap
[SPHERE]^C^Csphere
[SPELL]^C^Cspell
[SPLINE]^C^Cspline
[SPLINEDIT]^C^Csplinedit
[STATS]^C^Cstats
['STATUS]'status
[STRETCH Crossing]^C^Cstretch c
['STYLE]'style
[SUBTRACT]^C^Csubtract
[TABLET]^C^Ctablet
[TABSURF]^C^Ctabsurf
[TBCONFIG]^C^Ctbconfig
[TEXT]^C^Ctext
[TIFFIN]^C^Ctiffin
[TILEMODE(sv)]^C^Ctilemode
['TIME]'time
[TOLERANCE]^C^Ctolerance
[TORUS]^C^Ctorus
[TRACE]^C^Ctrace
[TRIM]^C^Ctrim

***POP9
[UVWXYZ-3D]
[U]^C^Cu
[UCS]^C^Cucs
[UCSICON]^C^Cucsicon
[UNDO]^C^Cundo
[UNION]^C^Cunion
['UNITS]'units
['VIEW]'view
[VIEWRES]^C^Cviewres
[VPLAYER]^C^Cvplayer
[VPOINT]^C^Cvpoint
```

```
[VPORTS]^C^Cvports
[VSLIDE]^C^Cvslide
[WBLOCK]^C^Cwblock
[WEDGE]^C^Cwedge
[WMFOPTS]^C^Cwmfopts
[XBIND]^C^Cxbind
[XLINE]^C^Cxline
[XPLODE]^C^Cxplode
[XREF]^C^Cxref
['ZOOM]'zoom
['ZOOM Window]'zoom w
['ZOOM Previous]'zoom p
['ZOOM All]'zoom a
[3DARRAY]^C^C3darray
[3DFACE]^C^C3dface
[3DMESH]^C^C3dmesh
[3DPOLY]^C^C3dpoly
[3DSIN]^C^C3dsin
[3DSOUT]^C^C3dsout

***POP10
[Parts]
[Threads]$I=THREADS $I=*
[Fasteners]
[Springs]

***ICON
**THREADS
[T H R E A D  S Y M B O L S]
[thdsld1,Internal]^C^C(thd1)
[thdsld2,External]^C^C(thd2)
[thdsld3,Hidden]^C^C(thd3)
[thdsld4,Thru-visible]^C^C(thd4)
[thdsld5,Thru-hidden]^C^C(thd5)
[thdsld6,Blind-visible]^C^C(thd6)
thdsld7,Blind-hidden]^C^C(thd7)
```

Extracting Attributes & Post-processing Attribute Files

This appendix shows how to extract attribute information from a drawing and how to convert an attribute file into a parts list. The process of producing a parts list, or bill of materials, is diagrammed below. See Chapter 37 for a discussion of the ATTDEF, ATTDISP, ATTEDIT and ATTEXT commands.

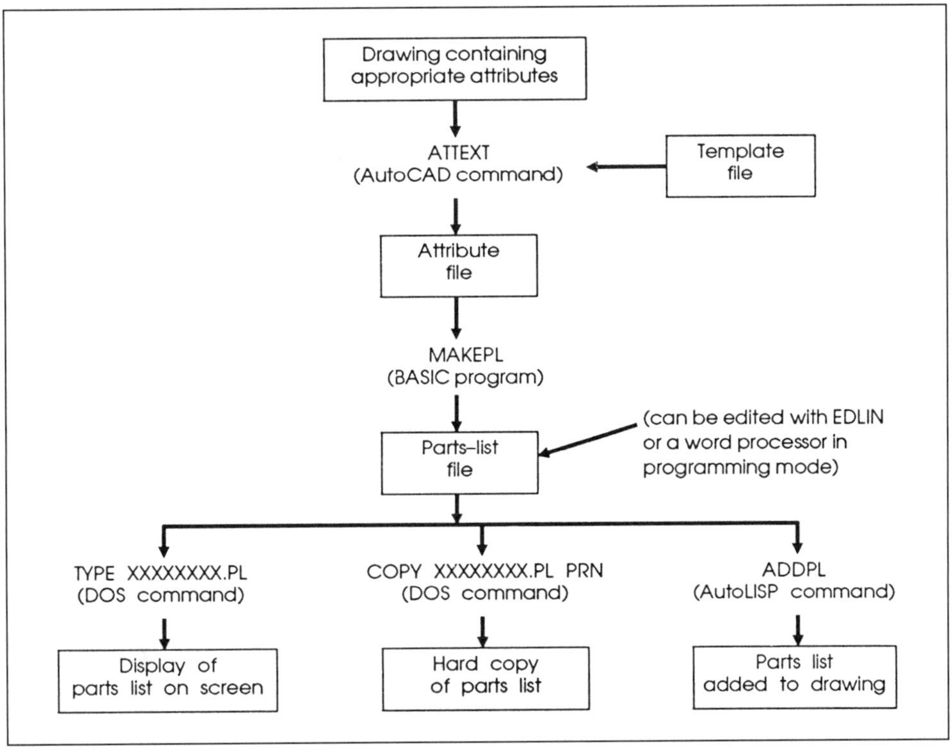

Figure B-1: Attribute processing flow chart.

Following these steps can ensure that assembly drawings and parts lists match. It can also speed up producing and revising parts lists, especially if predrawn blocks with the appropriate attributes already exist in a parts library.

The next two figures provide plottings of an outlet box. The drawing file is named OUTLETBX.DWG. The first plotting shows the drawing with its attributes (ATTDISP is on) ready for extraction and post-processing. When the drawing is at this stage it's represented by the top box in the diagram above. The second plotting shows the completed drawing (ATTDISP is off).

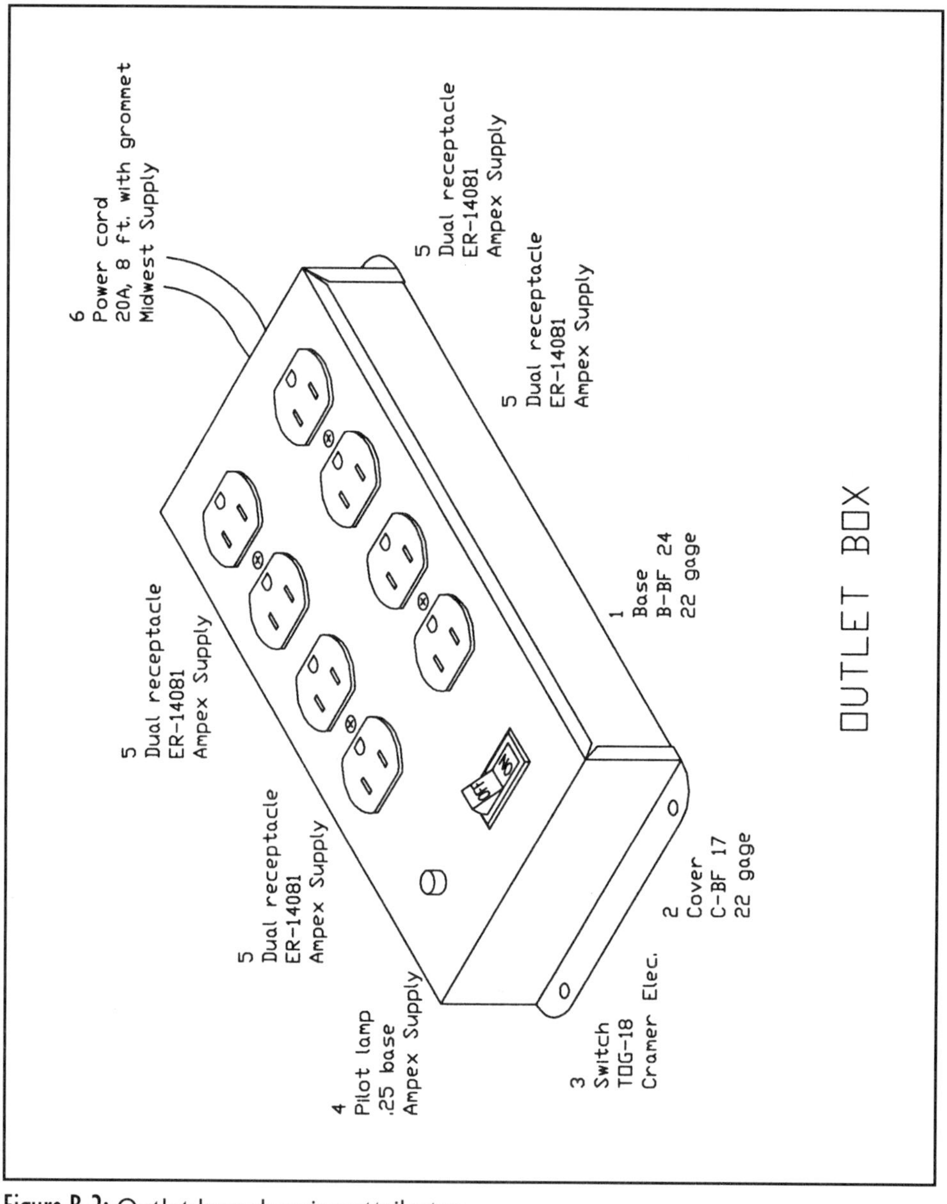

Figure B-2: Outlet box showing attributes.

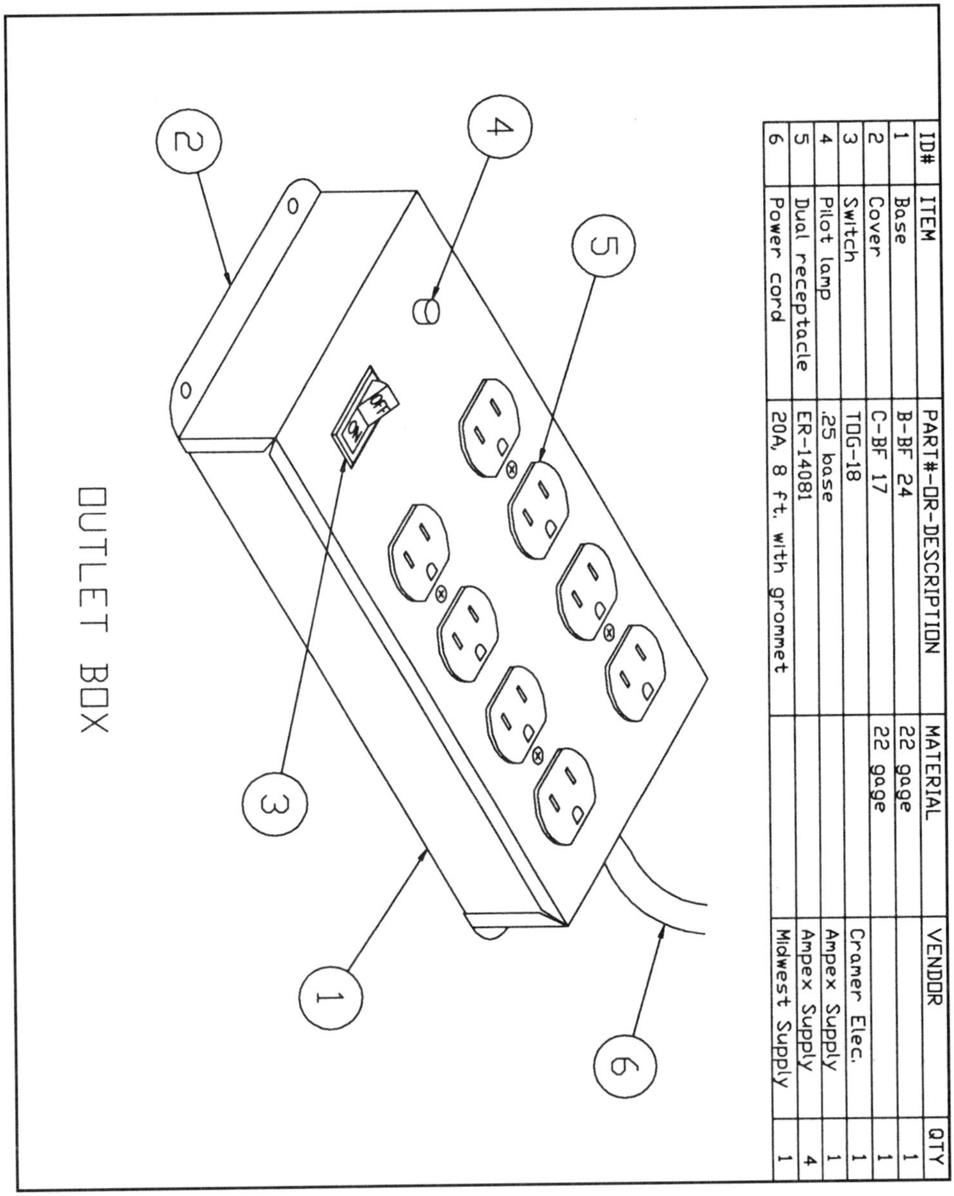

Figure B-3: Completed outlet box.

There are six blocks in the drawing: base, cover, switch, pilot, cord and recep ("recep" is the block name of the dual receptacle and appears four times in the drawing). Each block has several attributes (tags). For example, the switch block has these: ID#, ITEM, PART#-OR-DESCRIPTION and VENDOR. The cover block has these: ID#, ITEM, PART#-OR-DESCRIPTION and MATERIAL.

Attributes can be created so that they're large enough to read without zooming in. This often means that they have to extend outside the geometry of the block with which they're associated. There's no problem if they overlap other geometry, even other attributes, because they can be turned off with the ATTDISP command. In the sample drawing, some of the attributes have been moved from their original positions with the ATTEDIT command for the sake of clarity.

Another approach is to make attributes so small that several of them will fit entirely inside the associated geometry. In this case it's usually necessary to zoom in on the block or part of the block to view or edit the attributes.

You extract attribute information with the ATTEXT command. In this example, the extract file is in the SDF format. You must create a template file before using the ATTEXT command. The following file, named ATTTEMP.TXT, can be created with EDLIN or a word processor in programming mode. It's designed to extract up to five attributes from each block. A block can have either more or fewer attributes than those listed below.

```
ID#                        C003000
ITEM                       C015000
PART#—OR—DESCRIPTION       C023000
MATERIAL                   C014000
VENDOR                     C014000
```

ID# stands for identification number (balloon number).

Later we'll use a BASIC language program to post-process the attribute file that's extracted using the above template file. In order for that BASIC program to operate correctly, each block must have the ID# attribute (tag).

Notice that the column widths in the file are 3, 15, 23, 14 and 14, a total of 69 characters.

After all the blocks have been inserted in the drawing with the appropriate information in the attributes, and after the template file has been created, we can extract the attribute information and place it in a file. To do so, use the ATTEXT command and enter the following information when prompted:

`CDF, SDF, or DXF?`	Enter **s** (for SDF format file).
`Template file:`	Enter **attemp**.
`Extract file name:`	Enter **outletbx**.

This will produce an SDF format (random access) attribute file named OUTLETBX.TXT which, when typed on the screen, looks like this (order of the lines may vary):

```
5   Dual receptacle ER-14081                             Ampex Supply
5   Dual receptacle ER-14081                             Ampex Supply
5   Dual receptacle ER-14081                             Ampex Supply
5   Dual receptacle ER-1408                              Ampex Supply
4   Pilot lamp      25 base                              Ampex Supply
    Switch          TOG-18                               Cramer Elec.
6   Power cord      20A, 8 ft.                           Midwest Supply
                    with grommet
1   Base            B-BF 24             22 gage
2   Cover           C-BF 17             22 gage
```

For this file to become an acceptable parts list file, it must be modified (post-processed) as follows:

1) Sort lines according to ID number.

2) Combine identical lines.

3) Count identical lines so the quantity can be included.

4) Put spaces between the columns.

5) Add column headings.

6) Add a header line to identify the parts list file.

You can use the BASIC program below to make these modifications. It's intentionally written short and simple so you can alter it to suit your needs. This program is designed to work with extract files that are in SDF format and that are created using the ATTTEMP.TXT template file given earlier. If a different format or a different template file is used, you must adjust the BASIC program accordingly. The program will handle an extract file of up to 1,000 lines.

```
100 | MAKEPL.BAS, written by R.W. Leigh.  Ventana Press
200 | Reads an SDF format attribute file (XXXXXXXX.txt), sorts the
300 | file, combines identical lines, and creates a new parts list
400 | file (XXXXXXXX.PL)
130 | Variables:
140 | C counter for identical lines  L$ line of file in buffer
150 | COMP no. of comparisons        L$ (I) array of lines in files
160 | CR$ carriage return/Line feed  MA$ MATERIAL  tag info.
170 | F$ file name                  NLC new line count
180 | F1$ file name with .TXT       PASS no. of passes
190 | F2$ file name with .PL        PA$ PART#-OR-DESCRIPTION tag info
200 | HL$ header line               QU$ quantity
210 | I index                       SF swap flag
220 | ID$ ID# tag info.       TEXT$ first 4 lines/parts list file
230 | IT$ ITEM tag info.      VE$ vendor tag info
240 | LC line count
250 |———GET ATTRIBUTE FILE————
260 SCREEN 0 : WIDTH 80 : KEY OFF : DEFINT C,I,L,N,P,S : DIM L$(1000)
270 INPUT "Name of SDF format attribute file (do not include extension): ",F$
280 PRINT "Header to identify parts list file (up to 78 char.,enter below):"
290 LINE INPUT "",HL$
300 F1$ = F$ + ".TXT" : F2$ = F$ + ".PL"
310 OPEN F1$ AS 1 LEN = 71 : FIELD 1, 69 AS L$ : I = 0
320 PRINT "Getting attribute file " F1$
330 I = I + 1 : GET 1
340 IF ASC(L$) > 31 THEN L$(I) = L$ : GOTO 330
350 CLOSE 1 : LC = I - 1
360 |———SORT ATTRIBUTE FILE————
370 PRINT "Sorting "; : COMP = LC
380 FOR PASS = 1 TO LC - 1
390 COMP = COMP - 1 : SF = 0
400 FOR I = 1 TO COMP
410 IF L$(I) > L$(I+1) THEN SWAP L$(I+1) : SF = 1
420 NEXT I : PRINT "*";
430 IF SF = 0 THEN PASS = LC - 1
440 NEXT PASS : PRINT
450 |—COMBINE & COUNT IDENTICAL LINES, CREATE PARTS LIST FILE—
460 PRINT "Combining/counting/filing ":
470 OPEN F2$ AS 1 LEN=80 : FIELD 1, 78 AS TEXT$,2 AS CR$
480 LSET TEXTS = HL$ : LSET CR$ = CHR$(13)+CHR$(10) : PUT 1
490 LSET TEXTS = "" : PUT 1
500 LSET TEXTS = "ID#  ITEM   PART#-OR-DESCRIPTION   MATERIAL  VEN DOR   QTY" : PUT 1
510  LSET TEXTS = STRING$(78.45) : PUT 1
520 FIELD 1, 4 AS ID$,16 AS IT$,24 AS PA$,15 AS MA$,15 AS VE$,4 AS QU$,2 AS CR$
530 C = 1 : NLC = 0
540 FOR I = 1 TO LC
550 IF L$(I) = LS(I+1) THEN C = C + 1 : GOTO 600
560 LSET ID$ = MID$(L$(I),1,3) : LSET IT$ = MID$(L$(I),4,15
570 LSET PA$ = MID$(L$(I),19,23) : LSET MA$ = MID$(L$(I),42,14
580 LSET VE$ = MID$(L$(I),56,14) : RSET QU$ = STR$(C)
590 PUT 1 : NLC = NLC + 1 : C = 1 :PRINT "*";
600 NEXT I : CLOSE 1 : PRINT
610 PRINT NLC "Lines written to file " f2$
620 END
```

To try the program, enter **basic** from the System prompt, then enter each line. Lines 100-240 are merely documentation and need not be entered for the program to run. Then save the program by entering **save "makepl"** (short for MAKE PARTS LIST). This saves the program in the file MAKEPL.BAS. To return to the System prompt, enter **system**.

To run MAKEPL.BAS from the System prompt, enter **basic makepl**. When the program prompts for the name of the attribute extract file, enter **outletbx**. The program will also prompt for a header line to identify the parts list file. The program will produce a file named OUTLETBX.PL, similar to the one shown below. To return to the System prompt, enter **system**.

```
Webber National Products, Job No. 85227B, KRV, 11-91
ID# ITEM             PART#-OR-DESCRIPTION MATERIAL VENDOR        QTY
1   Base             B-BF 24              22 gage                1
2   Cover            C-BF 17              22 gage                1
3   Switch           TOG-18                        Cramer Elec.  1
4   Pilot lamp       .25 base                      Ampex Supply  1
5   Dual receptacle  ER-14081                      Ampex Supply  4
6   Power cord       20A, 8 ft. with grommet       Midwest Supply1
```

You can display this OUTLETBX.PL file on the screen by entering

type outletbx.pl

or send it to the printer by entering

copy outletbx.pl prn

It's a regular ASCII text file, so you can edit it with the Windows Notepad or the DOS EDIT. If you edit this file, don't change its basic structure, or the AutoLISP program described below won't work properly.

The AutoLISP program listed below is called ADDPL.LSP and is used inside AutoCAD to add the parts list to the drawing, as illustrated in the second plotting earlier in this appendix. The program is designed to work only with parts list files created by the MAKEPL.BAS program.

The ADDPL program prompts for the name of the parts list file, then the location of the lower right or upper right corner of the parts list box, then the distance between lines. (Text height is automatically set at one-half the distance between lines.) The program then draws the outline of the parts list box and asks if you want to continue, or if you want to specify a new location and line spacing.

The program doesn't use the header line from the file. That sort of information would usually appear in the title block of the drawing. It ignores the blank line and line of dashes, since the remaining information is placed in a typical parts list box.

```
c:addpl—Add parts list. Adds a parts list file
; that was produced by MAKEPL.BAS to a drawing.
; Variables:
; c Y or N for continuation    n Number of lines
; f Filename            p Starting corner of parts list box
; fr File descriptor       s Line spacing
; h Height of text         x1-x7,y1,y2 Coords.
; line Line from file
(defun c:addpl (/ c f fr h line n p s x1 x2 x3 x4 x5 x6 x7 y1 y2)
    (princ "\n** This program works only with files created with
MAKEPL.BAS **")
    (princ "\n** Current text style should have a variable
height. **")
    (pl-sizefile) (setq c "N") (setvar "cmdecho" 0)
    (while (= c "N") (pl-getbox))
    (pl-lines-text)
    (setvar "blipmode" 1) (setvar "cmdecho" 1)
    (princ))
(defun pl-sizefile ()
    (while (= "" (setq f (strcase
         (getstring "\nName of parts list file (w/o extension):
")))))
    (setq f (strcat f ".PL") fr (open f "r") n -3)
    (while (read-line fr) (setq n (1+ n)))
    (close fr) (terpri) (princ n) (princ " lines in ")(princ f))
(defun pl-getbox ()
    (setq p (getpoint "\nUpper right or lower right corner of
parts list box: ")
         s (getreal "\nDistance between lines (pos. up, neg.
down): ")
         h (abs (/ s 2.0)))
    (setvar "blipmode" 0)
    (setq x7 (car p) x1 ( - x7 (* 84 h)) x2 (+ x1 (* 5 h)) x3 (+
x1 (* 22 h))
    x4 (+ x1 (* 47 h)) x5 (+ x1 (* 63 h)) x6 (+ x1 (* 79 h)))
    (setq y1 (cadr p) y2 (+ y1 (* n s)))
    (command "line" p (list x7 y2) (list x1 y2) (list x1 y1) "c")
    (command "zoom" "c" (list (/ (+ x1 x7) 2.0) (/ (+ y1 y2)
2.0))
    (max (* 1.5 ( -x7 x1)) (* 2.0 (abs ( -y2 y1)))))
    (while (not (member (setq c (strcase
         (getstring "\nContinue? (Y/N): "))) (list "Y" "N"))))
    (if (= c "N") (progn
         (command "erase" "L" "" "erase" "L" "" "erase" "L" ""
"erase" "L" "")
         (setvar "blipmode" 1))))
(defun pl-lines-text ()
    (command "array" "l" "" "r" n 1 s)
    (command "line" (list x2 y1) (list x2 y2) ""
```

```
                    "line" (list x3 y1) (list x3 y2) ""
                    "line" (list x4 y1) (list x4 y2) ""
                    "line" (list x5 y1) (list x5 y2) ""
                    "line" (list x6 y1) (list x6 y2) "")
    (setq x1 (+ x1 h) x2 (+ x2 h) x3 (+ x3 h)
        x4 (+ x4 h) x5 (+ x5 h) x6 (+ x6 h)
        y1 ( -(+ y1 (/ s 2.0)) (/ h 2.0)))
    (setq fr (open f "r"))
    (read-line fr) (read-line fr) (pl-printline) (read-line fr)
    (repeat (1<196> n) (pl-printline)))
(defun pl-printline ()
    (setq line (read-line fr))
    (command "text" (list x1 y1) h 0 (substr line 1 3)
                "text" (list x2 y1) h 0 (substr line 5 15)
                "text" (list x3 y1) h 0 (substr line 21 23)
                "text" (list x4 y1) h 0 (substr line 45 14)
                "text" (list x5 y1) h 0 (substr line 60 14)
                "text" (list x6 y1) h 0 (substr line 76 3))
(setq y1 (+ y1 s)))
```

Using DXFIX

Dxfix is a means of converting Release 13 files downward to Release 10, etc. You will need to locate the dxf files in your \ACADR13\COMMON \SUPPORT directory.

Early shipping versions of AutoCAD Release 13 contained a bug in the dxf translators that prevented files from being exchanged between Release 13 and earlier versions. By the time you read this book, chances are that the bug has been fixed. This appendix describes how the dxf translation routine should work.

About DXFIX

Dxfix is a dxf translator. It is an open architecture (FORTH-based) language toolkit used for dxf files; being aptly named ATLAST. (The full name is Autodesk Threaded Language Application System Toolkit.)

One of the problems with using dxfix is that drawing information will be lost because of differences between the different releases (binary drawing file creation) and new updated commands in them. Dxfix is mainly a means of deleting new commands and new dxf tables or entities. A dxf file consists of certain levels within the following sections:

HEADER

TABLES (This section has subsections LTYPE, LAYER, STYLE.)

BLOCKS

ENTITIES

EOF

The open architecture of dxfix can be programmed to let you translate drawings into AutoCAD versions earlier than Release 10. For example, you can translate

Release 13 to Release 11	or	Release 13 to Release 10	or
Release 13 to Release 9	or	Release 13 to Release 2.6, etc.	

If you know your client is using a version of AutoCAD earlier than Release 9 and a dxf translation will be required, consider how to input your drawing in Release 13.

Input the drawing to be dxf translated as follows:

1. Keep the text left-justified. (Do not use MCenter option.)
2. Do not use or create any Dimstyles. (Keep all text standard.)
3. Do not create any polyface mesh. (If you do create polyface mesh you must explode it before creating the dxf file in Release 13.)
4. Do not nest any blocks. (Do not have a block within a block.)
5. Do not use Z-coordinates. (Use simple X and Y input.)

Using DXFIX to Convert Drawings

Use dxfix as follows:

First, complete the drawing, following the guidelines listed above. Keep everything standard. If you're using Release 13 run the AUDIT command in your drawing file and check it for errors.

Second, as you use the DXFOUT command, keep the default number of binary places as 6. Do not change the number.

Third, copy the DXFIX.EXE and DXFIX.DXT files into your AutoCAD drawing directory.

Finally, run the DXFIX translator file. If you're using Release 13, this is run as described in the following examples.

Examples

For the first example. I'll assume you've created a file called: TEST13.DXF

Run the DXFIX command input/output at the DOS prompt—all on one line:

```
DXFIX XXXinput file YYYoutput file
```

XXX is the name of the input file, and YYY the name of the output file.

Here's a second example of a file called TEST13.DXF that has to be converted. Notice on the line below you don't need to put the .dxf extension in.

At the DOS prompt type:

```
DXFIX TEST13 TEST11
```

As an alternative you could use the .dxf extension. Type:

```
DXFIX TEST13.DXF TEST10.DXF
```

In this last example you'll force DXFIX into a specific ASCII mode with six binary characters as follows.

At the DOS prompt, type:

```
DXFIX -a6 TEST13 TEST10
```

Using DXFIN to Insert a DXF File Into AutoCAD

If your client has asked you for a fixed dxf file and uses an earlier AutoCAD release, fax the person the following advice on how to insert the dxf file correctly.

1. DXFIX the file (as described earlier).

2. If you are using Release 9, 10 or 11, as you start AutoCAD you enter a menu screen.

    Press 1 to start a new drawing.

    Name the new drawing and add an equals sign to the end.

    For example, the name of your dxf file is TEST10.

    Therefore, after pressing 1 to start a new drawing you'll name it:

    ```
    TEST10=
    ```

    The purpose of the equals sign without any statement after it is to disallow any prototype drawing interference. Thus the = sign prevents any prototype drawing from entering the program.

3. Immediately upon entering the the drawing editor Graphics Screen, enter DXFIN and provide the name of the dxf file you wish to use.

4. Save the file.

Metric/English Conversions

If you know the number of British/U.S. units and want to find the number of metric units:

Millimeters = inches x 25.4 (exact)

Centimeters = inches x 2.54 (exact)

Meters = feet x .3048 (exact)

Meters = yards x .9144 (exact)

Kilometers = miles x 1.609344 (exact)

Square centimeters = sq. inches x 6.4516 (exact)

Square meters = sq. feet x .092903

Square meters = sq. yards x .836127

Square kilometers = sq. miles x 2.5900

Hectares = acres x .404686

Cubic centimeters = cubic inches x 16.3871

Cubic meters = cubic feet x .0283168

Cubic meters = cubic yards x .764555

Grams = ounces x 28.3495

Kilograms = pounds x .453592

Metric tons = tons (short tons) x .907185

Milliliters = fluid ounces x 29.5735

Liters = quarts x .946353

Liters = gallons x 3.78541

Meters/second = miles/hour x .44704 (exact)

$$\text{Centigrade} = \frac{5}{9}\ \text{Fahrenheit} - 32$$

If you know the number of metric units and want to find the number of British/U.S. units:

Inches = millimeters x .0393701

Inches = centimeters x .393701

Feet = meters x 3.28084

Yards = meters x 1.09361

Miles = kilometers x .621371

Square inches = sq. centimeters x .15500

Square feet = sq. meters x 10.7639

Square yards = sq. meters x 1.1960

Square miles = sq. kilometers x .38614

Acres = hectares x 2.47105

Cubic inches = cubic centimeters x .06102

Cubic feet = cubic meters x 35.3147

Cubic yards = cubic meters x 1.30795

Ounces = grams x .035274

Pounds = kilograms x 2.20462

Tons (short tons) = metric tons x 1.10231

Fluid ounces = milliliters x .033814

Quarts = liters x 1.05669

Gallons = liters x .264172

Miles/hour = meters/second x 2.23694

$$\text{Fahrenheit} = \frac{9}{5}\ \text{Centigrade} + 32$$

Estimating Your AutoCAD Skills

Name _______________________ Date___________ Latest version _____

Place an X in the box that represents your level for each skill.

LEVELS

1 Partial Familiarity Level—I've tried this skill (or some aspects of it) a few times with fair success.

2 Mastery Level—I've used most aspects of this skill many times with good success.

3 Teacher Level—I could demonstrate and explain all aspects of this skill.

SKILLS **Level:**	**1**	**2**	**3**
DOS commands and subdirectories			
Using the keyboard to enter AutoCAD commands			
Using the screen menu & pull-down menus to enter commands			
Using a tablet overlay to enter AutoCAD commands			
Using dialog boxes			
Rendering drawings			
LIMITS			
GRID			
POINT			
Relative rectangular & relative polar coordinates			
SNAP including rotation & style			
SETVAR various system variables (PDMODE, PICKBOX, etc.)			
LINE			
Manipulating SNAP, GRID, and ORTHO from function keys			
NEW, OPEN, QSAVE, SAVE, END, QUIT			
UNITS			
Interactive item selection			
ERASE, OOPS			
Using the File Utility menu			
STATUS			

SKILLS Level:	1	2	3
DRAGMODE			
ARC			
ZOOM, PAN, VIEW and VIEWRES			
OSNAP, APERTURE			
ID, DIST, LIST, DBLIST			
AREA			
MOVE, COPY			
MIRROR			
OFFSET			
FILLET, CHAMFER			
ROTATE, SCALE			
U, UNDO, REDO			
GRIPS			
TEXT, DTEXT, MTEXT			
STYLE using various text fonts			
Using prototype drawings			
CONFIG			
PLOT			
BREAK, TRIM, EXTEND			
CHANGE			
STRETCH			
DIVIDE, MEASURE			
TRACE, SOLID, FILL			
LAYER			
COLOR, LINETYPE, LTSCALE			
ARRAY			
POLYGON, ELLIPSE			
BLOCK, INSERT, EXPLODE, WBLOCK, BASE			
PURGE			
xrefs			
DIM (linear dimensions)			
DIM (all other dimension types and dimensioning variables)			
Dimension styles			
Editing dimensions			
Drawing/plotting at various scales and using metric units			
HATCH			
BHATCH, BOUNDARY			

SKILLS Level:	1	2	3
TABLET			
SKETCH			
SHELL, Advanced DOS commands, etc.			
MSLIDE, VSLIDE, and using the SLIDELIB program			
PLINE, PEDIT, DONUT			
Isometric drawings			
User Coordinate Systems			
Cylindrical and Spherical coordinates			
VPOINT, PLAN, HIDE			
TILEMODE and Paper Space vs. Model Space			
Wireframe modeling			
3DFACE, 3DPOLY, PFACE			
Surface Modeling			
DVIEW			
Using point filters			
Meshes			
Solid Modeling construction			
Solid Modeling analysis			
Extracting 2D views from solids			
Shading and Rendering			
SCENEs			
Attributes, ATTDEF, ATTDISP, ATTEDIT, ATTEXT using template file			
Custom linetypes			
LOAD, SHAPE			
Creating custom shapes			
MENU and creating custom screen, tablet and pull-down menus			
DXFIN, DXFOUT, IGESIN, IGESOUT			
PSOUT, PSIN, PSFILL			
Using the ACAD.PGP file			
UNDEFINE, REDEFINE			
AutoLISP programming			
Post-processing			
Toolbar Customization			

INDEX

A

B

D

E

F

G

H

I

J

K

L

M

S

T

U

V

W

X

Z

Colophon

This book was produced on Apple Power Macintosh computers using PageMaker 5.0. PostScript files were printed to disk and output directly to film using a Linotronic 330 imagesetter.

The body text is set in Palatino. Subheads, running heads and folios are set in varying weights of DTC Classical Sans and DTC Classical Condensed Sans. Sample code sections are set in Courier. Illustrations were produced using AutoCAD and Adobe Photoshop.

The AutoCAD Reference Library

NEW FOR RELEASE 13

AutoLISP in Plain English, Fifth Edition

$27.95

352 pages, illustrated

You don't have to be a programmer to customize AutoCAD for top productivity. The classic guide to AutoCAD's internal programming language, revised and expanded for Release 13 for Windows, features six new chapters of advanced techniques for users of all levels. All without conventional programming! The companion disk contains all 15 practical programming examples from Chapter 17, plus programs from each chapter and sample entities and blocks.

1000 AutoCAD Tips and Tricks, Fourth Edition

$34.95

650 pages, illustrated

No more hours of figuring out AutoCAD's quirks—the most popular selection of shortcuts on the market, rewritten and fully updated for Release 13 for Windows. Features advice and undocumented techniques for editing, viewing, 3D, AutoLISP, system variables and more. A proven productivity builder! The companion disk includes all the AutoLISP programs and drawings from the book.

Many of Ventana's books include a free Internet *Online Companion™*, featuring archives of free utilities plus a software archive and links to other Internet resources.

THE WINDOWS INTERNET
TOUR GUIDE
CRUISING THE INTERNET THE EASY WAY
FULL STARTUP KIT & ROAD MAP INSIDE!
INCLUDES ONLINE COMPANION
SECOND EDITION
PHIL JAMES
VENTANA PRESS

VENTANA PRESS
WINDOWS
SHAREWARE
500
4 DISKETTES ENCLOSED
The last word on the best virus-free Windows shareware
America Online Special Offer
John Hedtke

M·O·S·A·I·C
QUICK TOUR
FOR WINDOWS
FREE! ONLINE COMPANION INCLUDED!
SPECIAL EDITION
ACCESSING & NAVIGATING THE INTERNET'S WORLD WIDE WEB
VENTANA PRESS

Looking Good in Print, Third Edition

$24.95

464 pages, illustrated

For use with any software or hardware, this desktop design bible has become the standard among novice and experienced desktop publishers alike. Now with more than 300,000 copies in print, *Looking Good in Print, Third Edition* is even better—including new sections on photography and scanning. Learn the fundamentals of professional-quality design along with tips on resources and reference materials.

The Visual Guide to Microsoft Access

$29.95

664 pages, illustrated

The Visual Guide to Microsoft Access makes traditional text-heavy tech talk obsolete with a presentation as visually based as Windows itself. Illustrations on virtually every page highlight this handbook, designed for beginning users through intermediate database developers. Learn how pictures, icons, buttons, graphics and more have transformed complex database development into simple drag-and-drop operations. Includes a companion disk with sample files from the book and a fully functional database application.

The Visual Guide to Paradox for Windows

$29.95

682 pages, illustrated

Whether you're a DOS veteran or a newcomer to Paradox, this *Visual Guide* will help you with your Windows database management and programming. Covers all the new graphical capabilities of Windows as well as the latest features of Paradox, including the graphic Query Editor, BOCA (Borland Object Component Architecture) and ObjectPAL, Paradox's new object-oriented program language. The companion disk includes all the macros, reports, tables and queries needed to create an initial working database.

Check your local bookstore or software retailer for these and other best-selling titles, or call toll free: 800/743-5369

THERE'S MORE TO THIS BOOK THAN THE PRINTED PAGE!

http://www.vmedia.com/autocad.html

Do you have an Internet account and a World Wide Web browser? Then Ventana has an additional resource for you!

Part of the popular Ventana Visitors Center on the Internet, ***The AutoCAD Online Companion*** provides FREE instant access to a variety of utilities available over the Internet and links to newsgroups, mailing lists and other valuable AutoCAD resources.

The *Online Companion* also gives you access to other resources on Ventana Online, including regularly updated listings of the latest Net hotspots and link chapters from the book online.

So join us online today FREE. We're just a URL away!

Ventana Online

http://www.vmedia.com/autocad.html

VENTANA ONLINE